"IT'S UP TO OURSELVES"

A Mother, a Daughter, and Gurdjieff

A SHARED MEMOIR and FAMILY PHOTO ALBUM

by

JESSMIN and **DUSHKA HOWARTH**

Gurdjieff Heritage Society

FIRST EDITION#............

Published by
GURDJIEFF HERITAGE SOCIETY
New York, New York

Printed in the United States of America

ISBN: 978-0-9791926-0-9   0-9791926-0-9

LIBRARY OF CONGRESS CONTROL NUMBER: 2008927138

"We were blessed in our lives to come close to some special human beings. Special, yes, because they had more _being_ than the rest of us. But that doesn't mean they were any the less _human_. Quite the contrary!"

Dushka Howarth

"Religion without humanity is more dangerous than humanity without religion."

A. R. Orage

"I cannot develop you. I can only create conditions in which you can develop yourselves. ...Take the understanding of the East and the energy of the West and then seek!"

G. I. Gurdjieff

"The stature of Gurdjieff, the man and his life, was of sufficient magnitude in itself not to require superstitious embellishments."

William J. Welch, M.D.

"You sit around waiting for pearls when what you should actually be doing is not to be swine."

Sophie Grigorievna (Mme. Ouspensky)

"Mr. Gurdjieff could hit you over the head and catch you before you hit the ground. These people only know how to hit you over the head!"

Olga de Hartmann

"Everyone of you is a disciple of the Truth if you understand the Truth and do not follow individuals."

Jiddu Krishnamurti

"Remember, dear, you don't have to judge 'The Ideas' by the people who believe in them."

Jessmin Howarth

CONTENTS

THE FIFTIES

THE LATER YEARS

ACKNOWLEDGMENTS

I am exceedingly grateful to so many of you for your practical help and valuable advice, permission to use letters and photos, and especially for kind encouragement and support when my hopes and health were flagging or my convictions were in doubt or being criticized!

You know who you are, but so others will also —

TO GENEROUS FRIENDS —
Gert-Jan Blom, Ernie Haim, Doug Sprei, Vasken Kalayjian, James Ehlers, Lise de Etievan, Tania Nagro, Eve (Petey) Chevalier, Nicolai Stjernval, Vivien Elliot, Martha Heyneman, Kenneth "Kip" Page, Lillian Firestone, Richard Lipton, Greg and June Loy, Laura Lelievre, Elizabeth Evans, Carmela Mercuri, Robin Smith, Patty (Welch) de Llosa, Bob Gerber, Victoria Orfaly, Tom Daly, Clodagh Simonds, Dr. Barry Spector, James Sarfati, Michael Benham, Marianne Levin, Bob Schneck, Kathryn Arizmendi, Hane Selman, Joanna Schlesinger, Herb Cohen and many others.

AND THE HEIRS OF —
Mme. Jeanne de Salzmann, Dr. Michel de Salzmann, P.D. and Sophie Ouspensky, Alfred Etievant, Ethel Merston, Stanley and Rosemary Nott, Thomas and Olga de Hartmann, Nathalie de Etievan, Daphne Ripman Matchelajovic, Terry Winter Owens, Lord John Pentland, Annette Herter, Dr. William and Louise Welch, Evelyn Sutta, Margaret Capper, Louise Goepfert March, Bernard Metz, Sylvie Anastasieff, P.L. Travers, A. R. and Jessie Orage, Solita Solano, Emile Jaques-Dalcroze, George Bernard Shaw, Jacques Copeau, Suzanne Bing, Bess Mensendieck, Lizelle Reymond, and Maud Hoffman, etc.

THE GURDJIEFF HERITAGE SOCIETY, INC
Susan and Bruce Thompson, Meg Sinclair, Nella Liska, George Mobille, Paul Beekman Taylor, Robert Hohenberger, Linda Spitz, Walter Driscoll, Stephen E. Foster, Enid Langbert, Peter Rogen, Tim and Barbara Cook and the Church of Conscious Harmony, the Rochester Folk Art Guild, and many others world wide.

Many warm thanks,

Dushka

PREFACE

References to "The Fourth Way," "The Enneagram," "Harmonious Development," and so forth, appear everywhere nowadays and the name of G. I. Gurdjieff, the man who originally introduced most of these concepts to the West in the early 1900s, is often used as a commercial attention grabber.

The 1985 publication of *Gurdjieff: An Annotated Bibliography*, a 363-page volume, drove this home to many of us. Identifying and briefly summarizing the existing books and articles about this philosopher and writer, who had died in 1949 almost completely unknown except to a small coterie of pupils and admirers, it lists the astonishing number of one thousand seven hundred and forty-three publications (in English and French.) And every year the list increases.

Unfortunately, of the now almost three thousand publications about Gurdjieff and his work presently available, one can with discrimination and a clear conscience recommend only a very small percentage to the serious reader. Most of them are inept, misguided or, worse, sometimes really destructive. The saleability of the Gurdjieff name has resulted in an avalanche of spurious imitations. Hundreds of writings and public presentations are offered nowadays by people who never knew the man himself or had direct experience of his teaching. However they realize that by using his name they increase credibility and sales for their own work.

For years many of us laughed at this profiteering, clumsy and blatant as it was. However such shameless exploitation not only produces ugly distortions but is cruelly unfair to those many good people who have worked quietly and faithfully for years to preserve the integrity and continuity of this valuable, and, to them personally, sacred system of ideas.

In the Americas and in Europe of the 1920s, Asian and even Near-Eastern culture, thought and religious practices were almost unrecognized, or were, at best, suspect. But the "Gurdjieff Teaching," reconciling as it does Eastern spiritual ideas and contemporary scientific discoveries, was practical and free of mystical trappings and cultish atmosphere. It attracted the attention and active participation of educated, successful-in-life adults, and evidently satisfied a deep need in an era of weakening traditions and modern challenges. Today that interest intensifies and continues.

In more than twenty-five countries around the world thousands of serious, discriminating people come together regularly in large, active groups to support each other's attempts to verify and put into practice "The Work," as it has come to be known. In truth, it is no easy panacea! So for many of these pupils it has been dif-

Dushka
♦

ficult to accept that what started out as such a private, if not downright secret personal study is now widely discussed, and eagerly investigated by the media. It is publicly revealed internationally not only in numerous books and magazines but also in TV documentaries and feature films, (notably the award-winning *Meetings With Remarkable Men* directed by Peter Brook), and ever more widely (and mostly inaccurately) on the Internet.

Despite increasing popular interest in Gurdjieff, much less is known about an essential part of his rich legacy: the extensive and exacting series of physical exercises now called simply "The Movements," which have been variously described as "Sacred Dances," "esoteric gymnastics," or, as Jacques Maritain, the French theologian called them, "meditation in motion."

In order to introduce his new ideas to the West, Gurdjieff briefly showed his Movements to the general public in Paris in late 1923, and then in cities in the United States in early 1924. He presented skillfully prepared, elaborate theatrical performances in colorful ethnic costumes, with a thirty-six-piece orchestra and an informed commentary by the respected English editor and critic, A.R. Orage. An article or two appeared in the American and European press at that time (see Chapter 4) but another twenty-five years would pass before any further mention of Gurdjieff appeared in print.

In certain circles these demonstrations attracted attention and comment and people who expressed interest were offered the opportunity to join small study groups. However as soon as the American tour was completed, those early Movements (and another hundred or so that were developed later) were withdrawn from public access.

Since then Gurdjieff's students have maintained a constant effort to preserve and protect the Movements undistorted and to prevent their indiscriminate use. These are strong methods which must be used in the context of an ongoing practice of self-observation, "work on oneself," and a careful synthesis of physical, emotional and psychological experience.

Gurdjieff's emphasis after 1917 on Movements as an integral part of his teaching greatly discomfited some of his more intellectual followers. This included the Russian P.D. Ouspensky whose scientific mind demanded (and then was fully satisified with) logical, precise explanations and formulas, which precious material he accurately reformulated both orally and in voluminous writings, thereby earning gratitude from many followers and readers.

However, it was often the Movements that attracted Westerners to the Work, and many of these gained understanding, and often had profound experiences from working with Movements long before they learned of the "Ideas" through verbal expositions. Notable among these were my mother, Jessmin Howarth, and her friend and colleague, Jeanne de Salzmann, both of whom, after being exposed to Movements, abandoned successful dance and teaching careers to devote their lives to Gurdjieff's "System"— before reading any books, hearing any lectures or group discussions. They continued actively instructing and preserving the Work, especially the Movements, until their respective deaths at the ages of ninety-two and one hundred and one.

When my mother first encountered Gurdjieff in 1922, he and a group of thirty or so followers had just arrived in Paris by a long and difficult route, driven out of Russia by the Revolution. Though formerly of the intelligentsia and aristocracy, these "refugees" had few European contacts or readily marketable skills and no financial resources. They spoke little French or English and even their legal status was uncertain.

Mother, on the other hand, orphaned at an early age and having endured a grim childhood in Victorian England, had the good fortune and talent to be sent as a teenager to cosmopolitan pre-World War I Dresden for advanced violin studies. There a multi-national community of avant-garde artists and performers at the Dalcroze Institute in Hellerau welcomed her into their midst. With their encouragement and collaboration, she developed her other talents in the fields of dance, pantomime, and physical therapy, changing her life's direction.

Ten years later, at the time of Gurdjieff's arrival in France, Mother, then thirty, was already at the peak of a career as choreographer for the Paris Opera, a sought-after teacher of Dalcroze Eurythmics and pantomime, and an esteemed veteran of the history-making theatrical experiment, Jacques Copeau's *Vieux Colombier*.

How unlikely the meeting, much less the relationship, of these two, Gurdjieff and Mother! And how difficult for me, a result, to understand years hence!

When asked, Mother was always happy to share interesting and often hilarious anecdotes about personages — many now quite famous — and places she had known in her long life. Yet she rarely talked about herself and her own personal life, not even — or perhaps, as I now recognize — *especially* not to me.

However, in later years, when her teaching schedule became less frantic, and she had time alone while I traveled the world as an entertainer, she began to write down some of her reminiscences and inner thoughts. Several completed essays were neatly typed, hand-bound, and shyly included amongst my holiday or birthday presents. For one example of these see Appendix 1, *"For My Daughter at Christmas,"* an amusing but poignant account of her Victorian upbringing at the turn-of-the-century.

Then after her death I found many more intriguing items among Mother's papers and private letters. I was moved by her personal dichotomy about Gurdjieff — private wariness side by side with an unwavering fidelity to his "Teaching"— and motherly attempts at objectivity when, in 1948, as a young adult, my encounters with Gurdjieff required me to recognize him as my father and join him in France for what turned out to be the last year of his life.

Once Mother's writings were put into a semblance of order, our closest friends — especially the Welches, Dr. William, his wife Louise and daughter Patty all three published writers — insisted that they should be rounded out and made into a book. I worried that the very personal nature of some of this material might be considered gratuitous. Later I came to agree that a larger context demanded the sharing and could help towards a better understanding of the complex, sometimes maligned, persons involved. Especially as so much else of what was being published grew more and more specious.

Thus, in spite of so many conflicting versions, and often mistaken interpretations of certain past events and the people involved in them, here is yet another account. But, hopefully, this one is mostly from a clear-sighted first hand witness, my mother. Her open, unprejudiced viewpoint, and her ability to describe people and situations with refreshing skepticism, frankness and wit make her a unique observer, one of the last from whom we can glean real glimpses of the past.

Gurdjieff's *Meetings with Remarkable Men* and hundreds of other books are by men and about the men in the Work. But what about the women? This account of Mother's life, her friendships and collaborations, offers also an opportunity, long overdue, to meet and appreciate "remarkable women." Rarely mentioned elsewhere, many played crucial roles in supporting and continuing Gurdjieff's work during his lifetime and afterwards: Mme. Ouspensky, Jeanne de Salzmann, Olga de Hartmann, Olgivanna Lloyd Wright, Rosemary Nott, Annette Herter, Nathalie de Etievan, Louise Welch, P. L. Travers, Ethel Merston, Carol Robinson, Peggy Flinsch, A. L. Stavely, Evelyn Sutta, Lizelle Reymond, and many more.

I also hope that perhaps some of Mother's own special common sense, humor, moral fiber and mature wisdom may be understood and appreciated, and even, God willing, emulated as time goes by.

Although wishing to leave most of the original writings unedited, (including Mother's English spellings, etc.) I felt I should arrange them in a sequence for the sake of clarity, and have added remembered conversations, my own comments, stories and descriptions of our later lives as well as the many photos and captions. And it was a real struggle for me to learn modern computer techniques so as to salvage all these hundreds of very old photographs, many faded, neglected, often torn and water-stained, so that we could better show you what mere words might have failed to express.

I have done my best to thank the original writers or heirs of those whose letters to Mother and myself have added much to this narative.

Gratefully,

Dushka Howarth
New York City, 2008

INTRODUCTION

I pondered the suitability of adding an "Introduction to Gurdjieff" for the benefit of those readers who might require some background about the man, who he was and what it was he taught and wrote about. But even considering my closeness to the situation and my many years of observing what we sometimes call "the Gurdjieff Phenomena"— *i.e.* the effects of this ordinary/extraordinary being on the world around him — I decided that I, for one, would never attempt such an overwhelming task. Especially since, frankly, I still need to resolve some of my own questions about him, his life, his work and his relationship to my mother and to myself.

Heaven knows there are hundreds of other people who evidently feel perfectly well qualified to "explain" Gurdjieff once and for all and who claim authority, and, even worse, "authorization," to pass on his teaching!

Dushka
♦

George Ivanovich Gurdjieff in Paris, 1949, shortly before his death.

And how to discriminate between the myriad of writings about him? Even his own books raise many questions. As Gurdjieff himself, from the beginning, warned his readers, his writings were intended to challenge on every level. To be "difficult." They demand much special attention, time, dedication and real effort to master his style, to separate allegory from fact, as well as truly absorb his new and difficult ideas – both spiritual and practical – so as to use them as tools for self study.

Many authors whom we may admire for their faithful, exhaustive "Gurdjieff research," have, to my mind, then proceeded to flaw their results by mixing in their own questionable conclusions and philosophical pontifications. As someone who has long been openly critical of such efforts, I don't want us now to commit the same error.

Here Mother and I are simply offering a selection of personal glimpses of the past, a necessarily subjective overview with frank, often humorous, impressions and reactions. We include family scrapbook fragments, various letters, articles, quotes from "friend and foe" alike, and some of the memorabilia and old snapshots that we have been collecting through the years. Their interpretation or significance we leave to you, the readers, realizing that it will undoubtedly be colored by your valuation of us as witnesses and chroniclers.

Recognizing, however, that some readers will be served by an introduction to the basic facts about Gurdjieff, I have appended an article, *Gurdjieff, An Original Teacher*, one of the more worthy offerings to be found on the Internet. (See Appendix 2, page 495.) I found it well-researched, seriously considered and modestly presented.

In pointing out how Gurdjieff attracts contemporary attention, we should add that besides the notoriety of the man and the legends surrounding him, there is also a lot of confusing minutiae that clouds a clear picture of him.

First of all, the name itself.

Because of the difficulty of transcribing the Russian Cyrillic alphabet, it has been spelled in many different ways, i.e. Gourdjev, etc., which has sometimes caused imaginative writers to falsely identify Gurdjieff with someone completely different like the notorious Tibetans "Lama Dordjieff", and Ushe, or Dordje, Narzunoff. In fact, Gurdjieff's father's family name was originally Georgiades, a common Greek name which acquired a Caucasian version when the family moved eastwards.

Gurdjieff and his siblings adopted Russian usage for their first names. Thus we used to hear Mr. G. being called by his family and close friends what sounded to us like "**Gur**givantch," but was really Georgei Ivanovich. This is the Russian way of saying "George, son of Ivan." His brother was Dimitri Ivanovitch, and the feminine patronymic used by his sisters was Sophie Ivanovna, Anna Ivanovna, etc. So his father's name was Ivan – the Russian form of "John," or Greek "Ionas" – not George as wrongly attributed by various writers. A seemingly minor inaccuracy. But sometimes such a clue can reveal the dubiousness of a work like the fictional *The Teachers of Gurdjieff* which purports to describe the origins of Gurdjieff's system and those who taught him in the early years. In this case the author, (actually Idries Shah), calling himself "Rafael Lefort," claims that many of these supposed teachers knew Gurdjieff by a special name, "*The Armenian Jurjizada*," (footnoted as meaning "*Son of George in Persian*"!)

The habit of calling him "Mr. G.," or just "G," probably started when P.D. Ouspensky's unpublished manuscript of *In Search Of The Miraculous* was first read aloud. Ouspensky never refers to his rather mysterious "Teacher" in any other way. In the Twenties many people felt that the Work should be "protected from the public" and hesitated to use actual names. So in England and the U.S. the term "Mr. G." came into common usage. The French didn't have the same qualms and to them he was always "Monsieur Gurdjieff."

This name confusion made possible one of the more blatant and exploitive distortions, an anonymous book called *Secret Talks With Mr. G.*, in which the actual author (whose name, conveniently is Gold, so there is no legal liability) even posed for photographs copying existing pictures of Mr. Gurdjieff. Unfortunately, many people, including long-time Gurdjieff pupils, were deceived. But E.J. Gold's answer, when questioned about it twenty very profitable years later, was a bland: "I don't believe that prank, *Secret Talks with Mr. G.* hurt anybody. It was just intended to prod some people into doing the right thing." *(Gnosis, 1998)*

And the ramifications continue! Most recently Rosemary Hamilton in her book about life with "Osho" (formerly Bhagwan Shree Rajneesh) acknowledges: "a special thank you to those early **Gurdjieff teachers** [sic] without whom this tale would not have been conceived: Ray 'The Fake Sheik' Walker and <u>E.J. Gold</u>." [!]

Also Colin Wilson's lengthy introduction to *People of the Secret* by an Ernest Scott gives another reinforcement, possibly innocently, of Gold's charade: "In writing a short book on Gurdjieff — which necessitated reading everything that has so far been published about him — perhaps the most convincing and impressive of all these books is a recently published volume called *Secret Talks With Mr. G.* issued anonymously in America."

To no one's surprise, "Ernest Scott" is another of Idries Shah's pseudonyms!

As to confusion about Gurdjieff's age? An old passport once showed his date of birth as 1877 and for many years this was accepted. Then the dust jacket of the first edition of *All and Everything* gave it as 1872.

But in recent years the consensus seems to be 1866, affirmed by remarks G. himself made to his Paris groups in '43, and again in '49 to John Bennett as quoted in *Witness*, and to Elizabeth Bennett in *Idiots In Paris*, "I have already eighty-three years." His niece Luba wrote, "He died when he was eighty-two." And he himself writes in *Meetings With Remarkable Men* that he was seven years old when his father was ruined by the loss, due to drought and disease, of the herds and flocks in his charge. This catastrophe has now been dated to 1873-4.

Everything that he had obviously experienced and accomplished in his early life, though undocumented before his arrival in Moscow in 1912, certainly tends to confirm the earliest birthdate. And in 1949, even taking into account that he had recently undergone a second (or third?) serious automobile accident he appeared to us all to be a man in his eighties rather than early seventies.

P.D. Ouspensky first met Gurdjieff in 1915 and described him as "a man of an oriental type <u>no longer young</u>." Would Ouspensky, then himself 37 years old, have said that about a 38-year-old? And *The Prospectus of the Institute for The Harmonious Development of Man of G. Gurdjieff*, issued in October 1921, states that the eminent scholars known as the "Seekers after Truth" formed their group in 1895 — *with an <u>eighteen year old</u> Gurdjieff?*

Having finally settled all this in my own mind, wouldn't you know a recent visitor from Armenia, Gurdjieff's birthplace, brought me photocopies of state census records.

Presumably, since I could only read the dates, not the Russian text, they showed that "furniture maker" Georgiades had two sons, one, Georgei Ivanovitch, born in 18<u>80</u> and the other, Dimitri, born in 18<u>83</u>. A marriage certificate for the parents was dated 1875! So...?

In any case, such "nit-picking" and historical uncertainty can make no real difference to a true valuation or active practice of Gurdjieff's teaching, and perhaps, after all, it is not so surprising that there is no accepted, definitive Gurdjieff biography.

In the tense days immediately after G.'s death in 1949, there were many urgent discussions and excited arguments about how and by whom this responsibility of a biography should be undertaken, but nothing was resolved.

I, myself, argued with youthful conviction that the only valid, truthful way to attempt this nearly impossible task would be to ask not one but a great variety of people to combine their many different personal impressions and experiences — and even that would be just a beginning.

To experience the variety of reactions which I foresaw — and thus point up one of the most important aspects of the "*<u>real</u>*" Gurdjieff, or at least the one <u>we</u> thought <u>we</u> had known — just glance at a few samples:

<u>WHO WAS G. I. GURDJIEFF?</u>

<u>JOHN. G. BENNETT</u> (Mathematician/Philosopher):
"Gurdjieff was a very great enigma in more ways than one.
"First and most obvious is the fact that no two people who knew him would agree as to who and what he was."

<u>DR. WILLIAM J. WELCH</u> (Physician/Author *What Happened in Beween*):
"To some he was a libertine and a Middle Eastern rascal; to others he was a teacher of such stature and impartiality as to rank among the authentic avatars."

<u>HENRIETTE LANNES</u> (Journalist/Author *Inside a Question)*:
"I saw him as he was to the extent I was able to see myself... But to recognize Mr. Gurdjieff truly is not an easy thing."

<u>JANE HEAP</u> (Editor):
"He is a multitude... But, if you watch, sometimes you see the sage pass by."

<u>J.B. PRIESTLEY</u> (Author):
"Whether Gurdjieff was a new prophet and teacher or a Near Eastern original, two thirds genius, one third charlatan, he certainly knew a great deal more about our common humanity than most of us know... a very remarkable man."

<u>LOUISE WELCH</u> (Author *Orage with Gurdjieff in America*):
"An unknown spiritual teaching rooted in timeless esoteric ideas, its founder G.I. Gurdjieff, a stocky, swarthy, shaven-headed, heavily-mustached Georgian,

handsome in his way but definitely not Western. His behavior, too, seemed incomprehensible, since it was soon evident that he was indifferent to what people thought of him. He came to shock us awake, and shock us he did."

CLAUDIO NARANJO (Gestalt Therapist):
"As a single individual he managed to administer the European and American world a shock perhaps more significant than any other until the cultural wave of the early sixties."

JERZY GROTOWSKI (Theater Director);
"C'etait une sorte de volcan." (Tr: "He was a sort of volcano.")

HENRY LEROY FINCH (Professor of Philosophy):
"Gurdjieff brought to life again, in a protected form which people would have to work to find, surviving knowledge from Egypt, Sumer, Babylon, Greece, Central Asia, and Tibet."

JAMES MOORE (Author *Gurdjieff, The Anatomy of A Myth*):
"He coaxed from archaic sources a major critique which speaks authentically to the condition, suffering, and spiritual aspiration of modern man. For thousands of sensitive and intelligent people, who had the wit to see beneath his occasional mask of fraudulence, he came to represent the breathing embodiment of authenticity."

JACK DREYFUS (Founder, The Dreyfus Fund):
"Gurdjieff, a superbrilliant man, extraordinary in many ways."

ROBERT TODD CARROLL (Author The Skeptic's Dictionary):
"George S. Georgiades [sic} was a Greco-Armenian charismatic con man who was born in Russia [sic] but made a name for himself in Paris as the mystic George Ivanovitch Gurdjieff."

GORHAM MUNSON (Literary Critic):
"...he was all that a writer should be: indefatigable, living life to the fullest, inspired with the highest aim in literature — the writing of a modern scripture."

THE REV. TIM COOK (Pastor: The Church of Conscious Harmony):
"...God dressed up in the form of a man we call Gurdjieff."

GEORGE LATURA BEKE (Author):
"...called everything from an incomparable spiritual master, to one son-of-a-bitch whose feet of clay booted many away."

HENRY MILLER (Author):
"...of all the Masters...the most interesting."

WALDO FRANK (Author):

"I think you are the Devil!"

WHAT IS "THE GURDJIEFF TEACHING?"

EDWIN WOLFE (Radio Director):
"Mr. Gurdjieff replied: 'What I try do? I try show people when it rains the streets are wet!'"

DR. MICHEL DE SALZMANN (Psychiatrist):
"The teaching ...does not call upon any belief, any cult or worship, or any ritual. At first it simply proposes that one should know oneself as one is. It cannot, in its essence, be in contradiction with any traditional teachings."

JEANNE DE SALZMANN (introducing the *Third Series*):
"The aim of his teaching is that man should become aware of the meaning of his presence and of his place in the scale of Being."

TERRY WINTER OWENS (Composer):
"In confronting the huge body of literature now available about the teaching of Gurdjieff, we will be lost without some discriminatory powers. Counterfeits and cults dot the landscape."

RENE ZUBER (Film Producer):
"This teaching is a virile version of the Gospels."

ROBERT S. DE ROPP (Bio-chemist):
"Neoalchemy is the basis of Gurdjieff's teaching."

Z'EV BEN SHIMON HALEVI/WARREN KENTON (Kabbalist):
"The closeness of Gurdjieff's System to Kabbalah can be perceived."

IDRIES SHAH (Author *The Sufis*):
"G.I. Gurdjieff left abundant clues to the Sufic origin of virtually every point in his system."

WILLIAM SEGAL (Publisher):
"No doubt there is a profound connection between Zen and the teaching of Gurdjieff."

JOEL FRIEDLANDER (Publisher):
"...anticipates the holistic approach of contemporary body-centered therapies like Bioenergetics, Hakomi Therapy, and Core Energetics."

BORIS MOURAVIEFF ("Esotericist!"):
"In its historical frame the message brought by Gurdjieff roots in the ancient beliefs of the Slavs and Scythians which still survive in the traditions of Byzantine

Russian Orthodoxy."
DR. MAURICE NICOLL (Jungian Psychologist):
"Esoteric Christianity, as Gurdjieff called the Work, is not a religion, but it is the inner meaning of what Christ taught."

SRI ANIRVAN and LIZELLE REYMOND (Authors *To Live Within: Teachings of a Baul*):
"Gurdjieff has been a pioneer in the West, far ahead of his time...
"He has at least three different sources in the East - Vedism, Buddhism, and Islam."

JEAN TOOMER (Author *Cane*):
"Here was a discipline, an invitation to conscious experiment, a flexible and complete system, a life and way to which I felt I could dedicate my whole mind and heart and body and soul."

JEAN VAYSSE (Surgeon/Metaphysian):
"...Gurdjieff's ideas contain what is probably the truest answer to the question raised by the tremendous material power now in the hands of modern man...."

DR.TRIBHUWAN KAPUR ("Reader in Sociology"):
"It is rare for a mystic to provide a full-blown system of ideas and methods, leading to a vast expansion of awareness. This is rarer still in modern times. Gurdjieff was one such mystic and sage...."

ALEXANDER PHIPPS/SRI MADHAVA ASHISH (Aeronautics Engineer/Hindu Monk):
"If you want to pursue in a Western way the path that we follow here..., you need to study and work with the Gurdjieffian teaching."

BHAGWAN SHREE RAJNEESH/OSHO ("An Enlightened Master"!?):
"...nobody has tried to understand the phenomenon of Buddhahood in scientific ways. Gurdjieff was the first man in the whole history of humanity who tried...
I am Gurdjieff plus Ouspensky!"

WILLIAM PATRICK PATTERSON (Founder/Editor, *The Gurdjieff Journal*):
"Gurdjieff's goal/mission was to establish the ancient teaching of the Fourth Way in the West so the world would not destroy itself."

OSCAR ICHAZO (Founder, Arica School):
"I am the root of a new tradition.
"My teachings have no link and could not be inspired in any way by the naive, materialistic cosmology and the very old 'ideas' presented by Mr. Gurdjieff."

FRANK LLOYD WRIGHT (Architect):

xx   IT'S UP TO OURSELVES

"In Gurdjieff the ancient teachings of Lao Tse, Jesus and St. Augustine all have fresh import and find valid scientific support. Ancient wisdom of the East not only intelligible to the thought of the West but... a way of WORK."

WHAT WAS GURDJIEFF'S EFFECT?

LINCOLN KIRSTEIN (Founder/Director, New York City Ballet):
"As in everything I do, whatever is valid springs from the person and ideas of G.I. Gurdjieff."

HENRI TRACOL (Journalist/Photographer):
"Is it not a fact, for instance, that for a number of our contemporaries the encounter with this man was the major event in their lives?"

MICHAEL MURPHY (Co-Founder, Esalen Institute):
"The older I get, the more I respect Gurdjieff."

COLIN WILSON (Author):
"Russia tends to produce mages — men or women who impress by their spiritual authority... certainly no other nation has come near to producing anyone like Madame Blavatsky, Gregory Rasputin or George Gurdjieff. The achievement of Gurdjieff was to raise such matters from the realm of 'magic' and 'the occult' to the realm of scientific common sense."

PETER BROOK (Theater/Film Director):
"...the most immediate, the most valid and the most totally representative figure of our times. More than anyone, he built the bridge between something higher and something in everyday life..."

PIERRE SCHAEFFER (Ex-Director, Office of French Radio & Television):
"...as dangerous as Everest or the Orinoco, as expensive as aureomycin, as exacting as a lover."

CLAUDE IDOUX (Painter):
"Gurdjieff's teaching forced me to take another look at my conceptions about art and my capacity to express something real,"

THOMAS DE HARTMANN (Composer):
"Mr. Gurdjieff knew how to bring a man from his ordinary state to a higher level."

EDGAR VARESE (Composer):
"Quel m'as-tu-vu!" [Tr:"What a ham!"]

A. R. ORAGE (Editor):

"True, I had found some of the ideas earlier. They were beads and some of them pearls. But before I met Gurdjieff I had no string to hang them on. Gurdjieff gave me the string."

KATHERINE MANSFIELD (Author):
"Mr. Gurdjieff is not in the least like what I expected... But I do feel absolutely confident he can put me on the right track in every way."

D.H. LAWRENCE (Author):
"I have heard enough about that place at Fontainbleau where Katherine Mansfield died, to know it is a rotten, false, self-conscious place of people playing a sickly stunt."

MARGARET ANDERSON (Publisher/Author):
"How distressing it is, (and how unsurprising) to discover the number of intelligent people to whom Gurdjieff is unknown and by whom, in consequence, he is vilified."

TCHESLAW TCHEKHOVITCH (Author):
"How sad, how sad not to have known him; but more, how sad to have known him and not to have understood him.

"And above all, how sad to have understood him and not to have served his work."

MOSHE FELDENKRAIS (Body-Mind Psychotherapist):
"....the person I feel I have the most kinship with is (G.I.) Gurdjieff.

"DENIS SAURAT (Professor, French Institute):
"Gurdjieff's teaching will have a profound effect on men's thinking a hundred years from hence."

WHAT WAS GURDJIEFF LIKE IN PERSON?

JAMES WEBB (Author *The Harmonious Circle*):
"Unless the inquirer is aware of the concept of 'playing a role,' he risks misinterpreting the story of Gurdjieff and his followers altogether."

C.S. NOTT (Author *Teachings of Gurdjieff*):
"Gurdjieff gives shocks, makes difficulties, plays roles both for his own development and for those around him. He lives the Teaching while we talk about it."

A. L. STAVELEY (Author *Memories of Gurdjieff*):
"In all the books and articles... not enough has ever been made of the humor — the delicate jests, the broad jokes, the gales of laughter — that sometimes swept through the room easing unbearable tensions."

THORNTON WILDER (Playwright):
"His anger was controlled. He used it for pedagogical emphasis."

BASIL TILLEY (Manufacturer):
"I see now why he shouts at people.
"He does not require a servility, but he can see when he shouts how long it takes to dissipate any inner collectedness which we may have."

JANET FLANNER ("GENET" of *The New Yorker*):
"...a very wise old man in his rich pantry of food and thoughts."

MARTIN SEYMOUR-SMITH (Author *The 100 Most Influential Books Ever Written. The History of Thought From Ancient Times To Today*):
"Of all this century's spiritual teachers, Gurdjieff was unique in that he determinedly sought to undermine his pupils' devotion to him personally — to the extent of renouncing their genuine love for him — in order to make them think and act for themselves."

CARL LEHMANHAUPT (Designer)
"In the mid-Thirties Mr. Gurdjieff, on one of his periodic trips to America, attended the wedding of his long time pupils Martin Benson and actress Rita Romilly Benson. Asked by the officiating minister what was his relation to the couple he answered: 'I father to them both!'"

(Above) Mr. Gurdjieff in the Thirties at the wedding of his pupils Martin Benson and actress Rita Romily.

ROM LANDAU (Author *God Is My Adventure*):
"Evasiveness, contradiction, and bluff — formerly the weapons in a most complicated system — seem to have become part of Gurdjieff's very nature."

DOROTHY CARUSO (Author *The Great Caruso*):
"Gurdjieff was gentle with my soul... gave it courage.
"From his mysterious and conscious world he guided it with a kind of understanding he called objective love."

MARGARET CROYDEN (*The New York Times*):
"The mysterious Gurdjieff was a marvelous cook."

EDGAR TAFEL (Author *Apprentice to Genius, Years with Frank Lloyd Wright*):
"The thing we all remembered most clearly afterwards — more than his music or philosophy — was that he taught us how to prepare sauerkraut."

BERNARD METZ (A translator of *All and Everything*):
"Ouspensky loved ideas as ideas — with G. they were merely a means to an end."

KATHRYN HULME (Author *The Nun's Story*):
"He uncovered in me a longing I never knew I had — the desire for an inner life of the spirit — and taught me how to work for it as one works for one's daily bread."

KENNETH WALKER, F.R.C.S., F.I.C.S. (Surgeon):
"Gurdjieff used strong medicine and I doubt whether I should have stomached his very drastic treatment had I met him at the beginning. I owe a great deal to Ouspensky...during those earlier years."

IRMIS B. POPOFF (Author):
"If I respected and feared Mr. Ouspensky, I respected and loved Mr. Gurdjieff."

RODNEY COLLIN (Author *The Theory of Celestial Influence)*:
"....I believe the Work to be one, though Ouspensky's and Gurdjieff's ways to be distinct and unmixable in themselves."

GARY LACHMAN (*Gnosis*, Spring 1996):
"For Gurdjieff loyalists Ouspensky was a thief peddling a teaching he never truly grasped."

TONY SCHWARTZ (Author *What Really Matters, Search for Wisdom in America)*:
"Ouspensky continued to believe in the authenticity of Gurdjieff's vision and teaching... but found the man himself more and more intolerable."

P. D. OUSPENSKY (Philosopher/Author):
"Gurdjieff had gone off the rails — become mad... — and I wanted to save the system."

SOPHIE GREGORIEVNA OUSPENSKY (Teacher):
"All that I know is that he is my teacher... and I refuse to enter into any discussions about him."

FRITZ PETERS (Author *Boyhood with Gurdjieff*):
"With Gurdjieff, we never knew what was going to happen next... and when it did, it was usually exciting and almost always amusing; sometimes he made it a magic world for children...
"Imagine a man wild enough and wonderful enough to buy two hundred bicycles and make everyone ride them. What child could resist that alone?"

PAUL BEEKMAN TAYLOR (Professor/Author):
"Amongst the many men in my mother's life. She repeatedly expressed, according to the occasion, scorn, amused detachment, or distant respect: 'He was... not a '*n i c e*' man!' "

LUBA GURDJIEFF (Restaurateur):
"Uncle George? For me, he was a man who so much loves life.
"He loves everything in life, everything about life. He loves females... children... dogs and cats... And now they are making him a saint.
"He was not a saint. He was a very, very good philosopher."

GEORGE IVANOVICH GURDJIEFF (?.....................?):
"I must, in respect of my own signature, be very, very careful...
"Very well then...
"Simply...
"Teacher of dancing!"

* * * * *

All his life Mr. Gurdjieff quoted the wise, witty sayings of Mullah Nasser Eddin (or "Nasreddin hodja") whose likeness is still found everywhere throughout the Middle East. (Above) A typical clay figurine from Istanbul, Turkey. (Right top) Nasser Eddin dinner bell (middle) A silver ring (bottom) Puzzle ring instruction book

But why is the beloved Mullah always shown riding his donkey backwards?

Well, when Jessmin and Dushka once bought gold puzzle rings in Kusadasi, Turkey, the booklet of instructions for "solving" the puzzle ring also included this explanatory story:

"WHY TO RIDE BACKWARDS? One day on his way to the mosque with his students Nasreddin hodja answered their questions about this:

"If I rode the normal way and you walk behind me we can not see each other.

"If I follow you riding the normal way the situation is the same.

"This way I am riding before you as your teacher and we are facing each other at the same time.

"Now you should decide which way a person in my position should ride on his donkey!"

CHAPTER 1

THE VIOLINIST MEETS DALCROZE, 1912

"It is necessary that in education intellectual and physical development should play an equally important part."

Emile Jaques-Dalcroze, 1910

Dear Dushka,

In order to tell you how, and through whom I first met Mr. Gurdjieff, I need to go back to about 1910 when I was studying violin in Dresden.

At seventeen, I was the youngest of various music and dance students boarding in a pension (at 22 Werderstrasse) owned by Frau Sonntag, a Viennese pastry cook whose daughter, Lizerli, soon became a close friend.

I was fresh out of English boarding school, still wearing out the school uniform blazer of bottle-green serge, with my hair in pigtails but proudly worn on top of my head (doorknocker style), the prerogative of a prefect. So, to me, Lizerli seemed the epitome of feminine elegance. She had been educated in a convent school and then given a year in Paris to study languages and ballet. Called home when her father, a wealthy pork butcher, died suddenly, she had been followed by a Greek engineering student, Nick, with whom she had fallen deeply in love.

At first, Frau Sonntag had disapproved of Nick's courtship. But, when he assured her that once his courses were completed he would take her and Lizerli to Greece to meet his family and secure his parent's consent to a marriage, she allowed them to be engaged.

All this Lizerli told me as I listened, wide-eyed. How romantic, and rather wicked, it seemed!

Between sawing away for hours on Kreutzer studies and violin concertos, I used to watch her daily doings with fascination.

Now, looking back, I think that Nick really regarded Lizerli as a charming doll. She was a pretty, winning little creature, small boned and *"rondoletta."* He insisted on having a suite of rooms in the pension remodeled for her with flowery wallpaper, flounced curtains and light-painted or gilt furniture with lace spreads... it delighted me. Such a contrast to the red-plush overstuffed furnishings dear to the German hausfrau.

I spent many hours in this dainty suite with Lizerli. She loved to show me her possessions. Although she made a pretense of sophistication, she still, at twenty, had her schoolgirlish moments. She was proud of her linen, hand-stitched and tucked, and embroidered underwear, products of hours of fine sewing at the convent under the Sisters' eyes. Her closet was hung with beautiful dresses.

When Nick took her out in the evenings it was quite a ritual. He would oversee her preparations and then marshal her round to her mother's room to ask her approval.

I looked on with envy. How heart-warming it must be to have a devoted admirer interested in dressing you like a doll and proud to show you off to his friends!

Lizerli took pity on the dowdiness of my English wardrobe. First, with laughter, she encouraged me to throw away my Jaeger underwear. She and I would spend lazy afternoon hours leafing through fashion magazines and looking over the materials collected by another friend, Selma, an Austrian milliner-dressmaker, who enjoyed carrying out Nick's ideas for Lizerli's clothes.

In the mornings when I just had to practice and attend my various classes at the *Konservatorium*, Lizerli would do her "barre" exercises and go on with her sewing. If she could override her mother's objections, she would go into the kitchen and cook up some substantial dish. To see her demolish a big plate of wurst and sauerkraut was a shock.

That first year in Dresden was a happy time. The city, with its spotlessly clean streets, its spacious park, and the beautiful Palace, Church, and Opera House roofed with verdigrised copper, had the South German quality of *"Gemütlichkeit."* The Saxon people were easy-going and well disposed toward the many students who came from all over Eastern Europe to enter the Polytechnic, or the Art and Music schools. In my master class there was one Berliner, a Bulgarian, a Russian, a Dane, a Montenegrin, a Polish Jew, and myself from England.

The violin classes were deadly, for our teacher was a pedant. Every pupil had to study the same list of technical exercises and concertos— and he insisted upon the same fingering for everyone whether your hands were large or small. Sometimes, the two and a half hours of listening to the different pupils attacking the double-stopping in the Mendelssohn Concerto would be torture. It was a joy to escape to chamber music sessions or orchestra rehearsals.

Otherwise we were especially favored. Master class students were admitted free to most concerts and to the opera on condition that we sit way up under the roof on the side. There we saw more of what went on in the wings than what took place up stage. Somewhat disillusioning to see the swan in *Lohengrin* getting stuck on its rails and needing a quick squirt of oil and a hefty push before gliding along to Lohengrin. Or to watch the solo prima donna making a scene before her entrance, because, perhaps, the lighting was not to her taste.

Our teacher was the leader of the first violin section in the *Stadtorchester*, and at their concerts we were expected to dress up and sit in the first row of stalls to watch his feats of bowing. So, eventually, without serious effort, we became conversant with an extensive repertoire.

When winter came there were weeks of snow. I can remember waking in the mornings while the sky was still deep blue, crawling out from between the warm feather mattress and down comforter, to watch, through a frost-flowered window, as the children went to school. They would look like little gnomes, with their peaked caps wound about with woolen mufflers, humped over with their school satchels.

Some of them would carry little lanterns, others would pull sleds, and all wore wooden snow skates, which made a soft swishing sound as they slid down the sloping street.

Afternoons, a group of us might venture to the city square which was lined with prosperous stores. Long before Christmas these would have richly decorated window displays. One, in particular, was unforgettable. It featured two buxom mechanical lady mannequins, wearing low-cut evening dresses which revealed pink satin bosoms which rose and fell as their heads turned jerkily from side to side. Portly gentlemen would stand in the cold fascinated by this marvel.

We younger onlookers preferred to patronize the *Konditorei* and eat thick slices of *Baumkuchen* (cakes) served with *Schlagsahne* (whipped cream). Or we would drop into one of the coffee houses where some acquaintance might be playing with a small band for a *"Thé-Dansant."* Toward evening the boys would go off to a *Bierstube*, and the girls return home, or, in twos or threes, repair to the Public Baths for a soak and a shampoo. (There was just one bathroom in our pension.).

On the weekends we would often go tobogganing or cross-country skiing. Such fun in the crisp cold air, but against rules, for members of a master class were not allowed to engage in any sport which might lead to accidental hand injuries.

With springtime we used to meet early in the *Grosser Garten*, to play ball and breakfast on bran muffins and yogurt from the *Molkerei* kiosks dotting the arbors. If the guard looked the other way, we didn't hesitate to pick a few flowers and steal branches of lilac, arriving at our music lesson as gay harbingers of spring, thus putting our teacher into a furious temper.

Summer was the season for steamer excursions up the Elbe to "Buda Pesth" to hear gypsy music and sample Middle-Eastern foods. Or for *"Bümmel"* (outings) in the *Sachsiche Schweiz* forests where on weekdays one would meet only woodcutters and charcoal burners. On Sundays there would be the typical German families taking the air. Father in a bowler hat and stiff-collared shirt, leading the way and pointing with his umbrella to anything of interest. Mother in a batiste blouse with boned lace collar, jabot, and a wide skirt held up in scallops by an elastic suspender arrangement hanging from her waist. And then the children, dawdling behind, with their bulky packages of *"belegte Brötchen"* (sandwiches) — only interested when they came to a little waterfall which would be turned on by a guard on payment of ten pfennigs.

After these months of spending twenty hours a week in lessons and practice, plus many evenings' attendance at orchestra rehearsals and concerts, I was tired and had developed an inflammation in the shoulder of my bowing arm. The doctor advised some weeks' rest. What to do?

At the suggestion of some older music students who had visited it, I went out to see the Institute of Dalcroze Eurythmics in Hellerau, a suburb of Dresden.

The Institute was part of a model village for workers, envisaged and financed by Polish brothers Wolf and Harald Dohrn, millionaire philanthropists. They had installed a factory specializing in silk weaving, a modern school for the workmen's children and a Cultural Center with a large central auditorium for concerts and plays, flanked on each side by meeting and class rooms. The young architect, Henri Tessenow, became famous overnight for this auditorium he designed which was so ideally suited to the experimental presentations of the other artists who were recruited: Emile Jaques-Dalcroze, his advisor and collaborator Adolphe Appia, the noted set-designer from Geneva, and, from Russia, a painter Alexandre de Salzmann, who was also a virtuoso of theatrical lighting.

I went to see their first public performance, of "Rhythmic Gymnastics" and a musical pantomime, "*Echo and Narcissus*." The leading roles were taken by Annie Beck, a fey, fragile ash-blonde as Echo, and as Narcissus, a Swiss girl who, I was told, had been a pupil of Dalcroze since the beginning of his teaching in Geneva; the handsome, dynamic brunette: Jeanne Allemand (later de Salzmann).

I watched some classes and was fascinated. The work combined gymnastic movements, very attractive to an English product of drill meetings (in which I had formerly won medals), and free interpretation of music, besides Solfege and Harmony instruction. I returned to the pension enthusiastic, and set to work getting my guardians' permission to register as a full-time student.

◆◆◆

Dushka
◆

Emile Jaques-Dalcroze (1865-1950), was a composer, educator and theorist, who invented "Dalcroze Eurhythmics" and had a great influence, especially in the early 1900's, on the surging new trends in theater, music and dance through his writings and teaching, and by innovative collaborations with foremost artists in every field.

Note: "Eurhythmics" should not be confused with "Eurhythmy" which was developed by Rudolf Steiner (1861-1925) and is still used in the Waldorf schools and as part of anthroposophical therapies.

Emile Jaques-Dalcroze.

In addition to his revolutionary work with children, Dalcroze attracted many adult pupils including such noted musicians and dancers as Mary Wigman, Uday Shan-Kar, Hanya Holm, Michio Ito and Miriam Ramberg, 1888-1982, (who later, in England, became Dame Marie Rambert); and today thousands of teachers of his system continue to disseminate his ideas throughout the world.

Born in Vienna of Austro-Hungarian parents, Dalcroze studied at the Conservatory in Geneva (to which he returned later as Professor), with Leo Delibes in Paris and with Anton Bruckner in Vienna.

He also studied theater arts and at the age of twenty went as a theatrical director to Algiers, where the native percussion instruments brought home to him the inadequacies of most Europeans' rhythmic sense... the need to use and develop it and relate it to physical movement (not just instrumental technique), ear-training, and improvisation.

By 1910, "his name had spread throughout the European music world as a result of his work with the psychologist Edouard Claparide on the relationship between body movements and responses to music, especially rhythm. Based on this research, Jaques-Dalcroze came up with a system of movements, called eurythmics, that would have a strong impact on ballet and modern dance." [*Keyboard Magazine*, Oct. 1984]

His ideas and work came to the attention of Prince Serge Wolkonsky, superintendent of the Russian Imperial Theaters. Wolkonsky became an enthusiastic champion, writing and lecturing about these new ideas, and pledging his time, labor and money. Why? "Because," he said, "I hadn't the right to do otherwise. I had under-

The Dalcroze Institute at Hellerau, outside of Dresden, Germany

One of Adolf Appia's innovative stage sets

Alexandre de Salzmann

stood that *éducation rythmique* develops the entire man, that it represents a benefit to humanity."

Wolkonsky helped establish "*rhythmique institutes*" in St. Petersburg, Moscow, and Riga, and arranged two Russian tours for Dalcroze and a group of his pupils, during which, in Moscow, they were the guests of Stanislavsky's "Théâtre des Arts" and the Conservatory (where Rachmaninov greatly admired their performances.)

Soon after this Serge Diaghilev visited Hellerau with Vaslav Nijinsky, and after watching the lesson given by a young Miriam Ramberg (c.p. Marie Rambert), hired

Hellerau dancer Miriam Ramberg.

Serge Diaghelev (left) with Vaslav Nijinsky in Venice, 1911.

her as a *"professeur de rythmique"* for his Ballets Russes, and to collaborate with Nijinsky on his historic version of Stravinsky's *Sacre de Printemps (Rite of Spring.)* This went very well though the other dancers in the company were much less interested in these new ideas and rarely came to her classes.

In May of 1913, Miriam Ramberg worked again with Nijinsky on Debussy's *Jeux* (Games.) But this time the composer's reaction was rather less than enthusiastic. In fact, on June 9 Claude Debussy wrote to a musicologist friend:

"Among recent pointless goings-on I must include the staging of *Jeux,* which gave Nijinsky's perverse genius a chance of indulging in a peculiar kind of mathematics. This fellow adds up triple crotchets with his feet, checks them on his arms, then suddenly, half-paralyzed, he stands crossly watching the music slip by. It's awful. It's even Dalcrozian - for I consider Monsieur Dalcroze as one of the greatest enemies of music and you can imagine what havoc his method can create in the mind of a young savage like Nijinsky."

But Emile Jaques-Dalcroze had been developing very interesting ideas about music, dance, and education. Already in 1914 he had written: "The aim of all exercises in eurhythmics is to strengthen the power of concentration, to accustom the body to hold itself, as it were, at high pressure in readiness to execute orders from the brain, to connect the conscious with the subconscious, and to augment the sub-

Nijinsky in his famous role as the faun.

Composer Claude Debussy.

Nijinsky in Debussy's *Jeux* (Games.)

conscious faculties with the fruits of a special culture designed for that purpose....to purify the spirit, strengthen the will-power and install order and clarity in the organism. The aim of eurythmics is to enable pupils at the end of their course to say, **"not *'I know'*, but *'I have experienced!'"***

In 1919 he wrote his friend Jacques Cheneviere: "How can we expect a child's sensibility to flourish if we do not cultivate his elementary vital manifestations from the first, and throughout his school training? Surely it is the most bizarre of anomalies to teach him the rhythms of the speech and thought of others before enabling him to sense those of his own organism."

After World War I, greatly concerned for the future he pleaded: "It is not enough to give children and young people a general tuition founded exclusively on the knowledge of our forebears' activities. Teachers should aim at furnishing them with the means both of living their own lives, and of harmonizing these with the lives of others. The education of tomorrow must embrace reconstruction, preparation and adaptation; aiming, on the one hand, at the re-education of the nervous faculties and the attainment of mental calm and concentration, and, on the other, at the equipment for whatever enterprise practical necessity may dictate and at the power to react without effort; in short, at the provision of a maximum force with a minimum of strain and resistance...More than ever in these times of social reconstruction, the human race demands the re-education of the individual. Our children...should be enlightened as to the relations existing between soul and mind, between the conscious and the subconscious, between imagination and the processes of action. Thoughts should be brought into immediate contact with behavior - the new education aiming at regulating the interaction between our nervous and intellectual forces."

The similarity of many of these beliefs and aims of Dalcroze to those of Gurdjieff is striking, especially as they were formulated many years before Gurdjieff arrived in Europe.

Compare Gurdjieff's remarks in March of 1924: "Education is a very complicated thing. It must be many-sided... Generally speaking a child's education must be based on the principle that everything must come from his own will. Nothing should be given in a ready-made form. One can only give the idea, one can only guide, or even teach indirectly, starting from afar and leading him to the point from something else. I never teach directly or my pupils would not learn. If I want a pupil to change, I begin from afar, or speak to someone else, and so he learns. For, if something is told to a child directly, he is being educated mechanically and later manifests himself equally mechanically."

Some writers have claimed, mistakenly I believe, that the two men, Gurdjieff and Dalcroze, knew each other. This confusion probably arose because early in 1922 Gurdjieff, encouraged by the de Salzmanns, seriously considered the Hellerau site of the former Dalcroze Institute as a new home for his own Institute (and there exist photos of him taken during a visit there.) But after unresolvable legal difficulties with Harald Dohrn these plans fell through, and Gurdjieff with his group continued on to Paris. But Dalcroze himself had not returned to Dresden after the war and in 1922 was living in Geneva. So the two men never actually met. But it is interesting to note how previous exposure to the work and ideas of Dalcroze may have prepared some people for the teachings of Gurdjieff: Mother, Alexandre and Jeanne de Salzmann, Annette Herter, Rosemary Nott, etc.

Years later British director, Peter Brook, and Romanian director, Andrei Serban, both studied the Gurdjieff Movements with Mother, and if they were able to get her alone, away from classes and filmings, they would question her avidly about the theater and dance worlds she had known. They were particularly intrigued by her accounts of the Copeau and Dalcroze eras.

British director Peter Brook.

Jessmin being interviewed by Roumanian director Andrei Serban, Summer, 1983.

Andrei Serban remembers that she told him about one "Dalcroze incident" that had never come out in her conversations with the rest of us. Evidently, on the occasion of Gurdjieff's first Movements Demonstration in Paris in 1923, ardent supporters and pupils of Dalcroze turned up outside the Theatre des Champs Elysées and chanted: "*Tricheur! Voleur!*" ["Cheat! Thief!"]

But if one looks closely there is little real similarity between the two methods as to aims, choreography or music. Only a common interest, revolutionary for its time, in observing and understanding the relation of the inner to the outer, mental to the physical, etc. (And some shared appreciation of Eastern cultures since over the main door at Hellerau then, and in Dalcroze schools to this day, the insignia displayed is a "yin-yang" sign.)

The "yin-yang" sign.

◆ ◆ ◆

By the time I moved into the student hostel at Hellerau, in the autumn of 1912, Jeanne Allemand, to be my friend and colleague for the rest of our lives, had been married to "Herr von Salzmann" and lived in a small house nearby.

Jessmin
◆

Lizerli took great interest in this new venture of mine to leave my violin studies and go to Hellerau. I could not convince her that the Dalcroze School was seriously designed for teaching music. She thought of it as a new type of Dance Academy. Remembering her own pretty tutus, she was stunned to learn that the rhythm pupils exercised in bare feet, and black two-piece bathing suits, (known as "Annette Kellermans" after the famous swimmer).

My guardians would have been even more stunned!

Once settled into the schedule in Hellerau, I was not able to go to Dresden often. Sometimes, after a shopping trip, I would take one or two of my new companions to call on the Sonntags. Lizerli was always very glad to welcome us and her mother would bring us

Swedish gymnastics on the outside terrace in shocking "Annette Kellerman" bathing suits.

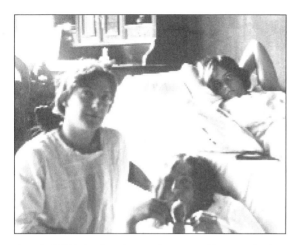

Jessmin (left) in her Dresden pension room with guests Crosby and Clegg.

"Annette Kellermans" were also worn for public presentations.

some of her delicious Viennese pastries. But these meetings were not very pleasant. The English or American girls did not conceal their disdain of any Germans who were not artists, and I had an uncomfortable time explaining to Frau Sonntag that they refused the cakes because they were experimenting with a *"Roh Kost"* diet.

My fellow students were a very mixed group, mostly composed of earnest music students, German, Swiss and Scandinavian, with a few Middle-Easterners, one American, and four English girls (of whom I was one). The youngest of these last, Elsa Findlay, and I found most of the others very stodgy, as did Crosby, the pretty, bohemian New Yorker who became very friendly with the Salzmanns and later married a close friend of theirs, the Polish Baron Bechtieff.

In any case, the Dohrns and the Salzmanns were amused by our giddiness, invited us sometimes to their homes, and even played practical jokes on us. Salzmann, on whom I confess I had a schoolgirl crush, was quite avuncular with me. He sympathized with my boredom in the Solfege classes and showed me a way to slink out a rear door into the theatre where I might wait out the end of the hour watching him experiment with his lighting.

In the spring of 1913, Lizerli let me know that her mother was not well -- also that Nick had been called home to Greece.

As soon as possible I went in to see her, knowing that she must be feeling lonely.

I was met at the door by their grim cleaning woman who said that the *"Gnädige Frau"* was in bed and that Lizerli was having treatment for a severe cold and could see no one.

It seemed to me that I could hear Lizerli crying, so I pushed my way in and ran to her room. I found her sitting in a steaming hot sitz bath, her face all blubbery with tears. Selma was mopping her forehead and a strange woman was forcing a drink on her which Lizerli tried to push away — sobbing that it was too bitter. I was indignant and cried out, "What is the matter? Whatever are you doing to her?"

Selma, when she saw that Lizerli couldn't talk and that I looked determined to stay, pulled me out of the room and whispered, "You shouldn't be here, Jessminchen.

We are only doing what is necessary and Lizerli wants us to help her. You see, she has missed her period and what with Nick gone and her mother bedridden...." I stared, not understanding until Selma added, "Oh, don't you see? She may have started a baby and we've got to stop it."

I went away, deeply shocked and grieved. Although the scare turned out to be a false alarm, it was little relief to me. I think I really grew up at that moment. I had never realized the full implication of Nick and Lizerli's relationship. Relations between the members of our music group had always been innocent and comradely. I felt embarrassed to have been so naive and immature.

In the early summer of 1913, I went to England at my brother's request to meet his fiancée and her family. While I was away Frau Sonntag died of a heart attack.

When I next saw Lizerli she was trying to keep the pension running, although, during the vacation months, few students stayed. Her brother, who had inherited their father's delicatessen, kept an eye on things and looked after the accounts.

Herr Salzmann invited me to join a pantomime class he was starting for five or six people (including Michio Ito, to be my future partner,) who had registered for a so-called "Theater Course" which had never been finally organized. Of course, I was thrilled to do so, and in this way got to know him and Jeanne much better.

Japanese dancer Michio Ito.

That winter in Hellerau was very busy. We were preparing a production of Gluck's *Orphée* (Orpheus) using Appia's mise-en-scene of stairs, platforms and columns, and Salzmann's lighting. This was quite extraordinary, for the steps, pillars, walls, and even the ceilings were equipped with hundreds of electric bulbs behind muslin, which could be turned on or off in sections and glowed with a diffused light.

We students rehearsed hard and long. Even the workmen memorized the musical score and could be trusted to manage the lighting to accompany any crescendo in the action, or pinpoint an outstanding figure.

The performance was a huge success. Our last evening was like being transported into a fairy tale, for the Dohrn brothers ordered huge hampers of flowers, which were tossed down on us from the wings.

And then things came to an end and most of us went to Geneva to take part in a pageant Dalcroze was directing.

◆ ◆ ◆

Those innovative experiments going on at Hellerau were described by the acerbic British playwright, George Bernard Shaw in witty correspondence with his special actress Mrs. Patrick Campbell.

Dushka
◆

"The Dalcroze school at Hellerau, which is what we came to see, is very interesting. The theater has walls and roof of white linen with the lights behind the linen... The children can beat four in a bar with one hand and three in a bar with the other simultaneously, and they can change instantly in marching from four and three and six (and such rhythms as you and I can manage) to five and seven. Tots as high as your a - - ...take a stick and conduct like Nikisch, only better. There is no discipline, absolutely no nervousness, though there are seven hundred strangers looking on.

You should have come. We should have brought Pinero [Sir Arthur W. Pinero, playwright] and then we'd have got you on the council of that silly Academy of Dramatic Art and revolutionized artistic education in England.

British playwright
George Bernard Shaw.

"The evening finished up with one of the best performances of Gluck's *Orphée*... the production most remarkable; it only needed a few rehearsals by Barker [Harley Granville-Barker, actor-director] and myself to be perfect!

"This afternoon we went again and saw the lighting installation, acres of white linen and the multitude of lights behind and above it.

"Also we saw two examinations of grown up pupils. Both examinees confronted the examiners, a row of elderly gentlemen... in a bathing singlet without an inch of sleeve or leg drapery. Each had to take a class of other victims in singlets, and to play rhythms for them on the piano and make them march to it. Then they had to pick up impossible themes written on a blackboard, and harmonize them on the piano straight off. They had to improvise variations on them, to modulate into all keys on demand of the examiners, then to listen to Dalcroze modulating wildly and name the keys he had come into. Finally they had to conduct a choir, first with a stick in the ordinary way, and then with poetic movements of the whole body. This last was extraordinarily effective... Yet I am told that this was a wretched display of second raters and that we must go again when the examinations are over and see Dalcroze give a lesson.

"They have twenty movements and when they have learnt them, the first variation they are asked for is to give them in canon; that is, when the right hand has finished Number One, left hand begins it and accompanies Number Two, etc. All these games, instead of driving them mad, seemed to come quite easily to them. I shall try and learn some of them. Then I will buy you a singlet and teach them to you. Then we will give public demonstrations of the new art............ GBS"

◆◆◆

Jessmin
◆

Summer of 1914 — I took what I thought would be a quick trip back to England, but no sooner there than the war broke out. My brother went off to join his regiment and I never saw him again. It was not until 1923 that I was finally able to go to Ypres and locate his grave in the War Cemetery there.

I also never saw Lizerli again. There were no answers to my many letters. Did she ever join Nick in Greece? Did her brother apprentice her to a couturier in Vienna as he had wished? I've never known.

There was no longer any question of returning to Dresden. M. Jaques had been forced out of Germany when he, with many other well-known artists, signed a manifesto against the German bombing of Reims Cathedral. He had returned to Geneva and I joined him there to complete my Dalcroze diploma and do some teaching at the Lausanne Conservatory of Music.

I missed the Salzmanns who had returned to Georgia, in Russia, and we heard nothing more about them. In fact, everyone feared that they might have perished there during the Revolution.

Dalcroze Institute Pageant
(in more typical Greek-style costumes.)

Outdoor rehearsals for a pageant.

Dalcroze dancers.

(At right and below)
Dalcroze students leaping.
That's Jessmin leading!

Dalcroze "al fresco" with some of his students.

Children's eurhythmics.

"M. Dalcroze " with members of Jessmin's children's class ("next to Stravinsky's house.")

...and in his later years.

(Below) One of Jessmin's few remaining photos. On the back she wrote: *"Summer, 1914 Geneva Centenary, Group of Dalcroze pupils improvising dance."*

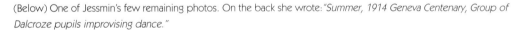

(Above) 1914 Passport.

(Below) Time out in Geneva.

I settled into life in neutral Switzerland, and shared an apartment with another Dalcroze pupil, the vivacious and popular Annette Ponce. Later she married Jean Herter, and later still became your Godmother. Our little apartment was a gathering place for crowds of students and artists.

Annette was so pretty that when we needed extra funds she would go off and work as a photographer's model. She was particularly successful posing for romantic colored photographs which were made into the popular postcards of the period. I still have one of them.

Two years later I was left on my own when Annette went to Paris.

The Dalcroze "gang" in Geneva, 1916, including Annette (back row third from left), Jessmin (middle fourth from left), Micho Ito (bottom fourth from left), etc.

Jessmin in Geneva....

....serving tea in the apartment she shared with Annette.

Annette the model.

Jessmin the "cut-up."

The roomates clowning around with some of their many artist friends. (Jessmin on right knee, Annette on left.)

(Above) One of the postcard modelling jobs resorted to when Annette and Jessmin needed funds. Annette inscribes it "**Gagne-pain in extremis**" (Bread-earning in desperation.)

(Above) Even before arriving at Hellerau to join Dalcroze, Alexandre de Salzmann had had his work published in Europe. In 1909 this cartoon appeared in the German magazine *Jugend* (Youth) entitled "*Liebhaber Theater*" (Connoisseur's Theater), it was captioned [approximate translation]: **"If we don't soon arrange another charity affair, I really don't know how I will pay my dressmaker."**

CHAPTER 2

THE "VIEUX COLOMBIER," GURDJIEFF LEAVES RUSSIA

1916, Dear, dear Annette.

Jessmin
♦

I am so happy to have your letter and that you are going to come. Hurrah! But it's sure isn't it? I have so much to tell you and to ask you.

First, though, I'm going to scold you. I don't care a bit about those stupid two hundred francs. I had thought to ask you to keep them for me until September so I could be sure of having something to move again, and other than that I didn't think about them. This time it's you who are not being simple "*vieux tortue*!" Don't think of it any more. Later, if you insist on that pride that I like so much...

It's true that I've had terrible months since the beginning of the year. For the first time I realized seriously how I am in myself.

I have been tired though I've done nothing. I detest the future because I must earn my living and economize, and I've been very alone and discouraged. I still am, but I'm not going to write you all that. I'm trying to pull myself together and stop pitying myself, and I know that you need to read more positive things. When you come I will be so happy to confide in you.

I wanted to write you in any case since there is the slightest little chance that I may come to Paris for the holidays.

It's like this. Since my guardians wrote me at Easter from England **that we have lost nearly all our money,** I have had to decide if I want to become a professor or an actress. It was a terrible struggle. I like *La Rhythmique*, but I feel fatigued and without the will to work on all the things I need to earn my diploma... and after that to begin again to become more of an "artiste." But where to go to work in Theater during the war, and above all to find the idealistic, impossible expression that I wish, all without a penny, and without too much talent.

So it is decided that I am going to Lausanne next year again to teach at the Conservatory of Music and to give private lessons and "*des Cours de Plastique*," etc. enough lessons to earn the money to pay for my pension and my studies, but still have the time to work seriously for the diploma. But I am disgusting... I like giving lessons, if it weren't for this damn money business. But I am so fed up, and tired of little towns and little people. So in the end it is up to me to become bigger myself and not to lose my little grain of "*loofokerie*". [?] I'm really very ungrateful.

But after all was arranged, I was sad. Then Jeanne de Lanux arrived from Paris. You remember her. She was once at Hellerau with her sister. She is a very nice girl, a painter, and full of good sense and gaiety. She did me good. I was able to speak to her as she isn't part of all this milieu and she understands. She so wanted that I should go to Paris next year where they need a professor above all to give courses for Jacques Copeau (I attach an article about him). But I can't change things now.

Copeau came here with one of his actresses and they gave two plays at the "*Comédie.*" It was original and good, a bit poor and badly finished, but the two of them play marvelously and I was very attracted to them.

Jeanne tried to interest Copeau in me. He was very nice and came to visit me. It was like a breath of fresh air, this change of conversation. As a man he is inferior to what he is as an artist, a bit familiar, but not a "*roué.*" And Suzanne Bing, (who was married to Edgar Varèse), is a charming little personality, sweet, humble, modest—but can she act!!!

So Copeau said that he hadn't a "*sou*" at present, or pupils, or collaborators and that he was looking for a job for the summer. If he didn't find one, then I should go and work with him and Suzanne Bing and her children. We would exchange all that we could, and at the end he would tell me if I should continue. And when he has his school reestablished, perhaps he would take me to teach Gymnastics, etc. But they were all dreams and I don't believe that I'll go. I'm waiting for his letter. In early July I will know if I will come to Paris, or if I'll have all the summer vacation to myself. If so I may go to the mountains with the little Brookes and in August be here for the summer course since several nice people are coming, Paulet Thévenaz, etc..

But in any case I must arrange to see you.

I've seen nobody of your old friends, but one evening when I was with Jeanne de Lanux, Jean Binet, Copeau and Suzanne Bing, I spoke with Carmen d'Assilve about you. She gave me a mixed impression. I think she, also, has had a very hard year, she was thinner, more made-up, more ordinary and a bit false. She was with a horrible little man though she is in the midst of a flirtation with Copeau. She treated me like a child, but she spoke nicely of you, and she admires your courage, as we all do.

I do so want to see you. Try to rest and come soon to Genève.

Love J.

◆ ◆ ◆

Dushka
♦

Jacques Copeau (1878-1949), had great influence on the theater worldwide, and in France in particular. In fact Albert Camus is quoted as saying: "In the history of French theater, there are two periods: before Copeau and after Copeau."

His innovative methods of working with the group of actors and technicians that he gathered together under the name of the "Vieux Colombier" in 1913 brought French theater into the modern age and launched the careers of many luminaries of stage and screen like Charles Dullin, (1885-1949) and Louis Jouvet (1887-1951). Many of the "modern" trends in stage technique, set-design, directing, etc. owe much to him.

In the late 1980's Gallimard Press published a series tracing the history of French theater directors in four volumes, two of which are devoted to Copeau. One of the authors, Norman Paul, a theater professor at New York's City College, asked Mother's cooperation. He sent her pertinent questions about Copeau's goals, methods and successes and she roughed up answers which are presented here. But in the final publications one also finds further references to "Mlle. Jessmin."

For example I notice Copeau's diary entry in 1916 when he visited the Dalcroze

School in Geneva:

"Conversation with Jessmin, young Irish [sic] girl who would like to come with me. Beautiful grey eyes, a charming, fine mouth, (twenty-two years old they tell me), but a large nose which seems out of character in this face and makes it unusual but not unattractive. She pleases me. Immediately I say: 'Come... I will make you into a clown...'"

Copeau had already gone to Switzerland in 1915 and met Jaques-Dalcroze and Adolphe Appia at the suggestion of Gordon Craig, the English theater designer (father of Isadora Duncan's first child). He was evidently most impressed as he indicates in this letter:

"Dalcroze has unquestionably and to a very high degree, the gift of humanity, love and understanding of human beings and a faculty for communicating with them... No dogmatism... Nothing fixed, crystallized, always experience and discovery. He requires his pupils to instruct themselves. He questions them, consults them. As a result there is an ease, a humanity, a lack of affectation and stupid *amour propre*, and in the entire group a joy which strikes one from the very beginning. He knows how to live with them.

"The link which exists between my actors and me, that indefinable something 'real,' on which I have begun to build, I find between Dalcroze and his pupils. And that is what is important above all. To awaken a 'collection' of people to a new life.

Dancer Isadora Duncan with Gordon Craig in Berlin, 1904.

"I am now certain of the point of contact and agreement between the methods of Dalcroze and what I am 'meditating on,' the virtue of a general *rythmique* education as a base for the professional training of actors."

When the Vieux Colombier was finally reformed and started work together in Paris, Copeau's favorite actress, Suzanne Bing wrote in her diary:

"August 1917. Since several days rehearsals have been suspended due to the *patron's* [boss's] travels and replaced by lessons with Jessmin from three to five-thirty—body technique, some eurythmics, beginnings of solfege, games, pantomime, dance.

"I can never say too much about Jessmin's lessons, but they are too long. The *patron* had told her to work with the actors: vanquish their pride, their fear of ridicule, their preconceived idea that this had nothing to do with the theater. Jessmin even had to deal with stubborness and impertinence. But the majority already realize.

"The first exercises: 'Hear! Listen! Be blind!' Jessmin asked us to observe until Monday, especially the elderly, so each can mime a different old person."

◆ ◆ ◆

Norman Paul, City College, N.Y.　　　　　　　　　　　　　　　　　　**Jessmin**

Dear Mr. Paul,　　　　　　　　　　　　　　　　　　　　　　　　　　◆

Actress Suzanne Bing...   ...and her husband composer Edgar Varese with their daughter.

In answer to your inquiries about my associations with the Vieux Colombier

Early in 1916, Jacques Copeau and Suzanne Bing visited Geneva. They attended some parties with friends of mine who were much addicted to charades. Our "goings-on" amused and interested Copeau and he came to watch us also in Eurythmic classes. He spoke to us of his wish to form again his theatrical company, La Compagnie du Vieux Colombier, disbanded at the outbreak of war, and to add "new blood". In order to revitalize his original group's acting, and to train younger actors in a freer way, he had come to the conclusion that lessons in certain aspects of the Dalcroze teaching, gymnastics, rhythm, dancing, and pantomime would be required. And he asked me to go to Paris during that summer to be in touch with all that he was preparing (including a possible season in America) and to hold myself in readiness to work with his people as soon as enough of them had reassembled.

I joined the company not only as instructor but as a trainee in the special line which it was Copeau's great wish at that time to develop. He believed that experience in improvisation was essential and he had a great respect for the "*lazzi*" traditions of, for example, the Fratellini clowns, and, further back, the Commedia del Arte players. He used to say that despite all the modern psychology and complication of motives put into words in present-day plays, all the essential types and plots existed in the "cameras" used by the old Italian travelling troupes.

When the war had separated them all, Copeau had asked his "*anciens*" (particularly Suzanne Bing, Louis Jouvet, Romain Bouquet, Charles Dullin, Jane Lory, and Valentine Tessier) to be creating their own "*personnages*," these to have definite characteristics, habitual ways of moving and reacting, etc. And he was preparing situations to be given them as themes for improvisation

For example, my own "*personnage*" was to be "*L'Espirit du Vieux Colombier*" [The Spirit of the Vieux Colombier] whom he saw as a mime, a silk-overalled, neutral, masked figure providing a link between the actors and the spectators at all times- a mixture of sprite, buffoon, Chinese Theater property-man, and so forth; who might intervene in the action on the stage, or just sit on the edge of the proscenium after opening the curtains and lead audience reaction.

Much of Copeau's correspondence with his leading associates during the first three years of the war was on this theme. Certainly Copeau had hoped, in arranging the Company's trip to the USA, not only to succeed in winning goodwill for France but also to have time with his pupils to work along these lines.

As things turned out, this never really became possible. I believe that the *"Amis du Vieux Colombier"* organization had intended to have a house ready for us in New York where we could all live together and work in an experimental way. But on arriving we were placed in Broadway hotels from whence we quickly scattered all over the city. Gaston Gallimard, Jouvet, Dullin, Valentine Tessier and I, together with two Swiss scenic and costume designers whose names I cannot at the moment recall, formed the largest group living in any one place who could easily come together.

◆◆◆

And to this paragraph as printed in their book, *Les Registres du Vieux Colombier*, the authors added: "... and by this time Jessmin had become Jouvet's *'amie'* [lover]."

Dushka
◆

Hidden away in Mother's old papers I found a fading black and white postcard, of the famous French film star. On the back she had written:

LOUIS JOUVET
Born at Crozon, Finistere (December 24, 1887)
Lived in the Ardennes
Studied Pharmacie and with Leloir
Theater d'Action d'Art with Noel
*   then at Chatelet-Odeon with*
*   Rouche Theatre des Arts*
Joined Copeau 1913
Le Limon, 1912
Married Copeau's "mother's helper" Danish Elsa Collin
Mobilized 1914, Out Spring 1917
To USA Summer '17 etc.
Died Aug. 16, 1951 of a stroke
Buried in Montmartre cemetery   "'64..."

[Presumably re-interred belatedly in a cemetery dedicated to France's honored dead?!]

* * * * *

Mother's postcard of Jouvet

Otto Hermann Kahn (1867-1934), the son of a comfortably upper-middle class family from Mannheim, Germany, was trained as a banker, and moved to New York in 1893. He became a partner in the prominent financial firm Kuhn, Loeb & Co., but having been, himself, an amateur musician and playwright, he devoted much of his life and fortune to the arts, and to raising levels of culture internationally.

In 1908, as chairman of the Board of Directors of the Metropolitan Opera, he was responsible for bringing to America conductor Arturo Toscanini and director

Giulio Gatti-Casazza, thus transforming the Met into one of the world's greatest opera companies. He sponsored the US tours of Diaghilev's "Ballet Russe" with Nijinsky, Stanislavsky's "Moscow Art Theater," Gémier's "Theatre de l'Odeon," "The Abbey Players" from Dublin, "The Kabuki" from Japan, "The Habima Players" of Tel Aviv, and artists like Pavlova, Chaliapine, Isadora Duncan and Paul Robeson. In literature he helped support, among others, Margaret Anderson, whose *Little Review* published the first works of Yeats, Ezra Pound, T.S. Eliot, and especially James Joyce, which daring effort (publishing *Ulysses*) resulted in jail sentences for Margaret and her partner Jane Heap, both of whom, coincidentally, later embraced the Gurdjieff Teaching.

Publishers of the *Little Review*:
(Above) Jane Heap ....and Margaret Anderson.

Author of the controversial *Ulysses:*
James Joyce.

In 1917, with the U.S. having entered World War I fighting side-by-side with the French, there was a general movement in America to promote closer relations with France and a better appreciation of French culture. Otto Kahn spearheaded a group called *"Amis du Vieux Colombier,"* [Friends of the Vieux Colombier], who invited Copeau to bring his company to New York for two theatrical seasons, 1918-1919.

When its first season opened at the Garrick Theater on Thirty-Fifth Street, the Vieux Colombier attracted a prestigious audience that included French nobility, ambassadors and diplomats, and the high society of New York.

First on the program (which noted that the choreography was under the direction of Miss Jessmin Howarth) was *L'Impromptu du Vieux Colombier* by Jacques Copeau. It opened with Suzanne Bing greeting the audience. Then the entire cast and the director Robert Casa (Casadesus), in various costumes and work clothes, were seen preparing for the performance. At this point "Jessmin comes on stage dancing..." and Copeau addresses her:

"Ah! There you are, you little dancer, sprite, house spirit, quicker and purer than we, who shames us when you appear in our form, imperfect, with lifeless graceless gestures. Go! Flee while this thin curtain still separates us from illusion. From top to bottom of the hall, to all those presenting the show, inspire rhythm. Go! My flame, my spirit, my joy!" (Jessmin exits dancing as the music fades.) *"Curtain."*

The evening proceeded with Molière's *Les Fourberies de Scapin* and concluded with *Le Couronnement de Molière*, a procession of characters richly costumed representing the history of theater from ancient times, Aristophanes to Shakespeare, Cor-

Louis Jouvet in various roles.

neille, etc., all paying homage to Molière (a bust of whom was seen on a platform center stage). The music stopped. Jessmin, still as the "Spirit of the Vieux Colombier," danced. The dance ended in the middle of the proscenium, Jessmin stretched her hands to the courtyard and garden where Copeau's two little daughters, Maïène and Edi appeared. Each held in her hand a wicker cage containing a dove which they carried up onto the platform and offered to Molière.

The opening night press was glowing: "Greetings And Long Life To The New Theater Of The Vieux Colombier!" "Finally A Real French Theater For America!" "Copeau's Debut, An Artistic Triumph!" "Public Welcoming And Enthusiastic!" etc.

◆ ◆ ◆

Jessmin
◆

Copeau found that the calls upon his time in order to attend social gatherings for publicity, fund raising, propaganda for the Allied war effort, etc. were very great.

To the disappointment of all of us also, the number of spectators who could understand French well enough to follow the plays was really too small to warrant the running of any one play for longer than two or three weeks. Jouvet was still redesigning the stage of the Old Garrick theater. It had to be, so to speak, rebuilt for each new play. (As a rule, work on the stage settings went on without break from Saturday eleven p.m. until Monday eight p.m.). Also, the former members of the Vieux Colombier, although they had played some parts before, had been separated for some time, were feeling the results of front-line war experiences, and were having to help integrate the new members of the company. So every moment possible was needed for rehearsal and plans for other experimental work had to be postponed.

To begin with I was entrusted with putting on a short introduction to the Theater's first performances, a kind of stylized "walk on" of all the members of the company...called *Hommage à Molière*, and performed to beautiful music provided by the group of French players of ancient instruments under Henri Casadesus. During the first season I arranged any dance sequences or crowd scenes needed and played miming roles added by Copeau to plays like *Les Caprices de Marianne* (Alfred de Musset), *Le Mariage de Figaro* (Beaumarchais), and *L'Amour Médecin* (Molière).

In the early summer of 1918, Otto Kahn lent Copeau a large house, Cedar Court, near Convent, New Jersey. This huge, Italian Renaissance-style mansion was usually run by a staff of about twenty servants, but for our arrival had evidently been stripped of practically all its staff and furnishings!

We could now try to make a few experiments and I must say that Copeau gave me every help and encouragement. I gave the men, women, and children a class in, I suppose I should call it, "gymnastics" every day before breakfast, and we managed to get in a few sessions of improvisation, pantomime and dance instruction. Copeau was not able to be with us all the time, but Suzanne Bing and Dullin were particularly keen, and, in fact, Dullin used a lot of the material we sketched out there, later in Paris in his courses at the Gémier school which I also supervised on occasion.

However, again, there was a killing winter program to prepare. Stage- and costume-designing had to be speeded up. The company's schedule called for the mise-en-scene and rehearsal of one act a day during the summer break.

Copeau's New York backers had persuaded him that he must appear in as many plays as possible, acting rather than just directing. I always thought of him as more of a dramatic critic than a performer or innovator.

Later, when I watched Firmin Gémier work, it seemed to me that Copeau needed material set before him which he then cut into a new shape, whereas Gémier knew at once what he wished and could ask for it before anything had been shaped, but did not arrive at anything very new.

Copeau's method, then, was to have the play read on the stage, each actor sketching out, in tone and movement, his own conception of the part, while Copeau would keep saying: "Go ahead. Do something. Do anything!" At a certain moment, (sometimes it took days before this moment came), Copeau would withdraw. He would return with a detailed, written mise-en-scene, complete down to the number of steps to be taken in any direction, in which he would have developed, reinforced and much improved each actor's idea of his part and pulled them all together into a possible dramatic whole.

When he himself had to carry the principal role, the mise-en-scene was apt to suffer. Although gifted, he was after all a beginner in acting. I think it was at this stage that Copeau probably found his oldest people unwilling to adapt, and while appreciating the fact that they were the Vieux Colombier and his loyal supporters, he began to realize that his new ideas on acting and modern theater would have to be worked out with younger people.

Copeau was brilliantly intelligent and could extract diamonds from what appeared dross. His sense of theater was innate, but as yet untrained. He had wonderful flashes, but it was not to be expected of him that he should have the day-to-day "*métier*" that the experienced actors had gradually acquired, and so he was erratic.

There was disaffection in the company at the end of that summer in 1918, but certainly not caused by Copeau's being a hard taskmaster.

I have never, before or since, seen people who would work as long, as intensively and as willingly as Jouvet, Suzanne Bing and Dullin, and they set the tone for the younger members of the company.

But life in America was unsettling. We have to remember that some of the men were just released from the trenches after terrible times. Everyone was homesick, as

Copeau's Vieux Colombier rehearsing *Twelth Night* outside Otto Kahn's house in Convent, N. J. (Jessmin center right)

only the French can be. We had lived that summer in New Jersey, voluntarily cut off from any other activities and recreation. No one possessed a car. Otto Kahn had left one couple to do the cooking, etc. so we were very poorly fed. We received $5 a week for personal expenses, and we finished up with four cases of typhoid!

In short, circumstances were against Copeau's original plan being realized.

It was more or less understood at the beginning of the second season (1918-1919) that Otto Kahn would not continue to finance the theater after spring 1919. So it would be necessary to present first the plays in which the largest casts appeared, and the company would then gradually disband. Charles Dullin had married and was among those whose principal roles fell among the first plays given in the season, and he was anxious, after the Armistice, to be back in France to live his own life and for his own ideal. He and Jouvet had, in a way, found themselves. Although I know they suffered when the original plans for the continuation of the Vieux Colombier had to be changed, and when their strong tie to Copeau as their *"cher patron"* was somewhat weakened, the fact of their becoming less dominated by Copeau enabled them to do a very great deal for the theater in France later.

In this way, they were fulfilling much of what Copeau had wished, and perhaps forseen.......

Sincerely,   Jessmin Howarth

◆◆◆

And in later years another luminary of the French theater, Jean-Louis Barrault, would concur:

Dushka

◆

"All our youth was formed, strengthened and protected by three men: Jacques Copeau, Charles Dullin and Louis Jouvet. Each of these men brought his own particular teaching that corresponded to his own nature. Copeau taught us the rules, Dullin injected us with the passion, Jouvet constantly tested its resistance."

* * * * *

Meanwhile in far away Tiflis, Russian Georgia, Mother's friends and colleagues from the Dalcroze Institute, Alexandre de Salzmann and his young wife Jeanne now with a little daughter Nathalie ("Boussik") had met someone called George Ivanovich Gurdjieff. They had joined forces with him a couple of years earlier in his search for a place to establish his own "Institute of Harmonious Development" where he and some followers could live and study together.

The group was already being talked about. On Dec. 14, 1919, a Georgian journal, *The Devils's Whip*, ran a cartoon by de Salzmann showing the difficult conditions Gurdjieff and his followers were undergoing. [See opposite.]

Years later, Mother would laugh at her own Victorian fastidiousness in general, but especially the kind of professional disdain she exhibited in 1922 when Gurdjieff and the others finally arrived in Paris. For in fact, by 1919, his followers were already a distiguished group that included:

Thomas Alexandrovich de Hartmann (1885-1956), an acclaimed composer and protégé of Czar Nicholas. He had studied music with Arensky and Taniev, piano technique with Esipova-Leschitsky, and conducting with Wagnerian conductor Felix Mottl. An important early success for him was *The Scarlet (or "Pink") Flower*, a ballet featuring Nijinsky, Pavlova, Fokine and Karsavina. While in Munich in 1910 he collaborated with noted artists of the period, writing articles for the *Blau Reiter* and composing music for *The Yellow Sound*, a revolutionary multi-media experiment by Kandinsky, which was successfully revived in New York by Gunther Schuller a half-century later!

His wife **Olga Arkadievna (de Shumacher** or **Shoumatoff) de Hartmann** (1885-1979) was a singer with blue-blood lineage. She later proved a great aid to Gurdjieff as a devoted secretary, especially as her upbringing with governesses made her one of the few in his entourage who understood any European languages.

Pyotr Demianovich, "P. D." Ouspensky [or Uspenskii] (1878-1947) was a philosopher/writer already well known outside of Russia for his scholarly treatise *Tertium Organum* that had been translated and published by Paul Bragdon and for studies of the Fourth Dimension, the Tarot, etc. The detailed personal record of Gurdjieff's teaching that he had started keeping in Moscow, published posthumously as *In Search of the Miraculous, Fragments of an Unknown Teaching* proved invaluable to later generations of pupils of Gurdjieff's system.

Sophie Grigorievna Ouspensky (? - 1961) known as Mme. Ouspensky (although her relationship with Mr. Ouspensky seemed to many very distant) had had two earlier marriages, one of which resulted in a daughter, **Lenushka (Elena Gorb Savitsky)** who travelled with her small son,**"Lonia." (Leonide)**

Olga Ivanovna Milanova Hinzenberg, later famous as **Olgivanna Lloyd Wright** (1898-1985) was the ninth child of a Supreme Court Justice, and an army general. Her <u>mother</u> had been a general and her <u>grandmother</u> the Commander-in-Chief of the Montenegran army during fierce fighting with the Turks!) She had a small daughter **Svetlana**, (probably Gurdjieff's daughter.)

Dr. Leonid Robertovich Stjernvall had left successful practices in St. Petersburg and in Finland, and was accompanied by his wife **Elizabeta Grigorievna** and her little boy **Nikolai Leonidovich**, who in later life was recognized by Gurdjieff as his son (and wrote a book *"Daddy Gurdjieff"* under the pen-name "Nicholas de Val.")

Julia (Yussovna) Osipovna, Gurdjieff's "wife" but always called **"Mme. Ostrovsky"** or **Ostrowska** or **Ostrovska**. She was aristocratic, Polish and twenty-three years his junior. No one seems sure where, how, or if they were married, but her cruel death from cancer in 1927 in spite of all Gurdjieff's heroic attempts to cure her was a terrible blow to him.

Others included the Armenian **Elizabeta "Lily" Galumian**, or **Galumnian**, who married a diplomat, **Chaverdian**, a noted St. Petersburg lawyer **Alexei Yakovlevich Rachmilievitch,** an artist **Adele Kafian** among others and, of course, the **de Salzmanns.**

* * * * *

De Salzmann's 1919 cartoon in *The Devil's Whip*. (Left to right) Thomas de Hartmann, G.I. Gurdjieff, an unidentified couple, Dr Leonid Stjernvall, and seated far right Alexandre de Salzmann, the artist himself at work.

The caption in Georgian read: "**A voice from the window**: '*Somehow he found space for his work.'*"

(Above)

In Tiflis Alexandre de Salzmann had been recruited to design a cover, in Russian, for the prospectus of Gurdjieff's Institute. In it he portrays Gurdjieff surrounded by all sorts of allegorical creatures and symbols including the enneagram, but also musical instruments, carpentery tools, a cooking pot, a sewing machine, an iron, a microscope, a telescope, a scale, a T-square, a saw, an axe, a painter's palette, books, etc.

Then, it is interesting to note, as plans for the Institute changed and the group moved West, de Salzmann had to do a new version of the prospectus. This cover of this one (Above) shows nearly all of the same items but it is in English and there are now a few slight differences in the art-work. The second version turns the standing globe on the right to show more of Europe than Asia and the Far East. The phrase "Western Section" originally written in Russian at the bottom is omitted, and the word "Harmonious" would have been better translated from Russian as "Harmonic."

(Above) A third version of the de Salzmann cover for a Gurdjieff Institute prospectus. This time it is in French. The translation is roughly "To Know - To Understand - To Be" and "The Science [sic] of the Harmonic Development of Man Method G. I. Gurdjieff European Section."

TIFLIS STATE OPERA THEATRE

On Sunday, 22 June 1919

PROGRAM

2nd Evening of the School of
Jeanne Matignon-Salzman

Part I.
The Method of **Jaques-Dalcroze**:

Children. Rhythmical exercises.

Accelerando & Rallentando.

Realization of Rhythms, dividing a rhythm.

Circle of speed.

Independency of limbs.

Double rhythm.

Nuances (pathetic accent).

Solfege, improvisation.

Rhythmical group exercises:

    1) Pulse/accent.

    2) Moment musical

    3) Syncopation

    4) Accelerando

    5) Sudden liberation and effort.

Part II.
The System of **G. I. Gurdzhiev.**

    1) Exercises of plastic gymnastics,
       Nos. 3, 9, 12, 15, 17, 21, 23.

    2) Exercises for ancient sacred dances,
       Nos. 23, 24, 25.

    3) Stop

    4) Fragment of a Round Dance from Act
       3 of *The Struggle of the Magicians* by
       G.I. Gurdzhiev.

    5) Fragment of the mystery *Exiles* by the
       same author.

ГОСУДАРСТВЕННЫЙ ТЕАТРЪ

Въ Воскресенье, 22-го Іюня 1919 г.

ПРОГРАММА
2-ой ВЕЧЕРЪ ШКОЛЫ
Жанны Матиньонъ-Зальцманъ.

Отдѣленіе I.

Методъ **Жака Далькроза.**

Дѣти. Ритмическія упражненія.

Ускореніе и замедленіе,

Реализація ритмовъ: Дѣленіе ритма,

Кругъ быстроты,

Независимость членовъ тѣла,

Двойной ритмъ,

Нюансы (патетическій акцентъ),

Сольфеджіо. Импровизація,

Групповыя ритмическія упражненія:

    1) На удареніе.

    2) Momentmusical.

    3) Синкопы.

    4) На ускореніе.

    5) На внезапное освобожденіе и напряженіе.

Отдѣленіе II.

Система Г. И. Гюрджіева.

    1) Упражненія пластической гимнастики
       №№ 3, 9, 12, 15, 17, 21, 23.

    2) Упражненія къ древнимъ священнымъ танцамъ
       №№ 23, 24, 25.

    3) Стопъ

    4) Отрывокъ хоровода изъ 3-го акта балета
       „Борьба маговъ" Г. И. Гюрджіева.

    5) Отрывокъ мистеріи „Изгнаніе", его-же.

(Above right) The 1919 program of a public performance in Tiflis, Russian Georgia of Jeanne de Salzmann's Dalcroze pupils sharing ["on the second evening"] the stage with Gurdjieff's Movement exercises and excerpts from his ballet *The Struggle of the Magicians.*

(Above left) Translation of the Russian text.

Travelling out of Russia

(Above) Gurdjieff (right) with Dr. Stjernval (center).

(Right) Gurdjieff's Armenian Passport issued in Batum, 1920. (This time his age was shown as 43!)

(Below) Gurdjieff in a typical moment with various animal friends.

(Above) The young Mme. Ouspensky.

(Below and right) Snapshots of Mr. Ouspensky apparently taken during his travels to India and Ceylon (circa 1913).

Gurdjieff (right) and his followers travelling out of Russia by foot include Olga de Hartmann (left, in a big hat) next to her husband.

(Above left) Olga and Thomas de Hartmann when first married and (right) later in Munich.

Munich friends, 1911. (Left to right) Maria Marc, painter Franz Marc, Bernhard Koehler, Heinrich Campendonk and Thomas de Hartmann (Seated: Vaslav Kandinsky).

Vaslav Kandinsky in Munich, c.1912.

(Above) Thomas de Hartmann conducting his orchestra in Constantinople 1921. Special performances were given for ladies who were not permitted in a mixed audience.

(Right) The Armenian priest/composer Komitas Vartaped about whom de Hartmann wrote articles and gave lectures. With his singer wife, Olga, M. de Hartmann presented concerts of Komitas music in Georgia and Armenia helping to fund the travels of Gurdjieff and his followers.

(Right) Tiflis, 1919. Newly-born Nathalie de Salzmann (foreground) with admirers (left to right) Gurdjieff's wife Mme. Ostrovsky, Mr. Gurdjieff, and the proud mother, Jeanne de Salzmann.

(Right) Swiss-born Jeanne Allemand de Salzmann who accompanied her Georgian-born hus-band Alexandre to his homeland just before the outbreak of WW I.

Mme. Ouspensky's earliest photo album contained snapshots marked "Constantinople 1921" showing Gurdjieff and others in a railroad yard. The group appears to be on the point of departure. It has been said that they all travelled "in a freight train" but these pictures look like they are boarding actual boxcars!

On the opposite page (Bottom right), Gurdjieff stands next to Mme. Ouspensky, while (Bottom left) a young Jeanne de Salzmann can be seen at the back holding her small daughter Nathalie (Boussik).

Still moving westward: Photos found in Mme. Ouspensky's album marked by her at the bottom "**Berlin Juillet 1921**."
Apart from Mr. Gurdjieff the only person we can identify with certainty is Dr. Stjernvall (Above far left).

Das Institut
für
harmonische Entwicklung
des Menschen

Nach der Methode
von
G. J. Gürdschijew-Georgiadis

1921

Buchdruckerei Otto Hellwig, Berlin-Wilmersdorf, Uhlandstraße 61

(Above) 1921 Prospectus in
German for the Berlin branch of
Gurdjieff's Institute for the
Harmonious Development of Man.

In 1914, a Moscow newspaper announced a new ballet "written by a Hindu," entitled *The Struggle of the Magicians*. Ouspensky, who was at that time very interested in India and Theosophy, was sufficiently intrigued to agree to a meeting with the author — who turned out to be no Hindu, but the Caucasian Greek, G. I. Gurdjieff.

In light of later events this proved an historic meeting! P.D. Ouspensky later recalled:

"I understood from what he said that the important scenes represented the schools of a 'Black Magician' and a 'White Magician' with exercises by pupils of both schools and a struggle between the two schools... with sacred dances, Dervish dances, and various national Eastern dances, all this interwoven with a love story which itself would have an allegorical meaning.

"I was particularly interested when G. said that the same performers would have to act and dance in the 'White Magician' scene and in the 'Black Magician' scene, and that they themselves and their movements had to be attractive and beautiful for the first scene, and ugly and discordant in the second.

"'You understand that in this way they will see and study all sides of themselves; consequently the ballet will be of immense importance for self-study,' said G."

Though to our knowledge this ballet was never actually presented, in Russia or elsewhere, then or later, it was talked about for years.

When Gurdjieff brought his group to Tiflis in 1917, much of their work apparently centered around this ballet. Special dances and music were composed for it, but incompletely preserved, and elaborate stage props were constructed and then abandoned.

For a scene in which a magician casts a spell, Thomas de Hartmann remembers: "Mr. Gurdjieff himself made a doll of *papier maché* with little lights inside that shone through tiny holes. The brilliance of the lights was controlled by a rheostat also made by him. It was wonderfully effective... but then destroyed because: 'Only the effort is necessary and not the thing itself.'"

So there is little real evidence as to what Gurdjieff really intended to present to the public, if he intended to present anything.

A preliminary scenario exists (thirty-four pages translated by whom?) describing the settings and action of five acts built around a sketchy plot in which a jaded young aristocrat, Gafar, attempts to win over Zeinab, a beautiful girl who is the pupil of a "white magician," in the course of which he recruits the aid of a "black magician".

Alexandre de Salzmann did paintings of several scenes from the ballet. The most effective and interesting of these depicts the moment the hero first sees his heroine in the open-air market of a town still recognizable as Tiflis, now called Tbilisi. (See cover.) Three examples of this painting are owned by members of the de Salzmann family, two of them copies made by a pupil of de Salzmann's, Adele Kafian, which are indistinguishable from the original.

Exactly reproducing, in every detail and color, Gurdjieff's explicit written descriptions, de Salzmann portrays passers-by from many countries in their typical costumes. Thus, a century later, it is like seeing that part of the world and its extraordinary diversity of inhabitants through Gurdjieff's youthful eyes.

But some of the characters shown are also de Salzmann's witty portraits of his companions, members of Gurdjieff's original entourage, the artist himself, his wife

Jeanne, Mr. Gurdjieff, M. de Hartmann, Dr. Stjernvall, P.D. Ouspensky and Mme. Ouspensky, (and probably several others whom I can't identify, though Tom Daly tells me that Olga de Hartmann, still beautiful and electrically energetic in her late eighties, was proud to have been included! She said de Salzmann assured her the monkey climbing high up the building on the right side was supposed to represent her!)

* * * * *

Segments of Gurdjieff's original scenario of his ballet
"THE STRUGGLE OF THE MAGICIANS"

"Act 1 takes place in the market place of a large commercial town in the East (Tiflis/Tblisi?) where several streets and alleys meet. Surrounding it are shops and stalls with every kind of merchandise, silks, pottery, spices, open-fronted tailor and-shoemaker shops. There are two- and three-storied houses with flat roofs and many balconies, some hung with carpets and others with washing. At the left, there is a tea shop on a roof. The mountain can be seen behind the houses, winding streets, mosques

(Above) An early photo of Tiflis (now Tbilisi) as it was when Gurdjieff was a boy, the inspiration of his ballet setting. (On opposite page>) Alexandre de Salzmann's painting of the market-place as described in the opening scene of the ballet scenario *"The Struggle of the Magicians."* Here the hero, Gafar (standing center), first sees the beautiful Zeinab (right) kindly giving a poor beggar boy her scarf. At the upper left on a small balcony a musician, (a very recognizable portrait of **Thomas de Hartmann**, plays a flute while at his feet a dark-eyed, bearded man (**G.I. Gurdjieff**) reclines intently watching the scene below him.

minarets, gardens, palaces, Christian churches, Hindu temples, and pagodas.

"In the crowd moving about the alleys and the marketplace are types of almost every Asiatic people, dressed in their native costume: a Persian with dyed beard... A proud Afghan all in white... a Baluchistani wearing a white turban with a sharp peak, a short white sleeveless coat with a broad belt, from which stick several knives... and a half-naked Hindu Tamil, the front of his head shaved and the sign of Vishnu, a white and red fork painted on his forehead... a native of Khiva wearing a thickly padded coat and a huge black fur cap... a yellow-robed Buddhist monk, with shaven head and a prayerwheel in his hand... an Armenian wearing a black silver-belted 'chooka' and black Russian hunting cap... a Tibetan in a costume bordered with valuable fur similar to the Chinese... Bokharis, Arabs, Caucasians, etc.

"Merchants are hawking their wares.

"Beggars with their whining voices beg for alms.

"A vendor of shaved ices amuses the crowd with a witty song

"A street barber, [a self-portrait of **de Salzmann**], while shaving the head of a venerable old 'hadji' [**Dr. Stjernvall**] gives the news and gossip of the town to a tailor who is eating in the shop next door.

"On the right, a fakir with outstretched arms, his gaze fixed on one point, sits on an antelope skin. A humpbacked old woman stops near the fakir and with a devout air puts money into the coconut alms bowl near him.

"Across from the teashop, a snake charmer [**P.D. Ouspensky**] sits down, and is at once surrounded by a curious crowd.

"Donkeys pass, laden with baskets.

"Women walk along, some wearing the 'chuddar,' and others with unveiled faces [**Mme. Ouspensky**].

"Two men separate themselves from the crowd. Both are richly dressed. One of them, Gafar, is a handsome well-built wealthy Parsi about 30 or 35 years old, clean shaven with a small black moustache and close-cut hair. He wears a light yellow silk coat belted with a pale rose-colored scarf and blue trousers. Over them a brocade robe, with the cuffs of the shirt faced with embroidery in silver. He wears high boots of yellow leather, the legs embroidered in gold and precious stones, his head is covered with a turban of a figured Indian material, its predominating color is turquoise blue, on his fingers are rings with large emeralds and diamonds.

"The other man is his confidant, Rossoula, also richly but carelessly dressed. He is short, stout, subtle and cunning — the chief assistant of his master in all his love affairs and intrigues. He is always in a sly and merry mood. On his head he wears a red skullcap wrapped round with a yellowish turban, in one hand he fingers a short red rosary.

"Two women come into the square from a side street. One of them, an Indo-Persian type, is young, about 20 or 22, of middle height and very beautiful. This is Zeinab [**Jeanne de Salzmann**]. She is dressed in a white tunic, with a green scarf round her waist, her smoothly dressed hair parted in the middle is bound with a gold fillet. Thrown over her head she wears a *chuddar* but her face is uncovered.

"The other is her confidante Khaila short, plump, middle-aged and good-natured. She is dressed in a blue velvet coat under a violet *chuddar*. Her mouth is covered with a handkerchief.

"Zeinab holds a roll of parchment wrapped in a silk handkerchief. She passes

(Above) Detail of center right, Gafar listens as Rossoula tells him about Zeinab who is seen at the right binding up the beggar boy's arm with her scarf, while Khaila holds the unwrapped parchment. (Below left) Musicians on a balcony entertain lounging teahouse customers. (Below right) The gesticulating story-telling of the barber seems to discomfit his

(Above left) A seated snake charmer is regarded by a Tibetan, while an unveiled woman stands by as does a Beluchistani with white turban and knives in his belt. (Right) A woman gives alms to an Indian fakir while a monkey climbs the wall above.

across the square, graciously giving alms to the beggars whom she meets... [She] goes up to a beggar-woman near whom stands a half-clad boy about seven to nine years old, with an open sore on his naked arm. Zeinab wishes to bind up the boy's arm but she has nothing to wrap round it. She unwraps the silk handkerchief from the rolls of parchment and binds it around the sore.

"The painting shows Khaila holding the parchment.

Act 2 takes place in "The large auditorium of the White Magician."

There is an armchair with a high back like a throne at the top of which is the sign of the enneagram. Men and women are dressed in white tunics. "The girls have their hair dressed smoothly and bound with gold fillets; the men wear silver ones. All wear scarves around their waists; the girls' scarves are yellow, orange and red, while the men wear blue, green and light blue scarves." The magician's assistant wears "the symbol of the heptagram" (a seven-pointed star in a circle) while "the White Magician wears the symbol of the enneagram, worked in precious stones."

All gather around and the magician directs a telescope toward the sky. "The chief idea of his exposition is that what is above is similar to what is below, and what is below is similar to what is above. Every cosmos is a unit. The laws which govern is below is similar to what is above. Every cosmos is a unit. The laws that govern the Megalocosmos also rule the Macrocosmos, the Aiocosmos, the Deuterocosmos, the Mesocosmos, the Tritocosmos, and others down to the Microcosmos. Having exactly studied one cosmos you will know all the others. The nearest cosmos of all for our study is the Tritocosmos, that is Man. And for each one of us the nearest man of all is himself. Knowing yourself completely you will know all, even God, for you are created in His likeness.

The beggar-woman from the market scene in Act 1 brings her boy in and the Magician cures him with a mystical ceremony.

Then "at a sign from the Magician, they [the pupils] execute various movements resembling dances. The Magician's assistant walks up and down making corrections.

"These 'sacred' dances have always been considered, both in ancient times and today, to be one of the principal subjects in all Eastern esoteric schools. Such movements have a double purpose; they contain and express a certain knowledge. At the same time, they serve as a method of attaining a harmonious state of being. Combinations of these movements evoke different sensations, produce different degrees of concentration of thought, require special efforts in various functions, and show possible limits of individual force."

"The White Magician goes to the window and raises the curtain.

"It is early morning and the sun is rising. All fall on their knees.

"They pray. The curtain slowly falls."

(Above) Another painting by Alexandre de Salzmann based on the scenario of Gurdjieff's ballet. Act 3 finds the jaded Gafar lounging in his luxurious home while his musicians (seated far right) play and young women in colorful costumes try to entertain him with dances from their various homelands.

(Above) Mme. Ouspensky saved this newspaper clipping of one of the women's costumes used for the ballet excerpts that were included in Gurdjieff's Movements Demonstrations in 1923 - 24.

So as not to generate any more strange myths and rumors about Mr. Gurdjieff it should be noted that the swastika motif used on this costume was first used in neolithic Eurasia, and appeared on pottery from around 4000 BC. In antiquity it was used extensively by the Indo-Aryans, Hittites, Celts and Greeks among others and is a sacred symbol in Hinduism, Buddhism and Jainism. It occurs in other Asian, European, African and Native American cultures, sometimes as a geometric motif, sometimes as a religious symbol.

Act 3: A room in the house of Gafar. All attempts to attract the attention of the beautiful Zeinab seem to be failing.

"Gafar remains seated on the divan. Rossoula tries offering him various distractions.

"Musicians with Afghan, Indian and Turkestan musical instruments enter. The music begins...the dancers of the harem enter... All of them are dressed in thair native costumes."

This part of the ballet gives an opportunity for a series of beautiful solo women's dances for which Gurdjieff composed special music. In 2005, these pieces were recorded by the Metropole Orchestra and are part of the recreation of the 1923 demonstrations in Paris at the Theatre des Champs Elysées.

Also recorded was strange disturbing music used in Act 4 which takes place at "The School of the Black Magician." In this Act the Black Magician wears "a golden pentacle" and his throne is decorated with a "lighted pentegram." There are signs of the Zodiac, Kabalistic symbols, a thick book with "strange hieroglyphics and the symbol of the hexagram." The Black Magician casts a spell on Zeinab which is counteracted by the White Magician in Act V for a happy conclusion for all.

* * * * *

Soon a century will have passed since Gurdjieff wrote this scenario evoking the Middle-East of his youth. And although his later writings have been so widely read and discussed, few people ever mention the allegorical and philosophical content of this, his first published work that he climaxed with a scene in which:

"...the White Magician whispers as if in prayer: 'Lord Creator, and all you His assistants, help us to be able to remember ourselves at all times in order that we may avoid involuntary actions, as only through them can evil manifest itself.'
...and then he blesses them all raising both hands saying, 'May reconciliation, hope, diligence and justice be ever with you all.'
"All sing 'Amen.'
"(Curtain)."

* * * * *

CHAPTER 3

THE CHOREOGRAPHER MEETS THE "TEACHER," 1922

Jessmin
♦

During the second season in New York, I took time to prepare and give dance recitals with Michio Ito and Paulet Thevenaz, both talented colleagues from the Dalcroze days. I worked again later with Michio Ito in California. But Paulet, a very gifted painter (he once did a very flattering portrait of me) as well as dancer, died at the early age of thirty-one in 1922 of appendicitis.

Jessmin with her dance partner Paulet Thevenaz, New York, 1918.

New York, Feb. 23, 1919 Recital program.

Paulet's portrait of Jessmin.

I also started some dance classes and a class for volunteers who were mainly from Columbia and New York Universities, and used as "*figurants*" (extras) when crowds were needed in the Vieux Colombier productions.

In March of 1918 I had moved into the Dalcroze School at 9 East 59th Street, and when I had finished my two years with Copeau, could only expect to earn my living in New York by taking more responsibility for the school.

But Jouvet wrote from Paris advising me to try to stay with theatrical activities — to go to Paris and try my luck, since he knew that one possibility was open — Charles Dullin wanted me to help teach gymnastics and pantomime with him at the Ecole Gémier.

So I did go, and I was very lucky indeed, for on my arrival, the director of the Paris Opera, **Jacques Rouché** (1862-1950), whose daughter was an ardent "*rhythmicienne*," asked me to go to see him. He told me he was considering some operas with more modern music and felt that his dancers and extras were not capable of moving in the more natural way required. His daughter had persuaded him that courses in Eurythmics could solve this problem. He asked me whether I, who had theatrical experience, was willing to form a special new "*corps de ballet*" and prepare them for eventual performance.

This was a marvelous challenge, but I would never have dared to accept it if I had not had Jouvet's encouragement and Rouché's permission to bring in two devoted and gifted American Dalcroze pupils, Esther Whiteside and Evelyn Latour who championed me at every turn. My own pianist, Rachel Pasmanik, a well-trained musician studying at the Dalcroze School, could read orchestral scores, prevent me from doing anything too unmusical, and sometimes had brilliant ideas for choreographic details.

So for nearly three years I was at the Opera and my group was used for various ballet sequences in *Herodiade, Falstaff, Les Troyers, La Petite Suite*, and others.

Of course, in the beginning the other ballet corps resented Rouché's modernizing ideas and considered us foreign interlopers. But the various frictions smoothed out and I was having an interesting time, also teaching children's classes at the "Dalcroze Club," and managing a rather skimpy living.

During the summer, there were no Dalcroze classes, so I was left in charge of the studios on the rue de Vaugirard opposite the Jardin de Luxembourg to do any Opera rehearsing or give private lessons there.

One day, toward the end of the summer in 1922, I was going back to my hotel. Feeling very tired and rather ill, I sat down on a bench in the Jardin to gather strength for the remaining few blocks' walk home. As I sat there, a couple came walking by and as they passed it struck me that they looked like Jeanne and "Sasha" de Salzmann, but somehow diminished, dingy and grey. By the time I realized this, they seemed to have suddenly disappeared. "Oh, Lord," I thought, "I really must be sick, I'm having hallucinations. Everyone knows they must be dead!" So I hastened home and got into bed.

When Jouvet happened to telephone, I told the hotel porter to say I was ill. In a while Jouvet arrived to find out what was wrong. I told him of my strange experience and was furious when he burst out laughing. "Hadn't I told you," he said, "that Salzmann has just come to the Théatre des Champs-Elyseés to do the lighting for *Pelleas and Melisande*?"

He told Salzmann what I was doing in Paris and I was asked to go to see them at the theater.

♦ ♦ ♦

Jeanne later told us that the intervening years had been spent mainly in Tiflis in Georgia. After a difficult time during which Salzmann was a kind of forest warden, he regained a theater position at the Tiflis Opera House. To help them out financially, especially when their daughter Nathalie ("Boussik") was born, Jeanne started giving Dalcroze lessons to a group of young women.

It was this class that G.I. Gurdjieff came to watch, asked to experiment with, "to give them some exercises of attention."

Although for some time G. had been giving his followers examples of what he called "gymnastics" accompanying them with his guitar, here, with Jeanne to improvise at the piano, "Movements" developed further.

♦ ♦ ♦

I was so happy to talk with Salzmann again. He must have had trying times, for he had grown much older and quieter. He said that he and Jeanne had met and were keeping close to the most wonderful Teacher, an extraordinary man who had true secret knowledge. As an example he drew an "enneagram" for me, expecting me to be dazzled by its magic. I'm afraid I wasn't!

It took years for me to begin to appreciate this esoteric symbol and the laws it represents.

He said that Jeanne was looking for a hall to rent where the pupils could work on their dances for a while. She came to see me and I arranged for her people to be allowed to practice at the rue de Vaugirard studios. Before this was finally decided her teacher said he must see me. I was instructed to meet Jeanne one evening outside the Café de la Paix.

We waited for a while in the chill and then were quietly joined by a stocky man whose astrakhan coat collar and pulled-down hat almost hid his face. All I could see in the Boulevard lighting was sallow skin and a large moustache. He did not really greet me at all but just told Jeanne that we would be taking a taxi to a restaurant he liked. I've often wondered since why I, unlike so many others, was not more deeply impressed. But, of course, I was feeling very shy, and I was a little embarrassed for Jeanne, whose lover I was guessing he was and of whom she seemed rather afraid.

Once under the dim lighting of the restaurant interior I saw that this man was not as furtive as he had seemed when muffled in his outer clothing. But still for me, he was just another type of Levantine. All conversation at the meal had to be conducted through Jeanne's translation to and fro. I did not enjoy the food — very rich, undercooked duck (I was a vegetarian at that time) relieved by sprays of dill and mint. At last we got through, and Jeanne and I were allowed to leave. She told me with some relief that "Giorgei Ivanovitch" (pronounced "Gurgivanch") had given permission for the pupils to use my studio, which I thought was rather patronizing since I felt that I was the one who was doing them a favor.

The day came when the group was to come for the first time to rue Vaugirard.

Dushka
♦

Jessmin
♦

The symbol of the enneagram.

The studios there were set back of a square courtyard, with the concierge's loge at the front entrance. When I arrived I was met at the front gate by an excited and twittering concierge. "Oh! Mlle. Jassmine, some very strange people have come and said they were to be let in to wait for you." I calmed her down explaining that they were some refugee Russian dancers.

I soon saw what had upset dear Mme. Renaud. It was certainly a strange looking assembly. One or two of the men wore business suits, but shirts without ties, the others had nondescript outfits, corduroy trousers with worn tuxedo jackets, or layers of grubby sweaters with thin cotton trousers. Most of the women wore *babushkas* (headscarves), and skirts almost to their ankles with different, shoddy, ill-fitting coats. But they were pleasant, courteous people who got themselves politely installed in the studio where they were soon joined by Jeanne, M. de Salzmann, two or three Russians — and by Mr. Gurdjieff.

I left them to get started on their work and went to my own room. Soon, M. de Salzmann came to find me and "bring me an invitation" to see the dancers. The studio was already a mess, the corners piled with crumpled coats, dusty shoes and shopping bags. The men and women were lined up in strict rows, and at a grunt from Mr. G., began taking gymnastic positions, very tense and brusquely it seemed to me.

After watching this practiced for a little while, I left the studio. M. de Salzmann ran after me saying, "But Jessmin, you must not leave until Mr. Gurdjieff tells you to." I answered, "I'm sorry, but you and Jeanne told me that these were wonderful esoteric dances. All I can see are some unattractive people who look more like cleaning women and day laborers than dancers, and all of them scared out of their wits. I don't want to watch any more."

Finally I was persuaded to return and the group proceeded to do some more interesting exercises. It was the music that appealed most to me. Mr. G. asked me if I could understand the rhythm of one of the dances, *The Sacred Goose*, and seemed quite surprised when, with one of the Russians, a M. de Hartmann, beaming at me, I marked time to it correctly.

Well, they continued to come in each day. Sometimes I watched and sometimes not. Once, to my horror, I found them all painting fabrics on our spotless white linoleum floor. They were making costumes. Mr. G. showing great skill in cutting out and fitting some quite beautiful Eastern outfits.

By this time I had started to learn what they called the "Obligatories" myself and found them not at all easy and very challenging to one's coordination.

After seeing the men practice whirling, the Dervish exercise turning on place, I stayed after they had gone to see whether this was really so difficult. I got started and went on quite happily feeling serene until the thought entered my mind, "How do I stop?" And when I did, I found myself lying gently on the floor. For the next hour or two the world spun around me counter-clockwise.

◆ ◆ ◆

Dushka
♦

What Mother refers to here as "Obligatories" are a special series of six dance-type exercises meticulously worked out by Gurdjieff, not just to be shown in the demonstrations, but offered as fundamental, practical tools to anyone interested in working on his ideas. First-time visitors, skeptical beginners or devoted followers, all were encouraged to make use of these potent, non-verbal, and therefore universal.

means of self study. They required no special training or understanding of esoteric ideas, only a sincere effort to master, while observing oneself doing so, challenges that were new and simultaneously physical, mental and emotional. Most evening classes, and later the public demonstrations, began with the six Obligatories. When practiced conscientiously in the complete prescribed sequence, (unfortunately a rare occurrence these days), they are capable of interupting people's usual everyday confusion, dispersal and passivity. They can lead one through developing stages of attracted interest, then growing awareness, brief moments of sensation and inner observation, and for certain persevering students, a real "taste," at least, of active "*paying of attention*"... a primary aim of Gurdjieff's "System."

◆ ◆ ◆

During the next few weeks I came closer to the group. I would be invited for Sunday lunch at the house in Neuilly where they were all installed. I really began to like them all very much. Also, Mr. G. would sometimes send to ask me whether I could go for an hour or two to his "office," usually a café, as he was seeing some English people, and Jeanne and Major Pinder were not free to help translate. I learnt a great deal in those sessions. Mr. G. seemed to answer a lot of the English people's questions in a very direct common sense way.

One woman, a teacher of philosophy, was always begging for information so that she could write a book about him. Mr. G. asked, "How can you understand me enough to write about me until you have learnt, at least, to do the First Obligatory?"

Another younger woman was movingly eager to stay near and study with Mr. G., but her husband was not in favor. So Mr. G. said, "You come work when you can, and if your husband sees that you change in any way for the better he will be glad to let you stay."

One day, at the end of one of these meetings, I think that Mr. G. saw I was in a very negative state. He teased me, saying that I looked as if life was not worth living. I sulkily replied that that was exactly true. He felt in his pocket and brought out a capsule and told me that if I would swallow this, I could end my unwanted life. Of course, out of pride, I took the thing and gobbled it. Mr. G. then very angrily shouted,"If I know you so stupid, I would have given you a pill which would have made you suffer as you never have" — and sent me away.

He asked Jeanne what was wrong with me. She told him that I had an unhappy love affair. For nearly three years I had waited to see whether Jouvet could arrange for us to have a life together. He was working harder all the time becoming quite well known, meeting all the important actors, musicians, and writers in Paris; and could never find leisure to see much of me or even consider what should be our future plans. I was very depressed and disillusioned.

Mr. G. sent a message by Jeanne to say that he felt I was living the wrong kind of life and that now he was going to have a house in the country and do interesting research, he invited me to live there. I told Jeanne I had so little money that I could not afford to do this and she said, "But Jessmin, Giorgei Ivanovitch invites you to be one of our family!"

The prospect of getting out of my daily grind was tempting and I was not too upset at giving up my Opera job, which was really very ill-advised of me for I was just beginning to be accepted and have good notices from the critics for my choreography. My pianist, who had been such a valuable collaborator, was leaving to get married and I knew I would be lost without her. Other pianists at the Opera were unsatisfactory and irregular, so I had just engaged Rosemary Lillard, a former pupil and fine pianist.

I explained to Mr. G. that I was not altogether free to make this decision. If I left, Rosemary would be stranded and I felt I could not do this until something else was worked out for her. And if I were away from Paris, I would have to come in sometimes to rehearse my ballets if they were to be performed, since the teachers, who could replace me otherwise, did not know the choreography.

Mr. G. said these were not difficulties. I could always come in to Paris when necessary, and if my friend Rosemary would like to come to the Prieuré, the estate they had taken over near Fontainebleau, she would be welcomed and could decide later whether his work would interest her. This generosity shamed me, and when I had the blow of learning that Elsa, Jouvet's wife, was pregnant again, I just gave up on every hope and let everyone know that I was leaving to study elsewhere.

Considering that I did not join Mr. G. for any other reason than disappointment in a love affair, I must be grateful for having learned from him what I did.

* * * * *

Jessmin's Dalcroze Studio in Paris, 1922

Watching a Movements rehearsal in the Dalcroze Studio in Paris, 1922, (Left to right) G.I.Gurdjieff, Mme. Ouspensky, Catherine and Dr. Maurice Nicoll. (Standing behind the piano), Alexandre de Salzmann with Thomas de Hartmann barely visible, seated at the piano.

Gurdjieff (Left) paints colorful costumes with Dr. Kissiloff's help (right) while Dr. Stjernval (standing) watches.

...and others join in. Alexandre de Salzmann (center) Dr. Young, (right).

Sewing costumes. (Back row, left to right) Olgivanna, Jeanne Lily, and Olga. (Front row, left to right) Dr. Young, unknown woman, and Bernard Metz

(Above) Everyone tries out their new white costumes, including Jessmin already in the front row, far right!   (see detail at right>)

...and everyone rehearses *"The First Dervish Prayer."* In the front row (Left to right) Olgivanna Hinzenberg, Lily Galumian, and Jeanne de Salzmann doing the special women's part known as the "camelwalk."

(Below) Lily Galumian leads "*Copying Positions in canon.*" (Jessmin writes on the back of this photo "For the demonstrations it was more or less arranged (?!) for effect.") Note the small boy far right.

(Above left) Cutting cardboard....folding it into tubes...(watched by a small boy on the right).. then (right) the women cover the tubes with fabric, fit and finish them.. .and (below) the musicians have their Dervish high hats.

(Above) The men, including the small boy (right) try out their dervish robes and hats. The boy is unidentified, remembered by Boussik only as "an orphan who lived with Gurdjieff's family at the Prieuré." Probably one of three young Kozlonski brothers listed on the ship's manifest two years later in 1924 as part of the group accompanying Gurdjieff to New York. (Below) Rehearsing *The Great Prayer"* as usually done — in blindfolds!

(Above) The women's dance *"The Sacred Goose"* evokes every stage of a woman's life.

(Above) At the order *"STOP"* all freeze to study their inner and outer states.

(Below) A discarded "mysterious" photo of Gurdjieff (Center...twice..!) working with the Movements class. Another *"STOP"* ? or a double exposure? No blurs?

(Above) Assembling scraps of material to be sewn together into colorful combinations.

(Below) The women and two boys aid with the sewing by hand and by machine. At the back of the room Mr. Gurdjieff works with one of the women to ensure the shoulder fit and ease of movement of a man's costume.

(Above) Work continues, sometimes with one sewing machine, sometimes (Below) with three. Mme. Ouspensky sits at the third machine from left.

(Above) Men working. At the right food and wine?
(Left) Painting hats.
(Below) Another hat in preparation. But is the woman in charge of refreshments or using wine bottles to mix paints?

(Above) Finishing touches are put on a costume and turban-type hat.

(Above and below) Another thirty or so costumes are finally completed and rehearsals begin.

CHAPTER 4

GURDJIEFF'S INSTITUTE AT FONTAINEBLEAU

Jessmin
♦

FOR ADAM AND JIMMY NOTT:

Your mother, Rosemary, and I first met at the New York School of Dalcroze Eurythmics in 1918. She was enrolled in a Rhythmic Gymnastics class I was teaching. I remember her as being about seventeen then, pretty, flaxen-haired and chubby. She was also lymphatic and sometimes, when I would ask her, please, not to drop out of some quick, active rhythm sequence, she would answer mildly in a voice tinged with a slight Southern accent, "Ah jest cayant."

In later years she would often amuse her friends describing how her parents, the Lillards of Houston, Texas, had attempted to cure her of an essential indolence. They would have her walk up and down a flight of stairs several times, pick up a deck of cards from the floor one at a time, or exercise on her bicycle, which she confessed she was always falling off of because she pedaled so slowly.

However, in New York there were reasons for Rosemary's lack of energy. It seems that when her father died he had left his family in difficult circumstances. He had been a doctor who, all too often, had allowed his patients not to pay him. So his widow, Mrs. Lillard, decided to move to New York, invest in a pleasant three-story house on the West Side of Manhattan and run it as a boarding home for Southern girls studying in the city and needing "chaperonage."

This venture proved quite successful and her rooms were always filled, so much so that Rosemary never had a room of her own, just a cot and a chest of drawers placed behind a screen in a storeroom. She acted as housekeeper, rising early to go out to do the shopping, and at mealtimes supervised the colored help in the kitchen, while the boarders, all rich girls, were served by a white-gloved butler.

The only relief she had was to go for piano and eventually *Rhythmic* lessons. This was insisted upon by her godmother, who had been her piano teacher in Texas, and later came into a lot of money when oil was discovered on her family's land. Named "Ima" by a father whose last name was Hogg, she later became famous and beloved as "Miss Ima," Houston's foremost patroness of the arts.

◆◆◆

Dushka
♦

Ima Hogg (1882-1975) was born in Mineola, Texas, and from an early age was interested in music. She played piano at the age of four. Later she studied at the National Conservatory of Music in New York City, and in her twenties for two years in Austria and Germany. In 1913 she became the founder of the Houston Symphony Society.

The Hogg Family   The grown "Miss Ima"

     Her father was Jim Hogg, a self-educated man. He became a newspaper editor, a district attorney, and in 1891 the first native-born governor of Texas. Involved in the early stages of the oil industry, he bought the 4100-acre Verner Plantation confident that oil would be discovered there one day and stipulated in his will that the property must not be sold until fifteen years after his death.

     In 1918, twelve years after he died, oil was found there and this new found wealth allowed Ima and her brothers to bestow enormous cultural and charitable gifts upon Houston, their adopted "home town."

     It appears that "Miss Ima" acquired her surprising name from a poem written by Jim Hogg's brother in which the heroine is called "Ima" short for Imogene. Despite rumors that have circulated for decades, her brothers' names were William, Michael and Thomas, not as many would have you believe "Heeza" and "Yora!"

◆ ◆ ◆

     Until I left New York in early 1919, Rosemary and I often talked together. I was really distressed that her mother expected her to live like a kind of Cinderella.

     In 1922, Miss Ima arranged for Rosemary to come to France for a month's "Master Course" with the celebrated pianist Blanche Selva. When this ended, Rosemary wrote to me in Paris and told me that she longed to stay in Europe, and could I help her do so? Fortunately I could, and she was engaged at the Opera. The stipend was not large, but with help from Miss Ima, who was all in favor of her godchild continuing studies in Paris, things worked out.

     When I told Rosemary about Mr. Gurdjieff and his invitation, she bravely accepted the offer, and we both moved to the Prieuré.

     We were, at first, treated as Mr. Gurdjieff's guests. We shared a room and took our meals in the "Ritz" dining room where the English visitors who were providing money were regaled with rich eastern dishes.

Jessmin
◆

For the first month I was supposed to rake the extensive lawns and hold myself in readiness, at a moment's notice, to ride with Mr. Gurdjieff to and from Paris to translate at the tollgates and otherwise be inconspicuous.

Rosemary, meanwhile, was free to work on her music. We both attended the classes of "Movements" held every evening.

One day Mr. Gurdjieff discovered Rosemary at the piano in the drawing room rippling off scales and arpeggios with a novel open on the music stand, her usual way of letting her fingers get warmed up. He told her that if she would trust his advice, he would guarantee that her playing would improve one hundred percent. He asked her not to touch the piano for a month and then resume practicing for only as long as she could listen attentively to every note she struck.

This really did have a profound effect, as did her contact with M. de Hartmann, whom she greatly admired as a musician and adopted as her mentor. I had come to know and depend on the brilliant and kindly English editor, A. R. Orage. So we felt we had friends in the Institute.

Gradually we undertook daily tasks like everyone else. But, I'm afraid we still often acted like schoolgirls. One so-called "task" Mr. Gurdjieff had given me was to care for a baby hedgehog that had been picked up on the grounds. The poor thing just wished to hibernate, I think, but anyway, we corralled it in our bedroom and tried to feed it. So that it should not be let out we placed a notice on our door which read: "Please be careful when opening door that Mr. Hodgkins does not escape."

Mme. de Hartmann was very shocked by this and instituted a system whereby Lily Galumian was ordered to call frequently at our room to see what we were doing. When I told Mr. Orage that Lily was apt to barge in at intervals and say: "What are you doing?" he told me to answer: "I am milking a cow."

After this we were moved away from the visitor's wing, but we were still recalcitrant about certain rules. At one time no one was allowed to have butter, which Rosemary particularly craved. So, since Mr. Gurdjieff had been at times concerned because I ate so little, I went to the "kitchen ladies" and said that Mr. Gurdjieff had told me I should have butter. When he later found out that it was sufficient to tell any of the Russians "Mr. Gurdjieff had said so" to get anything one wished, he told me: "If they such fools, continue!"

As Christmas drew near that year, Rosemary and I were somewhat tamed. With our taskmaster, Lily, we did all the laundry. This meant putting sheets, shirts, etc. to soak with wood ash in barrels, then boiling, rinsing with a hose, and carrying the loads in a wheelbarrow about three blocks' length to Paradou, the other house, to hang them out to dry. We also took turns, but separately, in the "worker's dining room,"— a six-thirty a.m. to eight p.m. job — setting, serving, washing up and cleaning three meals a day plus afternoon tea.

We had been amused and interested by the high-flown philosophical and psychological talk in the "Ritz" dining room, and learned a lot when Mr. Gurdjieff sometimes joined the visitors for a meal.

We also had opportunities to talk with Katherine Mansfield who would sit on the stairs in her red jacket, and with wonder and laughter, go over some of the esoteric conversation that had taken place at the table. We were always glad that we had gone into her room and had given it a "spring cleaning" before her husband was to arrive from England. She died the next day.

But we asked to be put with the other "workers," glad to make friends with them.

For Christmas, Mr. Gurdjieff insisted that the English people should prepare a traditional celebration for the Russians. He allowed a tree to be brought in and trimmed, and he joined in when the plum pudding was stirred.

◆ ◆ ◆

Katherine Mansfield, the noted New Zealand author, also describes this scene in her writings adding that Mr. G., apparently having heard of an old English tradition, included a silver coin in the mix promising "who gets the coin gets our darling newborn calf for a present." The calf, one day old, was led into the salon to the beating of tambourines and to a special melody composed for it.

Dushka
◆

◆ ◆ ◆

The English women including Mrs. Page, Mrs. Young, Mrs. Nicholls and others laid in a stock of provisions. But on the last day they found that not one of them knew how to stuff and roast a goose, make mincemeat pies, heat a plum pudding, mix hard sauce, or prepare a trifle. So they were much relieved when Rosemary offered to take over. This she did most capably with Mme. Ostrovsky, Mme. Ouspensky, and Nina Mercuroff, the usual cooks, taking orders from her and good-naturedly helping.

Jessmin
◆

Mr. Gurdjieff was pleased about this and from that time on encouraged Rosemary.

And so she stayed.

"Miss Ima" and a friend from Texas took out time from a tour of Europe to come to the Prieuré to see what Rosemary was doing.

Mr. Gurdjieff, having been told that Miss Ima was rich and influential, decided to be benevolent. When he came downstairs and was introduced to them, he said carefully, in his newly acquired English, "How do you do?" and then added, "And what do I do after that?" Miss Ima answered patiently, "Now you take off your hat!"

The two ladies stayed for a few days and insisted upon being given some work to do. They mended all the men's socks and shirts so beautifully that Mme. de Hartmann stored them away with the new things.

I was still very spoilt and determined not to kowtow to Mr. Gurdjieff or to any of the Russians "peasants" as I thought of them then. To the eye of a young woman who had lived in Paris for some years, they took no care of their appearance. In fact, it seemed to me, they were not even quite clean. So when, that Christmas, Mr. Gurdjieff had gifts bought for everyone by Mme. de Hartmann, it was rather a shock to see that every woman had been given a cake of what I considered my special brand of scented soap.

Meeting Mr. G., I blurted out: "Well, now I shall be able to smell myself everywhere."

"Oh, no!" said Mr. G., "You know that same perfume smells quite differently on different skins –," and he walked on.

Mr. Ouspensky passing nearby halted for a moment and looked at me enquiringly. I sulkily said:

"You see, Mr. Ouspensky, Giorghivanch has given every single woman a cake of my own special soap!'"

There was a moment's silence and then Mr. Ouspensky said:

"I think Mr. Gurdjieff is very generous." I truly felt ashamed.

Later on, when it had been taken for granted that my chief interest and task was to be the study of the Movements, Mr. G. told me to learn from Jeanne de Salzmann the part she did during the Warrior Dervish intended to represent a young Dervish in a state of frenzy. Something in me rebelled at trying to let go in that way. So, for two or three weeks I did not take part in the Movements at all. In fact, I sulked.

Finally, one weekend, Mr. Ouspensky came to me in the Study Hall and said: "Jessmin, I no longer see you in Movements." I answered: "I do not want to pretend that I am an epileptic." Mr. O. looked at me for a long moment and then said:

"You know, Jessmin, you are in your own way."

On thinking this over, I began to face my vanity and "considering." I am so grateful to him, for I learned more in making myself do that part than during all the other long practices for the demonstrations we gave.

◆ ◆ ◆

Dushka
◆

One of the things that Mother, in her later years, obviously wanted to set straight was an old rumor about the Prieuré dredged up again in the book, *The Harmonious Circle*, by James Webb.

Referring rather avidly to a "suicide of Mrs. Y," the author (who, himself, had mental problems and committed suicide soon after the publication of his book), repeats third-hand hearsay and imaginatively draws dubious conclusions such as: "Orage always maintained that it was Gurdjieff's 'near rape' of Mrs Y. that finally decided Ouspensky..." (*i. e.* to make a complete break with Mr. G.)

Mother painstakingly wrote out the following on yellow sheets of a legal pad and placed them (for me to find?), at page 333 of James Webb's big book.

◆ ◆ ◆

Jessmin
◆

Re: pages 335, 362, 384– About "Mrs. Y"... I could add something which casts another light on her "suicide."

Doris Tyndall was one of my Eurythmics pupils in Paris. Irish, about twenty years old, very pretty, and charming, and naive, she and her mother, a widow, also pretty, charming, and naive, lived for each other. I have never seen mother and daughter so devoted to each other.

Toward the end of my time at the Opera, I allowed Doris to join the class. She and her mother were enjoying life in Paris, and although Doris was supposedly engaged to a decent, well-bred Englishman, she gave the impression of being in no way anxious to settle down to married life yet.

A few months after I entered the Prieuré, Doris and her mother came to see me. Mr. G. met them and invited them for a visit.

Doris was fascinated by the Movements and in a little while she more or less stayed at the Prieuré. Her mother stayed nearby in Fontainbleau and often joined us.

Doris found the farm life congenial. She had been brought up in the country in Ireland. She looked like a happy peasant in her cotton dresses and headscarf, and all the young men found her adorable. I don't think she flirted intentionally. She was really serious about the Movements, especially when Mr. G. announced that he would be taking some pupils to America.

But finally Mr. G. said he was tired of all the men at the Prieuré looking at Doris like hypnotized sheep, and that it was time Doris learnt that she could not behave in her flirtatious way and not expect someone to call her bluff. He advised Mrs. Tyndall to get her married and withstood all her and Doris' pleading to be allowed to be part of the Movements group going to America. This was a terrible blow for Doris.

Anyway, Doris did marry early in 1924. After a year or so her husband had a temporary job abroad. Since Doris was expecting a child, she did not go with him, but went back to live with her mother again and insisted on staying with her even when her husband came back.They realized that she was really disturbed (schizo-phrenia?) and when the mother, Mrs. Tyndall, wanted to marry again, the doctors advised her to put Doris into a nursing home for a while to accustom her to the impending separation.The doctors at the nursing home finally advised Mrs. Tyndall that it would be better if she discontinued her visits. Doris saw her leaving and became distressed because she had not come in to say "Goodbye."

According to an attendant who was in her room with her, Doris leaned out of the window and shouted: "Mama, come back! Mama don't leave me here." Then fell (?), jumped (?), or threw herself (?), from the second-story window.

This happened in 1927, almost three years after leaving the Prieuré!

It is true that Mrs. Tyndall made a point in 1923 and 1924 of telling a lot of people in London that "Mr. G. had invited Doris into his bed," and the Ouspenskys may have heard the gossip.

The scandal reached New York when we were there and Mr. G. upbraided me one day, saying the "trouble" was my fault for having brought to the Prieuré "two such idiot women."

◆ ◆ ◆

Dushka
◆

In later years many people wrote their own accounts of the Prieuré and its activ-ities.

I suppose Mother was conscious of this and so, regrettably, except for these few personal anecdotes, she wrote little about it. She did write a lot about the specific Movements work they did, but that material doesn't really belong here.

For more background I include some selections from contemporary periodicals, but especially a little known, but to me fascinating, contemporary description that has been lying deep in the archives of the *New York Times* for eighty years.

This article was obviously prompted by the interest Gurdjieff must have aroused in the U.S. with his Movements demonstrations, as it appeared less than three weeks after the first performance took place in New York on January 23, 1924.

The writer, was a Maud Hoffman. One perceives, she was more than a casual observer. In fact, she must have been a participant. She describes the previous year's arduous preparations in France with marvelous objectivity mixed with respectful understanding.

I find myself wondering whether, today, any *Times* writers or editors would give this kind of attention and space to such a subject.

TAKING THE LIFE CURE IN GURDJIEFF'S SCHOOL

An Intimate Description of the Russian's Institute in France, Whose Aim Is the All Round, Harmonious Development of Man

BY MADD HOFFMAN

DURING this last Summer the in-

your business. If you are a Summer visitor wanting to see the demonstration

The New York Times, **February 10, 1924**

"During this last Summer the inhabitants of Fontainebleau and Avon in France, and the Summer visitors at the hotels flocked to the old Prieuré des Basses Loges to see the Saturday evening demonstrations of the work done there by the pupils of the Gurdjieff Institute. The demonstrations are given in a large aerodrome [sic], erected by the pupils, which comfortably accommodates more than sixty pupils and several hundred visitors. The stage is large enough for forty people to take part in the exercises at the same time, and a large space covered with Persian carpets remains free in the center.

"The pupils sit around this square space on goatskins and cushions in the Oriental fashion. The interior of this study house has been decorated with color, drawings, stenciling and designs. The whole of the extensive canvas ceiling – and every buttress, beam and space is covered. The colors are rich and vivid, as are the windows. All the work of painting and designing has been done by the pupils themselves.

"The demonstrations are unique in their presentation. They consist of movements which include the sacred gymnastics of the esoteric schools, the religious ceremonies of the antique Orient and the ritual movements of monks and dervishes — besides the folk dances of many a remote community.

"The movements are not only bewildering in their complexity, and amazing in the precision of their execution, but rich in diversity, harmonious in rhythm, and exceedingly beautiful in the gracefulness of the postures, which are quite unknown to Europe. To the accompaniment of mystical and inspiring music, handed down from remote antiquity, the sacred dances are executed with deeply religious dignity, which is profoundly impressive.

Philosophy of the Movement.

"You may or may not know about the philosophy which lies at the back of all the activities of this unique community. The American papers have called them the "Forest Philosophers" and you listen carefully to catch any of the teaching. But the nearest that you get to philosophy for many days is to make the acquaintance of a good-natured, but not well-pointed, fox terrier, with a large body and a small head, named "Philos."

"You venture to ask if there are any lectures or classes. Quietly you are told, without further comment, that there are none. After this you think a while and observe the people around you. They are all English and Americans. Where, then, are the Russians – that little band of people whom Gurdjieff led safely out of Russia when the revolution broke out?

"Later you find that everything that is done in this place of work has a meaning. You work hard – not for the sake of the work – but for the sake of what the work evokes in you, for the sake of activity, for the purpose of making efforts, and for the purpose of self-observation. You soon begin to suspect that this place may be an outer court of one of those old mystery schools about which you have read, over the portals of which were always the words 'Know Thyself.'

"The Gurdjieff system aims at an all-round and harmonious development of man. It is a place where everyone can be an artist or an artisan, and the material with which he works are his own mental, emotional and instinctive energies. As most of the energy in modern life flows into mental activity, much physical activity is needed, and many acute emotional conflicts are required to divert this energy into instinctive and emotional channels.

"The claim made by the Gurdjieff Institute is that, by the reactionary effect of harmonious movements on the psyche, man may hope to progress to that balanced development which has been arrested by the cramping of an unnatural and mechanical civilization.

"But the process toward a balanced development of being is not confined to gymnastics and dancing. Every kind of manual labor, within doors and out-of-doors, is performed by the students, both men and woman doing all kinds of work. Combined with the physical work are difficult mental exercises: and the emotions are kept active by the natural reactions in each person to an environment and conditions that are in many ways the reversal of most of their fixed ideas and habits.

Irregularity a Principle.

"If you wish to visit the Gurdjieff Institute, you would, on leaving Fontainebleau Station, turn down the hill to the right toward Avon and old Prieuré des Basses Loges instead of to the left toward Fontainebleau and the Palace. At the foot of the hill at the crossroads on the right hand corner is the gatehouse of the old Prieuré, now known as the Gurdjieff Institute, and Chateau du Prieuré. You will see the little door in the wall and you will know it is the door you are seeking, because over the bell on the right are the words '*Sonnez-fort*' (Ring loudly). It will be well if you take the advice and ring loudly and long. Your arrival may correspond with that phase of the life within which does not provide an attendant at the gate. Unlike other communities the gatekeeper is not a fixed and invariable post. Had you arrived any time between the end of last August and the middle of October your ring would have been instantly answered. During that period the gates had keepers, both the front gate and the back gate at the end of the far garden, six minutes walk from the chateau. Before that time there was no gatekeeper, since that time there has been no gatekeeper.

"In the meaning attached to this irregularity, which arises at the very entrance to the Gurdjieff Institute lies a crucial principle of the enterprise. It is a place where habits are changed, fixed ideas are broken up, mechanical routines do not exist, and adaptability to ever-changing forms and modes of life is practiced. So, '*sonnez-fort*' and wait. Someone passing within may open for you. It is really the 'kitchen boy's' duty. There is a different kitchen boy each day and it is the most onerous job in the place. He may not be able to drop what he is doing at once. Presently he will appear with a large apron tied round him – possibly not a clean apron. He may be anybody, the editor of a London paper, a Harley Street specialist, a court musician or a Russian lawyer. England, America, Russia, France, Poland, Georgia, Armenia and several other nations are represented here.

"To some one of these you will state your business. If you are a summer visitor wanting to see the demonstration you will be asked to come on Saturday evening at nine o'clock. But if you have come all the way from America solely for the purpose of living at the institute you probably are expected and you will be admitted at once into the courtyard with its fountain and duck pond and the old chateau standing there close to the gate. As you cross the courtyard, and as you enter the house, you will have a feeling that, at any rate, there will be esthetic satisfaction here, for you see at a glance that the house is an excellent example of the smaller type of French chateau.

"You probably have already heard that it was formerly a hunting lodge belonging to Mme. de Maintenon, (a royal mistress), before that there is the tradition of a Carmelite monastery. More recently it was the property of Dreyfus, who gave it to his avocat (lawyer), Labori, in payment for his defense in the famous trial. For several years past it has had the fate of so many historic mansions and has been let as a summer residence to wealthy Americans.

"You are left to wait in the first salon, one of three which is furnished in the Empire period, and you go at once to the window, where there is a lovely view of the terrace in the extensive lawns beyond, with their fountain surrounded by beds of flowering plants and great forest trees, for the whole of the estate of forty acres is a part of the forest.

"Beyond the lawns is a long alley of formal lime trees, leading to a round bathing pool in a basin of stone. From here short paths lead to the top of a little knoll where you can sit and view the grounds and the chateau on one side and the meadows on the other.

"During the warm days of July and August the piano was brought out of doors and we practiced our gymnastics and dances in the shelter of the lime tree alley. From ten to eleven – from three to four – from nine to any hour in the night.

Pay According to Means.

"Presently some one takes you up to the 'Ritz' corridor, so named because of its beautiful furnishings, or in the beautiful 'Monks' corridor above, so named for its cloisterlike appearance. In the Ritz the rooms are luxurious, while in the Monk's corridor they are comfortable and quaint. All pay according to means. Those who are rich must pay very well indeed, for there are many among the pupils who cannot pay at all.

"Round about midday there is a meal. At noon, if you have risen at six, at one if at seven, at half-past eleven if you have risen at five. You have probably arrived in time for this meal. If your room is in the Monk's corridor you take a hasty glance round at the red brick floor, the old French chintzes on the walls and furniture, and the heavenly forest garden without, before you hurry down to the dining room. This is a beautifully proportioned room with red hangings and fine old paintings. Three windows overlook the grounds and a door leads on to the terrace.

"If the day is warm you can have your bread and soup on the terrace or in the dining room, or you can take it to your room, or to the garden or the pantry – where or how you like. The food is nourishing and sufficient, but useless conventions of service and elaboration of dishes, food and courses are absent. You receive your food from the hands of the cook in the kitchen, and after you have eaten it, you wash your plate and cup, and there is an end of it. In the matter of food there is an opportunity to 'change habit.'

"As you are a visitor your soup has been brought to you, but you decide to fend for yourself for the pudding or fruit, and make your way through the pantry to the kitchen. Seated at the kitchen table, with his hat on and an overcoat, is Mr. Gurdjieff. He is having his dinner, one dish only, and coffee, surrounded by the noise and bustle of the kitchen. It is crowded with people, among them the Russians, whose dining room is on the other side of the kitchen, past the dairy, to what was probably the servants' hall.

Work and Effort: Nothing Easy.

"When you enter, Mr. Gurdjieff greets you and makes you welcome, with a smile that has both sweetness and spirit-quality. You get a first impression of a nature of great kindness and sensitiveness. Later you learn that in him is combined strength and delicacy, simplicity and subtlety. That he is more awake than any one you have ever known.

"Your first evening in the study house is a never-to-be-forgotten experience. Here from nine o'clock to twelve, to one perhaps to two o'clock the work goes on. When the obligatory exercises begin you receive a shock. You find yourself sitting up, leaning forward and receiving impacts from that moving mass of energy on the stage. The obligatory exercises contain every movement which is later worked up and used in the various special groups and dances. After the first hour of exercises — when the blood is tingling in every accustomed and unaccustomed cell of their bodies – the pupils rest on the goatskins and this is the moment chosen for the most difficult kind of mental concentration.

"The key words of the Gurdjieff Institute are 'work,' and 'effort.' Nothing is made easy in this place. Always the task is a little beyond your strength – you must make an effort; the supply of work material runs short, you must invent – make effort; the time is curtailed – hasten! make effort; you have reached the limit of your strength and are exhausted – then is the moment to make effort – and tap the higher energies and the source of Will.

"Those who are intellectually powerful and physically and emotionally weak cannot be considered successful. Their structures are top-heavy. The Saints found only incomplete illumination by means of an over-developed emotionality on the path of devotion. Exquisite movements alone, or physical strength alone cannot give knowledge or perfect being. At the Gurdjieff Institute an attempt can be made to fill in deficiencies, correct heredity and habit and to balance knowledge and being. Incidentally and as a by-product of these efforts you renew your energies and your youth and make yourself more efficient for life."

* * * * *

An English publication, carried an article by Dr. James Carruthers Young who visited from London:

<u>**New Adelphi, September 1927**</u>

"The Dalcroze Institute in the Rue de Vaugirard in Paris was taken temporarily during the summer vacation of 1922 and there, in August of that year, I, with a number of English people, joined up. The exercises were soon in full swing...

"...The other main activity of this period in Paris was the making of costumes which were to be worn in the public exhibitions of the exercises and dances given later at the Institute. Gurdjieff cut out the materials with great skill, and the members were employed in sewing, hand-painting and stenciling designs on them. Metal ornaments for such things as buckles and belts were also fashioned with varying degrees of skill. Other things were made or improvised, dancing pumps, and Russian boots, for example, which called for a knowledge of various handicrafts... This work was carried on with feverish activity, and occupied, together with the exercises, thirteen or fourteen hours every day....

"In due course, Gurdjieff found and rented a suitable place for the Institute. Although left fully furnished except for the servant's quarters, it had not been occupied since the beginning of the war. The grounds were overgrown and neglected... ...A multitude of activities were soon set afoot by Gurdjieff... But the *piece de résistance* was the building of the 'study-house.' An area of ground large enough to accommodate an ordinary aerodrome [sic] was leveled after exceedingly strenuous work with pick, shovel and barrow. The framework of an old aerodrome was erected on this, fortunately, as I thought, without loss of life or limb.

"The walls were lined within and without between the uprights with rough laths. The space between the laths was stuffed with dead leaves. The laths were then covered over inside and out with the material of which the Hebrews made their bricks, a mixture of mud and straw, or hay chopped very small. Stoves were then put in the building and the walls dried and hardened before painting them. The roof was made of tarred felt nailed on to the joists; glass extended all the way round the upper half of the walls. This glazing was improvised from cucumber frames — a really good piece of work. After these had been fixed in position the glass was painted with various designs. The lighting effect was very pleasing. The floor, which was the naked earth pounded thoroughly and rolled, and dried by means of the stoves, was covered with matting, on which were placed handsome carpets; the walls below the window were hung with rugs in the Oriental fashion. A stage was devised, and a kind of balcony for an orchestra; also two tiers of seats all around the walls, padded with mattresses and covered with rugs and skins, for the accommodation of visitors."

* * * * *

Dr. Mary C. Bell also visited and reported:

"... on Christmas Day, 1922...I went over for a week. ...At that time the Study House had not been acquired, and the evenings were spent in the large salon of the chateau — a spacious room with a beautiful parquet floor. And yet there was no sense of incongruity when the door opened and a bewildered day-old calf pushed its head in, gently propelled from behind by Mr. G. ...

"When I returned in March the Study House was being erected. It was an old hangar. Passing through a small lobby, one entered an almost square space with a low stage thrown out at the further end. Against the walls were couches for any who wished to rest and a six foot foyer to which strangers were admitted, but the center portion, divided from the foyer by a low partition was reserved for the pupils alone. Against the partition were slightly raised seats, each covered by a goatskin, which were allocated to the pupils, men on the right and women on the left. Mr. G.'s seat was a tented divan on the right side of the entrance into the central square. The floor of the square was covered with Eastern rugs, and in the center was a fountain with a slowly revolving disc of many-coloured glass and the colour of the water appeared to change from minute to minute. The piano was in the foyer at the left of the stage. The stage was raised about fifteen inches and covered with linoleum, and the front sloped in a gentle curve to the floor. Again there was no sense of incongruity when a kid, that was being brought up in the kitchen came to the Study House one evening and, having discovered the slope, spent a happy hour slithering down it again and again."

* * * * *

A London newspaper printed four lengthy articles about the "new cult," "the forest philosophers," and the wonders of the Study House.

Written by E.C. Bowyer, the pieces were accompanied by photographs of Gurdjieff, Ouspensky and people in costume doing movements. They were featured on the front page coincidently sharing this honor with the historic archaeological discovery of Tutankhamen's tomb.

Daily News, February, 1923

"... Imagine a plain, square building, to hold, perhaps 300 people. In the center a fountain, illuminated by constantly changing colored lights and making pleasant music, the floor carpeted with costly Eastern rugs. Around the walls are divans, with here and there an alcove with rich tapestries. The windows are painted over with Arabic designs, and soft light comes from hidden electric globes. Some sweet perfume pervades the whole interior...

"... Around the walls of the Study House students reclined on the divans and watched their fellows, men and women, on the slightly raised stage at one end of the hall. The illuminated fountain threw up a head of glowing water which fell back with a pleasant murmur into the carved basin and filled the interior with a faint odour of attar of roses.

"The Study House is not yet complete, gorgeous as is the interior. Gurdjieff told me that he is having built a special organ, unique in Europe, with the octaves in quarter tones. Much also remains to be done to other parts of the House. Soon the fountains will diffuse a different perfume for every hour, and other fountains are yet to be installed.

"By his elaborate combination of appeals to the senses Gurdjieff believes he is providing many aids to meditation. 'The senses should be gently distracted,' he said, 'and then the mind itself untrammeled by the senses is free to work. Only by such means can it be brought into the way of harmonious development together with the body and with the emotions. It is indispensable to develop new faculties which are not given to man in life and cannot be developed by him, in himself, by the usual methods.'"

* * * * *

♦♦♦

Dushka
♦

Yes, the Study House got a lot of publicity, but Mother always laughed that, despite all these marvels, they never really did seem to solve the problem of omnipresent mildew smell from the damp straw matting under the floor carpets

London's _Daily News_ front page Feb. 17, 1923 — announces the discovery of Tutankhamen's tomb and a "New Cult." During the next four days two-page articles and photos about Gurdjieff and the Prieuré continued to appear.

"Le Prieuré des Basses Loges," Avon, Fontainebleau. 1923

(Left) One of the first photos of Gurdjieff at the Prieuré,1922. Note: Gurdjieff on the steps surveying his new domain. (Detail above)

(Right)
Front driveway

(Below)
The rear facade
and the "Avenue
of the Lime Trees."

(Above) Mr. G. roams the grounds of the Prieuré planning where to install the old airship hangar he has bought, had disassembled and will have delivered in sections to be reconstructed as the basis for his "Study House."

(Left) The pupils start breaking ground so that a foundation and floor could be laid.

(Below) Planks to support the sections are brought in.

(Above) Putting up the framework.
(Right) Propping up the first section.
(Below) Artist de Salzmann

(Above) An old greenhouse provides glass frames that are recycled to provide windows.

(Above and left) More separate sections of the hangar are raised and attached and the building begins to take shape.

(Below and left) Work proceeds on the interior design and painting the windows as Mr. G. supervises.

(Above) Gurdjieff does much of the work himself, teaching by example. In hat and coat he nails to the Study House ceiling draperies handed to him by a pupil.

(Below) He takes out a moment for coffee.

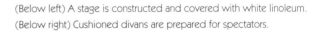

(Above) Valuable oriental carpets are laid to cover the rough floors of earth padded with straw.

(Below left) A stage is constructed and covered with white linoleum.
(Below right) Cushioned divans are prepared for spectators.

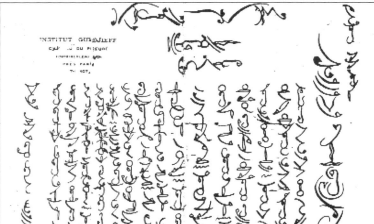

(Above) Aphorisms are painted on the Study House windows. in a decorative "secret code" script.

(Left) The same script is used by Alexandre de Salzmann to write out a Russian folk tale on a piece of Gurdjieff Institute stationary.

(Below) The last carpets are laid down.

(Above) The perfumed fountain Iluminated by changing lights is installed in the center.

(Below) The Study House is ready for a party/dress rehearsal at whch everyone wears their new Movements costumes.

(Above) As a young man, Gurdjieff loved horses,
(Right) and he rides horseback at the Prieuré.

(Below) Then, after buying himself an automobile, he teaches himself to drive "by experiment, with much grinding of gears and squeaking of brakes." [Dr. Nicoll]

(Left) In July of 1924 Gurdjieff suffers a nearly fatal automobile accident.

(Right) Even while he is still convalescing and should only be supervising from the special white chair provided for him, he can't just sit by and watch others work.

He gets up to climb into the ravine (Above) and personally handle the dangerous task of felling a tree that will be sold for timber to raise much needed funds to keep the struggling Prieuré going. Note at far left his vacated chair with a second chair beside it for his coat and coffee.

(Detail at right) As Gurdjieff (center) works, one of his helpers standing right, holding the end of the rope, is young C.S. "Stanley" Nott who has just met his future wife, Jessmin's Dalcroze pupil Rosemary Lillard at the Prieuré.

**And, yes
Gurdjieff did actually have a driver's
license...** (Right) **...but it's dated 1935 -
nearly twelve years later!**

(Above) Dr. Maurice Nicoll minding his daughter and, (Above right) — busy in the Prieuré workshop.

(Above) Jeanne de Salzmann's young charges include her daughter Nathalie (Boussik), Leonid "Lonia" Savitsky, Nicolai Stjernval and Yvonne Pinder.

(Below left) Lonia hides from his grandmother, Mme. Ouspensky.

(Above) The children play outside the bathhouse.
(Right) "Gurdjieff got bicycles for everyone!" including his sister Sophie and her husband,
— and visitors from England and America. (Below)

It is a wonderful life for children at the Prieuré.

They have their own activities and projects but are included in everything and watched over carefully by the adults. Note the overseers in the window, (Above) and Mr. G. (Right.) (Below and right) Many of the farm animals roam the grounds freely and even the smallest youngsters interact with them and learn to care for them.

The children at the Prieuré share physical work and outdoor picnic meals with the adults, but also have their own responsibilities and fun.

(Above left) A pause for lunch for workers includes de Salzmann and a small girl, perhaps his daughter Boussik.

(Above right) P.D. Ouspensky in an unusually tender pose with his cat and Lonia. Gurdjieff favored dogs, but P.D.O. nearly always through the years had a pet cat.

(Left) The children in their own donkey-cart!

(Below) One of the little girls valiantly does her share of farm chores.

Mother Evdokia

Sister Sophie

Niece Luba

G.'s father Ivan (Ionas) Georgiades,
well-known as "Ashogh Adash."

Brother Dimitri

Nephew Valentin

Cousin Mercuroff

GURDJIEFF'S FAMILY:

**Although his father and cousin did not
survive the 1915 massacre, G. was able to
bring the others to join him at the Prieuré
in the Twenties.** (Above right and below)

Seated left to right: Gurdjieff's wife Julia
his mother Evdokia, and sister Sophie
Ivanovitch Kapanadje. Standing:
Nephew Valentin "Valia" Anastasieff, niece
Lucie Devouassoud (née Anastasieff),
and Sophie's husband, Mr. Kapanadje.

(Right)
Sophie and her
husband flank
nephew Valentin
relaxing on the
grounds of their
new home, the
Prieuré.

Mr. & Mrs. (Katherine Mansfield)
John Middleton Murry

Thomas de Hartmann

Bernard Metz

SOME OF THE PRIEURE RESIDENTS circa 1925 All nationalities, all types...
(Foreground left to right, one of G.'s nieces, Lonia Savitsky, and Mme. Ouspensky.)

Kapanadze (G.'s brother-in-law)

Jean Toomer

Lenushka Savitsky

Lily Galumian

Julia Yussovna Ossipovna, called "Mme. Ostrowska"

Jeanne de Salzmann

Olga de Hartmann

Jessie Dwight Orage

Katherine Mansfield

Olgivanna Hinzenberg

Edith Taylor Swaska

Elizabeta Stjernvall

The women and girls work with the men indoors and outdoors and tend the children and the chickens used for eggs and meat.(Below left Jeanne de Salzmann center.)

There are the vegetable gardens to plant, water, and weed and their produce to harvest to feed the hungry community,... babies to rock... various farm animals to feed, or harness up to work in the fields...

(Above right and left) Members of Gurdjieff's family newly arrived from Tiflis enjoy the Prieuré and its grounds but also take an active part in the kitchen and meal preparations.
(Right) One of the goats provides fresh milk and (Far right) Mme. Ouspensky helps supervise the kitchen workers.(See below).

(Above) Gurdjieff oversees work on improvised forges.   (Below) The men and boys prune trees.

(Below) Indoors the grand piano is often used as "Gurdjieff/de Hartmann Music" is composed and notated.

(Above, left to right) Editor A. R. Orage, with diplomats Frank Pinder and Rowland Kenny.

(Right) Journalist/author P. D. Ouspensky.
A verification of Ouspensky's actually having spent
time at the Prieuré although it may have been brief.
This photo was marked by his wife in her album (see
top) "F'bleau, august 1924."

(Below) Physician Dr. Leonid Stjernvall.

F. bleau, august 1924

(Above) When years later Mme Ouspensky's granddaughter Tania (Titania Nagro) passed on to Dushka one of her grand-mother's earliest photo albums it contained this page. The center picture is recognizable as the Study House during an evening's celebration. Or was it a dress rehearsal? The other photos surrounding it show a professional theater's prosce-nium and were probably taken in 1923 at the Theatre des Champs Elysées during the Paris Movements Demonstration that took place in December of that year before Mr. Gurdjieff and his troupe left for demonstrations in America in 1924. (Below left) Another old photo showed the ship's arrival in New York on January 13, 1924. Passengers crowd the deck but at back in the center one can just see a quiet Mr. G. waiting for the gang plank to be lowered. (See detail at right.)

CHAPTER 5

THE MOVEMENTS DEMONSTRATIONS IN 1923 AND 1924

We know that already in 1917, in Tiflis, Mr. Gurdjieff was creating Movements. His followers were working with them, and demonstrations were given in the Caucasus and in Constantinople with specific music composed with the aid of Thomas de Hartmann who describes:

"...new, not very complicated exercises all connected with developing the attention. The marvelous combinations occupied the whole of one's attention and the mechanical flow of associations ceased to bother one."

But Ouspensky, otherwise such an accurate recorder of the early days of Gurdjieff's teaching, has surprisingly little to say about any of this work with Movements. He emphasized the philosophical challenge: "....the central part of your own work is understanding of the fact that we cannot 'do,' of why we cannot 'do' and of what it means that we cannot 'do.' How can you understand that? Either by trying to do what you have never done before or by doing things in another way. Then you will see whether you can 'do' or not." But Ouspensky, unlike his wife, never seems to have realized the practical value of Movements in relation to all this or how they can give one an organic experience of this basic aspect of the Work.

So the few quotes we have from Gurdjieff himself about Movements were noted by other people.

In Paris on February 29, 1924, Gurdjieff is quoted as saying:

"If our aim is a harmonious development of man, then for us, dance and movements are a means of combining the mind and the feeling with movements of the body and manifesting them together." (*Views*, page 183)

Berlin, November. 1921:

"Taking new unaccustomed postures enables you to observe yourself differently from the way you usually do in ordinary conditions. This becomes especially clear when on the command "Stop!" you have to freeze at once... not only externally but also... all your inner movements" (*Views*, page 167).

Paris, 1944:

"You understand now why I repeat always among other things, do not, for example, make a movement with the leg which should be made only with the foot. Perhaps you will need that leg for something else. You must do everything exactly from the beginning... One movement not exactly executed among seven persons and the result would be cacophony. Everything depends on the totality." (*Views*)

In December of 1923, after weeks of showing the Movements to special visitors

Dushka
♦

who came out to the Prieuré Study House on Saturday evenings, Gurdjieff was ready to present them to the sophistication of Parisian audiences. Public demonstrations took place in the famous Théâtre des Champs-Elysée, with a large orchestra, rich costumes, and special effects like a fountain of wine in the lobby!

One might have wished that a little more attention had been paid to preparing the printed program two pages of which attempted to explain in both French and English what was being offered and why. A combination of poor writing, bad translation, and a French-speaking typographer, makes the English version particularly difficult to read, but since the original source was obviously Mr. Gurdjieff, I find it an interesting document to present here.

WHAT THE GURDJIEFF INSTITUTE
HAS SOUGHT TO PRESENT US

It is practically impossible to find an epithet [sic] that will aptly describe the subject of the present programme. It is something so peculiarly new, so out the [sic] ordinary run of what we are accustomed to see, that the word "demonstration" renders very imperfectly the character of what Mr. Gurdjieff is now setting before the public. If we stretch a point and grant that it recalls the choreographic art, since we are shown movement ritual, subtle rhythms and transpositions of music into corporal expressions, still it were [sic] puerile to be satisfied with the definition of "dances" in explanation of these exhibitions. As a matter of fact we cannot fail to observe that these movements and rhythms are but a part of a tremendous whole, and that the conception of it is sheer genious [sic]. And yet it is all only one of the numerous branches applied by the founder to what he calls the Harmonious Development of Man. And the form presented has only been chosen in preference to another because it illustrates perhaps clearly and more esthetically the idea — in other respects more abstract — that underlies this Development the fact is that we have to realize that we are face to face with a gigantic synthesis of all the harmonics in the new gamut [sic, "scale"?] to which new man must vibrate — the Ideal gamut of the good and the beautiful. While it would be a difficult and hazardous task to present at once to an unprepared public subjects that can only be approached through a course of serious lectures; religion, magic, ancient art, philosophy, mathematics, all of which take share [sic] in this great re-moulding of our "Self" the explanations to this same public of the wonderful results that an entirely fresh method of education has succeeded in producing on bodies such as ours was easy and most convincing. And from the body, we are brought back to the soul...

Thus we should keep constantly in mind the principle that we must not simply admire these dances, these attitudes of ritual, these almost electrical reactions merely in themselves and for their esthetic beauty - as we might do a choreographic show - but that we must also give a thought to the new soul that makes these bodies live.

And, in this way, we shall merely hark back to the ancient wisdom of the East, according to which a dance is a prayer, a manifestation of God, a mystery. It is in this that Mr. Gurdjieff, with the insight worthy of a great prophet, has made vigorous hold of the teachings that he has brought back from his numerous travels in the East, not the East of the literary world, but the East that hides even today the most astonishingly philosophic religions amongst the secret peoples, so to say of Thibet, Upper India, Turkestan, Afghanistan. The wisdom of the thinkers of those regions has appeared to Mr. Gurdjieff to be the sole means of restoring in us the energies which western civilization is crushing out of us for ever. The more perfect and more harmonious combination of all our physical and spiritual possibilities he sought in an entirely different organization of our psychological and material temperament, and this organization was distilled into him drop by drop by the extraordinary work that went on in him after his mind had hearkened to the pre-ancient voice of the Hindu Gush [sic] and the Pamir.

We will not unnecessarily weary our readers by explaining the principles that are clearly set forth in Prospectus No. 1, presented with this programme. For the sake of greater clearness now we will merely observe that, in Mr. Gurdjieff's view, our threefold system of perception, reaction and emotion has been completely

Ce que l'Institut Gurdjieff
a voulu nous présenter

The French program for the 1923 demonstrations.

thrown out of gear under the action of modern life. The functions of each of these systems are exercised independently of one another, and this has brought about the complete incoherence of our psycho-corporal machine.

Since long before the war, Mr. Gurdjieff has devoted all his energy to the re-education of these complex mechanisms — receiving — emotional — transmitting and executive — and it is mainly to this end that he has just completed the organization of his model Institute for the Harmonious Development of Man. An almost super-human task, whose noble ideal will come right home to every thinking being. Let us hope that he will meet with ever more and more sympathy and real help on the part of all who yearn to heal humanity of the malady that afflicts it. It is signal merit to have sought the remedy in balancing our faculties anew. Does not this seem, upon reflexion, to be the most efficient and radical solution?

We trust that the circle of those who are convinced of the necessity of this total reform of our "self" will continually widen. Will not those present at the performance of to-day's programme begin by acquainting themselves, by a careful perusal of the above-mentioned prospectus, with the essential details regarding the preliminary organization of the Institute, which is fitted up with extraordinary richness and beauty, as well as with the profound causes of the need felt by Mr. Gurdjieff to change completely our relations with the external world and with our fellow-beings.

H. Br.

As previously pointed out a more accurate translation of the Institute name would have been to use "harmonic" rather than "harmonious" a subtle but interesting difference. Especially considering that in 1919 the Russian-speaking journalist C. E. Bechhofer Roberts called it Georgiy Ivanovich's Institute for Harmonic Human Development.

Soon after the Paris demonstrations were completed, everyone involved, except the orchestra, packed up and sailed for America arriving in New York on January 13, 1924. For the Russians it was an auspicious day, as according to their Julian calendar, it was January 1, the start of the new year.

Missing from the group, an exception notable in retrospect, was Jeanne de Salzmann who was unable to participate in the actual demonstrations, both in Paris and in America, as her son Michel was born on December 31, 1923.

On Feb. 28, 1924, *The New York Times* printed this letter to the editor:

"The growing body of those who are aware that 'we are in for wonders' in the realms of psychology and of feeling are not always able to recognize one another in the mass of cults and curios which these days offer. It may thus be that hundreds in New York who are interested in the idea of the extension of human consciousness to new levels will not connect this interest with the Gurdjieff Institute of France, whose founder is now in New York. Yet the free demonstrations which have been given in the last month at the Neighborhood Playhouse, and the final formal demonstration to be given at Carnegie Hall next Monday evening, Mar. 3, preceding the return to Fontainebleau of the twenty-five teachers and pupils of the school, have as their basis this ancient wisdom. The Asiatic dances are very beautiful but these are merely an introduction to the technique developed by Mr. Gurdjieff, whose Institute, now established in the chief European cities, may in another year have an American branch.

ZONA GALE"

* * * * *

On Monday, March 3rd, 1924 the Carnegie Hall program read:

DEMONSTRATION BY GURDJIEFF'S INSTITUTE

for the Harmonious Development of Man, of some of the material collected by the Institute in the East and not hitherto published

PROGRAMME

I

1. Explanation.
2. Six different gymnastic exercises of esoteric schools.
3. The Initiation of the Priestess, a fragment taken from the mystery "The Truth Seekers."
4. Stop exercise.
5. Ritual movements of the Mevlevi dervishes, known as the Whirling dervishes.

II

1. Ritual movements of the dervishes of Matshna.
2. Ritual movements of the dervishes of Majar-i-Sherif.

3. Ritual movements of the dervishes of the Takmur-Bogaeddin Order.
4. Ritual movements of the dervishes who call themselves "They who tolerate freedom."
5. Funeral ceremony over a deceased dervish of the Soukhari Order.
6. Ritual movements of Christian monks tinged with Sufism.

III

1. Four different ceremonial rites.
2. Three groups in which work is performed while dancing.
3. A few popular Oriental round dances.
4. Ceremony for inducing the prophetic sleep of the Pythoness.
5. Various exercises for the development of memory, hearing, sight, attention and concentration.

* * * * *

It should be remembered that these demonstrations were put on a scant two years after Gurdjieff arrived in France. He knew as yet little French and even less English. He had to depend on those around him: Russians, Armenians, Englishmen who had learnt some Turkish, etc. to do amateur translations. As they gave so much time and trouble trying to really understand him, this all succeeded better than one might have thought.

But I notice that de Hartmann writes that he had to hire "only Russian musicians in New York" so that "Mr. Gurdjieff could 'communicate' with them!"

Although the English editor A. R. Orage knew no Russian or Armenian and very little French, Gurdjieff came to depend on him for any presentations to the American public, such as the written programs, interviews and spoken introductions, and to help turn his profound but rough manuscript, *Beelzebub's Tales Tis Grandson* into an acclaimed literary work of art.

Alfred Richard Orage (1873-1934) was born in Yorkshire, England, to a simple working-class family that wasn't able to afford him a higher education. At twenty he became an elementary school teacher but was also able to indulge his avid interest in Theosophy, Plato, Nietzsche, and Socialism. He became known as a writer and speaker and helped found the avant garde Leeds Art Club.

In his early thirties, he ended an unsuccessful nine-year marriage and moved to London, where after three years as joint editor of the periodical *The New Age*, he took over as sole editor in 1909.

Under his leadership, *The New Age* became an influential journal that launched many famous writers, including T.S. Eliot, who called Orage "the finest critical intelligence of our day" and George Bernard Shaw, who said he was 'the most brilliant editor for a century past!"

Yet in 1922 Orage gave up *The New Age* and moved to Fontainebleau to join Gurdjieff which is why my typewritten copy of the following document is titled "Written by A. R. Orage." However we don't know how often it was actually used.

INTRODUCTION TO 1924 DEMONSTRATIONS

"The program of this evening will be chiefly devoted to movements of the human body as shown by the art of the Ancient East, in sacred gymnastics, sacred dances, and religious ceremonies preserved in temples of Turkestan, Thibet, Afghanistan...

A. R. Orage

"A few words of introduction are necessary to assure a correct understanding of our demonstration.

"Mr. Gurdjieff with other members of the Institute pursued during many years, through the countries of the East, a series of investigations which proved that Oriental dances have not lost the deep significance — religious, mystic, and scientific — which belonged to them in far off ages.

"Sacred dances have always been one of the vital subjects taught in esoteric schools of the East. Such gymnastics have a double aim: they contain and express a certain form of knowledge and at the same time serve as a means to acquire a harmonious state of being.

"The farthest possible limits of one's strength are reached through the combination of unnatural movements in the individual gymnastics which help to obtain certain qualities of sensation, various degrees of concentration, and the requisite directing of the thought and the senses.

"As for the dancing itself, it has in that form quite another meaning from that which we of the West are accustomed to give it. We must remember that the ancient dance was a branch of art; and art in the early time served the purpose of knowledge and of religion. In those days one who devoted himself to the study of any special subject, expressed his knowledge in works of art, and particularly in dances, just as we, today, give out our wisdom through books.

"Thus the ancient sacred dance is not only the medium for an aesthetic experience, but also a book as it were, containing a definite piece of knowledge. Yet it is a book which not everyone may read who would — which not everyone can read who will.

"A detailed study extended through many years, of sacred gymnastics and sacred dances, gave practical proof of their great importance in connection with the all-round development of man, one of the principle aims of Mr. Gurdjieff — the parallel development of all man's powers. The exercises in sacred gymnastics are used in this system as one of the means of educating the student's moral force, and of developing their will, their patience, their capacity for thought, concentration, hearing, sight, sense of touch and so on.

"We will also demonstrate some of the so-called "Supernatural Phenomena" — one of the subjects studied by the pupils of the Gurdjieff school. A few explanations of these phenomena will be found useful:

"Mr. Gurdjieff classified all phenomena under three categories. Tricks, the phenomena which are brought about artificially, whereas the performer pretends that they result from this or that source of natural force. Semi-tricks designate phenomena which are produced neither by deceit nor in the way in which they are explained produced through laws different from those to which they are ascribed and at the same time not artificial in their essence. The third class of phenomena are those having as the basis for their manifestation laws explained with difficulty by official sciences.

As regards the tricks, their study is considered necessary both for future investigators of genuine phenomena and for every pupil of the Institute, not only for their cognizance to free a man from many superstitions but it also introduces in him

BOSTON POST. FRIDAY

GURDJIEFF
WORK WELL
RECEIVED

Group of Pupils May
Return to Hub
Later

Impressed by the reception his prize dancing pupils received last night at the Fine Arts Theatre, Georges Ivan Gurdjieff, exponent of the harmonious development theory for the perfection of man and the dissipation of his troubles, will leave for Chicago today with a promise to return to this city, if possible, and give a third demonstration of his method, and to appear before the students of Harvard as the guest of Professor William McDougall, eminent psychologist.

AUDIENCE OF 400

An audience of more than 400 nearly filled the seats in the small theatre last night, and as on the night before, when but 100 distinguished celebrities witnessed the spectacle, they greeted the strange Asian dances and the weird musical accompaniments with hearty applause.

In the orchestra were groups of students from Harvard, Boston University, Radcliffe, Wellesley, Simmons and other educational institutions of this city and its environs. And among them were a number of psychology professors and other educational instructors.

In addition to the programme of the previous evening, Gurdjieff had his pupils perform some of the unusual tricks of fakirs, as well as actual phenomena. To the dances he added the "whirling dervish" and other steps, which far surpassed in sheer beauty of muscular precision the popular Dance of the Wooden Soldiers.

The master produced one of his pupils who was greeted as a musical marvel. With one hand he played desired parts from any opera, the name of which was written upon a slip of paper by a member of the audience and given to an attendant who held it. Without seeing the writing and ap-

Gurdjieff's Dances Amaze Boston

**Morgan Memorial
Anniversary Today**

The birthday anniversary of Henry Morgan, founder of the Morgan Me...

March 7, 1924. Newspaper clippings
from the Boston papers.

a capacity for critical observation indispensable to the study of real phenomena which requires a perfectly impartial attitude, a judgment unburdened of the pre-established beliefs.

"The phenomena of tonight will be given as if all were genuine, though in reality they will consist of the three kinds — their classification we shall leave to your discernment."

* * * * *

Jean Toomer, a budding writer, still in his twenties, but already a leading figure in the Harlem Renaissance, describes seeing the Movements demonstrated in New York first at Leslie Hall and later at the Neighborhood Playhouse: "There was no printed program. You were not given through the mind the slightest idea of what to

Jean Toomer

expect. You did not know what to call the various exercises and dances. You were in no way helped to label and classify. Not until I had seen several demonstrations did I learn that the group of exercises with which the demonstration invariably began were called 'The Obligations' [sic] and that another exercise was called 'The Stop' exercise and that one of the dances had the title "The Initiation of the Priestess." The movements... [of] the dancers caught hold of me, fascinated me, spoke to me in a language strange to my experience but not unknown to a deeper center of my being... Though I could have listened to it again and again, I had a sense from the very first that the music had not been composed to be listened to, but to be enacted. It was a call to action in those very moments that were being performed on the stage or in a march of men and women towards a destiny not even foreshadowed in the ordinary world. And

so it moved me."

Carl Zigrosser points up Gurdjieff's commitment to the Movements as an integral part of his "System" when he discusses the early days of the New York groups: "Gurdjieff later censured Orage — while admitting partial responsibility — for the mistakes he made in expounding the Method, such as not stressing sufficiently the urgency, the "terror of the situation," and *neglecting **the special educative value of***

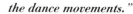

the dance movements."

Dr. William Welch

Many years later there was still the difficulty of explaining to those unfamiliar with the Gurdjieff teaching what were the Gurdjieff Movements, the "Sacred Dances," and especially their function, value and place in the Work. Scores of them were documented in beautiful films exquisitely performed by Jeanne de Salzmann's Paris classes, (usually assisted and polished by Mother). But there was no explanation of what the executants were really striving for, their inner as well as outer work, the intensity of their personal efforts, and why they felt no need of "commercial theatrical" facial expressions audiences had come to expect.

For example, once when Joseph Campbell and some of his fellow scholars attended a screening of one of these films, Dr. Welch had the unenviable task of offering them a brief introduction, reducing to a few words an immense and complicated subject.

He put it this way:

"Sixty years ago, more or less, in the Caucasus, Gurdjieff, who had come out of Russia with a small group of people, first introduced his pupils to the study of movement by means of sacred dances. These dances which he developed, and those he saw in the Middle-East and during his travels in Asia, are not ceremonial rituals, but rather a precise means of self-study based on ancient principles and knowledge, quite remote from the contemporary idea of 'the dance as self expression.'

"Gurdjieff saw the sacred dance as a way of giving an organic experience of the essential substance of his teaching — which can be, perhaps, subsumed under the term 'self-remembering.'

Joseph Campbell

"'Man in motion', according to Gurdjieff, 'is a Man lost.' It is possible to make a persuasive case for the statement that 'the essential dilemma of the human condition lies in the fact that Man in repose — 'Man the Thinker' — 'the Planner' — 'the Artist' who knows where he is going, is curiously out of contact with himself once he is in motion.'

"A position of repose is quite clear, but what happens in going from one point to the next is a mystery that clearly has influenced his direction and his destination. His attention, his presence and awareness undergo a change when he is in motion and the result, more often than not, is that he arrives at a place unanticipated by his thought and his feeling. And the movements of the body are not the only mystery. The movement of emotions, moods and feelings are equally mysterious.

"These sacred dances are designed to act simultaneously on all three parts of the human being: the mind, feelings, and body, and to discover the inner conditions that are necessary for the experience of self-awareness. Each dance has its own center of gravity that calls into play the organic experience of a particular state and its concomitant understanding.

"The dancers are focussing their attention not only on their bodily gestures which constitute a language of expression, but also on their own inner experiencings at the moment of movement.

Lord Pentland

"Here then is one aspect of the work of self-study according to the teaching of Gurdjieff."

Lord Pentland once explained Movements in another way to an open class given in San Francisco in 1963:

"In the Movements given by Mr. Gurdjieff, the succession of outer postures and attitudes, and the changes of tone and rhythm are arranged to correspond with the development of an intended inner experience.

"The attempt to keep adjusting myself to the outer and inner requirements of the movements acts as a direct help in my search for my presence. This produces in me that miraculous experience of unity which we began by calling self-observation."

And Hugh Brockwill Ripman wrote:

"I had never seen anything like this. It was not gymnastics. It was not any ordinary kind of dancing. The movements of the participants

Hugh Ripman

had a clear-cut quality, the postures were taken and held with a precision whose beauty wrung the heart.

"From the very beginning, the 'Movements' as they were called made a demand on my attention that was different from anything I had ever experienced — one couldn't hide, one couldn't go to sleep. The moment my attention wandered, I made a mistake. It was in this way that I first tasted in my own experience the force that is generated by attention which is directed by an effort of will for a long time. For myself I could hold my attention steady for a few minutes: but here, where the outside demand was added to my own efforts, and constantly renewed for an hour or an hour and a half, the results were of quite a different order.

"For this I owe my teacher, Jessmin Howarth, a never-ending debt."

But Mother herself perhaps said it best to some of her Movements pupils in a talk I once recorded.

◆ ◆ ◆

Jessmin
◆

Mr. Gurdjieff gave us a system of ideas. Why did he also put his teaching in the form of Movements? What did he mean us to learn from them? Why were the study of ideas and the practice of Movements always treated as complementary? Do we find that the Movements really are a means towards eventually gaining consciousness?

It has been said of Mr. Gurdjieff's system that 'it is a system of shocks.' And when one first begins in the work, the first shock comes when we are told to verify this statement: "You are asleep. You are entirely conditioned as a creature of habits. You are a machine. You never live with conscious intention for two minutes at a time."

We don't know ourselves so we don't really accept this. But most of us have found that through the practice of Movements one has direct experiences which lead through the body and feelings to an understanding of the Work ideas which might, lacking this means, have remained simply as theory.

Never forget that the Movements are a means. Also the inner exercises are a means; the readings are a means; physical work is a means; personal 'tasks' are a means, etc. All are means to the same end. They complement and cannot contradict each other. One means may be more helpful to one person or during one phase than another, but all are part of the Work. Without any of the other means, some people, including Mme. de Salzmann and myself, and our daughters Dushka and Natalie, have arrived, solely by doing the Movements under Mr. Gurdjieff, at understanding of awareness, directed attention, separation, the meaning of "I" and "it," and levels of consciousness.

We realize in Movements that we rarely awaken to our own life — inner and outer. We see that we always react in a habitual and conditioned way; we become aware that our three main centres, head, body, feeling rarely work together or in harmony; we begin to try to move always intentionally, not mechanically. And we discover in ourselves many hitherto unexpected possibilities; we find that one can collect one's attention, that one can be 'awake' at times and have an overall sensation of oneself. That quietness of mind, an awareness of body and an interest of feeling can be brought together and that this results in a more complete state of attentiveness in which the life force is freed and one is sensitive and open to higher influences. Thus, one has a taste of how life could be lived differently.

Because that is so, the Movements are sacred for us, and we try to keep them as pure as when they were first given and protect them from distortion and superstition.

◆◆◆

In the first few years between escaping Russia and having his Teaching recognized in the West, Gurdjieff obviously accomplished something pretty extraordinary. It was a time of dire national crisis, and burdened as he was with disoriented followers and family members all completely dependant on him for safety, support, and direction, it is amazing that this one man with no tangible resources somehow achieved the birth of a now widely recognized Teaching.

Dushka
◆

Under those most adverse conditions he managed to recruit suspicious strangers and mould them into groups of devoted pupils. In alien cities he gathered communities and materialized Institutes. Challenged by new languages, he developed non-verbal teaching methods. In foreign capitals he inspired sophisticated intelligentsia to re-evaluate discarded spiritual traditions. He weathered jealous bigotry and narrow-minded complacency. On top of it all, he underwent a catastrophic motor accident.

I find it amazing, therefore, that P. D. Ouspensky, considered by so many as Gurdjieff's primary "Boswell" could just gloss over this entire period with the following few casual and self-centered dismissive words found in the original 1925 manuscript of *In Search of the Miraculous* in the Yale University archives:

"[At] about this time I explained to him [Gurdjieff] my idea of a book which would set forth his system with my own commentary. He approved the plan and gave me permission to write and publish the book. Up until then there had been an agreement between us that I should publish nothing about his system without his consent. In May 1920, I began to work on the exposition of G.'s system and the present book took shape. In August I went to London and G. remained at Prinkipo, and shortly after went to Germany where he tried to open his Institute. In the summer of 1922 he moved to France and in the autumn of the same year opened his Institute for the Harmonious Development of Man at Fontainbleau. I must say that in the course of the following years i.e. since 1922, G.'s work was chiefly dedicated to perfecting methods of the study of rhythm and plastic art. He never ceased to work at his ballet, introducing in it the dances of various dervishes and Sufis, and restoring from memory the music he had heard in Asia many years ago.

"He moved to France in the autumn of 1922 and opened his Institute of the Harmonical [sic] Development of Man at Fontainbleau. The program of the Institute was conceived on very wide and interesting lines; and the Institute provoked a great deal of expectations among people who were interested in G.'s ideas and were following his activity. But these expectations were not justified and the proposed program was not put into practice. Besides from the very beginning there came into [the] life of the Institute many strange currents incompatible with his ideas, aims, and plans, and very soon made quite impossible any further development of these ideas. In my opinion the chief cause of this was the unfortunate choice of people whom G. admitted to the Institute. In this case it looks as if G. acted against the principles he himself had so insisted upon from the very beginning of my work with him, and the results did not fail to become very soon quite evident [to become very soon manifest.] Soon after its inauguration the Institute attracted the attention of the press and for a

MR. OUSPENSKY.
"Daily News" photograph.

month or two many articles appeared in the French and English papers. They called G. and his pupils 'The Wood Philosophers' from the Fontainebleau woods. They interviewed them, printed their photographs, etc. In December 1923 G. gave a demonstration of eastern dances and rhythmic movements at the Theatre des Champs Elysees in Paris. But I must say that the reproduction of the dances and ritual ceremonies was very uneven in these demonstrations; and while some of the dances arrested attention, others, as for instance the movements of the whirling Mevlevi Dervishes, [gave the impression] not of a reproduction, but simply of a superficial imitation without even an attempt at an exact reproduction of the movements.

"Soon after these demonstrations in the beginning of 1924, G. went to America with some of his pupils and organized lectures and demonstrations in several towns of the United States. In the autumn of 1924 the Institute at Fontainbleau was closed owing to G.'s illness. Later when I finished this book in the spring of 1925 I heard he was better and writing his memoirs.

London, 1925"

* * * * *

Another indication of Ouspensky's early attitude toward Gurdjieff can be intimated from what he says to the *London Daily News* in 1923 in a brief interview included at the very end of the four days of articles and photos of Gurdjieff and the Prieuré.

"My book, telling of our [sic] discoveries so far as they have gone, should be out this summer. I am thinking of calling it *'Fragments of an Ancient Teaching.'* In the meantime I am lecturing before small private classes, which is as much as my command of English permits.

"When students have once got over the initial difficulty of thinking along new lines and grasping the meaning of the terms employed — which may sometimes take a good many weeks — they make steady progress in quickness of perception and understanding, even without taking a course at the Institute.

"The difficulty on our side is to translate our discoveries into modern forms, but I hope that there, too, progress is being made."

* * * * *

P.D. Ouspensky's interview in the
London Daily News, February, 1923

CHAPTER 6

THE DAUGHTER

In the spring of 1923 Mr. Gurdjieff had ordered almost everyone at the Prieuré to fast. He had Rosemary keep this up for nineteen days paying her constant attention. She was really wonderful, but when she was due to break her fast, she happened to displease Mr. Gurdjieff because she went to Paris to be at the wedding of our close friend, Gert Dana (Parlier). I think Mr. Gurdjieff thought she had eaten some refreshments. He said this was a wrong and dangerous way to act after a long fast and that he, henceforth, washed his hands of her.

It was true that she had lost a lot of weight and was moving faster, but it seemed to me that her health was not good. When I went to Mr. Gurdjieff to tell him of my concern, he snubbed me roughly saying that I should let Rosemary face her own difficulties, and that to do otherwise was to be a bad friend and hinder her development.

When it was certain that we were to go to America to give demonstrations and that Rosemary would not be included in the company, I took her to see an old friend, Dr. Schlemmer, a pupil of Dr. Paul Carton who said that her metabolism had been disturbed. As a "nature" doctor he was interested and undertook to care for her until she was ready to return home.

Jessmin
♦

◆ ◆ ◆

Dr. Schlemmer was also, by coincidence, treating a young Indian visitor, one Jeddu Krishnamurti, and his tubercular brother, Nitya.

Krishnamurti was proudly living on his own for the first time in his life, in a small apartment at Number 4 rue des Colonels Renard, by further coincidence wall-to-wall with Number 6 which would later be Gurdjieff's home for many years.

Dushka
♦

◆ ◆ ◆

In February of 1924, when we were busy with the Movements demonstrations in the U.S., Rosemary came back to New York. And thank God for that — for by March I knew I was pregnant!

I continued taking part in the Movements until the Chicago date, but then I had a case of food poisoning and could no longer function. So I was shoved off onto a slow train to New York — a journey that I remember as a nightmare of everyone eating oranges, bananas, hot dogs, peanuts and popcorn, strewing the floor ankle-deep with refuse. Rosemary met me at the station, took one look at my grubby state and insisted that we brave her mother and go to their house. She proceeded to scrub me from head to foot, shampoo my hair and put me to bed with some soda water to drink. I can never forget her Guardian Angel ministrations that day.

Jessmin
♦

When Mr. Gurdjieff vetoed my plan of going to live with friends in Italian Switzerland, and went off without leaving me a return ticket, Rosemary had me stay with her until I went up to be with Esther Whiteside and her family in Ogunquit, Maine. Mrs. Lillard was not too difficult about this since she knew I had helped Rosemary out in Paris, but we had an anxious time concealing from her that I was more than five months pregnant. We knew she would fuss and be very resentful because Mr Gurdjieff had not, at least, provided transportation back to France for me.

◆ ◆ ◆

Dushka
◆

Only years later, after Mother died, reading over the de Hartmanns' reminiscences published as *Our Life With Mr. Gurdjieff*, did I myself have second thoughts and get another sidelight on this apparently shocking callousness exhibited by Mr. G. and what his circumstances were at the time. And my heart breaks now to realize that my mother died at 92 without ever knowing about these early financial dificulties of G.'s. and understanding the reasons for his treatment of her.

In describing the demonstration group's departure from New York in April, 1924, the de Hartmanns recall how Olga "had to pawn her mother's wedding ring since there was not a single dollar left once the tickets had been bought."

This is supported by a letter from Bernard Metz to his brother.

"...Then Fritz's (Peters) story that G. returned from America with $100,000.!! As a matter of fact G. returned broke from his first visit to America. We were in Chicago stranded. Our return tickets were bought for us out of the city's charity funds — what they call the Community Chest — or Traveller's Aid."

Certainly Mr. G. himself wasn't able to go back to the Prieuré with everybody else, but stayed on in New York with just one person. Since Olga had refused to be separated from her husband, and insisted that they both stay or return to France together, Mr. G. sent them off and kept Lily Galumian with him.

Thomas de Hartmann describes how: "...in order to dictate some recollections of his youth in the Caucasus. He scraped together enough money to rent two small, cheap rooms, where they began as energetic a work as only Mr. Gurdjieff knew how to create — dictation, transcription, typing, revision, again dictation... For a while they literally starved, not having the wherewithal to buy food. But the work had to go on, and it did. And when it was finished, money appeared from lectures given by Orage and Movements classes given by Mme. Galumian."

They returned at the beginning of June ("in first-class cabins."!) And then within a few weeks of his return to France Mr. G. suffered the serious automobile accident from which he almost died and which caused him to completely change his life and the activities of the Prieuré.

◆ ◆ ◆

Jessmin
◆

I spent the last weeks before Dushka's birth in Philadelphia with Mary Henderson and her friend so it was there in Samaritan Hospital that Dushka was born on September 16, 1924. As she was to have two godmothers, we gave as her name for the birth certificate "Cynthia Ann" (for Rosemary whose middle name was Hyacinthia after her patron saint, and Ann for Annette), but immediately and from then on we called her Dushka.

We returned to New York and were taken in by Annette and her French husband Jean who were running an antique store.

1924, Sailing back to the Prieuré after the the last US Movements demonstation: Thomas de Hartmann (back row center), his wife, Olga directly in front of him, and Mme Ostrowska (second row right) The three young Polish Kozlonski brothers are first row left, third row left and third row third from right. The man with life-buoy is Bernard Metz. Probably Ivanov on third row right, Merslioukin on de Hartmann's left and pianist Antoine Konstant/Tony Finch front row right

My few attempts at helping them out in the store were catastrophic. I have never had a head for business. I didn't even spot as con artists three "clients" who came in when I was alone and gave me their names as Mr. White, Mr. Black and Mr. Grey!

◆ ◆ ◆

Louise Welch later described how:

Dushka
◆

"The need to earn money for the support of the Gurdjieff work led Orage to undertake a series of lectures on literature. The sessions were held on the second floor of an antique shop on East Fifty-third Street belonging to Jean Herter, the son of a Brittany painter, himself knowledgeable in the fine arts, and his wife, Annette, a talented exponent of Dalcroze eurythmics."

◆ ◆ ◆

In addition to teaching at the Dalcroze school and various private schools, I was giving classes of Gurdjieff Movements in a hall at the Walden School. Many people had

Jessmin
◆

(Above) First photo of mother and daughter 1924.

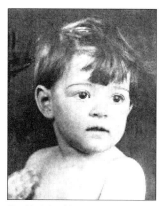  

"Dushka" Cynthia Ann Howarth. (Left)   with "Mama Schneider" (Center)   and godmother Annette Herter (Right).

been attracted by the demonstrations at the Provincetown Playhouse and Carnegie Hall, and groups were formed under the guidance of Orage who stayed on in the U.S. when Mr. Gurdjieff returned to France.

The next year, 1926, I went to Kansas City to help Dorothy Perkins' Dance School give performances, grudgingly leaving Dushka in Wantagh with a motherly "Mama Schneider," who permanently influenced her food habits by giving her pumpernickel crusts to teeth on.

By 1927, Rosemary was successfully teaching at the Mannes School and other private schools including Rosemary Junior in Connecticut. When Mrs. Lillard gave up her house, Rosemary and I decided to share an apartment on West Eighty-Third St. Dushka was finally able to be with us thanks to "mother's helper" Adela Gorska, a Dalcroze student who looked after her when she came home from nursery school and helped make us all comfortable. And this was also when I was able to study with Dr. Mensendieck and earned my diploma in her method.

◆ ◆ ◆

Bess M. Mensendieck (1863-1957), an American by birth, went to Europe to study at the Academy of Sculpture in Paris in the late 1800s. Her fascination with the obvious relationship of health to the beauty of the human body led her to go to Switzerland to study medicine and become one of the world's first female physicians. After many years researching "kinesiology," the science of human posture and motion, analyzing in minute detail the individual functions of every bone, joint and muscle and their intricate interactions, she developed the "Mensendieck System of Functional Body Education."

The System was established in Europe by 1905 and grew rapidly there, but in the U.S. the "Comstock Laws" hindered publication of her books which contained forbidden illustrations of unclothed bodies. It wasn't until the 1930s that Dr. Mensendieck really became known in her own country and began a private practice in New York which continued until her death at ninety-four in 1957.

Dalcroze had been an admirer of Mensendieck and present day holistic attitudes and methods like Alexander and Feldenkrais owe much to her. And Mother remained faithful to her training. Throughout her life, whatever form of dance, mime or physical therapy she was teaching, "Mrs. Howarth" always insisted on the constant directing of attention to one's own correct posture. This proved especially helpful to her pupils in the Gurdjieff Movements, and often when she was training instructors she would refer them to the writings of Dr. Bess Mensendieck such as:

"TOWARD PERFECTION,
EACH OF US THE ARCHITECT OF HER OWN BODY.

"In the slow evolution from the horizontal animal posture into the erect human posture, the stage has not yet been reached when the body will, entirely of itself, remain upright. On the contrary, we always have to be on the alert if we would maintain, in fine erect alignment, a structure constantly menaced by the habits and occupations of civilized life, as well as by the encroachments of age... Only by an alert and informed mind can this "floating" human architecture be maintained in perfect alignment. We must be ever conscious of our responsibility...

"Within the framework of its skeletal structure, you can sculpture the shape of your own body at will... but the primary exercise anyone needs is the maintenance

Dushka
◆

of correct posture during normal daily activities. No daily half-hour or any periodic physical exercise can ever create a balanced musculature if the muscles are not properly used the rest of the time. Correct posture and the relief of pain that is caused by a faulty posture, can only be achieved when all muscles are used in accordance with their anatomical functions and the laws of mechanics.

"The most common defects in posture are toeing-out flat feet, saber-shaped calves, knees locked in hypertension resulting in bow-legs, slack buttock muscles, potbelly, sway-back, hunched back, stooped shoulders resulting in sagging breastbone and thus caved-in chest, 'dowager's hump', and sagging crown resulting in a compressed vertebral column...

"The habit of 'toe-ing out' makes it impossible to position one's various body masses properly... Start always placing your feet parallel and exactly below your hip joints by positioning the balls of your feet almost two inches apart, toes pointing straight ahead, and your heel about three inches apart so that they point straight backward...

"Never straighten your knees all the way. Bend them ever so slightly. Raise your pelvis in its hip joints by tucking your buttocks firmly together and slightly under. Contract your abdominal muscles firmly while maintaining a tall stance (especially to stand correctly on one leg.)... Rather than allow your legs to drag your body along, it is the body, tall and thus well-aligned shifting its weight forward in the ankles that should carry your legs with it."

◆ ◆ ◆

Jessmin
◆

During some time, Rosemary had been courted by an Englishman, Stanley Nott, and Mr. Orage encouraged her to become engaged to him. They were married in the summer of 1927. Because Rosemary was Catholic and Stanley was not, no Catholic priest would perform the marriage ceremony for them. It was finally arranged in the Russian Orthodox Church.

Mrs. Lillard had been very much against everything and I had to beg Mr. Orage to come with me and persuade her, at least, to appear at the service. He charmed her into acceptance, reminding her that Stanley was an old friend of his. Later, we laughed together for I discovered when I went to help Mrs. Lillard dress that she had her hat, gloves and handbag all laid out ready.

The day of the wedding was the same day that Lindbergh came back to New York after his record-making flight across the Atlantic. Traffic in many parts of the city was held up by the crowds (reported by the media to be "two-thirds of the total population of the city".) gathered for his Welcoming Parade. Rosemary and Stanley had to wait for an hour for the priest to get to the church. Stanley's best man and the chief usher were even later, and a disappointed little Dushka, who had looked forward to being the flower girl, arrived with her nurse when the ceremony was almost over. On the way downtown to the wedding luncheon arranged by Larry Morris, Sherman Manchester's car ran into someone (who was not badly hurt), and some of the wedding guests who were with him had to sit around for hours in the police station. So it was a day to be remembered by us all as well as the newly-weds.

My memory is hazy about why and when Rosemary and Stanley went to Europe. It must have been early in 1929, because I then took over her job at the Rosemary Junior School and we moved to Connecticut for a few months until I decided to try for a better life for us in California.

◆ ◆ ◆

Mr. Gurdjieff made another visit to New York about this time. I myself have no clear memory of our encounter, but I'm told that some of the Orage group people evidently decided that I should be taken to him, and since Mother refused to go, her friend Louise (later Welch) and some others were recruited to escort me.

Dushka
◆

Mr. G.'s first reaction was an immediate objection to my being called "Dushka." He decided that my name should be "Sophie," (whether because my birthday occurs near to a St. Sophia namesday, or because it was his maternal grandmother's name, I've never known.)

I thereupon proceeded to appall everyone by scowling and arms akimbo, digging my fists into sturdy hips, (see photo at right) loudly objected that I would not "be called a sofa!"

I further disgraced myself by refusing something Mr. G. offered me. It was probably "*loucoum*" (Turkish delight) which through the years he loved to hand around to guests, especially children, but which I have never liked. He immediately scolded me saying that it was not polite to refuse something without at least trying it.

I was tightly hugging to myself a bribe that Louise had given me to ensure my good behavior, one of those "circus cage" boxes of animal crackers. When, and very generously I thought, I held them out and offered them to Mr. G, he just waved them away.

I later reported smugly to Mother and everyone else: "That man wasn't polite,"

Another glimpse of that period is given by Bernard Metz, one of the original translators of *All and Everything*, and one of the few still staying on at the Prieuré in 1929. I still have a copy of a revealing letter he wrote on June 8 to Orage in New York City.

Dushka/Sophie.
Early attitude!

"Dear Orage,

"As promised I am sending further 'report.' G. has gone ahead with 'improvements'– gone whole hog — and still going on with the postage.

"Monk's corridor 100% renovated, you can guess what that means, all down to details, even new furniture, new lights, lino. And how richly painted! Corridor is going to be surprising — enneagrams painted on every arch and other things — what? I don't know yet. Elsewhere — perhaps angel and devil on each side of each arch?

"Over each door is black skull and crossbones beneath which are words '*Memento Mori*'. This will be over every room in Prieuré..."

[Metz explains elsewhere this use of "*Memento Mori*" quoting Gurdjieff saying that: "One of the strongest motives for the wish to work on yourself is the realization that you may die at any time — only you must first realize this."]

Louise Welch in the Twenties.

Bernard Metz at the Prieuré.

Painting of Orage in New York.

"Paradou too is being done. English corridor rooms also and even attic rooms. All old furniture repaired and upholstered, all beds painted, etc. etc. Concierge is painted in oils and new furniture is being put in, also expensive anthracite stove... all this not for boy on duty... does G. expect many enquiries in winter?

"Does this mean first volume will soon be published — who knows? Also library painted in oils, 'very special' room for private interviews with G.

"What's in that head of his? He's preparing for something — improving fountains, buying hundreds of roses and other plants, beginning a swimming pool just outside Bath, ('will all be covered in — ') and so forth and so on.

"He is personally attending to all as of old. He is here four days a week. Not yet been on a trip. Two days to Vichy and one day to Rouen, that is all. Yet he is still revising. Goes to 'office' at Y. in the morning till midday, again in evening.

"I've not touched Book since my return. Too much to do out of doors — we're hard at it. My brother has returned — felt there wasn't much purpose in 'ordinary conditions of being-existence,' however rosy they may be.

"[Allan] Browns are here. G. taking a lot of trouble with them. They're very comfortable. Live on ground floor, old billiard room. He is daily massaged by hand and machine under G.'s direction. Also gets it 'hot and cold' in the Bath. David is a changed boy, happy and eager. They all seem contented. Mrs. Brown fits in well; difficult at first but now even works enthusiastically... G. is good to them.

"When are others coming? Caesar [Zwaska] I hear is in Paris, may be here soon.

"Great pity people are not yet here. Weather is perfect for work. Spring here is fresh, air filled with 'Okidanokh,'' plenty to do, and spirit of activity is infectious. It helps.

"G.'s threat of 'thorns, thorns' did not materialize. I didn't give him a chance. I pricked myself before he could. Result, he saw no further need, nor do I, so again it's '*roses, roses.*' After all, hard physical work can be a great pleasure, for a period — this period is now. Something like the first autumn, but, of course, not so strenuous and not so much friction.

"No 'Enos' [outsiders] here, not one, only family.

"And how are you? And your 'Result?' [New baby, Richard] And Jessie? All well I hope. I'd very much like to see him. I wonder when.

"My greetings to Jessie and remember me kindly to all there, particularly to the 'Gods' and [Hugh] Ferrisses, and the Schindels and Rita [Romilly]. Is [Paul] Anderson coming? And the Orages?

"Well, au revoir

Bernard Metz"

* * * * *

In another letter written to his brother Louis many years later (August 8, 1961), Metz revealed something else about activities at the Prieuré:

"Yes, I translated *Remarkable Men*. It was so easy compared to *Beelzebub*. G. wrote it just once in comprehensible Russian, but as for Beelzebub, he wrote and rewrote it several times and each time it had to be translated anew. And he wrote it in a deliberate, obscure style. Many a time I asked him what he meant and he said 'Ask Dr.' Dr. S. [Stjernval] puzzled over it and said 'damned if I know,' then I'd ask Hartman [sic] and he gave up.

"You know the first version of Beelzebub G. dictated to Mme. Hartman soon after his accident when he was too weak to write. It was about 25 pages, then it grew and grew with each re-writing. I must have translated that book about 7 or 8 times, and as for 'THE Warning,' he revised it at least 20 times.....

"...No, I'm not writing about G. There is an old Buddhist saying: "He who knows not, speaks; He who knows, speaks not." ....I'm working on a historical-religious novel...."

* * * * *

When Gurdjieff visited New York in the winter of 1930 he was accompanied by several people. One of them, Louise [Goepfert] March [quoted by Beth McCorkle in *Recollections*] described how:

"Mr. Gurdjieff said he wanted to have photographs made 'by the best photographer in town'... First shots of him alone were taken and then it was time for the group photo of all of us: Mr. Gurdjieff, Dr. Stjoernval, Mme. De Salzmann, myself, Michel and Nikolai. Such a fuss! Who should stand? Where to sit? How to be?

"In the end Mme. De Salzmann and I stood while the others sat — the two bearded men, one at each end of the couch, the two boys in the middle.

"The next day Gurdjieff shaved off his beard.

"That was the reason for the picture!!"

* * * * *

On arrival in New York on one of these visits in the Thirties, Mr. Gurdjieff had more trouble than usual going through customs. He made the officials furious and suspicious by declaring, of all things, large quantities of — eyelashes!!

But, again, this is one of those stories that has had all kinds of versions and ramifications through the years that had a very simple, practical explanation. And I have the proof — a little box the top of which reads:

New York, 1930 (Left to right) Mr. Gurdjieff, Louise Goepfert March, Nikolai Stjernvall, Jeanne de Salzmann, Dr. Leonid Stjernvall. (seated in foreground: Michel de Salzmann.)

(Above) The box of XENICILS marked "Les filles D. Gurdjieff, FONTAINBLEAU (FRANCE) which when opened (Right) reveals a tas-selled vial of dried up adhesive and two wooden cylinders on which are affixed eyelashes made by Dimitri Gurdjieff's daughters

"Les Filles D. Gurdjieff
FONTAINEBLEAU, (FRANCE)"

Mr. Gurdjieff's younger brother Dimitri had three daughters living at the Prieuré, Luba, Genia (Eugenia) and Lida (Lydia), who made eyelashes out of their own hair. Packed in specially made boxes also containing an attractive tasselled vial of adhesive, the girls' "Uncle George" had brought a supply of them along to sell to the Americans.

Nicholas de Val in his book *Daddy Gurdjieff* remembers that a frequent visitor in those days to Gurdjieff's Paris apartment was the viscomtesse Ksenia de Nozzolini. A sub-contractor for Elizabth Arden, Ksenia was probably closely involved in the eyelash project, hence the name "Xenicils." And it was she who recruited the young Nicholas to help with the publicity (as he later described in his book) – by wearing them in public on the sidewalks of the Champs Elysees.!!

Luba later wrote that: "She [Xenia] was French-Russian – a funny woman. During the war, that woman was making false eyelashes. I worked wth her some, and

The German Consulate in New York City issued this "identity" card (passport?) to Gurdjieff (date?) The entries in German approximate: "Stateless ...previously Greek"..."a writer"..."born in Alexandropol 28.12.77" {sic} [!?!] ... "strong build"..."oval face"..."brown eyes"..."grey hair" (!?!). The signature is simply "G. Gurdjieff".

I learned. Gosh it was difficult work. So minute. We used to use our own hair and fastened it to little wooden mats..."

Gurdjieff was often the victim of countless rumors and an easy target for dubious stories. Two examples of this kind of thing that I had to listen to through the years were "that he had once almost been deported from the United States," and, worse yet, "that he was working with Hitler which is why he stayed on in Paris during the second World War." But these two rediculous stories can also now probably be explained by an old document found amongst the Gurdjieff family papers.

Paul Beekman Taylor, doing research for his books, recently came up with the piece of information that Gurdjieff had travelled to America in those days using a "Nansen passport." (Named after Fridtjof Nansen, a Scandinavian diplomat who developed this document, thereby winning a Nobel Peace Prize, as a solution to the problem of countless stateless people needing identity and travel papers after the eruptions of the first World War, and the Russian Revolution.)

But later Paul also noticed that these Nansen passports ran out in 1934.

So if Gurdjieff was on one of his visits to New York and his travel papers were suddenly no good it explains why he would have to apply for new ones.

Though it doesn't explain to me why he went to the German Consulate to do it. (Though probably it had something to do with the fact that the influential Schwarzenbach family were part of the New York groups.)

What other plans did he have in mind then? Where was he hoping to travel to next? In fact, where did he actually go in some of those years when there is no clear record of his activities? Yes, Louise March said somewhere that "Gurdjieff once arrived on her doorstep in Germany in the mid-Thirties travelling on a German passport..." but otherwise??

And when a real emergency did come, such as the German occupation of Paris, surely an experienced veteran of other international upheavals, revolutions and wars would know how to pull out a German passport when necessary!

* * * * *

CHAPTER 7

THE THIRTIES IN HOLLYWOOD… LYNE PLACE, ENGLAND

In the summer of 1929, Mother packed us up and we set off for California which meant many days of train travel, but we broke up the trip twice. First, we stopped off in Chicago so that Mother could give Movements classes to a group of people working on the Gurdjieff ideas with Jean Toomer, acclaimed as the author of *Cane*.

(Arna Bontemps, in his book *The Harlem Renaissance Remembered*, describes how "…in 1925, at the Gurdjieff meetings in Harlem, Wallace Thurman soon met Jean Toomer, Dorothy Peterson, Eric Walrond, Langston Hughes, Dorothy West, Countee Cullen, Aaron Douglas and other eager and talented young black artists like himself.")

We also stopped for a couple of weeks in New Mexico where Mother worked on pantomime with the Santa Fe Theater Group and visited her old friend Mary Henderson who was working with the Indians there. Mary arranged for me to spend my days with the Navajo children in their one-room schoolhouse. You can imagine my envy at seeing them arrive in the mornings, riding their own horses.

One school project there that we all joined in on was making adobe bricks for a new building. Adobe is the reddish clay found locally which is mixed with water and chopped-up straw, put into small molds and baked in the sun. The mixing part involved us all treading barefoot in a big vat with the pink mud squooshing up deliciously between our toes. Then, to reward us for our work in the glaring sun, we were given huge pieces of watermelon. Unfortunately no one noticed that we then innocently spat the seeds into the mud mixture. The result of this was that the next year, as Mary Henderson wrote us, the building which had been made from "our" bricks was cracking and buckling as those melon seeds sprouted and expanded with nature's irresistible force.

Mother had a bad shock when we arrived in Southern California. She had been promised Movements classes that never materialized, and the place we were to stay, Kevah Griffis' small house in Dana Point, was still under construction. Luckily Michio Ito, now a successful "modern dancer of Japanese origin" had also moved west. He had known Mother at Hellerau and given dance recitals with her in New York in 1918-19. He asked her to join him running a dance studio in Hollywood.

They were also joined by Jon Caldwell, a talented young dancer and later NBC-TV producer. Jon earned extra money working for cartoon companies where his work consisted of dancing as certain characters while the artists drew him as the basis for their animations. (I think it is called "live action reference.") He began to have ideas

Dushka
♦

THE "HARLEM RENAISSANCE" GURDJIEFF GROUP IN THE TWENTIES
SOME OF THE MANY NOTED WRITERS AND ARTISTS WHO GATHERED AROUND JEAN TOOMER
(WITH VISITS FROM A.R.ORAGE AND JESSMIN HOWARTH)

(Left and above)
Author Jean Toomer, 1894-1967.

Arna Bontemps 1902-1973.

Wallace Thurman, 1902-1934.

(Above) Langston Hughes, !902-1967, as a young man in 1923 and

(Right) as a national treasure memorialized on a US postage stamp in 2002.

Dorothy West, 1907-1998.

Countee Cullen, 1903-1946.

Aaron Douglas, 1898-1979. A poster extolling his art work.

about basing his dancing and their cartoons on classical music.

To try out the effect of this on a child, he would use me as a guinea pig, much to my delight. When Mother was busy teaching, Jon would sit me in the back room of the dance studio and play me phonograph records. As the music played, he told me stories and described characters whose actions and moods synchronized exactly with each note and effect of the music. He had hoped to interest Walt Disney in his stories but had no success, until he finally interested Leopold Stokowsky who had better access to Disney. And so, Fantasia was born.

Michio Ito (ca 1892-1961) came from a samurai family in Tokyo. His father was a well-known architect who knew Frank Lloyd Wright and Michio's six brothers were all active in the arts. Michio originally left Japan for Paris at 18 to study singing and there met Debussy and Rodin. But seeing Isadora Duncan dance led him to the Dalcroze school where Mother met him. World War I took him to London where he began his career as a solo dancer, meeting and collaborating with members of the artistic community notably Ezra Pound, Yeats and George Bernard Shaw. In 1916 he moved to New York where he again met and danced with Mother. Many such famous names as Martha Graham, Pauline Koner, Lester Horton, and dance-mime Angna Enters danced with him early in their careers during the 1920s. His successful teaching and performing career in California ended in the 1940's when, after being interned here during the war he returned to Japan until his death in 1967.

THE NEW YORK T

E VIEW

io Ito

from Page 10

"In performance, Ito kept his face immobile so that personality was excluded and idea enhanced."

From the Times review of *"Michio Ito, The Dancer and His Dances,"* 1978

When Jon Caldwell's sister Helen Caldwell, also a dancer who worked with Ito, published her book *Michio Ito, The Dancer and His Dances* in 1978, the *New York Times* review headlines called him 'An All-But-Forgotten Pioneer of American Modern Dance.'"

Mother was also giving private Mensendieck lessons at home. Since these sessions involve the pupil and teacher studying all parts and actions of the body, the pupil usually works nude. I would giggle to myself when I saw movie luminaries like Lili Damita, Nancy Carroll and Mrs. Samuel Goldwyn arriving in chauffeur-driven limousines at our house for their early morning classes. I knew that often the big fur coat and high heels were the only clothes that they had thrown on for the trip.

Mrs. Goldwyn recommended me to her husband for a role in a new movie he was casting. It was to be the life story of the famous opera diva Mme. Schumann-Heink and they needed someone to play her as a child. I sulked when Mother turned down my "big chance." It was years before I relented — when I finally saw actual photos of the famed prima donna! She really did look like the character she presumably inspired, Disney's hilarious "Clara Cluck," the full-chested hen that sang duets with Donald Duck.

Mother tried her hand at various other things as well. She wasn't allowed to teach in American universities since she didn't have the required accreditation. But that didn't stop them from putting her in charge, one summer, of teacher training (!) at the University of Southern California. How to understand the vagaries of education and bureaucracy that sanctioned that!

There were visits, I vaguely remember, to Ojai to listen to someone called "Krishnamurti" and in Los Angeles we met a "Rajgopal" whose small daughter, "Radha," I could play with.

In 1931 Mother joined with Leah Lovell, wife of the noted health food pioneer, Dr. Philip Lovell, and some other educators to start their own experimental school, The Children's Workshop. Up until then I had been happily fooling around at the Hollywood Progressive School where I was allowed to go barefoot and keep a pet, a slim little brown pig that followed me to all my classes.

But the originators of The Workshop had many very innovative ideas of education. We children were kept busy, alert and happy while really learning a great deal. The French classes were given as an outdoors recess activity where all the games and songs were in French. We eagerly and quickly learned our multiplication tables since there was a daily contest with a prize for the first one to solve the problem: 123456789 times 987654321. Mother taught Dalcroze eurythmics and pantomime, and many parents, whether teachers or not, spent time with us and joined in various activities. Even the smallest children were encouraged to "write." They could always go to a nearby adult who would seriously take down their dictation.

We studied various sciences during weeklong camping trips out of doors. By day as we roamed the desert our enlightened science teacher aroused our curiosity about geology, meteorology and biology. Anthropology and history were linked as we discovered Indian mummies in hillside caves. At night, under the open sky, we learnt astronomy.

But the most unforgettable lesson of all, and I still wonder at it, was visiting a huge construction site where grown men, presumably educated and intelligent, were building a dam right next to the San Andreas fault!

I spent much of my time when Mother was busy, with the Lovell family in their special new house on the top of Dundee Drive which overlooked Ginger Rogers' house and busy tennis court. The Lovell House became famous as one of the outstanding modern designs by the architect Neutra. But when I first visited it, like the Dana Point house, it wasn't finished. The house consisted of huge slabs of concrete terraced into a steep slope of bare earth down which dust and dry leaves blew to settle on the surface of the swimming pool. The pool was built in directly under the living room and was therefore always in the shade. On the other hand, the living-room draperies had to be kept drawn so that the bright sun wouldn't fade the royal blue carpeting!

The Lovells also had an avocado ranch where we spent two summer vacations with the icy irrigation tank as our swimming pool. Dr. Lovell was one of the first nutritionists to extol avocados and I heard later that he made a big contribution to the emerging state of Israel by sending them shiploads of avocado seeds.

In 1934 we spent a wonderful summer at a cattle ranch in Santa Susanna where the owners were trying to survive the Depression by taking in paying guests. The

(Above) Neutra's acclaimed "Lovell House." . The terraced garden (Below) provides a setting for a production offered by "The Children's Workshop." Dushka (center) tries her first acting role, as a poppy!!!

(Clockwise) Amerlia Earhrdt (left, in 1932) rents Jessmin her cabin in Eagle Rock where Dushka visits her mother. When they vacation on a ranch in Santa Susanna Dushka is a proud participant in the Rodeo parade, wearing borrowed finery and riding a borrowed mount.

matriarch of the family, old Mrs. Gillebrand, enjoyed reminiscing with Mother about the North of England. She had been born there but had left as a 15-year-old bride to accompany her husband across the United States to California in a covered wagon.

The big ranch and its livestock had been used in recent years as a location for filming cowboy movies. One surprising result of this was that the older horses, which we children were allowed to lasso and ride bareback, might suddenly remember some former training. Then a bare toe touching the withers in a certain way, or a careless yank on the reins, could unwittingly signal the animal to do any of a variety of sudden disconcerting tricks from jumping or bucking to collapsing down acting dead.

(Twenty years later, when Fred Clark and Benay Venuta drove me up to revisit that area, I was so saddened to find that the ranch I remembered so fondly had already been turned into a huge community of bungalows.)

About this time Orage got in touch with Mother. After years of running the Gurdjieff groups in New York, he had returned to England in 1931 and established a different kind of life for himself, his wife Jessie, and their two young children, Dick and Ann. He had started a successful literary journal, *The New English Weekly*, and was an active propagandist for Major Douglas' *Social Credit*. But he had not, in spite of how some people have misinterpreted these activities, *left* the Gurdjieff Work. On the contrary, he asked Mother to come to London to work with him and a group of pupils, both adults and children.

A. R. Orage and his new son Dick.

Louise Welch writes "Orage had undertaken to supervise special work in Dartington Hall, having always felt the importance of right education for the very young – and now with a boy and a girl of his own, his interest was personal as well... When Mrs. Howarth arrived in London, she and Orage talked together, leaving her with the impression that he intended, with Gurdjieff's permission, to have children in the school learn the Gurdjieff Movements suitable for the young."

So, at the end of the summer of 1934, Mother and I found ourselves in San Pedro Harbor boarding the *Villanger*, an old Norwegian fruit freighter that took us down the Mexican coast, through the Panama Canal to the Caribbean and across the Atlantic during a month of dreary sailing. There were only five other passengers, a strangely assorted and boring group. I managed to pass my time hanging around the patient crew, "helping them" with their work of scrubbing, painting, splicing rope, etc. They were a kindly group of tough old Vikings whose main pastime, oddly enough, was doing beautiful flower embroidery.

But I don't know how Mother endured the tedium. I know she must have been pretty desperate because for the first and last time in her life she joined in our card games. We usually played rummy, and surprisingly she always won. Only years later when she was watching a game and said, "Oh, is that the way you count the cards?" did I realize we had been rather trusting in letting players figure their own scores.

◆ ◆ ◆

During those years that we spent in California, Rosemary first spent some time in France, studying with M. de Hartmann to whom she was devoted. He passed on

Jessmin

to her and taught her how to play the music for Mr. Gurdjieff's Movements, which she herself preserved and passed on in the last years before her death, by recording an extensive series of about sixty pieces. She saw a lot of Edith Taylor, stayed with her now and then, and cared for her before and after Edith's baby, Eve (later called Petey), was born. The Notts' first son, Adam, had already come on the scene, and when they moved to London, a second son Jimmy, was born.

I don't think that any of Rosemary's English familiars have ever understood how very difficult those first months of London life were for her. She was homesick for the freedom and vitality of existence in America. Stanley was often abroad, travelling for his family's hat business. She had to keep house on a limited income, and Stanley's parents accepted her rather grudgingly. She told me that they would always introduce her to friends apologetically, saying: "And this is Stanley's wife. She is American and plays the piano."

But, at least she had the Orages close by and some fulfillment in her teaching in one or two progressive schools — including the Russell School run by Bertrand Russell's wife, Dora. Stanley tried to encourage her to meet people and invite guests in. He was naturally gregarious and a good host, very proud of Rosemary's cooking skill and always showing off her piano playing.

When we arrived in London in the Fall of 1934, I found Rosemary not very happy. We stayed with them in Hampstead for a week or two and I saw that the strain of keeping house, caring for two active boys with little help from a series of young, untrained Irish maids, as well as her teaching, really exhausted her.

We renewed our friendship as we were always able to do immediately whenever we could come together. I moved out to Buckinghamshire and Rosemary would come out often on Sundays sometimes bringing Adam or driving with Jessie Orage. The following summer, when the Notts were staying on a farm in Hertfordshire, we also lived near and were able to see them often, and Rosemary let me take Adam and Jimmy along with Dushka on a vacation in Brighton.

By then, Mme. Ouspensky had heard that I was in England and asked me to go to see her out at Lyne, the beautiful property Ouspensky's English pupils maintained for him. She wanted to persuade Mr. Ouspensky to have the Gurdjieff Movements taught to his pupils there. She was very kind to me and relieved, it seemed, when I somehow managed to give a right answer to Mr. Ouspensky's grim question: "Why do people do the Movements?" and I could only say: "To help develop their attention."

So it was arranged, and for several years Rosemary and I went out to Lyne regularly every week, and always had the privilege of talks with Mme. Ouspensky. We both learnt a great deal from her. It was a happy teaching time, for Rosemary did not just play the music for us. She felt exactly how best to support me and was sensitive to the pupils' state. I never had to suggest to her to slow down or speed up, to play more loudly or more softly — she always sensed when this might be helpful. And I never since have had a pianist who understood as she did, that the physical tonicity of the executants was directly influenced by her touch.

◆ ◆ ◆

Dushka
◆

Mother and her pupils gave Movements' demonstrations at Lyne in 1938 and in London's Colet Gardens in early 1939.

Mme. Ouspensky's photo collection that Tania, her granddaughter, passed on to me, contains 145 large pictures of the Colet House event and indicates that what

The Nott Family (left to right) Rosemary, Adam, C. S. (Stanley) Nott, and Jimmy.

Adam (left), Dushka and Jimmy by the pool in Brighton, 1935.

they presented then was a pretty accurate recreation, about fifteen years later, of Gurdjieff's original 1923-24 demonstrations.

It might be noted that among the dedicated, hard-working participants were: Dr. Maurice Nicoll, John G. Bennett, Dr. Francis Roles, Lord John Pentland, Rodney Collin-Smith, Pierre Elliot, Hugh Ripman, Robert S. de Ropp, Thomas Forman, Aubrey Wolton, Capt. Vivien Wolton, Reginald Hoare, Geoffrey Palmer, Lonia Savitsky, Daphne Ripman (later Matchelajovic), Dorothy Darlington, Lesbia Kadleigh (Kadloubovsky), Irina Valnieff (later Hoare), Eve Pryor (later Princess Galitzine), and others. Most of these were influential in the later continuation and spreading of the Gurdjieff ideas, and I'm sure this experience was significant in establishing Movements as an important part of their work in spite of Mr. Ouspensky's reluctance.

In fact, I notice that in one of J. G. Bennett's many books, *The Sevenfold Work* on p. 122 he points out:

"We can understand these ideas better by taking the example of the movements… There are three different ways in which the movements are significant and they illustrate how a practice from the tradition of the Work can enable us to make a transition from one line of work to another… This was most impressed on people in London in the winter of 1938-39, just before the war, when they were working on a demonstration of the movements. The people who taught the movements — far more than in the much more free and easy approach at the Prieuré – insisted on treating them as something sacred and that it was a privilege to be expressing through the movement."

◆ ◆ ◆

The demonstration at Colet Gardens included the "Hoya Dervish" exercise in which most of the participants are men. But at the edge of the big grouping there are two kneeling women, in this case Daphne Ripman and Irina Valnieff. The deep prostrations they had to do were exhausting and I told them to arrange together some signal to use when they wished to stop for a breather.

Jessmin
◆

Margaret Capper

Robert de Ropp

Mme. O. with her granddaughter Tania Savitsky.

(Above) Sophie Gregorievna Ouspensky at the head table during a party at Gadsden .

(Left) P.D.Ouspensky (Above) Mme. O. at Lyne with old friends the de Hartmanns.

(Above) Young Tom Forman, a dashing private pilot and horseman whose regular duty at Lyne was to bring Mr. Ouspensky (far right) his favorite horse for his afternoon ride .

Lyne Place, Virginia Water, Surrey, England

On the evening, no one sat in the first two rows of the audience, and Mr. Ouspensky asked me to sit with him in the third row.

All seemed to be going as planned when, suddenly, to my astonishment, in the middle of the Dervish, everyone on stage froze immobile. After a moment or so I felt I had to call up to the stage "Enough!"

Later, I learnt that Daphne, growing out of breath, had meant to whisper "*Stop*" to Irina but it came out in a squeak that all the group on stage heard and obeyed.

The next day Mr. Ouspensky called me to him and said:

"Jessmin, I will show you how superstition begins. You remember that last night we sat together and you made no sign to the pupils and yet they suddenly stopped. Today, already, many people from the audience have called me saying: 'Wasn't it extraordinary how Mrs. Howarth was able to give a *Stop* without any of us being able to see how it was done.' And we laughed together.

◆ ◆ ◆

Going out to Lyne sometimes took more time from her small sons than Rosemary would have wished, especially at weekends when Adam and Jimmy were free from school. She later told us of the salutary experience she and Stanley had when they decided to sit the boys down and explain to them what it was that took her away. They tried to explain "how Man could improve himself," "the importance of an opportunity to work on oneself," "the possibilities of human self-development," "the seriousness of what they were studying," "the depth of their commitment." All this kind of thing was discoursed upon at length.

Dushka
◆

Finally, the two youngsters just looked at each other and then back at their parents and said:

"Crikey! What were you like <u>before</u>?"

Rosemary's husband, Stanley, (C.S. Nott) was certainly a good, kind man, but as Mother suggested, one who "might have needed a little more success." Even the nicest people may suffer personal bias that should be kept in mind when evaluating them as witnesses. (Did you see *Rashomon*?)

An example is Stanley's version of how Mother came to be at Lyne:

"When they moved to Lyne Place I had suggested to Ouspensky that he should

Jessmin's Movements pupils give a demonstration at Colet House, London, 1939. (Above) *The Hoya Dervish.* in which the men shout "Ho! Ya!" while in the foreground Daphne Ripman and Irina Valnieff do energetic prostrations. (Below) One of the touching friezes of *The Women's Prayer.*

let [!] Mrs. Howarth and my wife teach his pupils some of the dances that Gurdjieff had shown in the demonstrations. He agreed to consider it. Much later there was a big "do" at Lyne at which some of the Movements were shown. I very much wanted to go and was somewhat chagrined to be told that it wasn't possible. Madame had decided to punish me, I gathered, because I would not take an active part in their work."

A quite different character can be felt in this modest account of some activities at Lyne, by someone who became one of Mme. O.'s closest caregivers, Margaret Capper:

"...Then we moved from the small house (Gadsden) to Lyne Place, a lovely house with beautiful surroundings: a lake, a rose garden, a ravine with a variety of rhododendrons ablaze with colour. Mr. O. had a quiet apartment with a small tiled hall where, on a table, there was an impressive figure in bronze of a warrior. Passing this one day, I met Mr. O. and asked: 'Why do you have that figure, militant? fighting?'

"'War necessary' he said, 'inner warfare.'

"But so much has been forgotten... Alas. Lessons without words, depending on one's state of awareness.

"Madame had asked the men to dig a trench, a large one, for storage of our possessions or even for shelter. The men set to with a will. Mr. O. passing by this activity told the men to stop. 'But Madame said... etc., etc.' Mr. O. disregarded this and left them to their misery.

"What, oh what to do?

"So a procession started along the corridor of the house from Mr. O.'s room to Madame's room. White-faced they went from one to the other. Madame: 'Continue! It has to be done.' Mr. O.: 'I told you to stop...'

"What a lesson!

"I witnessed this interesting procedure sitting in a corner waiting for Madame's bell. After a very long afternoon of anguish, all was peace. Exactly how that came about I never heard, for the next day all was 'normal,' and what was necessary was done. More than one trench was dug."

However, Robert de Ropp, who was one of those diggers, comments in his book *Warrior's Way*:

"Actually Ouspensky was quite right. The outdoor bomb shelters that the British people were feverishly digging were completely useless. They filled with water in the wet weather and turned into swimming pools." I also would later find that out at my English school, St. Christopher's.

Margaret Capper also described the first meeting she attended, which had referred in part to the native people in far off countries:

"Mr. O. advanced the theory that, maybe, they were not 'savages' as we called them, but remnants of a very old forgotten civilization. This sounded most realistic to me.

"The rest of the meeting I have forgotten, only that at the end Mr. O. said: 'There will be no more meetings. You have enough material to continue for yourselves if you wish, but I have work to do to continue my writing and can no longer give time for meetings. That is all.'

"Many were stunned, including myself. I hastily wrote a note asking I know not what, but with much anguish. I had a telephone call by return and was invited to meet Mr. O. 'This was not intended for YOU,' he said. 'There are many people who come as a matter of course and this is one way to get rid of people who are not serious.'

"After this I was privileged to be given small assignments and errands. Unlike most people, I was quite "free," someone therefore always available.

"One time I was asked to go to a meeting place and announce, 'there will be no meeting tonight.' I was a little puzzled at the seeming lack of interest or comment by the recipients, until having expressed this on my next meeting with Mr. O. he said: 'Oh, I daresay they had been given the message many times before. Always I give such messages to several people. In that way I am sure of achievement. Why? People are asleep. You cannot depend on them... so...'"

* * * * *

CHAPTER 8

THE SHADOW OF W.W. II

Dushka

♦

Orage had died unexpectedly soon after we arrived in England, thus changing all Mother's plans to immediately begin teaching Movements in London. So after those first weeks spent with the Notts, she moved us out into the country, to Wendover in Buckinghamshire.

She rented a picturesque little cottage that was covered with roses on the outside with the result that there were hundreds of earwigs on the inside. A big rock garden had been lovingly created by the previous tenants, two elderly bachelors. The plumbing was primitive even for pre-war England; the bathtub placed in the middle of the kitchen with a wooden top on it which served as the table. The outhouse was exactly that. Out! But poised on the hillside so that one could open the door and gaze out at a beautiful, uninhabited expanse of valley and fields filled with black-faced sheep and rabbit warrens.

I bicycled daily to my new school, the all-girl Mayortorne Manor, which professed to be a "farm" school. That sounded fine in principle. Like most kids I loved animals and regretted that our travelling around so much made it difficult to keep pets. But I was unprepared for this English version of farm education that was apparently intended more as an aid to snobbish families who couldn't cope with realities like telling their daughters the facts of life. Here any animals "in heat" or about to produce young were spirited away out of our view. The only reproduction we learnt about were amoebas dividing or the albumen in eggs. We did lug around heavy pails of slopping bran mash, and swept out dusty, cobwebby pigsties while piglets nipped our legs even through our high rubber "Wellington" boots. When I once reacted with a good old American "damn it all!" I was almost expelled. On occasion we paraded two by two "in crocodile" on walks through the countryside wearing our required school uniform: a "beaver" hat and navy blue, pleated gym tunic over a navy sweater over knee-length woolen "knickers." Strangely enough, for gym period we took off our gym tunics. That was fine for leaping over the leather horse but when we learned folk dances it was difficult to feel graceful skipping and curtseying in those long knickers.

So I wasn't too sorry when it was arranged for Mother to teach at Lyne Place for Ouspensky's people and later the groups of Dr. Maurice Nicoll and Mrs. Allen as this necessitated our moving to Wimbledon on the outskirts of London. I transferred to the Beltane School, a very progressive co-educational school. But the kids there did anything they liked, which I found very boring. One saving grace was the forge where I spent hours pumping bellows, heating, melting and hammering horseshoes into knives — and vice versa.

This period of Mother's teaching is referred to by the author Samuel Copley in his *Dr. Maurice Nicoll: Portrait of a Vertical Man.*

"Great Amwell House. Here the Work began to assume a perceptible 'Nicoll' character... From time to time we performed some of the first six of Gurdjieff's 'Movements' known to us as the 'Obligatories'. These had been given to us in pre-war days by Mrs. Howarth with Mrs. Nott at the piano. The services of these ladies, pupils of Mr. Gurdjieff's, had been lent to the Nicoll group but were promptly withdrawn when it was observed that notes were being made of both the movements and the music. This was against the rules.

"Some of us who later joined the Gurdjieff Society, found that our aim should not have been to 'Learn' the movements, but to learn to work on ourselves by means of the movements. In fact, if we did master a movement to the extent of being able to perform it mechanically, it would no longer be of any benefit to us. The demand for attention in all parts of our being was of prime importance. Sometimes a posture or a movement, never made in ordinary life and outside the scope of our habitual associations, would give us a new impression of ourselves and a sense of wonder."

Soon we were moving again — now to Wandsworth, a London suburb, where Mother rented the ground floor of an old house owned by the Brays, two elderly sisters and their even older brother. These three were very English, but had been brought up in Czarist Russia where their father had managed a remote estate. I would sit upstairs with them in the evenings helping to braid red, white and blue cords and sew them onto strips of elastic to make patriotic headbands which were to be sold at King George's upcoming Silver Jubilee celebrations. The Brays recounted fine stories of Russia, things like wolves chasing their sleighs or the first time they were served blinis with red caviar and couldn't understand starting with dessert pancakes and why did the raspberry jam taste so fishy! — or the neighboring Countess who heard that bathing in milk was good for the health and complexion — but it took so much trouble and expense to bring in all that milk that she couldn't waste it, so she drank it.

Stanley Nott describes going to see Mr. Gurdjieff in Paris about this time and that he was given three huge boxes of sweets, sausages, and preserves to bring back to Madame Ouspensky, his own little family, and Mother and me. I remember a box filled with chocolate liqueurs shaped like bottles, Turkish delight, litchee nuts, halva, gold coins of foil-covered chocolate, mysterious unknown things from a mysterious unknown person — who was, I gathered, my father— but I let it pass!

Our new address, 91 West Hill Road, even got written up in the newspapers. This residential back street was sometimes used by the royal motorcades as a shortcut to Wimbledon tennis events, and we would hurry out to watch. Once we were shocked to see one of the big Rolls-Royces take a corner too sharply, and right in front of our house, ease over onto its side with a dull crunch. The anguished chauffeur and other attendants leaped up on top to pull open the door and lift out an old lady with lots of white curls, none of which seemed disarranged. It was Queen Mary! Everyone was much more shaken up than she seemed to be. We rushed to bring out a chair and she graciously sat in our little front garden to wait for another limousine. The Press appeared out of nowhere and the papers next day were full of pictures of the Queen in spotless white gloves sipping a cup of tea sitting on our chair!

King George celebrated his Silver Jubilee in May 1935, but then died in January 1936, and the popular Prince of Wales became King Edward Vlll.

People had always spoken of the Prince fondly and I only remember hearing one criticism — that "he sometimes made God-awful noises." Evidently he had been trying to learn to play the bagpipes!

But soon there was turmoil in the government and within the Royal Family about his relationship with the American, Mrs. Wallis Warfield Simpson. Many people were appalled when she got her divorce and Edward wished to marry her.

But London Cockneys had their own loyalties. One day Mother and I were on a London bus which was held up by a huge, noisy crowd gathered at the gates of Buckingham Palace. We finally made out what they were chanting: "We want Eddie and we want his missus too! We want Eddie and we want his missus too!"

But by mid-December, Edward had abdicated in favor of his brother, George VI (Elizabeth's father), after making a moving announcement on the radio.

Queen Mary

King George V

Mrs. Wallis Simpson

The Duke and Duchess of Windsor

About this time Mr. Gurdjieff was sitting in a cafe in Paris with Kathryn Hulme and Alice Rohrer. These were two members of "The Rope," the special group of women, mostly Americans, and mostly writers, who studied with him at that time writing down verbatim whatever he said. And one notices that they begin to adopt some of G.'s speech mannerisms in the process.

Kathryn Hulme

Kathryn reported in her diary that she had commented on Edward's speech saying: "Now King has left — says in radio speech not for long time will he return — he is like man without a country."

Gurdjieff's reply was:

"This case, he is my colleague."

When Alice sympathizes with Queen Mary who has seen her first-born son fail, Mr. G. says:

"No, not be sorry. Those people quite exceptional, not like ordinary man on earth. EARLY SHE TAKE HABIT OF VANITY — all humaneness go into ego. She have pride for class, only people who REPRESENT SOMETHING can be important for her. Already now she turn to this next son, he is now King."

Another time G. talks about "King business," this time about the new King, saying: "...he is nonentity, but different kind than was brother. New King is such nonentity that if, for example, he wish kiss your hand, between arising of wish and expressing it, a thousand times he forgets, and when he speak he says 'I wish break your rib.'"

And about the departed King, now the Duke of Windsor, G. says: "Only in one case I have pity for him — if he NOT marry her. Only then..."

In 1949 in Gurdjieff's Paris apartment I met a tall Englishman, Russell Page, about whom an American newspaper once wrote : "...(he) is to landscape gardeners as Isaac Stern is to violinists or Rod Carew is to hitters."

Russell Page and his wife Vera in 1949 at Gurdjieff's funeral.

When the Windsors took a house in Gif, near to Paris, Russell had been the obvious choice to design the gardens, which became an important hobby for the Duke, and he developed a lasting and close relationship to the exiled couple.

Russell's American wife, Vera Milanov (Rene Daumal's widow), once told me that at the weekends she often accompanied Russell to Gif. One day when Russell and the Duke were busy outdoors, she found herself alone with the Duchess, and couldn't resist asking her: "Tell me! As one American to another! Really... How has it been?"

She told me the Duchess sighed and said: "Well! It's not easy keeping a romance going for eighteen years!"

For my summer vacations, no matter where we were living, Mother always tried to send me away to somewhere "different" and "interesting." As I look back on it now, I think this was her attempt to put me in touch with some male authority figures to help round out my adolescence.

Whatever the reason, one year, since I was a typically horse-mad teenager, she arranged a junior apprenticeship for me in a racing stable. Unfortunately there was practically no riding, but a lot of manure shoveling.

Then there was a summer on a fishing trawler in the Norfolk Broads. But the boat had engine trouble and never left the dock. Nevertheless it required a great deal of scrubbing and mopping starting at five o'clock on cold, misty mornings, and eating fish three times a day.

A third year she sent me to a boys' (sic) camp in the countryside near Hastings. The director, a Major Curry, was a "pukka sahib" type who had been in "Indjah," and had, to his chagrin, no sons, only two daughters. So that summer he included me so as to keep them company. We three girls were segregated at night in a separate field where our individual pup-tents were set up. I found my tiny tent stuffy so I would lace up the flaps at my neck and sleep with my head outside. That is, until the morning I awoke thinking I was being attacked by a hideous, huge-eyed monster. A farmer had let a herd of cows into our field to graze, and one of them was enthusiastically licking my face. Another time I woke up to a strange musky smell, a scrabbling down my body and over my feet, and a horrendous noise of barking and horn-blowing above and all around. A fox-hunt had chased its poor quarry into our field and the fox had tried my tent as a place to "ground."

Finally in 1939 Mother managed to save up enough for us to have a summer vacation together and we went off happily to France. She had somehow located an inexpensive pension in Moulleau on the outskirts of Arcachon, a seaside resort on the Bay of Biscay. It was surrounded by tall pine trees and nearby there were large sand dunes. A popular local sport was to ski down the slopes of the dunes that were coated with pine needles. The aroma of the bruised needles and the sound of the cicadas in the vibrating heat were a wonderful change from England. So was our first lunch at the pension, so thoroughly French with lashings of garlic in the lamb and the cake sodden with rum. But at the next meal, the meat was also redolent with garlic and the dessert strong with rum, and so it continued for our entire stay. On the other hand, we never had too much of the ripe peaches that everybody sliced into glasses of white wine with a little sugar. Even we children were allowed to share in that and our own special treat was afternoon *goûté*, hunks of crusty *baguette* bread eaten with big blocks of dark chocolate.

It was an easy walk down to the beach where instead of cabanas for changing, all the mothers had huge sack-like robes tied by a drawstring at the neck, under which, with some strange bumps and contortions, they dressed themselves and their children.

Further along the shore there was an inlet where the famous Arcachon oyster beds were tended by men and women all wearing the traditional big black lace headdresses to protect them from the sun.

I made friends with the little daughter of the pension owner. She was home on vacation, and despite some language difficulties, we compared notes about our respective schools. By this time I had transferred to St. Christopher's in Letchworth, and she was shocked to hear that it was co-educational, Quaker and vegetarian. The idea that our school uniforms were a hideous color combination of olive green and murky gold also understandably offended her pubescent French taste. She, on the other hand, was smug about her strict convent school and profoundly shocked me when she casually said that the nuns required that even when she was at home she had to wear a long gown in the bathtub so that she wouldn't see her own naked body.

Our idyllic holiday was suddenly interrupted!

War had been declared and general mobilization was urgently under way!

Everyone congregated in the narrow streets gesticulating, yelling and pushing to read notices that were being posted up everywhere.

In a few hours the tourist hotels along the beachfront were unceremoniously emptied out, so as to be converted into hospitals. The bedding was carried outdoors to be aired and draped over all the lawns and bushes, so it looked like snow had fallen. Almost immediately the first wounded soldiers started to arrive "from the Maginot Line," said hushed unbelieving voices, for the French had had complacent faith in their "Line" as an ultimate protection against invasion.

Mother and I needed to return to England, but there were difficulties, not least of which were the special documents that were immediately required for any kind of travel. The local police station soon ran out of the necessary application blanks, and we were told to ask for some in one of the other towns. The only problem was that getting to another town also required special papers, and so it went.

Finally, we were able to get under way. The first part of the journey was to Bordeaux where we waited all day for space on a train to Paris. The station was like a madhouse, noisy and crowded with hundreds of frightened and irritable vacationers frantically trying to get home. The only ones quiet and calm were a company of statuesque Senegalese soldiers, so tall that their finely chiseled black faces stood out high above the crowd. It was a shock to see, as we approached them, that a very small, arrogant, white officer was in charge of them, strutting about, prodding them with his cane and being altogether loathsome.

Mother managed to push through crowds around a refreshment stand to get some fizzy lemonade which in those days came in a bottle with a cork, and gave it to me to hold. Imagine the effect when, shaken up too much in the heat, the lemonade exploded with a loud bang and projected its cork right into the officer's cheek. Convinced, evidently, that he had at last really been shot by one of his own men, he yelled, scrambled over a ticket counter, and cowering behind it, waved his pistol in all directions. After a moment of shocked silence, the entire station-full of worried people started roaring with laughter at him while his delighted soldiers tried to keep straight faces. For the rest of the afternoon, the mood was relaxed and everyone was pleasant and friendly.

Our overnight train ride to Paris was slow and uneventful, except for the crowded conditions, blacked out windows, and dim lighting, all the light bulbs having been hurriedly painted blue. But our arrival in the huge city was extraordinary. Paris was a ghost town. The Parisians had rushed to leave, fearing immediate bombings, and they only returned gradually in the ensuing weeks. At that moment the streets were quite deserted. The stores were empty and dark, all the windows criss-crossed with paper tape to keep them from shattering if there were explosions nearby.

When we did manage to reach the well-known Hotel du Quai Voltaire where, presumably, we had reservations, everything was locked up and vacant-looking. Finally an old watchman answered our anxious ringing and reluctantly let us in to the dark lobby, directing us up to a third floor linen closet so that we could make up our own beds.

The next day we hurried to leave on a boat-train to London.

Once we were back in England and for the next few months, the war seemed remote with just a few hints of the big troubles to come.

My school, St. Christopher's, patriotically dug up its treasured cricket field to install a huge underground bomb shelter, only to find during the first formal Air Raid Drill, when teachers and pupils all obediently lined up and marched out in formation, that the shelter had completely filled up with water.

Then the government distributed gas masks. Each person was assigned one and required to carry it at all times in a square cardboard box also provided.

In the family where I lived as a day boarder, Mr. Reece had also purchased a special dog version for their beloved spaniel. The first and last time we tried on our masks was an event. The Reeces, their two children, the dog and I all became monsters resembling black faced pigs. And the noise! For after having sucked in foul, latex-smelling air one had to blow it out through the rubber flaps against each cheek which made the most rude sounds. The poor dog barking and honking in his, and our choking laughter in ours made us glad we never had to use them seriously.

In the meantime, Mother was still living in London and also coping with gas masks. She had felt it incumbent on her to join up as one of the Wandsworth Air Raid Wardens. She was trained, uniformed and given a heavy metal helmut as well as all sorts of cumbersome equipment which included a First Aid Kit, a flashlight, a gas mask, a whistle and a large wooden ratchet noisemaker that she was expected to twirl loudly in case of a gas attack, while holding the light, giving instructions while whistling, etc. One of her first duties was to canvass the neighborhood, going door to door intoning the recommended inquiry as to whether the inhabitants had "receptacles for their respirators?" It didn't take too many blank stares from our Cockney neighbors to make her abandon the official jargon and ask simply if they had "boxes for their gas masks."

On many of the London streets First Aid stations were being set up and protected by piles of sand-bags. One of our friends passing by stumbled on a protruding bag and grazed his leg. The fledgling paramedic recruits rushed out and begged him to let them practice their new bandaging techniques. Unfortunately, one of them, solicitously leaning over his patiently reclining form, allowed her heavy metal helmet to slip off, falling on his face and breaking his nose. That wasn't enough! The ambulance they called to race him to the hospital had a bad accident on the way.

In the winter of 1939 Mother had decided the time had come to leave London and join me in Letchworth, a town designated as a "Garden City", so that we could live together without my changing schools yet again. But many people were trying to leave the big cities suspecting the bombings to come, and accommodations were hard to find.

So we were glad to accept the only empty cottage in Meadow Way Green even though it was very reluctantly offered. In the 1920s, "The Green," a cluster of two-story cottages, had been planned and financed by two retired suffragettes to provide a haven where single "gentlewomen" and widows could live together in a friendly atmosphere. To that end a condition imposed by the well-meaning founders was that all the residents must come together for lunch in the communal dining-room, and each in turn take on the task of planning a week's menus. The tight-knit community of elderly ladies must have realized that the alternative to accepting us might mean being forced to include "some of those noisy evacuees," the city slum children who were being billeted wherever possible in the country.

By this time, Rosemary, whose family, the Lillards, still lived near New York, had taken her two boys to America. They were waiting for Stanley to join them there. Little Jimmy was recovering from a tragic accident with farm machinery which took his leg. Then and for the rest of his life he overcame this loss amazingly well, even, as an adult, becoming a foremost teacher of Gurdjieff Movements.

The Herters, Annette and her husband Jean, were also in New York but no longer had their antique business. Annette had opened the "American Conservatory of Music, Drama, and Dance," an impressive title for an old East 64th St. brownstone with a little stage in the basement. She hoped to recruit old friends like Mother and Rosemary as teachers and in the meantime printed up an impressive list of "participating faculty," including Robert Porterfield of the Barter Theater, dancer Hanya Holm, composer Edgar Varèse, and others. How much their participation was active and how much was moral support we never knew, but she did, later, get me into the Edgar Varèse Chorus for performances at the World's Fair.

❖ ❖ ❖

Meadow Way Green, Letchworth, Herts.
To Annette Herter, New York, December 13, 1939
Dearest Annette,

Jessmin

◆

It seems less absurd to wish you all in the USA a "Merry Christmas and Happy New Year" than to say it here. Now that I've heard from Rosemary that you and the Conservatory are still hanging on courageously, I can send you the usual greetings with less anxiety and with all my love.

I looked forward to writing to you, and suddenly there seems nothing to tell. If we want to try to "carry on as usual," then talk, and even thought about the war has to be cut out, and I would go melancholy mad if I let myself dwell on the future. So we behave and exist as if Dushka were to be able to live out a useful youth in a constructively-minded world.

It is not so difficult to pretend here in this suburban "Garden City" where only minor things fret us. The school carries on normally and most of the children are too absorbed to be conscious of any changes. Dushka has gotten over her first upset and is completely busy all day and some evenings with

Meadow Way Green,
Letchworth, Herts.

lessons and friends, and dancing and class performances and earning swimming medals. She is going through a rather frivolous stage, a little late, and rather inconveniently as this is School Certificate year, but I take it as normal. In fact I've gotten over my excessive maternal cycle and feel more detached from her than I could ever have hoped. But existence being so precarious, we have to live together and just wait to see what can happen.

I hate the idea of returning to the USA as I can't get one idea for how I might earn my living there. However, Dushka is slowly orienting herself towards trying to get into Antioch College which Mary Henderson recommended. And, if things are as horrible next Spring as we have every reason to expect, somehow, if it can be accomplished at all, I must get Dushka away. At the moment she blindly plans on at least one year here, perhaps more, and some more time in France which she loves. I say nothing, for what can one advise? At least she is not wasting time, and she is still only fifteen.

Our new home is still looking like a poor student's quarters. I've had to bring the furnishings people have lent me, mostly old and ricketty, and try to fit them into three rooms about nine by nine feet. The result is not too handsome, but we are really more comfortable than in London, and shall be living more cheaply, despite new wartime prices, once we get settled and have provided heating and black-out necessities like thicker curtains, and so on.

You would be able to make a play out of the inmates. There are the two retired nurses, efficient and Rabelaisian, in constant friction with two poverty stricken "ladies" who are hopelessly loud-voiced and Bohemian, using their hunting habits to screen the windows, and hopefully digging straw into their garden, evidently believing this to be manure. And a fragile wee thing who is stone deaf and makes enough clatter with her table utensils and size-three walking-shoes to make one fear that a milk cart pony is loose, and so forth.

We see them all daily because we have lunch all together in a big dining room, and everyone has, in turn, to manage meals for a week. Anyway, one can't feel isolated here, and Dushka doesn't mind being the only youngster, so we'll get on all right.

As for the place, in winter it is ugly and has a vile climate. It is set so high there is always a bleak wind and rain and sleet quite five days out of the week.

I busy myself arranging, painting, altering curtains, and doing stupid work for the Parent's Circle. But once Christmas is over I have other schemes, but alas, no hopes of earning money. So I don't know how we shall finish out the winter.

What news have you from France? Jouvet wrote me when war was declared saying that he would not be called up, (yet), but that his son had gone. He seemed confident that Paris would come back to almost normal. I just hadn't the courage to meet him, as he asked, in Paris. He is too startlingly successful, and somehow the same romantic *tendresses* hardly ring true after twenty-two years. He had better be left with his sentimental souvenir and illusion.

Rosemary will have told you about the Ouspenskys, and G. And although I think she and I find different value in the system, she in making effort and being active in doing, and I am trying to observe and learn to be, not do; still I believe we feel exactly the same about both and I won't add anything. I am just more convinced than ever that having "power" is a white hot danger. And pride, possessing and excluding, can poison anything.

Anyway the three Jessmins — one who does housework meticulously and is polite to her neighbors — one who teaches the G. Movements feeling really sure and knowing certain possibilities, though entirely inarticulate — and the other that very few people know of (Rosemary never at all), who gets wildly furious and suicidally lonely, and madly set in certain loves and ideals — these three just won't tie up together. And I know I have to go on secretly watching, for superficially acting is far too easy. And such a relief I found this summer in Arcachon when I went back to being a gregarious chatterbox with the nice, warm, demonstrative French people. It struck Dushka dumb and she hasn't forgiven me yet!

There I go, babbling on, so as to tell you something different from the less intimate news I'm writing to Rosemary and Mary Henderson.

Rosemary tells me that she is so happy to come over to work at the Conservatory, and that there is life and promise there. This must cheer and encourage you, as it does her. She has had a hard row to hoe since Jim's accident, even if success seemed to be with her, and I do trust that her friends will all help, as you have. Hasn't she developed delightfully?

For Stanley it will be more difficult to make the change. He has lost his spring and is apt to pity himself and shirk responsibilities. And too he has, somehow, the Jewish sensitivity, and way of not being able to be on the same level. Either he feels superior and "manipulates" people, or inferior, and then he is either resentful, or he becomes negative. But he is a very good organizer, full of ideas, and he is tremendously fond of being with people. Just a little success and he will be radiant. So if you or Jean can give him a tiny encouragement, please do.

In any case, don't worry about us. For the present it is all right. I'll watch out for Dushka as best I can, and be joyful for any unexpected pleasures like, for instance, a nice long letter from you.

With all my love... and your godchild's greetings...

Jessmin

◆◆◆

In Meadow Way Green, Mother and I, the only child, were considered strangers and foreigners to be regarded with curiosity and suspicion. But there was a special tenseness about what Mother might do when it came time for her lunch planning.

The two main leaders among the tenants were: the purposeful, overpowering Miss Rolfe (whose insignificant sister followed her around like a pale ghost), and her great rival, a Miss Kilgall whose brother was a missionary overseas. The latter was a dainty but determined little woman who, being very deaf, wore an electrical "hearing apparatus." This was considered very modern then when many old people still pointed silver hearing trumpets at you. But she was very stingy with her batteries. As a result, Miss Rolfe, who usually got her own way merely by insisting on it loudly and at much length, had met her match in Miss Kilgall who triumphed by simply turning off her "apparatus."

These two constantly tried to outdo each other and build their social reputations by producing interesting possessions and giving competing accounts of their travels abroad. But their biggest bone of contention was – Yorkshire Pudding! Each had her own pet recipe that she actively campaigned for and tried to convince other meal-planners to use for Sunday lunch to accompany the traditional roast beef that was usually served.

We found on our arrival, not the friendly community hoped for by its founders, but two armed camps, those who would use Miss Rolfe's recipe when it was their turn to be planners, and those who chose Miss Kilgall's.

Excitement grew as Mother's week approached. Whose recipe would she choose? When Sunday came, the problem was sneakily circumvented by Mother who took

Dushka
◆

advantage of the nearness of Christmas to serve them turkey and stuffing.

From that time on we were accepted by both groups and were much in demand as tea guests. The same old stories which had palled from being told to the same reluctant listeners were joyfully dug up for this new audience. Beloved souvenirs were dragged forth from musty corners for our inspection, and often as we entered a cottage (always, of course, suitably dressed up for the occasion) we would find all the inside doors slightly ajar revealing little treasures carefully placed so as to catch the eye. We soon learned the art of balancing a teacup and cinnamon toast in one hand while admiring some handmade lace or watercolor miniature held in the other.

The way was not always smooth. Miss Rolfe, who, as she casually but elaborately informed us, was directly descended from "*Princess* Pocahontas — <u>that</u> Captain Rolfe, you know," had arrayed her room with old dance programs and photographs of a well-known regiment. She kept leading the conversation back, so as to stress the importance and exclusiveness of this regiment, her way of impressing on us what high circles she had once moved in, and showing us, semi-heathen foreigners that we were, how condescending she was to honor us with her invitation. Unfortunately, at some point Mother unthinkingly revealed that her brother Wallace had been a Major in that regiment, a fact which undermined Miss Rolfe's entire campaign and caused that party to end on a rather sour note.

We also had a little difficulty with Miss Kilgall. We had been invited to have after dinner coffee with her. Mother refused cream and sugar in her cup so that Miss Kilgall exclaimed: "Oh! So you like it black as we used to have it in Cairo." Mother nodded violently, glad to have the matter settled. Ever after that Miss Kilgall was firmly convinced that Mother had lived in Cairo, while everybody else secretly suspected her of deliberately deceiving the old lady.

But it was Annie, our pert little charlady, who really saw to it that we were kept in our place and conformed to the high standards of "The Green." She was an institution in the place and had been there as long as anyone could remember. She knew just how everything had always been done. If Mother so much as put some firewood on a different side of the fireplace, Annie would deliberately pile it back in its original place saying: "We always keep it here!"

Annie belonged to a vanishing breed. Later, when we were back in New York, she sent a letter to us painstakingly thanking us for a gift we had sent her. Then, to explain how busy she had been, she said that she had started "Spring Cleaning" early this year. It was mid-winter! She had heard that the Germans were a "very cleanly people." And with all the newspapers full of dire warnings of a imminent Nazi invasion, she had firmly resolved that "no foreigners were going to arrive and find her ladies dirty!"

One day, coming back from school as usual to have lunch in the dining room, I found Mother looking anxious. She explained that she had just received a phone call from the American Embassy advising her to get me to Galway, Ireland, in two days to board the *S.S. Washington*, the last ship that would be transporting civilians for the duration of the war. It was already crowded with almost three times the passengers it was intended to carry, even first-class ticket holders gratefully accepting cots in the baggage hold.

Being American born I needed no visa, but Mother had always carried a British passport and the British quota into the States had long ago been filled. The shock of hearing about this sudden up-rooting and the idea that I would have to leave Mother and make such a trip alone evoked one of my rare fits of weeping. Everyone in the dining-room stopped talking and looked over at us, concerned. Miss Kilgall got up and hurried to our table asking what the trouble was, and Mother tried to explain into the hearing apparatus.

Miss Kilgall gently patted my shoulder and cooed: "But dear, I always thoroughly enjoyed my sea voyages. Just be sure to take a nice fancy-dress costume as there will surely be a lovely ball."

Mother tried to suggest that, perhaps, considering war conditions, this might not be quite the usual crossing. Miss Kilgall paused to consider this and then said brightly: "Well, isn't it good that Dushka swims so well..." Mother's face blanched, "...although I have heard that it's most difficult to swim when there's oil on the water." That finished Mother completely.

With only a couple of days left she bravely started preparing me for my trip. We went up to London for some last minute shopping in Selfridge's Department Store. Everyone was commenting that today's fog was "a real pea-souper!" Even indoors it was difficult to see across the room. Only later did we learn that, this time, the "fog" had been smoke from fires at Dunkirk where hundreds of gallant small boats were evacuating trapped English soldiers from the French coast.

Then, wonder of wonders, the next day some unknown young man at the American Embassy (Bless him!) called to say that he had just noticed on my travel documents that Mother's place of birth was South Africa. Did she realize that this made her eligible for the South African quota which was still open, and since as a minor I was allowed to have an adult accompany me, she could therefore leave with me on this last sailing?

What a rush! Even with Annie's valiant help we only just managed to throw together a few clothes into a couple of small bags, and left the rest of our belongings, everything we owned, to be professionally packed, crated and consigned to some future transatlantic freighter sailing.

Little had we imagined that the English customs officials, in meticulous conformity to petty wartime restrictions, would demand that the huge crates containing our things be reopened to locate and remove one old Roman coin someone had once given me, "since no currency might leave the country." They were then reopened yet again since the shipper's detailed bill of lading listed my old Mickey Mouse watch and "no jewelry is permitted out." The resultant months of delay meant that all our things were still there waiting to be loaded onto a ship when the London Docks were so terribly bombed, destroying everything.

Grateful as we were to sit out the war safely in the United States, we missed these links with our past and family. There were many times, as the years went by, that Mother regretfully referred to certain keepsakes and heirlooms, letters from Adolph Appia she had collected intending to put together a book, and so on.. We were lucky that Annette was a conscientious godmother. As Mother had sent her various photos she had put them into an album that I later inherited, our only mementos of all those early years.

So in June of 1940, Mother and I together travelled to Galway to board the

Washington, and we set off across the Atlantic. But soon there was an atmosphere of uneasiness. A rumor began to spread amongst the passengers that our ship was being followed by a German submarine. This was finally confirmed by the Captain who announced on the loudspeaker, "Everything necessary is being done." However, this merely meant that he had ordered his radio officer to repeatedly send out the message: "We are American... We are neutral... We are carrying only civilians... We are American... We are neutral...."

Most of the people aboard had recently been through very difficult times, only just keeping ahead of the Nazi advances to get to this, the last ship's sailing that could take them out of wartorn Europe. Mother and I had only seen in newsreels what many of them had personally experienced; escapes on foot along roads strafed by German planes, indiscriminate bombings and much more. Not surprisingly, they mistrusted the submarine's intentions and the Captain's casual assurances. So they pushed up from the crowded depths of the ship wearing their life jackets and spent nearly the entire transatlantic crossing out on deck as the submarine continued to follow us, ominously, day and night.

On June 14th., I also was up on deck when the Captain made a special announcement, this time in a choked voice.

I can only guess what it meant to the adults milling around me, how it must have epitomized to them the probable fate of all Europe.

To this day I can feel the palpable emotion around me and see those hundreds of faces, all, whether men or women, with tears streaming, as the loudspeakers broadcast:

"At this moment German Forces are marching into Paris!"

* * * * *

CHAPTER 9

RE-ADAPTING AS
AN AMERICAN "CO-ED"

Once we arrived in New York, the war in Europe began to seem more and more distant. Annette and Jean Herter welcomed us and installed us in an upstairs floor of "The American Conservatory of Music, Drama and Dance."

Dushka
♦

After the months of blackouts and restrictions we happily re-accustomed ourselves to bright lights and American extravagances, but especially to lightheartedness, humor and optimism in people around us, recently so rare in England.

While Mother started trying to get herself established professionally, I joined in the productions the Conservatory students presented in the basement theater, practiced the piano, and rehearsed with the large chorus of young people that Edgar Varèse was presenting at the World's Fair.

What appeared later on my first job resumé impressively as "part time secretary and receptionist" was really just an attempt to be generally useful to Annette. I was definitely miscast for one task my godmother set me. She needed to audition ballet instructors for the next season and asked me to be a beginner's ballet class for them to use to demonstrate their teaching abilities. Poor applicants! This was a talent Mother definitely hadn't passed on to me. The only thing balletic about me was that my feet turned out. I don't think Annette hired any of them.

In September, we found that although I had completed my final year at St. Christopher's, I was still too young to be accepted for the work and study program at Antioch College. So, as there was a good public high school in nearby Huntington on Long Island, Mother rented rooms for us there and enrolled me for a repeat senior year.

In those days, but no longer I'm afraid, Huntington was a comfortable country suburb where many of my fellow seniors drove their own station wagons. Most of my classes were pretty easy after my English preparation. So the hardest part of high school life for me was simply fitting in.

I was hardly ready to be a typical U.S. co-ed. This was the epoch when American girls wore those two-toned saddle shoes with ankle socks, a string of pearls over sweaters buttoned down the back, and long swinging hair.

I had few clothes except my horrible green and gold school uniforms. My hair was dangling in schoolgirl braids, and being shortsighted, a London doctor had condemned me to ugly little round "specs." My English spelling, putting "u" in words like colour and honour, irritated the teachers. And worst of all, since when we had first arrived in England and many of Mother's friends had been reluctant to expose their children to my "terrible American twang." I had proceeded to develop a super-British accent, and yes, probably, a prissy attitude to go with it.

Godmother Annette tried to help by making that year's birthday present a new hair-do by Antoine du Printemps in his exclusive Fifth Avenue salon. My dreams of a long sweep of hair were dashed when, with one swift chop Antoine sliced off the first braid up near my ear. I let out such a yell and floods of tears that the whole establishment came to a standstill and people were sent scurrying to buy me placating presents and roses.

So, if nothing else, that extra year of high school helped turn me back into an American. A convincing final touch was my being awarded the gold medal at an American Legion Oratory Contest, where I piously declaimed the virtues of "The United States Constitution!" No mean feat considering I had never even read the thing until I entered the competition.

St. Christopher's School uniform.   Huntington High School senior.   Godmother's birthday haircut!!

Huntington, Long Island visitors: "Godmother Annette" Herter (Above left) with Jessmin.

"Godmother Rosemary's" husband Stanley Nott (Above right) and their son Adam.

Now the question of college came up again, but this time we had help from one of Mother's old friends from the Orage groups, Boardman Robinson. Now head of the art department at Colorado College in Colorado Springs, his advice (and probably his influence) got me accepted there and granted an art scholarship. I was soon averaging twenty hours a week of life-drawing, and enthusiastically experimenting with lithography, oil and water-color painting, and sculpture under various instructors: Adolf Dehn, Arnold Blanch, Doris Lee, Bill Dozier, and of course the well-loved "Mike" Robinson who really was a special person and inspired teacher.

Boardman "Mike" Robinson (1876–1952), born in Canada, had studied art in Paris where he was greatly influenced by French political cartoonists, especially Daumier. An early supporter of women's suffrage and a socialist who went to Russia with John Reed in 1914, he became known for his cartoons in radical journals. But when Mother met him in the Twenties he was teaching at the Art Student's League, and becoming famous for his book illustrations, cartoons for the *New York Times*, *Tribune* and *Morning Telegraph*, magazines like *Harper's* and mural paintings especially those at Rockefeller Center. He founded the Colorado Springs Fine Arts Center and directed it from 1936–47.

My respect for him as a teacher increased through the years as I came to realize more and more how he had resisted imprinting his own style and ideas on his students, but had pushed each one of us to discover and develop our own individuality. At his New Year's Eve party he asked each pupil to seriously write out for him resolutions. And then the next year he found out where we were, and mailed them back to us with encouraging wishes!

Boardman Robinson

Located in Colorado Springs, a charming little town at the foot of Pike's Peak, Colorado College seemed like a story book, or perhaps *Saturday Evening Post*, version of American campus life complete with Sorority and Fraternity houses, giving out of "Frat" pins, serenades, Homecoming Games followed by victory parades and bonfires and Freshmen hazings. The first weeks I had to wear a little green beanie and scrub the front steps with a toothbrush in between classes.

But there was also a real cultural life there. The clear mountain air and peaceful surroundings had apparently attracted sophisticated residents from big polluted cities, and for a small town (about 45,000 inhabitants) there was an amazingly large audience for concerts (Egon Petri and Jose Iturbi came up) and theater performances. The college was affiliated with and used as its art departments the Colorado Springs Fine Arts Centre, which attracted all types of artists and teachers. Dancer Hanya Holm and composer Roy Harris held their summer sessions there, and guest lecturers like actor Maurice Evans, dancers Valerie Bettis and Jose Limon passed through or attended conferences.

I was studying piano with James Sykes and had developed my own method to practice sight-reading – turn the music upside down and then read it. This can have very interesting results.

Dushka, Colorado College freshman.

Depending on the key signature, and whether you respect it or not, the left hand accompaniment now becomes your melody line and you are apt to achieve strange modes, syncopated accents, eerie harmonies – all sorts of effects.

One day, when I was doing my usual upside down experimenting using a simple setting of a folksong, I think it was *Annie Laurie*, the door of my practice room burst open. It was Roy Harris who said: "Oh, it's you, Dushka. What was that you were playing? Very original! Was it something of your own? Wouldn't you like to join my composition course?" I gladly accepted, never explained further, and had an interesting time at his lectures!

My professors for theater arts were Ernst Lothar who had worked with Max Reinhardt in Germany, and Arch Lauterer, a noted lighting- and set-designer, and I was happy to be part of a drama group that was formed combining college and local townspeople. When the question of our working on pantomime came up, Mother sent

Ernst Lothar

me some of the exercises she had used with the Vieux Colombier. Lothar and Lauterer were fascinated and set us all to working on them.

Then came December and the bombing of Pearl Harbor. Now the U.S. was also in the war.

Mother came to join me in Colorado and was able to get a job helping Enid Curry run the Country Day School. But she had to live in someone's abandoned mobile home roughly furnished with car seats and shelves made by laying wood planks over small piles of bricks. As the winter progressed her little wood stove was hardly sufficient.

As an example of the sub-zero temperatures in this mountainous region, picture the Colorado College football field on Saturday afternoon. The entire student body turns out. So do I, shivering in the bleachers, not because I give a darn about the game, but to applaud my fellow piano student, Roger Willams, as he makes his debut as drum-major of the marching band. My shy freshman companion, who keeps tropical fish, has suddenly been glamorized by a natty uniform and tall, fur "busby" helmet. There he comes, leading them all out, strutting as he pumps a huge baton up and down. I'm so impressed as they proudly advance across the field in formation until the music begins to... falter... and honk... and fade out... After only a few moments of being blown into, breaths condensed and soon the wind instruments all seized up – frozen solid!

Pianist Roger Williams as a drum major.

So, by comparison with Mother I was very lucky to be living in an art student rooming house, simple but well heated, and provided with a good lunch every day in the College dining room.

But, finances were very tight for us both. Supper for me was often a ten-cent vegetable beef soup eaten straight from the can. I don't know how Mother managed.

I did make some pocket money coaching fellow students in subjects that I wasn't too sure of myself, discovering that the best way of learning something is to teach it to somebody else. Years later I found out that this was one of Mr. Gurdjieff's favorite aphorisms. Mrs. Curry also gave me a chance to try out as an art teacher at the Country Day School. In this I was a roaring success. I simply played phonograph records to the kids, and told them to paint what they felt. That kept them wonderfully quiet, and produced a lot of original, colorful works. What more do you want?

When the College put on a production of *Carmen*, as a member of the Chapel choir I was assigned to the chorus as — what else — but "a gypsy woman." We were asked to take our show up to the mountain town of Leadville and give a performance for the local ranchers in the old Tabor Opera House.

On sketching trips as art students some of us had visited the picturesque remains of old mining towns like Cripple Creek and Victor, but nothing compared to Leadville as a real ghost town. Evidently, it was subsequently used as a training area for ski troops, re-occupied, and probably "tourist-ized." But when we arrived in our buses and trucks, it seemed just as it must have been when it was abandoned many years earlier. The houses had those false fronts that made little shacks appear to be two- and three-story mansions. Through dirt-coated windows one could see the remains of meals, discarded toys and clothing, left behind who knows when and who knows why. As it was summer we found the narrow streets ankle deep in dust, but one could well imagine how in winter they must have become rivers of mud and ice, explaining why, in place of sidewalks, there were four-foot high wooden boardwalks with steps at the crossings.

Broadway and Hollywood (*e.g. The Unsinkable Molly Brown*) have dramatized the story of silver prospector Jim Tabor who spent some of his multi-millions building Opera Houses in the old West. Though uncared for and rarely used, the Leadville example was still an imposing and luxurious theater. On the walls of the large lobby were displayed fading photographs of boxers in long trunks posed with both fists held up stiffly in front of them. Inside there were plush seats, a proscenium framed with painted, ivy-entwined columns and sagging curtains. Where we were accustomed to space at each side to use as wings, here we had to descend a clumsy spiral staircase to a dim cellar under the stage itself. But as one's eyes grew accustomed to the gloom there was mute testimony to the past generations who had also waited here for their cues. Carved into the wooden supports were their signatures "General U.S. Grant" "Jenny Lind," and so on.

We had a good audience of local families, children and adults, who arrived in pick-up trucks and on horseback, but I'm afraid they saw one of the worst public performances ever given anywhere.

When we arrived for afternoon rehearsal, the only local establishment open and functioning was a small bar into which we all trooped to order sandwiches and beer. Alas, no one had thought to warn us that, having just come up to an altitude many thousands of feet higher even than Colorado Springs, any alcohol, even a beer, could have a drastic effect. We all got completely smashed. The show was a shambles! For years Mother teased me about my inelegant arrival home, the first and only time I ever got drunk.

One aspect of the war that greatly changed Colorado Springs was the opening of Camp Carson. This huge, sprawling collection of prefabricated barracks, sentry towers, prisoner compounds, etc.,was hastily erected just outside of town, and soon accommodated fifty thousand men, more than the town's entire population. At least the flimsy construction had one good result. When a fierce *"chinook"* wind hit one night, the strong gusts just blew away the barrack roofs and all the walls tilted over to the ground. The next day the walls were simply propped up again, and the roofs, still whole, were trucked back, hoisted up and reattached. The only real damage was to the round observation posts in the prisoner section. These broke off and rolled away, down, it was said, "to Santa Fe."

With the opening of the Camp, about fifty of us college girls were signed up as U.S.O. hostesses. With the ratio of one thousand men to each girl, we were naturally asked to come out to the Camp as often as possible. They picked us up in canvas-sided army trucks, bumping us over the unfinished dirt roads, as we shivered patriotically in our party dresses and ankle-strap dancing slippers.

We were certainly appreciated when we arrived. Since Army policy appeared to be designed to break down regional differences between draftees by mixing them up as much as possible, we had to hostess a wide variety of men. Some of the soldiers were homesick Manhattanites who sought me out and flattered me with their attention, because I was "the only one who could do a real New York jive." But at the other extreme were the "Oklahoma muleskinners" who wouldn't give up their chance for some female company, even if they didn't know how to dance, had just spent the whole day climbing mountains and still had on their cleat boots. To keep our slippered feet from being nailed to the floor by these fellows, we girls soon developed a survival technique. We would sing in their ears: "Hup, two, three, four!" hoping that this would help coordinate our steps more safely.

Then the U.S.O. asked us to a party honoring the winners of the Camp's athletic competitions. One of these was a pleasant, black, second Lieutenant. After some time in casual conversation, he and I got up to dance. In a moment one of the woman chaperones pushed through the crowd of dancers, disapprovingly tapped my shoulder and ordered me to leave the floor.

I did!

I left the floor,

        the hall,

                - and the U.S.O.!

* * * * *

CHAPTER 10

FRANKLIN FARMS,
FREE FRENCH VOLUNTEERS, CURC.

By the fall of 1941, the Ouspenskys had also come to the United States with some of their followers. After a brief sojourn in Rumson, they were invited to occupy Franklin Farms in the, then, small rural community of Mendham near Morristown, New Jersey.

Their pupils Rodney Collin-Smith (later Rodney Collin) and his wife, Janet, (née Buckley) made this possible by putting at their disposal an old estate that had once belonged to a Governor of New Jersey but retained only vestiges of its former glory. Huge falcon perches tipped into clogged fishponds, and rare bushes were choked by poison ivy. But its big main house with three floors of spacious rooms and huge basement, various barns and cottages, and about three hundred acres of rolling land, provided the elements of a "Work house," a place where people could live or visit, have meetings or classes, share unaccustomed farming and housework tasks, arts and handicrafts, including the shearing, carding, spinning, dyeing and weaving of wool from their own sheep.

Dushka
♦

Rodney Collin-Smith

(Above) **Franklin Farms, Mendham, New Jersey** From the front driveway.

Franklin Farms (Left) Front entrance, (Right above) The "Turkey Cottage," (Below) The barnyard.

While Mr. Ouspensky spent most of his time in New York City concentrating on his writing and lecturing, Mme. Ouspensky supervised the new community and wrote this letter to the pupils left in England at Lyne.

"Franklin Farms, New Jersey
September 18, 1941

"We are hurrying with cleaning, painting and furnishing in order to have a party on the Fourth of October.

"I hope that you, too, are going to gather together to celebrate the opening of our house here and can combine it with the celebration of Pentland's [John Sinclair, Lord Pentland] marriage.

"Tell everyone that I do not feel that we are separated. Only the thing that interests me is what they will get during this time and to what conclusions they will arrive.

"I have received the translation of St. Maximus the Confessor. I read him very often, and I would have translated some other bits from his writings. All my extracts follow the line of work and the principles of knowledge about Man. His Trinity tries to show that things do not get done by themselves, that it is insufficient to feel for a few moments and then have everything rubbed out again.

"I would not translate emotional parts because they do not linger in a man, for these impressions are superseded by a series of other impressions.

"I am striving to show to our mind the necessity of work on oneself. I try to give our mind new material and to show where our profit lies. I am trying to teach people to reason and not to trust passing and impotent good intentions. Our intentions have no force and Hell is paved with them.

"It is necessary to realize our place in the Universe and to admit that we are atoms and not worlds. But everyone feels his own 'I' as the whole world and takes the world in relation to himself or herself, instead of taking oneself in relation to the world. St. Maximus shows things on a different scale. He shows the place of Man and the necessity of knowledge.

Little John Sinclair (foreground) and his sister returning to the family seat.

Portrait of Lord Pentland's family, (many wearing the traditional family tartans. (Back row, second from left) University student John Sinclair later Lord P.

(Above)
Lady Aberdeen, Lord Pentland's grandmother.

(Above)
John's grandfather, Lord Aberdeen, (right) hosting the three royal princes including the future King Edward VIII, (second from right.)

(Left)
Lady Pentland (née Lucy Elisabeth Smith) and their daughter Mary Sinclair on a Paris balcony in 1949.

(Above) Lord Pentland (Henry John Sinclair) sails transatlantic on the Cunard Line.

"Remind everyone that we are together as long as, and as much as we strive towards the same thing: to a way out of the contemporary and the illusory, at the same time doing our duty in life."

Mme. Ouspensky continued to counsel her oldest pupils still remaining in England by dictating personal letters to them pertaining to their individual work like this one to Ronny Bissing at Lyne in June of 1945:

"All your mistakes are because you do not know what work is, and what work is for. Work begins only when you know you are nothing, and have nothing, and need help.

"In order to know what work is you must have aim, a large aim. If you make small efforts, or efforts for some small aims, you will get results only on the same small scale. The distant aim must be kept in mind, and the way to it is shown by nearer aim becoming clear, and then nearer aim still; and so on like lamp posts (only we must remember these are only lamp posts and not to be confused with real aim.)

"Desires pulling in different directions, without aim there is chaos. Like creation of the world: God divided light from darkness, we must divide in the same way right and wrong. What would seem wrong from ordinary standpoint, if done because of aim, is right if it leads towards that aim. Whatever is against is wrong.

"Direction must be checked... everything turns aside. Motives must be examined.

"Effort from wrong motive, small motive, is without result.

"Depression must be fought. One must be resilient. A spring must bounce up again when pressed!

"Never say 'I.' Observe who speaks. Remember principles!"

With their people established at Franklin Farms, Mme. Ouspensky (Note! Once again not Mr. Ouspensky) wished for them to work at Movements.

So Mother agreed and moved us back East from Colorado to Manhattan.

Mother's old friend Mary Henderson was in New York with her partner Helen Howard, a professor emeritus at Barnard College. Advised and undoubtedly helped by them both, I was accepted with a tuition scholarship into that venerable institution, the female undergraduate part of Columbia University. Mother took over a small apartment on nearby Claremont Ave., borrowed furniture, and painted, and the two of us started our "New York Experience." From then on, in spite of much travelling apart and together, New York was our home, or at least, legal residence.

At this stage of WW II, France was fiercely divided between "Vichy-ites," Frenchmen who were reconciled to cooperate with their German occupiers and the "Free French" who weren't!

The latter, proclaiming General Charles de Gaulle as their leader, and the "Cross of Lorraine" as their symbol, set up separate headquarters in various capital cities. In New York they occupied offices in Rockefeller Center and sent out requests for volunteers. An old Dalcroze friend of Mother's, Jeanne de Lanux, was already very involved and roped us both in to help.

What started out for Mother as a little volunteer translating became a real, and often difficult job in the Press and Information Service and its Overseas Department, at which she struggled for many years so as to earn our livings.

My own contribution didn't last long. It was supposed to be simply helping out in a sort of seamen's canteen set up at the Free French Consulate in Rockefeller Center. But when a huge French warship the *Richelieu* docked in New York, we heard that the men aboard were also fiercely divided in their loyalties. Most of the officers accepted the Vichy regime, but many of the crew took the opportunity of shore leave in Manhattan to defect. They would walk away from all their possessions on board, risking court-martials and bloody fistfights with rival seamen so as to come to the consulate and sign up with De Gaulle.

So my simple task of dispensing *café* and *gateaux* began to include First Aid, laundering bloody uniforms — the regulations for ironing were very strict requiring two exact vertical creases on the big collars — and being a kind of big sister and mediator.

One misunderstanding I had to smooth over especially often was due to an old French tradition. Generations of *matelots*. French sailors, allowed pretty girls to touch the red pompoms on their cute little hats, "for good luck!" But then, in return, the sailor is allowed to kiss the girl. Alas, most American male escorts, unfamiliar with this tradition, were apt to react violently, greatly adding to my laundering chores.

Being a fine arts major at Barnard ("The Barnyard") was certainly different from my bucolic experience at Colorado College. Here the teachers seemed to me determined to produce museum curators rather than artists. We were asked to study and identify black and white slides, endless details of tombs and sarcophagi, memorize dates, write scholarly essays, all so mental and uncreative. The exception was a wonderful graduate course on iconography given by the late Meyer Shapiro. Worse yet, the credits I had earned in Colorado for life-class and painting were drastically cut and I faced many months of extra study to make them up.

Funnily enough, it wasn't scholastic credits that caused the most trouble, it was gym! In Colorado, gym was only required for freshmen. Barnard demanded four full years so that even after I had all my other credits for a B.A. degree, I still lacked six months of gym. This is why, twice a week I had to invent an excuse to get away from my first job as "Assistant Publicity Director of Radio Station WHN" (impressive title, only thirty-five dollars a week salary!), to rush uptown by taxi or subway, put on a little green gym suit, play idiotic badminton and only finally graduated a year later than the rest of my class.

Barnard College gym suits for badminton.

On Graduation Day, I sneaked out of work for the last time and as I panted out of the 116th St. subway station, I found patient Mother waiting for me at the entrance with my rented gown and tasseled mortarboard. I threw them on as I hurried across the Columbia campus, and after queuing up with a lot of strangers from the Class of 1947, I was handed my diploma, bundled it up with my gown and "board," thrust them at Mother and rushed back to WHN.

It was a sad culmination of all Mother's years of planning and struggling to provide me with a "real education." Especially since, in all the ensuing forty years in many different jobs, nobody ever asked me if I had a college degree.

Well, not quite true! An employment agency did once ask me, because they were sending me out for a job as assistant to the editor of a movie magazine. They then told me to redo my résumé without mentioning my degree since the lady editor was not herself a college graduate and might object.

Nevertheless, those years at Barnard really did influence the direction of my life.

At first I had little success making friends. Many Barnard girls were boarders, and as such, they were an insular lot whereas I went home every night to our Claremont Ave. apartment. Extracurricular activities didn't help much. The Barnard clubs were stuffy, and in those days, before the changes to coed campuses, strictly for girls. The clubs at Columbia College were strictly male, except for CURC, the Columbia University Radio Club. Need I say I suddenly developed a keen enthusiasm for radio in all its aspects?

The club operated an ambitious campus radio station that was part of the "Ivy League Network." This meant that on certain occasions, like the Presidential Election, or important football games from Baker Field we were linked by telephone lines to other eastern university radio stations, not often but enough to justify selling airtime to commercial sponsors. Otherwise, our listenership was limited to a few blocks of upper Manhattan since the broadcasts were transmitted through the campus power lines. However if you equipped your radio with a new device that cut out static interference, you didn't get us at all. CURC has since expanded and is now the successful FM station, WKCR.

Pianist/Musicologist Billy Taylor

I spent more time at the station than I did studying. I announced, engineered, disc-jockeyed, directed and acted in some Norman Corwin plays, had my own comedy show "Dopey Dushka" (sic!), and took on the job of Publicity Director.

My main publicity stunt was to create a version of the Stage Door Canteen for the Navy V-12s, officer candidates being trained on campus. We recruited Barnard girls as hostesses, convinced neighborhood stores to donate refreshments and door prizes, and managed to attract visiting dance bands and guest entertainers like Billy Taylor, Willie "The Lion" Smith, Jo Stafford, and best of all, Louis "Satchmo" Armstrong who, between shows at the Apollo, brought along his entire orchestra to play for us. "The CURC Canteen" was extolled in the *Columbia Spectator* as "the outstanding creation of wartime Columbia."

For the first time I discovered that I could be glib, had a knack for public relations and selling, and had a solid instinct for what would please and entertain other people. I developed a life-long enthusiasm for good jazz, and met an energetic gang of creative youngsters who wrote and performed Varsity shows and programs for the radio station. Notable amongst these was a shy teenaged pianist, Dick Hyman, who I kept urging to become a professional musician since he could play and compose in any style with a brilliance that has since brought him worldwide fame.

Meanwhile, my job at WHN was leading in a like direction. To compete with other radio stations who filled the mornings with soap operas, WHN had inaugurated a daily four-hour variety show called "*Gloom Dodgers.*" A live orchestra, well-known comedians, and an endless parade of singers and instrumentalists of all nationalities were brought together by the director, Edmund Anderson.

A devoted fan of jazz and life-long friend of Duke Ellington, Edmund made a specialty of presenting the best jazz artists even if some of them, like Erroll Garner,

(Above) WHN's *Gloom Dodgers'* regulars: (Left to right) Bandleader Don Bestor, violinist Eddie South, singer Don Arres, M.C. Ward Wilson, singer Brad Reynolds, comedy star Morey Amsterdam and director Edmund Anderson. (Right) Ed Anderson at St. Peter's Church fifty years later.

had trouble getting up that early!

Forty or so years later, when Ed started the "Midday Jazz Concerts" series for the St. Peter's Church Jazz Ministry, he looked me up again and I enjoyed many years as his eager assistant.

In the Forties my boss at WHN, George Q. Lewis the Publicity Director, didn't like music at all and, happily for us both, assigned me to cover all such programming. Some of the jazz artists began to pay me on the side to do personal publicity chores for them. There I was on my way to an unexpected profession – "press agent."

I am still proud that my contact with Dan Burley, editor of the *New York Amsterdam News*, got Dick Hyman his first job, a booking at Wells' Lounge in Harlem.

On June 12, 1945, Burley enthused in his column ***BACK DOOR STUFF***:

"Dick Hyman, Columbia U. music major and perhaps one of the greatest piano stylists to come around in years, started his first nightclub engagement Tuesday when he opened at Wells Music Bar where the enterprising Joe T. Wells, bossman, has successfully instituted an interracial entertainment policy.

"Hyman, who is just a kid, strongly reminds listeners of his idol, Art Tatum, plays organ, composes and stands out like a sore thumb among his keyboard contemporaries."

And sixty busy years later (April, 2006), at one of his many concerts I attended, the extensive laudatory program notes included: "DICK HYMAN is a pianist, organist, arranger, conductor and composer. He has recorded more than 100 albums under his own name and even more in support of other artists. While developing his own improvisational piano style, he has also investigated and recorded music from the earliest periods of jazz and ragtime. In 1975 he conducted the New York Jazz Repertory Company on a State Department sponsored tour of the former Soviet Union. As a busy studio musician, he has won seven "Most Valuable Player" awards from the National Academy of Recording Arts and Sciences. He has acted as music director for radio and television, including the 1989-90 *In Performance at the White House*. He has written numerous scores for dramas and documentaries for which he has received Emmy awards for both composing and musical direction. Dick has orchestrated Broadway musicals and composed scores for films including many for writer/director Woody Allen. He composed and performed the score for the Cleveland Ballet's *Piano Man* and for Twyla Tharp's *The Bum's Rush* with the American Ballet Theatre..."

Of course, my own personal favorite composition of Dick's is ***The Dushka Stomp***!

* * * * *

Dick Hyman at his very first job, at Wells Lounge in Harlem, 1945.

Dick Hyman with new wife Julia "on the night before I went into the Navy."

Fifty or so years later (Left) star at one of many jazz Festivals.
(Left bottom) in 2004,
and (Below) with an old friend, Dushka!

CHAPTER 11

THE FORTIES IN NEW YORK... NEW JOBS AND LIFE STYLES

New York, Nov. 24, 1944 [To Dushka's Godmother #1 recently returned to England.]
Dearest Rosemary,

At last news from you... How grand... It was the short note which you must have finished on the *Queen Mary*. Of course by now you will have realized that your trip was slow because of the storm and the danger of floating mines. It was in the papers and we were quite worried here and that was why I am extra glad to hear from you.

It is good to know that, although things move slowly, life and the possibility of getting settled in your own home does not look too difficult. It is especially encouraging to have Mr. Desouter's opinion about Jimmy's walking. That in itself must make you feel that the ordeals of preparing and travelling back to England were to some very worthwhile purpose.

I have not seen Mme. Ouspensky except for a few minutes since you left. She is really suffering from nervous exhaustion, I think, and whenever she accumulates a little energy she passes it on immediately to other people (like Mrs. Evans who has had a frightful cold, Mrs. Nicolls and Miss Capper who have just arrived from England, Mrs. Sutta who has had worry about her boy running around late at night with some queer characters, etc.) The lessons at Mendham continue, with, at the moment, a new lease of life, mostly, I think, from some new "recipes" or "tricks" I am trying.

Our office is in a state of upheaval as all the bosses are being recalled to France. But we, the personnel, have been given a small raise in the meantime (before being axed perhaps?) so we hold on awaiting future developments.

Dushka is adventuring since a week. The editor of a Harlem paper offered her a temporary job doing publicity for the opening of a new Club in the old Cotton Club quarters. That is, he asked her to make the contacts among white papers, etc. Her boss told her that she would be a fool to pass up the experience and even let her be free afternoons for her last week at WHN.

Bill and Louise were darlings and accompanied me to the very noisy opening of the Club on Thanksgiving Eve. You would have had fun seeing your godchild in action and all the Harlem élite in satin, feathers and diamonds. We only got away about four in the morning. That, I hope, will be the last time she will need to go up there in the evening or that I shall need to act as chaperone.

But, as she says, even if the job only lasts the three weeks for which she made the arrangement, it will have been fun and paid her twice as much as the other place — at least IF she gets paid! — she did receive her first $60 in advance which made it possible for her to buy an evening dress, rent desk space for a month and meet a lot

Jessmin
♦

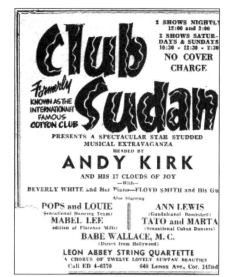

A newspaper ad for the newly opened Club Sudan in Harlem (formerly the Cotton Club).

Annette in Germany in her censor's uniform.

of people "in the business." Her next role is Vice-Chairman of the Harlem Benefit at the Apollo Theater on Dec. 1. Her first duty is to persuade Mae West to come and wriggle her hips in front of the colored hip connoisseurs. You remember how they used to say that Lonia wanted to begin his army life as a retired general? I think Dushka, without being aware of it, is beginning her professional life as a retired Madame!

Anyway, she certainly needed a rest and, as she chooses her own hours for this job, the change has already done her good. I just coast along to see what next and where the next slippery place may be!

Annette has written from Germany twice, the first letter a long account of misery; their whole set-up sounded dreadful, unheated barracks, no light, no warm water, long trips on foot through mud and by bug-infested trains to an office with stone floors and again no heating. But the second letter said things were much improved and she had hopes of going to Geneva to see her mother before Xmas. Husband Jean lost his chicken farm in the Florida storm and in that quarter things sound worse than ever.

Much love to you all.................

Jessmin

January 10, 1945 [To Dushka's Godmother #2, now a uniformed U.S. censor in Munich, Germany.]

Darling Annette,

A wonderful letter came from you. Although you had a dreadful cold when you wrote, you did somehow sound a little more cheerful about conditions and that was a great relief to us here who love you and often feel worried about this terrific job you have undertaken. I do so hope that your leave was granted and that you were really able to get to Geneva. Everything else seems comparatively unimportant. But I can guess too that whether you find your mother better or the same it will still be an upsetting experience to meet after so long. Only she will be so delighted that you will feel that you did the right thing to go over.

Despite everything the days are not too dreary. At the office we have had an interim period — the various bosses recalled to Paris, new ones to arrive soon, credits halted and many people very uncertain as to their immediate future. Our own very nice *Patron* will be back in a few days, thank goodness, and, as we are somewhat independent of the Information Office, being really subordinate to the Ministry of Colonies, we are trusting that not too many changes will be made in our status. I am still translating and writing reports on places I had previously never heard of and never hope to see.

Dushka has been adventuring for the last three weeks. Some time ago she had occasion to meet Dan Burley, editor of the *Amsterdam News*, one of the big Harlem papers. She evidently was able to formulate for him and realize for herself that she wanted to try freelance publicity and that she felt from both a business point of view and from the tolerance point of view (about which she feels quite strongly) her best bet would be to begin by representing colored artists and musicians. This evidently impressed Burley for he suddenly phoned her one day and told her that he had a job she could grab to start this line of work, to handle publicity downtown to the white papers for the new night club "Sudan" which is being opened in the former Cotton Club quarters and will attempt the same kind of wide popularity.

Her boss at WHN, George Q. Lewis, who has been very nice to her lately, helped her decide to try this thing out, since there was no possibility of advancement for her there. He had never been able to keep a promising assistant longer than six months. So Dushka got the Club to pledge her a month's guarantee at twice the salary she was getting at the radio station and has been barging around like a tank ever since.

I don't think the work can continue long and I frankly rather hope it doesn't. The people and the place are quite nice, they appreciate her and try to see that she is all right — BUT — it is no life for a young girl to be racing up to Harlem most nights of the week to meet columnists and press agents and get home at four a.m. at the earliest, and then get up in time to contact people at regular office hours. I have a tremendous exercise trying not to worry and after three weeks I am just beginning to be able to sleep before she gets back, so that I can get to my office.

Anyway, Dushka is not really losing by the experience and she is a good kid. She even turned to and helped the cook, a white soldier veteran, wash dishes the other evening. But her difficulty is that the owners (two white, one West Indian) are inexperienced and poured so much money into decorations and the floorshow that they are now retrenching on quite important items. Except for one insertion in papers before the opening at Thanksgiving they have done no advertising whatsoever. Naturally they cannot expect crowds and, in these days with stories of Harlem muggings being brought up at every oppor-tunity to discredit La Guardia's administration and give O'Dwyer's Irish supporters new jobs in the Police Department, a club catering to a mixed clientele with money won't find it easy.

I got Bill and Louise Welch to chaperone me to the opening and we had fun. The nightclub was pleasant and large with a big stage. I had never seen the prosperous mid-dleclass of that section. They are really as comfortable, good-natured and conservative as, say, some southern France shopkeepers. All resplendent in tuxedos and the wives in satin, feathers and diamonds. I wouldn't have missed the robin's egg blue W.C. complete with silver cupids for anything; espe-cially as on opening night there were huge bottles of perfume

Bill (not yet "Doctor") Welch and Louise courting in the old Cotton Club days.

(a local favorite called "Christmas Night"), and a dozen assorted shades of lipstick (for common use!) out under the mirror.

Louise and Bill had evidently done some of their courting at the Cotton Club and indulged in some reminiscing and a few dances. I met the owners. The West Indian has more of an Oxford accent than any Britisher I ever knew, and the other two are young soldiers whose fathers used to have interests in the Cotton Club and have allowed them too much money to try out the venture again.

Dushka hopes by February to make what she needs to pay for her own office, send out regular releases and clear enough so that she can take the two half courses to finish up the degree loose ends at Barnard.

Will you be in Geneva at Christmas I wonder? We shall only celebrate by trying to sleep a few hours longer, I think, but we shall certainly think of you.

All my love and Good Courage...   A big hug from Dushka.   Jessmin
p.s. later: ...as for your news of Germany — yes! we do read much of this in our newspapers. But everyone is "tired" of other people's suffering. They want to ignore and forget things, and they do. Even the threat of terrible and rapidly arriving horrors caused by this indifference seems to be pushed away and we all close our eyes.

Of course, at the office we hear more about France's problems. The black market and a preoccupation with politics seem like a cancer and an itch that the sick country cannot cut out or clean up. The complications, inefficiency and lack of vision as far as French Gov't offices abroad are concerned, are really spectacular, but I suppose the reasons are very simple and human in the end. I know I asked our nice director why we had been compelled to spend $1000 cabling the text of the constitution, etc. to various colonies in time for the elections. Why had the text not been sent with the colonial representatives who were traveling from Paris to their constituencies? He said: "Probably somebody got his nephew a job that doesn't pay enough to support his family. And maybe he had to choose between racing to the airport with the briefcases, or standing in line to get something to eat for them and he chose the latter. Can you blame him?"

I sometimes wonder whether all the people who had truly great souls, the ones who could feel responsibility for bigger things than their own affairs, have not been killed off. I know my instance is a stupid example, but I think in all countries there must be that struggle for immediate self-preservation after these years of misery, which blinds us all to some degree, and we cannot imagine how our present behavior is already affecting the future for all. Things now move with such speed, we are too little to cope with them.

I shake myself after such realizations and remind myself that there have been such tragic periods before and men won through them. I try to keep my faith in French genius, British steadiness, American large-mindedness. But, of course, I am talking away through my hat! We know nothing and can take refuge in nothing. All one can do is to see one's life and job as a minute fraction of the whole set-up. I think that your job is in this way necessary for the future, not as censorship of people's letters, but as an attempt to understand what they are thinking.

In the same way I felt that my work in the Overseas Department might be legitimate since I worked for a man who believes in trying to help the Colonies attain what they want, not in exploiting them. Alas! This is considered too democratic, even slightly "red." Result! Paragraphs from his book are quoted without mention of the author everywhere when the French Colonial Department wants to prove to the UN or USA how marvelously disinterested France is. But any economies needed are made in our department, and after five months of struggling to get the funds to publish reports, etc. (*i.e.* to obtain the last quarter of credit needed, three quarters of the work being already done and paid for) — the department was liquidated at a month's notice.

I was really sorry because our little group was working hard and happily. There was so much to do I hadn't time to realize that I was soon to be jobless. I had the wrong reaction, a sick longing to be free of ties and hours, and subways, and strain — and my own old wish for "change." However two possible opportunities came up. The head of the Child Adoption Dept. at the American Relief for France (a friend of Suzanne Ferrieres, whom I once knew in Paris) asked me to go train as her assistant and take over for her when she left for a two-month visit to France. I would have liked this work although there might have been a number of personal mix-ups involved — but the salary was small — and the possibility of doing anything better there, or of it lasting longer than Christmas seemed very remote. Then everyone I had known at the office said "Try to get into the UN." That also seemed a pipe dream, considering my age and lack of specialized training, but, at least, it was the only place where my former bosses and their friends could help me at all.

One unexpected thing in my favor is that the employment quotas for American, French and British people are filled, but I count as a South African, which is an asset. Of course it means making applications, passing tests, staying in a dismal "pool" until you can be placed in some special department, when it is eventually organized — going out to Long Island (Lake Success) to work from nine to six daily...

Anyway, I decided that I would try this as soon as I was free of the office on June 1st. Two days before, my old boss Mlle. Daumarie came to me and said, "Have you got yourself a better job? If not, will you consider staying on and coming back to work for me? I must know within three hours." She is more domineering and

Jessmin at work for the Free French Press and
Information Service in Rockerfeller Center, N. Y.   ....and her boss, Mlle. Daumarie.

personally chaotic than ever, and the work she does on a limited budget is quite poor. But she has had four different assistants, young and clever, who have all quit, since I left her. So I accepted. But I am still going to apply at the UN as I have a feeling that even the French Press Office may not last long, and I intend to try to protect myself in case of further possible explosions.

Perhaps from this you'll understand why jobs and material ways and means come crowding into the letter at every line. Even though I didn't have to face it out, it was a fear experience to know that we only had enough in the bank to tide us over one month of careful living. I've always known this but saw no way to change it except by doing my best where I was.

I'm so glad I'm not out of work at once, as I particularly wanted Dushka to feel rather free this summer. Dixon Gayer, a publicist/writer, took her into his Scope Public Relations mainly to do outside client- and press-contacting while he stayed at the typewriter. For her, an ideal set-up! But he has now spent about $1,000 moving to a larger office on Broadway. Some shrewd crook fooled him into expecting his cooperation, a well-paid hotel publicity account, office furniture for nothing, etc. and then having collected some advance checks, disappeared and can't be found.

So economy is the order of the day there too. The secretary and the office worker (who did the typing, multigraphing, mailing, etc.) were fired, and Dushka took on their chores, thinking it was a temporary arrangement and all good experience. Gayer had given her hopes of representing him in a small branch in Los Angeles and she would go through almost anything to make that come through. But after five weeks' grind she realizes that he doesn't know one third of the daily office jobs that have to be done. He takes her completely for granted, expects her to be at the office from nine-thirty to seven, and expects her to feel all right about everything because she is his "Assistant," not an "employee."...

◆◆◆

Dushka
◆

Imagine how satisfying it was, twenty years later, to be the "star"on a Carras Line cruise ship when Mr. and Mrs. Dixon Gayer came aboard as paying passengers!

◆◆◆

Jessmin
◆

...Evidently, in this field, one must either write very well in a special way and be capable of thinking out weird stunts, or there are two other avenues open. One: to do managing on the side. This can be lucrative, but one needs licenses, experience and plenty of toughness to take all the legal responsibilities. Or two: to try to do something oneself in radio or club or show business. This may not bring in any money, but it is a personal satisfaction that "selling" someone else's talent cannot give you, and it might fulfill something in Dushka. As long as she is still young and has some ideas, and as long as I can help her out, I would love to have her try something along this line, even if it is only giving jazz record programs on a tiny station. She has spent all her money on dozens of jazz records and has met most of the New York musicians with whom she gets on marvelously.

There is a possibility that a chain of Negro Colleges down south will arrange for her to travel and give illustrated lectures on jazz!! Can you imagine that?

Anyway the colored artists are sweet to her. One, Bob Howard, made himself late for his radio broadcast driving her to the hospital when she swallowed some wire (in a serving of pasta) that stuck in her tonsil. And the last time she took the King

Cole Trio from the Zanzibar to NBC in the small hours of the morning, they drove her home afterwards, but called Gayer the next morning to say they appreciated the service, but "if it meant bringing Miss Dushka out in the rain in the middle of the night they could do without the escort – Thank you!!"

Dixon Gayer (left) and his wife with cruise ship "star" Dushka

So, the poor dear is like I have been, with no time to lift her head out of the rut. But, if we can work it, I'll try to get her a little time off to take either piano or broadcasting lessons, and Madame Ouspensky knows a "big pot" at NBC who would advise Dushka if she asks him. (She, Mme., rarely sees Dushka now, but is unfailingly kind about her – says she respects her for trying her own way and will always help her to speed the whole experience of this phase.)

Anyway, at the moment, Dushka is still a hard-working woman and I don't really see much of her. Her latest outside interest is trying to clinch some deal for a Norman Granz and a jazz group to go to Paris for some concert festival in connection with the UNRRA. She hopes to make a little extra money and gain prestige. If she does make any money, I shall compel her to take some days at the seashore as she is physically awfully done up.

Bob Howard

We hear that G. has his visa to come to N.Y. and is only putting off his visit hoping to obtain a re-entry permit also before leaving France. It shows what a bad state I'm in, since I dread his coming. As for Dushka, she never asks me anything, and still seems to shy away and even resent anything to do with the "Work," Mendham people, or any esoteric ideas. I don't know whether what she may have gathered about her father is the cause of a certain insecurity and solitariness that I see in her.

I hope if he comes he will not begin to "work upon" her unless she is really ready to learn and profit, rather than just be hurt and pay too dearly.

The groups on Wednesdays and my classes at Mendham continue and both help me a lot. God knows I need help, or I sink completely. But there is just a slow movement, nothing striking. A lot of visiting Britishers, otherwise no extraordinary happenings in this connection.

Annette dear, did you receive any magazines and a parcel from me? You know we always have to have a letter at the Post Office to prove that you have "asked" for anything we send, and that limits our sending. I forged the last one to show as I'd lost your original.

Jessmin

* * * * *

CHAPTER 12

THE BROADWAY PRESS AGENT

Dushka
♦

Mother's comprehension of my professional activities in those days was understandably a bit hazy.

Even amongst ourselves in the press agent business we differed as to what our real function was. We would sometimes say "Publicity is getting your client's name into the papers. Public Relations is keeping it out!"

To be a good press agent or "p.r." (press representative), I learned, wasn't just to represent one's client to the press, but rather to serve as an active assistant to all media people; dreaming up new ideas that they could claim as their own, providing appropriate facts, photos and often complete pre-written copy: facilitating personal interviews and usually picking up extravagant bar and restaurant tabs.

All the newspapers in New York (many more then than nowadays) had to be serviced daily. In the entertainment field that Dixon Gayer and I specialized in, columnists like Walter Winchell, Earl Wilson, Ed Sullivan, Louis Sobol and Dorothy Kilgallen were a kind of "royalty." We might earn about $100 a week doing a "quantity" of general publicity for a client, but we could snap up $250 for a brief column mention...*quality!*

I spent hours doing the columnists' work for them, combing the city for interesting news items and gossip, cultivating informants (head waiters, desk sergeants, society matrons), or simply originating material based on the barest skeletons of fact. For instance, when a Mr. Goldman rented desk space from us at Scope Public Relations, to broker coal by the truckload, I sent Winchell the item that "the President of the Goldman Coal Co. warns East coast residents not to delay getting in this winter's supply..." I wonder what the effect of that was nationally, or when he printed my "Why has the —— factory, supplier of military uniform accessories, suddenly resumed full production?" which I based on someone's moving into the empty premises of a small plastics outfit in New Jersey that had once stamped out buttons for the Army.

The trick was to send each columnist every day at least a page of presumably exclusive, "free" items (most of them got revamped and recycled later,) Then, to each page of "freebies" you added an underlined client item. Every three or four free items used earned you one mention of your client. At the end of the week, with all my carbon copies in front of me, I would have a telephone conference with each columnist going over which items would be used and why, or which would <u>never</u> be considered, because they mentioned some person or nightclub he/she disliked, or

Tex Beneke and the Glenn Miller Orchestra. The young pianist with all the hair (detail below left) is Henry "Hank" Mancini.

(Right) Beneke vocal group "The Mello-Larks " with their press agent. (Left to right): Bob Smith, Tommy Hamm, Dushka, Jack Bierman and, at the piano, Ginny O'Connor, soon to be Mrs. "Hank" Mancini.

how other stories or gags could be salvaged with a different presentation. For example Winchell's secretary Rose would have me resubmit some things over and over, with slight changes of wording since much of her work was simply to cut out approved items and paste them, "as is," onto a master script, like a roll of shelf paper.

You could usually spot "client" items, as they were pretty weak, like "Orchids to——," or really corny jokes. I got a lot of mileage out of a series: "Nat Cole knows a turtle who wears people-necked sweaters," or "The Modernaires saw a pigeon which walked people-toed," etc.

Nat "King" Cole was a favorite client of mine.

On the day his Trio opened at the Club Zanzibar on the same bill as the Duke Ellington Orchestra, I was there making final arrangements, verifying guest lists and so forth. I happened to introduce Nat to the tall, elegant girl currently singing with the Ellington band, whose name was Marie Ellington although she was not a relation. Later when Nat decided to marry her, he

Nat "King" Cole.

(Above) The King Cole Trio.
(Below) The unfortunate publicity picture. Sorry Bill Gottlieb!

allowed me to use the occasion as a publicity opportunity, teasingly saying that after all I was the one who had started it all.

In addition to a lot of other coverage, I got *Life Magazine* to do a multi-paged photo spread of this "Showbiz wedding of the year" which took place Easter Sunday, 1948, with the ceremony in Harlem, Adam Clayton Powell presiding at the Abyssinian Baptist Church which was lined with lilies, and rocked with the singing of the Hall Johnson Choir. The reception was downtown at the Belmont Plaza Hotel and seemed like an extension of the Easter Parade. All the top entertainers, black and white, dressed in their festive best, and a tiny flower girl who danced with... who else?... Bill "Bojangles" Robinson. I was also all dolled up and hopefully edged into various group shots, but naturally got cropped out of all of them.

But another picture opportunity with Nat didn't turn out so well. The Trio was appearing at the Paramount Theater where there was a well-equipped gymnasium backstage to which, one day between shows, I hustled Nat and a photographer, Bill Gottlieb. It was December so I had thought to combine the publicity hooks of the upcoming "Sports Week" and the Christmas season, and had rented a Santa Claus outfit and a big sack filled with sports equipment, like boxing gloves, and tennis rackets. Nat patiently let us dress him, hoisted the sack over his back and posed riding an exercise bicycle.

As hoped, it was enough of a gimmick for hundreds of small regional newspapers to run the picture. But what a shock when the clippings started coming in! No one had noticed until the newsprint exaggerated it, that the bicycle-saddle, a large shiny metal spring, protruded in a most embarrassing way. Years later, photographer Gottlieb, who loved and respected gentlemanly Nat as we all did, said that he immediately destroyed the negative and had finally with great difficulty managed to collect and burn all the prints... Well, not quite!

At the end of my day working at the office I would rarely go home. Freshening up my make-up and putting on long fancy earrings to dress up my basic black outfit, I set out on evening rounds that often didn't finish until daylight. Song pluggers, road managers, and journalists were also "night people" and roamed the theater district until all hours, but they were nearly always men. I had heard of only a few other female press agents and they usually had dubious reputations. I was determined to compete on a purely professional basis.

Scope Public Relations, which usually consisted of just writer Dixon Gayer and myself, handled a long list of big bands and jazz musicians. So I had to make almost nightly visits to the Paramount, Strand, or Roxy theatres where,

Orson Welles (left) with Nat Cole who, sadly, died of lung cancer in his middle forties.

between showings of a movie, there were stage shows featuring our clients: Cab Calloway and his Orchestra, Tex Beneke and the Glenn Miller Orchestra, Bill Doggett and the Jimmy Lunceford Orchestra or others. Then I rushed a few blocks up Broadway to the ballrooms like Roseland and Arcadia to check in with any of the dozen or so bands we handled who were currently in town, enjoying an urban respite after months of provincial "one-nighters." Then there were the rounds of the 52nd Street jazz clubs to touch base with our jazz musicians, often having to track them down at the White Rose Bar around the corner! My special favorites there were Slam Stewart, Tiny Grimes, Earl Hines, Cozy Cole, Trummy Young, Billy Daniels, Una Mae Carlisle, the Phil Moore Four, the Dardanelle Trio, Bill Gooden, and Eddie South. Oh, so much great music!

Often in the early morning hours I dragged myself to radio stations located in darkened, locked-up office buildings, lugging heavy cartons of records, or shepherding bleary musicians to be interviewed. There was always some intense negotiating to get past the uniformed security guard at the street door and make it up to

the top floors where all-night disc jockeys like Symphony Sid, Fred Robbins, Barry Grey, Bill Gordon, or Art Ford were on the air. About the only way I ever used feminine wiles as a publicist was when I started frying up batches of crispy chicken in the middle of the night so I could take it, hot and fresh, to late-night deejays. I never had any trouble gaining access after that.

In between these other duties I might have to escort a newspaperman to one of the big hotels to hear Hal McIntyre, Ray Anthony or especially popular Vaughn Monroe.

As I had to learn to match these reporters drink for drink and still keep a completely clear head, I've never enjoyed hard liquor since. It did pay off years later when I was in France with Mr.

The Modernaires and their press agent. (left to right) Vic Dickenson, Dushka, and Mrs. "Paula Kelly" Dickenson.

Gurdjieff and challenged by his "Toasts to Idiots"ceremony!)

We once pretended to Earl Wilson that Vaughn Monroe regularly went from home to the Commodore Hotel dressed for the stage in his white tie and tails, riding down Park Ave. on his motorcycle. So Earl put on his tux, and gamely hitched a bike ride hanging on for dear life behind Vaughn and wrote a hilarious column about it.

Dixon Gayer had discovered four wide-eyed, talented co-eds who were music majors at North Texas State College. When we played Vaughn a recording, he hired them sight unseen as his new singing group. Then with a fifth girl added they became "The Moonmaids." (Monroe's famous theme was *Racing With The Moon*.) who turned out to be sweet and pretty, but home-spun. Part of my job became glamorizing them, with make-up, new hairdos, and lowered necklines. I was predictably opposed at every

(Above) Southwestern "glamour" in *GRIT* magazine.
(Left) Vaughn Monroe and "The Moonmaids" on the cover of *Downbeat*.
(Below left) The Harlem Midnight Benefit announcement.

The Ames Brothers. (Clockwise from top left)
Vic, Gene, Ed, and Joe.

turn by <u>Mrs.</u> Monroe, who preferred the girls just as they were.

But I did get a photo of them all in bathing suits running on the beach with Vaughn which earned us a coveted cover of *DownBeat*.

Another vocal group just starting out was ambitious to do something more than merely sing with a band. Joe Urick, the eldest, was a trained singer who had recruited his three younger brothers, rehearsed them and managed to get Art Mooney to hire them for his Hotel Lincoln booking, dubbing them, imaginatively "The Four Brothers." When I was able to arrange for them to appear at the Apollo Theater "on their own" they were thrilled even though it was only for the Midnight Benefit. It took a few years, some nose bobs and a name change for them to become the successful Ames Brothers. Much later, when I became a singer myself, one of my first important European TV appearances was in Germany on the popular "Joe Ames Show," accompanied by the USAFE Ambassadors, the superlative U. S. Air Force Band then stationed in Weisbaden.

When the Roosevelt Hotel decided to bring in a new orchestra from the Midwest that they hoped would please their faithful Guy Lombardo audiences, Dixon and I contacted all the print media but were worried about radio coverage. Most of the disc jockeys were jazz-oriented and we'd already had real trouble getting even Vaughn Monroe's bestseller hits played. In this case I had finally resorted to making a running gag of it with Barry Gray. I took him extra cartons of Vaughn's records, and every night he would announce and play one, and then halfway through, take it off and loudly smash it on the floor. In his autobiography *My Night People*, Barry recalled: "Monroe threatened to punch me in the nose, but then he saw the humor of the situation (or it was pointed out to him), and his record sales started to climb. He once wired me that my rapping of one particular dog he had recorded sold 45,000 copies."

But I was stuck with what to do with an unknown, what we called "Mickey Mouse-style" band whose only record so far was the forgettable opus: *I'm just a lonely little petunia in an onion patch. Boohoo! Boohoo!* A press agent hero of mine had been Jim Moran, a very nice guy who was famous for clever publicity stunts. He's the one who actually sold refrigerators to Eskimos, by convincing them that this way they could avoid their food being frozen solid. He found a haystack by a highway, printed up and sold thousands of brochures containing "a straw from the proverbial haystack

Dushka, "The Duchess," (right rear) keeps a maternal eye on her clients trumpeter/violinist/vocalist Ray Nance, (left) and guitarist Tiny Grimes jamming at the *Club 845*. (Below) My publicity stunt using the popular champion Joe Louis to help promote Ray Nance.

1945　**Amsterdam News**

New York

"Champ" Plays Farewell Ditty

RAY NANCE, THE GREAT VIOLINIST-CORNET playing star of Duke Ellington's band doesn't seem to approve of Joe Louis' musical talent when the "champ" played a farewell ditty before leaving out the Century for Chicago and then to California. But maybe it's only professional jealousy as both are stepping out in the music field, Ray to do a single as a comedian, and Joe to make appearances in the Southland with Luis Russell's band and Ralph Cooper. Incidentally, Louis won't be waving a stick in front of the band. Instead it will be, according to Ralph Cooper, a dignified job of selling tolerance on the part of the champ to folks down yonder.

Bandleader 'Summit" at the Roosevelt Grill. (Left to right) Lawrence Welk, Guy Lombardo, Jack Edwards, and Vincent Lopez.

BONES FOR BOWSER ... Lawrence Welk, band leader at the Roosevelt Grill, is setting up nothing but the best for his canine pal, as the two dine in the grand manner at the Ziegfeld Restaurant.

"I Got My Start in Music This 'TEACH-YOURSELF' Way"

...says famous orchestra leader
LAWRENCE WELK
Television Star of
"The Lawrence Welk Show"
MONDAY AND SATURDAY EVENINGS-ABC-TV

(Above) One of the Lawrence Welk "girlie magazine" covers we had to buy back.

(Left) Borrow a cute dog for the day, call in favors from editors and get publicity for two clients at once: the new Ziegfeld restaurant and Lawrence Welk.

with a needle in it!" He also inaugurated carpet sales in Madison Square Garden with salesmen on roller skates.

But I had also noticed that another P.R. guy, a real creep called Milton, had an even greater success just by being so obnoxious and annoying that people agreed to whatever he wanted, just to get rid of him. So I started a similar campaign. Every day the deejays got all kinds of junk in their mail: strings of onions, petunia seeds with fertilizer, sink stoppers labeled "here's a plug for you, how about a plug for me?" and so on. It worked! Phone calls flooded in, "O.K. Dushka. Enough! Cut it out! We'll play the d--- thing."

And that's how Lawrence Welk's music was first heard in the New York area!

And Welk was the only client a press agent ever had to pay money for to get his picture <u>off</u> a magazine cover.

Before coming to New York, Lawrence had happily agreed to pose for a full-page ad showing him playing his accordion. But as this ad was for cheap music lessons from a "teach yourself" correspondence course and appeared on the back covers of movie and "girlie" magazines, we had to buy back the testimonial to protect the new image we were building for him.

What we called our commercial clients – restaurants and schools, etc. – were even more difficult to place material on. What to do for "Maurice and George," an elegant hairdressing salon, for instance? Well, I did manage one good stunt. I got the necessary permission to sneak the two owners and some models into the Metropolitan Museum after closing hours. My idea was for them to invent hair-dos on-the-spot, inspired by the Old Masters' paintings. The newsreels loved it, covered the event as a fashion feature-, and we got worldwide coverage.

But I was greedy for more, and sold the newsreels on yet another idea: Maurice and George designing special coiffures for a bearded lady! But I had underestimated the effects of modern treatments and hormones. Even with the help of *Billboard's* circus desk, I was never able to find the necessary model.

Another new band I spent a lot of time with was "King Guion's Double Rhythm Orchestra." King, a sax-playing veteran of the Hollywood studio orchestras, had planned for years the ultimate big band that would be perfect for both dance music and stage shows. He commissioned first-class arrangements and sought out attractive, talented musicians, adding an extra four musicians: a piano-organist, a drummer-percussionist, a guitarist and a second bassist. Most of the personnel played in a variety styles and on different types of instruments and could thus create specialty groups within the band, making feasible effective stage presentations of Dixieland jazz (with battles between the drums), Bluegrass and Country music, (with fiddles and banjos), Continental Gypsy (with accordion and violin), Bebop, and especially authentic Hawaiian productions as Guion's lovely, longhaired vocalist, Angel DeShay, came from Honolulu and did a mean hula.

King Guion, leader of the unique Double-Rhythm Orchestra and his versatile vocalist/dancer Angel DeShay.

I loved helping design and order their band uniforms (we had a different color of the spectrum for each section of instruments, with white for Guion as leader) portable music stands and elaborate presskits.

But on one occasion getting equipment for them proved to be difficult both for me and a storeowner. The horn-players needed more mutes, so I went to a local hardware store. Naturally the owner couldn't understand why I was buying eight rubber toilet plungers but refused to take the long wooden handles!

The band finally opened at the Rustic Cabin in New Jersey. Although it was a long trip from the city, this place had become well known because radio remotes were broadcast from there. However what any new band really needs most of all is recordings and the infamous "recording ban" was about to go into effect. None of the record companies were even considering new artists and the only solution was for Guion to rush to do his own recording session independently, which meant borrowing a lot of money quickly. He made an unfortunate agreement with some Englishman, a fan who had been hanging around being enthusiastic. After various tribulations and fighting our way through a snowstorm to bring the instruments into Manhattan, we managed a wonderful session, recording four great numbers. I had also managed to get Guion to hire Dick Hyman for the piano solos so this was Dick's very first professional recording. He was, of course, sensational.

So what ever happened to such a great band? How come you've never heard of it? Well, the Englishman's check bounced! The musicians and the studio never got paid. As a result, King Guion lost his all-important musician's union card. The entire project sank without a trace. Not even the recordings existed to bear witness. I believe the masters were seized when taxes weren't paid, and although Dick Hyman and I searched for years for his first professional recording, no one heard anything of it.

Until 1999! Fifty-two years later, Dick called me to say a record collector just found an old 78-record of that session on a small label and sent him a cassette of it. And my old friend, now a mature world-renowned artist with more than 200 best-seller albums added modestly: "Hey, Dush, you know...those solos weren't bad!"

I have always had a frisson of guilt about all that. I really knew there was something rather wrong about that Englishman, but I was too young and naive to know what to do about it. I was in no position to force Guion to turn down this one possibility of getting a record made, and I just couldn't go into the personal reasons for my strong distrust of this so-called backer.

About the only time I had even talked with that Englishman was one rainy night at the Rustic Cabin when things were slow and instead of waiting for my regular ride home I had accepted a lift from him. As he drove, I began to notice that we weren't heading for the George Washington Bridge but in quite another direction. We ended up on a hillside out in the country where I finally had to get out of the car. My usual tactics for dealing with...er... "fresh guys" just didn't work this time. Once having proved I was serious, I expected him to accept it, even if albeit grudgingly. Instead, this wierdo drove off and left me there alone in the dark. Somehow I struggled down the hill in the rain and finally found the town of Little Falls, N.J. where the only lights showing were at the police station. There the astonished night-duty officers kindly offered me a cell to nap in until they could put me on an early morning bus into New York.

Yet in certain ways I was more sophisticated than all that sounds. I had certainly never told Mother that while I was at the Club Sudan the owners had taken out a permit for me and presented me with a small pearl-handled revolver to carry. I pushed it back at them in horror. But a few weeks later our doorman there was shot dead. I had realized that there was more going on in Harlem then than the politics Mother attributed all the problems to. To get up to the club, I had to take taxis from downtown, which refused to go further than 110th Street where one had to transfer into a Harlem cab for the rest of the way. To get me home, the Club owners had arranged for a nice young man with a large black limousine to wait for me every night. I once asked him if it was his own car and he told me: "No, it's my family's. They have two others like this and three hearses."

Sometimes late at night when I felt the need of air, I would duck out of the Sudan and stroll along Lenox Avenue, or visit other clubs where the headwaiters would welcome me even though I was unescorted, and install me at a ringside table. And I always felt perfectly safe, even more so there than downtown. I now realize that being Dan Burley's protégé must have had a lot to do with that.

I did worry a bit when two of the Sudan's "Twelve Lovely Sun Tan Beauties" drew me aside and warned me that one of the other chorus girls had been bragging that she was "carrying a knife" for me. Apparently she was Trummy Young's bitter and jealous ex-wife, who had seen us together and thought ours was more than a business relationship. (A lot of fans did find him quite attractive.)

But I certainly never felt that what was going on in Harlem at that time was really due to racial tensions. Many of us were beginning to make black friends and had "colored" heroes and believed we were building the right kind of community at least in New York. However the advent of black militantism caused most of us to lose our friends who felt obliged to take sides and withdraw from us.

The rumors I heard in those days were that the troubles were being stirred up by the downtown club-owners and/or the "syndicate" who were afraid of uptown competition. They wanted to keep people from patronizing Harlem establishments as they had in the days of the original Cotton Club. Back then, it should be remembered, although all the entertainers were black, the numerous wealthy and enthusiastic patrons were strictly white. At any rate, as a campaign it worked. Soon after I felt I had to quit the Club Sudan, like many other uptown businesses, it was forced to close.

Sadly, to this day, many people avoid that part of the city.

Nor was I blind to other things going on around me. It was a common joke that shaking hands with musicians at Birdland would leave a strange sweet smell on you. Most of the players, hoping to hide the odor of the "pot" they were smoking, saturated their systems with *Sen-Sen*, popular breath freshener tablets that came in strong and horrible perfume flavors. And the worst language I have ever heard was one day at the Brill Building, known as "Tin Pan Alley," when a police raid was rumored. All the song publishers' staffs shoved into the men's rooms to flush away their illegal stashes, only to find out later it had been a false alarm.

I had visited clients in horrible mental wards in Bellevue, and been invited to participate in "round robins" or "daisy chains," fortunately checking around to find out what they were before accepting. I even finally figured out why, when we were driving to Long Island for jam sessions and had to go through policed toll-gates, the musicians would ask me to hold their "special cigarettes" in <u>my</u> cigarette case.

I had already lost a lot of my naiveté when I worked long and hard with an international singer, John Paris, to put together a most original radio program, *Around the World On Records*, using foreign songs, anecdotes, unusual records and guests. We recorded sample shows and for weeks I slogged around town trying to sell the concept. We finally hooked an advertising agency that had a client who might sponsor a network version when everything was suddenly ruined. A local radio station, WNEW, aired a new program *Records 'Round The World*, almost identical to ours, shamelessly pirating our ideas and material, even playing special

Singer John Paris being accompanied by Maria Grever, composer of *Magic is the Moonlight*, while fellow composer Roberto Unanue listens appreciatively.

segments of our audition recording. The sponsor immediately backed out. Of course we sued and won, although awarded little more than what the lawyers had cost. But what really shocked and disillusioned me about this business I had chosen to work in, was that it wasn't even WNEW or the culpable program director who paid. It was an insurance company. The station carried a big policy against being sued for stealing program ideas!

While I was doing publicity for Sterling Records, I was happy when the owner Al M. started a subsidiary company, Bandwagon Records, and appointed me "A and R" (Director of Artists and Repertoire). I didn't begrudge the extra time and energy it would take because it seemed like something much more creative. I was to help M.'s assistant George Bennett put out cheap versions of overnight hits, what is now known as "covering." If a record suddenly starts selling well in one part of the country and the original producers can't keep up with sufficient distribution, someone else imitates the arrangement and rushes out copies to the stores. We had no budget to hire people, so I did much of the singing myself and still cringe at my ersatz versions of "great hits" like, *The Woody Woodpecker Song, My Happiness,* or *Mother Never Told Me It Was Anything Like This,* using exotic pseudonyms like "Dorothy Howe," "Alice Nelson," and "Betty Beaver."

I felt much better about a series of children's records I did. Having noticed that even toddlers knew the words and sang along with those bouncing-ball film shorts that usually featured popular songs, I thought "Why not make pop records for kids?" It was a very original concept for that time! So I gathered together some cooperative, (that is, inexpensive and available,) instrumentalists and vocalists, improvised introductory skits with animal characters and turned out novelty versions of *"Baby Face," "Mañana," "When You're Smiling," "You Were Meant For Me,"* etc. But the secret ingredient was that I had rented from Nola Studios a transcription table which could be adjusted to turn at any speed. After I got an engineer to attach a recording arm to it, we were able to record everything at a very slow speed. These masters then went to our regular pressing plant and were processed just like other records. The only difference was that, played on a normal phonograph, the music and voices were speeded up, and sounded toy-like and "cute," living up to our name *"The Menagerie Series."* We sold a lot of those records and even earned prestigious ratings in *Billboard Magazine.* This was years before anyone had even thought of Alvin or his Chipmunks!

But everything for both Sterling and Bandwagon Records was done on a royalty basis, no fees or salaries. I soon found out why. At the end of the year, when I was looking forward to big royalties from my various successes, Al M. declared bankruptcy. None of us received a cent! On checking around about him later, I heard that Al M. then opened another business at the same address, importing English lawn-mowers. With his staff working on royalties, he again declared bankruptcy at the end of the year. Then he opened another, and so on.

What really got me, though, was that in 1953 when, with Fred Clark and Benay Venuta, I moved into the very elegant and pricey Hotel Carlyle, who did I find there as long-time residents but Mr. and Mrs. Al M. They had been luxuriously installed there during all those years, in a big suite, with a private limousine all in the wife's name, safe and untouched by Al's activities — including their elegant Madison Avenue fur store!

* * * * *

CHAPTER 13

ETHEL MERSTON AND "THE INDIAN CONNECTION"

On Mother's death in 1984, I found many old letters from "Ethel" in a handwriting almost impossible to decipher. But in a large spiral notebook accompanying the collection, Mother had copied many of them out in her clear rounded script under the heading:

"FOR DUSHKA: Extracts from my letters written to Ethel Merston — between 1948 and 1957 — which she returned to me before her death — saying she had kept them, thinking they might one day interest Dushka."

Of course I was passionately interested in the extracts, only regretting that many of the original uncut letters were missing. (Did Mother edit much?) They give a first-hand picture of that period, in America and France, and personal glimpses of Mr. Gurdjieff, Mme. Ouspensky, and others which should correct and add dimension to other second- or even third-hand reports as well as failing memories, including my own. More important to me, since Mother shared so much with Ethel through the years, she reveals in these letters thoughts and feelings to which even I had never been privy.

Many people have looked to Fritz Peter's book *Boyhood with Gurdjieff* for personal glimpses of the 1924 Prieuré. However cooler heads may question his ability as a lonely eleven-year-old to understand all that was going on around him.

He describes a rather formidable, from his childish point of view, "Miss Merston." She was renamed, for reasons known only to an editor, "Miss Madison" in the American edition of his book.

Gurdjieff was then recovering from his near-fatal automobile accident and had decided that many changes must be made. So Fritz Peters describes:

"As part of the 'complete reorganization' of the school, Mr. Gurdjieff told us that he was going to appoint a 'director' who would supervise the students and their activities. The director turned out to be a certain Miss Merston, an English bachelor lady (as the children all called her) who had, up to that time, been mainly in charge of the flower gardens. She was tall, of uncertain age, a bony angular shape topped off by a somewhat untidy nest of fading reddish hair."

Mother met **Ethel Merston** (1882-1967) in those days and for years they remained friends. Although they rarely saw each other, they continued an intimate correspondence. They shared an admiration and appreciation of Jiddu Krishnamurti,

Jiddu Krishnamurti.

Helene Blavatsky founder of
Modern Theosophy.

and in the summer of 1938, they went together to his camp in Ommen, Holland.

Jiddu Krishnamurti (1895-1986) was born in Colonial India to simple but well-born Brahmin parents. His mother died when he was ten and four years later his father, a rent collector for the British and a long time Theosophist, retired and moved with his four sons to the International Headquarters of the Theosophical Society in Adyar, Madras. There young Jiddu was chosen by Charles Leadbeater to be the "vehicle" for the World Teacher (the Lord Maitreya, the Christ), given an English education and an intensive physical and spiritual training.

Annie Besant, one of Mme. Blavatsky's successors, adopted him and placed him at the head of the Order of the Star of the East, a large international organization she formed in 1911.

For years Krishnamurti accepted his role and the leadership of thousands of devotees. But finally, in 1929, he formally dissolved the Order and resigned from the Theosophical Society, causing great rifts among his legions of followers.

From then on until his death, he travelled widely giving public talks and private interviews always stressing the importance of independence and personal responsibility. For example, he sometimes said: "The teacher is not important; use him like a telephone, but live the teaching." (Quoted by Sunanda Patwardhan in her book.)

I remember Mother returning from that 1938 visit to Ommen. She told me about the Castle Eerde and its beautiful estate, originally made available to the Theosophists by its owner the Baron van Pallandt, and subsequently offered to Krishnamurti — how every effort had been made to accommodate properly the thousands of people who had gathered, even providing wonderful vegetarian food supervised by the Swiss Birsher-Brenner Clinic. (This clinic was later well-known for inventing "Müssli," a nutritious breakfast food of grated apples, raw oats, yogurt and honey, at least that was how later we were taught to make it at St. Christopher's, my vegetarian school. Now, of course, a packaged version is sold everywhere.)

According to Mother, after the first few days at Ommen, it became apparent that the crowds of visitors were littering and dirtying the lovely grounds, and that something must be done. A mass meeting was called, and everyone came together and started endless discussions, setting up rules, electing committees, and assigning inspectors.

Krishnamurti, strolling by, was surprised to see everybody having a meeting without him, so he eased into a seat at the back. After listening for a while, he got up and was quietly leaving when the organizers noticed him and asked him to stay and participate. He just said: "I'm sorry. I don't understand all this. When I see paper or something where it doesn't belong, I pick it up." Then he left.

I was a skeptical thirteen-year-old then, quite uninterested, even leery of some of these "esoteric" interests of Mother and her friends. But when she told me this story it made a huge impression on me, and helped make me also a life-long admirer of Krishnamurti.

KRISHNAMURTI THROUGH THE YEARS

Krishnamurti age 5, c 1900   and later In 1910.
(Below) With Charles Leadbeater and Annie Besant c 1911.

With his beloved brother Nitya. (left),

In his teens

Illness!   Ommen, 1930.   Education in London,1929.

With Annie Besant before the break.

Talks in India.   In later years.   Summer lectures in Saanen.

When that summer at Ommen was over, Miss Merston sailed to India as a tourist and visited another camp being held by Krishnamurti near Benares. She wrote: "By chance — I heard that a College there, run by some friends of his, was badly in need of someone to grow their vegetables. Outdoor life and gardening were my hobbies, the College people seemed nice and we had interests in common, I was at a loose end — so why not offer to fill the gap?"

That casual decision changed her life and from then on India was her home, although she traveled back and forth to Europe and America to keep in touch with many friends, especially those who, like Mother, also shared her varied spiritual interests.

The vegetable gardening turned out to be a much greater challenge than she had dreamed. Already middle-aged, she found herself working hard physically, night and day, in primitive conditions, and at first almost without help.

Village Life By The Ganges, a small book she later published anonymously, is a record of the six years it took her to make friends with the local people and train them to be independent. In the process, she had to act as arbitrator in caste disputes,

Bhagavan Sri Ramana Maharshi.

(Above) The original Ashram Temple, Tiruvanamalai, Sri Ramanasram, India.
(Below left and right) The ashram today still attracting many visitors, as photographed by Michael Begeman in 2003.

judge in criminal matters, and fighter against widespread corruption.

When she found the **Ramana Maharshi** and his teaching [not to be confused with the Beatles' guru "Maharishi Mahesh Yogi"] she made him the center of her life and work, and even after his death stayed on at his Ashram until her own death of cancer, twenty or so years later.

Though Mother often mentioned "Miss Merston" to me through the years (and I gathered that in a couple of especially dire emergencies she had even helped us out financially,) I only really remember being with her a couple of times, one of them in pre-war England when I was a schoolgirl.

Then, evidently determined to help Mother give me the widest education and formative experiences, Ethel took it upon herself to help me overcome "fear of snakes" and swept me off to the London Zoo.

What she didn't realize was that, coming recently from California, I was used to lizards, horny toads, tarantulas and snakes as pets. At the Gillibrand ranch the cowboys had taught us children how to kill a snake by holding it by the tail and cracking it like a whip. I don't think any of those men seriously expected us to try that on rattlers of which there were many, especially, as we were warned, under the elderberry trees. (Not that snakes like berries, but they hunted the mice who came after the fallen fruit.) The main danger of snakes there was that if they crossed your path when you were out riding, your horse would "spook" and throw you.

So in the Snake House at the Zoo I was quite calm when Miss Merston sought out the keeper and asked him to let me touch a snake pointing out to me how they were not cold and slimy, but warm and dry and so on. The keeper took out a fat, old seven-foot python and with great jocularity hung it around my shoulders. Then he strolled away with Miss Merston as they compared at length their experiences in India where he had also once lived. Unfortunately, the python was fat and so heavy that it painfully pinned down my schoolgirl braids, and from living in captivity it was slimy — and smelly! For a long time they left me alone with this thing completely circling my vulnerable throat, waving its head just four or five inches from my face, eye to beady eye.

As a result I have since then been really scared of snakes!!

Looking back at Ethel's *Village Life* book, I am amused to see that her section on Indian snakes and traditional cures for their bites finishes with:

"My parents in London Town must have had some premonition that one day I should come to India, for they brought me up with small snakes as pets at home and to have large ones put around my neck at the Zoo, determined that I should not be afraid of any living creature; baby alligators were also playmates at home and all the young cat-tribe and polar bear cubs at the Zoo. Consequently I am more curious than fearful of any animal."

But I think an even more likely inspiration for this effort of Miss Merston's on behalf of my education is Gurdjieff's description of how, as a child, his father "...took measure on every suitable occasion so that there should be formed in me, instead of data engendering impulses such as fastidiousness, repulsion, squeamishness, fear, timidity and so on, the data for an attitude of indifference to everything that usually evokes these impulses... I remember very well how, with this aim in view, he would sometimes slip a frog, a worm, a mouse, or some other animal likely to evoke such

Fritz Peters, younger and older.

impulses, into my bed, and would make me take non-poisonous snakes in my hands and even play with them, and so forth..."

Inheritance or not, I still dislike snakes!!

When Ethel ultimately read Fritz Peters' book containing his description of her, she wrote to him the following:

"Your book just to hand in India. You do give a wonderfully vivid account of those Prieuré years, and pleasant or unpleasant, make one re-live them — I nearly said re-value them, but that is done already. I rather squirmed at your picture of me, outwardly to you all so cold and dictatorial, inwardly under the cold mask, an acute fear of the responsibilty Mr G. put me into. He knew that in giving it to me, accentuating my feeling of loneliness, but you couldn't know that, or that things like the 'little black book' and 'reports' were by his orders; as was also the restrictions on leaving the Prieuré.

"Also, what you could not know since it was done in private; several of the old students did not worship blindly, but stood up to him, including myself, using our own judgment, as you did when you decided to leave.

"Gurdjieff, as you say he himself said, was no God, but was himself learning - we were often his guinea pigs. But that he knew far more than we did is unquestionable, he was a marvelous instrument, even with occasional mistakes, for making us more awake, a necessary preliminary stage before real work. That he did fail sometimes for himself and others is for me equally undoubted.

"Many years later I realized how invaluable G.'s training of self-observation on the physical center was, and how it prepared one for Maharshi's teaching of self-enquiry, both have to be impartial, but both are the same, one more exterior than the other — G.'s at Prieuré was exoteric leading to mesoteric (as he said.) Maharshi is mesoteric leading to esoteric. I realized that but for Gurdjieff I would never have understood Maharshi's teaching, and at the same time until I met Maharshi I had never really understood Gurdjieff."

Ethel's comparisons of the teachings of her Indian guru and Gurdjieff reminded me of the experience of another of Mother's friends, Lizelle Reymond, and her mentor **Shri Anirvan**. After a long time in India, Lizelle had returned to Switzerland and then became active in the Gurdjieff work for the next thirty years. Asked to give a lecture in Paris in 1969, she explained: "I would like to talk to you about the life I led in a Himalayan hermitage, and tell you how Shri Anirvan, a Baul Master kept me close to him for five years, and then sent me back into the world to meet my destiny and fulfill my task. After he read at one stretch Ouspensky's *The Psychology of Man's Possible Evolution,* he pointed out to me the possible junction between his teaching and the Gurdjieff groups of which I am now a member. As he handed me Ouspensky's book he said: 'Read it attentively, for in it are ideas which are dear to

(Above) Lizelle Reymond.

(Right) Sri Anirvan, Lizelle Reymond's teacher.

us and which have nourished you these last years.'"

Through the years there has been considerable contact and travelling between India and the centers of the Gurdjieff Work.

For example, the English aeronautical engineer/Hindu monk, **Alexander Phipps/Sri Madhava Ashish** (1920-1997) was visited by many of our friends and colleagues in his ashram in the Himalayas. His writings and letters which were published after his death by Sy Ginsburg interested me as it is obvious that he was familiar with and an admirer of the Gurdjieff Teaching and Work books. He saw pretty clearly the situation in Gurdjieffian circles, and though he had certain criticisms he often advised visiting seekers to return home and find a Gurdjieff group to work with, understanding that few Westerners could adapt to life in India as he and his own guru **Sri Krishna Prem** (1897-1965) and also their mutual friend, Ethel Merston, had done.

My friend Victoria (Fewsmith) Orfaly, a pupil of Lord Pentland, whom I first met in the late 1950s, the early days of the New York Gurdjieff Foundation, recently wrote me a long letter answering my questions about how she made the first of her three visits to India:

"Olga de Hartmann's intention to visit India resonated with my strong desire to visit this country and meet men and women who had higher knowledge and who were considered 'enlightened' or 'saints'. We talked about this often. Tom and Ruth Daly and Peter Colgrove were part of the plan. While visiting Mme. de Hartmann in the Spring of 1961 in her home in Garches (just outside of Paris) she made a remark that seeing the Taj Mahal was not essential. I loved and respected her but realised that on such a trip she would make all the major decisions. This created a dilemma, but an interview with Mme. de Salzmann proved helpful. She remarked that there were advantages in going with the group but also

Sri Madhava Ashish.

Victoria Orfaly in India.

James George, retired.

Shivapuri Baba aged 112.

(Above) The Shivapuri Baba aged 129 (seen also standing at right!) with John G Bennett who would later describe his visits with the Baba in his book *The Long Pilgrimage*.

Olga de Hartmann in her later years.

Sai Baba.

advantages in going alone on such a journey.

"Eventually I went to India on my own. The impact of those three months of experiences, including profound encounters with **Swami Ramdas** (of Kanhangad), **Ma Anandamayee Ma** and the Sufi mystic **Raihana Tyabji**, brought on an emotional and physical exhaustion, and I looked forward to a refreshing visit with Jim and Carol George in Colombo. [James George was the Canadian High Commissioner in Ceylon] .

"Surprisingly, on the way in the Madras airport I bumped into Olga (de Hartmann) and Peter Colgrove who were flying to Nepal to visit the **Shivapuri Baba (Sri Govindananda Bharati**, 1826-1963, 137 years old!!) and they urged me to join them.

"I was unable to change my plans and went on to Ceylon [Sri Lanka] for a wonderful stay with the Georges but always regretted not meeting the Shivapuri Baba.

"Later back in New York Olga told me of her exchange with the Baba. She had asked him why he had not established a school so that his teaching and wisdom would have greater exposure. His reply was: 'One in a million is a true pupil.'"

Vicky also recounted a postscript to that India trip which points up Olga de Hartmann's independence and initiative. Evidently, instead of accepting funds offered by Gurdjieff pupils to help pay for her voyage, Mme. de Hartmann decided to sacrifice one of her few valuables, an authentic Kandinsky painting, (that was probably acquired in those early days in Munich when her husband was friendly with the artist.) But before parting with the precious work, to a purchaser who was a private collector in Manhattan for an amount that by today's standards would be considered negligible, she asked Vicky, a skillful painter, to make her an exact copy.

This was evidently accomplished with complete success. In fact when the India trip was completed Mme. de Hartmann was again visited by the same collector eagerly interested in another purchase. But many explanations were needed when he spotted what he thought was <u>his</u> unique Kandinsky still hanging over Olga's fireplace!

Other Indians such as **Sai Baba** noted for his apparently magical materializations of objects, and pseudo-Indians such as the American **Richard Alpert** who now calls himself "**Ram Dass,**" have figured in the experiences of people we have met. One with whom the Gurdjieff name is unfortunately often linked is **Rajneesh,** (Chandra Mohan Jain) or as he is now known, **Osho,** perhaps more widely known as "the one with all those Rolls Royces."

I was first alerted to this in 1990 when in Brazil my pupils questioningly presented me with a video entitled "Gurdjieff Sacred Dances" they had been able to buy in Brazilia, in the middle of the Amazon jungle. It was obviously widely distributed.

Put out by the people in Poona about the time of Rajneesh's death, it is a complete travesty as far as real Movements go.

Although in intervening years they have been able to track down, and pirate a considerable inexact repertoire which is now taught in "Osho" venues world-wide, the Poona people at that time had only been able to copy incomplete scraps of Movements that were included at the end of Peter Brook's publicly distributed film *Meetings with Remarkable Men.* Their music was odd, their costumes were similar in shape to the traditional white Movements costumes but here they were a dark red "Rajneesh" color. The only similarities to real Movements were a few arm gestures and positions seen in the film. Then in a final indignity, in the video their dancers finish by joining hands to run on and off stage taking smirking curtain calls to audience applause!

They didn't even respect the serious nature of Mevlevi Dervish turning, which they carelessly

I am again trying to work in the third dimension, and I have not taken the risk that Gurdjieff took. I am not depending on anybody; I am Gurdjieff plus Ouspensky.

(Above) Bhagwan Rajneesh, now called "Osho," addressing his devotees. (Right) Excerpt from his magazine *Sannyasin in* which Rajneesh is quoted: "I am Gurdjieff plus Ouspensky."

mixed in with so-called "Gurdjieff dances," with young girls tossing long blond hair in all directions.

And finally "anyone who wishes" was invited to "come and join in!" — and the spectacle of crowds of adults and very small children staggering around groggily was truly awful!

All of which launched me on an unsuccessful campaign to have the Gurdjieff Movements copyrighted!

Nowadays in Europe there is a lot of "Osho" activity, especially in Germany.

Richard Dill, the long time "responsible" in the Gurdjieff group in Munich has been watching it proliferate during the years. He recently sent me part of his large collection of Osho quotes and writings with this note:

Richard Dill.

"Dear Dushka

"I finally could put my hand on a dossier which contains most of what Bhagwan [Rajneesh/Osho] ever said about Gurdjeff. I had always assumed that he spoke a lot and in a friendly way about him but closer scrutiny reveals that his praise, (*e.g.* 'only enlightened Westerner,' 'only known man number seven,' etc.) is outweighed by conceit, (*e.g.* 'Gurdjieff may have been good, but now I am here, not to succeed him but to surpass him, and I am supreme.')

"He has apparently read Gurdjieff's books and studied his system, also uses him to illustrate his own biography, ('Gurdjieff was betrayed by de Hartmann, Ouspensky and others as I was betrayed by Sheela and her clan.')

"Interesting to peruse — then file!

Regards,

Richard"

A last example of a kind of "Indian" connection might be the following. For several years I have been in contact with Tim and Barbara Cook and the large active group they have in Austin, Texas, whose by-laws describe "A Contemplative Christian

Community." based on "the esoteric Christian school of the Work of G. I. Gurdjieff ...free to reach deeply into all religions and spiritual traditions for insight, wisdom and inspiration." This "Church of Conscious Harmony" constructed their own building making sure it included an impressive space for Movements, have monthly concerts of Gurdjieff music, and meaningful participation of a large youth group.

Amongst many interesting activities they have hosted was a "A Christian-Buddhist Dialog" featuring Brother Wayne Teasdale and "TC" [**Tenzin Choegyal,** the Ngari Rinpoche and younger brother of the **Dalai Lama**.]

Tim Cook, minister of the Church of Conscious Harmony

After hearing his brother's enthusiastic report of this event the Dalai Lama invited members of the church to Dharmsala in Northern India where he now makes his home. Six senior members arranged to make the trip. They had personal visits with His Holiness and described to us their two weeks of inspiring experiences in India. Nevertheless they all agreed that they now had an even stronger appreciation for what they were already receiving in their own church right there in Austin.

One member of the group added: "Yes, Mr. Gurdjieff may well have called his Work esoteric Christianity, but could it not just as well have been called esoteric Buddhism?"

The Dalai Lama in Dharmsala welcomes the six visitors from Austin, Texas.
Prepared for the Tibetan ritual they had brought with them and presented to him the traditional white scarves and were then photographed happily wearing the scarves he had blessed.
(Left to right) Doug Sanders, Michael Begeman, Pamela Gursey, the Dalai Lama, Mary Ann Best, Edward Pierce, Donald Genung.

CHAPTER 14

PRELUDE TO GURDJIEFF'S ARRIVAL, 1948

Jessmin
◆

New York, November, 1948

To Ethel Merston in India:

Since August there has been almost daily cable communication between Jeanne de Salzmann and Mendham.

Madame Ouspensky is completely bedridden [we understand "Parkinson's"] and she sees very few people. But she directs all the work and planning, and helps everyone who is working regularly as a member of the group, meticulously choosing readings from many different traditions and faiths, and dictating special messages to be read to everyone. We do not know whether this can continue for months and years. She has said that, if she were younger, she would take a few of the most serious pupils and go in a caravan somewhere else. The property, Franklin Farms, is a great burden and takes almost too much of people's energy just to maintain.

Madame has been working hard to unite people — one could almost say that the barriers are down, but this is not altogether true. At present no one new is accepted at Mendham and the younger people who have come out before are not allowed to come to live there permanently.

Some of the pupils who used to be in London have decided that they must still be loyal to Mr. Ouspensky's expressed wish that they have no contact with Mr. Gurdjieff, and so have cut themselves off, some starting their own small groups.

It is certainly a time of testing. I feel it might take very little to change some people's decisions. The important thing is that Mme. O. has prepared the Mendham group in a slightly different way than when Mr. O. directed them, to be open and capable of learning from anything Mr. G. or Jeanne de S. will teach them. Some of them have been encouraged to go to Paris, and sound enthusiastic about their contact there, yet hope to return before long if Mr. G.'s expected trip to the U.S. materializes.

About the recent accident, as far as I know it was fortunately not too serious for Mr. G. and the two people with him, but two in the other car were killed. [A drunk driver.]

Mr. G. had a cracked sternum but made an astonishingly quick recovery. He went back home from hospital in two days in spite of lung congestion, and the readings of his manuscript continued. However, later, he seemed to feel the effects more and at the moment we are told that he is rather low in vitality.

In the meantime groups in England conducted by John Bennett, Kenneth Walker and others are revitalized by direction from Mr. G.

But I don't know what will happen with the Ouspensky people still at Lyne.

Here the pupils work hard as ever. There are a number of book readings in the evenings at the Farm and some of us go out from New York for them. Certain chapters will always be associated for us with fatigue, cold feet, and hot heads from sitting in the Mendham chill!

In a way Franklin Farms is marking time. They are preparing as if some people might come over soon from Paris, and one wonders how they will continue if all the plans fall through. We all become a bit weary of the uncertainty which has lasted for more than a year, since Mr. Ouspensky died in October of 1947.

For my part, I don't expect things to be easy whether organized work continues under Mme. O. or not.

She asked me long ago what would be my reaction if ever Mr. G. came over here. I answered that I would probably hide under her bed. She laughed and said: "No, I think Mr. Ouspensky already there!"

But I have been working on my fear of the complications that may arise for Dushka and myself when he arrives.

It has been a long time since he suggested that the de Hartmanns adopt Dushka so that she could be brought up near him at the Prieuré. And, also, since I had to trust to the loyalty of Ada Potter, who was then my "mother's helper" to prevent Annette Herter from spiriting Dushka over to Mr. G. at the time when I had forbidden all contact. By now, after sixteen to eighteen years, he would probably have lost interest.

◆ ◆ ◆

Dushka
◆

This is the kind of unexpected remark in Mother's writings that really took me by surprise. Mme. de Hartmann had often offered advice to us younger women about menstruation and motherhood. For example, she was always suggesting to me a spoonful of glycerin as a guard against PMS! But to some of those closest to her, she revealed that she herself had never been capable of child-bearing. I had always somehow felt that this helped explain her extraordinary devotion to her husband and Mr. G. So it really shouldn't have shocked me so much that this adoption possibility was once considered. But thank God for Mother's fortitude!

◆ ◆ ◆

Jessmin
◆

One thing I find painful, is that some of the old New York group members, newly in contact with Paris, resent me very much because I continue with Mme. O. and have made no move in their direction. They begin to say that I should not go on teaching Movements at Mendham without receiving direct permission from Mr. G. Others are almost too "identified" with what they learnt through the Movements in Paris — and so it goes.

Mme. O. hardly ever calls me to her at this time. I'm afraid I have disappointed her by not going to live at Mendham. She is preparing herself for death and can no longer be responsible for pumping right wishes, right aims, and right efforts into "amateurs," among whom I count myself. The bond between us is one of constant gratitude on my part for all her help and teaching, and I am deeply touched to know that she said I was "better daughter to her than her own," for I have done so little to deserve that.

Now, I must try to tell you some everyday news. Yes, we did go to Ogunquit for a vacation. It was heavenly! We missed the worst heat wave in the city and had more than two weeks of perfect weather. I met old friends, a former pupil, and my old secretary and their families, who took us both right into their circle as if we had seen each other only the day before. Of course, they are the kind of people whose children work during the day in "Gifte Shoppes" and the like, but we joined them for lobster broils and evenings of charades and such. Dushka was rather surprised by it all, but I found it very refreshing indeed.

It is a lovely place, although it has changed so much from the quiet painter's resort that I knew in the summer of 1924 when I went to these same friends to await Dushka's arrival. I was glad that I had only good associations and that my friends were happy in their marriages and open to believe that I had not been harmed by the old experiences, but was seeing my way.

I am ashamed to say that I came back in a rather rebellious frame of mind. The city and the office, the impossibility of ever seeing any simple loving people, partly because of the Work rules and demands, and partly because we are all so busy and live so far apart make me feel that these last seven or eight years have been a prison stretch.

This was accentuated by the atmosphere in the office. My colleague, Sylvia, who is brilliant and ambitious, cannot get on with our lady director and they have had frictions while I was gone. Yet, if Mlle. Daumarie would admit it, Sylvia had done my work much better than I could and is capable of doing everything Mlle. D. does too. Perhaps Mlle. D. felt this. Anyway, she greeted me back with a complimentary "Thank God" and then proceeded to behave like a hypochondriac. She is going through the difficulties of middle age, and being rather masculine, she is as fearful about her health as a child. She was on top of me all day for two weeks talking about her health and then fainted one day, and got quite terrified. So she decided to go to Paris for two weeks to consult her own doctor.

She has been away all the time since, leaving the Bulletin to me to do. Since I find this really difficult, and have no protection against my colleague's devastating but quite justified criticism, I get rather paralyzed and very weary. I hate to confess after such an unexpected and enjoyable holiday, that I am hoping against hope that sometime soon this daily drudgery will end. I seem to have done Bulletins for years (it is six years) and they grow duller and more difficult every time. Yet I would be terrified to be without a regular salary, especially in these times when prices continue to rise and we all just manage to get through each month.

As for Dushka, she is also having a rather difficult time. When we got back she started to organize her work. It had been understood before leaving that she was to try and get radio and television programs for Freddie Bartholomew, and do what she could to promote outside engagements for Dione Lucas, the cooking expert who has the Cordon Bleu Restaurant and Cooking School, and comes regularly to Mendham.

The first job was all complicated because Freddie and his forceful wife, Maely, were quarrelling. While he was a child star, he led a sheltered existence with his ambitious mercenary aunt, and now finds making a comeback as an adult, after illness and a marriage of which everyone disapproves, very hard going. It is astonishing that someone, who, as a boy was for years a top moneymaker in Hollywood, now finds himself in debt and reduced to working for unscrupulous managers who keep him that way. In any case, charming and candid though he is, he needs to learn to act, not just, as when he was little, take direction well. But this he will not face.

Freddie Bartholomew in 1936. At twelve years old a child star and top Hollywood money-maker.

But in 1948 a struggling actor, newly married, touring in summer stock.

(Above) Freddie stars in *"Berkeley Square"* on the Trask Theaters' summer stock tour.

(Right) This photo of Dushka painting Freddie's portrait was released to newspapers all over the country by the Associated Press.

18— PASADENA STAR-NEWS
Monday, Aug. 2, 1948

ACTOR'S PORTRAIT—Artist Dushka Howarth touches up portrait of Freddie Bartholomew (right) as "Peter Standish," character he is playing in summer stock. Used as prop, portrait will be auctioned for benefit of Heart Fund.

However, she got one satisfaction from it all when she was commissioned by the producers of the play Freddie was to tour in, *Berkeley Square*, to do an oil-painting of him to be used on stage as an important part of the plot. It is the story, you remember, of an American who identifies with a portrait of his look-alike English ancestor, so it had to be a perfect likeness of Freddie but in Seventeenth Century costume, painted in traditional style. She managed it very successfully and when the play closed, the painting was sold at auction to benefit the Heart Fund and Dushka's picture was in the papers.

As for the other project, Dione is a person with every possibility of success, but as we in the Work see only too clearly, she is somewhat pathological in that she lies about all practical matters and spends hundreds on presents when she owes thousands. It had been suggested that Dushka not only act as her public relations representative, but also as her business manager. She postponed having Dushka do anything for her until three weeks ago when things got just too bad. With plenty of money in the bank she just won't write checks even to her wholesale suppliers, so they have cut her off. Supplies for the restaurant and classes now have to be bought at an expensive Lexington Avenue supermarket.

So Dushka is putting in long hours reorganizing everything, re-establishing credit, and so on. However, Dione is now bringing over from London her architect husband, Colin, to put Dushka's plans into practice. We are really not too disappointed, even though Dushka feels a bit let down, because we suspect that Dione doesn't really want to have her affairs put in order. She has some absurd arrangement about paying half her possible profits to a woman who once lent her $2,000. This is a sum Dushka could arrange for her to pay off within a few weeks, but Dione won't face it so I suppose she must "dree her own weir..."

For the moment, Dushka is having to take care of her health. Her tonsils have been very bad. As soon as the strep infection clears up, she will have to have them taken out as her ears and glands are affected. This has been a poor year for her and she feels badly about doing so little from the financial point of view. I am glad that you could argue that her friendliness and helpfulness must be useful in the world even if she does not make her fortune. But I am sorry that this makes her so dependent on me. At her age she should be free. But I do feel that she is learning discrimination and that she is fundamentally honest.

She recently confessed to her godmother Annette and me that her greatest disillusionment of the year had been something about which she had never told me.

I had asked her to try to save some of any earnings she managed, to help pay for the vacation with me in Ogunquit. It seems that she got together the equivalent of three week's salary, but when she took it out of the bank, preparing for our departure, someone stole it out of her handbag. So she rushed around and telephoned all the many people who owed her money and explained the situation. Not one of them even tried to procure for her what they had borrowed weeks and months before, and she felt very badly about it. She guessed that I would probably have given up my vacation if I had known of her loss. I did wonder why she didn't take any photographs, or go riding or anything. I think it was courageous of her to keep silent. Now I hope she can learn to strike a happy mean between being too interested in financial success and too generous to others in these horribly uncertain times. But above all I hope she can find a way of earning her living in which she can be both happy and respect herself. Otherwise my and your efforts will have been in vain.

I feel that for me this office work has been a time of frustration in one way only. I have learnt a tremendous amount and am getting over my besetting vice of sensitivity and its accompanying self-pity. So long as I can meet some of my old friends

Dione Lucas' Cordon Bleu Restaurant, 117 East 60th. St. New York City.

again and not have them treat me as the elderly drudge (as at the office), or the rebel (as at Mendham) but just sometimes simply and warmly as they did in Ogunquit, all will be well.

I do hope that all works out for you, that you will take care of yourself and progress happily along the path you have so bravely, and I believe, so wisely chosen.

Please write if it does not disturb your work too much. I love to hear from you.

Jessmin

◆ ◆ ◆

Dione (Norona Margaris Wilson) Lucas (1909-1971). How strange it was recently to turn on my TV set and see again Dione Lucas's familiar face, and hear her familiar voice with its youthful, very English accent explaining how to make wonderful, high-calorie gourmet delights. Only the lack of color and the huge amounts of butter and heavy cream being used would suggest that this wasn't a program taped nowadays, and if one hadn't known Dione well and remembered that she died more than thirty-five years ago.

The advent of a new "Food Network" was the occasion for re-airing a series of shows she made long ago when she was the first and only one to do a cooking show on television. Julia Child, though often referred to as the "doyenne" of such shows, didn't do her first "French Chef" program until 1963, and even she credits Dione with being the pioneer and setting the high standards for everyone who followed..

When I worked with Dione as her manager and publicist, her TV program was broadcast at eight o'clock at night (they didn't yet call it "prime-time") and everyone watched, men and women alike.

Dushka
◆

60   L+   *THE NEW YORK*

Dione Lucas, TV Cooking Teacher, 62

DIANA LYNN ACTRESS ...

Star of Light Co...
1940's on Film a...

By BURTON LINDHEIM

Dione Lucas, the doyenne of haut cuisine here, who had operated cooking schools and fine restaurants while writing gourmet-recipe books and demonstrating the culinary art on television, died yesterday of pneumonia in London. She was 62 years old and had lived at 200 East 31st Street.

Mrs. Lucas contended that American food was the best in the world, but very often did not taste that way. She maintained that the American cuisine suffered from a shortage of the essential ingredient of an epicurean meal: time in which to prepare it lovingly.

Throughout her career Mrs. Lucas, who loved to teach cooking, insisted on giving personal lessons. She preferred no more than six students in a class at any one time so that she could stand next to each and show each one hand to hand how to prepare a dish, how to stir, how to roll out pastry and line a flan ring, how to "serve up" a dish, to garnish it, to make it appealing to the beholder.

First Studied Cello

Mrs. Lucas was born Oct. 10, 1909, a daughter of Henry Wilson, British sculptor, architect and painter, and grew up in Venice, England and Paris. In Paris she first studied the cello at the Conservatoire and then took up the culinary art at l'École du Cordon Bleu under Henri Paul Pellaprat. After receiving the diploma of the cordon bleu, she gained a ...

Dione Lucas

... chef's apprenticeship at the famous Drouant Restaurant in Paris.

In the early nineteen-thirties with a friend, Rosemary Hume, Mrs. Lucas opened Le Petit Cordon Bleu Restaurant and Cooking School in London. She was married to Colin Lucas, an architect. The marriage later ended in divorce.

In 1940 Mrs. Lucas, with her two small children, came to America on a Liberty ship. Her first work was at Longchamps ...

... Restaurant on Madison Avenue, where she filled merchandise for the display window eight hours a day. She next cooked for cowboys on the Hope Williams Ranch near Cody, Wyo., titillating the palates of the Westerners with her pâtés.

In 1942 Mrs. Lucas opened her first Cordon Bleu restaurant and school in the East Sixties, where her dexterity in conducting omelets attracted crowds of dinner watchers. Joan Alsena, Harold Lloyd and Joan Fontaine, as well as society women, enrolled in her classes.

In the mid-nineteen-forties, Mrs. Lucas launched a cooking show on television. Her program was seen on the major networks and WPIX. Among the guests who "cooked with her," were Salvador Dali and his pets.

During the forties and fifties, Mrs. Lucas demonstrated, taught and wrote about cooking throughout the United States and made several trips to Australia and the Far East. In the early nineteen-fifties she moved her restaurant and school to 3 East 52d Street. In 1956 she opened the Egg Basket Restaurant and continued her cooking classes on East 60th Street and shortly afterward opening the Gourmet Cooking School on East 40th Street.

Created Gourmet Center

In recent years, Mrs. Lucas opened the Ginger Man Restaurant in Lincoln Center, established the Brasserie Restaurant in the Potters Yard art complex in Bennington, Vt., then created the Dione Lucas Gourmet Center on East 51st Street and the Heritage Village Restaurant in Southbury, Conn.

Mrs. Lucas and Miss Hume published "Le Petit Cordon Bleu Cook Book," which was reissued in 1956. In 1947 Mrs. Lucas wrote the original "Cordon Bleu Cook Book" in this country, which remains a best-seller.

Her other books included "The Gourmet Cooking School Cook Book," with Darlene Geis, and "The Dione Lucas Meat and Poultry Cook Book." At her death she had just completed with a friend, Marion Gorman, "The Cordon Bleu Cook Compendium," which is planned for publication next fall by Little, Brown.

During the last two years Mrs. Lucas had undergone serious surgery and last September she chose to live near her son, Mark, and grandchild in London. Surviving also are another son, Peter of Bennington, and a sister, a cellist professionally known as Orea Prencel of Ireland, and her ...

LOS ANGELES, ... Diana Lynn, the movie actress, die... Mount Sinai Hospital after having suffered ... She was 45 years o...

Miss Lynn played... star of light come... movies in the 194... "Our Hearts Were ... Gay," "And the An... Every Girl Should ... "My Friend Irma C... "Meet Me at the Fa... Never Too Young," ... ruckus" and "Anna ...

She was the wife ... Hall, treasurer of ... York Post.

Started as a ...

By WILLIAM M. F...

Diana Lynn brok... movies as a musi... age of 11. A child v... being auditioned fo... "There's Magic in ... film about Michig... kitchen Music Camp... agreed to accompa... the piano.

The girl did not ... but Miss Lynn was ... the role of a child ...

After that, roles ... what difficult for he... she remarked some... "By the time they ... — a role I had grea... more and was too ...

Her break came ... for and the Minor," ... ring Ginger Roger...

Dione Lucas obituary in the N.Y. Times, December 19, 1971.

It wasn't difficult to get her publicity. The newspapers and magazines were clamoring for interviews or to hire her to write columns. She was, at that epoch, supposedly the only person in America authorized to award the coveted French Cordon Bleu diploma. So her Cooking School was attended by professional chefs as well as celebrated amateurs, movie stars, and international personalities (Brian Aherne, Harold Lloyd, Joan Fontaine, Salvador Dali, etc.) who also guested on her TV programs.

When her show moved to ABC, the new producers planned to have Dione do her own commercials.

I was in the control room for that first telecast — all live, of course. A few minutes into the program there was to be a commercial for the Citrus Growers of Florida and a big glass of freshly squeezed orange juice had been put on the set for Dione to drink. She did — but choked on it! Another few minutes and it was a new Birdseye product. Frozen foods were just coming onto the market and people were still rather suspicious of them. So it didn't help a lot when Dione said about this frozen fish that she would be working out a recipe for the next week "to give it some taste." But the "coup de grace" was her third attempt, a promotion for a new powdered instant pudding about which Dione suggested: "You just mix with milk and then put it in the refrigerator and forget about it!"

From then on they hired an announcer to read the commercials!

The ABC producers also wanted to add some embellishments to the simple cooking demonstrations. For March 17th, St. Patrick's Day, the writers had prepared an elaborate program working for weeks on a special set of lyrics for Dione to sing to the tune of an old Irish folk song. Someone had mistakenly understood that Dione sang and played the guitar. Her husband, English architect Colin Lucas, did play, quite nicely, and that was probably the confusion.

I got a frantic call from Dione, who had sneaked away from the rehearsal, begging for help. I don't know if her idea was that I should dub in the sound from backstage, but I took my guitar and hurried along to the studio to see what could be done. I was relieved to find that Dione at least knew the old song and could hum it in tune. I decided to experiment. We worked until she could hold the guitar and keep time, albeit painfully with her soft un-calloused fingers, strumming up and down with her right hand thumb. Then I figuratively glued down two fingers of her left hand to hold the two strings needed to sound an E minor chord.

On the day of the show, the announcer gave a big build-up, and there was Mrs. Lucas, wearing an Irish costume, gracefully perched on a high stool, strumming that one mournful, monotonous chord as she sang the special lyrics, reading them from a big cue card behind the camera.

You can't imagine the mountains of mail they received for that show. Not only had everyone <u>loved</u> her singing, but <u>those in the know</u> were particularly impressed by the <u>simplicity</u> and <u>authenticity</u> of <u>her interpretation</u>!

Dione worked so hard all the time (one of her sons had been born needing extremely expensive medical care and the other was completing his studies in England) that she must have been exhausted. Certainly she often seemed a bit "dippy," and covered up embarrassing situations with elaborate fibbing. But she was endlessly generous and well-meaning, and really talented in what she did, so that people forgave her.

I was once with her in her apartment at the Dakota on the west side of Manhattan when the doorbell rang. Dione went back into her bedroom saying: "Oh, those are my pupils who come up from Philadelphia. I don't feel like teaching them today. Tell them I'm sick!" I was aghast, but had to do it, and the nice ladies meekly turned around and took the long trip back home.

Benay Venuta took some lessons with her and then decided to show off with a special dinner party for all her many Broadway colleagues, hiring Dione, at huge expense, to come and personally supervise and help. Benay ordered all the lobsters and other complicated ingredients and vintage wines necessary. The night arrived, the supplies arrived, the guests arrived - but Dione never did!

At one period Dione also managed to squeeze in weekly demonstrations in San Francisco, flying back and forth carrying the provisions she needed. Naturally she often dozed en route but on one trip she slept so deeply that she didn't notice when the dozen live lobsters she had with her managed to escape her carrier and roamed the aisles of the plane causing havoc among the passengers.

Dione quite often provided big quantities of meat much needed for Franklin Farms meals, claiming that she got it "almost as a gift" from her restaurant suppliers. Even Mme. Ouspensky didn't realize for a long time that this was pure invention. In fact, Dione had bought it at a high-priced Manhattan supermarket.

This caused a strange incident. In those days, the New York people who didn't drive out to Mendham took the ferry to Hoboken and then changed to a train for Morristown where they were picked up. One weekend Dione was in Hoboken struggling with a heavy suitcase on her way from the ferry to the train when a complete stranger kindly offered his help. But when she got to Morristown station the police were waiting to arrest her. Her "Good Samaritan" had reported her. That day's newspapers had carried headlines about a woman who had murdered her baby — and when the poor man had carried Dione's bag he noticed blood had been dripping from it. After much commotion, calm was finally restored when the suitcase was opened revealing scores of beef hearts that Dione was bringing out for Sunday lunch at the farm.

For several years I didn't see Dione until one day she called me saying she had a business proposition for me. When I got to her apartment I found her excited about a new project that she thought I could help with. She was going into partnership with someone who would finance a line of prepared foods under the Dione Lucas name. That seemed to me quite a good idea, but Dione and partners could be a volatile situation, so I said: "Well, I hope you have a really good lawyer." She said: "Oh yes, my partner has used him for years."

I patiently tried to explain that she should have her own lawyer to draw up such an agreement. But my heart really sank when she mentioned the partner's name, "Tiger" Morse.

A few years before, I had spent a summer in Cape Cod helping my ex-fiancé Alfred Etievant launch *Chez Alfred*, a restaurant he attempted in Provincetown, taking it over from our friend, Cordon Bleu chef Pablo Ford and his wife, Helen.

One day at lunchtime a nice-looking, well-dressed, very excitable woman, followed by a frazzled-looking man, rushed in insisting on talking to me right then. She said her name was Morse and that our mutual friend Emily "Jackie" Davie had recommended me as someone who could organize businesses and personal lives, so she had "flown right up to the Cape" with her boyfriend? — manager? to hire me.

Flinching from her energy, I managed to put her off until my return to New York.

Asking around about her, I soon found out that she was well-known as a high fashion dress designer with her own stores on Madison Avenue, the *A La Carte*, and *Gilded Cage*, for example. Jackie Davie also told me more about her. She was a good promoter for herself, (*e.g.* she had once, as a finale to a fashion show she was narrating in Tudor City, walked right down into the swimming pool, microphone and all!) and that her special designs, like skirts made from priest's robes, sold for thousands of dollars. I got the clear impression that she was a bit "kookie," and since fashion, high or low, is one thing I have little affinity for, I never got involved.

But now I was reminded of my reservations about this gifted but mercurial woman as someone to work with, and conscious of Dione's foibles, I predicted the combination of these two personalities might result in fireworks.

Apparently I was right. In a few months the partnership blew up, not surprisingly!

But the tragic thing was, that because what Dione had contributed as her investment in the partnership was the use of her name, from that time on, until her early death, she could no longer use it herself. She had to work anonymously.

This was what she was doing the last time I talked to her, when she was working in the kitchen of the *Ginger Man* restaurant near Lincoln Center.

* * * * *

CHAPTER 15

G.'S LAST VISIT TO AMERICA

Dushka
♦

Solita Solano, in New York, on December 17, 1948 made this entry in her diary:

"G. arrived yesterday on the S.S. *America* with Mme. de Salzmann, Lord Pentland, another Englishman and a Mr. Wolton who was at Prieuré and is now *tamada* [toastmaster].

"All old group at ship or Hotel Wellington to greet him. First coffee and armagnac at eleven, then lunch at two for twenty-five or more.

"He told us the English (old Ouspensky group) had paid his debts in Paris, 'millions of francs'... that he was to buy a large chateau for headquarters... that his health is now even better than before accident... 'All debts liquidated in France; I come to you pure, like newborn baby.' Big suite at hotel, prepared and stocked for him, his kind of food and drink.

"After lunch he went out with Donald Whitcomb to shop for salad materials, Donald carrying a shopping bag.

"Alfred [Etievant] had flown to New York earlier and had already begun to rehearse the new group of sixty at Carnegie Hall. G. went there the first evening to supervise the exercises."

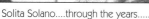
Solita Solano....through the years.....

◆◆◆

Jessmin
♦

New York, May 30, 1949
Dear Ethel:

As you know, Aubrey Wolton arrived in New York last November with a young Frenchman, Alfred Etievant, who had been sent over by Mr. Gurdjieff to teach the new Movements in preparation of G.'s visit.

He started at once. I had only been informed indirectly, so I went over to see on the second night, and on the third I joined the class without anyone telling him who I was. I found even the first exercises quite difficult for the elderly and inactive lady I had become, but liked Alfred's intensity very much.

Alfred Etievant, 1949

There were not many young people among the group that the New York leaders, Rita Romilly Benson, Wim Nyland and his wife Illonka Karasz, Louise Goepfert March and Paul Anderson, had been able to call together. So, on the Sunday, we took Alfred out to Mendham and I showed him the work of the Movements group there. He was surprised and pleased and asked to have everyone attend his classes. Mme. O. made it possible for two-thirds of them to go into New York every night, and it was arranged for the others to attend in turn.

Wolton helped me to persuade Dushka to join in, and since she was somewhat attracted to Alfred, she did so. To my surprise she moved very well and was very quick in grasping the exercises. They all seem very complicated, quite tiring physically, but extremely stimulating. What I could sometimes see was beautiful, although in some ways repetitious.

Quiet collectedness was out of the question for us older people in the back rows who had difficulty in understanding and following but were also determined to try and to endure. Alfred had been told to dictate the thirty-five Movements he knew as quickly as possible. My younger pupils in the first row enjoyed the challenge and said they felt their capacities and their brains "stretching in all directions."

Mr. Gurdjieff must have been pleased to know that, with the Mendham pupils, about fifty people were attending the class.

He arrived in New York, and that first evening came to the studio in Carnegie Hall, arriving halfway though the Movements class. Dushka was in the first row and I saw that he was looking at her a lot. When we all finally sat down, he called Jeanne over, and asked her in Russian who the "Dervish" in the back row was. I took it that this must mean me since he looked, and had her look, at me and I was wearing a kind of turban.

◆ ◆ ◆

Dushka
◆

We often teased Alfred later about that first evening when Mr. G. came to watch.

Alfred had been working hard with us every night preparing for just this moment. Naturally he wished us to make a special effort and he walked between the rows encouraging us in a soft whisper.

All of a sudden a strange noise started to grow at the back of the room. A wailing kind of "lalala" trying to match the piano accompaniment spread through the class until Mr. G. raised his hand and told Mme. de Salzmann to stop playing. He looked as puzzled as many of the rest of us in front were.

Days later it was explained. Alfred had a charming but strong French accent and he had walked through the class exhorting his pupils to: "Think! Think! Think!" But some of them had misunderstood and tried obediently to: "Sing! Sing! Sing!"

◆ ◆ ◆

Jessmin
◆

At the end of the lesson, Mr. Gurdjieff informed everyone that he was staying at the Hotel Wellington nearby at 56th and Seventh Ave and he invited anyone who wished to come over for supper.

I was changing into my street clothes when a message came "that Mr. G. wished to speak to me." I went to him (not too willingly) and he said: "Jessmin, I not know

The Hotel Wellington at
Seventh Ave and 56th Street

you. You grow so stout and solid. I never can thank you enough for preparation." (I still don't know whether he meant the Movements pupils or Dushka.) "You please come to apartment," (which I hadn't intended to do), "I wish to talk seriously to you." He then pushed into my hand a gold wristwatch and said "Give this to daughter."

We all went over for supper (served then and each day thereafter, from the extra bathroom where some boards over the bathtub supported a two-burner alcohol stove.)

Mr. G. then made a great to-do in front of everyone, sending to the secluded corner I was in various tidbits from his dishes, and I'm afraid I liked him less each instant. He felt this, because, about 2 a.m. I got up to leave and he stopped me saying he wished to talk to me. Someone else just then greeted him with a kiss and he said softly to me: "You see, you only one here who not glad I came."

When almost everyone had left, he brought out a big box of Russian cigarettes and some handsome embroidered Swiss overboots, and candy. He began by saying that he had noticed that Dushka smoked. I was to give her the box of cigarettes and tell her to smoke them but to please him by never smoking any more afterwards. If she had will power to do this thing, he would reward her by paying a great deal of money into her bank. He gave me the shoes for her or for me; saying to take measurements so that he could have others made for us.

Then he said: "You know, now I am an old man. This summer nearly die. Also, I now rich man. Much that I never able to do before is now possible because in England are hundreds of pupils who pay, and soon I publish book and become millionaire. I will take big chateau in France. Already I pay much money down. And now I am not interested in many people, only interested in a few young people. Your daughter also. You please give her to me while I am here. I am impartial parent, not kind, but I will teach her. As for you, you rest. Later, I oblige her provide for you."

◆ ◆ ◆

Dushka
◆

He also asked her, apparently referring to me, "whether it was reward or punishment?" Mother answered rather grimly: "Reward! But only because I made it so." He nodded slowly and said: "Yes. You speak true."

(Above) Gurdjieff lighting
a cigarette.

And now, fifty years after this little incident, it may seem ridiculous to dwell on what he said about cigarettes. Yes, I remember those particular ones. They were specially made, probably by hand, and were two-thirds filter with a bare inch of fragrant tobacco. I did smoke them all ultimately and although I "disobeyed" his suggestion and occasionally smoked socially in later life, I never really acquired a habit. But considering the strange stories and superstitions that are increasingly attributed to Gurdjieff these days, I feel I should point out what he said about cigarettes and other people's (at least his daughter's) smoking. Especially after hearing my musician friend, Gert-Jan Blom describe a recent visit to the Gurdjieff group in Holland. Apparently he was shown through a long hall, thick with smoke, on either side of which were benches filled with grim-faced people avidly puffing on cigarettes. Surprised, he asked about this and was seriously answered: "But you know Mr. Gurdjieff always smoked." (!!)

Now — as for that *chateau*! Mr. Gurdjieff extolled it to me also saying;"It will one day be yours!"

He then gave me impressive photographs of a luxurious estate. I later learned that this was the "Château de Voisins" at Rambouillet which he was presumably trying to buy.

But all I ever saw of it were those snapshots.....!

Photos of the chateau which Gurdjieff presented to Dushka.......   The photos, that is!

◆ ◆ ◆

Dushka was by now quite interested in doing the Movements although she was not a bit well. She ought to have her tonsils out, she has a recurring streptococcus infection. She was interested in being around the apartment and trying to help Alfred because she felt that no one seemed to be capable of organizing things, and that is true.

The Wolfes had left Mendham to run things for Mr. G. They were feeling very important, but were, alas, at first often drunk, and identified, resentful about their responsibility being shared. Mr. G. was always complaining about "hysterics," bad food, disorder, etc. Jeanne sat by and patiently let things happen.

The New York group members were nice to me personally, but a bit peeved that the Mendham pupils seemed to be getting so much attention in the Movements classes. Later too, when Madame Ouspensky brought in some people with money about whom a fuss was made, the New York people sat by glumly and seemed to think that, if they were not being taught anything special by Mr. G. it was the fault of Mendham. "Too much importance being put on Movements!" and so on.

Mr. G. continued to come around to Movements every evening. We worked from eight to eleven every night and then went up to the Wellington, forty to sixty of us at a time and had supper. A chosen few sat at table with Mr. G., and the rest, sitting picnic fashion, were tightly packed into the living room.

The meal would consist of a special salad, soup, a meat dish with rice, and dessert, accompanied by endless toasts drunk in Calvados and Armagnac to the various "Idiots." This was followed by readings of his manuscript being prepared for publication, conversation, and music that Mr. G. played on his Asian hand harmonium until three a.m. or later. He was still coughing terribly from the pleurisy following his accident.

Jessmin
◆

He looked very old but the old vitality shines through sometimes. He seems a little more benevolent, rather than the passionate shock-giver of the Prieuré days.

After a day or two Mr. G. spoke to Dushka and told her that her "sister" (Petey Taylor) was coming into town and that he wanted Dushka to buy her some clothes and also help her to buy presents for everyone for Christmas. He added that he did not like what Dushka was wearing, that, as his eldest daughter, she was to buy herself something to wear for that evening, and handed her $500 for each of them.

Dushka (who till then had never spent more than about $10 on any outfit) called me to come and help find a dress in the couple of hours left of the afternoon. Nearby on Fifty-seventh Street, at a sale at Jay Thorpe's, we found her a dress of deep-blue velveteen with a big circular skirt. It was very plain, with long sleeves, but when she turned up the little collar and fastened it across with a small brooch, it took on an old-fashioned and Russian look. She wore it that night and Mr. G. was evidently very pleased and said that it, and Dushka, reminded him of his sister when she "graduated," or something. We had also rushed over to La Vieille Russie on Fifty-ninth Street and found a real Russian dress, black silk with the traditional collar buttoned down one side, embroidered in red, which served for some of the other evenings, and still we had not spent half the money.

Petey "Eve" Taylor

Dushka did meet Petey Taylor, a sweet quiet girl who has worked as a model, and the two of them arranged to go shopping several times when Petey came in from Westport, Connecticut. She lives with her mother Edith Taylor (who is working as a kind of Recreation Director for the very chic mental Sanitarium out there).

By now Mr. G. had become angry about the way the apartment was run and had told Alfred to take over entirely.

Dushka saw her opportunity to share in this. She loved the idea of lavishly feeding so many people, felt that Alfred was given too hard a task and elected herself his assistant. The two did the best they could, but Dushka told me that sometimes they were not sure that what they prepared would be edible. In fact, one day they dropped the can of the tomato puree they were adding into the huge vat of stew. They were able to fish out the can — but never did find the label!

Next Mr. G. called Dushka to him and said he would not have Alfred falling in love with her; that she was "Miss Gurdjieff" and too good for Alfred, that she was to treat him like a "louse that one makes chik" (crushes between one's thumbnails.) Dushka answered that there was no question of a love affair. She said frankly that she went up to the apartment perhaps more because she enjoyed working with Alfred than for any other reason. But, though she was sorry not to do as Mr. G. said, she could not treat another person unkindly without understanding why. She then added that she had found herself a new job now and would not be able to come up to the apartment as much anyway.

Well, that raised a storm. Mr. G. said he was her father and that he expected obedience. Dushka answered that she had only known him since three weeks, that she had learnt to be independent in her twenty-four years; that she was not yet able to understand what he wanted from her, or even his right to impose it! Mr. G. told her to talk to me.

She came home and I thought she was really wonderful. Although I had guessed that he would be talking to her and rather dreaded how he would do it, Dushka had never told me anything.

But now she said that, although she had had a real shock when he informed her so casually that she was his daughter, she had tried to give herself time. She understood perfectly why I had never tried to explain all this to her and was really grateful that I had let her see him for herself. She said that of course he was a most interesting man and that life around him at the apartment was exciting, especially after the dull and frustrating period she had just been through. But, frankly, she did not care if she never went up there or set eyes on him again.

I talked to her as best I could, being quite honest, I think, about my own reservations, confessing that I was prejudiced and a little afraid. However, I managed to advise her to try to learn as much as she could from this special opportunity and to try to see straight about Alfred and what was her interest there.

I next had a talk with Jeanne who could hardly believe that Dushka had not known about Mr. G. being her father. I think she may have told this to him and he was also surprised at the way Dushka had taken it, and at my permitting her to be with him. From then on he would have Dushka go shopping with him and take her along when he went to see old friends like Romany Marie.

◆◆◆

Dushka

◆

Describing Greenwich Village in the Twenties, Edgar Varese's widow (in her book, *A Looking-Glass Diary),* asks: "I wonder if anyone still remembers Romany Marie? For years her restaurant was Varese's café where he could go to find concordant spirits or argumentative minds in Marie's friendly ambiance... into the early hours of morning in endless talk over her innocuous Turkish coffee (no alcohol)."

But my friend, Edgar Tafel (Frank Lloyd Wright's biographer and another patron in those days) recently told me that his "coffee" cup always contained whiskey.

In fact, "Romany Marie's" was a speakeasy!

Romany Marie in 1928

....and her pencil sketch of her "coffee house!"

So, whether it was the special clientele (explorer Stefensson, sculptor Zorach, writer Theodore Dreiser, Georgia O'Keefe and Stieglitz, Buckminster Fuller, Mark Tobey, mime Angna Enters and others) that drew Gurdjieff, or other attractions, he evidently often spent time in the restaurant during his first visits to the U.S.

Mrs. Varese describes Marie as a "Rumanian Jew and self-styled 'gypsy', dressing the part, and telling fortunes in coffee grounds. She was a handsome, dark woman with so deep a voice that when she telephoned I invariably mistook her for a man."

In 1949, when Mr. G. took me downtown to meet Marie in her small dark apartment, her "restaurant/coffee-house/speakeasy" was long gone, but she was still dynamic and had that amazing bass voice. I didn't get the impression that she knew or cared anything about "Gurdjieff, the Teacher," she was just delighted to see her old friend.

Mr. G. never mentioned our two visits with her to anyone else!

He did take a few others along with us when we revisited his other favorite "restaurant" (?) from the early days, Frank's Steakhouse on 125th St. in Harlem.

◆ ◆ ◆

Jessmin
◆

Dushka saw G. spending money lavishly, handing people hundreds of dollars at a time. She watched Petey buying expensive clothes and jewelry, and the strangest types and hangers-on being flattered, while loyal pupils like Alfred and others were working themselves to a frazzle without being given a kind word, money or a present.

She sat during meals at a small table on the side with one or two of the other "calves" (as Mr. G., and thereafter, of course, everyone referred to some of the younger ones) watching and listening to his behavior with the older guests. After a while, she told me how clear it was to an onlooker that Mr. G. acted in order to tease, provoke, and test people. She was astonished that we all took everything he did and said so heavily. But, naturally, she did not realize how strung-up we all were and how avid for some personal directives.

By this time I hardly went around to the apartment at all. My boss was away and I had a lot of extra work at the office. I did attend all readings and Movements classes, but went home at one a.m., possibly missing much that Mr. G. might say to those who stayed on. On Saturdays I would go to lunch.

Edith Taylor had come in from Connecticut and was staying in the hotel, and pleased Mr. G. by profiting of the rest, ordering breakfast in bed, and taking advantage of the beauty shop and massage services one could have there. But, at Saturday lunch, Edith and I would be put through the same old routine of disapproval. We were not to call our daughters "Pity" and "Dushka" (but Eve and Sophia!) One time we would be shouted at "*Svolotch!*" "*Balda!*" [Strong insults, difficult to translate. Approximately: "lowest of the low;" and "dullard"]. Another time treated with much special attention, extra food and commands to the girls to "love their mothers." Edith, who had always been a good companion to Mr. G. managed to be undisturbed, tactful and good-humored. I just curled up inside and froze. At least Mr. G. had finally realized that I was earning our living by carrying out a task at the Free French Information Service which was quite difficult for me, and otherwise he left me alone.

I had let Dushka move into the hotel so that she could get a little more sleep at night, between sitting around until 2 a.m. and getting to her new job in the mornings on time. Everyone was trying to function on about four or five hours rest a night. The Mendham people slept in the truck driving home, for Mme. Ouspensky had made it clear that if they went evenings to the Movements in New York, they were not to neglect any of their usual daily duties at Franklin Farms. We all began to be very doped, and I think, highly suggestible.

Dushka began to think that Mr. G. was not as "impartial" as he made out. He seemed really hurt when Petey showed plainly that she did not want to be around. Edith will not tell her that she truly is Mr. G.'s child, and encourages her to be independent. She is a sweet and honest girl. I was touched and grateful when she showed Dushka and me some affection, for otherwise she did not include many people. It must all be very hard for her because she was in no way prepared to think of Mr. G. as a teacher and on a different level.

The sore spot of friction between Mendham and New York was now being exacerbated by Mr. G.

He went out to see Mme. O., and she told me that "she felt the innocent joy of a baby recognizing its mother" when he walked into her room. She was in bed since some months, and he said he would give her treatment, injections and such, and that she must practice getting up and walking. He told her he needed her to get better to help him in his work. (The injections he prescribed for her were given her with heartfelt trepidation by Irene Tilley, who tried to learn to do it painlessly by endlessly experimenting on her long-suffering nice husband, Basil.)

The New York people, and I think Jeanne also, felt that the Franklin Farms property ought, at once, to be passed over to Mr. G.

Mme. O. told me she had offered him the use of it as long as he was in America, and even said she herself would move out into a small cottage nearby. But she tried to explain that since Mrs. Collin-Smith had deeded it to the grandchildren, Lonia and Tania, with Mme. O. allowed to use it for Work purposes as long as she wished, she had no legal right to give it away. But also she made it clear that, although she still believed in him as her Teacher, she did not yet understand the lines along which he was working. After all, although she had considered herself always only as a "nurse" to help people along so as to bring to him pupils of Ouspensky's like Wolton, Bennett, Walker, Pentland and many of the other English people, she could not entirely desert a number of the younger people who had been doing all the labor involved in keeping the property going, and helping her to pay the taxes on it. She had arranged everything so that Gurdjieff had pupils prepared to take over responsible jobs; Wolton as his book agent, Pentland as his representative, and various other people who helped with money.

People were only too ready to report to her how Mr. G. complained in New York that she and Mr. O. had never helped him, but, "with crumbs from his table" had gained money and luxury for themselves. This, after she had given him Mr. O.'s book (*In Search of the Miraculous* about which he said he could hear himself speaking), and had turned away a big money contribution from Mrs. Pearce, advising her that she would get a better return for her generosity if she handed it to Mr. G. And he was very pleased to get it and said that it permitted him to "teach" instead of having to give all his time and energy to raising money.

I think the New York groups realized that they were poorly prepared for any study together and that Mr. G. felt no urge to teach them anything special. They had all been working on their own, but they were not in sympathy with the discipline of Mendham. So they were gratified when Mr. G. seemed to disapprove of all that was done there.

If ever the subject of Mendham came up at meals I would try to assert that I considered myself a Mendham pupil, that I was able to learn best from Mme. Ouspensky and that I would not have been alive and at Mr. G.'s table now if Mme. O. had not helped me. Jeanne upheld me in this. Mr. G. would just snort, and the others either look at me pityingly or glare.

One Saturday night when he was really completely exhausted, this all came to a confrontation. Dushka and I were finishing clearing up the apartment alone, it was nearly 4 a.m. and Mr. G. came out to the kitchen. He told me to go home but come to see him the next day without fail. Like a fool, I said I was going to Mendham as I did every Sunday. He then made a noisy scene saying that I was never to go to Mendham again, that the Ouspenskys had used me very cheaply and that he would provide for me better, twenty-five years I had looked after Dushka and now, for twenty-five years I was to rest, have nice house of my own, etc., etc.

As usual, he managed to upset me. But Dushka, on the side lines, realized how he was forcing himself, for he was obviously tired out and she said to me: "Just keep quiet, and of course, go to Mendham, and I will be around here and get in touch with you if really necessary."

I didn't relate the whole storm to Madame, but she advised me to return Sunday afternoon to New York and plan to spend all following Sundays at the apartment in case Mr. G. truly did wish it. Of course, when I got there I was completely ignored.

The days went on with the same rhythm. I think individuals were given "inner exercises," but otherwise, beyond serious work on the Movements, Mr. G. seemed to confine himself to preparing for the publication of the books, and gathering people together for meals with him. A lot of money was spent. He had sent me $500 which I returned, only learning later that he had passed it to Dushka to deposit in my bank account.

By now other youngsters, Mme. Ouspensky's granddaughter, Tania (recently married to Tom Forman), Frank Lloyd Wright's daughter, Iovanna, and the Sutta's daughter, Marian, were being welcomed and encouraged.

Dushka was active and never otherwise than herself. Even when Mr. G. railed at her for singing while she worked in the kitchen, saying: "What will people think — that I have a 'light woman' in my apartment?" She answered: "No, they will just think there is someone happy here!"

Fortunately, most people began to feel kindly towards her even if she was not, like Iovanna, "serious" about the Work.

Mr. G. made her read from the publisher's drafts of *Meetings with Remarkable Men* sometimes, and this was difficult for her and painful for us, because although she was intelligent about it, to us it seemed empty. We did not know that he gave her certain instructions; for instance, when she read about his "Workshop" that she should make people laugh or he would "punish" her.

Next, Mr. Bennett arrived from England. He had been an eager student of the Movements at Lyne, and I suspect that he asked whether I could go over to teach again, for suddenly Mr. G. seemed to become aware of my presence again. He asked me to choose a first row of six pupils to be trained to give Movements demonstrations in London. He found fault with everyone I suggested, but in the end, they were the ones he took over to Paris, except for two, a slightly more mature woman who couldn't leave Mendham and one young man. They were all young women of varying sizes and shapes. He called them fondly the "monsters," and gave them lovely silk material, each slightly different, to have made up into tailored suits "for travelling," and explained that they were the "calves who needed to be nourished."

Mr. G. also talked about the Movements with me and began the old story again, that I might ask him anything, for now he could give me a "whole town" if I wished it, and so forth and so on. I was in a very negative mood and felt that he really had no genuine kindliness toward me, probably because while I was seeing that there is so much more in the teaching than I had ever realized, I just couldn't arrive at complete trust in him.

One evening when I happened to be in the front row of the Movements class, and feeling quite ill from eye strain (some little blood vessel had broken behind my eye, the doctor said, after long hours of proofreading at the office) I just couldn't balance or follow and stepped out. Mr. G. asked me why I had stopped and I answered that I had missed seeing the Movement demonstrated, so did not know it and shouldn't be in front. He then said: "You come out and watch. Make notes of exercises to be used when Alfred no longer here."

This did not please me much, because the one thing I was getting out of the practices was a certain stimulation of energy which I valued overmuch. Sitting in the office for months on end seemed to have deadened everything in me so that there was no joy in life.

Then Mr. G. announced: "You are now Director of Movements in America. You will teach when I leave."

Since there were a dozen people who already could do the Movements better than I, two of them women who had previous experience in teaching dancing, I thought this choice was rather silly. I know he had asked the Wolfes who could assume responsibility for the classes and that they had said: "Only Jessmin." And it is possible that Jeanne reminded him that I had taught at Lyne, before that in New York since 1925, and since 1943 in Mendham.

◆◆◆

This "making of notes" led to hours of work with Alfred to make sure that the Movements that Mr. Gurdjieff had started the Americans on were completely understood and accurately recorded since, as Gurdjieff had firmly instructed: "Movements must be the same everywhere, in America as in Europe!"

In fact, when Gurdjieff and his entourage went back to France he had Alfred stay behind to help Mother finalize this material so that she (and many of us in the ensuing years) could refer to it and be confident that what we were teaching was accurate and as Gurdjieff had advised.

This incident also belies what misinformed people have claimed, that Mr. Gurdjieff said not to make notes!

Of course he didn't want you to run home from a class to scribble intellectual formulas instead of gradually building a physical, mental and emotional comprehension and personal experience of an exercise. But once this total understanding

Dushka
◆

of an exercise was achieved, to guard against changes and distortions of his meticulously fine-tuned exercises that he was expecting us to share with future generations — of course he would expect the practical use of notation.

◆ ◆ ◆

Jessmin
◆

Then Mr. G. began to bring pressure on me to leave my job. He swore he would provide generously for me. As I look at it a few weeks later, perhaps it looks as if he were truly trying to fulfill some obligation. And if I bridled at the rather contemptuous way he offered this, it was because I was not interested enough in his teaching to throw up everything to serve it, without thought for the morrow. After all, I had tried that once. So I told him I did not wish to be a "Teacher" again — that I had had classes for many years and that this only fed my vanity. Most important of all, I did not yet know all these newer Movements well enough to judge whether they could bring good results, and how to go on with them.

Paying no attention, he told me to arrange to practice with Alfred every day. He would remember sometimes to bait me about this. He never talked to me about anything else. He would call me into his room and say: "Now you teacher of Gurdjieff work. You take money," and hand me wads of bills, saying I should count out $1000 for myself. This used to demean me so. After twenty-five years of providing for Dushka, often not having enough to eat, that he should act as if I were only interested in my own material security! In fact, on one occasion I felt so hateful that I threw the money in his face, and stood by with my heart sinking into my boots, as he had to pick it up from the floor.

He now behaved as if Dushka had nothing to do with me at all.

He was arranging to take some of the young people back with him to Paris. He told Iovanna, Tania and Marian Sutta, another American girl (whose father he wrongly believed to be a millionaire), and asked Edith to let Petey go, which she said would only be on condition that she go with her. He also spoke to Dushka about getting her travel papers in order and added: "Perhaps mother come too!"

Nothing was definite until the last minute. I was told that sometimes at a lunch, Mr. G. would speak of how his work in the U.S. was to be conducted: "the net was to be thrown wide," his book was to be read in large auditoriums, etc. He elected people to positions: tasks or titles (however you wish to look at it). John Pentland, understandably, was to be the figurehead, Wim Nyland, the Comptroller and "Kapellmeister" (whatever that meant), Rita Benson, the Reader, Carol Robinson, the Pianist for Movements Classes, etc. Edith was to be Custodian of the books, Donald Whitcomb in charge of recordings. I did not hear all this myself for, after one experience of Mr. G. calling a meeting in the middle of the day, ostensibly to give directions, an occasion when we sat around for hours with nothing happening, I did not go back for his lunches. I could not absent myself again from the office during working hours without a medical certificate.

But when I went in the evenings, I saw that he was packing trunks with appliances, provisions, and equipment to take back to France. Nothing more was said about whether or not I would accept to be responsible for the Movements teaching, and Dushka did not know what plans were being made for her.

We both felt that it would be a pity for her to miss the opportunity of going to France, and seeing more of Mr. G.'s ways of teaching, but we were both afraid of

Lord Pentland Wim Nyland Edith Taylor Rita Romilly Benson Donald Whitcomb
"Figurehead." "Comptroller." "Custodian of the Books." "Reader." "Recorder."

Aboard the *RMS Queen Mary* sailing from New York to France in February, 1949.
(Left to right) Tania Savitsky Forman, Mme. de Salzmann, Iovanna Lloyd Wright, Lady Pentland, Mary Sinclair, (a waiter), Mr. Gurdjieff, and Lord Pentland.

what this might lead to.

At one moment Mr. G. had said that Dushka was not to be like the other "calves." She was to live with and be part of his family.

I tried not to worry and felt that I could count on Madame Ouspensky to help me see what was the right thing to do.

Then, one morning, a day or so before Mr. G. was due to leave, I was going in a taxi to the office and we were halted for a moment at Fifty-fifth Street and Sixth Avenue. And I saw Mr. G. in his astrakhan cap and soft felt boots, picking his way across the street amid the mud and melted snow. And suddenly I saw him as an old gentleman, intent on his own concerns, still walking like a cat, but physically diminished. And the memories of his former violence were erased, and from one moment to the next, I felt sorry that I had not wished to be of service to his aim.

That night I went to him and said that I would try to do as he wished and teach the Movements, and that if he wished to take Dushka to France, I would encourage her to go. I asked him just one thing in return, to see that her throat (she was uncomfortably overdue to have her tonsils removed) was cared for. He answered that he promised and would ask Jeanne to remind him to send Dushka to a very good specialist they knew.

He then kissed me "Goodbye," and came out of his room to tell the men to give me $1000 to pay for Dushka's outfitting and ticket. She was to follow him in a couple of weeks.

This they did at once, but then followed me out into the corridor to ask me if I could please give it back for the moment as otherwise they would be without cash for last minute expenses. I confess that this tickled my sense of humor, and of course I handed it back. And of course, later they got Dushka her ticket.

As soon as Mr G. had gone on February 11th, the conflicts began. It was evident that all the "old" people in New York had strong memories of former associations with him, and felt a strong personal bond that made their approach rather subjective. He stirred everyone up more than is believable and left an exhausted group with nothing really to cooperate on. Everyone was overwrought, disappointed at not having been welded into one real group, and yet each one believed that he was the only one capable of taking charge of everything.

They were also afraid that I would go back and teach the new Work only to the Mendham pupils. While this period lasted, it was very painful, even though one could realize that it was only as Madame O. said, "just scum coming to top." The various disputes that went on are now almost inexplicable.

Alfred came out with Dushka and me to Mendham on weekends. The young people remaining there were in good state and made us happily welcome.

Dushka was one of the few people who were asked into Madame's room, and she heard some of *Fragments* read and was enthusiastic, and began to think she would rather stay at Mendham than go to Paris. She really loved Madame who was always wonderful to her, direct and humorous.

Madame gave me courage to supervise the practices and encourage Dushka to get off.

She left, sailing with Edith and Petey on the *De Grasse*, on March 7th.

* * * * *

CHAPTER 16

PARIS 1949,
"SOPHIE," "THE CALVES," AUTO TRIPS

"I ask you to believe nothing that you cannot verify for yourself." G.I. Gurdjieff.

Jessmin
◆

New York, Spring, 1949
Dear Ethel,

Dushka is living in a Paris hotel, (the "Belfast," near the Arc de Triomphe). She is being kept busy at the Movements which they do every night for two hours before going to the apartment nearby on the Rue des Colonels Renard for long dinners after which she has her special responsibility of recording Mr. G. playing his hand harmonium. They have been taken on trips to Geneva, Cannes and Dieppe, and Dushka went to Brussels once with Michel. (She was at once told by Mr. G. that Michel was her brother, although Jeanne will not acknowledge this to anyone.)

◆ ◆ ◆

Dushka
◆

No, actually Petey and I weren't "at once" told he was our half-brother. Years later, as old ladies comparing memories, we admitted to each other that for the several days before this fact was revealed to us, we both thought Michel was one of the most attractive men either of us had ever met. Mr. G.'s announcement, therefore, was a surprise to us that mixed disappointment with pleasure.

As to my personal dealings with Mr. Gurdjieff, it is true that for the first few weeks in Paris, I struggled with conflicting feelings. What to believe? How to behave? Mother had tried to prepare me for all this, suggesting I be open to new experiences while also discriminating in what I accepted and obeyed. But once there, it was difficult not to be influenced by other people. They flocked around Mr. G. Most knew him so much better than I did, and unfortunately, many of them brought with them an atmosphere not just of respect or even of awe, but sometimes, I didn't know why, even of fear.

So one of the first times that I was summoned into his "private office," a tiny closet-like room stuffed with supplies and exotic foods, I was really frightened when I found myself defying some order he was giving me, that I didn't feel right about. I don't even remember what it was, only that I refused and then worried and fretted about it for hours.

Dushka's snapshot of a young Dr. Michel de Salzmann on an airplane trip to Taliesin East.

The next day, Mme. de Salzmann, who may have realized the state I was in, helped me to understand something very important about Mr. G., which influenced all my subsequent relationship with him.

(Above left) 6 rue des Colonels Renard in Paris. Mr. Gurdjieff's small crowded apartment is on the first floor over the pharmacy. The black Citroen parked in front is probably his. (Right) And around the corner, the venerable Hotel Belfast.

Taking me aside she said that M. Gurdjieff had told her about our confrontation.

Then she amazed me by adding that contrary to what I might have feared, he had in fact been very happy with me saying: "Now I know I can trust her!"

Mr. Gurdjieff's name for us, "The Calves," evidently needs more explanation, especially as I was appalled recently to read how James Webb in *The Harmonious Circle*, refers to "calves as he called his children, their mothers were cows." This is a completely silly and insulting misinterpretation.

When Mr. G. talked about "his calves," it was an affectionate name he used for the six young women whom he invited to Paris in 1949 to be trained as the first row for a future Movements Demonstration. These were Petey and myself, yes, but also Tania, Marian, Iovanna and Lise, though sometimes other young visitors were added temporarily to our group. We certainly never heard him refer to any woman as a cow!

He would give extra meaning to this name for us by repeating a special "teaching story" we often heard him tell at the long dinners we attended every night in New York and then in Paris.

Through the years, even at the Prieuré, people remembered him using "the cow story" to point out how someone was staring at him stupidly and wide-eyed. In 1935, he was still using it and it was noted down verbatim in the diaries of "The

Rope," the group of women working with him at that time.

Kathryn Hulme in Paris, in 1935, made this diary entry:

"Sunday, October 27 at Fontainebleau ...with him... He turns on me and gives me a terrible test I cannot understand... I do self-observation while attack goes on to stop flushes or tears, and keep my eye on him, eye to eye with him. Afterward he, looking me in eye, laughs, then turns to others, says, 'See, she look on me like cow at new-pan-door.'

"(We all have to think what 'new-pan-door' can mean. Finally realize he means new '*peint*' door, newly painted door.)

"'Cow in morning..' he says, 'goes out from barn... live always in same barn... go down same road to field... stay all day... eat. Man, while cow gone, paints door of barn. Night... cow comes home, same road she knows, to same barn... but now barn has new '*peint*' door... cow stands looking, looking, at new '*peint*' door. Not know her own home. That how she look on me now. You see?'

Kathryn Hulme.

"Tuesday, June 9: Margaret's animal has been named this afternoon. 'She Thibetan yak. She look at new '*peint*' door... think like business-man about cost of new paint, how long will last, etc. so that forget self. Interested surface detail. Even a cow concerns itself with only one question: is that my home or is it not my home?'

"Margaret's effort to mentate about detail leads her away from the principal subject — the relation of the thing to herself."

So we "calves," often heard versions of this story directed at various victims and we delighted in the pantomime that accompanied it, Mr. G. with his mouth gaping open, his eyes popping, craning his head from side to side in imitation of the poor bewildered cow.

Margaret Anderson.

But sometimes it was <u>we</u> who were the butt of the story. Then with an even more exaggerated pantomime, teasingly and kindly aimed at us, he would add: " ...and behind her follows calf... not know own way home... not see door... not understand why, but do same, copy cow..."

Evelyn Sutta, who had accompanied her young daughter Marian to Paris well understood how Mother who had remained back in New York was concerned about what might be going on with me. She tried to keep her informed:
"Dear Mrs. Howarth,

"Dushka left early this morning for Brussels with Michel. She went to get tapes for the recording machine. She seemed awfully pleased at the idea yesterday and looked forward to the change. She insists that she hasn't lost weight, but she looks lovely and slim these days.

"Last night, she walked home with Vera Daumal (one of the older French group, Rene Daumal's widow) and me, and we began to talk about the reading. I spoke about what I remembered Mr. Ouspensky saying about the moon. Dushka seemed very animated and said 'Why can't we have talks like this after the readings? I'm beginning to see something. I've wasted five months not understanding a thing because there are never any discussions. I can't get a thing out of listening to the readings, but I felt I understood a lot the other night when I was assigned to read out loud.' (Chap. 48 of *Beelzebub* "From the Author"). Vera told her that Mme. de Salzmann had a

Rene Daumal.

group that discussed the ideas and suggested that Dushka speak to her about it. I felt that Dushka really was interested for the first time.

"She feels much better although she still has a slight cough and said that she would see the specialist again today and the date for the operation might be arranged. She had a pleasant weekend. Alfred took her to the movies and to the theater to see *Ondine* in which his sister Yvette also appears, and yesterday he took her to the country which she enjoyed enormously.

"Undoubtedly, she is very wary of me now, but I tried to lighten the situation by saying in an off-hand tone, 'Come on now, Dushka, give me a full report of everything so I can write your mother about you.' As you say, she chatters away about superficialities and one can only piece together a few comments here and there to guess about what she is thinking. There is no doubt in my mind that she adores you and misses you dreadfully and hates to admit it. She must be disturbed about the past from the way she spoke about Eve. She had said (that one late night when we talked) that, contrary to what Tania had given out, Eve did know that she is his daughter, but that it hasn't sunk in yet... that she is naive, that she hasn't begun to visualize her mother in this situation, that she hadn't thought deeply about what such a relationship meant, and so on. I felt, from this, that Dushka was revealing her own thoughts. But it must be so, don't you think, and fortunately Dushka is sane and levelheaded and I am convinced she will 'manage' beautifully, even if she decides 'the Body Kesdjan' [A Gurdjieffian term, *c.p.* 'astral body'] is not her dish.

"The Vichy trip was superlative from beginning to end. How wonderful it was to see him and Mme. de Salzmann 'on vacation.' I even found it possible to tease him (very gently) a few times, and it seemed to me that he enjoyed it for he expanded and talked a lot, and joked and kidded us.

"There are three more movements that I need to work out; the problem is time. Solange is very busy and then it takes me ten times as long to understand her as it would anyone else; not because she speaks French, but because she is somewhat *mélangée*.

"Three Germans appeared last night at supper, the leader being the son of Count Kayserling. I suppose you know he has translated *Fragments* into German, and Peggy said that Louise March has been sent for especially for the purpose of checking the translation with him. Louise later said that the emphasis is now on *Fragments - Beelzebub* waits.

"Mr. Hoare is coming next week and bringing some new people from that group.

"I hope you're well and not worrying...

Much Love,

Evelyn"

Solange Claustre

◆ ◆ ◆

Dushka
◆

Going to the theater to see *Ondine* was especially interesting since it was at the Theater Athenée and starred the theater's director who I had admired in many French movies — Louis Jouvet! Yvette Etievant, Alfred's sister and Jouvet's leading actress, (and she took over as directrice of the Athenée when Jouvet died), had evidently told him about my being in Paris and he invited me to sit in his private box.

After watching the wonderful performance (that starred Pierre Blanchard's daughter, Dominique, as the water nymph,) I was led backstage. Jouvet received me in his office, sitting behind a big desk still in his make-up and black knight's costume, a huge dog sitting obediently on either side of him. Darkly handsome, he was friendly and asked about Mother, sending good wishes, etc. It was all rather casual.

But I felt warmed when, on leaving his office, two elderly stagehands rushed over to me, and patting my arm, both talking at once, gushed on at length about "Jassamine." They had evidently also been with Copeau's *Vieux Colombier* those thirty years earlier, and hearing that I was her daughter, wanted to be remembered to Mother.

(Above) Alfred's sister, Yvette Etievant, with Jean-Louis Barrault in *Elle Magazine*.

(Above right) Yvette as Charlotte and Louis Jouvet as Don Juan in the Moliere play at the Theatre Athenée, 1949.

(Left) Jouvet (right) and his close colleague Jean Giraudoux.

◆ ◆ ◆

Dear Ethel,   **Jessmin**
    At the moment Dushka sends little real news. Her first test was when Mr. G.   ◆
wanted her to become engaged to Alfred at a few hours notice...

◆ ◆ ◆

    This was done in what I was beginning to learn was a typical Gurdjieffian   **Dushka**
manner. After lunch one day, Mr. G. suddenly announced that there would be a   ◆
special dinner that night for the announcement of "Sophie and Alfred's engagement,"

Alfred's actor father known to us all as "Papa Cherie."

Alfred during the war in his French navy uniform.

and that he had already invited the Etievant family, Alfred's parents, who everyone called *Maman Cherie* and *Papa Cheri*, and his sister Yvette. (His younger brother, Jacques, was away in South America, and I didn't meet him until many years later when he had married Mme. de Salzmann's daughter, Boussik.)

As Mr. G. hadn't discussed Alfred with me at all since that time in New York when he shouted at me that I should have nothing whatever to do with him, I was stunned by this complete reversal. It is true that I had not really "obeyed" that prohibition and sometimes went out with Alfred. I liked and appreciated him, and especially when we got to Paris, was grateful for his company and some sight-seeing excursions, a welcome change from Mr. G.'s apartment and the daily long Movement classes. And I was flattered that he had enough interest in me to always insist on seeing me back to my hotel even late at night when this might result in his missing the last Metro train. Since his acute shortage of spending money didn't allow him taxis, this meant a two-hour walk home for him.

But we were completely different types. Alfred would refuse to go to a party if he didn't know everyone there, while that was just the kind of thing I loved, a chance to meet new people. If we had been somewhere together before we were due at Mr. G.'s, Alfred would insist that we separate a block away so that we didn't enter the apartment together. How I hated that!

So I certainly wasn't ready to be "engaged." Especially not forced into it in this high-handed fashion. But how to defy Mr. G.? I could only think of one solution. Passive resistance! I simply stayed away from dinner that night and only came in two hours later. I found everybody calmly finishing eating, chatting casually over coffee, and nothing at all was said — except a soft *"svolotch"* to me from Mr. G.

◆ ◆ ◆

Jessmin
◆

...Since they are as yet nothing but good friends, Dushka managed to laugh this off. I suspect that Alfred, who has no money and no training for any profession or trade (he was in a German labor camp during the war when he should have been studying) may have hinted that he needed to be less occupied with the classes and apartment chores so as to find a way to earn his living.

Otherwise Dushka seems to be left rather free. She is trying to practice the piano, renting one by the hour at the Salle Pleyel which is where they go for Movements, and when Rosemary went over, she gave her some lessons.

Dushka visited the de Hartmanns in Garches. They were very sweet to her, and she says, extremely curious about Mr. Gurdjieff and what he was doing since they haven't seen him in perhaps twenty-five years.

◆ ◆ ◆

Dushka
◆

Olga de Hartmann wrote Mother from their little house in Garches, just outside of Paris:

"My Dear Jessmin,

"We were very happy to see Doushka. One Sunday she phoned herself and came by herself. It was so nice. The first moment certainly it was so strange to see a beautiful girl and think it is little Doushka. But in half an hour she was already quite simple, she felt how glad we were to see her. Thomas told her she must be happy to be so beautiful. Really she is. And even not looking thik [fat?] at all, just a good, great young girl!

"We invited her to our musical evening (with the Blochs); she came, everybody also found she was beautiful and clever. I regretted she had another dress, a blue velvet one, but in it she looked a little heavy. I will tell her to change it.

"We have a feeling as it is our daughter; just such a near feeling. I hope it makes you pleasure that Doushka made such impression. G. does not allow to call her 'Doushka' but she has to be called 'Sophie.' We certainly did not know that and she was so glad we called her Doushka.

"I think she and two other young girls will study music (*harmonie*) with Thomas. But that has nothing to do with G. because we do not see him and are quite independent, although we never dinie [deny?] all the "great" we learned through him, and are always working on ourselves.

"Will you come over? It would be so good to see you. You can always live with us. Our best thoughts to you and I am happy that you have such a beautiful daughter.

Yours with love,

Olga"

◆ ◆ ◆

Dear Ethel

Jessmin
◆

Dushka is collecting impressions. Being of a down-to-earth nature she finds it very difficult not to be given anything definite to go on. In her last letter she said that the three months she was supposed to spend in Paris were almost up but that Mr. G. had been so occupied with visitors and the book that she felt he had not been able to do with the youngsters what he wanted. That she really did not know what was expected of her. Someone else wrote me that Dushka wanted badly to come home but felt she had a job to finish.

Anyway, it is all gain for her. This experience should heal the sore place in her psyche about her heredity and parentage. She recognizes something of herself in him. If it is to prove only a holiday, it will still have been something very special to understand better, perhaps, in the future. I just hope she will not be cast off eventually like a squeezed orange.

Maybe Mr. G. will come here in August and travel, maybe in September to stay. No one knows. He says that when his book is published, he will have to hide, and that America is a good place to hide in as it is also the back door to Asia.

We hardly expect any cataclysmic effects from the publication of the book, but he also talks of great clubs in various towns with public readings, Movement demonstrations, etc. At other times he says that we must provide him with money so that he can devote himself to teaching a few young people. This seems to be what Jeanne and Mme. O. understand his aim to be.

The young people are, however, allowed to lead a very social and amateur kind of existence.

It seems to work out like this: Petey and Tania are indulging their healthy young animal instincts, showing little interest in anything but the Movements, horseback

Petey and Tania.

riding in the Bois, going to the movies, and now swimming. (Have I explained that Tania is Mme. O.'s twenty-year-old granddaughter, Lenushka's child by her Ukranian husband, Savitsky, who is still in Paris? Tania was married last summer to Tom Forman, an old pupil who was at Lyne and now manages Franklin Farms. It was pretty much arranged by Mme. O.)

Iovanna, Olgivanna's twenty-four-year-old daughter with Frank Lloyd Wright, the "apple of their eye," was miserable at home after a divorce (a runaway marriage after the war). She tried to get away from her parents who demanded so much from her after her mother's first beautiful and gifted daughter, Svetlana, was killed in an automobile accident a couple of years back. Olgivanna has seemed stricken since. Svetlana, I take it, was Mr. G.'s daughter.

Through her mother, Iovanna has a sense of other than ordinary life values. She slogs along slowly with a feeling that the time her mother can spare to have her away is limited. She seems to "imagine" a great deal, and has no common sense or sense of humor, and can be a little hysterical.

◆ ◆ ◆

Dushka
◆

Years later, reading this remark of Mother's about Svetlana's parentage, I was totally surprised. But it made sense in various ways.

I did agree with her about Iovanna, a sweet girl, but hard to figure out.

Iovanna Lloyd Wright.

For example, one night we were all in the Movements class at the Salle Pleyel. Mr. Gurdjieff was teaching us a beautiful big grouping that involved semi-circles of people prostrated, gradually rising to an erect tableau, and then reversing the positions back to the floor. He asked us all to try adding a singing accompaniment, repeating "Allelulia" on each note of an ascending and then descending scale.

He walked among us as we worked, listening carefully. Then returning to the front of the class he gestured to us to stop and fixed on Iovanna one of his deep long looks. "You, you like sing, eh?" he said and she gushed: "Oh yes, very much Monsieur Gurdjieff."

"*Nu*, good. Tomorrow you come apartment ten o'clock and I give special exercise in singing — only for you."

Then, turning to Mme. de Salzmann who, as usual, was playing the piano for us, Mr. G. muttered something in Russian which I couldn't understand. But I was very curious and as soon as the class was over I asked Tania, who understands Russian from talking with her grandmother, what he had said. It was evidently something about this girl's voice spoiling everything so that he would have to do something about it.

Svetlana Lloyd Wright.

Unfortunately, Iovanna took it in quite another way, as an indication that she had been chosen for a special mission. From then on, anywhere and everywhere, when we were walking in the street with her, sitting in a café, riding in the Metro, while the rest of us moved to the other end of the car — Iovanna sang!

Doesn't this explain author Paul Beekman Taylor's description in *Shadows of Heaven*, of us all on our trip to Geneva "with Iovanna Wright who seemed always to be singing softly to herself."

In fact, some years later when the Taliesen Fellowship attempted (much to some people's dismay) an ambitious public demonstration of Gurdjieff Movements, I understand the program included Miss Lloyd Wright in a long white gown, seated at her harp — singing!

◆ ◆ ◆

Marian Sutta is the youngest, only seventeen or so, daughter of a Russian-Jewish-American real estate lawyer, Maurice, a nice ordinary, kind man. His wife, Evelyn, has progressed from Spiritualism to Theosophy, then to teaching yoga exercises, and now to Mendham, while remaining in some ways a frustrated, golf-playing, country-club matron. Marian, with a precocious intelligence (she entered Chicago University at fourteen) had already attended lectures. She has been amazing in her devotion to Mr. G., tries to understand what he means by "work," and is held closely to it by her mother who is in Paris with her. She is almost too clever, industrious and reasonable, but she will get something and Mr. G.'s presence is all she demands at the moment. However, she apparently told Dushka that she really does not understand anything Mr. G. says to her personally.

Jessmin
◆

The other "calf" is a young French girl, Lise Tracol, the orphaned niece of one of Mr. G.'s closest Paris pupils, Henri Tracol. She has lived in Mr. G.'s household for some time. Dushka describes her as "sweet, serene and inarticulate," and says: "She does the Movements beautifully, so serious and exact; no one else is like her. But she is so devoted in her personal attendance on Mr. G. that she does not mix much with the Americans."

As for Dushka, her going to Paris was, she felt, a "family" matter, a way to put her relationship straight. She is, of course, a bit older than the others and has learnt to be self-reliant. I cannot guess what Mr. G. thinks of her. One person writes me that he is very fond of her and therefore rather less generous and easy-going with her than the others! But he doesn't seem

Marian Sutta.

Lise Tracol, (to be Mme. Alfred Etievant

Tania (right) and Iovanna becoming friends with Lise (left).

Sophie/Dushka

to have been interested in her reactions to the ideas. Every now and then he checks up on her relationship with Alfred, but he gives her nothing to do beyond certain errands usually connected with the recording machines which he intends to use for making tapes of his hand harmonium improvisations.

She is somehow closed to "phenomena" and to seeing Mr. G. as a different order of being, which Mme. O. warned her that he truly is. She wants all the time to get a "sensible program of study" organized. She has come to respect Mr. G. and can absorb anything that is "directed to essence," and she is overjoyed to hear readings from *Fragments*. But she can make very little of the readings from *Beelzebub*, and none of the "calves" get anything from the long sessions which have been the daily and compulsory routine since their arrival, hours shut up in the dark, dusty apartment waiting for visitors to finish their meals (and toasts!) listening to the same things (they think) being said "over and over and over again."

The few trips they have had, have been attended by the usual frustrations, but this amuses Dushka. She tells how Iovanna can never be found in the early morning when the car cavalcade is ready to set off from an overnight stop, because she is out "Communing with Nature." This in spite of everyone else knowing from experience that whatever time Mr. G. said they would leave it always turns out to be an hour earlier.

Marian, on the other hand is always right there and manages always to travel in his car, and has a title of "Navigator."

Mr. Gurdjieff driving his Citroen with Marian beside him as "Navigator."

Dushka is grateful for this since I think that was to be her place. But after the first couple of days of travelling and seeing how he drove, (in the middle of the road, mostly in second gear, and nodding with fatigue and illness), she goes to great lengths to avoid being in the same car.

She triumphs when she is proved right for having provided herself with extra sweaters, snacks, medications, etc. But some of the older pupils who went on the trips were scathingly critical of her for "not having faith in Mr. Gurdjieff," and being "only concerned for her own physical comfort." Then, after the first day or so of difficult travelling, missed meals, faulty directions, changeable weather, auto break-downs, etc., these same older pupils were the first to ask to borrow or share what she had prudently brought with her.

◆ ◆ ◆

In the Twenties, Dr. Maurice Nicoll had been at the Prieuré and later recounted to Beryl Pogson and others how:

Dushka
◆

"Gurdjieff bought a car which seemed to give him great pleasure. He taught himself to drive it by experiment, with much grinding of gears and squeaking of brakes. To drive with him was terrifying!"

When Kathryn Hulme first met Gurdjieff in February 1932 they were in the Café de la Paix. He then instructed her to follow him out to the Prieuré. She said: "He drove like a wild man, cutting in and out of traffic without hand signals or even space to accommodate his car in the lanes he suddenly switched to — until he was in them, safe by a hair."

Dr. Maurice Nicoll.

And even faithful Olga de Hartmann later wrote stories of hair raising drives with Gurdjieff.

Once, for example, when she informed him that he must wait until the service station attendant finished repairing the brakes, Gurdjieff said: "Why lose time? I will go all the time in second gear." Olga reminded him that the road was very winding and steep, but:

"As soon as we were on the road, he of course drove in high gear and we went twisting down the road at a terrible speed... since Mr. de Hartmann was not in the car and I knew that he would not be killed, I sat still and did not say anything. But as soon as we came down near a café I asked Mr. Gurdjieff to stop and he, probably thinking I wished to use the ladies' room, stopped the car."

She took her little suitcase, refused to get back into the car, and telephoned her husband.

"Mr. Gurdjieff got very angry and rode away. In five or ten minutes, (he) came back and told me he would drive at the speed I wished if only I would come..."

"When we got home," she adds: "Madame Ouspensky and Mme. Ostrovsky told me that they were absolutely appalled that I would dare teach Mr. Gurdjieff how to drive... They reproached me for trying to order Mr. Gurdjieff to travel at a certain speed. I told them if they believed he could drive on clouds it was alright, but I did not wish to be on such a trip!"

◆ ◆ ◆

Dear Ethel,

Jessmin
◆

I hope Dushka hasn't missed too many opportunities by putting on a flippant mask. It is possible that she sometimes amuses Mr. G.

I'm told that once, at a halt during an auto trip, she went wading while she was waiting. Afterwards, standing barefoot by the roadside, she was idly picking up and throwing pebbles with her bare toes when Mr. G. strolled by and called out "Bravo, Sophie" (as he named her, refusing to call her Dushka, a "light" name). She finds it pitiful because some of the older people came to her later in the week, asking her to help them learn how to do this. In fact, she sometimes asks how Mr. G. can be such a "Great Teacher" when he has gathered such poor pupils around him.

Of course, she has suffered from the constant gossip. And it is amazing that a grown woman like Peggy would still go to Dushka, of all people, and pump her about

"Sophie" goes wading during a "siesta" stop.

the "fatherhood" of one of the French girl's expected child, saying that: "Of course we thought it must be Mr. G.'s!" Dushka wrote me of this saying: "He's a very sick, old man. I hope you won't be angry, but I was so shocked that I told her they all had dirty minds."

I was proud of her. Why does there seem to be this growing idiocy, the idea that no woman can hope to gain a "Body Kesdjan" unless she has had sexual intercourse with a "Master."

Alas for "higher emotional center," and for Mr. G. with all he wishes to accomplish in his state of health. And alas for his possible hopes for training the "calves" to carry on some of his work.

As far as Dushka is concerned my feeling is strengthened: she can have gained nothing but good from the contact with Mr. G., and observing him at work.

As can well be imagined it seems that Mr. G. has left the "calves" very

On the auto trips the "calves" can relax: Marian in Cannes.

(Above, left to right) "Sophie," Petey and Tania go for a swim in Chamonix.

"Sophie" (left) and Tania find the water refreshing but cold!

Sight-seeing on an auto trip (Left to right) Pat Healey, "Sophie," Petey, Vivien Healey (later Mrs. Pierre Elliot), Lady Lucy Pentland with (in foreground) her daughter Mary Sinclair.

much to themselves in the flurry of trying to get Mr. Ouspensky's book (*Fragments/In Search of the Miraculous*) translated and published as a forerunner to *Beelzebub (All and Everything)* which should appear this fall in English, French and German — as well as the necessity of suffering constant invasion by various groups from England who provide him with money.

Jeanne is still trying to do the work of four men and can find little free time to counsel them.   Love   Jessmin

* * * * *

"Polo" (Paul Beekman Taylor) visited his half-sister, Petey, in Paris and Mr. Gurdjieff invited him on our Chamonix trip. "Sophie" snaps him by the swimming pool with Petey and Tania (foreground).

Fifty-two years later we all have lunch together in New York. Petey (left) comes in from Connecticut, Tania from New Jersey and Polo from Geneva, Switzerland. Dushka snaps them outside her apartment.

(Above) G's sister Sophie and her husband Kapanadze watch departure preparations from the first floor apartment window. (Below) Niece Luba (right) joins Sophie to watch.

Collecting supplies for the trip, Lady Pentland carries the bread and Lise (Left) laughs as Mr. G. teases little Mary Sinclair.

(Above) Mr G. consults Mme. de S. Tania and Lise wait.   Henry Tracol (Right) and his wife "Nano" (left).

Getting ready to board their assigned automobiles.

(Left to right) Marian, Tania, Mr. G., Lady Pentland, Iovanna, Edith Taylor, Mary, Alfred, and Lord Pentland.

Mr. G. ready to lead off in his Citroen.

But sometimes, en route, there is a change of plan, the map must be checked. (Left to right) Mme. de Salzmann, Mr. G., Mrs. Pearce and "George."
(Below) Everyone waits to set off again after a leg-stretching break.

(Above) Jojo (Left), her mother Peggy Flinsch, her sister Anga, and (in back) Iovanna wait while Mr. G. and Mme. de S. consult a guidebook. (Below left) Mr. G. in Cannes.(Right and bottom) Most meals on trips are picnics improvised along the way, or in small cafes.

The only photo of G. with Dushka (on right). Anga (left) and Jojo in the Alps, and Mary (Right) enjoys a rain shower.

Dushka/"Sophie" and Petey/"Eve"

One of our last trips was to visit *La Grande Paroisse*, the *Restaurant-Cafe de la Gare* that Mr. G. had plans for.

(Above) One of many photos taken by Dushka of Mr Gurdjieff (with Mme. de Salzmann at right). This one helps answer everyone's question: "Did Mr. Gurdjieff really know you were taking pictures of him?." **Well! See detail at right !**

CHAPTER 17

PHOTOS OF G.

Evelyn Sutta in Paris reported again to Mother in New York: "Dear Mrs. Howarth,

Dushka

♦

"Last Tuesday night at the Movements class, G. put all the calves in the first row, with instructions to the former first row to observe and correct everything. I feel that this is an intensive preparation for a first row for America. He speaks all the time about coming to America. He told Eve that she is to drive him in the Cadillac in America. He spoke of the Wellington and said he wanted to go back there again, it was very good, he said, one hundred twenty people could be served there! At lunch with Mme. de Salzmann at her apartment, during the sewing, we all talked quite informally and I asked her if she felt he would come in September. She was absolutely certain that he would. (We finished the costumes in eight days, thirty-one of them.)

"G. complained the other day at lunch that he had so much difficulty out-fitting the calves with chic Parisian ensembles. 'You know,' he said, 'I have harem (pronounced Garem). Such monsters you never saw. One have big buffers here, and another—buffers absent.' Another time he told the calves that they must take turns working in the kitchen, that he gives them everything and they must also do something. The girls all shrugged it off and said, 'Oh, he's said that before.'

"Tomorrow he's taking them to Fontainebleau for coffee—the last trip of the Cadillac before it goes back to America. It looks as if the Pentlands are really going this time.

"Dushka took some wonderful pictures on the Cannes trip and Marian and Lord Pentland wanted copies. I asked Dushka if I could take the negatives and have some enlargements made and I would order sets for the others. Marian showed her set to G. today and he commented on many of them and asked Marian to get three for him, one with George, his old Russian friend, and Mme. de S., one with Mme. de S. 'looking angry,' and one of Marian. Referring to the one I sent you where he is sitting at the table wearing the fez, he said to Marian 'There I more drunk than usual.'

Evelyn"

I suppose I was one of the few who dared take snapshots of Mr. G. and I only did it on the trips, the apartment was too dark in any case. Bill Segal took some nice ones when he came to Paris with his wife Cora and their daughters, Liz and Margaret, but most people probably thought it disrespectful. Of course there was no journalistic interest at that time, so there are few good pictures, especially of Mr. G.'s last year. I don't mean good technically, but which give a truer impression of what he was really like.

I have eight or nine minutes of home movies that Mrs. Sutta took of us all, also outdoors during the trips. As far as I know, these may constitute the

Bill Segal and his family.

Bill Segal snapped this wonderful moment between his daughter Margaret and "fierce ogre" Mr. Gurdjieff.

Evelyn Sutta with her movie camera.

only moving picture record of Mr. Gurdjieff, and show him relaxed, happy to be with a few old friends and a group of youngsters, away from the usual pressures. This is certainly not the "ferocious Master" described in some books, but the much more kindly, humorous old man that many of us remember. So many published writings seem to concentrate egoistically on the author's personal battles with himself and his teacher, exaggerating the difficulties that had to be overcome in the course of this work. The result is that for many younger people that I talk with, Gurdjieff, as that "Teacher," has emerged as some kind of ogre. So I cherish these few moments of film which show the other side of Gurdjieff the man. And since "a picture is worth a thousand words," I include some stills of them in this book to make my point. Although some of the photos I took myself have appeared in innumerable books, (and on four or five covers, uncredited, of course!) there are, sadly, no really good reproductions or prints of them. The two rolls of film I took in France of Mr. G. were developed in a local shop and I received the usual set of little prints. When I returned to the U.S. and started going out to Franklin Farms, Lonia offered me the use of a rough darkroom that he had in the basement and I started experimenting with the old enlarger there. But after my first few trial prints, most of which I casually gave away, the negatives disappeared and have never reappeared. So heaven knows where all the publishers get the pictures they have reprinted. I myself don't even have a print of some of them.

I understand, and suppose I'm flattered, that so many people have used my picture of Mr. G. wearing his fez, lunching in a roadside café (with, as at home, bottles and fresh herbs by his place). Editors usually crop away the other half of the original photo which shows a collapsed Lord Pentland. John, the much younger man, had also been driving all morning but the older Mr. G. has apparently thrived on it.

What a shame that modern, professional techniques can't be used on all those missing old negatives to accord us clearer glimpses of that time.

For instance one tiny, hard-to-see snapshot that I would love to see enlarged is of Mr. G. sitting in his beloved Citroen with a magazine open on the steering wheel in front of him. It is a comic book! Probably he was just checking out something little Mary Sinclair (Lord Pentland's daughter) had brought along on the trip, but I guess I'll never know!

(Above) Dushka's "fez photo " of Mr. G. in 1949 lunching in a roadside cafe on an auto trip has often been reprinted But editors usually crop out the much younger "wiped out" Lord Pentland seen here in the original.

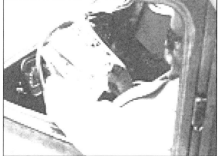

(Above left) Sometimes the only chance to snap a photo of G. in his Citroen was from the back seat.
(Above right,)...or at a rest stop where he was once caught leafing through someone's comic book!

In recent years a few more photos have surfaced. One source has been Sylvie Anastasieff, widow of Gurdjieff's nephew Valentin, and therefore one of G.'s main heirs. Negotiating for our projects to preserve the harmonium recordings required Gert-Jan Blom to visit Sylvie in Spain. She happened to mention that she had inherited some old Gurdjieff family photo albums and had instructed they should be burned at her death. Since she had just celebrated her 89th birthday, we were naturally grateful when she let us choose out some photos to use for this book and the one that accompanies the recordings. Although we have no way of being sure when and where any of these were taken they are a welcome addition to the Gurdjieff pictorial record.

* * * * *

SOME PHOTOS OF MR. GURDJIEFF THAT HAVE SURVIVED THROUGH THE YEARS

(FROM VARIOUS

SOURCES)

IN ROUGHLY

CHRONOLOGIAL

ORDER

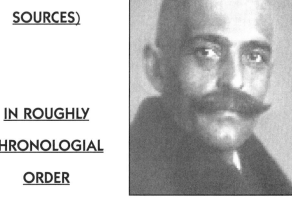

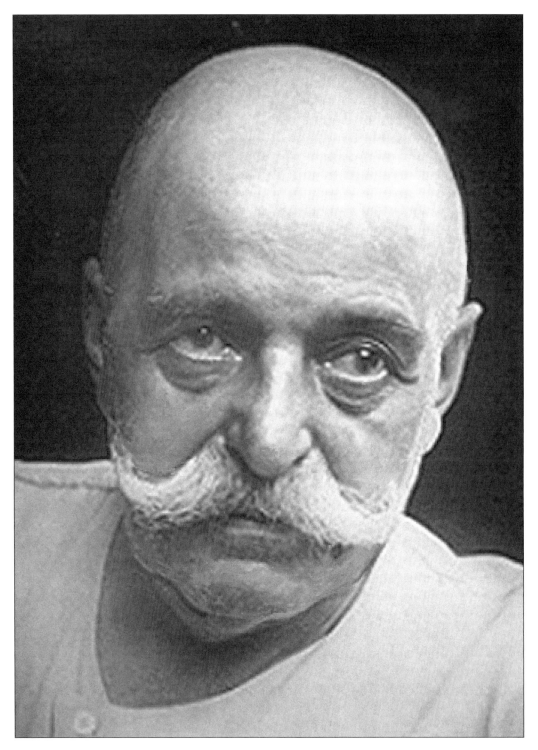

Perhaps the most often used photo portrait of Mr. Gurdjeff. Taken in his last year by French photographer Andrieu.

SYLVIE'S PHOTOS-

Sylvia **ANASTASIEFF**
V / Valentin ANASTASIEFF
Neveu de **GURDJIEFF**

(Above) Sylvie Anastasieff...   ....and her house and swimming-pool in Malaga, Spain.

Mr. Gurdjieff in a pensive mood. Where? When?

(Above) Another pensive moment.

(Below) This old railway station hotel was apparently bought and planned by Gurdjieff as the site for a new "Study House" to be designed by noted architect Clive Entwhistle. Later it was occupied by Gurdjieff family members.

(Left) G.'s sister Sophie, with her dog and husband Georgilibovitch Kapanadze in their new home, "La Paroisse."

(Right) Mr. G. strolling jauntily... where?...when?

(Right and below) Another picnic. This time on an auto trip with French and Russian friends.

(Above) We haven't been able to date or place this photo which is so intriguing because for once Mr. Gurdjieff is sitting so anonymously in a back row, (chatting with an Indian looking man). (See detail left.)

It is not even sure which country this might be though the formally dressed men, dated hair-dos and dress styles on the women, and greying moustache of Mr. G. give some clues.

(Below) Construction at the Prieuré. Luba doing the work watched by the men (Jean Toomer ? at right.)

MME. OUSPENSKY'S PHOTOS

Another source of photos in these last years has been Tania Nagro (Mme. Ouspensky's granddaughter) who has kept in touch with me since our days together as "Mr. G.'s calves." I had once made her promise she would never throw anything of her grandmother's away — that there might be treasure in what she might see as "junk." Indeed I have often found very valuable as documentation other people's old scraps of letters, notations or photos, especially when these are compared or put together with someone else's "trash," or posthumous "garbage!"

Just recently, when this book was almost finished, Tania mailed me yet another little old album of her grandmother's that she had come across. Though water-stained and mildewed, the tiny, torn and faded photos were of the early days, Mme. O.'s young friends, the children at the Prieuré, especially her grandson Lonia and so forth. A few of them are marked with a date "Berlin 1921"or "F'bleau 1924," so after much work scanning, retouching, increasing contrast and adjusting the arrangements of the early chapters, I have been able to add them to the book. But as in the case of photos that Sylvie inherited from her husband Valia, many of them are unidentifiable. Who remains who would know who,? when? where? they were taken.

For example, where to place several snaps scattered throughout the album but obviously taken at the same time and place... an outdoor picnic somewhere? The cooking is being done by Mr. Gurdjieff and a very young Mme. Ouspensky over an open fire. But what is fascinating to me is that of all the over 900 photos I have been able to locate and clean up to include in this book, these are the only ones to show Mr. and Mrs. Ouspensky together — and even more amazing — the only pictorial record I have ever seen of Gurdjieff and P.D. Ouspensky together!

(Left and below)
Mme. Ouspensky tending the cooking
fire.

(Bottom left) Mme. O. joining in the
picnic.

(Above) Mme. O (center) serves from a casserole while Mr. O. waits. (At back left) (Insert) The Ouspenskys.Where? (Below) Having hung up their overcoats on the tree, Mr. Gurdjieff (center) eats while Mr. Ouspensky sits behind him, still waiting to be served? . Olgivanna is in the striped headband.(Third from left)

(Above) A clipping from the Chicago Daily News, Sunday, March 21, 1924 reporting on the Movements Demonstrations tour. Caption reads: "LEFT TO RIGHT - MME. HINZENBERG, MISS HOWARTH AND MME PALE-OLOQUE OF THE GURDJIEFF INSTITUTE AT FONTAINBLEAU, FRANCE

(Clockwise from top right)
Mr. G. in 1924, yes, but where? Also Chicago? Doing what?
Mr. G. young but where? When?
Gurdjieff's wife but where? When?
Mr. Ouspensky on a ship, photo dated "August 1921 Constantinople",
This might be when he travelled alone to London. Or?

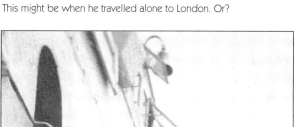

CHAPTER 18

MR. G.'S SPECIAL MEALS AND TOASTS

"There is more than one kind of food at my table. Let the food you eat here stay in memory only, but the other kinds of 'food' carry with you." G.I. Gurdjieff

Dushka

♦

As the years pass, I become increasingly, and painfully, aware of how few of us are still around who actually knew Mr. Gurdjieff, spent time with him, shared meals, or traveled with him. Simple, human aspects of his life are being forgotten, misconstrued, or blown up out of all proportion. Even something as natural and normal as the food he ate or had served to large groups of guests, and its relative importance in his daily routine and his teaching, is being given all kinds of false interpretations. As is his practice of having "toasts to idiots" at mealtimes.

Through the years I had been asked so often by various groups or Foundations, and personal friends to help them in preparing Mr. Gurdjieff's "Special Salad," that I originally simply planned to put in a recipe, (see Postscript 3). and leave it at that.

But even the "Salad" and why it is "special" seemed to call for so much explanation that I ended up wondering if the whole subject of Mr. Gurdjieff in relation to food and drink didn't merit some discussion and putting in perspective.

Nowadays, especially in most religious or spiritual contexts, actual physical food seems to be considered something one should ideally try to restrict, certainly not relish. Mr. Gurdjieff, on the other hand, one came to realize, always accorded food, its preparation and distribution the greatest respect. There was nothing hedonistic in this attitude. It came from his esteem for our marvelous human bodies and a belief that we are obligated to provide them with the best possible care and nourishment, including sense impressions! He only advocated fasting for special people under special circumstances, closely supervised.

In the early years, first in Russia and then in Europe, though often coping with severe financial set-backs, he always felt required to provide generously for those around him, his family, various followers, and even (especially during the war) complete strangers.

But he insisted: "Man should eat, not as an animal but consciously."This concept itself is not unique to Gurdjieff, only the importance he accorded it. Almost every religion advocates prayers before meals to remind one of this, but

Another of Dushka's photos of Gurdjieff lunching in a roadside bistro in France, 1949.

the reason itself has almost been forgotten.

Of all the examples Gurdjieff might have used to illustrate the essential aspect of his teaching, "quality of attention," he chose the one experience that all human beings share: "When you do a thing, do it with the whole self. One thing at a time. Now I sit here and I eat. For me nothing exists in the world except this food, this table. I eat with the whole attention. So you must do — in everything. To be able to do one thing at a time, this is the property of MAN, not man in quotation marks."

At another time he was quoted as saying: "If one knows how to eat properly, one knows how to pray."

And yet again: "It is important to compose a dish in its correctly-blended elements as a composition of music or the colors in painting. Harmony in scale. Must have much knowledge to be a good cook. A culinary doctor."

Louise Goepfert March, one of Gurdjieff's secretaries at the Prieuré, remembered that in those days he was usually quiet at the table. He would say, "When I eat, I self-remember." And he chided people who insisted on talking during the meal: "Idiot God made only one mouth. Should have made two."

Thomas de Hartmann also tells us that: " ... to taste life fully was one of Mr. Gurdjieff's principles. During our life with him we tried every sort of eastern dish, some very exotic. He told us that in the East they have always paid particular attention to the refinements of food elements. The aim is not to gorge oneself under the table, but rather to sample, in tiny portions, all kinds of variation of taste experience... I can still see him vividly, his muscles completely relaxed as always. Slowly he lifts to his mouth a very good pear, not peeled. Unhurried he takes a bite of it as if striving to absorb its entire aroma, its entire taste."

Louise March in later life.

In 1935 and 1936 the group of women known as "The Rope," spent a lot of time with Gurdjieff. Almost all of them later wrote books concentrating on their own lives in relation to the work, and what Mr. G. said to them. However, in Margaret Anderson's collection of their diaries, that Gloria Caruso passed on to me, I see that many of their daily notations were never included in any book. But these mundane, everyday descriptions that were discarded, are just what I personally find so fascinating as glimpses into G.'s private life.

For example, Kathryn Hulme wrote:

"Sunday, October 27, 1935. He (Gurdjieff) went to the Russian shop in Montparnasse. He has brought a great spread — caviar, salmon, meat cutlets, sausage from Latvia, animal feet in jelly, a 'favorite weekly dish at Prieuré,' he says, black bread, white bread, cheese, olives, pickles, Vodka and a bottle of white mustard and one of horseradish which he mixes together.

"January 26. Dinner in G.'s apartment. He has made special boiled potatoes for Jane [Heap]. Also an egg dish, a kind of omelet with asparagus stuffing, sugar on our portions, none on Jane's. [She was diabetic.]

"Today at lunch we ate 'Twenty-First Salad in Third Series!'

"I could identify tomatoes, parsley, leek, onion, horseradish and

Kathryn Hulme in later life.

preiselberry sauce, some curry, etc.

"He comes from Rouen, phones from the café at seven-thirty and says: 'Come at eight-thirty!' Since there is no food in the house, for this dinner '– all new, begin from new–' In one hour he has bought and prepared: hors d'oeuvres, baked dish (pasta and meat), saffron potatoes, baked baby lamb, soup, a thin pudding (best ever tasted).

"June 5. There is a general strike. With food shortage threatened, this is what we have: Hors d'oeuvres (platter of fresh greens, Kurdistan cheese, pastourma, fresh cucumber, canned eggplant with stuffing of pimento and carrot), two soups (one a 'phenomenon' soup), special rice made with apricots and raisins, etc., roast baby lamb, '*fraises des bois*' with fresh cream, Latvian chocolates and Syrian loucoum, fruit, Turkish coffee, special individual honey cakes AND Armangnac– 'My restaurant is good.'

"June 11, Dinner. He returns from Rouen with much food. 'Fiancée chicken' for us and also for another dinner party going on simultaneously with ours. He visits back and forth between his two '*salles*' and Valya carries his brioche back and forth.

"G. says: 'Practique show that man who eat rice take force only for working like donkey with body. But for man's mentation he must eat green things, eat vegetables, for making active his mind.'

"June 12, Lunch. Roast goose and preiselberry sauce and potatoes roasted with cinnamon and butter. Caviar and green onions.

"Thanksgiving. Turkey at his house with dressing made of chestnuts and sturgeon. For himself, sturgeon soup. For us also, after the turkey.

"December 8, Dinner. Menu like old times; Smoked herring hors d'oeuvre, then baked fish dish, then soup (fish consommé), Russian cutlet ('Officer cutlet' as known in Russia, as opposed to 'Soldier cutlet' which is five parts black bread to one part meat), melon (two kinds), candy (new kind), then raspberry 'sausage.'

"March 2. He calls me to peel potatoes – one bushel. 'Enough for twenty people.' They are hot, just boiled. He squeezes them in his hands 'Ekh. Ekhing' for the burn. Then he squeezes in four pounds of butter, then a quart of brown liquid ('eighteen spices cooked together'), then grated hard eggs and a bowl of chopped onion. This is the dish called '*caravanpashi*' (King of the Caravan) – it is as hot as hinges.

"At the hotel in Vichy. Boiled eel for fish course. G.: 'Why you give such thing? Is not fish – is serpent! Is m- - - - ! Normal man not eat such thing. Here we are English, American. This for us like oyster – only idiot and German eat such!'

"But one dish, the salad, is very good and we comment.

"G: 'When you travel with me and have any good thing, always you must thank Mme. de Hartmann. All the year she traveled with me, everywhere she go in kitchen and tell just how must be for Mr. Gurdjieff. Have much suffering then. But now, even after all these years, whenever I go place where she was with me, they always remember, so good she tell. She never thinks of self, but always of me. I give example, something I not know about then, one of my people tell me after. You know how woman carry always small valise. Once some of my people see she have in this bag a box of hemorrhoid medicine, because five year before that, just after accident, once I have hemorrhoid. Mme. de Hartmann always remember that and for five year she carry, just in case, if ever I have again she can give to me. That is why she First

Friend of my inner life. Such thought she have for me."

Nikolai Stjernvall, using the pen-name "Nicholas de Val," wrote about Gurdjieff and his kitchen in his book titled *Daddy Gurdjïeff.* [sic!]

Originally in French, a translation into English was started by Paul Beekman "Polo" Taylor who sent me a few chapters. They concern the same period in the Thirties described by "The Rope" as seen from the viewpoint of a rather obtuse, teenaged Nikolai. They suggest another aspect of Mr. G.'s trips to Rouen, and his bringing back those "fiancée chickens" and another example of G.'s kitchen skills.

In 1932 "when it was their turn to leave the Prieuré," Nikolai, his mother, Elizaveta, and her husband Dr. Stjernvall (whom Nikolai called "Papoussia") had moved to a small village near Rouen. Here they started a simple rooming house and raised chickens and geese for sale.

Nicholas de Val [Nikolai Stjernvall] writes:,"...Gurdjieff, on his way to Rouen, liked to enter without warning, leaving his entourage – sometimes two or three automobiles – outside... Very often G.I. bought chickens for his own use.

"Without doubt Georges Ivanovitch's visits were motivated principally by... the state of Papoussia's health which began to decline seriously... His cancer of the prostate had progressed and caused him great suffering. Georges Ivanovitch stopped by more often, visibly preoccupied by the state of the health of his most faithful and valuable collaborator. He tried to spoil Papoussia by every means. One day when Papoussia let him know that he'd appreciate some fruit juice, cases full of juice arrived on Gurdjieff's orders...

"Some time later, in 1937, according to his habit, Gurdjieff arrived... After the customary small talk there was a brief consultation apart with my mother, whom he

had drawn aside. I guessed right away that what they were talking about concerned me directly. To both my surprise and my satisfaction, G.I. had need of me in Paris for a few months, mainly to help him take care of his domestic affairs. I ran to Papoussia to tell him the news and I saw him break out in tears in front of me. After drawing me into his arms, he gave me a sign to leave him... To this day I cannot yet understand the true sense of his great sorrow...

"Soon after my arrival [at the rue des Colonels Renard] Gurdjieff charged his nephew, Valia, to roast four appetizing capons in the oven. 'Uncle' was expecting some important guests at noon. When he came in with his guests, I went up to him and whispered in his ear: 'There's bad news. We forgot to take the chickens out of the oven!'

"Papoussia," Dr. Leonid Stjernvall.

Dr. Stjernvall in the Study House at the Prieuré.

"Mastering his rage and disappointment, Gurdjieff strode off toward the kitchen. With a quick twist of his hand he tore off the skin which stuck to the burnt carcasses of the birds. A few spoonfuls of butter, some cream, onion, garlic powder and some spices transformed into a delicacy what was a hopeless disaster a few moments ago. Turning to Valia he said 'Serve this in a crown of basmati rice. This will be a Georgian specialty *chokhom bili*!'...

"...The day finally arrived when Georges Ivanovitch told me quite simply: 'Your mother asks for you. She needs you in the country.' My turn with Gurdjieff had come to an end. It was Michel de Salzmann who succeeded me...

"...George Ivanovitch cut down severely his trips to Normandy after the death of Papoussia."

When I first read the above description of how Nikolai's real father, Gurdjieff, so often visited his "legal" father, Stjernvall, it made me wonder how much else went on behind the scenes that we don't know about, or was hidden from Prieure residents. It also reminded me of something touching Mr. Gurdjieff's niece had said in her book *Luba Gurdjieff, A Memoir with Recipes.*

Around 1925 Gurdjieff's brother, Dimitri, had brought his wife and their three daughters, Luba, Genia, and Leda, from Tiflis to live at the Prieuré. So some of Luba's modest "memoirs," especially of those days, contain clues for the careful reader.

For instance, I was intrigued by her brief mention of how her father, by three years the younger brother, was the one who financed Gurdjieff's travels with "The Seekers of the Truth." No one, as far as I know, has ever considered that side of things, or how it happened that two brothers were treated, educated and developed so very differently.

But what Nikolai's account brought back to me was Luba's remembering: "When I was about twelve I began to have this pain in the back... it was tuberculosis of the bone. They put me in plaster for four years. I went to Berck Plage — it was a place specially made for treating that kind of illness, near Calais. For four years I was there. Nobody was with me, it was just a big hospital but... My Uncle would come every week — my father came — they brought me fruit and flowers and spoiled everybody."

Visiting New York 1931: Nikolai Stjernvall (left) and eight-year old Michel de Salzmann

Calais is on the coast of the Straits of Dover — a very long way from Fontainebleau!

As early as 1916, in St. Petersburg, P.D. Ouspensky had described that G. "liked to arrange big dinners, buying a quantity of wine and food of which however he often ate or drank practically nothing. Many people got the impression that he was a gourmand, a man fond of good living in general — -although all of us already saw that this was 'acting.'" [!!]

In 1948, the noted British surgeon Dr. Kenneth Walker remarked:"...old men are inclined to hesitate and to fumble, but Gurdjieff possessed an extraordinary control over his body. He was preparing a salad for us and was cutting slices off a cucumber, fishing for small onions in a bottle, dividing up gourds, and he was doing all this with the assurance of a skilled surgeon engaged in his favorite operation. The whole work of preparing the salad was done without one false or unnecessary movement. It was also done speedily, but without any vestige of hurry."

Even during the German occupation of France, despite difficult conditions, Mr. G. had continued his generosity and hospitality. Henri Tracol noted: "To see him in the early morning busying himself in getting the rarest and most exotic provisions the market could produce and preparing with such care, on his old charcoal stove, the most harmoniously audacious meals, was to realize what importance he attached to the patriarchal custom of welcoming guests."

Mr. G.'s crowded supply closet and "private office" in 1949 at the time of his death.

John G. Bennett recalled an occasion in Paris in July 1949, when Mr. G. announced that he was going to make some Persian pilaf with real Persian rice which had been flown to him from Persia: "Now we were quite used to Gurdjieff informing us that he was going to bring in some exotic fruit that had been flown to him from the Solomon Islands, when people present in the room had been with him that morning in the Halles market where he had bought it. And when he said that the *brinza* cheese was specially flown to him from the Caucasus, we knew that he always bought it from a particular Jewish shop. So we were naturally inclined to doubt that rice would have been flown to him from Persia. However, when I went into his kitchen, I saw twenty or thirty little sacks all with labels and Persian stamps on them. He had, indeed, received by airmail a consignment of Persian rice!"

But even more telling is this description of Mr. Gurdjieff (no name is mentioned, but it couldn't be anyone else). I came across it by accident in a paperback novel *Group Feast* by Josephine Saxton, published 1971 by Doubleday Science Fiction. Nothing further is gone into about him, just this one paragraph on page 34, but imagine finding the following written by a complete stranger!

"Nicolette ... had seen the effects of poverty in old people; her own mother had died lonely and cold in a small dirty room in the back streets of Paris during the war. But there had been 'Le Vielle [sic] Marchand du Viand,' the strange Armenian who had conjured up foods from nowhere, right under the noses of the Occupation Forces, and had given food parcels to her mother. It had always been an occasion of joy to go and visit him. There he sat in his 'office' in the Rue des Colonels Renard with strings of sausages hanging over his head, jars of strange fruits and pickles, whole sides of smoked salmon, sweetmeats, hams, herbs, garlic, strings of onions, cream, eggs, oh, riches in the wilderness! And much of this he would give to the poor of the district, the poor and the old. And he would play tunes on an ancient accordion, tunes that wrung the heart and said things to a person that could not be spoken. And it was because of him that her mother had said she was content to die and was not in anguish. Some kind of love had passed into her stricken old life along with the food parcels. And when he died there had been thousands of people at his funeral, a long train of weeping people. A strange man, a strange man. And as Nicolette thought about that old man she, too, became filled with an inexplicable nostalgia..."

And I often thought to myself: "..and so might we all."

But then, in January 2002, after so many years wondering how this paragraph happened to appear in a Science Fiction paperback, I finally found out that "Josephine Saxton" was a nom-de-plume for the English author Mary Howard, who replied to a letter I then wrote her:

"I had forgotten about Nicolette, 30 years, many happenings. No, my mother did not know Gurdjieff. My former Teacher in the Gurdjieff Work knew him, she is now dead several years, Rina Hands. But she was not 'Nicolette'. That was a fabrication of mine, hinting at the meaning of my books of which *Group Feast* is the 3rd part, as I thought of it at the time."

In his last years, when more and more people wished contact and instruction, only very few, or those with serious problems, were privileged to have private conversation with Mr. G. The Movements classes and long, almost ceremonial meals became the main opportunity for teaching. Much that was said at table had very personal application to the person addressed, but it could also be understood on different levels, in various ways, (or maybe not at all!) by others present.

When Carol Robinson, a concert pianist who had been at the Prieuré came to the Wellington in New York, Mr. G. said to her: "If you wish, advice I give you. Now must begin to eat for quality, not quantity. If not, you will soon resemble wife of merchant, each time see, more big is. And for your profession, think how will be if fingers four times bigger, like elephant. You know even elephant have five fingers."

In 1949 when I was with him in New York and then in Paris, there was always a crowd invited for lunch and dinner, as many as could possibly fit, some of us regulars, others special guests, or visitors from abroad. The food, though of necessity

... "oh, riches in the wilderness!"

cooked in large quantities, was amazingly good. This was a tribute to the attention and care with which it was prepared, for, excepting gifts that people sometimes brought or sent him, — hard-to-get avocados or melons, hot peppers, sometimes caviar or camel sausage, (ugh!), all apportioned and shared — Mr. Gurdjieff's meals were based on the simplest, most economical of ingredients. They consisted of a first course: tasty soups or hors d'oeuvres; and then meat and vegetables, usually cooked together for many hours, blending and caramelizing, intensifying the flavors enhanced with fresh herbs, spices, fruits, etc. and tenderizing ordinary cuts of meat or fowl into something of gourmet quality. This was followed by fruit, sometimes a "sweet," and coffee which we learned to drink Russian style, sipped through a sugar cube held in our teeth, or Middle-Eastern style, with a hunk of sweet sesame halva.

Through the years he trained and supervised various people to oversee preparation of the kind of meals he required for his guests (at the Prieuré; Mme. Ouspensky, his sister Sophie, and niece Luba; in Paris, Lise Tracol and Alfred), but he never completely gave up doing some actual cooking himself. When Alfred and I took over a lot of the food preparation at the Hotel Wellington, Mr. G. was terribly busy and really not well. But he still participated in the planning and shopping, made suggestions, came in to taste and adjust, and even took over and prepared complete dishes.

I have always tried to re-create one amazing lamb stew with a lot of mint and dried apricots that he made, saying it was "Tibetan!"

When I accompanied him in and out of the hotel, it always amazed me that the hard-boiled, New York elevator men and doormen weren't furious with this elderly client for pulling out of his pockets and distributing, not always money tips, but often candies! They loved it and him!

But I soon learnt that this was nothing new. People repeated old stories to me, or I read about past incidents when: "...the waiter brought his bill. To a generous tip G. added, from his pocket, a handful of small wrapped candies which the gray-haired waiter gathered up with a pleased expression. 'Like a small boy,' Gurdjieff said as the waiter went off. 'Always I take bonbons in my pocket, chiefly for children. They call me Monsieur Bonbon. Even here in café by such name I am known. So I must give, always. They expect...' A sound of deep inner mirth escaped him."

In this blurred detail from a 1926 photo of Gurdjieff in a café, he appears to be giving a "bon-bon" to the little girl,

But imagine our surprise, in a serious Carnegie Hall Movements class, after working for hours on a difficult new exercise, and, yes, probably tying ourselves in knots of stress, to receive finally, not only a grunted "Bravo!" from Mr. G., but also handfuls of dried litchi nuts in spiky brown shells which he pulled out of his pockets and rolled across the studio floor at us.

Many of us never forgot that moment; the shock, the laughter, the scrambling, the delight, the overdue release from tension. So when, a few years ago, I was asked to suggest desserts or "sweets" for a "January Thirteenth" celebration at the New York Foundation, I mentioned halva and litchi nuts as things which Mr. G. sometimes used to give us. On the night, in a well-meaning effort to recreate a Gurdjieffian atmosphere, the food planners finished the meal by passing around, without explanation, a huge bowl of dried litchi nuts still in their prickly shells! I watched with horror as two hundred earnest guests, all evidently unfamiliar with such things, each took one and obediently, as if it were a communion wafer, placed the whole thing, shell and all, in their mouths.

I will always remember, with sympathy (mixed with impatience), the pained, martyred expressions on their faces.

Through the years that most people knew him, Gurdjieff always celebrated January 13th. There were often discussions as to whether it was his birthday or his namesday, or — ? What should be remembered, however, is that Mr. Gurdjieff's Orthodox Church follows a different calendar than we do in the West. Therefore those who believe that Gurdjieff's actual birthday was January 1 (in 18....?) should remember that in the nineteenth century January 1 by the Julian calendar was by our Gregorian calendar January 12. that it became January 13 in the twentieth century... and now, since 2000, it has been January 14th.

I, myself, never believed that Mr. G. would celebrate his own birthday. (He never allowed toasts to be drunk to him personally or that sort of thing.) I always took for granted that we were joyfully and meaningfully welcoming the first day of the New Year!

(Incidently, the Orthodox Easter also differs from ours. It changes from year to year. But this date depends on which Sunday follows the first full moon after the Vernal Equinox, and thus relates every year to the Hebrew Passover, the biblical "Last Supper" having been a Seder.)

If one watched carefully through all the pageantry, Mr. G. himself ate and even (despite some accounts, his own included) drank very little, although an integral part of the meal, lunch or dinner, was a series of toasts. These were drunk in a strict order from small glasses, usually of old Armagnac, but sometimes of home-made red pepper Vodka.

This latter, made with cayenne pepper, developed a pink color that I happily succeeded in imitating convincingly by putting into water a few drops of Cassis black-currant liqueur that I found in Mr. G.'s kitchen. For weeks I raised glasses of this mixture, matching toasts with everyone, till one day Mr. G. reached over, took my glass and tasted it. I braced myself for a huge explosion. But with a long look at me Mr. G. just muttered "*svolotch*" and no further comment. So I continued.

Since it was expected that everyone drink honorably and we women were supposed to control the amount we sipped to exactly three toasts per glass, I did feel a bit guilty. But I figured I had already had my "alcohol experiences" back when I was a Broadway press agent matching drinks with hard-boiled newspaper men!

The seat next to Mr. G. was assigned to a "M. le Director" who was responsible for reciting the toasts (in a strict order and using a traditional wording whether in French or English) and seeing to it that the glasses were properly filled.

Sometimes referred to as the "Science of Idiotism" (using the word in its Greek sense, meaning "one's own," "being oneself" as in "idiosyncrasy"), these toasts honor each different category of "idiot" (Ordinary, Super, Arch, Hopeless, Compassionate, Squirming, Square, Round, Zigzag, Enlightened, Doubting, Swaggering, etc.) and anyone present at the table who has recognized himself as belonging to it. Most people took the responsibility of choosing their own category with Mr. Gurdjieff's agreement. But, sometimes he identified your "idiot" for you.

That is what happened in my case. I myself vacillated too long and was told to consider myself "squirming!" Later I took note when he told somebody else in my category: "Squirming! Soon you must change. Squirming only is passing state for man. Is state like fish out of sea. Man must not stay long, or man die, or obliged be born again. Man can stay squirming two, three months, but not for a year." To someone else he once said, "Squirming idiot... not yet ready for help."

Ceremonial Toasts are an old tradition in Georgia, but John Bennett, who often functioned as Director when he came to Paris, believed (possibly prompted by his friend, Idries Shah) that Mr. G. adopted "Idiotism" from the Sufis. They, Bennett told us, used it as a teaching method to "trace the path of man's evolution from a state of nature to the realization of his spiritual potential. There are twenty-one gradations of reason from that of ordinary man to that of Our Endlessness, that is, God."

We never reached half of those. I don't remember that even the longest "feasts" went beyond the "Zigzag" toast (or three women's glasses consumed with much rich food and hours of conversation) and despite stories, there was rarely anyone who was obviously affected by the alcohol, at least while still in Mr. G.'s presence.

Afterwards...

...well...!...?

* * * * *

CHAPTER 19

MENDHAM AND NEW YORK, AFTERMATH OF G.'S VISIT

New York, Summer, 1949

Jessmin

♦

Dear Ethel,

Jeanne is under tremendous pressure and has to carry too much. She has grown enormously since I first knew her at Hellerau in 1912. I just hope she does not become so depleted that she gives up her own common sense and good judgment. Mme. O. once said to me that she felt Jeanne was the only person who had the capacity for work and at the same time the "mask" which would enable her to carry on for Mr. G. She asked me if, in that case, I could accept Jeanne's direction willingly, for she would never require this from me in what had to do with the Movements teaching for her pupils.

I do like Jeanne very much and admire her even more. I think that, perhaps, she still looks at Mr. G. as a man, excuses certain of his actions on this ground, and maybe expects certain things from him as if he cared about people.

For myself, I still do not trust him at all in everyday or personal things but I am much more certain that real work exists. I no longer resent his treatment of me although the dent it has made in me will always remain. On the contrary, I realize that as long as I can learn anything for myself by trying to be useful to him or his work in any way, this is good. And I am sure that when I am not learning anything for myself, he will be the first to take away any function I have.

In any case, I feel much freer and more trustful in Mme. O.'s way of refusing to see anything in him but "the Teacher," and insisting that there can be no personal relation with him. That his "weaknesses" are our own laid at his door and that he cares not one speck for any one of us; and that he is working towards his next life on earth. Her way, although beyond my range, is a sounder position to work from.

It would be too long to try to describe what has been going on here at Mendham during the last three months. Madame Ouspensky was left with about ten younger people living at Franklin Farms and an income (from them for their board) completely insufficient to cover the property taxes. Her old people are all away, most of them losing their heads entirely in their new roles as Mr. G.'s "Chosen." As usual, there has been "dirty linen" to deal with — stories about money and sex mix-ups — two young people here have had nervous breakdowns. But Madame is a fighter, she continues a grueling series of injections and this miserable period only stimulates her to hold on to what she has learnt from Mr. G. and struggle to try to help him.

I have taken my cue from her and am continuing the Movements classes. As the New York people wish to be separate, they are taught in New York in two groups on Wednesday nights. On Friday evenings, after the reading at Mendham, we sometimes practice the Movements without music, and on Sundays in the late afternoon we have a long workout. It is not easy because we rarely have any music (Carol Robinson has gone away) and I have to teach the new exercises and I do not feel confident. But I won't pretend that I don't enjoy teaching and studying some new material. But it is very bad for me to have my vanity flattered by the pupils' expressions of gratitude. It is only good because it is a Godsend to me to be kept so busy: otherwise I would miss Dushka too dreadfully.

Mme. O. was afraid of that. She knows how suicidal I can become when physically down and emotionally depressed. She asked me to go and keep her company at Franklin Farms, and has been unfailingly kind even when I am stupid and not working rightly at all. I wish I knew how to do something for her.

If Mr. G. had kept his word and sent another instructor here after three months, I might have risked the plunge and resigned from the office to do only part-time work at home for my boss who is taking a lot of sick leave. I don't have quite as many expenses with Dushka away. But Mlle. Daumarie may also quit, and then I would not have a champion to insist on my seniority and see that I was guaranteed employment when I needed it. I have a long bulletin to finish and see through the printers and the New York classes must be kept on at least until we have information about Mr. G.'s coming. So — must hold on —

Possibly Mr. G. thinks that I am taking money from the pupils and so can be free to do as I wish. But such payments would be collected from people who work just as hard as I do, and who have already done their part giving money to Mr. G., some even borrowing from their banks to do so and being burdened with repayments for the next twelve months or so. Rosemary tells me I should pay myself a small salary and take the money and go right away for a month. I can only see that I must somehow hold on.

I was pleased when Mr. Bennett asked again if I could go soon to England to teach, but I'm sure Mr. G. would want to send one of his Paris pupils. I can only see him sending me if he brought Dushka back here and wanted to separate us again.

I can't say I'm happy but at least I realize that peace of mind is one thing that one can never have in this method. I know how little I really work, being, as they say, just a "hanger-up of coats."

I have to wait to see what happens to Dushka. That is in Mr. G.'s hands. No use my "identifying," and writing him. I sometimes feel that I shall never see Dushka again and I can face that better since what I had to hide from her is now being made clear to her.

She will make her own plans. I hope that Mr. G. has not acknowledged her existence too late for it to be of real help to her in finding herself. She is really a good girl, honest, energetic and talented. Everyone writes me that she is the only "calf" who behaves in the same way when Mr. G. is there and when he is not. This, unfortunately, also shows that she has not gained enough discrimination yet to try not to be her mechanical self in his presence. But I hope it means, as well, that she trusts him to understand her and will not let herself be constrained, because she is afraid of Mr. G., or thinks to please him, to act in any way that she does not understand.

That can be the kind of stupid mistake which was my undoing.

July 26, '49

...I hope that you are really strong enough to put yourself through this long period of study. You have not said very much about your program at the Ashram and I have difficulty in imagining your life there. I do hope with all my heart that the effort is bringing you what you desire. You say you are not detached and that you are so often distracted. It cannot but be so for us who have been conditioned by an active life, yet I feel in you a determination and a new kind of stability. So I cannot ask the question that is often in my mind, "When do you think of coming home?" Home must be for you where you can get the impression nourishment and meet the understanding you need. Someday, please, if you can, tell me a little of your work.

It was very discerning of you to sense that I needed a little "building up." But if I believed that you could really see in my letter all the progress and comprehension you speak of, I would, indeed, feel very guilty. There is no such "Jessmin" as you think, dear Ethel. Sometimes, the older one, who realizes that one must try and understand principles and not stick at everyday complications, is uppermost. But, much more often, there is a very provincial and resentful creature. In fact, were it not for Mme. O.'s constant prompting, these would certainly submerge any other "I"s.

* * * *

Dear Ethel,

Dushka's health in Paris was not too good and, finally, after waiting for three months she was taken to a good throat specialist. He operated first for a large polyp in her nose, and then treated her for three weeks to clear up some bronchial trouble and the worst tonsil infection. She had the tonsillectomy on July second in a charming nursing home in Neuilly. As everyone paid attention to her, Alfred played chess with her as long as she couldn't talk, and so on; she didn't really have a bad time.

She was kept in and away from movement and excitement for almost two weeks, fortunately for my peace of mind, because after the first little bit of surgery, she had gone out and then had a terrific nosebleed, which thoroughly frightened everyone. Now she is well and I do hope this will make a great difference to her. It was long overdue.

It is most generous of you, Ethel, to think about helping me with the costs. I do have hospital insurance paid up and this will apply for the nursing home expenses, even in Paris. For the rest, I shall pay off Mr. G. as quickly as possible.

Jessmin.

◆ ◆ ◆

Dushka
◆

I must confess that the nosebleed was a result of Alfred's solicitousness. He had escorted me to the doctor when the polyp was removed, and afterwards was sure that the one thing I needed was the typical French remedy for everything – a big brandy! He didn't realize that this would counteract the medicine I had been given to reduce bleeding. In an elegant restaurant, while Alfred raced through the neighborhood to find a *Pharmacie* and tissues, I ruined white linen napkins by the pile. Alfred finally got me back to the hotel really weak and pale, though I think he was even paler. Then he went off to the evening at Mr. G.'s apartment. Unfortunately his explanation of why I was absent got misunderstood. Mr. G. thought that it was my tonsils, not just my nose polyp that had been done, and gave stern instructions that I was not to eat anything, even sent someone over to the hotel to forbid them to serve me anything even if I asked. Of course, the one thing I knew I needed was some real nourishment, and I finally sneaked out by the back stairs and service entrance and went to the nearest restaurant that would serve me a huge, gory *Steak Tartare*!

About this time Lord Pentland wrote me a letter from his new apartment at 235 E. 48 St. in N.Y.C.

"Dear Sophie,

"We heard from Mrs. Pearce and others that your throat, etc. had been giving you trouble and after the movements class in New York last night your mother told me what she knew about your operation which sounded rather unpleasant, particularly if you had anything like our heatwave.

"Now I want to ask you to do a few small things for me, and if you aren't well enough, not one of them really matters, so you can forget if you like or work them in later.

"First, about Mr. G.'s Cadillac. In the rush of getting away, I never gave instructions for it to be shipped over here, although I found out how this could be done. It is still at the Garage Carnot (presumably it is) in the Rue des Acacias and to bring it over here all that is needed is to post the enclosed letter. From what I've heard since we left, there is very little point in leaving it in France and of course Mr. Gurdjieff told us to bring it along with us and keep it for him here. Maybe you could think yourself or even ask Madame Salzmann, if there is any fresh light to be thrown on this problem, because if not there is no point in garage charges

Lord Pentland, the usual chauffeur for Mr G.'s Cadillac, and his regular passenger, Tania Savitsky Forman (Below)

mounting up any more in Paris, and the letter might as well be posted and the car shipped over here and serviced ready for him to use when he comes.

"We've had more prints made of the photographs we took and there is a complete set here for you and for Marian, a practically complete one for Iovanna and a few for Eve, who wasn't there in most of them. They will seem very out-of-date to you all, but maybe you would like to have them. I'll give Tanya's to her when she comes or to Forman. Also there are a few odd ones for people like the doctor and Mr. Gurdjieff's sister. If you're not at the apartment maybe someone else would take them over, as they were asked for and we had no time to get them done before leaving.

"There's been rather a run here on the enlargements, which seem to come out much better than the prints, but I'm sending a few we have, to you or anyone who wants.

"Just one other thing on the subject. Madame Ouspensky saw the enlargement you gave me of Mr. Gurdjieff sitting at table with the bottles, and asked for a copy to keep. I will give her mine, but if you ever can get another one made and send it, please do, as we should like to have it.

"I expect you get a good deal of news from New York. I think Alfred would be interested to hear about the movements classes, which we go to here and at Mendham. Your mother is wonderful — she shines on our collections of ragged people 3 or 4 times a week and always keeps control of us, but of course without Mr. Gurdjieff we somehow never get beyond a certain point. She seems to have been talking more about the inner side of the exercises lately, particularly to the New York group, which, although less well together, for some reason I find the more interesting and useful of the two movements groups. Mr. Wolfe plays well now, if only he can hear what is wanted.

"We ourselves settled down to a very luxurious — when there is time — New York apartment, furnished. It has everything except an electric fan which we have bought. When I'm not in Washington on business, we have this one free evening (Tuesdays) and as there is a big gramophone and a large library

Other regular Cadillac passengers on the auto trips, "Sophie" (Dushka) and Lord Pentland's young daughter Mary Sinclair.

of records we have spent some time tonight introducing Mary to the *Mikado*. We tried to get her to dance appropriate steps to the Lord High Executioner, Wandering Minstrel, I, etc. and of course it all ended up by my demonstrating how this should be done!

"Mrs. Howarth told me you've 'invited' her to come over to Europe. I wonder whether she will. Of course, I don't have any idea. It would be wonderful for her and a disaster for us to lose her even for a week, but there are always many ways of looking at a thing.

"About Mendham, there is not much news that will interest you. Lonya is, as usual very well. He sometimes asks for news of Eve. He has been watching tennis at Forest Hills and has got very sunburnt.

"I'm sorry about this letter, it's got very late, and I shouldn't have started on it without having more to say to you, but I did think about you and wanted to write. Mrs. Howarth told me you were staying till September, it's none of my business but that is very good and I do hope you'll be quite better and lively soon. No use asking you if there is anything you want from here, is it? I'll send you C.S. Lewis' version of travelling through space to another planet, if I can get it tomorrow. It is very light but why not sometimes?

Love,

John Pentland

"P.S. Please tell Marian I was so glad to get a letter from her. I'll write in a day or two. I hear her mother is expected back here next week."

◆◆◆

Jessmin
◆

Dear Ethel,

The immediate future is full of plans, but that is also a feature of Mr. G.'s work.

At the moment, in England, three groups, Bennett's, Walker's and Jane Heap's, plus the Hoares and Wolton, are joining forces and will use the former big Ouspensky house at Colet Gardens for lectures, etc. If Mr. G. cannot get visa permission to go to England, Jeanne will probably go with the calves to initiate the new project. In the meantime, *Fragments* and *Beelzebub* continue to be worked on in America, England, France, and just recently, in Germany. We are told here that Mr. G. will come over at the end of September and stay in America for six to eight months, although not all the time in New York, and not always "in public." In the meantime, he has refurbished his Paris apartment, bought furniture, and settled his sister in the country (near Fontainebleau). All will depend upon whether the books create a furor, as he pretends to expect, or not.

As for the work here, two separate groups continue. The one in New York helped by Pentland who tries to walk the tightrope of constructive relations with Paris, London, New York and Mendham. At Franklin Farms, Mme. O. has taken the line that Mr. G. told her to stay out of things and look after her health. For the time being, the house is open to anyone who expresses the wish to come to readings, and the Sundays of outdoor work, discussion at tea and Movements.

Extracts from Mr. O.'s book, *In Search of the Miraculous*, are being read at Town Hall. Mr. G. seems to be pleased by this activity. It is rather a shock to hear people being interviewed on radio programs about "consciousness," etc. We are supposed to understand that the teaching is to be spread as widely as possible and that when Mr. G. gets here, he will winnow out the chaff and choose people to work with him.

Marian's mother, who has been a teacher of Yoga, is back from Paris with all the latest information on the Movements and tells me that Mr. G. says she is to be my "official assistant." I am relieved to have her for she is a very clear and energetic instructor. She has free time, pep, money, and friends; and a real desire to accomplish things for Mr. G. So, as soon as the worst summer heat is over, we may be able to build up the classes a little.

These newer Movements are certainly interesting and varied but I feel they are for young people, quite fast in tempo, strenuous and complicated. It seems that, in Paris, people are allowed to do them as they have understood, without a lot of correction. There are so many given, that it is a real challenge. I am told that the result is rather disorderly. This way of working is quite different from our practices at the Prieuré when we were gradually preparing for public demonstrations and needed to be "drilled" so as to work exactly together. I see that this experience had guided my teaching and I sometimes wonder if I have been working on them in an outmoded way. After all, most of the New York pupils are elderly, (four sixty-year-olds in the first row!) and are not demonstration material. However with Mrs. Sutta to inject new life, I trust that we can keep from de-naturing the new exercises.

Annette Herter has developed a new talent. She is playing piano, which means literally improvising music for our classes. This is the greatest help. This is the weak point in the work. We have had to use some dreadful accompaniment by a well-meaning amateur [Edwin Wolfe] which has a disastrous physical effect on certain people, including, I am ashamed to say, myself.

* * * *

New York, summer, 1949

Dear Annette,

You spoke to me about coming out to Mendham on Sundays, saying that you had heard that one must ask to do so, that I had given you no encouragement, but rather led you to understand that one could only be invited. I knew that Mr. Sutta must have been talking to you because he knew I would love to have you. He probably forgot to explain how difficult work on Sunday is. In fact, he may not have realized it himself!!!

I sent a message to Madame asking her whether it would be a convenient Sunday to allow certain people to watch the Movements, and if, in this case, I might have you play.

She said yes for the visitors, and "Why Jessmin ask me about Mrs. Herter? I already say she may come if Jessmin feels right to ask her to play."

When I saw her at the weekend I asked her whether someone else could explain to you about Sundays, conditions, etc.

Annette Herter in the 1940s.

Mme. said, "No. Your friend. I feel nice creature. You explain. Already I tell Mr. Bissing. She come. If she foolish, must then be ready take slap like other people in work. I only know her from what you tell me. I understand what she said about wishing to say the right thing but everything coming out upside down. So, perhaps, suggest that for her, Sunday work begins here. Not to talk. If necessary for politeness to strangers, discuss weather. But no mention of whom she knows, of anything of work in different groups, different readings, etc.

"Here we prepare for Mr. Gurdjieff's coming in September. Now our organization different than before when we did not know whether he would ever come. We try to open our place to new people. We offer grazing ground for sheep. If, when Mr. G. comes, he wish shear or train, this is his business. For the moment we do not wish to antagonize anyone. Everyone new who comes out is friend of some friend of ours. This friend is responsible."

Now I see that you really had meant that you would like to come out on Sundays to the readings and stay to do movements or play the music in our class there. I think this is quite a feasible idea. However, I really must see whether this is acceptable to Mme. And there is nothing personal in it, but we have found during the last few weeks that to have visitors staying around after the readings immobilizes the people who are considered the older ones. Frankly, we have a lot to do on Sundays. For your ear alone, there has been work on the *Fragments* publication, etc. to be done together.

Otherwise, as I have always understood it for people coming out to Mendham at first, they are supposed to understand that they do this primarily for their own sakes — to be able to do physical work of another kind than they are accustomed to — and in conditions that make it possible to try to do this activity for experiment in awareness and observation of oneself. I assure you that everything is carefully planned and that the Mendham people spend a lot of time preparing, and, in fact, especially at this moment, when there is no one there who has any money, they also stint themselves a lot so as to be able to provide everything necessary for the work.

(By the way, Mr. Ouspensky's way of supporting groups carries over in a certain degree. It was that the older people provided what was necessary for a new group of people. When the new people began to understand and expressed a wish to carry certain expenses etc., they were allowed to carry the expenses for a new group, and so on. This will perhaps explain to you why Mme. will never argue with you or with me, even if she realizes that you are not regularly salaried at the moment, if you want to give your time to the newer people for nothing. I have never allowed the old "house" people to pay for movements. A special group who first invited me there, have always carried that responsibility. Now, none of them are in America.)

No indications are given to people unless they ask. The only thing is that they are instructed what physical activity to engage in. The rules are, as always at Mendham except on special occasions, "no unnecessary conversation." Try to ask one person and talk to one person, usually the one in charge of the work you are engaged in, what to do and where to go. She will try to be responsible for you. If she doesn't know how to answer one of your questions, she won't, since this comes under the heading of "lies."

Mostly, people do not start coming unless they expect to be regular. This is very important at the moment. You can understand that the number of newer people cannot be too large for the few older Mendham people to manage. Also, at the moment too, work is difficult (I mean the farm and gardening work) as they are shorthanded, and it is really very complicated to teach a different person everything about a job, where tools are kept, etc., etc., every Sunday. Especially since *Fragments* readings now break into the time formerly allotted for work.

Most people arrive ready to begin work at ten a.m. They work until lunch at one p.m. return to some job between three fifteen and five p.m.. They are supposed to arrange their own transportation. Those who get lifts in cars are specially chosen. We none of us really wish, when leaving in a car, to revert at once to ordinary life and conversation. But, for instance, I, as an older person, am not supposed to cast a gloom on the party by keeping silence if they begin to talk. However, if questions about the ideas come up with people younger in the work, we are in honor bound only to say what we feel we really know, and to leave other explanations to the person at Mendham who is in charge of talking to a new pupil.

You don't come under any of these categories. But you still have a role to play if and when you are out there. For instance, I have not yet carried through what the rest of us always do at Mendham, even Bill and Louise [Welch]. While there, and in front of other pupils, we address each other by our surnames, and do not mention any of our social ties in town.

We are different people, all pupils when we are at Franklin Farms.

There is also the question that no one at Mendham has business dealings with other pupils unless this is first reported to Madame. This is to prevent people getting into mix-ups by being too familiar, and to prevent people using each other. Sometimes, just the mere fact of reporting a proposition of this kind makes one see that it is not right.

For instance, Mr. Sutta reported that he wished to take French lessons with you. I would never have known about it, however, unless I had not had to explain that you were really ill at Easter and that I thought you had done too much at Mrs. March's. Madame said she realized that you were trying to make your living in such a way as to be free to be as much with the Work as possible, and she said that she had approved Mr. Sutta's wish to study, as useful to him and suitable for you.

But, until you began to insist on speaking French to Mr. Sutta before Mrs. Varin and others, no one else knew who was teaching Mr. Sutta, and, according to Mendham usage they need not, and even should not know. In this connection, for instance, as a general rule, if someone, even an old friend had asked me, as you did, whether Daly came regularly to *Fragments* readings, I would not have answered. You can ask him yourself and he can answer you. It is not for me to say to anyone.

I assure you this is a good and constant reminder and very useful. It prevents all kinds of mix-ups. I know it is something that may seem very arbitrary to you.

In the beginning I also used to feel a little restricted or curious or even hurt by this custom. Now I find it so peaceful and so wonderful to be assured of everyone trying to be silent on what does not directly concern them in the work, and to be able to count on people's discretion. I have had a bad weakness with you about this because I felt you would think I was trying to be mysterious with you or something. But once you understand that it is all done for a constructive purpose, I know that this would appeal to you too.

I know of no other conditions. Madame only suggested your working on "silence."

Still, now that your life is not arranged in such a way as to allow you to come every Sunday and give the energy and the taxi fares etc., and as long as you cannot see that it might be right for me to make this money available to you from the Movements Fund at Mendham, I think your whole question is settled for you.

Whatever you want to do, I shall be delighted to help you do. You must feel that. But Mendham work is not a thing to begin with fervor and drop suddenly because it takes a very long time for this to become useful to one. And, although a strong relation in the work is created, there is never, never, never any question of "friendship" and "helping one another" (except for the work) or identification with one's friends, and absolutely no outside social connections.

In haste...

With Love...

One thing I should confess — Once speaking to Madame about Dushka's god-mothers I said I liked Rosemary but couldn't love her — yet it was pleasant to be with her — that I loved you, but often didn't like you and that we were never together without disturbing each other. At that time, years ago, Madame said, "You coward, you like peace. Your friend Annette have all impulses and enthusiasms — but perhaps not enough common sense. Life will teach her discrimination — must teach you courage and not to consider people wrongly and be 'nice' and indirect with them. Then you will both like and love both your good friends."

Jessmin

* * * * *

CHAPTER 20

SUMMER OF 1949

Jessmin
♦

New York, 1949

Dear Ethel,

"They" say that Mr. G. is planning to send Marian and her mother with Iovanna to help Olgivanna with groups in Wisconsin and Chicago. I think he will probably bring people from Paris to take over the Movements here, just as he will do in England. So things are uncertain for me.

"Tim" Dahlberg (the former Mrs. Kenneth Walker) evidently told Mr. G. that I was teaching in New York and at Mendham, and also that I was having to work hard at the office. Jeanne sent me a telegram telling me to go over there, but I felt I could not. I can learn best from Mr. G. by taking him carefully in small doses. But neither can I decide to fit completely into the Mendham life. Mme. O. treats me as one of the family. Whenever I stay overnight I am given Mr. O.'s nice room and, unless I am dressed in time to prevent it, someone trudges up with a breakfast tray.

I feel that Mme. O. suffers. Even I feel a certain lack. No really serious work can go on under present conditions. The young people run the house and farm as best they can, and at least they do not fool themselves about the quality of their effort. The more responsible pupils, two or three, are very busy with the New York publication business and the public readings. There is a constant coming and going.

Fortunately Mme. O. bears up under the hot and humid weather better than most of us. She confesses that, whereas last year she was preparing daily for death and had not much desire to postpone it, now she is still expecting death but is interested in living as long as Fate allows, since she still wants to see what Mr. G. accomplishes.

I suspect that she is a little disappointed in the visible results on people who have been to Paris, the English crowd and those of us who were around Mr. G. here. Yet she has always taken the long view. She says that Mr. G. is evidently "cooking." Each pot gets a different treatment. It may be allowed to cool off, or boil up, perhaps simmer until the scum rises to the surface, or it gets a vigorous stirring. Each pot may think that it contains the whole supper, but only Mr. G. knows whether he really is going to serve the meal sometime, and what it will consist of, and whether it will all be ready at the same time. I see this clearly when he is away. When he is here I shall probably freeze up again.

I can't say truthfully whether I believe, with Mme. O., that Mr. G. is a truly great teacher, or as Mr. O. did, that he was once on the way to being one, but is now "insane." I do know that I can find something to believe in the Work, and, as I told you before, some justification for all the painful friction. I no longer want to pretend to anything I do not feel, and this makes the way a little clearer in some ways, but rather separate, since I cannot subscribe to the devoted enthusiasm of some of the old and the new pupils here.

I do want to say something to you about Jeanne, since you ask and seem to have some reservations about her. She is truly the center of the work for the young people in Paris and has had a wonderful influence on them. It is her groups that feed Mr. G.'s. It is a long time ago, I think about 1936 or 1937, when she came over to Lyne and we went over the Movements we remembered together. She talked then with Mme O. who advised her to go and live close to Mr. G. again. At that time he seemed to have quite small groups, and Jeanne's return must have been very profitable to him. She has been working under terrific pressure for so long now. She has tried her best to keep her promise to me to watch out for Dushka, but I can't expect her to pander to my identification when she does not even have time to sleep properly.

When I first knew her she was a very attractive young woman and brilliantly gifted in the Dalcroze Eurhythmics. She could have done anything.

I'm sorry but I don't see your point about Olga and Jeanne using "de" in front of their names. This is the accepted translation of the "von" their husbands were entitled to (as aristocrats of German origin in Tsarist Russia when French became the official court language) and certainly a better kind of name for Mr. G.'s representatives than "Smith" or "Jones" would be. (Salzmann always signed his cartoons in that way.)

Mme. feels that Jeanne, like Olga de Hartmann in the old days, may feel that she is indispensable and take on more than her health can stand. I admire the force in her, and feel very stolid and inert, and exceedingly lazy, when I compare my greatest effort with her least. But, with the role she has to play, one cannot be on very warm, friendly terms with her and I am glad to have Mme. O. to talk to.

* * * *

Ogunquit, Maine, September 4, 1949
My Dearest Ethel,

Thank you for the books on [Sri Ramana] Maharshi's teaching. I gave them to Madame [Ouspensky] at once after one evening of study. She is most interested... used them herself, and has recommended them to two of the older pupils. I would have liked to have brought them up here, but, as these two people were badly in need of them, I will study them on returning. Madame O. was appreciative of the parts of your letter about work (I read her excerpts) and spoke of what you said to the few pupils she sees regularly. To me she mentioned the simple, quiet, friendly tone of your letter. She seemed to understand that work in the Ashram milieu must be quite difficult for any European, but, she said, you evidently had found a "way" and she was happy for you.

I meant to write you at once, but the last few weeks were unsettled. I had to regain some peace of mind. You think I have won to non-identification about Dushka, but I find I am not at all big about understanding Mr. G.'s motives in his dealings with her. Dushka's last letters have been disturbed.

First Mr. G. had been violent in insisting again that she marry Alfred at once, so that the two could go soon to England (with Jeanne initiating things for the first week or two). Dushka managed to get him to accept a compromise, i.e. an official engagement, but finds the prospect of so many roles terrifying: "Dochter" (Daughter) of the Master, conventional fiancée, sponsor and protector of Alfred, etc. She then heard that Mr. G. says he will probably sail for the U.S.A. on October 20th., a date which hardly allows any work to begin in London since there are studio re-model-lings and music preparations to do that can take weeks. She rather dreads England, and I guess that her feeling of duty to Mr. G., and of concern for Alfred's future are not as strong as they should be to offset her wish to be back in America when everyone else is.

I think a phase is past. The youngsters are all restless. Tania has come home, more or less unchanged. Olgivanna is still ill and has sent for Iovanna. Edith expects Eve (Petey) home in October.

For Marian and Mrs. Sutta, at least, their interest in G. has been constructive. Their family is now united for the first time. I have the sixty-two-year-old grand-mother, Mrs. Frankfurt, and the fifteen year-old brother, Elihu, in the Movements class. Mrs. Sutta now assists me (Marian does the Movements very easily and she and her mother have clear, tidy minds) and Mr. Sutta can afford to be "sheared."

Another thing that has upset Dushka is that Mr. G. took her (and others) to Geneva, and there acknowledged Nikolai Stjernval as another son (though Mme. O. tells me there are doubts about the blood relationship). Dushka says that he is the first young man that she has ever thoroughly disliked. She felt he reacted very coarsely. After Mr. G. gave him money, he took her and Petey out to his "club," a late-night bar full of prostitutes, got very drunk, and disappeared with one of the "girls."

Lonia, Lenushka's son, also went over to Paris and announced to Dushka that "his mother had told him that he was also a 'Beelzebub brat.'"

Before going he had asked me whether it was true. I said that I had no way of knowing; he must trust his mother. Then Mme. O. told me that her first disillu-sionment about Mr. G. was when he told her daughter, Lenushka, that she was a "hysteric," needed to have sex, and offered himself to initiate her. But Mme. O. says Lonia's father was certainly Rachmilevitch, and that Lenushka just told this tale to give Lonia a little more confidence about being with Mr. G.

Dushka says that Lonia finally went to Mr. G. and asked straight out whether he was his son. I think Mr. G.'s answer was a marvel, for it did not demean Lenushka. He said: "You can tell your mother that if you are not it is her fault." But Lonia will not look at or speak to Rachmilevitch who often goes to see Mr. G..

I don't dare tell Lonia that once, when Lenushka had long since married Savitsky, Rachmilevitch wanted someone to help him get to America and he wrote me a letter, quite obviously copied from a French *Manual of Polite Correspondence*, proposing marriage!

Fortunately Dushka and Lonia can get on together, though she admits that a lot of it comes from her feeling that his life is so lonely and artificial at Mendham, that someone should get him out into ordinary life. They both love and respect his grandmother and Dushka knows that Lonia said it was a pity that I was not his mother, and Dushka Lenushka's daughter. His reason: That I liked to be with his grandmother, whereas Lenushka always criticizes everything Mme. does, and he says his mother would just love to make dresses for Dushka, etc. now Tania is married.

◆ ◆ ◆

Yes, I really did feel sorry for Lonia. During those few weeks he was in Paris he didn't make a place for himself with us all. He completely ignored Rachmilevitch

Dushka
◆

who was, it is true, a poor, unprepossessing little man, obviously not up to Lonia's snobbish ideas about himself, though the resemblance between them was striking. And even later, when we were all back in New York, I had little success trying to draw Lonia into my business and social circles.

Sturdily built and well dressed, Lonia wasn't bad looking in spite of having to wear small, unbecoming glasses. But he wasn't used to being with strangers. It didn't work to invite him to parties or double date situations. He was like a fish out of water. With no job to go to, and few normal hobbies, he lacked any topics of conversation, much less amusing repartee. And it was understandably very hard for him to pull off the role of country squire or man of leisure with limited spending money, and the obvious difficulties of inviting anyone to his home or introducing them to his "family."

Just once did he manage to fit into the social background. The occasion was a la-di-dah New York party we were both invited to by Mendham pupil, Clive Entwistle, a noted architect.

Clive's brother, society photographer Anthony Beauchamp, (for some reason pronounced "Beecham"), was visiting from London with his wife, Sarah (Winston Churchill's daughter). But then that was the kind of affair when nobody listens to what anybody else says anyway!

Mother had told me that she felt that Mme. worried about Lonia's emotional stability, which is why she always kept him near her (not insisting that he continue an unsuccessful university experiment, or be drafted into the army, etc.). It was true that he was protected in a certain way in the Franklin Farms "Work" environment. Certainly everyone always made a special effort near him (even when at times they were sorely tempted to punch him in the nose), but how depressing it must be to serve as a soul-developing "special task" for the people around you.

I'm afraid that in this instance I questioned Mme.'s decision. I certainly didn't know all the circumstances and though I felt strongly, "in my gut" that both Lonia and Tania would have benefited from more normal surroundings and being forced to make the usual adjustments and relationships with other people, I said nothing. After a few more attempts I stopped inviting him to my parties in town.

But still I was one of the few people at the farm who had free time to spend with Lonia. Sometimes in the evening he would invite me to watch television with him (his was the only set in the house), and a couple of times he took me with him to his "club" to watch him play tennis, his current major interest. (He had already given up on golf.) Everyone had heard a lot about all this during monologues he often went into at mealtimes, so once there, it was embarrassing; his "friend Prince Oleg Cassini" barely recognized him, and the other country club members pointedly avoided him.

Then he got a big, new car (while I wondered which of Mme.'s devoted pupils had made it possible) and I agreed to take a ride in it and even to try driving it, until he put his foot heavily on top of mine forcing the accelerator to the floor. After a few terrifying moments roaring along the country road unable to stop, something, fortunately, gave me the idea to turn off the ignition. Lonia treated it all as a big joke and I tried to forget about the incident.

Next he got interested in flying, and at Mendham mealtimes this was all we

Lonia Savitsky at the Prieuré.

Lonia at university in England.

Lonia's mother "Lenushka" Savitsky.

Christmas at Franklin Farms. Lonia celebrating with Lord Pentland looking on.

Being uncooperative with the photographer (Dushka) at the gift-giving Christmas breakfast.

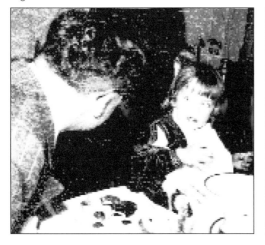

Trying to be avuncular with a suspicious Dolphi, Jim George's small daughter, (later Mrs. Chris Wertenbaker).

Society photographer Anthony Beauchamp with his wife Sarah (neé Churchill) at the Stork Club.

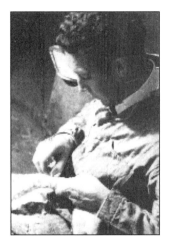

Plucking geese in the basement at Franklin Farms. (Left) Architect Clive Entwistle (Above, left to right) Barbara Mills (later Mrs. Pierce Wheeler) Betsy Bonbright, Countess Marie-Claude Jallu, and Lady Lucy Pentland.

heard about. He finally got his license and I was invited for a ride. It is true that the Morristown airport was small and green like the surrounding fields, but dear Lonia almost couldn't find it again. I just thought his nervous whistling and mutters of "Where's the bloody airport?" were meant to be amusing.

A few months later the extremely chic and attractive Countess Marie-Claude Jallu came from Paris to stay for a time at Mendham. She was a good sport and took Lonia's clumsy attentions in her stride. We all remember the night at the dinner table when Lonia was being especially obnoxious and Marie-Claude calmly and elegantly poured a huge pitcher of milk over his head. But even she got discouraged after her first (and last!) plane ride with him. This time Lonia not only didn't find the airport, but he flew so far in the wrong direction that the plane ran out of gas over Manhattan and they had to make a tricky emergency landing on Governor's Island in the East River!

So I suppose I should have thought twice about his birthday present to me one September. It was a trip to the Princeton airport where he had arranged for me to have a flying lesson. But, no! I was thrilled, and while Lonia sat in his car reading, I happily climbed into the small open plane with the instructor behind me shouting instructions. As we took off and flew around for awhile, I thoroughly enjoyed the feeling, the freedom, the three-dimensional sensation that was like my favorite activity, underwater swimming. More shouted instructions and we landed moderately smoothly.

It was only when the instructor and I went into the little shack that served as an office, so that he could fill out the receipt for my hour of instruction, that we both had a bad shock. With a big smile he said, "Well, what does that make now, ten or eleven hours?" When I casually answered, "No, that was my first time," the poor man's face went gray and he gasped: "But I would never have let you take off and land and so forth — except your friend told me you had already had about ten hours flying time!"

At the end of 1961, when it was finally evident that Mme. O. could no longer sustain her valiant hold on life, Lonia was apparently unable to face an existence without his grandmother and the identity and support she always provided him. He chose not to try.

He was found in his bedroom at Mendham, having shot himself.

The devoted older pupils who nursed Mme. O. during the remaining months of her life made great efforts, up to the very end, to keep this tragedy from her. They have always wondered how well they succeeded.

And I will always wonder if there wasn't something I could have done!

◆ ◆ ◆

Ogunquit, Maine

Dear Ethel,

Jessmin

◆

Dushka is a bit fed up with all the strange people who come up to her and say "How does it feel to have a father like that?" and she was relieved when Mr. G. told her to pack, give up her room at the Belfast Hotel, and go to the seashore, Deauville, to stay with Boussik. She loved that life. Michel, Alfred and his sister Yvette, and Tolik Mercuroff swam, played chess, and were young. Heaven after being shut up for almost six months in the apartment and the Cadillac. But after just three days she was ordered back to Paris for a motor trip which did not materialize, and found herself with no place to live, no money, and finally had to camp out in someone's half vacated apartment. So possibly her "Roses, Roses" period is also coming to an end, and she will need to take stock and ponder her immediate future.

If she does come back, there will be readings and Movements to follow, with or without Mr. G., and Madame really helps one to understand — not him — but how to work with him. As for practical life, I don't know. I still wish she would study cookery and the restaurant business. She loves feeding people, has a natural gift for it and loves to be gregarious. If she eventually marries Alfred she will need a real metier.

Alfred playing chess.

Vacation in Deauville: (Above) Dr. Michel "relaxes" playing volley-ball. (Right) Alfred and "Tolik" watch. (Far right) Michel gives Alfred a light.

Mme. O., unfortunately, still seems disappointed that I do not see living at Mendham as my way. I regret too, for this is a rare opportunity to see more of her, since there are so few people left there. But I cannot honestly choose that life.

The break with the office was accomplished very easily. My director insists on regarding it as a "three-month leave of absence" and hopes to call me back for something by Christmas. But, of course, I cannot live without earning for so long, especially as, since I chose to leave, I am not entitled to the extra month's "severance pay" I had expected after six-and-one-half years' service.

Well, all this, with the continued heat, a recurrence of colitis and the possibility of another Gurdjieff "stirring" this winter, decided me to risk a week's holiday. I am staying with my Ogunquit friends, the Whitesides. Esther was a Dalcroze pupil, at the Opera, and her mother brought me here for three months before Dushka's birth. We have a long relationship, all gratitude on my side. On returning, we will be active organizing more and better functioning Movement groups. Then I will see how the rest of my life must be oriented.

Ethel dear, I do hope that the Maharshi's health has improved and that you have not again been uprooted. But, if a change has come, I trust that we shall see you before too long. I realize that the money complications connected with living in the U.S.A. are almost prohibitive, and I wonder whether you could find anything with the groups in London. I think Mme. again put her finger on the difficulty when she used the image: "Yes! Many quite solid bricks there, with which Mr. G. can build, if he wishes. But I think, more necessary, to have seeds with possibility of germinating."

I don't know, Ethel, if it can be true, what you say about accomplishing little. We cannot judge of our own states until we are out in ordinary conditions without the constant help of our teachers. I show up very poorly indeed in such circumstances, and I know I am self-indulgent and lazy about real and continued effort. But if I can stay somehow in relation to Mme., or G., or Krishnamurti, I hope not to be engulfed entirely, and I can push down many useless and petty desires. But I am in no sense ready for a life uniquely consecrated to "Work." I feel I could learn more in work with People. Above all I have to go on trying to separate the "Work" from Mr. G. and striving to see him without resentment, self-defense, or the opposite, infatuation. I can go ahead only a crumb at a time.

But, I do trust, that if events cause you to leave the Ashram, you will please continue to write, and perhaps, keep in more frequent, close contact with us all. Mme. O. asked me to send you a "good message" and a real thank you for the books.

Mr. O.'s book *In Search of the Miraculous* will come out here in October. It is a great help to me and will, I think, be a wonderful preparation for most people. Mme. O. has told me how he sat down to write this, at a moment when he was very unsure about the direction in which Mr. G.'s teaching was moving, and yet he managed to be objective and set forth the system impartially. What an admirable effort!

* * * * *

Late September, 1949

Two letters from Dushka too long to copy.

The first telling how she was commanded to present herself at Mr. G.'s apartment for lunch on the 16th, her birthday. During the meal Mr. G. announced that Dushka and Alfred were now engaged and that he would be sending them to London to unite the various groups and start Movement classes there. Dushka, as his personal representative would be "Head of Work in England."

It must have been almost as much a surprise to Alfred as to Dushka for it was Mr. G. who produced an "engagement ring" which she describes as a heavy gold ring with a ruby in a square of diamond chips; more like a man's ring. I'm afraid Dushka had to hide her feelings which were indignation at Mr. G.'s highhandedness and regret because I was not there and had never been consulted. But after all I had not gone over when invited by cable and I took all this as "window dressing." And, in fact, as I suspected, when Dushka talked to him privately later, Mr. G. said that he needed the two of them to go to London together but that to "English" it wouldn't look correct unless they were engaged.

Dushka made it clear that she still wasn't ready to commit herself but agreed to the arrangement if amongst themselves and Alfred's family they all knew she was just "engaged to be engaged."

◆ ◆ ◆

So many people who knew and admired Alfred in later years, especially the women, were puzzled about our relationship and why I could have any hesitation about him. Certainly the Alfred they knew then was a very special being, an attractive gentlemanly "gentle man," and extraordinary teacher. But in 1949 he was really just starting his life as an adult. The war years and his imprisonment had taken a serious toll on his health, psyche, and self-confidence. He was sensitive about his interrupted education and lack of professional skills, but proud, even arrogant, about his "Frenchness."

I, on the other hand, was a self-sufficient, self-supporting, self-mocking American who had spent years in "client management" making a profession out of directing other people's actions and opinions, and I knew it was the last thing I wanted to do in my own personal life. I craved the opportunity to be "feminine" and to fulfill what I was always convinced was my real destiny, to have a large family. But I needed a "Father" for that family especially since I had seen clearly, at first-hand what strength and courage it had taken Mother to do it alone.

But the mainstay in Alfred's life in those days, as later, was the Work and especially his devotion to, almost fanaticism for Mr. G., while I was still just trying to understand and find my way in all that. I struggled against any real emotional commitment because of an intuition that Alfred wasn't so much in love with me as with "Mr. Gurdjieff's daughter."

So when one day, out of the blue, Mr. G. announced at lunch that there would be an "engagement party" for us that night it was a shock for everybody.

The afternoon was spent in a bustle of activity to prepare for the evening. Alfred's family was invited, as they had been once before, when I had intentionally avoided the announcement being made by arriving late, but this time I tried to cooperate. I even dressed especially for the occasion.

As Mr. Tilley wrote in a letter to his wife Irene who was back in Franklin Farms helping care for Mme. Ouspensky:

"Friday we had a special time in celebration of Alfred and Dushka's engagement. Alfred's parents and sister were there and many French people.

Dushka

(Left to right) Petey, Alfred and "Sophie" celebrate wth champagne.

"Sophie's ring is very nice, and Mr. G. gave them both a wad of notes. After the cake and congratulations the meal developed along its usual lines, and it could not be called a party in the sense that you are used to. Later I acted as chauffeur to the couple and we went to one or two clubs and got home about six-thirty a.m.

"Sophia looked quite lovely in a white suit with white flowers."

* * * *

Well, that was the first and last time I ever wore that suit. It was made from the special silk that Mr. G. had bought for the "calves," giving each of us a bolt of a slightly different shade of cream or grey. I was the only one who had had mine made up. Unfortunately Mr. G. had insisted that I go to one of his old Russian cronies, whose only tailoring experience had been with men. He used prickly stiffening inside big shoulder pads and wide lapels which pierced the delicate material and didn't adapt to my contours, the masculine styling totally wrong for my very female shape.

The ring was also a problem. Mr. G. presented it to me with great ceremony while Alfred looked on, a bit embarrassed. What he himself had given me was a beautiful, small heart-shaped diamond locket on a chain, a family keepsake. But the ring was so big and heavy that even when I wore it on my middle finger it was perilously loose. I still believe it was some man's cocktail ring. I remember looking around and speculating which visitor Mr. G. might have commandeered it from at such short notice.

◆ ◆ ◆

Jessmin
◆

Dushka's second letter after their arrival at Colet Gardens in London was sour-humored.

The engaged couple have a dance. (Note the too big engagement ring on the wrong finger!)

Evidently, the day they had to travel it had been arranged that Alfred would get the taxi and pick up Dushka and her luggage quite early as they were supposed to have breakfast with Mr. G. on their way to the boat train. When Alfred did not appear, Dushka made her way out to a telephone, called him and found that he was still asleep. She then had to tug all her luggage down three flights of stairs alone, and they finally had to race for the station only having time to pass by for a minute to wave "goodbye" to Mr. G.

After the crossing they were separated to go through English Customs and Passport Control. Dushka waited and waited as all the trains to London left and then had to insist on joining Alfred to vouch for him and prevent them deporting him back to France.

He had been saying all the wrong things: "He didn't know how long he would stay... No, he had no money with him but would work... No, he had no work permit but would teach... He would teach but really didn't speak English," and so on."

Dushka had to use all her public relations techniques and acting ability to find excuses for him, saying: "...they were newly engaged and it was she who had insisted that he come with her to England to meet all her friends there, and as for needing money...if they just stayed a few days with each of all the English people who, during the war, had accepted her family's hospitality in America, they would be taken care of for years!"

Arriving late at the London House, where the first big reunion had been called (and Dushka was to play recordings of Mr. G.) they found that the necessary equipment had not been installed. Dushka buzzed around while Alfred, already homesick and somewhat bewildered, moped in the background,

"And that," says Dushka, "was my first day of being cherished by my fiancé!"

* * * * *

CHAPTER 21

THE FINAL WEEKS

Of all the older people who gathered around Mr. Gurdjieff during that last year, perhaps the one I was most grateful to was the tall, patrician-looking John G. (for Godolphin!) Bennett. I think he had only recently begun to make a relationship with Ann, his daughter by a former marriage, who was about my age.

Ann and her husband, actor Donovan Ubsdell, later became good friends of mine. I felt in Bennett an empathy and that he, at least, understood that this experience of suddenly being Mr. G.'s daughter wasn't all "roses, roses." He would sometimes take me out to a Paris café and it was a relief to talk on a more equal basis than I found possible with many others.

He often brought his elderly wife (the former Winifred Elliot Beaumont) with him to G.'s apartment or on our automobile caravans. But when "Polly" as he called her wasn't there, it seemed quite obvious to the "calves" that the young English girl, Elizabeth Mayall, was her replacement. And, in truth, at the end of his life these two married, worked together and had tall, handsome children.

When Alfred and I were sent to England together, again people treated us artificially: either critical, or embarrassingly servile. But Bennett would breeze in and take us out for a break. We once even went as a foursome, Bennett and good sport Polly, Alfred and I, and danced for hours at the Hammersmith Palais de Danse. How his many pupils would have been surprised!

One of the few times we got out of London was the weekend when Bennett took us to Stratford-on-Avon to stay with one of his pupils, Col. Flower and his family. The drive took us through lovely country with thatched cottages, flowered hedgerows, and the university town of Oxford where we stopped to sightsee. I happily snapped pictures with my little "Retina 1" camera which my Godmother Annette had brought me back from the PX in Munich.

Bennett c. 1918

Bennett in 1949.

(Above) Bennett's daughter, Ann, (center) and her husband Don Ubsdell in their London "flat" during a visit with them in the Sixties. Jessmin (Left) doesn't seem too sure about their dog!

(Above) While Mme. de Salzmann is responsible for checking out the bill for lunch, Dushka leaves the table to snap some photos of the group which includes (Below from left) John Bennett, "Polly" Bennett, Cynthia Pearce, Mr. Gurdjieff, Mary Sinclair, Lord Pentland, an old Russian doctor, and Lady Pentland.

Against a college stained glass window, Alfred in his wartime duffel coat with a hood, came out looking just like the monk that I sometimes, unkindly, accused him of acting like.

But my favorite photos were of Alfred grudgingly posing on one of the various empty pedestals that were left when statues were removed during the war to be melted down for their metal content. Bennett, on the other hand, loved the idea and needed no urging.

Col. Flower had, I believe, once been the Mayor of Stratford and he took us to visit all the usual tourist sights, such as Ann Hathaway's cottage. But I was really disappointed when we attended the famous theater, since their Shakespeare company was absent on tour and was replaced by a musical comedy production starring musical comedy star Jack Buchanan.

Queen Victoria statue

Alfred statue

Bennett statue

(Above from left) Dushka (in her first and only "fur" coat), "Polly" Bennett and Alfred in Stratford with the Flower family.
(Right) Alfred in Oxford before stained glass windows, "like a monk."

Alfred was just as happy. In spite of having a father and sister who were both theatrical celebrities and an elder brother, Jacques, who was in radio before moving to South America, due to his war experiences Alfred was sometimes culturally naive. He was musical and played the piano quite well, but in London I had to drag him to things like the Sadler's Wells Ballet. Once there of course, he loved it, but during the curtain calls, when the conductor in evening dress was called up out of the orchestra pit, Alfred turned and asked me: "Is that Mr. Wells?"

We were living in the big "Work" house in Colet Gardens with the Woltons as our hosts. I had known Mrs. Wolton at Mendham, where she was always "Miss Bissing" (Tosca von Bissing), then a rather grim spinster, especially as her role at that time was as Mme. O.'s representative and required her always to be carrying a huge bunch of keys. I couldn't ignore the resemblance to the housekeeper in Du Maurier's

Rebecca. But recently she had married nice middle-aged Aubrey Wolton, gained weight, and softened into an eager, if impractical new bride. She and her husband both tried really hard to make us comfortable, but the food,

Dushka and Alfred try "Polyfotos," (multiple poses), London"s latest fad.

I'm sorry to say, was a disaster. Tosca's previous experiences had all been organizational and she had little personal know-how for keeping house or preparing meals. For example, since meat was still rationed in England, I was naturally depressed to see our entire week's allotment of beef cut into thin strips, and shriveling up in a pan till it looked like black shoelaces. She proudly informed me that she was making *Boeuf Stroganoff* using a Dione Lucas recipe. I suggested, gently I hope, that an important ingredient was lacking, sour cream. At that she grabbed a bottle of solidly soured milk from the windowsill and plopped it all in. Ugh!

Another time, having served us a very English boiled fish, she carefully saved the cooking water for a soup ("after all it contains all the vitamins and goodness") but failed to refrigerate it. The next day we all, including her patient husband, left it untouched. The next meal she tried again, having added curry powder to mask the bad taste. The final time it was presented, we really rebelled and demanded to know what she had done with it. "Well, I thought maybe I had used too much curry, and I know in India they counteract the heat of the spices with sweet chutney. But since I didn't have any chutney, I put in strawberry jam!"

So I wasn't really surprised at the deep, nauseous feeling I had been living with for two weeks. But even when we were invited out to nice restaurants, I didn't enjoy it, and decided that English food as a whole was even worse than its world-wide reputation. Until one morning when I woke up to find that I was completely yellow. Even the whites of my eyes were deep golden-colored. A dignified Harley Street physician was quickly summoned and his only question to me after one look was "Do you feel depressed?" At my heartfelt agreement he beamed and rubbed his hands. "Ah, yes. Classic symptoms! Hepatitis!" I was thankful to be confined to bed with a strictly fat-free regime, even though Mrs. W. made more boiled fish! Alfred hovered over me like a mother hen, but couldn't bring himself, Frenchman that he was, to allow me the one thing I craved — probably due to my California upbringing — a sharp, clean orange. "Non! Non! Trop acide! Trop acide!"

◆ ◆ ◆

Jessmin
 ◆

New York, October, 1949

Dear Ethel,

Just when we were imminently expecting Mr. G.'s arrival, probably on the twentieth, we heard that he would not be able to leave as planned. The postponement of his trip might have no significance or be due to many factors, but the truth is that Mr. G. is really ill. I think anyone with any experience could see that he must be suffering from a liver ailment as well as the results of over-exertion after his automobile accident last summer which left him with a serious bronchial congestion. The cirrhosis developed recently in an alarming way, and he had dropsy. No one in Paris could induce him to have the fluid drawn off from his swollen belly and legs.

At last this week, my nice doctor Bill Welch was sent for to bring a special medication from New York. He managed to get off within eight hours. Immediately on his arrival, Mr. G. consented to go to the American Hospital where Bill was helped to make the necessary puncture, drawing off unbelievable quantities of fluid.

Of course, there must follow a first reaction to the shock, and fatigue. But they can now proceed to try a new and rare medicine with the definite hope of cooperation on Mr. G.'s part and the possibility of quite extraordinary improvement. Only a few people here know what is going on, and we have to hold ourselves in readiness for anything while trying to keep the most constructive thoughts for him.

He has against him his age, his misuse of his body, and the suspected presence of a blood clot somewhere. But, as you know, he has with him unpredictable forces, aided now by the best professional care.

At the same moment I was first told that Mr. G.'s condition was bad, I also had a cable to say that Dushka was in bed with hepatitis. She had been feeling ill for a couple of weeks but it took a long time for the jaundice to show so that she could be correctly diagnosed. She is living in the Colet Gardens house with the Woltons and I know they and the Phelps will look after her well. She is depressed, feeling that she has lost the opportunity to be of any use in England, having missed meetings and classes for nearly three weeks. I understand that she wants to come home to get some perspective on things. She can leave Alfred with a wonderful vista of activity opening up for him there; about two hundred people doing the Movements with fresh enthusiasm, and Mr. Bennett charged by Mr. G. to find him a good job as his independent *gagne-pain*. In the meantime, Dushka has taken out the last money we had in the London bank to outfit him with a warm overcoat, and pay for some dental care, etc. So, I see that she does care for him.

* * * *

October 31, 1949

Mr. Gurdjieff died two days ago. Jeanne and Dr. Welch were with him all the last hours.

As most people knew, his liver was badly affected. Also, when he was in New York, he had a dreadful cough and my doctor said he must not only be suffering from cirrhosis of the liver but also a deep lung infection besides the chronic bronchial congestion. Although insisting on having large, rich meals served to his guests, he himself managed, mostly without people realizing it, to eat very little. And, at that, he often complained of indigestion and kept himself going, more vigorously than nearly everyone else, by drinking quantities of coffee and Armagnac. During the summer, his strength must have been gradually leaving him, although reports differ. Some days his complexion was as clear as a child's and he was full of energy and good spirits. On other days, he would look very old indeed with big brown patches on his face and hands and a bloated look to his body.

In August and September he complained of having "ruptured" himself, wore an uncomfortable truss and blamed his discomfort and digestive disturbances on this. When a leg swelled so badly that he had to be helped to lift it across the other, he insisted that this was just the effect of his injury in last summer's automobile accident. However, the various doctors who saw him, and whom he sent away disgruntled, diagnosed the trouble as an accumulation of fluid in the leg and abdomen, which any layman could see! Finally, it seems, Mr. G. agreed to try to treat the liver condition, went on a diet with no stimulants, took some medication and submitted to some massage. This was not enough to cause any real improvement, and, of course, if he did feel a little relieved, he would immediately go off to the Turkish baths and the Movements lessons, and eat and drink again. Then his state would become worse.

Jeanne sent over to New York for some special medicine. And when, last Tuesday, Mr. G.'s condition seemed grave and it was obvious that he was agonizingly uncomfortable, she telephoned Dr. Welch to ask him to fly over. As I have already told you, this was done quickly, and, at the American Hospital, they did what was necessary to relieve him of the pressure of a large amount of fluid. It seems that he went through this quite cheerfully, rallied well, drank coffee with Dr. Welch and saluted him with "Bravo American!" He listened with seeming interest to a description of the special medical treatment he was to receive. Now, Bill Welch suspected that there was a clot of blood not far from the heart, and he began to feel that Mr. G. knew perfectly well that he would not really last out to undergo the treatment. All we have been told is that after talking with Jeanne in Russian, he died, with Jeanne and Bill beside him. We do not know why he gave up.

Of course, some of the old people, and other doctors begin at once to find fault with what was done, and say he should never have been taken to the hospital, that the tapping was too strenuous, etc. But, all that is over now. He was probably spared much pain and I am sure he would not have consented to these measures unless he felt that some medical attention was necessary. He had fought alone long enough.

◆ ◆ ◆

Dushka

◆

Later, people who were there at the hospital, Solita Solano, Vera Daumal Page, et al, reported that the actual cause of his death was cancer of the liver.

◆ ◆ ◆

Jessmin

◆

After the first grievous shock, for Mme. O. had really had faith in his surmounting this last misery, she reared up and insisted that life must go on as usual. She sent down a message which I had to read to the people present at Franklin Farms, saying: "This is no time for weeping, but for work. Mr. G. gave us so much; we must repay by trying to understand and hold to the best part in ourselves," and we were given a quiet time to attempt to examine ourselves and try to realize what had been of most import and value to each of us personally in Mr. G.'s teaching.

I think you would be pleased to know that Madame spoke to me of having used the Maharshi's book (*The Questionnaire*) on Saturday. Evidently she values it and turns to it in moments of difficulty.

For some weeks at least, I think things at Franklin Farms will continue as before. Time will be needed to put everything in order. We hope there is provision for G.'s immediate family and for those whose lives have been given to his work. Jeanne will surely continue the groups in Paris. Although Mr. G. had not asked for them, Jeanne sent for the de Hartmanns in the last hours. Perhaps their old friendship will support her. Mme. O. will decide upon her course when she sees what is possible and helpful.

For me, I finish out the month and await Dushka's return. I want to study and show some gratitude to Madame by staying close to her, but I do not want to be pushed into the position of a teacher or a guide, someone who takes responsibility for what she cannot truly pretend to know or value properly herself.

LATER: There was a most impressive and crowded funeral service in Paris at the Russian Orthodox Cathedral on the rue Daru, and the burial was in the cemetery at Fontainebleau-Avon, where his mother and Mme. Ostrovsky rest.

Although she was still quite sick, Dushka went over to Paris. Bill Welch is our doctor and he looked after her. She wrote that he had helped her tremendously by explaining to her that there had been no hope for Mr. G.'s recovery, that he could only have existed longer in increasing pain and helplessness. Dushka was regretting that there had not been time for her to understand her father better, but concluded that it would be cruelly selfish to wish him to live longer under such conditions.

Now she just longs to be well enough to travel home.

◆ ◆ ◆

During those weeks of being ill in London, I felt guilty that Alfred had to take all the Movement classes alone. I would lie in my second floor bedroom and watch the old ceiling pulse up and down as fifty or so people over my head would tread out foot rhythms: "One, Two, and Three!" And any visitors who sneaked in to see me were evidently reluctant to give me any bad news such as the reports of Mr. G.'s worsening illness.

So it was a terrible shock on October twenty-ninth to be told that he had died at 10:30 that morning.

Alfred and I flew immediately to Paris and I checked into the same Hotel Belfast near Mr. G.'s apartment, but then collapsed into bed. In the chapel of the American Hospital, people of the Work were keeping round-the-clock vigil by an open casket and Alfred went right off to join them (Solita Solano describes him arriving "looking like alabaster") He just couldn't understand that I wouldn't go with him. It wasn't only that I was still so ill, though I was, but I couldn't make myself relate what was in that chapel to the vital force I had known as Mr. Gurdjieff. The memory of him that I wanted to keep, and have for all these years is very different.

I did, of course, join everybody for the moving service at the Russian church on the rue Daru, of which one of the priests said there had never been such a funeral before "except Chaliapin's in 1938." Then a long procession of automobiles accompanied the hearse to Fontainebleau where the burial took place in a grave near to those of Mr. G.'s mother and wife.

One of the lighter but still poignant memories of that part of the day, was the sudden arrival of Olga de Hartmann, who hadn't seen or spoken to Mr. G. in over twenty years. But she immediately reverted to her old role as his secretary, ordering everyone about, assigning seats in the limousines, and so on.

Photographs taken that day remind me of another example of Mr. Gurdjieff's rather special kind of "gift giving." In the Spring when I had sailed from New York to Europe I hadn't taken with me anything more than a thin light-colored coat. But when Alfred and I were sent to London that Fall; Mr. G., sure the weather would be dreadful, (he disapproved of many things "English") dressed me in a very large and painfully heavy black Persian lamb coat. At last, my first real fur coat! What I didn't know was that it was something he had simply appropriated suddenly off the back of his poor sister, Sophie. She immediately demanded it back the moment Alfred and I landed in Paris. This explains why I am about the only person in the funeral photos not wearing black, and looking very cold!

Dushka

◆

HERALD TRIBUNE, MONDAY, OCTOBER 31, 1949

Georges Gurdjieff, Paris Cult Leader

Set Up Plan for Harmonious Development of Man

Georges I. Gurdjieff, eighty-three, founder of the Institute for the Harmonious Development of Man, died Friday in the American Hospital in Paris after a short illness.

Mr. Gurdjieff, who claimed followers in Europe, North and South America, and Asia, taught that in every man there are three persons, one that thinks, one that feels and one that acts, and that the three elements of his nature should be developed harmoniously.

Born in Alexandrople, in the Russian Caucasus, of Greek parents, Mr. Gurdjieff studied medicine and for the priesthood. His earlier work with an organization known as The Seekers of the Truth was interrupted by the Russian Revolution, and he went to Paris, where he founded his institute in 1922.

In 1924, he brought a group of his pupils to the United States and gave demonstrations of sacred dances and exercises in New York and Chicago. As a result of injuries suffered in an automobile accident, he gave up plans for establishing branches of the institute in America and elsewhere, and devoted his time to writing and teaching in France. A book "All and Everything," is scheduled for publication in New York this

Founder of New Religion

Georges I. Gurdjieff

New York obituaries (Below) N.Y. Times

G. I. GURDJIEFF, 83, FOUNDER OF CULT

Rites Today for Mystic Whose Devotees Found Calm Through Exercises—Died in Paris

Memorial services will be held this morning here and in Paris and London for G. I. Gurdjieff, explorer and founder of a cult, who died Friday night at the American Hospital in Paris, after a brief illness. He was 83 years old.

The service in this city will be at 11 o'clock in the Greek Orthodox Cathedral of the Holy Trinity, 319 East Seventy-fourth Street. Burial will take place today at Fontainebleau, France.

His early career somewhat of a mystery, Mr. Gurdjieff began attracting attention in Constantinople shortly before the first World War as organizer and high priest of a new religion whose devotees found calm and self-control through a system of exercises involving 6,000 different movements, which they performed to music.

Mr. Gurdjieff established a similar group in London, but his cult did not receive much publicity in the United States until the early Twenties, shortly after he had set up his Institute for the Harmonious Development of Man at Fontainebleau.

In a rented chateau thirty miles from Paris, Mr. Gurdjieff presided, amid Oriental trappings, over a congregation of seekers after peace and happiness from many lands. Katherine Mansfield, the novelist, spent her last days under his roof, and the late P. D. Ouspensky, mathematician-philosopher, was among his pupils.

Mr. Gurdjieff brought forty of his pupils to this country in 1924, and gave demonstrations of cult dances and exercises in New York and Chicago. He planned to establish an institute here, but abandoned the project after he had been injured seriously by an automobile. He continued the Fontainebleau establishment for several years.

His last years were devoted to writing about his philosophy, which held that every man was made up of three different men who did not understand one another. One of his works is to be published this winter in New York.

Mr. Gurdjieff was born in Alexandrople, in the Caucasus. He described himself as of Greek ancestry and told interviewers that he had been trained for medicine and the priesthood. He said also he was a survivor of a group of archaeologists, explorers and philologists who traveled through Tibet in the early Eighteen Eighties and learned much concerning early teachings about man's inner life.

(Above) Pall-bearers Dr. Michel de Salzmann and Valentin Anastasieff.(Left)

(Left and below) Russian priests officiate.

Gurdjieff's funeral at the Russian Orthodox church on the rue Daru

In the church:
(Above, detail at right)
Mme. de Salzmann

The casket and flowers.

(Left) Dushka and Alfred
       (Right) Exiting the church.
(Below)
**The cortege gathers for
the trip to the cemetery
in Fontainebleau.**
 Dushka (Below left) in her
light-colored spring coat.

The Fontainebleau cemetery: Following the hearse ...

(Above) Approaching the gravesite....   The final ceremonies....   Mme. de Salzmann with
(Below) Laid to rest!   her daughter and son.

The Gurdjieff family grave in the Fontainebleau cemetery

This earliest photo of the family gravesite was apparently taken in 1924 when Gurdjieff's mother died. There is only a single dolmen gravestone arround which the children of the family are gathered (probably after an Orthodox church service since her granddaughter Julia, third from left, is still holding a handful of half burnt candles.) But notice that there is an inscription carved on the stone (and later removed, when? by whom? Gurdjieff himself?) which translated from the French reads: (See detail at right.) "**Here rests the mother of he who finds himself forced by this death to write the book entitled "*The Opiumists.*"** (Might this be "***The Cocainists***" referred to in the ***Herald of Coming Good***?)

A photo taken a few years later shows a large dolmen-like stone without adornment or identification (added in 1925 when Gurdjieff's wife died?) facing the one over his mother's grave (and the original orientation of the grave has been turned to accomodate it.) The stone bench remains and the small tree planted behind it begins to show itself.

(Above) Another early photo shows Katherine Mansfield's headstone in left forground. (Below and right) The site as it is today ...

...now over-shadowed by a large, almost ninety-year-old tree.

November 6, 1949,

Belfast Hotel,

Dear Mrs. Howarth.

I am writing this in Paris at a spare moment because I think you will be interested to hear someone's account of the movements class here on Friday, the first meeting of people together for 10 days or so.

I'm sure that Mme. de Salzmann, who started the class with a silence, chose numbers which Mr. G. most often asked for and liked to see. They were these and roughly in the following order.

French No.	17	Multiplication 2 1/2 times through
	19	Clock
	11	Seigneur ayé pitié
	2	Prayer first part, turning, quick, Intermed. quick, turning, quick, fourth part, quick.
	32	Note values
	5	Pointing
	39	The last movement he gave
	1	Automat
	36	(which I didn't know)
	6	The Cross, for a long time
	3	Three tableaux
	4	1 hup
	18	for a very long time
	38	which I didn't know

Arms out sideways, in which the spectators joined.

It was a very ragged performance, of course hardly anyone had had much sleep or been leading their normal lives...but it showed.

At Madame de S.'s beginners class yesterday, there was a much stronger and exceptional level of attention, which, although the work she gave was very simple, produced a remarkable effect on everybody.

I have got [Emil] Hana to show me 36 and 38 and it seems to me that 36 is a particularly good "dervish," one which you would like to see done as you tried to get us to do the old dervish movements.

Sophie went back to England with Alfred today and looks forward to seeing you about November 25th in N.Y.

Yrs,

Pentland"

* * * * *

CHAPTER 22

NEW BEGINNINGS, RECORDING G.'S HARMONIUM MUSIC

"Music alone cannot separate the whole of our unconscious automatism, but it is one of the aids to this." (G.I. Gurdjieff, 1923)

Dushka
♦

In the autumn of 1949 Ethel Merston wrote to Mother from Sri Ramanasram, India:

"Jessmin dear,

Thank you for Ouspensky's *Fragments* just arrived. I am so grateful and a little conscience-stricken for it cost, I see, the "eyes of the head." I fear that you will have deprived yourself of some necessity to get it for me. I've dipped into it already and it is truly a monumental work and testament to G., and invaluable. What reviews has it had? How much will the teaching be accepted?

Here things are, I think, coming to an end. The Maharshi has a fresh tumor above the old wound not yet healed, and this is to be reoperated tomorrow. His general condition is so poor that there is little hope for any permanent recovery and I, for one, hope that he may quickly pass before the lungs or heart are affected and the body has to suffer tortures. This is purely selfish because it is awful to see anyone suffering daily and hourly before one's eyes and be unable to do anything – let alone one's Teacher.

What makes me think that he will leave soon is that Chadwick and I, both in Madras, and an Indian devotee living there, all three dreamt at the same hour, the same morning, that he had departed. Since it did not actually materialize then, I think it may have been a sign. There has been a general refusal to face his condition. He himself is completely serene, though weaker.

The five days in Madras, three at a hotel with Chadwick and two with the Raos, were a real sadhana [walk of self-observation.] Chadwick went in for the dentist, and I got too tired, combining my necessary shopping with his various wishes, really to enjoy it. He did though. Which was a pat on my back that I had managed to keep detached enough not to be cross or answer back when he blamed me for this, that or the other. He was very sweet and concerned about me but I realized that I am not cut out for a life "à deux," and am thankful that I don't have to cater to a husband.

I'll write again when anything new, one way or the other, happens here.

Yours ever,

Ethel"

[The Ramana Maharshi, after several other unsuccessful operations, died quietly April 9, 1950.]

◆◆◆

New York, March, 1950   **Jessmin**

Dear Ethel,   ◆

    Jeanne de Salzmann did come over and stayed until February tenth. She set herself the task of raising several thousand dollars to pay for the further expenses of publishing the books, making records of Mr. G.'s harmonium and the piano music, and preparing to give the Movements demonstrations that Mr. G. wished. It is all very hard.

    Mr. G. had arranged nothing in regard to his money affairs. Everything available went to the family (who aren't at all interested, much less knowledgeable about the "Ideas"). It is fortunate that his sister does not distrust Jeanne too much and allows her a certain freedom about what is necessary for the continuation of Mr. G.'s work. Jeanne managed to see everyone and talked often and at length with Madame Ouspensky. She succeeds very well with people about material things. She had hoped to bring about some working arrangement whereby the New York and Mendham groups would combine under Mme. O.'s eye until, if ever, she can complete her tasks as administrator and travel around to inspire and hold things together.

    It did not work. Mme. O. says it was not realistic to expect people to come and be willing to learn anything from her when they don't really trust her, and when she only has strength to see very few people and now has near her no people prepared enough to act as her intermediaries.

    But, more than that, most of the New York people, like the Nylands, Wolfes etc., seem to me to take their "positions" too literally. (After all, Dushka's "position" is that of "Head of the Work in England.") Mme. O thinks of the tasks and titles handed out by Mr. G. as "pegs to hang one's own work on," while the others are convinced that the last phase of Mr. G.'s teaching, i.e. the new Movements and the "inner work" (more or less exercises of "meditation" which only Jeanne can now give), have taken place of and cancel out, all other work on attention. So they feel that they have understood Mr. G. better, and that conditions like those at Mendham are no longer necessary.

    One cannot deny that Mme. O. is, at times, a hard taskmaster. She says her time is so short that she can only help by "beating." Some find this cruel, but, for my part, she has never rebuked me when it was not entirely deserved.

    If the whole of the work and teaching does not become distorted at once here, it will be, I believe, because Mme. O. is here as a touchstone. She will always fight for her Credo. After some weeks of confusion and self-searching, I think I begin to see her line. It is this, perhaps. There is and can be no one who can now fill Mr. G.'s place. Each of us can only continue with his own work. If this work has been with people, then it continues with people. But to imagine that we are ready to put through immediately all Mr. G.'s grandiose schemes for huge book distributions, public readings, Movements demonstrations in many countries, and concerts of his music, may lead to just exhausting ourselves in outside activity and not truly studying to represent Mr. G.'s teaching.

    This does not mean that Mme. O. does not see and understand what Jeanne feels she must do. Certainly she will help her in every way she can to accomplish what she was charged to do. However, she advises all her own pupils to act only after serious thought, to remember that we now have the books as tools, but that any new people we bring in now cannot be promised a real Teacher, but must be able to study the books and work for themselves. A few of the older ones must be content for now to try to understand and guard the ideas from wrong interpretation and too easy and casual dissemination.

Jeanne is at the start of a long job and will carry a great deal of it through. She has been honest and kind in trying to help all Mr. G.'s dependents (in all senses) and former followers. And Mme. O., as always, is carrying her part.

While she was here, Jeanne played for nearly all my classes which was like manna from heaven. She took very little responsibility for criticizing or suggesting anything to me. She did see, however, that all the Movements and the music for them must be, so to speak, "officially" set so that they can be taught everywhere in the same way. So since returning to Paris she has been working on this with Alfred and some of the older pupils.

De Hartmann had already started composing while Jeanne was here, as Mr. G., when he was in hospital, had left a message that M. de Hartmann could help by making music for these newer Movements "which any idiot could play." Some of this new music has been sent to me and I find it very disappointing, scraps of Balinese, Chinese and Middle-Eastern themes, somehow too "ethnic" or "literary" for the pure abstract Movements Mr. G. had been teaching in those last years. The worst of it is that people will adhere to these short indications for each exercise from now on, play them ad infinitum, regarding them as gospel, and never be capable of or willing to try to develop them somehow.

Besides this, Jeanne and Carol Robinson have made a number of recordings of Mr. G.'s music for piano and these will be sold when the copyright has gone through. Dushka is to be in charge of their distribution. She has also been busy having copies made of all the music Mr. G played on his hand harmonium during the last year, that he ordered her to record on tape. These she feels are not well recorded. Already, after a few months, much better machines than the ones she had to use are now available and would have made a great difference to the quality of the sound.

◆ ◆ ◆

Dushka
◆

Naturally I have always regretted that the recordings I made of Mr. G. in Paris, every day after lunch and dinner, weren't of better technical quality.

I was an amateur but did my best. We had brought to France three machines, (two Brush tape recorders and one wire one) which were apparently, in 1949, the first magnetic recorders anyone had seen in Europe so I could find no one who had the experience to service them. I soon gave up on the wire. It would tangle up in a metal ball and couldn't be rewound or mended. But when even the better of the two tape machines began to have difficulties, I asked around until someone suggested that the Radio Diffusion engineers might be able to repair it.

Putting in an empty tape to be used for testing, I lugged the heavy suitcase-sized recorder to the studios.

Several days later I was summoned to pick it up. Various engineers had tried and failed to correct the problems, but one of them had evidently been unable to resist this new toy and had taken it home with him. The test tape was filled with French comments, laughter, a "*grandmère's*" story, a toddler's singing, and so on.

(Above) One of the Brush tape recorders purchased in New York and taken to Paris so that Dushka could record Mr. Gurdjieff's daily harmonium playing.
(Right) Gurdjieff's harmonium (with his fez and glasses.)

Afghan musicians practicing on traditional instruments (a harmonium at right) in "an unheated room in Kabul."

Holy woman "Amma" (Mata Amritanandamaya) with a harmonium common in India.

I finally diagnosed for myself one of the reasons for the poor quality and fluttering vibrations. The felt pad which presses the tape to the recording head was almost worn through.

Since new empty tapes were taking so long to come from New York, Michel had offered to drive me to Brussels, one of the few places in Europe where such things might be bought. Someone suggested that the special carpet factories there might also provide the extra-fine type of felt I needed for the repair.

What we were able to find helped only temporarily and would wear out again in less than a half-hour. So, from then on, twice a day, before each lunch and dinner, I had to cut out a tiny square of felt and glue it on — in time to dry — with enough glue to hold — but not so much that it would soak through and stiffen the pad —and then hope that Mr. G. wasn't inspired to play more than the safe twenty to thirty minutes. When he did, the music gradually acquired an increasing vibrato as the tape got looser against the head. I'm sad that later generations of listeners seem to love just that effect and react emotionally to the flutter with ecstatic sighs or tears, while, I'm afraid, I just glower at them.

An additional problem was that the apartment at 6 rue des Colonels Renard,

The elevator at rue des Colonels Renard
(Photo: G-J Blom)

was in a very old building and the rickety elevator rarely worked. When it did, it drew off so much electricity that my recorder would slow down. So I was never sure when Mr. G. finished playing and asked, as he usually did, to hear it played back, whether there might not be a sudden burst of speeded up tinkling. At this point, of course, all the listeners' soulfully closed eyes would pop open to glare at me as if I had done it intentionally.

At times, in fact, nothing recorded at all, and while everyone waited I would hurriedly sneak on a tape from another day and pretend it was the playback. Nobody else ever noticed, I don't think, but I often wondered if Mr. G.'s usual "Bravo, Sophie!" wasn't sometimes ironic.

In her *Diary of Madame Egout Pour Sweet:* Rina Hands writes that:

"His devotion to Sophia is lovely to see — she is Directeur Music and each night before going home has played us some of his music recorded on the "wire." Often it ends with him exclaiming, "Bravo, Sophy — for this I show you genuine forged thousand franc note!" To which she replies, "Oh, that's all right — I've got one too!"

In *Idiots in Paris* Elizabeth Bennett quotes Jeanne de Salzmann as saying:

"...If we read and understand the chapter on the Law of Seven, [in *Fragments*] we will understand also about his music. It is all concerned with the octave. By *'clef'* he does not mean what is meant in ordinary music. This has great significance for him and the movements also are based on this same octave. Sophia knows a lot about ordinary music but she does not understand the Law of Octaves. So when he tells her to play two pieces of music, each in a different key, she sometimes fails to do what he wants, and he tells her that it is the same key, and to him it is, though to her understanding it is quite different."

I finally left Europe at the end of 1949. I sailed on the *Queen Elizabeth* from Southampton so as to join Mme. de Salzmann, Lise Tracol, Cynthia Pearce and Bernard LeMaitre who had boarded the ship in France. Jeanne asked me to include in my own baggage a huge footlocker containing the whole collection of recorded harmonium tapes. They had a plan to edit them and make some recordings to sell as part of the funding for the publication of Mr. G.'s books.

So on arrival in New York, I guess I wasn't quite honest when the Customs man asked me if I had anything "commercial" to declare and I answered: "No! Nothing!" Of course, just that big footlocker was the one the official noticed and demanded to have opened. His shocked reaction and angry: "What the H— are those?" when he saw a couple of hundred tapes made me realize I was in real trouble. I desperately sought for a way out.

Then I had a flash of inspiration and putting on an injured, vapid expression said: "Well... you know... er... I spent this whole year in Paris studying singing... and I worked very hard... but my mother just wouldn't believe I wasn't fooling around over there... So to prove to her that I was seriously working and doing my practicing... every day when I did my vocal exercises I recorded them. Would you like to hear?"

He quickly slammed down the lid and waved me on through!

Aboard the *Queen Elizabeth* sailing to New York, 1949 (Left to right) Dushka, Cynthia Pearce, Lise Tracol, Mme. de Salzmann and Bernard LeMaitre.

◆ ◆ ◆

Dear Ethel,

Jessmin

◆

Before Jeanne sailed home, Mme. O. told her that the New York and Mendham groups must be separate and Jeanne agreed. Maybe they both think that the New York leaders will eventually feel a need and draw near to Franklin Farms of their own volition.

I was bitterly disappointed at this at first, but now begin to see many constructive possibilities in this arrangement. However it did make one thing impossible for me. Jeanne had spoken of my going to Paris for a month or so to work with her on setting the Movements and music. I need the new impressions very badly but there is no one here to take over. Certainly Dushka and Boussik (as we call Jeanne's daughter Nathalie) could have held the Movements classes together very well under normal circumstances, but the separation of the groups made everything too complicated. The New York people were delighted to have Boussik and though she reveres Mme. O., she could not help but feel that they were closer to her mother and to the recent teaching she had had herself. And Dushka felt the opposite. So, though I can't pretend to be impartial myself, I felt that, by staying put I could help them to be.

But I realized that my vanity was really very hurt being shown that New York people who had learnt Movements from me since 1925 might be ready to be rid of me. I asked Mme. O. whether she thought I should stop taking those classes, and she answered: "Nu! Already with first unpleasantness you give up. What you think

Jeanne Yulovna and I must bear? I advise you wait until she makes such decision. And you, ask yourself whether something wrong with your way of teaching."

There are only about twenty pupils in New York, most of them elderly. They work faithfully twice a week. I thought I was trying to help them understand the Movements as a means, and to know how to use them for their own self-study. Also, to get them to develop a group spirit so as to be responsible for their own organization and to contribute money in order to pay for a hall and a pianist.

Weeks pass by and Mendham is in a strange state of suspense. The house is dreadfully short-handed and Mme. O. tries to run it on about $300 a month, all she can count on regularly.

At least the weekends have been full of life with Lonia and Dushka taking some part in things, and Boussik and her family there.

One amusing scene was when Mme. O. asked Dushka to think what kind of presents should be given to Boussik's children, Anne Marie, Serge and Olivier. Dushka suggested kittens or puppies (she probably would have liked to have one herself), but Mme., who had been lying limply in bed, at once reared up and exclaimed: "I not allow!" Later it was understood that she had foreseen that the little animals would be spoilt over the weekends, then left out there, and probably neglected, when the family went back to the city during the week.

It now appears that Boussik will go to Venezuela for a time. Alfred's younger brother, Jacques Etievant, is there in Caracas.

As for the "calves," they have scattered. Petey, in a very unsettled state was invited to Jamaica in the West Indies by Anci Dupré, one of Jeanne's rich Paris friends whose husband, Francois, owns the George V and other hotels. Lise is teaching with Iovanna at Taliesin West, the Frank Lloyd Wright Fellowship in Arizona. Marian Sutta has gone back to college. Tania has been doing a lot of riding but has just had a fall from her horse and is in bed with a concussion. She hasn't settled back into any kind of married life with Tom Forman, whom, as a youngster, she was crazy about and to whom Mme. O. had her married as a "safeguard" before she went off to Paris.

Dushka is still suffering from the low emotional state that I'm told is usual after a case of jaundice, and there was not only the shock of Mr. G.'s death, but also her separation from and uncertainty about, Alfred.

From much that has been reported to me I understand that Mr. G. wished her not to "drift" any longer and suggested marriage, any marriage, as a way of gaining stability. She sees this, but I'm afraid the "engagement" to Alfred won't be the answer. He is working well, at last, in London, and she could, he says, help him there. But despite difficult conditions here, she seems in no way tempted to return to England.

She finished the tape recordings by working long hours before Jeanne left. She has a good relationship with Jeanne who seems to trust her honesty and common sense and enjoy her company. She has also been trying hard to find a job. We all want to help her to take time so as to go into an organization and work her way up since she has no wish to return to the kind of unsatisfying independent work she tired herself out with before. She may be hired by the new Butlin's Holiday Camp which is to open soon in the Bahamas. She has a champion in Keith Thorburn, Butlin's Chairman of the Board whom she met at Mr. G.'s apartment, and he arranged a successful meeting for her.

Dushka
♦

◆◆◆

The good impression I made on Mr. "Billy" Butlin during that meeting was certainly helped by a lucky coincidence.

My first personal contact with him was when he stopped off in New York on his way to the islands. He suggested that we talk over lunch at the Twenty-One Club. This is a most exclusive celebrity hangout, and never having been there in my life, I was feeling a bit intimidated as we approached the entrance. But as luck would have it, one of the brothers who own it was standing by the door, and as we entered he greeted me effusively saying: "Oh, we haven't seen you in far too long!" I managed to carry off an airy: "Oh, yes... well... I've been very busy." I've never known who I was mistaken for, or if it was just the charm ploy of a clever proprietor, but Butlin was obviously impressed and immediately invited me to join his staff as a management trainee.

Unfortunately, the Butlin holiday formula so long successful in Europe didn't export well. In spite of considerable advance publicity including a *Life Magazine* cover story, something — the place itself, the folksy entertainment style, or the English food — failed to thrill American vacationers, and the project was closed before I could use the plane ticket they sent me. Someone else ultimately took over the new buildings and converted them into a luxury hotel.

◆◆◆

Jessmin
♦

Dear Ethel,

Mme. O. has been very kind to Dushka and welcomes her to her house insisting that Lonia has benefited from her companionship although they fight good-naturedly most of the time. He was feeling soured about the New York group's attitude towards his grandmother and it has done him good to try to be brotherly to someone. He and Tania aren't close.

I often wonder how much Mme. O., Jeanne, and Olgivanna are counting on Lonia, Michel and Boussik, and Iovanna to become leaders of the Work. I make it quite clear that I have no illusions about myself and about Dushka. We hope to remain friends with the mighty but are not convinced that we should try to join the hierarchy!

My heart is sore for Mme. having to pass her last days among such stupid and provincial-minded, unprepared people. The old pupils, from Lyne, etc., have little clear-sightedness about their motives, and she says they are endlessly playing a game of "musical chairs" in their efforts to "help the Work."

I'm mailing you a copy of Mr. G.'s book at last. What will be your impression to see *All and Everything* compressed into this small package of dynamite?

Mme. O. likes to hear from you and about you. Jeanne says she has the Maharshi's writings: "...but it isn't for her now."

By the way, Krishnamurti will be in New York in June lecturing on Sundays.

J̲

＊ ＊ ＊ ＊ ＊

CHAPTER 23

BOOKS, MENDHAM, 1950 DEMONSTRATION

Jessmin
♦

New York, May 16, 1950

Dear Ethel,

At the moment, with the onset of summer heat, groups are breaking up little by little, people going out of town, and the most active work on publicizing the books slackening off. I will try to get you copies of the few good reviews there have been. In some ways there seems to have been a conspiracy of silence. However, it is much more likely that the ordinary reviewer cannot read *Beelzebub*. As you say, this needs special preparation, or a special "magnetic center."

I suspect that the gap between Jeanne's and Mme. Ouspensky's points of view as to how to continue the work Mr. G. began, is gradually lessening. The books, the Movements, the music, and the "inner exercises" exist. What is lacking are people with "Being" to continue to sow the seed rightly, while reaping the results of Mr. G.'s fifty years of work, and the Ouspenskys' cultivation.

We have been shown that there is a purpose for man's existence but that he does not fulfill it. That being felt, there is no choice. Each for himself has to try to go on. But, as for guiding others, leading a popular movement, making a big splurge with Movement demonstrations, etc. there seems no one with the force and knowledge to do this.

Mme. O. is much less well lately. It is pathetic to see that both her English doctor and dentist, whom she learned to trust through the years, can pass through New York and never attempt to see and help her. Because, they believe, Mr. Ouspensky did not wish his pupils to be brought into contact again with Mr. G. or anyone believing in him! So she is not rightly cared for and is surrounded by very insufficiently developed people.

Jeanne, as you saw from the picture I sent you, is still very forceful and never spares herself. But she, also, is not strong, and she is the type who has to make her mistakes first and then remedy afterwards any hasty moves or too "considerate" an approach to people who need the truth hammered into them.

Olgivanna still cherishes her eighty-three-year-old husband and is startlingly young and identified in certain aspects of work organization.

Bennett makes things too easy.

The others, I feel, except for Dr. Nicoll, do not connect the everyday efforts and experiments sufficiently with the higher aspects and the aims that lift us.

No one else can, like Madame, relate the smallest household happening, the pettiest personal matter, directly to higher aim and basic principle. I have been real-izing all these last weeks in seeing her, what a stupid child I am in the Work and how un-alive, how intermittent, how "waterlogged" is my wish to hold on to the pos-sibility of growing somewhat more conscious, less mechanical.

I am sorry in some ways that Fate places me in the position of Movements teacher. By default I continue. I mean that there are just not enough people yet to teach the Movements other than as gymnastics. But my vitality is low, I am starved for impressions, and every lesson is a hill to climb. I do not find enough in myself to give.

But somehow we must continue until Jeanne can come in September, (I hope). Then we must see what can be done. I am punished every day for my inadequacy. Now, if ever, someone with more real weight could have helped. But I do see my level and shall not allow myself to be raised above it either through self-blinding or the necessities of the situation.

For June, Dushka and I remain in N.Y. with weekends at Mendham. Perhaps, thanks to you, we can go away a little in August. Where does not matter to me. I just need to see different surroundings and people for a while. Dushka "pants for cooling streams."

Much love from us both...

Jessmin

July:

The reviews of Mr. Ouspensky's book are very conflicting. Another attempt to publicize Mr. G.'s work has appeared in a big, so-called trade magazine, *American Fabrics*, a rather ambitious publication distributed mainly to fabric designers, cou-turiers, and interior designers. The publisher, Bill Segal, and his wife Cora are pupils and have printed in it several short extracts from *All and Everything*, hoping to interest some of their business acquaintances. This seems rather shocking, but is said to be in line with Mr. G.'s oft-repeated wish to "cast the net wide."

Mme. O gave me her last letter from Jeanne in which she speaks very seriously about her firm determination to prevent any distortion of Mr. G.'s work. She has many dependable pupils in Paris who will help her go ahead with plans for showing the Movements, in England first, in a small way, in order to see whether demonstra-tions will be feasible (using eight of her Paris pupils and the best of Alfred's London ones.)

She is putting all the Movement music, the Obligatories, etc. and M. de Hartmann's fabrications for what are called the Thirty-Nine, on sale everywhere, priced very modestly. She adds that she must work without break this summer on making more records and publishing more of Mr. G.'s music. Then she, and the de Hartmanns who are expected to visit Olgivanna for several months, should arrive in America at the beginning of October.

I do not agree with your London friend that the records of Mr. G.'s music are "awful." He dictated dozens of pieces that are perfectly well rendered on the piano. It is true that, as always in this work, somehow, those who knew the most in a pro-fessional way about recording were not given this task. And it is a pity that, although this was supposed to be her function, Carol Robinson was allotted the Movements music where her pianist's touch and technique is hardly needed and which she finds difficult since she has nothing like the instinctive body rhythm that is such a feature of Jeanne's playing.

I think the English people who used to go over to Paris liked to hear Mr. G.'s music on his harmonium. About this, I have mixed reactions. One listened to it quite differently in those days, but unless one took care it could become very soporific. It was usually played late at night when many people had drunk too much, and they have associations with released emotions. They are trying to persuade M. de Hartmann to edit the hundred or so tapes Dushka made during the months she was in Paris. But I cringe to think of records being perpetuated from these.

Iovanna has been here for three days and also for two at Mendham. I have passed half of each day coaching her on the Movements. She is a good and modest child considering the pampering she has had. Olgivanna is still the dominant person and

Jessmin at Franklin Farms in Mendham, N.J. appreciating the country air.

Iovanna quotes her mother continuously. They both urge me to leave the present set-up and go to them. They feel that people at Mendham have been crystallized and have no freedom of expression. They believe that they are working more as Mr. G. would wish. Perhaps so. Their young people need to work hard and play hard; and they are all, supposedly, craftsmen whose everyday interest is in "creating" with materials. There is no play and no skill in crafts at Franklin Farms. People are older, less impressed by artistic personalities, and duller by temperament, perhaps, partly, because they drudge and have only slightly varying conditions from month to month.

New York teaching is reduced to four evenings a week. Soon I shall go out to Long Island for two or three days to give lessons to people from the New York groups who are making a communal experiment in a large house belonging to someone's aunt.

Yes! I went to hear Krishnamurti in New York with Dushka. (It was a talk on "a quiet mind.") He was constantly heckled by strangers in the audience who do not understand his way of expounding through asking rhetorical questions. Each, in turn, would leap up to give an answer, using his own language of Zen, Vedanta, etc. The conditions were difficult; ugly hall, bad amplifying system, very hot, humid afternoon. Krishnaji himself looked nervous and tense and less detached. Some people described him as "querulous." But his mental processes are very clear, much more so than I remember. He communicates his ideas with more facility than when he was younger and almost embarrassingly poetic.

Dushka and I went round trustfully to speak to him having often met him in Ojai and Los Angeles, and of course, with you at Ommen. Dushka wanted to ask him about the daughter of his secretary Rajagopal, who was her playmate in California. But he seemed to be cowering against a back wall and unwilling to talk to anyone. So we just greeted him and left, disappointed.

I remember Mr. Ouspensky saying how he was drawn to Krishnamurti, that he "was Number Five man without having had to live the existences of Man One, Two and Three." And he added that the relationship they could have had together was spoilt by their pupils, "more Royalist than the King."

Mme. Ouspensky feels compassion for him, feeling that he was put through so much conditioning by Mrs. Besant, his English education, etc. She wondered if he would not have been supported by a stage with an Indian teacher.

Krishnaji onstage in Carnegie Hall.

What K. says does not really conflict with what we are aiming to become. I'm convinced that he is a higher Being and can touch some people directly. He has perception through the emotions and the years seem to have strengthened his opinion that it is only through the emotions that one can open up to an understanding of truth. He decries what he calls "effort" and tries to break down people's identification with words. It is as if he accepts that only a very few of those who listen to him can comprehend. And he lets the others go, except for warning them against methods and "gurus."

Krishnamurti once watched a Movements class at Lyne and afterwards asked me what the pupils were doing "here," pointing at his forehead. I made the mistake of saying (I really should have remembered his different way of using the word) that: "they were making an effort at attention." At the word "effort" he closed up and turned away.

In a way, although he gives much time to personal interviews, he has chosen an easier way than to let people be dependent on his constant help and advice. I feel that all he says is "Truth," but I know from talks with friends from the Geneva days that many of his listeners can be led to imagination and "self-calming."

◆◆◆

Years after his death, Jiddu Krishnamurti could be seen on television every week (at least in our part of the country). There is an avid audience for the video-tapes which were made of his talks in his later years, out under the trees in Ojai, California, at the Brockwood Park Educational Center in England, at the Rishi School in Andhra Pradesh, India, and in various television studios, (usually interviewed by professors of philosophy or religion like David Bohm, Jacob Needleman, and Allen W. Anderson.)

Dushka

◆

Just recently I heard an interviewer ask him: "It seems to me that you're saying something like this: That the key to doing this is a radical reversal in our point of view. It is as though we are prisoners straining at the (window) bars for the light, looking at the glimpse of light we see out there and wondering how we can get out towards it... while actually the door of the cell is open behind us. If only we would turn around, we could walk out into freedom. This is what it sounds like to me you are saying. Is it?"

Krishnamurti answers kindly: "A little bit. A little bit. Surely, Sir, in this is involved the everlasting struggle... conflict... Man caught in his own conditioning... and straining... struggling... beating his head to be free... So... Again we have accepted, with the help of religions and all the rest, that 'effort' is necessary, that it is part of life. To me, that is the highest form of blindness, of limiting man, to say that you must everlastingly live 'in effort.' But to live without effort requires the greatest sensitivity and the highest form of intelligence. You don't just say: 'Well, I won't struggle' and become like a cow. One has to understand how conflict arises... the duality in us... the fact of what is and what should be... Can we live in a different way...?"

Unlike Mr. Gurdjieff, (as well as Rajneesh/Osho, and many others), Krishnamurti didn't often tell stories and anecdotes to illustrate his points, but I remember one that he told years ago that I have often used. I say "used" because I find that I can usually guess the mindset or prejudices of new acquaintances by their reaction to this little tale:

"One day the Devil brought a friend down to Earth to show him around. He pointed out the varied landscapes and crowds of busy people. And the friend noticed that the ground glittered, covered everywhere with something bright. People hurrying by would pick up a shining piece and put it in their pocket.

"The friend asked the Devil: 'What is it that they are picking up?' The Devil answered: 'Oh, it's pieces of the Truth. It lies around everywhere.' The friend, amazed, exclaimed: 'But to just let them find it and take it like that. Isn't that very bad for your business?' The Devil shrugged: 'They're welcome to it. I'll only get involved when they start organizing it!'"

In her later years, especially when I was away in Paris or working on the cruise ships, Mother often spent her summer break in Switzerland. She was refreshed by the cool, mountain air, the off-season hotel rates, and, especially, the series of talks that Krishnamurti gave in Saanen, in a large tent erected in an open field. Sometimes I would join her, (though the grey and quiet that she so enjoyed soon palled for me... I preferred the baking heat and excitement of Greece). Amongst K's listeners I would recognize familiar faces from the Gurdjieff groups in New York, London or Paris. Even Mme. de Salzmann who usually vacationed in Crans, a long drive away around the mountains, was often there, Lord Pentland, Pamela Travers and others. It always interested me that although, as far as I know, Krishnamurti never referred to Gurdjieff (unlike Rajneesh who constantly quoted him), it was "Work" people whose questions he answered. It was as if he recognized the preparation, the personal commitment, something serious that separated them out from his other "hangers-on," whose questions he would listen to patiently, and then just say: "Next!"

One summer I traveled over with Mother and we stopped off in Paris on the way. I was suffering from a very painful, swollen foot and finally had to seek out a French doctor. I was surprised and rather humiliated when he diagnosed it as "gout" but I took the pills he gave me and the advice that, in spite of the pain, I could walk on it. After a few days we continued on to Switzerland and Mother's favorite Hotel Olden in Gstaad. The next morning, barely in time for the first Krishnamurti talk we rushed across the big field to the tent. That was just too much for my foot, and two brawny men had to help lift me up the steps to reach our seats. Apparently my problem was not gout at all, but an infection which finally opened and drained so that at the end of the hour's talk I walked out easily, ninety-percent recovered.

Ever after that I was pointed out with whispers and awed stares, Krishnamurti had "healed" me!

Poor man. It was just the kind of thing I knew he hated and tried to avoid.

◆ ◆ ◆

New York, July, 1950   **Jessmin**

Dear Ethel,   ◆

At Mendham we are now reading Mr. O.'s *Questions and Answers* written down in group meetings dating from 1922. They are very interesting indeed, a fund of material, almost more than *Fragments*. Perhaps much of it can soon be collated, indexed and printed. With it, Dr. Nicoll's *Commentaries*, and Solita Solano's diaries of those intimate Paris groups, plenty of documentation exists. There are scores of Movements too, besides what we have learnt here recently.

Jeanne has a whole series of "inner exercises" that she said she would share with me; but I don't seem to have any right sensitivity about them.

Also it is rumored that, when he was dying, Mr. G. gave Jeanne the names of "Teachers." This is spread about by the same people who say that Mr. G. was too ill to know what he was saying to her. They forget that he had been closely preparing Jeanne since years.

Well! "Everything comes to him who waits," it is said. And now it has come about that the New York groups have at last made a move toward Mme. O.

But "everything" can't come, for in the last few months she has become progressively more frail. She still has a keen eye and power when she speaks, but she easily and suddenly tires. She is a very modest old lady, and I'm afraid she "considers" a little for she will not face seeing anyone new, being shy about lying in bed and restricted in her movements.

This is very sad, for some people have worked conscientiously at Franklin Farms for years now, including a few from New York, and they have never laid eyes on her. She is informed about everything that goes on, by at least five or six people, and she sifts what they report according to what she knows about their characteristics. There is an emanation from her room, and her presence, though unseen, is felt.

So it is a pity that it is so late.

The Nylands and Mrs. Benson, with Peggy Flinsch asked me to go over to Brewster (where the Nylands have remodeled and built onto a house). They told me they wanted me to take a message to Mme. O.

After much thought and discussion it was this: They wished, for the Work's sake, to "cooperate with Mendham."

I told Mme. and her immediate answer was such that I burst out laughing. After all the preamble that we had gone through preparing the message, Mme. only said: "How?"

Naturally, she scolded me for my reaction and said: "*Nu*! What more necessary to say? We are not Royal Families sending diplomats to each other."

It seems that she will prepare a message and tell them they are welcome in her house at any time. But she warns us that she cannot consider meeting any of them.

So... it's up to ourselves!

◆ ◆ ◆

In the summer of 1950, Mme. de Salzmann wrote to Dr. Maurice Nicoll: **Dushka**

"...I happen to read two of your books, *Commentaries about Mr. G.'s Teaching*.   ◆

I give them a big value as the ideas are exposed in the genuine order in which they

Tom Forman, editor

Martin Benson, farm manager

Christopher Fremantle, painter

Blanche Rosette reads Walker's book

...and invites the Whitcombs, Donald and Lillian (left) to Woodstock.

Visiting the Suttas in nearby Farmingdale, New Jersey. (Left to right) Nancy Pearson, Maurice Sutta, Mme. de Hartmann, Martin Benson, Dr. Ralph Phillips, Jessmin. and Lord Pentland.

Christmas dinner at Franklin Farms in Mendham, N.J.

(Left to right) Mme Lannes, Lenushka Savitsky (Mme. Ouspensky's daughter), and the de Hartmanns.

Mme. de Hartman teases Lord Pentland.

M. de Hartmann plays Gurdjieff's piano pieces

Beatrice (Mrs. Frank Sinclair) Rego with puppets used to entertain the children.

Baroness Bissing tells stories of her huband and "the Kaiser"!

Barbara Mills (Wheeler) helps Mary Sinclair (Rothenberg).

...while Alfred Etievant chats with radio director Edwin Wolfe (Right).

Henriette Lannes and Tom Forman chat...

.... and open presents.

Nancy Pearson oversees
work in the kitchen

Dorothy Darlington runs
errands for Madame O.

Ronny Bissing discusses plans and makes lists with Mrs.
Howarth (reflected in the mirror).

Daphne Ripman acts as one
of the hostesses......

....and then volunteers as waitress
while Lady Pentland (Left) serves.

(Above) Henri Tracol and Mme. de Hartmann
send their old friend Mme. Ouspensky this
photo of them both relaxing in a Paris cafe,
writing on the back: "OUR WORK!"

were given out with the exact formulation without any distortion. The ideas-system appears so clear and understandable for everyone. For me, it goes side by side with Mr. Ouspensky's *Fragments.*

I will be very grateful to you if you could let me have your books so that I could read them to the group in Paris. I understand that the number is limited and I will be too happy to contribute to the expenses.

I am in London for about ten days. I wish to shew [sic] to a certain number of people the Movements Mr. G. has given in the last two years. They are really very exceptional. If you will be interested to see them and if you wish to bring some people with you, I will be very glad to see you. It takes place at Colet Gardens, the 10th of July, at 8.30 evening.

Sincerely yours,

J. de Salzmann"

Alfred was still living and working at Colet Gardens and wrote to me in New York about all this in his own special few-months-old English!:
"Ma chère Sophie,

"As I say in my previous letter, my classes are finish now for five weeks and I am preparing my voyage to France. I had some plans to go to southfrance or to the seaside but I don't think I will be able to do it for many reasons the first beeing the necessity to spare some money.

"I must say about money how much I would like to spend it for a nice wife and a home. I have lived here during that long time I haven't seen you, as a poor soul, bored to death, without "refuge" and nowhere to put one's head except this strange enormous house which I like as much as I hate it. I have a sort of impression that a time is over and I look forward for new things to happen. I must tell you frankly that I have been a littel (sic) desperate about us both, but now I have a new hope and all my thoughts are turned in a different way.

"To talk to you about my life here, the first thing will be Movements. As you surely know everything about it, I will try to say something you haven't yet heard. I know that will be difficult because I have noticed that there is a terrific Intelligence service, people writing to others about events even before they happen, spraying all news at a fantastic speed.

"We had, during the time that Mme. de Salzmannn has been here, a very good fortnight. The most important fact for the 'masses,' I would say, the most visible, has been the demonstration of Movements, which has been very useful on many points of view.

"First, it has shown us the power of the Movements that we didn't imagine. The fact that they were put before 'life' that is to say, before an audience without any relation with our work — instead to weaken them, to expose them has made them stronger. We have seen that they really were a powerful instrument that couldn't leave people indifferent.

"It has been very interesting for us to listen to the many opinions which have been uttered after the performance by the public invited for supper after. It was never indifferent — sometimes funny, or curious, or professionally interested, or even '*effrayed.*' Any way, not cold.

"We had choiced with some care the audience. There were industrialists, busi-

Thomas de Hartmann at the piano playing for the first time his new compositions. for the "39" exercises.

nessmen, dancers, ordinary people, Indians, etc. One of them said:

'Do you think it is necessary to do such work to live in a proper way?'

"They had been struck by the impression of effort and the sort of concentration you can feel in the performers... although we ourselves couldn't really feel anything else than an attempt in that way.

"Anyway we had the feeling that our inner and outer possibilities had been used as much as possible.

"The most impressive numbers were the #12 [The Alleluya] and the #11 [Lord Have Mercy]. During the #12 a woman went out. She said she couldn't stand for more.

"It has aroused a big curiosity. People want to know more about it. During the performance we had a fantastic silence. They didn't even cough, and that's a big thing for English people!

"You remember Colet Gardens. We isolated part of the hall by a curtain forming a frame, enough to hide the lights which were quite good. The decor was simple. The walls were masked by curtains, '*penderies*' and carpets. We tried to make something '*faisant ressortir*' [creating a background for] the Movements but at the same time very quiet and without '*chichi*.'

"De Hartmann played. Very well when he wants. I know you have been a little puzzled by his new music. You told me so in one of your letters. Personally it does not bother me at all in doing the Movements. But sometimes I'd like it to help me more. We musn't forget, de Hartmann didn't do Movements himself. It makes all the difference in the spirit of it. I think it shouldn't be played all the time. We do not use it for practicing.

"When the audience entered we just sat on silk cushions of different colours '*assis en tailleur*' [crosslegged] trying to work for ourselves. I say trying in order not to give you the impression of something smug. In fact, we had to hold ourselves very strongly in order to be able to do our work in an honorable way. It wasn't at all easy.

"First we had the six Obligatories after which we went out. Then we came back again and began, without any rest, my dear, our series of Movements. After the last one, #4 [The Prayer for Instruction], we sat again as at the beginning and waited for the people to go out.

"That last sitting gave to many of them, especially the people of Dr. Nicoll, the most strange impression of which they speak still. One of them said: 'It embarrassed me. It was as if I heard my own noise.' Very interesting, no? Without any pretension,

1950 Movements demonstration at Colet House in London. File leaders Alfred Etievant and Solange Claustres (Lubtchansky). Iovanna Lloyd Wright can be seen in the rear (far left).

Alfred as a dervish   John Bennett as the central "priest"   Solange in *The Women's Prayer*

it's true that we didn't move — simply because we had no wish for it. The work done had filled us enough for a certain time. It's true that the Movements had brought us something we didn't want to lose immediately in agitation.

"Otherwise it has been a very good experience — *'practique pour l'avenir.'* [practice for the future.] We needed very much to see what it could be and at the same time to study the way to present them, and what kind of practical arrangements to do. (How many rows for every Movement? What about lighting? How many men? How many women? and so on.) In general we needed to see them. We had never seen them really. It has shown us, too, what kind of work we still had to do, and in which way people did well or badly.

"Well, I missed you anyway. I'd like you to see it. I hope you will see much better. That time was just a very small beginning and merely an attempt. These things depend really upon the whole work done, not just a particular event. The English have done well. But they really do need a lot more of a lot of other things or different under-standings.

"We made a film also, on the Sunday between the two performances. Sure, we didn't work as well for the film as for the performances. You get dizzy and nervous with the lights, the re-shootings, all the fuss of that sort. I have seen most of it on the screen. It's very funny to see oneself even if you don't expect something very nice. All faults are awfully visible, as well as the funny side of your body personality and the mimic of the face. One sees very well the sort of work you do.

"Otherwise it is a very interesting document for us and very precise. We will have to bury it very deeply in case of an atom bomb. Certain close-ups are really beautiful. In the execution Solange looks far away as the best one.

"The difficulty will certainly be the music. It will have to be recorded with one of our pianists looking at the screen. If you take into account that sometimes the camera slows down, and the projection as well, it will be a nice sport for the poor guy.

"I am a little bit worried at the moment by one or two things. I am first very anxious about the next war which seems to approach very quickly. I am still in some difficulty obtaining a visa for the U.S.A. In my special case, I told you what happened to my brother and the consequences it had for me. I must produce documents, make a lot of translations, etc. But the documents I have, without someone knowing the atmosphere and the exaggeration of that period, seem awful. And if they refuse this [resident's] visa it would then be more difficult to get a visitor's visa. They do not like at all you change your mind that way.

"Dear Sophie, I don't know how you feel, but it is horrible to be alone. I manage to meet people but it always stays impersonal. Your absence has been very hard for me. And at the moment I feel much nearer to you although you are still very far.

"Do not write me in Paris because my concierge reads my letters.

"I will be back in England the ninth of November.

"*Bien des choses de ma part à Jessmine.*

Je vous aime,   Alfred

"(*Pardonnez mes horribles fautes, de linguiste et de typist.*)"

* * * * *

CHAPTER 24

FRANK LLOYD WRIGHT'S TALIESIN, A YEAR WITH MOVIE STARS

Dushka
♦

Returning to New York to pick up my life again in 1950 was a confusing time for me. Which "role" to play now?

For one thing, I had no idea what would happen with Alfred, whether he would be able to establish himself somewhere so that our "engagement" was meaningful. It wasn't only the question of where we would both end up, New York, London, Paris or...? Admittedly, after my spending so many months abroad I hoped that he would come to the U.S., rather than my having to join him again in London where I foresaw little future for myself. More important, I felt that he must create a more meaningful life for himself than that little room in Colet Gardens, and some Movements classes, everything dependent on a few English well-wishers, appreciative of him though they were. He needed to do this to be a husband for anybody, not only me.

So in the meantime I could only try to set myself up again in America, professionally and socially. My alter ego "Sophie" quietly disappeared. She got left behind in Paris in Mr. Gurdjieff's apartment when "Dushka" sailed back to New York. These days members of Gurdjieff groups may find mentions of her in books they are reading and wonder who she was and what happened to her.

For example, when a new book *Diary of Madame Egout Pour Sweet* arrived at the Foundation, I bought one remembering how the author Rina Hands had visited us in Paris in 1949. On opening it casually, the first thing I saw was: "Mr. Gurdjieff came in and taught a new Movement... a fantastic strain on memory and attention. When we saw them struggling with this wicked invention of Mr. Gurdjieff's it was in no way criticism of their efforts that was invoked, but only love and sympathy. There was one young girl who in the end won over all the difficulties and did them as if in an animated trance, and Mr. Gurdjieff's "Bravo, Sophy !" was heartily felt by all of us."

Flattered, I turned to a colleague sitting next to me, one of the current Movements instructors, proudly pointed to the paragraph and said: "Well, I guess I'm going to enjoy this book!" He just looked at me as if I were crazy.

The whole question of Mother and me in relation to Mr. Gurdjieff was never really mentioned again once he was no longer there to announce it to one and all. To give them credit, I'm sure that Mother's oldest friends and pupils felt that this was the kindest and most tactful way to treat the situation. But I know many "responsibles" who came along later can't understand why I get included on special occasions, ...if I do!

Rina Hands.

(Above left) Frank Lloyd Wright in the Ken Burns TV series about him. (Middle) A 1966 U.S. postage stamp (Above right) Mr. Wright with the model of his revolutionary Guggenheim Museum being built in New York City.

One vestige of my relationship to Mr. G., looking back now, may have been the reason for an invitation I received soon after returning home.

Frank Lloyd Wright's wife Olgivanna asked me to visit them at the Taliesin Fellowship in Wisconsin. Though I might have lunched with her daughter Iovanna if she visited New York, we had hardly become close friends in Paris and now, suddenly, I was invited to their home and installed in the Wright's special guest bedroom. This room is well-known and pictured in architectural journals because it is built around a living birch tree. The white tree trunk, a foot in diameter, passes right through the room from floor to a hole in the ceiling. It is very attractive until at night one begins to notice the parades of ants, spiders and other creepy crawlies ascending and descending it.

Mother, wishing me to take advantage of any interesting opportunities, had encouraged me to accept the invitation but had sent me off with a sort of "be open but be careful!" I don't know what she might have heard about Taliesin, or what memories she had of the Prieuré and Olgivanna, but she gently suggested that "Mrs. Wright" might have acquired a habit, from supervising her husband's young apprentices, of "being interested in" (i.e. interfering with) people's "personal" (i.e. sex) lives.

On my arrival I was warmly welcomed by everyone, but Olgivanna did immediately concern herself that I hadn't brought any long dresses. I didn't own any. Mother and I hadn't realized how really formal were the Wrights' weekend evenings when everyone dressed up and notable guests were invited for dinner and music. On my first evening, Dimitri Metropolis and Sessua Hayakawa were there among others.

Immediately a poor apprentice and his wife were sent all the way into Madison to buy me something suitable. This was no easy task, especially in the Middle West soon after the war. Lane Bryants didn't exist and my requirements,(size eighteen or twenty, young, dressy-but-not-bridal,) must have been daunting. The only one of their purchases that I haven't blocked out entirely was a monstrosity of pale blue taffeta with little puff sleeves. I suppose it wasn't "bridal" but it was certainly "bridesmaidal."

They also brought back bundles of red satin and white chiffon. Apparently there was to be a big outdoor party, an "Oriental Bazaar," at which everyone, myself included, had to be costumed. Under Olgivanna's Montenigran eye, lengths of red and white material were wound around me till I felt like a bulbous barber pole, but did look, I suppose, sort of "harem-esque."

Actually the event itself was wonderful. A large section of the property down by the lake was cordoned off, animals from the farm were let loose, and tents and banners flapped in the breeze. Boats floated nearby, hoses hidden at the tops of mountains of watermelons cascaded water down them, lambs on spits crackled over open fires and for a whole weekend we re-enacted a Middle-Eastern encampment. I have often been in costume but never for such a long time, night and day in the open air. A moment comes when you begin to live the part!

Olgivanna did, several times, ask me probing questions about Alfred, about our relationship, whether we had any definite plans, and my life and friends in New

(Left to right) Olgivanna Lloyd Wright, Mr. Wright, Svetlana Wright Peters, Wes Peters, Iovanna.

York. Then she introduced me to one of Mr. Wright's senior apprentices, Wes Peters, a tall quiet man, and she seemed to encourage our being together. Neither of us was very interested and nothing further happened there.

How many years later did I finally start wondering about all that? Probably not until the 1970s when so much publicity appeared about Stalin's daughter marrying a Frank Lloyd Wright apprentice, and our friends made comments about Wesley Peters and "another Svetlana." I hadn't thought too much about "Wes" having been the widower of Olgivanna's first daughter, Svetlana (1917-1946). I had never met her, and before reading Mother's papers had never heard any suggestion that there might be a relationship to me and Petey, (another Gurdjieff daughter?) Svetlana had died years before we all met Iovanna, She died in a tragic automobile accident that also took the lives of two of her children, one unborn. The remaining little boy, Brandoch, was being brought up by his widowed father, Wes Peters

Wesley Peters with his first wife, Olgivanna's Svetlana.

We had heard what a terrible shock it had all been to Olgivanna. As one of the Taliesin apprentices close to her later recalled in the documentary *Partner to Genius*: "Mrs. Wright, after Svetlana's death, was so unhappy and led such an inner life, that she couldn't break out of it. She gave up jewelry, make-up, meat, alcohol and coffee, for five years!"

I recently asked Petey, in one of our "old lady" talk sessions, what she thought about any possible relationship and she said: "Oh! Of course! Didn't I ever tell you about the scene we had with Olgivanna?" She went on to explain that in 1949 when we were all going daily to the Hotel Wellington, she and Iovanna began to be friendly, and one day Iovanna invited her to come to tea to meet her mother. When the two girls arrived at the Plaza Hotel, they went right up to the suite which the Wrights

The "second Svetlana," Stalin's daughter.

Dark Times

CELEBRATED FIGURES THE WORLD has long forgotten too often turn up in the most bizarre places. Case in point: Lana Peters, once known as **SVETLANA STALIN**, daughter of despot Joseph. After years of repeatedly migrating back and forth between East and West, Peters, 66, a mother of three children and author of two books, has wound up in a London charity hostel for those suffering with severe emotional problems. There, Peters apparently pays a modest $132 a week for her room and board.

Time Magazine, October 1992,

always kept as a New York base. They entered the huge living room and at the far end, on a big sofa, said Petey: "...sat this woman, Iovanna's mother, who took one look at me and began to scream. Hysterics! Crying and shouting, 'How could you? How can you do this to me? How could you? Get out! Out!' and we got out of there in a hurry. We went downstairs to have tea and Iovanna explained to me about Svetlana. How her mother, even so long after the accident, still hadn't completely recovered. Then Iovanna showed me some photographs of Svetlana and it is true, I look exactly like her!"

Stalin's "Svetlana," now "Lana Peters," I last heard of in October 1992, when *Time Magazine* ran a sad photo of her exiting her "London charity hostel for those suffering with severe emotional problems."

I, myself, found Taliesin a pleasant and interesting place to be, at least as a special guest. But I can imagine that it may have been difficult for some of the apprentices, and I heard some terribly negative stories about the place. But after having been around Mr. G. and seeing how this kind of thing could happen, I just figured these tales were spread by people who had never even been there, or those who left not having fitted in to the community, or understood what was going on. If what someone paid for, and expected to receive was a strictly traditional academic training as an architect, it's true, he didn't belong there. But if he was ready for all kinds of "life experiences" and willing to work and search, this was a unique opportunity.

Actual classes, as such, weren't taught, but technical questions were answered by senior apprentices and one "learned by doing." In fact, that was their motto. Mr. Wright's complete files were available for study. Anyone could trace the creation of a building from the first inquiring letter, through the rough suggestions, adjustments, expense details, additions, compromises, final plans and photographs of the completed result. A real education. And actively participating with Mr. Wright on his current projects was an invaluable opportunity. Hardly the imposition or "slave labor" cited by some of Wright's detractors.

But the young people did have to learn to fit into a communal life, and do a lot more than just sit at a drawing board. Apprentices did all the physical work on the farm, with its animals and crops, in the houses, cleaning and cooking, in the drafting room and on construction sites. Tasks were rotated on a weekly basis. and no matter what kind of work one had done, how "peasant" one had been on weekdays, on weekend nights one dressed up, dined and socialized like aristocracy.

That all seemed wonderful to me. And I loved it that an old stonecutter was invited to pass on to everybody his ancient craft, one of many skills Mr. Wright believed every architect should have. Walls built as demonstrations or by student's attempts were added to Wrights' own house until, finally, the building, added on to year by year, rambled all over a hillside with no apparent form. No wonder it was a strange example of a "Frank Lloyd Wright house."

(Above) Frank Lloyd Wright in the drafting room with two of his senior apprentices Wes Peters (left) and Eugene Masselink.   (Right) Olgivanna Lloyd Wright

(Above) When the Wrights were finally free to marry, (after divorces) their wedding invitations carried the picture of their 4-year-old daughter, Iovanna.

(Above) Doting father F. L. Wright with teen-aged Iovanna.

((Below) A postcard of Taliesin East, Spring Green, Wis.

THE "ORIENTAL BAZAAR" WEEKEND AT TALIESIN EAST, 1952

The Wright's tent at the party (Left to right.) Wesley Peters. Iovanna (from back), Olgivanna, (in tent) Frank Lloyd Wright.

Some of the architectural apprentices in costume.

The Wrights in a cart decorated for them.

(Left and above) Dushka in costume for the Oriental weekend which included coping with a whole leg from the roasted lamb.

(Below) Wesley Peters in costume.

(Below) Roland von Rebay (right) and Curtis Besinger take a break from haying work at Taliesin.

Taliesiin East in Spring Green, Wisconsin. One of the many red cars of the Fellowship.

Taliesin West in Scottsdale, Arizona. The Frank Lloyd Wright Fellowship's winter quarters.

(Above) One of our earliest photos of Olgivanna (Milanova Hinzenberg) seen here with her first daughter Svetlana. So this was probably taken in the Caucasus before arrriving in Europe with Gurdjieff's group in the early Twenties......

One of our last photos of Olgivanna as she continued to actively lead the Frank Lloyd Wright Fellowship for many years after her husband's death in April 1959.

I joined in various activities, including the haymaking where I made friends with attractive Roland von Rebay, nephew of Baroness Hilla von Rebay who had commissioned the Guggenheim Museum. Later in New York he invited me to their home for some private viewings of the Guggenheim Collection. Wow, some "etchings!"

And then, how you budding architects would have envied me! I was given a stint in the drafting room. The current project underway was the spectacular new Museum and I was given an actual task. I can now say: "I worked on the plans for the Guggenheim." For days I struggled to perfect the peculiar squared-off script traditionally used and then proudly lettered the linoleum specifications for a kitchen located somewhere in the depths.

Unfortunately that all led to a difficulty with Mr. Wright. Everyone agreed that he had a wonderful wit. In fact, for years I plagiarized some of his comments like "I learned early to value honest arrogance over hypocritical humility," and "The U.S. is a country that passed from barbarism to decadence without going through civilization!" Yes, he may have had a great sense of humor about most things, but I hadn't yet learned that this didn't include himself or his architecture. So when I first saw the Guggenheim plans, the innovative new circular building with its huge spiral ramp, and remembering the sore feet I suffered during so many school visits to museums, I had, to me, an amusing thought. I said to someone that maybe they

Taliesin West apprentices doing Movements out-of-doors led by Iovanna Lloyd Wright (above center)

should have a roller-skate rental on the top floor. This evidently got back to the Maestro and he cold-shouldered me for the rest of my stay.

On Sunday mornings there were late, lengthy breakfasts in the communal dining-room presided over by the Wrights. On my first Sunday there, I was touched by Mr. Wright's long talk to the apprentices about the effect Thoreau's *Walden* had had on him when he was young, and how he wished they could share it. A huge carton was dragged into the room and each person was given their own paperback copy to read.

The second Sunday was revealing of the relationship Wright had with his young people and why they were truly apprentices and not just pupils.

The night before, during the music after dinner, Mr. Wright had been called away when a group of people arrived to speak with him.

The next morning he explained to us that this had been a deputation from the Unitarians in Madison for whom he had designed a new church. In fact, many of the apprentices present had participated in the planning. The basic construction had been completed but now the Unitarian congregation was having difficulties raising the funds necessary to complete the building, and finish the painting and decorating. Mr. Wright detailed every dollar and cent, showed how they had sufficient money for supplies but not labor, and asked for suggestions. No one at the Fellowship wished to leave "their" building in such a state, and everyone volunteered to help with its completion.

The next day and from then on, groups of apprentices put in long days of work, driving to and from Madison in their little red cars.

Most of the Taliesin automobiles were repainted "Cherokee" red, slightly brighter than brick red. This was a Taliesin tradition, and the annual move to winter quarters in Arizona which everyone made together, driving in a caravan, must have been quite a sight.

* * * *

Finding the right job to settle into back in New York was a challenge. I could hardly put on a resume what I had been doing in Paris for the last year or so. I didn't want to go back to jazz things, and my art degree from Barnard wasn't much help.

I did take a course in advertising art and layout with Peter Piening at the Art Student's League and worked for a while doing ads in Rowland Brandwein's small ad agency.

Then Maely, Freddie Bartholomew's ex-wife, now married to writer Bill Dufty (she helped him write his book *Lady Sings The Blues*, about her friend Billie Holiday,) somehow got herself involved in a studio greeting card business. She called me to come and work as her assistant saying my art training and business know-how would both be useful. On my first day there she told me her grandiose plans and showed me all around her studio loft.

On my second day she phoned to say that she had had a heart attack and would I take over. She never came in again!

I discovered that she had two silent partners whose investment she had used up and three inexperienced employees who were helpless. Her not very good but complicated designs for cards each required a different expensive production technique (lithography, silkscreen, flocking, pasting on sequins and bits of fur, strange shapes and envelope sizes) and were all in various stages of preparation, none ready to ship, and all the suppliers unpaid. I almost had a heart attack too!

(Above) Dushka's photo of Mr. Wright's beloved Arizona desert as framed by a specially constructed, eight-foot high, wrought-iron enneagram. Significantly, although the Taliesin West property is preserved for tourists to visit, the enneagram and all that it represented of Mr. Gurdjieff and his Work,......has long since disappeared!

Lucette Heuseux and Tom Grey at Mendham breakfast.

At her partners' request I tried a salvage operation, completed what was viable, hurried together some cheap designs that could be printed eight up in two colors, went out selling to department and card stores, and maneuvered printers into delivering in time for the Stationary Show and Christmas shippings. Then I retired gracefully. Occasionally some new acquaintance of mine may receive from me a dated-looking studio card with an imprint on the back: Maely, Ltd.

A few pleasant weeks were spent with Lucette Heuseux, a Belgian painter, on an automobile trip to California, stopping to

(Above) Lucette (left) and Dushka (right) climbing around Grand Canyon looking for a good place to paint from..

One of Dushka's oil sketches of Grand Canyon. (Many were necessary because colors change drastically every couple of hours.)

English painter Theo Hancock with one of his popular watercolors.

paint along the way. All I had to do was watch the scenery since Lucette, who I'd met at Franklin Farms, did all the driving herself, proud of having been an ambulance driver during the war. We travelled by the Southern route, ("Route Sixty-six and all that!") and painted all kinds of Americana, including Grand Canyon, the Taos Pueblo, the Monterey mission, Carmel beaches and so on.

My big problem here was that Lucette used a palette knife and had such a quick experienced technique that she could produce an exhibit quality painting and be ready to move on, while I was still setting up my equipment. I soon tried following her example and learned to scamper, slash, scrape and splash, and ended up with some creditable paintings, a few of which were sold at the next Washington Square Art Show in New York.

Sadly I hadn't intended it that way. I did the show as a lark with a young English painter, Theo Hancock, and neither of us intended to actually part with any of our precious works, putting insanely exorbitant prices on them, chuckling all the while.

(Above) Fred Clark, one of his publicity headshots.

A movie magazine snaps a photo of Benay Venuta (left) with her best friend (and rival) Ethel Merman at the *Stork Club*.

Hollywood cohorts: (Left to right) Benay and Fred, Debbie Reynolds, Barry Sullivan and Frank Lovejoy.

Then some tourists really messed us up by insisting on buying them!

When we got back to New York, Lucette and I joined forces to try a window display venture. Lucette had the techniques for construction and decoration. I knew how to make an attractive display that would also actually sell something. We did projects for the Fifth Avenue windows of Swissair, a couple for the Swiss Bank in Rockefeller Plaza. We used all kinds of materials, did tricky carpentry so that things could be folded up and moved to other locations, or taken down and set up in the middle of the night. It was all interesting and well paid, but not a career.

So I was flattered to be offered the position of Director of Magazine Publicity, at the Mutual Broadcasting System and spent most of 1952 there. This involved lining up interviews and photo opportunities, mass-mailing bios or outlines for articles, and ghost-writing columns and stories. With an expense account for meals and drinks, I curried favor with publishers, editors, and columnists. I was really very successful dreaming up and placing reams of print for Mutual, especially considering that my competition at the other networks, CBS, ABC and NBC had dozens of people to do what I was handling all alone.

But one day I just couldn't resist answering a Help Wanted ad I saw in the Sunday Times for a "French-speaking person to travel in Europe, live in Hollywood and New York, excellent salary!" I was still nostalgic for California, loved to travel, and this was for good money, too.

But hundreds of other people had the same reaction and were mobbing the employment agency to answer that ad, so I decided to pretend that I was there for something completely different and just happened to have the right qualifications! I let them "talk me into" being interviewed by the clients and got the job. Maybe I really did inherit some things from Mr. Gurdjieff!

Fred Clark (1914-1968) the well-known film actor, and his wife, **Benay Venuta**, a successful musical comedy actress, needed a social secretary and travelling companion for their "second honeymoon" trip to Europe.

But this didn't turn out to be quite what any of us expected, because at the last moment one of Benay's two daughters by her previous husband, millionaire movie-producer Armand Deutsch, had to accompany us. This meant that most of my time would be spent being a governess to Patty, a strong-minded twelve-year-old with a reputation for terrorizing her caretakers.

Fortunately, a big breakthrough with the poor child happened at our first stop, London. Mother's old friend Pamela Travers, hearing I was in town, invited me to tea, and I was stuck with dragging along my young charge. I hadn't realized how Patty adored the *Mary Poppins* books that Pamela had written, and to visit the "Poppins" house on a Chelsea back street, to sit in front of a real English fire with a cat in her lap, drinking real English tea was for her an unforgettable event. This kid, who had been brought up knowing all the Hollywood greats suddenly treated me as a "familiar of the mighty," and from then on we had a close, if sometimes combative relationship.

The four of us dragged around sightseeing in to Europe for a couple of weeks, bumping into many of their Hollywood neighbors in Paris, and then visited Benay's family, the "Benvenutos" (hence her stage name) in Lugano, Switzerland.

We also went to the movies a lot since in nearly every town they would be showing some of Fred's many films. Dubbed for local consumption, Fred adored seeing himself and his actor friends spouting fluent French, Italian, Spanish or German.

When we got to Venice, we settled in for a few days of beach on the Lido.

The Hotel des Bains is a fabulous relic which was used for filming *Death in Venice* without changing a thing, string orchestra, potted plants, cabanas, all authentic. But it was rather pricey and suddenly Benay had the idea that we should economize by eating lunch from vendors on the beach instead of going into the hotel. So we sat with greasy snacks on the hot sand while above us on the terrace the rest of the guests were sipping iced drinks under shady parasols, or in the cool dining room. It was only when we checked out that Fred discovered that we had been on "full pension" which meant that each day's lunch in the dining room was included in the bill.

Then I came up with a solution for us all.

Fred Clark and his wife, Benay Venuta, leave for second honeymoon in Europe

(Above) Movie magazines cover the sailing, ...and the "Second Honeymooners" pose on deck with Dushka.

(Above) Venice, Italy. Patty Deutsch with her mother and step-father and (right) with her "governess" Dushka in a Piazza San Marco cafe.

(Left)
Fred provides "pedal power" for Dushka's "pedalo" ride on the lake in Lugano, Switzerland.

I found a place for young Patty in one of those Swiss schools that run special summer sessions for youngsters of all nationalities who come to work and play, perfecting their French in the process .

She loved it. And we adults loved it.

I went off to St. Jean de Luz to paint the Basque country, and Fred and Benay rented a car and set off for Spain, proud to be, for the first time, "abroad on their own."

After the summer, we all returned to New York to live at the Carlyle, famous as the Kennedys' favorite hotel.

I had my own tiny apartment there, and the family had a huge one. Each day I shepherded the girls, Patty and her younger sister Debby, to the Lenox School on East 70th Street in a chauffeur-driven car. Then I often got out and walked down the block to the new apartment that Mother had just found for us which we kept from then on, thanks to rent control.

Benay was playing on Broadway, in *Copper and Brass* and then in *Hazel Flagg* starring Helen Gallagher. Strangely enough when *Hazel Flagg* was made into the movie, *Living It Up*, writers changed the heroine into a hero so that Jerry Lewis could star, and Benay's part went to Fred Clark!

About this time, 1953, the New York Gurdjieff Foundation had opened up headquarters on East Sixty-third Street. In keeping with the usual "domestics" schedule, Fred and Benay allowed me Thursday afternoon and evening and every other Sunday off. So it was pretty devoted of me when I agreed to give my one free evening a week to the Foundation and undertook to teach a Movements class to younger, more active, pupils, many of whom are now teachers themselves. By this time Mother had introduced my godmother, Annette Herter, into the Work activities and, Lo and Behold, I ended up with her as my pianist. It wasn't always an easy partnership because, in my exigence as an instructor, I was unforgiving and apt to tactlessly stamp my foot

(Above) Sailing back to New York in first-class our shipboard companions include Rosalind Russell, Brian Aherne, George Murphy, Johnnie Mercer and others returning from a European film festival.

(Above left) Patty Deutsch a few years later, in her teens, and (Right) her sister Debby.

to keep the tempos steady. I think Godmother Annette must have really "worked on herself" a lot during these role reversals.

I had another problem on Thursdays, which also required great tact. Someone had told Benay that her floorlength, white mink coat wouldn't turn yellow if it was often worn outside, in fresh air even if not in sunlight. She got it into her head that I should wear it on my afternoons off. Every week I had to find excuses to convince her that I was just going to join friends in a hamburger joint where her long fur coat, (in which, incidentally, I looked like an old polar bear blubbered up for its hibernation) wasn't really quite suitable.

I could just imagine the effect on my Movements class.

When Benay's Broadway runs were over and her old buddy, Ethel Merman, had finally opened in *Gypsy* we all flew to Hollywood and the Clarks' Beverly Hills home.

This was a typical movie star house on North Hillcrest with flowering shrubs and palm trees, large pool at the back, and "five in help."

I foresaw a life of real luxury.

Then the staff began to shrink as I took over various functions, replacing the chauffeur driving the girls back and forth, doing cleaning, ironing, and so on. But I was especially appreciated when it was discovered that I could cook gourmet dishes that were low-calorie. This result of my Dione Lucas/Cordon Bleu experience combined with a life-long personal struggle with overweight, was a priceless advantage in Hollywood if you expect film people to attend your dinner parties.

The aged Dolly Sisters who lived across the street from us next to Stephen McNally staggered out of their house every afternoon for a drive around in a taxi. Claire Trevor was on one side and Benay's special friends, Frank Loesser and his wife were nearby. But the biggest gathering of celebrities was just down the block where there was a doctor who specialized in giving hangover treatments. At four or five in the morning, a few minutes of oxygen inhalation evidently helps prepare one for an early make-up call.

At Christmas time one of my jobs was to choose real fur bowties as Fred's gifts to his men friends. I seem to remember Humphrey Bogart got black seal, and Van Johnson got leopard.

Often when I got up in the early morning, Fred and his cronies were still playing poker downstairs, and above all the rest one could hear the familiar voice of "Mr. Magoo," (Jim Backus after a few drinks!)

If the girls, Patty and Debby, went to see their father, Armand Deutsch, or any of his family, Benay always asked me to accompany them. The divorce had evidently been bitter. Benay's comment to me once was: "Well, what can one expect from someone whose best friends at school were Leopold and Loeb!"

Mr. Deutsch's side of the family, the immensely wealthy Sears Roebuck heirs, (mother Adele Levy and various Rosenwalds), were suspicious of how Benay's girls were being raised and were apt to interfere. I guess my function was as a sort of peace-maker and someone who was able to help Patty control tantrums she had previously inflicted on everybody.

Armand Deutsch and his second wife, Harriet.

But I really appreciated Mr. Deutsch passing on to me his ticket for that year's Academy Awards. He wanted to watch it on television since his friend Johnny Green was producing. I was glamorously wrapped around with Benay's huge mink stole, and thoroughly enjoyed being part of the event. It was made even more special when I heard the name of our Mendham friend, Tom Daly, announced in connection with an Oscar for Best Short Subject for *Neighbors*, made for the Canadian Film Board.

With all this, I still had some free time during the day, especially when Fred started another film and Benay got a part in a Ma Kettle opus.

When I had first arrived, the Clarks had lent me a little convertible to drive around in, and in fact warned me that in Beverly Hills I might be arrested by the local police or security guards if I did the suspicious thing of walking anywhere.

On one of my drives along Beverly Boulevard, I noticed a low building with a large sign, "Academy of Spanish Arts." I went in to ask if they could teach me some Spanish songs, and was asked if I played an instrument. When I admitted to piano, they sighed and suggested a beginner's guitar class which had started several weeks before, "But our Mr. Gomez will give you some personal help to catch you up with the others."

And so it was that I lucked into private training with "Maestro" Vicente Gomez, who had just opened this Academy and decided to try out on me his new teaching techniques, original exercises and repertoire. Fresh from doing the music for the Tyrone Power film *Blood and Sand*, he kindly gave me a lot of attention and urged me along so that I was soon trying the tremolo solo *Romanza de Amor*, singing Rita Hayworth's song *Verde Luna*, and faltering through various Spanish and Classical pieces. I was exhilarated and practiced hard any place I could find any privacy, in the sauna-like greenhouse at the end of the Clark's garden, by the swimming pool or in the car that I parked on Mulholland Drive, which was unfrequented during the daytime, though busy as a "spooner's Mecca" at night. I never dreamed that all this

(Above) Fledgling guitarist Dushka practicing by the Clark's swimmng pool.

Master guitarist Vicente Gomez (Above right) with Tyrone Power during the filming of *Blood and Sand*.

might later lead to a twenty year performing career.

Another reason I have for being grateful to Fred and Benay is that they helped me finally get rid of an obsession I had nursed for years.

As an eleven-year-old, I was dragged away from sunny California and put in a strict and dreary English school. From then on I had longed to go back to Hollywood, and when, after college, my professional life took the direction of show business publicity, I was sure that my future lay in the West Coast film industry.

But by including me in their social gatherings, sometimes introducing me as a cousin and letting me visit their film sets, the Clarks gave me the opportunity to realize this wasn't at all an environment for me.

The work atmosphere of movie studios involved, it seemed to me, too much "gold-bricking." Most personal initiative and creativity gets stifled by the magnitude and expense of the productions, and the "stars" that I met, no matter how nice they may have started out, seemed to become either brash over-night successes, or disappointed, often alcoholic, veterans.

I had promised to stay with the Clark family a year. On the three hundred-sixty-sixth day, I flew off to Paris to see how long I could exist there.

I had only meager savings, so I had tried to line up some odd jobs before leaving Hollywood to help me get started.

For instance I arranged to escort King Vidor's daughter to a Swiss boarding school and get her outfitted in her uniforms. Someone else wanted a compatible French family to take in their rebellious teenager. A film crew on location in France needed suitable office space rented for them. Shopping requests added up to a long list of perfumes, gloves, art prints and sexy books to be shipped back,..... and so on.

These chores were what ultimately led to a successful multi-faceted business that I dubbed "Howarth Services" and continued in Europe for the next eight years.

Even nowadays I may reactivate it when I need a professional structure for some free-lance activity like party catering, entertainment booking, or record producing.

* * * * *

CHAPTER 25

TRYING A BUSINESS IN PARIS

"You are not alive unless you know you are living."
Written on the wall of one of Modigliani's studios

Dushka
♦

In 1953 tourist and business activities were increasing in Europe and the EEC and EU weren't yet functioning. So, though many local services and agencies existed in Paris, most Americans didn't know how to find or use them, and, moreover, were convinced that the French were all out to cheat them. So I found I could fulfill a need as a "fellow American" who would act as a liaison, or, when necessary, provide the help needed myself, "wearing my various hats," or by hiring staff, forming teams, even setting up an entire organization to handle any situation.

Not being able to afford salaried employees turned out to be a blessing in disguise. I was obliged to start collecting files of people, preferably bilingual, who might be available for part-time work. I had quite a choice, especially since I could usually arrange for payment in U.S. dollars, a rare commodity then. I ended up with over four hundred eager, grateful colleagues from whom I could choose any particular specialty I needed. They included the bored wives of U.S. Embassy personnel, ambitious Fullbright Fellowship students, talented but struggling painters, musicians and writers, titled French noblemen, Russian taxi drivers, and Vietnamese chefs.

Anci Dupré

Then I needed an address to work out of and to put on business cards. I gratefully accepted an offer of help from Anci Dupré in whose house I had stayed briefly in 1949. Her husband, Francois Dupré, owned the Hotel George V, and she thought that might make a good address for me. Wouldn't it just!

But I had barely had impressive cards printed when the embarrassed hotel manager, Max Blouet, called me in to his office. He had to ask me to make other arrangements as the police had brought up a problem. Apparently the French officials, in the course of legalizing prostitution and to curtail pimping had created regulations which forbade the taking of commissions from people you placed in jobs. Good for "girls of the night," but devastating for the kind of set-up I had planned. Later I found that even the important Paris couture houses suffered from the lack of model agencies due to this rule until a couple of enterprising American girls organized a model's club with a huge notice-board on which were posted job offers.

Francois Dupré (right) hotel owner and horse breeder at his stables in Haras d'Ouilly with his trainer Francois Mathet.

Another happy accident finally gave me not only a dignified address but wonderful facilities as well. Russell Page, who had at one time been married to Gurdjieff's niece Leda, had subsequently married Rene Daumal's widow, Vera, an energetic little American woman. They were living in Paris and had gathered around them an English-speaking group of young people interested in the Gurdjieff ideas. Some of these became my life-long friends: Ward Swingle of the Swingle Singers, Caruso's daughter Gloria, Alice and Herman "Shaef" Shaeffer from the American Embassy, Jack Mayer of UNICEF, and writer/model Matt Carney.

Idries Shah

When Vera died, Russell didn't feel he could keep the group together and suggested that those whose professions permitted it, move to London to work with Idries Shah, whose Sufi ideas some people, especially John Bennett, thought compatible with Gurdjieff's. Many did go and were quite happy, kept busy and fulfilled with ambitious business projects, and so forth.

However, a year or so later when I visited London, the Shaeffers admitted to me that Shah was constantly disparaging the work they had done for years in Paris (where Alice Shaeffer had been a Movements' teacher.) He complained that he had to "undo" all that they had learnt there. I asked them why then, if this were so, Shah was so actively proselytizing specifically Gurdjieff followers when he had even more accessible to him millions of unpolluted English who had never heard of Gurdjieff. They couldn't find an answer.

Herman and Alice Shaeffer

Alice and Shaef took me to have Sunday tea with Idries Shah and his family and group members. I found him tall and good-looking, most personable and well spoken, a completely Anglicized Afghan. But afterwards, in spite of not wishing to hurt the Shaeffer's feelings, I admitted that although he would certainly make a fascinating dinner guest, he didn't convince me as a "Teacher."

The Shaeffers also told me that Shah had recently announced to them that he was writing a book about Gurdjieff, whom I'm pretty sure he never met, to identify the sources of his teaching, but under an anagram pseudonym. So I was hardly surprised when the very imaginative *The Teachers of Gurdjieff* appeared authored by one "Rafael Lefort" ("a real effort?")

The connection of all this to my business situation in Paris was simply that another of Vera's young group was Jacques Abreu, a South American whose family owned a big, international travel organization, and Vera had the kind and practical idea that Jacques and I could be mutually useful.

And so it was. The Abreus provided me with my own office in their new building on the Rue Galilée just off the Champs Elysées, including the use of a conference room with facilities for simultaneous translations, furnished offices that my clients could rent by the day, and a telephone switchboard with multi-lingual operators. I, in return, served as the English-speaking representative for the S.V.P. (*Société des Voyages Parisiennes*) travel agency on the ground floor. I was also personnel director and copy writer for the car rental and auto-financing sections, and hostess for S.V.P. ("Service for Visitors in Paris"), the remnants of a tourist service operation once attempted by S.V.P. (*S'il Vous Plait*) a telephone company scheme.

The American Embassy seemed very interested in the idea of someone "from home" to whom they could pass on the many requests for information and aid that they received from U.S. visitors. Especially since, as I soon came to realize, almost nobody in our Embassy in Paris knew much about France or could speak French. This seems unbelievable but had something to do with a government policy of rotating staff to different countries every couple of years (to reduce fraternizing, or ??)

Mother's old connections at the French Press and Information Service were ready to write me up in their monthly bulletin. Countess Mab Moltke, one of Mother's grateful pupils, was an editor at *Vogue* which wrote me up, as did William Segal, publisher of *Gentry*, and I was making more friends and contacts every day. So all at once, with all this publicity, I seemed to have the possibility of a considerable enterprise. But, as an American, I had no legal permission to earn money or conduct business in France, much less promote and advertise.

Though I sometimes visited Mme. de Salzmann to keep her in touch with what I was attempting, I wasn't very close to anyone else I had met in Paris in 1949, and I didn't get involved with French groups or Movements classes.

Michel was now "M. le docteur de Salzmann" but just beginning his career as psychiatrist, and rarely had time to relax. When he did, he could be hilarious, and when I joined his gang of friends we clowned around like idiots, rushing all over Paris at all hours, trying to forget our usual serious professional selves.

He once told me a little about his internship in a government psychiatric hospital. Conditions must have been grim. He mentioned needing to keep on his fleece-lined coat when he made rounds, although the patients were almost naked. He was one of... was it four?... doctors for hundreds of patients. The young interns couldn't resist helping one favorite inmate, a country girl who was inconsolable being separated from her pet cow. To calm her and, they rationalized, thus treat her, they sneaked her cow onto the hospital grounds. In order to get the additional funds needed to buy hay to feed their bovine visitor they invented a flowery name and added it to the official patient's roster.

Determined bachelor though he was at that time, Michel had many girls after him. A leading contender and the ultimate champion, was attractive Josée Person. Hers was one of the first apartments I lived in when I got to Paris. It was in an old building above the Boulevard Montparnasse where the only running water besides the toilet was a cold tap in the kitchen sink. That was how I came to appreciate and adopt the Frenchwomen's ritual of a weekly pilgrimage to the "*hammam*" (Turkish bath) and extravagance with perfume.

This was also how I came to adopt Montparnasse as my "*quartier.*" Though my business kept me mostly on the Right Bank during the day, I was always glad to come "home" to the Left Bank. The neighborhood cafés, the "Dome," the "Coupole," and especially the "Select," became my clubs, sitting rooms, even subsidiary offices. Visitors to the area may be surprised at my omission from that list of "La Rotonde," the large corner café well known to tourists. They won't understand why we, the "real art crowd," would never go there! Oh, yes, I had soon learned and also respected the historic tradition. It dated back many years to when Modigliani, already acknowledged as a great artist, was

Josée Person de Salzmann.

Amedeo Modigliani 1884-1920

drinking himself to death. In order to save him, all the local bar owners banded together and agreed not to serve him. Only from the owner of "La Rotonde" did he get his deadly absinthe in exchange for priceless paintings and drawings. The artist community hasn't forgotten.

From then on I had a wide variety of abodes. Josée passed me on to her friend, the Princesse de Polignac, whose apartment was rather different, a gold-leafed grand piano and a diamond (rhinestone ?) crown (tiara, coronet?) in the bureau drawer.

The next was a real artist's studio on the Left Bank, rue du Dragon, skylight and all, rented to me by Odile Cayla and her architect husband. The six-flight walk up only bothered me when I gave big parties and had to lug up by myself huge quantities of food and wine. The studio was really like something out of *La Boheme* and inspired me to start painting again. In fact, when Rose Fried, owner of a prestigious gallery in New York visited me and saw my work, she offered me a show if I completed the number of paintings necessary for an exhibition. I well knew every other artist in Paris would have given almost anything for such an opportunity. Yet I never followed up on her offer. In spite of the years of studying and being told I had a "natural talent," I was evidently not destined to be a painter. That would certainly have been my moment, but it obviously didn't mean enough to me. After that my need for artistic expression took the form of music and entertainment.

Other rentals, or luxurious apartment-sitting for U.S. Embassy personnel on home leave, alternated with sojourns in affordable rooms. Café acquaintances taught me how to survive the winter months in the cheap hotels. Apparently the trick was to try for a room on the third or fourth floor of the hotels most patronized by the local prostitutes. These girls would only accept rooms on the first two floors since their clients wouldn't bother with more stairs. More important, their rooms were used several times a day and justified round-the-clock heat and hot water instead of the meager rationing usually offered, as well as superior cleaning and servicing.

I happened to be staying in just such an establishment, the old "Hotel de Blois," just around the corner from the Café Select, when Mother got a vacation and came to Paris to visit me. I met her at the Boat Train and tired out though she was, poor thing, I dragged her around for hours sight-seeing, having dinner, and so on — anything to put off her undoubtedly shocked reaction to my living arrangements.

I needn't have bothered! When we finally arrived at my hotel, she exclaimed: "Oh, I used to stay here in the Twenties. It hasn't changed a bit —" including, she confessed later, the special clientele downstairs, and the resultant advantages to young artists with limited resources.

With Mother's blessing and help, I continued my attempts to achieve a legal status. I made enquiries everywhere. What did one do in this country to put a project like mine on a sound footing? No one could give me a clear answer. In fact, the common reaction amongst the French was mild surprise that I should even wish to. One official shrugged and said: "You know, since the German occupation many of us still haven't lost the habit of considering conforming to regulations as rather unpatriotic!"

Sometimes Mother came along with me on my excursions. Even she, after years of working with the French Information Service, was amazed at the tangle of bureaucracy we faced everywhere.

We finally worked our way up to a crucial interview with the head of the Préfecture of Police. He sat us down in his office with much Gallic gallantry, obviously relieved that we both spoke French. Then he listened politely to my, by then, often repeated explanation of what I wished to do, my projected cooperation with the American Embassy and existing Paris organizations, my office arrangements, the type of clients I had lined up and the various services I might provide.

After long consideration, rubbing his chin and sighing heavily, he said: "You see, you make it very difficult. You wish to do so many different things for so many different clients. How can I know what specific kinds of permission you need? I can only suggest this. That you begin to work. Of course, sooner or later it will become apparent that you do not have legal permits. This is sure as some of the large American concerns already operating here, like American Express, retain private detectives to investigate possible competitors. They will come to us at the Préfecture and demand that we do a detailed investigation into your activities. Then, yes, it will be rather unpleasant. You will be brought before the Magistrate, who, based on the report we have submitted to him will say: 'Mlle. Howarth is doing such-and-such a thing without such-and-such permission, this and that without this and that permission,' and so on... Then, you see, I will know exactly what permissions to give you!"

Mother agreed with me that this wasn't the respectable foundation I wanted to establish my business on, particularly with the American Embassy as an important source of clients. She was also sensitive to another aspect to be considered in France considering Gurdjieff's various difficulties through the years with government offices, about passports, re-entry visas, and much else. As she wrote to Lord Pentland, the current Director of the New York Gurdjieff Foundation:

◆◆◆

Jessmin
◆

Paris, November 1954
Dear John,
I leave next Friday on the *Queen Mary* and hope to have three weeks intensive work with the classes before Christmas,

It is certain that Dushka will stay on until her very last cent has been spent. At best, two more months can make it definite whether it is possible for her to get the papers she would like to have, and, if not, whether she can find any kind of employment that will permit her to mark time for still a while longer. The scope of her activity seems to have been defining itself so that she can count on good cooperation from other tourist and travel agencies, and branches of "big business" here. This can be interesting if the right clientele can be contacted but this is only possible if she is allowed, and can afford, to do the necessary publicity and advertising.

One big obstacle for her, whether it is for procuring papers, or getting security clearance for working with the Embassy and so forth, is the impossibilty of giving the required details about her parentage. We have to accept that and try to get her established on her own in such a way that no complications arise.

Jessmin

◆◆◆

Dushka
◆

Mother soon had to return to New York and left me to continue my quest.
I heard that foreigners were sometimes granted a *"Carte de Travail"* [work card]. After much asking around I found out that this meant getting appropriate forms to

be filled out in detail, with letters of reference, proof that I had never been bankrupt, and the purchase of many special expensive stamps that were affixed throughout the large sheaf of documents.

I completed and submitted all this and then waited weeks. I was finally called in and told disdainfully that a "*Carte de Travail*" was only for those who work for someone. Since I was expecting to be self-employed, I obviously didn't qualify!

When I insisted, it was suggested that I might try for a "*Carte de Commerçant.*" Different forms, many more papers, and even more stamps and more weeks of waiting. This time it was a pitying: "But, Mademoiselle, the *Carte de Commerçant* is commercial permission. This obviously means that one buys and sells something. You don't! You will be providing services and that would be considered a "*Profession Libéral.*"

New form, more papers, stamps and various personal interviews. At last! An answer! "No! '*Professions Libérals*' are divided into definite categories: doctors, dentists, lawyers, engineers, etc. There is no category covering what you wish to do."

After many discussions with officials and their unidentified advisors, it was agreed that I came very well recommended and, more important, that I would obviously be helpful to visitors with "*devises fortes.*" (This much employed phrase simply meant those who would spend large amounts of money in France – very important to the government). So wouldn't it be a good idea to use my case as an example to legislate a change, create a new category to cover publicity and public relations?

You guessed it! More papers, stamps, interviews! Then I was called to a conference at the *Commissariate de Tourisme*. A regretful director explained that they all still wished my help with the "*devises fortes*" but the higher circles refused to create a new category which might serve as an entrée for other people's activities over which they could keep little control. It was true that I had heard stories, and seen examples in Montparnasse of young US expatriates who were financing their stays in Paris with various illegal activities including black marketeering and prostitution. As the director ruefully put it: "They say they will do public relations. But how do we know? Maybe it is private relations!"

The final verdict! There was just one way that had been thought of so that I could function legally, without their having to create the new category. They would get me special permission to be part of the team of "*Guide-interpretes de Paris*" that the Commissariate of Tourism trained and controlled. It had, until then, been reserved as an activity for "*Geules Cassées,*" mutilated war veterans. "But," the director said, "we will make a special exception and enter you in the six-month training course. Unfortunately, three months of the course are already over. However, you are a bright young lady. Just make sure to attend all the remaining sessions regularly and I'm sure everything will be all right."

Of course, I figured it was a "set-up" and all I had to do was to play the game a little so they could bend the regulations.

Not at all! After weeks of attending dreary lectures given in a wooden shack built into an unused Metro tunnel under the Parc Monceau, I had to take the two-hour written examination like everyone else. I was asked to answer, in French yet, questions like: "At what stage of construction was the Louvre when Louis the Fourteenth died?... Give a complete list of the mementos of Marie Antoinette presently

on display at the Conciergerie... Why is the door of the church in
St. Jean de Luz kept locked?...!"

The Eiffel Tower....
? feet tall?

And that was only the first, easy part of the examination. The
real test started early the next morning. We were all shepherded
onto a large tour bus that already contained a TV crew and two
dessiccated old men who turned out to be experts from the Louvre.
For the rest of the day we roamed at random around the city taking
turns extemporizing in French a travelogue whenever the microphone was handed to us, with the experts questioning and correcting us, and the camera recording every drop of cold sweat.

When the day ended and the bus dropped us off on a dark
street corner, I understood why someone might rush to the nearest bar for a stiff
drink. I did too! And after a few sleepless nights, I got the results of the examinations. I had passed by a bare point or two and was now *"agrée"* (officially permitted),
to work, to hire others and to advertise myself and my "Howarth Services."

As to all the historical facts, names and dates I memorized, they immediately
went completely out of my head. The only thing I do remember is – well, not even
the exact height of the Eiffel Tower – but the invaluable piece of information that
it varies, taller or shorter, according to the temperature – eleven centimeters!

* * * * *

(Dushka center with portfolio) At least it all turned out to be a useful publicity gimmick: "...Miss Howarth,
the only American licensed by the French Government as a guide of Paris..." (*Gentry Magazine*)

CHAPTER 26

HOWARTH SERVICES

Dushka
♦

So Howarth Services was finally established as a legal business in Paris and boasted a branch in New York. Of course, for the first couple of years this branch was simply my devoted "Mum" answering and passing on mail and phone inquiries from home. Even this was valiant of her for, truly, as she often confessed, she had no head for business. She was acutely uncomfortable with any kind of commercialism. Despite her theatrical training, she felt incapable of the kind of self-promoting, professional role-playing that I found so useful and natural, and I finally accepted that this must be one thing I had inherited strictly from my paternal side!

All of us knew how painfully correct about money matters she had always been. I remember her coming home one day, and on realizing that a department store had given her about five dollars too much change, she set out again, spending fifteen-dollars in taxi fares, to return it! She admitted, rather sheepishly, that this was an attitude typical of her "North of England" upbringing as was her obsessive cleanliness, and that Mr. G.'s reaction to it had been to call her an "upside-down Jew."

As the business progressed, I was able to negotiate a reciprocal arrangement with a similarly undefined group of people in London called Universal Mentors a take-off, I suppose, on the successful personal services agency, Universal Aunts. From then on I could happily refer to my fledgling operation as an "International Organization"!

Certainly life was never dull. I was asked to do all kinds of things and usually managed them pretty well. But, not too surprisingly, I couldn't control the number or quality of the requests. Sometimes I had hordes of clients, all arriving at the same time, but at others, slack periods with nothing to do but sit glumly in my office.

Another problem was that as the business grew, the whole idea I had based it on, my own personal versatility, was no longer so useful. Even in the busy times I was stuck in the office coordinating the work of others and not free to be personally participating. For instance, when Rose Fried first came to Paris to buy paintings for her New York gallery, what I made as her guide and interpreter was nothing compared to the commissions I earned on her subsequent trips when I knew just what she was looking for and procured the works for her.

This weakness in the plan was finally brought home to me one day. An English girl I had sent out as a secretary reported that she had now completed her job with my client, an American businessman, because he now "had to go to Germany to buy five hundred Volkswagens!" If I had been there, wouldn't I have promptly contacted the German automobile manufacturers and arranged, in return for a healthy "consideration," to "put them in touch with a very interesting prospect?"

The American Embassy did come through with plenty of referrals. Everything from former President Truman who arrived on a personal, not State, visit and was

Howarth Services Paris offices at 65 rue Gallilée, just off the Champs Elysées, sharing premises with other international businesses and services.

Client Richard Kaplan, filmmaker, being interviewed by Howarth Services.

Dushka (in her "Miss Howarth" hat) holds court in the *Cafe Select*, a popular Left Bank artists' hangout, where she can often recruit useful, multi-lingual helpers for Howarth Services activities.

...though some, like her friends Blanche and Ernie Massey can sometmes act a bit wierd!

therefore required to provide his own office and domestic help, to a seven-year-old boy in Texas who needed a small French flag for his school's "show and tell." (That request, elaborately expressed in official language, on Embassy letterhead, in triplicate, was rerouted through a long list of well-paid civil servants before it was finally referred to Howarth Services.)

Some of the other jobs that came in:

A Commander in the U.S. Navy, who, as a Catholic, had been unable to adopt a baby in a Baptist area of the South where he lived, rightly assumed that in France we could arrange it.

A missing husband was being sought by the Canadian Embassy. Sounds like a murder mystery? No! Rather... a romance novel. He had been waylaid by an attractive mademoiselle!

The movie company filming *Paris Story* assigned me as "bodyguard" to their star Steve Forrest. Actually I think they simply didn't want him on the loose in Paris at night.

UNRRA wanted a Soviet journalist introduced to Left Bank artists. The resultant conversations were difficult, not because of language, but because his idea of "very modern" art was Degas.

Another UN division needed help with a Panamanian sugar plantation owner who wished "to buy some inexpensive Old Masters!" That took me a while to figure out. But he was thrilled when I arranged permission from the Louvre for a young Italian painter to make him four copies of the Mona Lisa!

A very different kind of art negotiation was tracking down Salvador Dali in

Here's your "OPEN SESAME" to Europe

HOWARTH SERVICES

... a unique time-saving, money-saving organization geared to handle personal chores or business commissions with American efficiency and understanding.

Located just off the Champs-Elysées :

65, Rue Galilée
Paris 8ᵉ, France
Tel. Elysée 50-82

REPRESENTATIVES:

NEW YORK
226 East 70th. St.
New York, New York
Tel. Regent 4-3780

LONDON
c/o Universal Mentors Ltd.
4 Berkeley Street, W.1.
Tel. Mayfair 3482

HOWARTH SERVICES

FOR THE BUSINESSMAN
*Modern, fully-equipped offices and projection room.
Multi-lingual secretaries and executive aides on call.
Advance preparations, appointments set up, research.
Public relations, commercial and official contacts.
Conferences and cocktail parties arranged etc.*

FOR THE TRAVELLER
*Detailed personal planning for world-wide travel.
On-the-spot ticket booking, hotel, theater reservations.
Qualified guides and drivers to assist and accompany.
Rental and purchase of automobiles (and boats).
Special Paris tours, recorded for you on 16 mm. film.*

FOR THE FAMILY
*Help in apartment locating and domestic staff hiring.
Social secretaries and shoppers undertake any errand.
Introductions to schools, clubs, French families, etc.
Carefully chosen governesses and tutors to supervise
children's entertainment and trips.*

BUSINESSMEN, TOURISTS
and FAMILIES COMING TO EUROPE

**WANT AMERICAN
man-friday SERVICE in FRANCE?**

Contact

HOWARTH SERVICES

*... a unique money-saving, time-saving agency geared
to handle personal chores or business commissions*

FOR THE BUSINESSMAN — Offices ready to use.
Multi-lingual secretaries, executive aides on call.
Appointments set up; research handled. Conferences and cocktail parties arranged.

FOR THE TOURIST — Automobile rentals and purchases. Record of your Paris tour with 16mm. film.

FOR THE FAMILY— Help in apartment location and domestic staff hiring. Carefully chosen guides and shoppers to undertake any errand. Children's entertainment and trips supervised by highly qualified governesses and tutors.

HOWARTH SERVICES

**65, Rue Galilée
Paris 8, France
Tel. Elysee 50-82**

TRAVEL ISSUE

NUME   The current Gentry Magazine recommends:

In case you're rushed for time and need help, Miss Howarth, the only American licensed by the French Government as a guide of Paris, is a good friend to have. Her unique organization, Howarth Services (65 Rue Galilée, Paris 8), handles business commissions and personal chores for foreign visitors and introduces tourists to the real life of France.

THE SUNDAY STAR, Washington, D. C.
SUNDAY, MAY 13, 1956

DATELINE PARIS

By BRENDA HELSER

Pooled Talents

The young and pretty Duska Howarth, owner of Howarth Services, with offices in Paris, London and New York, was a girl who could do a little of everything and not enough of anything to get a job. She pooled all her talents and hired herself out to handle jobs too delicate or vague for impersonal travel agencies. Her main idea is to save her clients money, and her big trouble is collecting from them because she grows to like them.

"The better the job I do for them, the closer I must work with them; then the better I know them, the more I hate to ask them for money." She says that a European traveler can lose $300 on a trip by going just "slightly" wrong. Her job is to save them loss; but you see it's not a job one just walks into. ∗

Former Olympics swimming champion, columnist Brenda Helser, with her husband Comte Lorenzo de Morelos y Guerrero and their small son, (also addressed by their staff as "M. le Comte".)

Sheik Bakir El Suhail's visit to Paris includes Dushka introducing him to the famous *Lido*. He orders champagne for everyone (...though as a good Moslem, not himself!)

Spain to offer him a huge fee for designing the next year's Ringling Brothers' Circus. He wouldn't do it!

A filming expedition into the back country of Afghanistan (which included my friend, Jimmy Nott, Rosemary's son) needed thousands of dollar bills, the only useful currency there. I sent out word in Montparnasse and then sat for days on the terrace of the Select as my fellow Americans brought me greenbacks, and in the process almost got myself arrested as a black-marketeer. Years later Jimmy told me they had smuggled out forbidden photos they had taken by hiding the exposed film in his artificial leg which the superstitious border guards wouldn't touch!

The U.S. National Cotton Council assigned a director to four years in France, and he arrived with a wife and four young children. This meant arranging a house rental, furnishings, maids, schools, doctors, dentists, veterinarians, etc. and much domestic encouragement and hand holding.

Sheik Bakir-El-Suhail, having accompanied King Feisal to London on a state visit to Queen Elizabeth, stopped off in Paris on his way home to Baghdad. He said he had earned a few days "fun" because "that woman" gave such dull parties!

A Chicago college professor, paralyzed while on vacation, wasn't reacting to treatment in a French hospital and the doctors advised sending him home. But the resultant logistics, exorbitant expenses, requirements for a private physician in attendance on the flight, etc. were too much for even the Embassy to manage. Howarth Services to the rescue! Remembering my days as a press agent, I approached T.W.A. through its public relations director. Everything was taken care of. I got a heartfelt thank you from his family, and T.W.A. got heart-tugging write-ups in the Press.

Wilhela Cushman, *Ladies Home Journal* editor visiting Versailles with friends George and Dushka and admiring the outdoor sculptures.

Photographer Sperry Lea wanted to marry his Greek girlfriend in Paris. This meant three weddings to orchestrate: civil registrar for the young couple, traditional ceremony in the Greek Orthodox church for the bride's family, and a floating extravaganza on the Bateaux Mouche for the groom's family from Nebraska.

The Ladies Home Journal decided on bookkeeping supervision for their extravagant fashion editor, Wilhela Cushman.

Esquire Magazine needed research on Sidney Bechet's life in Europe so that Blake Ehrlich could write a detailed profile.

Gentry Magazine accredited me as their Foreign Correspondent and assigned me to write feature articles such as "The Breeding and Training of French Race Horses," and "Unusual Things for Tourists To Do in Paris."

Ebony Magazine wanted me to organize a special fashion issue for them based on the annual Paris *Collections*. But the only black models then available in Paris weren't tiny enough to fit into the original sample dresses without the coutouriers having to make alterations. By the time our turn finally came we had missed the deadline.

The young William Segal, publisher of *American Fabrics* and *Gentry Magazine*, with Zen monks on the first of his many trips to Japan where his business importing silk leads to a life-long passionnate interest in Zen Buddhism.

An encyclopedia commissioned translations including an article on French vintages. (Does it really sound the same in English to say that a wine is "witty," "mischievous," or "pretentious"?)

But one publication I disappointed was the *International Herald Tribune*. They assigned their hilarious columnist Art Buchwald to do a piece on me, figuring, I suppose, that an American girl doing business in Paris must have some pretty salacious stories to tell. My straightforward, strait-laced activities didn't fill the bill at all, and nothing ever appeared.

Horia Damian's critical acclaim as a painter wasn't paying off enough, so under a pseudonym, "Dominique," he started a commercial venture, the mass-production of easily saleable "hand-painted" Paris scenes. His skillful black crayon sketches could be convincingly reproduced by lithography. For a few francs each, a gang of us would color them, splashing big brushfuls of watercolor, a stroke of blue across the top for sky, blob of green for a tree, red on a parasol, etc. Attractive young girls were sent out to sell them in the tourist cafés. If the question ever came up as to whether they were authentically "hand-painted," the girl would just lick a finger and rub off a bit of color. One of these girls told me that this was how she supported herself and her illegitimate baby. With five or six others they lived in the Vert Galant park except when the police hassled them. Then they did their sleeping during the day on the banks of the Seine, in bikinis, pretending to sunbathe.

I was introduced to the Princess Aspasia by Dorothy Caruso, whom I had first met in 1949 when she came to Mr. Gurdjieff's apartment. Her daughter Gloria, about my age, became my good friend. A large fair woman, the real Mrs. Caruso was nothing like the little, dark Ann Blythe who depicted her in the Mario Lanza film, *The Great Caruso*. It was much easier to understand that the jaded, aging Italian superstar might be immediately attracted to the naive, young, plump blond that the real Dorothy must have been when they first met. I was always touched that although she married well three times subsequently, if she ever referred to "her husband" she never meant anyone but Enrico.

Mrs. Caruso's friend, Princess Aspasia, originally a commoner, had married into the Greek royal family, but her husband Alexander was short-lived. (It was said he died from being bitten by his pet monkey.) Their daughter, Alexandra, married King Peter of Yugoslavia.

World-famous Italian tenor, Enrico Caruso marries young American Dorothy Benjamin!

Dorothy Caruso in her later years retires to the South of France, to write.

Enrico Caruso and his family. One of the many newspaper photos published in the Twenties of the beloved tenor with wife Dorothy and new daughter, Gloria.

Mrs. Caruso (right) and "Sophie" in 1949 waiting for Mr. Gurdjieff to continue one of the auto caravans.

Gloria (Caruso) Murray (left) meeting two of her pal Dushka's Greek entertainer friends.

When Peter was deposed from his throne, the young couple took refuge in Paris. With very few resources, financial, educational or even personality-wise, they were ill equipped for real life in the big city. The paparazzi chased them but the result was mostly bad publicity, since they were apt to make social gaffes and run up large debts, especially Alexandra, who spent a lot of time in the top couture houses, ordering clothes she couldn't afford.

Although King Peter and his wife tried to keep in touch with some influential people, especially moneyed Americans who might one day aid them in retrieving the throne, practically their sole support was a monthly tithe collected from the many poor Yugoslav expatriates also living in Paris. Some of these worked in hotels and as taxi drivers, and Peter's reputation amongst his own people wasn't helped when they observed and reported back that he lived in the extravagant Hotel Crillon and was dining almost daily at deluxe Maxim's around the corner. His fellow refugees never understood the subtleties of public relations, and that these places offered free accommodation to a King and Queen for the publicity value.

Princess Aspasia decided something must be done to correct the whole situation and hired Howarth Services to:

a) Get the King a job (!)

b) Generate some good publicity for the young couple and...

c) ...move them out of the Hotel Crillon into an apartment, even if Mother-in-Law Aspasia had to pay for it!

Before going to meet my new clients for the first time, I asked various more social friends and acquaintances what I should be prepared for, how they thought I should dress, act, address them, and so forth. My biggest help was Brenda de Morelos, an attractive American, formerly the Olympic swimmer Brenda Helser, who had married "M. le Comte Lorenzo de Morelos y Guerrero" (or something like that). Determined to live up to the traditions of her husband's ancient family, and pass them on to their little son, Brenda became an expert practitioner in social protocol.

So she coached me to address the King and Queen as "Sir" and "Madame," since though Royals they no longer had a throne, decked me out in a hat and white gloves and sent me off to the Crillon. The guardians of the imposing front desk directed me upstairs, and, trying to remember all Brenda's instructions, I took a deep breath and rang the bell of the suite. No sentry, butler or even maid opened the door. Just a rather disheveled young woman in a plaid woolen dressing gown saying: "Oh, you must be Dushka. I'm Sandra and this is Peter. Come in! Come in!"

From then on they treated me like an old friend. In fact, they struck me as desperately lonely and rather lost. Any day that we didn't meet together, we had long telephone conversations. If they tried to phone me at my current cheap hotel in Montparnasse, the harridan of a concierge would come to the foot of the stairs and scream up three floors that some "*idiote*" [idiot] was calling herself "*La Reine quelque-chose*" ["Queen something"] and wanted me.

The first time I had lunch with them I was still struggling to be socially correct, especially since we were meeting at the Ritz, known to me only by impressive reputation. (It was probably another publicity "freebie.") Well, my fellow peasants, what do you think table conversation with a King consists of? Would you believe an hour's detailed description of how he suspected, had diagnosed, treated and finally got rid of — a tapeworm?

Years later the memory of that special lunch greatly helped me endure horrid treatments I had to undergo as a result of eating undercooked meat in Turkey.

At one time they sold capsules guaranteed to help you lose weight, and the secret ingredient was rumored to be a baby tapeworm. I can vouch for the fact that even dieting (that horrible word!) is preferable.

Well, I discovered that it isn't easy to get a King a job, especially this one! I had heard of Dukes and Earls who used their titles to help them work as Rolls-Royce salesmen, society photographers, and so forth. And I'd met Prince Obolensky, a hotel executive, Count George Gogh, the head-waiter at Mirko's, and Prince Oleg Cassini, a dress designer. But the only thing that Peter was interested in was automobiles. He would have adored being an auto mechanic, but that was hardly suitable, especially if he ever hoped to get back his crown.

He had once given some successful lectures to women's clubs in the U.S. and the provincial American ladies had been charmed to meet him, of course. But that made Alexandra jealous and she vetoed his attempting it again. So finally I suggested that they take advantage of that public in another way, and, together or separately, write articles, especially for womens' magazines, and later develop them into a book or two.

In spite of all my Broadway publicity experiences I wasn't able, however, to create much good press for them in Europe. So we concentrated on at least moving them out of the Crillon. Various housing agents I worked with regularly gave us suggestions and a bunch of keys and left it up to me to take my clients to visit apartments.

Wedding HM King Peter II and HM Queen Alexandra:

Standing (left to right): Duke of Gloucester, Duchess of Kent, King George VI, King Peter, King Haakon VII, Queen Alexandra, Princess Aspasia of Greece, King George II of Greece, Prince Bernhard of the Netherlands.
Seated (left to right): Queen Elizabeth, Prince Tomislav, Queen Wilhelmina of the Netherlands.

Doing this involved a special routine.

Peter did have one remaining asset. His favorite possession, a present to him from the manufacturers, was a big Jaguar limousine with the driver's seat separated from the passengers' by a glass partition. He loved driving it, which was fortunate since he could no longer afford a chauffeur. I knew that his wife was used to sitting in the front seat next to him. So when we were to check out an apartment, Peter would pick me up at my office, I would get in the back seat, and then we would start looking for Alexandra. This meant touring the whole area where the couture houses are located, and where some people knew me by sight.

Since I was still struggling just to make a go of my new business, imagine my astonishment when everyone started complimenting me on my obvious success.

Ultimately I understood their surprise and envy when some continued on making admiring comments about my "fine new limousine and handsome young chauffeur."

I naturally never admitted who that "chauffeur" was.

I met some of the other Yugoslavs who found themselves in Paris through another client and friend, Alexander V——. About forty, tall and broad-shouldered, with a big Balkan mustache, Alex was very attractive to women, including myself.

Someone had told him about my Services and one day he introduced himself to me on the terrace of the Café Select saying he had a job for me. He needed someone to arrange a numbered account for him in Switzerland, and he gave me about $12,000 worth of shares of International Nickel stock as a first deposit. It was only much later that friends of his told me, and by then I was really ready to believe it, that this was his payment for a political assassination.

In the weeks that followed, sober or maudlin drunk, Alex's stories and those of his friends were consistent and never contradicted each other, and amazing though some of them were, they were convincing.

Alex was born in a little Serbian village, and his father, who became police chief, was a strict, cruel man who often savagely beat his children. As Alex grew up he trained himself, learning to box and wrestle. His primary incentive, he told me, was to be one day big and strong enough to beat up his father in return.

His mother had been only fifteen, though tough and sturdy, when she married. The grown Alex grieved that "when he was little she never kissed him or took him on her knee." But she did pay him ten dinars to lie in her bed to warm it in winter, or to hold her cold feet.

His brother, Dushan, and a younger sister "had full educations." They went to business college. Alex didn't, but due to his height and strong features, he began to get jobs in theater groups playing old men, and Cossacks, etc. until, with three other boys who also sang and played guitar they toured as a group to "some twenty hotels."

This was all cut short when war was declared and the group was inducted, ultimately captured, and put in a concentration camp where the Germans used interrogation techniques of teeth-pulling and finger-breaking. (As a result, a Serb suggestion for finishing off an enemy was "break a finger, cut it off – and repeat – and repeat!")

Finally released from the camp, Alex brought his brother back from Bulgaria, saw to it that his father returned to his mother, and without a "goodbye," set off to join partisans fighting in the mountains.

The German enemy was gone, but had been replaced by Tito, whose government also considered Alex a war criminal, accusing him and his partisans of eleven thousand deaths. He said: "Not that many, but plenty" — seven hundred fifty in one troop train bombing — thirteen with a machine gun that he once manned for three days straight so that he couldn't lower his stiff shoulder for a month.

His group lived in the mountains for six months with no shelter, cooking for themselves whatever they could scavenge, mending their own shoes — but members of their families suffered reprisals. Alex counted that in all, eighteen people from his family and that of his fiancée had been killed. This was when and why he swore the revenge that shaped his later life. It took a long time for him to identify and locate the officials who were responsible, to make careful plans and ally himself to other anti-Communist forces who could help him, and whom apparently, he helped in return.

He admitted to me that he was in France illegally but had some kind of special arrangement with the police. He checked in with them each day and they closed their eyes to his lack of proper papers. And though we sometimes went out together, it could never be on a Saturday night. He had been warned to stay off the streets then, since there was too great a possibility of fights or brawls. If he were ever caught up in one of these or a "clean-up" raid, he would lose his immunity and his "friends" couldn't help him.

Alex had keys to several apartments scattered throughout the city where he could go during the day. Once I sat waiting for him during a couple of hours in a café in the Sixteenth Arrondissement while he went into a luxurious, big building to "freshen up for the evening." He came back with his shirt washed and ironed saying "the maid was very kind." He once mentioned that if ever he needed help and couldn't get to one of these apartments, he had been told to "go to the nearest Catholic priest!" (Which obviously suggested to me Vatican support for this avowed enemy of Tito's Communist regime!)

Of the original forty men who had fought together in Yugoslavia, eight survived and ultimately made their way to Paris, escaping by various routes, or deported after the war. Every year they gathered together for a reunion and once Alex took me along with him. In a small Russian nightclub in Montmartre they settled in for a night of reminiscences, drinking and nostalgic mountain songs. I remember that "Grischa" was a guitarist, and "Giko," the youngest, just fourteen when he fought with them, now sang in cafés.

As the evening wore on and the drinks took effect they became more and more insistent about how they would one day go back to their homeland, how they would risk their lives to throw out the Communists and restore the monarchy. And then, I was aghast but tried not to show it, they began to add that once they put their king back on his throne, after a few weeks they would assassinate him themselves.

It took me a while before I sadly understood their thinking. They despised Peter for many reasons but realized they needed him as a figurehead if they wished support from other countries, especially the U.S. But they did respect Peter's brother who worked in England as some kind of estate manager and their hope was for him to inherit the crown, and thus continue the monarchy.

Fortunately I never heard anything more about this plan and I gather that Peter and Alexandra moved quietly away from Paris, (to a house on the Riviera?) A Serbian acquaintance tells me that when Peter died, it was under a pseudonym in a California hospital where he had come, hoping for a special cure. (Though Wikipaedia states that he"died in Denver, Colorado on 3 November 1970 after a failed liver transplant.")

As for Alex... Who knows?

One Howarth Services client that I did accompany personally was Evelyn Sutta who had been with us in Paris in 1949 but hadn't then had much time to see the sights. During a summer visit a few years later she asked me to guide her around.

We were just coming down the hill on our way to the Place Pigalle after visiting Sacré Coeur, when I heard my name called and turned to see a familiar dark face with a big smile. It was Babe Wallace, the actor/singer whom I had met in Harlem when he was the M.C. at the Club Sudan. I introduced him to Mrs. Sutta who agreed it would be nice to rest our feet and all have coffee together on a café terrace. (Besides, that's still the best kind of sight-seeing I know.)

When I asked Babe what brought him to Paris, he said that he had been there for many months featured as production singer in the famed *Folies Bergeres* located around the corner. He was just coming back from rehearsal.

Babe was a very serious, well-educated man with a pleasant singing voice who, I'd always thought, should really have been a lawyer or doctor. But the times being what they were, like many blacks, he decided his chances were better in the entertainment field. And he did have a certain success and played opposite Lena Horne in the film *Stormy Weather*. Still, I was amused at the idea of him standing every night on the *Follies* stage singing while all those naked girls posed around him, especially when he insisted he was very unhappy and wanted to go back home.

Everyone had heard so much about Josephine Baker and others having great success in France, that it was a common belief that every American black would find a paradise of complete acceptance there. I had already had my doubts about that. I still remembered the surprisingly intense arguments I used to have with my French "fiancé" Alfred. In spite of his family's theatrical background and Mr. Gurdjieff's strong influence, Alfred still hadn't gotten rid of some of the attitudes and prejudices deeply engrained in many Frenchmen. I had found that this was often based not even on their own experiences, since they rarely met a "*noir*", but on those of their friends and relatives in the Colonies, who dealt with "primitive peoples."

So I was interested to realize that Babe was sensitive enough to be reacting to something of all this. Although he was constantly flattered and lionized by everyone in Paris, he felt it was on a false basis which left him feeling essentially lonely and homesick.

Babe Wallace

What made this brief meeting memorable was that Mrs. Sutta, in her frank, energetic way started teasing Babe unmercifully about the big, brown-paper-covered book he was carrying. In those days many American tourists bought and were asked by their friends to bring back the "special" books (Henry Miller, etc.) that were still banned in the U.S. but available everywhere in France.

So Mrs. Sutta was greatly amused that Babe, who spent so much of his life surrounded by naked women, was still embarrassed enough to want to hide what he was reading and cover it with brown paper. Still laughing she grabbed it and looked to see "which one" it was.. **It was P.D. Ouspensky's _In Search of the Miraculous!_**

Another friend from New York who became a sort of client was Yogi Vithaldas. A former dancer, Yogi was a skilled and articulate exponent of Hatha Yoga in India, and with the advent of psychosomatic medicine investigations, he had been invited to America to demonstrate and lecture.

Our friend Emily "Jackie" Davie offered him the use of her large Manhattan apartment for presentations to doctors, scientists and writers, and I was often invited. After a general introduction of the basic yoga positions, Yogi would also show startling internal cleansing techniques (which might include swallowing yards of gauze tape) and amazing examples of physical control and coordination (for internal massaging and organ stimulation.) He would then sometimes treat us to a vegetarian dinner that he cooked himself, and explain the effect and medicinal uses of the various ingredients.

Jackie's housekeeper was a "veddi correct" English lady who just cringed in the corner when Yogi took over her kitchen, mixing things with his hands, sometimes squatting on the floor, chanting, and often splattering staining saffron mixtures onto her spotless white walls. So after the first couple of times I offered to help with the cooking and learned to make some of Yogi's specialties and was pleased when years later a Susan Roberts collaborated with him and they published the useful little _Yogi Cookbook_.

As a result Yogi and I became friendly and I was happy when he began to have pupils and decided to stay on in America. A big photo spread in _Life Magazine_ which showed Yehudi Menuhin and "his Yoga teacher, Vithaldas," both taking the various traditional Yoga poses, really established him.

Yogi Vithaldas

I hadn't realized how near to us he lived until one summer day I went to check out the swimming pool in the nearby Julia Richman High School. I had heard that it was free of charge to the public but wondered about the question of cleanliness. I was enthusiastic when I found Yogi there doing laps in solitary splendor and reported to Mother that surely that was a good recommendation. She deflated me a bit when, with a twinkle in her eye, she reminded me that the Indians swim in the Ganges!

During one of the first years of Howarth Services in Paris when I was beginning to be very busy, I decided to take off precious time to go and help at the Billancourt Film Studios where Mme. de Salzmann was making one of the films of the Movements. Mother worked with her on most of the seven or eight that were done, and many of the rest of us were recruited to help with costuming, etc.

Imagine my surprise when one day the loudspeaker on the soundstage called "Mademoiselle Howarth" to the telephone. A faint, high-pitched voice said: "Hello, Dushka, this is me, Yogi. I am on my way to Bombay but thought I would stop off here in Paris and spend a week or so with you."

I was speechless! I was then living in a one-room studio with hardly enough space for myself, much less a guest, and I knew Yogi didn't have much money and spoke not a word of French. What to do with him?

So I asked him to meet me later in Montparnasse and told him how to get there. Then I rushed back to my *quartier* to arrange things and book a room for him in one of the cheapest hotels. But a big problem in that kind of place was to arrange for bath privileges. When I warned the concierges that this particular client of mine would need a bath every day, maybe sometimes even two, they went into shock.

Then I hurried around to some of the little neighborhood restaurants like my own favorite find, *Chez Wadja*, and prepared them, if Yogi were to come in, to give him vegetables, fruit, yogurt and water. He drank no wine, coffee or tea. Not from religious or health principles, he explained, but simply because after his intense internal cleansings such things were too potent, just as he required only tiny quantities of food as he assimilated it all.

Finally I installed Yogi in his hotel, with explanations and apologies, and rushed back to the filming.

The next day, to help him fill his time, since I still couldn't get away, I booked Yogi on an American Express sightseeing tour. Then a Paris By Night excursion from which he returned saying patiently: "You know, Dushka, girls same all over world!"

I struggled to think how I could provide him with some company, especially after returning to Montparnasse one evening and finding him sitting dolefully alone on the terrace of the Dome, perched cross-legged on one of their wicker chairs.

Then I remembered that Reid Hall was just down the block. This is a big residence hall for many nice young American college girls enduring their Junior Year in Paris. I spread the word there that if any of them saw this little, dark man wearing his national costume, they should just go up to him and say "I'm a friend of Dushka's," and they would find him charming and interesting to talk to, he had known Gandhi, etc.

Well, they really tried and they found lots of little, dark men in national costumes... African chiefs... Arabian sheiks...et al, all of them enchanted to be approached by pretty young co-eds.

But poor Yogi was still usually alone and it took me months to live it all down and explain away the rumor which quickly spread through the *quartier* about "the promotion-minded new Madame called Dushka."

The last time I ever saw Yogi was a few years ago, and something he said then about Krishnamurti stayed with me.

Anyone who heard Krishnamurti speak remembers how inspirational, but somehow at the same time intangible, and difficult to emulate practically, he could seem. Perhaps Emily Luytens, his foremost biographer phrases it better: "...one of the world's great religious teachers of all times. His message is simple to those who give it close attention, though extremely hard to implement."

Many people seem to have embraced the Gurdjieff Work because Krishnamurti inspired them, showed them what it could be to have real "being." But what came next? The Gurdjieff system offered a way to accomplish something real.

Well, some of his fellow Indians evidently felt the same.

One day I was escorting my ninety-year-old Mother through the traffic on East Seventy-Second Street. Coming through the cars was a small dark man in a white dhoti, with shoulder-length thinning hair. It was an older but still recognizable Vithaldas.

He beamed at us both saying: "Oh, it's Dushka! And Mama Dushka!" And almost immediately he was asking for news of Jackie Davie. I explained that Jackie now lived in Ojai, California, and only came to New York to accompany Krishnamurti when he gave public talks here.

Yogi nodded thoughtfully and said slowly: "Ah, yes... Krishnamurti. Very interesting man. Good man. I have conversations with him before. Very interesting. Yes. Ah, yes. But he like live thirty-ninth floor, no elevator," and he walked away downtown.

On reading this story, an old friend, Charles Campbell, now a Dervish, wrote me that once years ago he admitted to Sonan Kazi, a Tibetan Buddhist, that he could never grasp what Krishnamurti was trying to convey. Kazi said: "Yes, K is trying to hand you an egg with no shell!"

In his beautiful little book, *Krishnamurti: Two Birds On One Tree*, our friend Ravi (Dr. Ravindra) recalls many meetings and conversations with his countryman, Krishnamurti, but also that: "Once, not long before his death, he said to me, with his eyes full of sorrow. 'No one understands what I have been saying for the last sixty years. No one.'"

* * * * *

CHAPTER 27

ETHEL'S LAST LETTERS, BENNETT AND SUBUD

On October 19, 1953, Ethel Merston wrote Mother from Wellington Barracks, Nelgiris, South India,

"Jessmin dear,

"Are you going to Europe next summer? You must come. You have something in the bank and I can also help cover expenses, but come you must. From probably middle or end April, I shall be at Coombe Springs [J.G. Bennett's community at Kingston-on-Thames, outside of London, the full title of which was "The Institute for the Comparative Study of History, Philosophy and the Sciences."]

"Come and work there as well as in Paris.

"Your letter of June eighth was of great interest but I read through it desperate fatigue and loneliness and too much responsibility for your strength. Break through and come to Europe. The change of everything will act as the shock needed and help you regain your old friendliness and ease of contact. I don't believe that one can fight or sit on one's personality without creating an equally bad opposition. It is only by "seeing" one's personality in action, seeing down to the depths, that it, of it's own accord, without fight on our part, dissolves. The fight is to watch and see constantly, unbiased, impartial observation that is just as much effort but has not the negative consequences of disciplining, fighting the personality, or 'working against' it, as you say. If circumstances strengthen it, *tant mieux*, for then one can see it the more easily, but it makes the watching harder.

"I have to watch just the reverse from you, see myself going out right and left, see why I do so, the void in me, the fear of seeing it which makes me cling to people. Alternately I forget the way and try to curb this going out, then remember let the self go and watch it careening.

"Jessmin dear, I read disappointment that I did not come over to Mendham. Truly, quite apart from the question that I am not ready for that life yet, nor am I now strong enough, I don't even know how I shall fare at Coombe Springs in a community life for I can do very little physical work and people tire me still.

"Your letter found me in hospital soon after I had come up to the hills. Exhaustion culminated in a violent attack of nephritis. They very kindly took me in at the Military Hospital where the care was excellent and the six weeks were most happy except for a few uncomfortable tests at the beginning. I really enjoyed the complete rest. Now I am driving the car again, doing a little gardening, but can do nothing strenuous and spend the rest of the time feet up working on Bennett's book, and reading; some serious books, some modern novels. Working on Bennett's book

Dushka

◆

has been so reminiscent of work on *Beelzebub*. Endless typing and re-typing and discussions on use of words, and will be still more so at Coombe Springs.

"In one of my books I seem to find the source of G.'s teaching – not Tibet or Hindu manuscripts as I was always given to understand – or took for granted – but in the old Jewish mystical teachings of pre- and early Christendom handed down through the Sufis and Dervishes with whom G. was so much in touch. All the 'hierarchies,' the 'triads,' the 'sevens' are there in the *Zohar*. And now I am reading a booklet by Martin Buber, the Chassidic scholar, called *I and Thou* which gives all G.'s teaching about 'being' and 'function' in a nutshell.

"How is the Gurdjieff Foundation going? Will their house on 63rd. Street be in full swing this Winter? Are the numbers of new pupils drawn in by Jeanne and by Bennett's lectures, sticking to the Work? Who has come this year in Mme. Lannes stead? I felt about her just as you do – immature in the Work, and I would have little confidence in her judgement, but good for beginners and a nice woman. Mme. O. is so much the bigger woman and it sounds as if Mme. L was not yet ready for her.

"Who is there who is forceful in the Work anyway? Do teachers ever have forceful successors, except Vivekananda who even then deviated completely from his Master's lines? A Teacher is more for individuals than for a group, for Mme. Lannes herself rather than for her group, for Bennett rather than for his, for Jeanne rather than for the organization, for Mme. O. rather than for Mendham.

"Jessmin, why is there such mutual distrust amongst the leaders of G.'s (and O.'s) groups, Jane Heap, Maurice Nicoll, Ouspenskys, all keeping themselves apart and refusing to mix and cooperate? Why shouldn't you make friends of individuals? G. never prevented any of our friendships and kept himself separate. I like Mme. Lannes for that. She welcomed anyone to Cullingham Gardens.

"So Eve Taylor is married to a Frenchman. Does that mean in Paris? How I wish that Dushka could meet someone in Europe and marry. As you say, the average young American is much too immature for her. Perhaps she will meet someone this summer when over there.

"How is Mme. O., Sophie Grigorievna as I always think of her? You said she was getting progressively weaker and that sounds bad. How I would have liked to talk with her now. But it isn't to be, I know – not in this life. But I think we shall recognize each other wherever we next meet. Please greet her for me.   Ethel"

* * * *

Mother had a wide correspondence, and people would clip and send her articles they thought would interest her. On Oct. 29, 1950, a Madison, Wisconsin newspaper had reported on an event in Spring Green, with these headlines:

"TALIESIN DANCE DEMONSTRATION
MARKS IST ANNIVERSARY OF GURDJIEFF"S DEATH
Iovanna Wright Presents Students in Works of Mystic-Philosopher."

There followed a lukewarm but polite account of an evening presentation in the local Frank Lloyd Wright Fellowship "Taliesin Playhouse" and included a description of twenty-two dancers, "dressed in white tunics and trousers, with colorful sashes... women dancers with gold braid about their foreheads..." and quoted the program as saying: "An Inner Exercise in Concentration of Attention Within Oneself."

But three years later, Nov. 4, 1953, the *Chicago American* blasted forth:

"TALIESIN FAILS ON GURDJIEFF
by Ann Barzel

"Frank Lloyd Wright is a great architect and an indulgent father. He could not possibly take seriously the performance of his daughter, Iovanna Lloyd Wright, and her twenty-eight playmates who indulged themselves in ritual exercises and temple dances of the late George Gurdjieff at the sold-out Goodman Theater yesterday.

Respectful article in a local Wisconsin paper, 1950

"Mr. Wright's performance in the foyer before the show, greeting former students and current idol-worshippers, was as graceful as anything on the stage. His appearance before the curtain evoked an ovation. He gave the dancers a send-off with a few urbane and non-committal remarks.

"Daughter Iovanna is a pretty and very intense little girl who obviously takes herself and her cult very seriously.

"Philosopher Gurdjieff is purported to have found profound truths in the dance rituals of the orient. One is loathe to believe that disciples like H.G. Wells and Katherine Mansfield were taken in by a charlatan, but if what Iovanna Wright presented is simon-pure Gurdjieff, it doesn't have a dance leg, nor a philosophical one to stand on.

"The program notes reeked of numerology and such questionable metaphysics as, 'In the cosmic octave — the Ray of Creation, at the intervals between mi-fa and si-do, a slowing down of vibrations occurs.'

"The same kind of cosmic nonsense was repeated on the stage.

"The group danced out the patterns of Gurdjieff's pleasant music in the manner of Dalcroze Eurythmics."

* * * *

Another paper offered:

"TALIESIN DANCING GRIM, STIFF
by Herman Kogan

"'In the moving pageant of these dances,' read one of the few lucid sentences in the evening's program book, 'you shall see the reflection of truth and knowledge since time began.' Maybe so, but I reacted sensually rather than philosophically. Consequently, I experienced occasional excitement, occasional interest, considerable ennui ...

"Brief remarks by the great Frank Lloyd Wright assured us, among other things, that not many would understand what was going on. He was right.

"The dancers danced with grim, awful solemnity. Some of their sharply accented numbers stirred painful memories of hours of close order drill. Some, with their steady rhythm, manual gyrations and hip swayings, resemble the exercises at Charlie Postl's health club. A comely young woman proved fascinating in some Babylonian dances. A dancer with a heavy mustache counted his one-two-three-four visibly.

Clippings from the newspaper accounts of the Taliesin movements demonstration in Chcago, November 1953

"No one on the stage seemed to be really enjoying what he or she was doing. Maybe that's how Gurdjieff meant it to be."

Though she was never mentioned in the write-ups, it was obvious to Mother and myself that it was Mrs. Lloyd Wright who was the moving force behind these Movement performances and the way they were presented. Mother's reaction to all this was evidently written in a letter to Ethel who replied:

"Dear Jessmin,

"I'm simply horrified at Olgivanna. It is the evil spirit and is always the way that sacred teaching gets debased and perverted until it is lost. One can have energy and drive in the wrong as well as the right direction and Olgivanna has evidently turned left.

"One can't blame Iovanna. She is the product of two spoilt parents who exploit her. Olgivanna was always a lazy, self-indulgent woman at the Prieuré, and rather conceited, and now she is using the Work towards her own ends. But I am disgusted that she could descend to such depths as to get advertisement in such a way. It shows the danger of spreading the music, recordings and Movements wholesale as Jeanne has been inclined to do. I've always been against this because there is no one now with sufficient knowledge to control and know to whom to give and to whom not.

"Well, it is done, that is all there is to it. No wonder you are sick at heart over it.

"And now to happier sides of the Work! A Movement group of one hundred ten sounds really good... Is it so much smaller than the English ones? And also the working, talking and exchanging, in groups and as a group is so helpful. It is, (or was), one of the strong points of the Oxford Group (M.R.A. now). One can't go half so deep alone, anyway not until one is very far on. That is one reason why I want to work with Bennett's group this summer.

"You ask if there is a [Ramana] Maharshi group nearby. No, except for a few peasants whose language I don't know and who don't work in any way. They are just devotees who worship but do not work on themselves. The ashram at Tiruvannamalai is beginning to attract people for its atmosphere. But again... one of devotion and surrender.

"I am in touch with the Englishman who is one of the leaders there, but though he won't admit it our ways are different. He is a ritualist and I am not. He does not work on the self but lets it rip and loses it during meditation. It is not my way.

"Up here nearby there is no one interested at all that I have met. But a short trip away there is an Indian friend who has gone very far in 'non-identification' and he was galvanized into work by the terrible loss of his wife. I go up to spend a few hours with him every ten days or so and always come back refreshed.

"At Kotagiri there are many friends all interested in things of the spirit — earnest Quakers, earnest fundamentalists to whom God lovingly enters their lives, theosophists with, and without, occult leanings, amongst them all there is only one to whom I can talk occasionally and that not easily. But we just meet on the mutual level of an interest in the spirit, a God whoever or whatever he may be.

"What a good relationship you have succeeded in making with Dushka. You are marvelous. But one sentence makes me uncomfortable, no, not the right word, makes me 'questioning' is better, where you say 'Life alone seems so artificial, I have no impetus.' Doesn't that put the impetus onto an entirely wrong footing? On to that of vicarious living, which we don't recognize? If there were real living in oneself then one would have the impetus whether alone or not, and life would be no more artificial when alone than when with others. It isn't that life is more or less artificial when one is alone, but one notices its mechanicity usually hidden by the emotional content of a companionship.

"Jessmin dear, this sentence alone makes me still more say come to England this summer and don't feel that you are indispensable to the groups and Foundation. I felt I was indispensable to the garden and the feeding of the Prieuré and refused to quit when G. wanted me to go onto the book entirely, regardless of our food supply. Now I know I was wrong to have refused, I was too identified with growing vegetables for our needs.

"I'm glad you don't feel inclined to play the role of going round more to various places to start Movements. As I said above, the more you disseminate the more you lose or distort, and the Movements distorted can be very dangerous, e.g. Olgivanna's show, unless the disseminator needs the experience for himself and is capable of using it. I am convinced that many of the groups started by G. were for the learning of the leaders he appointed and not for the sake of spreading the teaching. Jane Heap's, Eleanor Crowdy's. John Bennett's, even Jeanne's work. Incidentally, in so far as each gains something for himself, so, incidentally to him, others can gain from his gain. I suppose that is one of the hardest experiences and tests of being a 'Teacher' and few can come through it. But as others can gain from his development, so others can go astray from his failure.

"Do you remember how in the demonstrations in the Champs Elysées Theater, G. played the buffoon during the interval and had a fountain of wine playing into a pool from which we handed glasses to everyone. Was that not the precursor of Olgivanna's show in Chicago? If G. really wanted to get the Movements over as teaching for others, and to as many as possible, why the buffoonery in the middle? I don't think he cared about others except the very few whom he saw had the possibility of development. And most of even those failed as far as one can see... But there one can't see the minute preparatory steps, so can't say."

* * * *

And a few months later Ethel wrote from Bennett's Coombe Springs in England:
"May, 1954

John G. Bennett

"Your letter did find me at Coombe and I'm thrilled to think that you are really coming over. Bennett went over to Paris to meet Jeanne on her return and says that all is fixed up for Dushka in Paris, so after the New York Movement groups are over you will come. And you must come here too for a visit because Bennett's is a most important part of the work with crowds flocking to his lectures and coming down here on Sundays.

"Bennett is very much as you describe him, immense kindliness, immense possibilities, great vitality and amazing knowledge, or, rather, learning. It is intensely interesting to see him work and he has given me the opportunity of seeing as much of the various groups as I have energy for.

"The whole place is alive and there is a spirit of friendliness and cooperativeness in this house which is rare in a hard-worked community. This is also largely due to Mrs. Bennett. She very nearly died last week, it was almost 'go' for four days, but on his return from Paris she licked up his vitality and has once more rallied and will live on for a time. She clings desperately to him, and because of him, to life, it is pathetic in a woman of her age.

"My position is queer, part guest, part worker, in the place, but not of it, given special privileges by Mr. B. and having to mind my Ps and Qs so as not to arouse resentment or jealousy. I have to watch out not to throw my weight about. It is all very good for me. So far all is well except for my memory which will not remember to remember the exercises and myself!

"All the first six weeks I was working weekly on Mr. B.'s lecture scripts, then typing out the first volume of his Turkish trip journal, then translating the lectures into French for Dr. M. Vernet, Mr. B.'s friend. Part of the day always gardening as recreation. This is a lovely place and at present the little wood is a carpet of bluebells, after yellow sheets of daffodils following a white sheet of crocuses. It is a joy to see the Spring again in England.

"Much love to you, bon voyage, and success to Dushka in her new adventure."

* * * *

"June, 1954
"Jeanne came down to Coombe and many of Bennett's groups were gathered

together for her to attend. Mme. Lannes and Henri Tracol with Bennett and I, went from room to room listening, spending about a half- to three-quarters- of an hour with each group.

"Jeanne never said a word at any of them, but at the end gathered the leaders together and gave her view as to their work. I had formed exactly the same opinion of it and was glad to hear her voice what I had felt for some time. Namely, that there was far too little stress given to impartial self-observation, and far too advanced exercises given which the leaders themselves did not understand. This last is Bennett's doing. He loves inventing exercises and is not good at preparatory work for beginners. He can enthuse and attract people, especially the young, but is less good at slow psychological work and has not trained his leaders. Jeanne's visit was very useful in bringing this out.

Stained glass window (enneagram design) made by Bennett's students for the special meeting hall at Coombe Springs, called the "Djameechoonatra," referring to what is described in *Beelzebub* as "a kind of terrestrial monasterial refectory."

"Bennett and I thrashed at the problem for hours the next day. He sees Work quae WORK with his people as pawns to do it. I see the Work for people, as the instrument by which to help humanity to be Men, Human. This is a crude way of putting it, but somewhat what it comes to.

"Where I so much admire B. is his capacity to take criticism unperturbed and give it real consideration. He is miles ahead of Jeanne in that way, and of most of us. He can see his whole edifice destroyed, and feel little but interest in re-building better. In other words, he is extraordinarily unpossessive whether of things, people, or ideas. That is a tremendous thing and means real inner security and a born leader.

"Jeanne is a far better organizer than B. but gives me the feeling of far less inner security, far less free, and so disliking criticism of any sort and possessive of her position. Both she and B. rouse hero-worship in people, though neither of them court it, both giving allegiance to G. Both are, I feel, being used, as G. himself was used, as Blavatsky and dozens of other 'formers of groups' were and are used, to awaken as many as possible of humanity to it's true position. B. has an inkling of a sense of responsibility for this. Whether Jeanne has I don't know, or whether she is just the disciple of G. Anyway, even so, she is very valuable and most instruments are not perfect especially in this dark age.

"As for the other leaders' groups (Jane's, Lannes', Crowdy's), I know little about them, or nothing. I found Mme. Lannes changed, rather dour-looking and one or two people have told me that she is not helpful about their problems, in fact that they no longer get anything from her. From what you said about her, it looks as if she were taking refuge from her shock and loneliness and broken life in a sense of power and position, I don't know but I'm sorry for her."

* * * *

In the summer of 1954 Ethel came through Paris where I was trying to get my "Howarth Services" project underway and on August 1 she reported to Mother:
Dear Jessmin

"...Dushka is a dear and how attractive. After calling around I finally got her phone number, reached her, and she came to Nina Mercuroff's (where I'm staying for a few days). Nina got home very late so we had a nice talk alone in my room before supper and your ears must have burned. She told me all about her plans and ideas, her horrid tour with the Hollywood family, Sophie Grigorievna's state, her longing for you to come over for a month while she has this flat, etc. etc.

"We had about an hour and a half together alone and then started to get supper. Nina arrived to give directions and Valerian joined us. Then I saw another Dushka, a more sophisticated one, and how she would be with clients, very feminine and attractive, but somehow not quite real, a part, a role.

"The whole impression I have is of great grit, of intelligence, of great need for affection, of emotional immaturity but carried on by mental maturity and courage in adult life and responsibility. How much of this is conscious to her I don't know, not entirely, I think. She needs to marry and to the right man, older than she, a responsible person, adult, not too rich (though she would like money and luxury) so that she could give something, or, rather, something be demanded of her. I hope she may meet such a man, a real man, dear Dushka.

"Last night Dushka, and today Michel and I lunched. I had not seen him since he was four years old (27 years ago?) and should never have known him again. We had a long talk on his career, on India... He has something special but not yet anchored, and is very young for his age. He might go a long way and be of much help in the world.

"What I feel about these young people is that there is no one now who can really direct them truly and that they won't be satisfied in the long run. But I may be wrong. I'm interested to find that some of G.'s old pupils, Nina here, and Miss Crowdy in England have turned back to their churches."

* * * *

Valerian Mercuroff worked as chauffeur to the U.S. Ambassador, Anthony Biddle, and his wife. His responsibilities included keeping their many fancy automobiles in a huge garage under the old apartment house where he lived with his family.

Apparently each morning the very fashion-conscious Mrs. Biddle carefully planned her complete wardrobe, decided which automobile matched her outfit and the occasion, telephoned Mercuroff at home and instructed him which of several uniforms he should wear to complete the ensemble. He somehow managed to keep a straight face, playing his part well for years, and was held in great esteem.

During a certain period I had the use of Betsy Bonbright's little studio on the rue Las Cases just down the block from the Biddle residence.

Several times Mercuroff picked me up on his way home after work and took me along to have dinner with his family (I already knew his son Tolik, a life-long friend of Michel's).

But a highlight of the evening always came at the end when I was led downstairs into the murky garage and given my choice of all those Bentleys, Cadillacs, Rolls-Royces, etc. to be driven home in.

* * * * *

In 1957 Ethel, en route back to India wrote Mother:
October 13,
"On the Red Sea,"

"....Once more on the bridge between West and East after a heart-twisting summer at Coombe, the doings of which will have been rumored across to you.

"It was so nice to see Olga de Hartmann once again. We lunched together and had a good talk. She is quick and lively as ever. Jeanne, too, I saw just before leaving and she looked much better for her summer in the mountains.

"You will soon hear all her impressions of the new teacher (Pak Subuh, his "teaching" is called Subud) at Coombe, so I will not say anything beyond that it is not my path. Most people at Coombe are under the influence of Mr. Bennett so accept enthusiastically, realizing that if they don't it means separation from him and many feel that they owe him so much that it would be disloyal to do that. But some are genuinely taken and helped by the method... the few....

"Because of everything, it was real work and I could see all my dependence, fears, and I didn't come out of it too well. Now I'm longing to get to Tiruvannamalai and settle for six months in the atmosphere of conscious work all round one."

* * * * *

"December 18, 1957)
"Tiruvannamalai, India,

"...Has Jeanne been with you? If so you will have heard more of Bennett's latest activities as chief propagandist for Subuh, the Indonesian he and the old Ouspenskyites imported as Mr. Gurdjieff's successor on a higher plane, and the reincarnation of Ashiata Shiemash or Jesus Christ depending upon whether B. is talking to Gurdjieffites or non-Gurdjieffites!

"The man himself makes an impression of simplicity and sincerity but with no knowledge, out to convert the world by his 'exercises,' definitely hypnotic and not spiritual in spite of what Bennett affirms. Psychic phenomena seems to play a big part in it if one is at all sensitive that way, and healing, especially if psychologically sick people.

"I left before all the publicity led by *The Daily Mail* burst forth, thank goodness, [the 'healing' and subsequent successful pregnancy of movie star Eva Bartok, etc.]

"I saw Jeanne just before leaving and she, after a couple of interviews with Subuh felt the same as I do about him. Miss Alexander, who actually attended the seances (exercises?... meetings?...they call them *latihans*, "trainings") for two months or more, feels the same too, that he is on a far lower level than G. and the work has nothing in common but is the opposite: everything to be done unconsciously, eyes physically and metaphysically shut. She has quit Coombe definitely now, as I have so long as Bennett is on this tack. But I am sorry for him and the crash that must come one day if not in this life, in the next, until he learns to face himself. Poor John. But he is happily revelling in the publicity, roping people in, talking, twisting, persuading.

Pak Subuh

Bennett being interviewed by Steve Allen.

John Bennett talking with Pak Subuh.

"Subuh is coming to America this winter to storm it as he is doing London, it seems. But whether he'll take Bennett with him or not, I don't know.

"It was joyous to get back to the clean and sane atmosphere of the Maharshi — for one feels him as much here now as when he was so in the flesh."

* * * * *

Ethel's two very last letters came from Kotagiri, India. In June she wrote Mother:

"Your news of the groups and Mendham is splendid. Jeanne is doing wonderful work all over the world; such vision and inner quiet: a power. Mendham should now become a real live center and training ground for the new 'Akhaldans' [a Gurdjieffian term for those 'striving to become aware of the sense and aim of the Being of beings'] who will be needed after next year.

"That Gurdjieff's and the Maharshi's teachings have come so close together as to be interchangeable, one throwing light upon the other, seems truly a plan of 'His Endlessness.' Krishnaji's too, though very inexplicit, has the same orientation. I see in them an intensive effort at the present to train small groups all over the world (the Maharshi's books are spreading over America) to form oases of knowledge to influence the world if only by their emanations.

"And not only these three, but evidently some Christian groups are also after the same inner centering on 'I.' I've just read a lovely book, *Bright Morning* by Derek Neville with the same theme. It plays in 1980 and shows how it might be possible, by rousing the masses to a feeling of the spirit or 'I,' to overcome war and evil.

"Of Subuh and Bennett I have heard nothing, nor know whether they came to India as planned or not. If they did, they made no stir."

* * * *

And finally on November 16, 1964 Ethel wrote Mother:

"Here, somehow, tho' so far away in mileage, I don't feel cut off from all the old group friends. I feel that we are all working on the same foundation and there is no disunity. In a way I feel closer to the group friends, because here very few people are working on the teaching line of the Maharshi. Most, perhaps all but two or three, are pure worshippers of his person. But with G.'s teaching as a basis and the Maharshi's further teaching, plus his emanations so strong here, this is the place for me to be. But I feel that G.'s groups have a tremendous place in the formation of the new era to come, and not so long hence either, though neither you nor I may see it.

"I certainly not... inoperable tumors! 'Nothing to be done, six months to live,' they said. That I'm going to beat, for after five months since then, I'm rather better and even had three days last week without any hemorrhage (the tumor is in the bladder) due largely to some Swiss-procured injections that I got from Geneva which cured a friend of mine of the same disease. Today the hemorrhage has started again probably because I stupidly sat up too late last night, was over-tired in consequence.

"There is no pain at all and in every other way but strength (easily tired) I'm O.K. It is marvelous. Let us see whether I don't beat surgeons and astrologer and see the New Year in joyfully. To look at me you would never know I was ill, so don't commiserate.

"You sound well and I hope you are, and Dushka.

"Much love to you dear Jessmin and do keep in touch.

"Affectionately,   Ethel"

To avoid confusion between the names: The real name of the Javanese man addressed as Pak or Bapak (an Indonesian form of respect) was originally Muhammad Subuh Sumohadiwidjojo. The shorter version, simply Subuh, is understandable.

But Subud the spiritual movement is "an acronym of the three Sanskrit words Susila (right living), Budhi (inner life force) and Dharma (will of God)."

John Bennett evidently did accompany Pak Subuh to America and they got considerable publicity. I even have an LP among my record albums entitled: "*What Is SUBUD*, A Discussion by John Bennett and Steve Allen." The liner notes include:

"This record brings together two unusual personalities with a still more unusual theme. Steve Allen is so well known and loved that he needs no introduction. John Bennett... is less known in this country, except to mathematicians who recognize in him the discoverer of a new geometry in six dimensions and to scientists in the Fuel and Power industries... [He] is the author of several books including his monumental philosophical work *The Dramatic Universe* and *Concerning Subud*.

"SUBUD, the theme these two men discuss, is a new spiritual movement that has no theory, no teaching, no dogma. Its universal appeal is proved by the fact that within two years of its first appearance in the West, Bennett was one of a small group who brought it to England in 1957, more than one hundred SUBUD centers have been established in more than thirty-five countries, and that there are thousands of SUBUD members who believe that SUBUD has given them the secret of a happy and useful life in conformity with the will of God."

Bennett's autobiography *Witness* discusses his relationship with Pak Subuh and others in a way that verifies what Ethel described as his "capacity to see his whole edifice destroyed and feel little but interest in re-building better." (And includes on page 159 the, to me at least, revealing comment about himself: "...Mixed with these emotions was, undoubtedly, a kind of spiritual ambition which made me long to become a superman...")

In fact, after a time he became disillusioned with Subuh, but the book he wrote about him led to a meeting with Father Bescond, a monk in the Benedictine monastery of St. Wandille in France. Bescond and other monks of the monastery wanted to meet Pak Subuh, realizing that experiences such as Bennett's book described could not be communicated in words. Bennett himself went and worked with the monks at various times through the years, in the process reinforcing his own Catholicism and a belief that it could be reconciled with Islam.

But the Gurdjieff Work seems never to have been far from Bennett's thoughts or actions in spite of a variety of other enthusiasms.

Predictably, after Subuh he made contact with other "Teachers" including Hasan Shushud (Turkish Sufi), Shivapuri Baba ("Right Livelihood"), and the Anglo-Afghan writer, Idries Shah, to whom he decided he should give Coombe Springs. (I still haven't really understood why. Especially when Shah turned around almost immediately, discouraging visits from Bennett or his people, and sold the property in order to buy one more to his taste near Tunbridge Wells, and Bennett seems to have accepted it all with surprising grace.)

Bennett continued to write and lecture in various countries.

The Shivapuri Baba

Gurdjieff Movements at John Bennett's Sherborne House.

Always a charismatic speaker, he had considerable scientific and professional credentials, fluency in many languages, and tall good looks; so he soon attracted around himself a new group of potential followers.

But now, increasingly, he felt an urgency about the future and the need for a nucleus of young adults "working on themselves," to act as a positive influence in the global catastrophe that he warned loomed ever nearer.

So, returning to England, he set up "The International Academy for Continuous Education" at Sherborne House in the Cotswolds. It was inaugurated in October of 1971 with ninety candidates enrolled for the ten month "First Basic Course," (and well-attended courses continued until a year after Bennett's death in 1974).

This general information about Bennett I gleaned from friends and writings about him. But since my own brief relationship with him was personal and social I wondered how Ethel's reactions to him compared with those who had known him longer and better.

When I showed these old letters of Ethel's to my friend Bob Gerber, (who has been in the Work for many years with Paul Anderson, at John Bennett's Sherborne, Pierre Elliot's Claymont, with Lillian Firestone in New York, etc.) he said:

"This does sound like a pretty fair criticism of JGB to me. In his defense a central element of the Sherborne experience was the thematic method which was based on self-observation. I think he came to understand some of these things about himself between the time of these comments and Sherborne House.

"JGB had Dick Holland, who was a very experienced teacher. Dick died part way through my course. I was fortunate to have gotten a good foundation from Paul Anderson before going to Sherborne.

"I must also say that at the end of his life JGB was a master of those exercises and he left us with a coherent set of practices that are

Bob Gerber at a "Work period."

Sherborne House in England, center of Bennett's activities in his last years. At the right, the proprietor, "Mr. B."

(Above) Elizabeth Mayall Bennett

(Right) Always friendly with Gurdjieff's family, Mr. and Mrs. Bennett are visited at Sherborne by Valentin Anastassieff (left) his wife Sylvie, (front right) and a friend.

Bennett with his wife Elizabeth in the grounds at Sherborne.
This is from one of the last groups of photos taken of Bennett. But since it was a windy day and wisps of his hair stood up on end...we retouched. Some of his faithful pupils have complained. Sorry!

very valuable. He taught the exercises to us but did not spend a lot of time commenting on them or presenting conceptual information about them. Those of us who continued to work with them after Sherborne were able to see what the exercises were about, how they could instruct us and what each developed in us. It is clear that each was taught for a purpose and that they were not taught randomly."

At the time of his death Bennett was also completing plans for an American community to be located on an estate in Claymont, West Virginia. One of my old friends who had been involved with both these projects had this to tell me:

"Bennett seemed to see the commonality in various paths. Although he was a practicing Catholic, he was as much at home in a mosque as in a church or a temple. People tend to forget that he was a philosopher, mathematician, and scientist in life as well as being a spiritual seeker. He had a formidable intellect, tremendous curiosity, he read and studied voraciously in both western and eastern traditions, reading much source material in the original languages. He did incorporate practices from non-Work sources that he found personally valuable, from such people as Hasan Shushud (zikr of absolute liberation), and was very much influenced by the Shivapuri Baba's teaching on right-livelihood, which seemed to flesh-out aspects of Gurdjieff's teaching, but he did not become a 'promoter' of any tradition other than the [Gurdjieff] Work after the Subud experience.

"Not only did he work with the 'candidates' at Sherborne, but he was able to work intensively with some of his long-time students who were staff. He sought to establish a nucleus of people grounded in the practice of the Work who could act as a positive influence in the World during the difficult times ahead. He planned five courses at Sherborne, with people returning to life in the world.

"Claymont was not an American version of Sherborne. The aim at Claymont

Pierre and Vivien Elliot during a visit to the Howarth apartment in New York.

was to establish a work community, which would be a new model for community life. The nine-month basic course would provide a foundation for life in a work community based on common practice and values and would be required for all who wished to join the community. No one ever 'graduated' from a course, a primary aim of which was to find out if one was in fact a real candidate for the Work."

Or as Bob Gerber described it, Claymont was to be "a self-sufficient 'village' community, the life of which would embody both Work principals and principles of environmental sustainability – technology that would serve a human scale community's sustainable position in the world's ecology. The project was intended to develop a balanced way of life which would address real human needs and the conditions of the future. The courses at Claymont Court existed to equip candidates to participate in the project."

Claymont was to open in March, 1975, but then Bennett died just a few months before this. His work in England was continued by his widow Elizabeth while his nephew, Pierre Elliott, came to America to supervise the first course. Pierre and his wife Vivien (née Healey, and previously one of Mother's gifted Movements pupils at Mendham) ended up staying on at Claymont for many years.

Unfortunately, it seems to me, the "courses" format of study sometimes had unexpected results. Such concentrated, secluded and, for some, expensive, "courses" led some people to feel that once having '"completed a course" they had somehow "graduated" and were now already capable, even obligated, to go out and become teachers themselves.

What Bennett envisaged as an introduction to a deep, lifelong search and way of life, was interpreted in other ways. especially when he was no longer there to

"The Mansion" at Claymont Court part of Bennett's projected American community in West Virginia

control things,

Bennett also, to my mind, unwittingly set an unfortunate example in regard to Gurdjieff's Movements. He allowed himself to add "improvements." In fact a big packet of papers I inherited from Mother was labeled by her: ***"Bennett/Sherborne Movements notes including Bennett's <u>dubious additions!</u>"*** and advocates Turkish or Arabic prayers to be recited, specific emotions to be "felt" in certain physical positions, etc. On the surface this seems a minor lapse of valuation, but I have seen that after many years it has had unfortunate results.

Because of my own special allegiance to the authenticity and proper use of the Movements, I had always been uncomfortable about so many "Gurdjieff Sacred Dance" seminars cropping up in unexpected locales like New Mexico, New Paltz, Germany, Santo Domingo, as far as Japan and Poona, India etc. These events were actively advertised and open to anyone prepared to pay the (often considerable) fee. no matter their preparation or understanding, They attracted all kinds of people who were obviously not involved in any unified, supervised ongoing program of Work and were offered by what one might, to be kind, just call: "Self-appointed Independent Movements Teachers" ("independent" of any real connection with the Work or personal contact with Bennett or any other direct source to Gurdjieff and his ideas.)

As my old friend reminded me: "The problem of authenticity cannot be laid totally at Bennett's door, although his distortions have had a major influence.... And no one acknowledges Pierre and Vivien's efforts over many years to try to correct the distortions both at Claymont and among former Sherborne students."

On occasion some of these independent Movement teachers have contacted me in New York wanting to share these things they are doing. Many of them seem to have the best of motives but appal me by their complacency about blatant innaccuracies in their Movements material and casualness in handing it out to unprepared strangers. They just shrug it off when I question many obvious mistakes, their confused teaching practices, their personal inventions, and indiscriminate mixing in of all kinds of other traditions and practices,

I sadly realize that many have come to believe that Mr. Gurdjieff himself left only vague and incomplete indications (..."if, after all, even someone like Bennett could improve upon them!")

So I've given myself a self-appointed task in recent years to convince as many people as possible that Mr. Gurdjieff really did bequeath us meticulously specific and carefully verified exact "formulas" for self study that a few of us are struggling to pass on authentically.

To explain all this I usually find myself using the metaphor of Movements being like a very potent and valuable drug. It must be most carefully prescribed for the particular "patient" (or to a carefully prepared class representing "patients at the same stage of ill-health") as part of a complete, complementary course of treatment. That was certainly what our months of working directly with Mr. Gurdjieff made us realize. Any other use of Movements is (apart from being downright dishonest) ill-advised, if not dangerous.

And for Heaven's sake, at least don't let the poor victimized pupils believe they are receiving authentic "Gurdjieff Work!"

From all corners of the hemisphere, we hear about strange situations, presentations and experiments occurring under the banner of "Gurdjieff." Many of them are hardly distinguishable from the wild distortions which we had come to expect from outsiders and mercenaries like Rajneesh/Osho (and his heirs who call themselves "Sannyasins"), the various "Enneagram people," Robert Burton and The Fellowship of Friends (the "bookmark people"), E.J. Gold, Boris Mouravieff protagonists, Idries Shah groupies, Spain's "Commander Clayton" and his "Institute for the Harmonious Development of Man, Order of the 4th Way," England's splinter "International Gurdjieff Society," various "Crazy Wisdom" projects... etc., etc.

Sadly many serious and eager new "seekers" have been confused, side-tracked even hopelessly discouraged by such pseudo groups and activities. Another regrettable outcome of such a "lowering of standards" is that it may arouse suspicion and cause withdrawal or rifts between older, more responsible leaders of the Work.

This has been especially disheartening for those of us who, like Mother, have long wished and worked hard for real unity and understanding between all true "Gurdjieffians" no matter how widespread geographically or different in circumstance or character.

* * * * *

<u>**CHAPTER 28**</u>

THE GREEK CONNECTION

Into the 1960s, Howarth Services continued to have busy summer and fall seasons in Paris. But the duller winter months made me think seriously about putting the business briefly in mothballs so that I could go home to New York and Mother for the holidays. At last this was made financially feasible when I managed to make a deal to act as a volunteer Recreation Director on Greek Line ships in exchange for my passage.

Dushka
♦

So I found myself sailing back and forth on the old *TSS New York* or the newer *Arkadia*, and working closely with very Greek captains and crews. Suddenly, out of the blue, I became conscious of and identified with my quarter of Greek blood! The other Scandinavian, English, even Armenian quarters of my heritage faded meekly into the background. I found I adored Greek music, and joined in the folkdancing on Crew Night. I gorged myself when there were ethnic specialties on the menu. I admired the men's fine heads and strong features, their practicality and humor, family values — and, yes, I suspect that a lot of it was that they found me attractive. My type of form and face had finally found its natural audience. I even started to learn a little Greek from the friendly officers until they sabotaged me! They got together and coached me in what was supposed to be a complimentary speech to recite to the young Captain when he came down that evening in a new uniform. Of course it was actually something totally lewd and insulting and so shocked the poor man that I was henceforth ostracized from the bridge.

Recreation Director on Greek Line ships.

But after returning to New York, I discovered that it was possible to take Greek language classes (presumably safer ones!) at the big Greek Holy Trinity Cathedral nearby on 74th Street. Well, that started a whole new social life for me. And very welcome it was too as I was beginning to find Manhattan a pretty cold and impersonal place after my busy popularity in Paris.

I did ultimately learn to speak a little Greek which proved useful in later trips to Greece and when Greek songs became an important part of my repertoire as a professional singer, but more important were the friends and contacts I made.

Nicholas J. Papadakos got me licensed as a registered representative of his General Securities, Inc., then trained me as his head cashier. Nick also, incidentally, taught me a most valuable business secret that I've used ever since: "Never sell something. Just help them to buy!" This basic concept also helped me really comprehend what Orage had meant when he described a "good teacher," not as one who taught well, but as someone who "knew how to help pupils to learn." That point of view has guided all my own teaching, and is one of the first hints I pass on to others.

Stellios Pappas registered me as an outside sales representative for his Greek Tourist Agency so I could earn commissions and get an agent's 75% discount on my own air travel.

When I was studying guitar with Vicente Gomez, he had often mentioned his friends in New York, the members of the Society of the Classic Guitar. But it was painter/guitarist Ted Anagnostaras who first took me along to their Tuesday meetings at Mirko's chic supper club. The relaxed atmosphere and the warm appreciation of SCG members gave me the courage to perform more and more often. But especially inspiring were the superb improvised accompaniments kindly offered me and others by great concert artists like Alirio Diaz, Ida Prestie and Alexandre Lagoya, Rodrigo Riera, Olga Coelho, Gustavo Lopez, Julio Prol, Anita Sheer, Jorge Morel, organist Ethel Smith and, of course, our talented host, Mirko Markoe. Word spread about this weekly gathering and though the impromptu entertainment was never promised, Tuesdays were always fully booked. Frequent visitors I remember were Mayor Lindsay, Prince Oblensky, Hoagy Carmichael (who played piano for me), Greer Garson, (who banged a lively tamborine with my Russian song), Theo Bikel, Dave Garroway, Eileen Barton, players of various stringed instruments from Japan, Hungary, and Turkey, and singers of all sorts from the Met to 52nd Street — a toothless old Spanish gypsy — a child prodigy guitarist encouraged to play Bach long after his usual bedtime, and so on.

My "pal" Gregory D'Allessio may have been a bit prejudiced but he included in the 1960 *Society of Classical Guitar Bulletin:*

"...The Guitar Festival at Greenwood Lake in June... Certainly there are some good singers with guitar, and fortunately just one of them was present at Greenwood Lake and entered the contest. This was Dushka Howarth who displayed a respectable ability on the guitar and an ingratiating manner... Worth listening to and looking at, anytime, Miss Howarth was so head and shoulders above her nearest competitor in the Folksinging Contest that the closest second was somewhere near Siberia."

Artist/guitiarist Gregory D'Allessio,

A talented young Greek singer, Paris Jamalas, joined forces with me and we started getting paid as a duet act, until he decided to concentrate on his day job and left me alone to handle our booking at Gerde's Folk City in Greenwich Village. I evidently did pretty well even on my own, because at the end of the first week the frugal boss, Mike Porco, actually handed me an extra ten dollars saying: "This is more of a

(Left to right) Dushka and some of her "Greek connections." Movie actor Tito Vandis, Miss Greece Corrinne Tsopei, and stockbroker Nicholas J. Papadakos.

Dushka's first ever singing job (at the *Club Thalami* on the Greek island of Mykonos) where she had to settle for a poster hurriedly painted over the previous month's attraction "George Zografos".

Later, in New York City, Dushka and Paris Jamalas, her duet partner, are advertised as the stars of the New Year's Eve Gala at the *Paradise Club*

compliment than you realize since you don't drink!"

I had to consult with the bartenders to understand what that meant!

Evidently most of Mike's usual performers ran up such big bar bills that at the end of the week they paid him!

I began going to the Sunday service at the Greek Cathedral pretty regularly, but mostly because I was accepted into the choir. (I love Greek, Russian and Armenian church music.) I would have had real trouble reading my part if the choirmaster, Nick Illiopoulos, to fill out the bass section, hadn't already hired some deep-voiced Russians formerly with the Don Cossack Choir. They, like me, could read the music but had trouble deciphering the Greek texts until someone wrote them out for us phonetically.

Voted the Social Chairman of the Cathedral's Young Adults Association, I became active running dances (in the process perfecting my own *kalamatianos*, *tsamikos*, and *hassaposervikos*) and organized bazaars and raffles which made a lot of money for the current Fund Drive, the major goal of which was to purchase a new baptismal font. I began to get general acceptance and appreciation in the Hellenic community but also a lot of teasing from some of my closer colleagues. Once they

Left to right: Mr. and Mrs. Lefteri Trihas, Goetze Claren, Dr. Arnold Benson, Sophi Nick Papadakos, Nai Bonet, Miss Dushka Vardar, Melba Macrygiannis, Kitty Papadako Howarth, Titos Vandis, Dr. and Mrs. Wolfrang and Father John Pallas.

A lovely cocktail party was given by Melba Macriyiannis Television Star Linda Show, Peggy Greer, Sophia Vardas, al Herald, and Bobby Mala fouris.

A clipping from the society page of a New York Greek-American newspaper.

Society of Classic Guitar (SCG) meeting at Greg D'Alessio's gallery (Seated from left) Olga Coelho, Society President Andres Segovia, Gustavo Lopez, Ted Anagnostaras, (In the background) Jesus da Silva, Etta Lopez, artists Giusti, Terry D'Alessio, and others.

(Above) Host Mirko Markoe and Dushka entertain at an SCG night at *Mirko's*. (This photo was used as a full-page ad for Guild guitars though we're both playing something else!) (Below) Dushka: Winner of First Prize at the First International Guitar Festival, Greenwood Lake, New York.

First singing job in New York...*Gerde's Folk City*.

Maestro Andres Segovia

Dushka at a guitar party with Ted Anagnostaras and Venezuelan guitarist Rodrigo Riera (right).....

...and Brazilian singer/guitarist Olga Coelho.

discovered how new I was to being Greek and that I had never even been baptized, they insisted my fund-raising was purely selfish and that I just wanted to make sure they could afford a big enough font, even for me!

Soon I was enough of an "expert" on Greek music for my old client Dick Hyman, who had by now become an icon in the music business, to refer ad agency people to me. I helped produce commercials, like the one for beer: "There are more Greeks in New York who drink Rheingold than live in Sparta..." and jobs for Betty Crocker, and Olympic Airlines, as well as a series of *"Recorded Live At A Party"* LPs, of which three were Greek and others Polish, French, German, and Latin-American.

A few years ago when I was teaching in Venezuela a fellow Grecophile played me a new Greek CD he was thrilled to have just bought in Miami. It sounded strangely familiar. Then I realized it was the original master of my *Recorded Live At The Athena East* album. The artwork on the cover was new (no photos of me and the original party guests), and no credits for the musicians, or me as female vocalist and producer. That the album was considered worth reissuing twenty years later was flattering to my ego and my two or three solo vocals sounded great on a CD player. But my friends still can't understand why I didn't "sue somebody!!"

Actually, when I made that album I had heard rumors about the recording company, and that their royalty accounting was questionable. So instead of the usual participation contract, I took a one time production fee with an added understanding that they would send me any copies I wanted for myself at the lowest wholesale price.

(Left) Cover of one of the three Greek "Recorded Live At...." albums.
(Right) Clipping from an Athens newspaper. *(Translation:* **"SHE SINGS IN 17 LANGUAGES.** These days visiting here in Athens, is the well-known, and beloved in the Greek community, artist and singer, Dushka, who sings with her guitar in...17 languages. The American artist is just passing through.")

So for years I bought carton after carton of those records, sixty-seven cents a piece, and, especially when I was a prima donna on Greek cruise ships, was able to autograph and sell them by the hundreds for ten dollars each! I really did very well out of it.

Why didn't it ever strike me as peculiar that year after year when I called to reorder I always got immediate delivery? That my records were always in stock? How often is an ethnic recording with no well-known name on it continuously produced, new pressings made every few months?

As "hostess" for these recorded "parties" my aim had been to create a natural, relaxed atmosphere, like a Saturday night club-date, rather than a recording session. To this end I tried to disguise the recording studio, converting it into a kind of bistro, and served a lot of food and drink to everyone involved. I sometimes personally prepared food for fifty or sixty people.

Recorded Live at a Greek Party album orchestra: (Left to right) Michael Daniels: leader/accordion, Paris Jamalas: vocals, John Yalenezian: drums, Dushka: guitar/vocals, Nick Rassias: clarinet, Grigoris Georgiades: bouzouki, Constantine Milanakos:bass

But the results were worth it. Whatever the nationality we were featuring, our "party guests" were chosen because I understood that they liked to sing and dance at social affairs. I knew this inspired the musicians, broadened the repertoire, kept the tempos danceable, and since I slipped a mike amongst the flowers at each table, provided us with fine vocals and improvised harmonizations — all without our having to pay any union singers.

I had always loved to give big, casual, "multi-cultural" parties, with lots of music and often with impressive guest lists. I had been proud of the variety of my international buffets: "hors d'oeuvres," "appetizers," "antipastos," "smorgasbord," "dim sum," "tapas," "zakuska," and the rest. But now, in my new "Greekness," everything was dominated by "***mezedakia!***"

Now the Howarth apartment kitchen bulged with gallons of olive oil, sacks of lemons, trays of ripening tomatoes and melons, vats of marinating lamb. I spent hours folding layers of ***phyllo*** dough into little triangles of ***tiropita***, and stuffing vine-leaves for ***dolmades***. I was even invited out to Smithtown, Long Island, so that Nick's brother, Peter Papadakos, designer and builder of Gyrodyne helicopters, could show me how to pick my own grapeleaves from wild vines, choosing not by eye for size or color, but by touch, testing each leaf for tenderness.

Manhattan's Ninth Avenue near Fortieth Street was my Mecca for superior varieties of ***feta*** cheese, barrels of ***elies*** (olives), different sizes of ***bulgur***, authentic ***loukaniko***, (sausage flavored with cinnamon and orange zest), sacks of mint (spearmint not peppermint), pistachio ***halva***, rose-petal jam, and ***tahini*** for ***humus***. My advisors from the ***Philoptohos***, the Greek Cathedral's ladies' organization, got into such heated arguments about whether one should make ***taramasalata*** using soaked bread or cold mashed potatoes that I tactfully developed my own version... I used both.

Interior of a Greek Orthodox church. showing the *Iconostas* or *Templo*n, the partition decorated with icons or sacred images, that separates the sanctuary from the nave.

And although I never quite trained myself to relish the turpentiny **retsina** wine, an **ouzaki,** (a little Ouzo), milky with ice, is a wondrous thing.

But the most lasting result of this Greek period was its effect on my attitudes toward religion, philosophy and the Gurdjieff Work.

Through the years, in many countries, I had visited churches, temples, all kinds of places of worship, participated in the usual college late-night "bull sessions," had profound discussions in Paris cafes, and so forth. Mother had never insisted on a religious training for me and while I felt comfortable in all these situations, it was only as a respectful, interested bystander or appreciative spectator. I had friends of different faiths and considered myself close to them until, in serious conversations, there would suddenly come a moment when they might say: "We believe..." at which point something in me would close up.

I could have understood a convinced: "I have come to believe," but not this group mentality, obedient, passive acceptance of other people's formulations.

As I got into conversations with more Greeks I found that this situation happened much less often. It seemed as though their Eastern Orthodox backgrounds still reflected old Asiatic traditions, Buddhist and others, which hold that Man is responsible for himself, for his own development. In Greek "to sin" translates to "miss one's mark," i.e. fail to accomplish one's goal. The theatrical ceremonial nature of a "liturgy" takes on a special meaning when you understand the Greek roots of the word that translate as the "working together of the people" or "common work." ("*Lit-*" as in "the people," *cp* laity, and "*ourgia*" to work).

And our careless everyday use of "to pray," with connotations of supplication, and entreaty, suggest a passive asking for something especially in certain Western churches. How different it sounded when one of our teachers, Father Kazanas, explained how old words can often be traced back to multiple roots, and then used "*prosevhi*" (Greek for "prayer") as his example. Pointing out that its four roots came from: "...my wish... is to put myself... in relation to... something higher," an aim completely compatible with all Gurdjieff's teachings.

Father Kazanas, realizing that most of the students in the Greek class weren't themselves Greek, and might be unfamiliar with the Cathedral, one day invited us all upstairs to look around. He led us down the long aisle and we lined up at the front as he explained the meaning of the icons that form a wall on either side of the central, arched doorway through which only ordained priests may enter as it leads into the sanctuary where the altar is located.

One of our group, evidently from a background different from this, exclaimed: "But with all this decoration, isn't this just like a Catholic church? What's the difference?"

After a long moment's thought, Father Kazanas (whose background had included not only the Orthodox Seminary but also Fordham University) stepped forward and mounted the several steps leading up to the archway. Turning, he looked down at us with his arms stretched low behind him, palms facing back, and said:

"This is the place of a Catholic priest..."

He then came back down to join us facing the sanctuary and with a hand on the shoulder of the person on each side of him said:

"... and this is the place of the Orthodox priest!"

Why should I have been so surprised that many things like this struck a chord in me, made sense, agreed with my upbringing, even sounded like something Mr. G. would say. After all, his formative years and schooling were deeply immersed in the Greek (Russian, Armenian) Orthodox tradition, and I have always felt that he never strayed far from those early influences, at least their principles and original meanings.

I find that many Gurdjieff group people I talk with have great difficulty accepting that Gurdjieff was truly a very religious man. But they forget the important difference, that *his* religion was one that most of them know little about: Greek Orthodoxy!

And I begin to wonder if, in this era, many "group people" weren't originally attracted, not so much to "the Work," as away from their own unsatisfying or constricting religious backgrounds. I found this especially true in Catholic South America.

Oh yes, people love to repeat stories about that "wicked old Mr. Gurdjieff" saying terrible things about priests. For example "The best way to lose your faith is to make a priest your friend." But they forget that he was probably referring to terrible priests! In fact, I remember that in Paris he had several Russian priests as close friends!

Certainly his often quoted aphorisms state clearly his attitude. "Respect every religion," "We can only strive to be able to be Christian," and "Here there are neither Russians nor English, Jews nor Christians, but only those who pursue one aim — to be able to be."

The titles of most of his musical compositions are also revealing as are the prayer words, inner exercises, body positions and hand gestures found in many of the most serious and beautiful of his Movements. And, of course, in his writings: "And here also is God!!! Again God! Only He is everywhere and with Him everything is connected... I am a man, and as such I am, in contrast to all other outer forms of animal life, created by Him in His image!!!" *(Third Series)*.

Just before Mr. Gurdjieff died, I was told, when he had finally accepted that he must be taken to the hospital, it was with the condition that first they would drive him to the front of the Russian church on the rue Daru (where his funeral was held a week or so later).

It was said he sat there silently for almost an hour.

* * * * *

CHAPTER 29

THE FILMS, MENDHAM, N.Y. FOUNDATION, G.'S FAMILY

"I am awfully sick of the comment that 'the harm has already been done' and that this kind of dissension and scattering has always followed the death of a 'teacher.'" Jessmin Howarth

Dushka
♦

Mother has described the soul-searching that she went through in 1949 when Mr. Gurdjieff went back to France leaving her as "Director of Movements in America." She hesitated about accepting such a task, but once having agreed, worked at it unremittingly for more than thirty-five years.

In addition to continuing her teaching in New York and Mendham, with special sessions in other cities, and helping Mme. de Salzmann and Mme. Ouspensky make plans for the Work, Mother decided that an important part of her responsibility to the Movements everywhere was to prepare for the future. She set about actively creating archives, coordinating the making of accurate notations, drawings, and recordings and was constantly training instructors, assistants and pianists. She held seminars for out-of-town teachers, travelled to visit and advise them, and wrote letters by the hour answering questions, correcting notes, arbitrating disputes, and helping with personal problems.

A lot of time was spent in France with Mme. de Salzmann on the preparation, rehearsing and photographing of the many valuable Movements films that were produced through the years. These were shown to select private audiences throughout the world, but made primarily to serve as all-important documentation.

She was also brought in to help with the making of the feature film *Meetings with Remarkable Men*, which the *New York Times Magazine* (8/29/79) described as:

"...a $3 million enterprise conceived and directed by the British director Peter Brook and produced by Stuart Lyons. It signifies a new departure for the Gurdjieff school whose exponents have always refrained from proselytizing and assiduously avoided publicity. Virtually underground until now, the movement has at last gone public."

But in this case Mother confessed to reservations. She wasn't at all happy about the Gurdjieff Movements being used in this way. Glimpses of them are shown in the final scenes, in brief incomplete segments, executed by young girls in snowy-white costumes, though presumably in a remote monastery. With her theatrical experience she

Jeanne de Salzmann on the film set.

Poster for the film *Meetings wth Remarkable Men.*

In an early scene from the film the young Gurdjeff questions his father, a furniture-maker and *"ashogh."*

The grown Gurdjieff on his journey as a "Seeker After Truth" (as played by the young Yugoslav actor Dragan Maksimovic)

During the filming at the Billancourt Studios in Paris, Peter Brook directs...

...while René Zuber discusses a production problem with Jeanne de Salzmann.

foresaw that the general public, accustomed to Hollywood dance routines, and not understanding the purpose or function of the Movements, might scoff at them and be uncomfortable with their serious, even grim, presentation. In many cases she was, unfortunately, proven correct.

As time went by more books were published and read, groups were started in many places, and the responsibility of disseminating Movements teaching of a high enough quality, and maintaining the necessary close supervision, became more and more difficult. Yet one thing that Mme. de Salzmann and Mother agreed passionately about was that work on "the ideas" should always be accompanied by participation in Movements classes and vice versa. More than that, they both decried an increasing tendency to separate Movements from "group work." As numbers increased, teaching became less personal, group leaders no longer took time to come and watch, much less themselves participate in Movement classes, and the essential basic experiences attained by pupils through Movements rarely got formulated and expressed in their group meetings and discussions.

Concerned about groups that began to draw away from the mainstream Mother would say: "I do not forget Mr. G.'s last words to me when leaving New York: 'And now, Jessmin, you are answerable to me for Movements in America... Must keep people together!'"

She worked hard to achieve unity, or at least understanding and mutual respect between older established groups and developing communities like "Wim Nyland's people" in Warwick, N.Y. (and California, Arizona, New Mexico, etc.) "Bennett's people" at Claymont, and groups in Washington, Toronto, Nova Scotia and elsewhere.

Mother later wrote Lord Pentland, then the head of the N.Y. Gurdjieff Foundation, who had doubts about continuing a connection with many of them.

◆◆◆

Jessmin
◆

"My own wish would be to seize any opportunity offered for bringing Movements teaching, in North America at least, into one harmonious organization, even though the system ideas might be approached differently and independently by various groups."

◆◆◆

Dushka
◆

Lord Pentland answered her from San Francisco:
"Dear Jessmin,

"Thank you for writing about your talk with Vivien [Elliot]. I realize my long hibernation in California has not been helpful, but away from these problems a bit, one or two probably obvious things have made an impression on me.

"I feel clearer about the 'heresies' which resulted in John Bennett and Wim Nyland leaving the main body of people which we are still a part of, Madame de Salzmann's people. The teaching they gave falls short, each in different ways, of what she has, and is, passing on to us. Altho' a greater deviation than Wim's, John Bennett's 'heresy' is the more difficult to see, and I think all his various posthumous books that are coming out will be attractive to some of our people, Annie Lou Stavely, for instance.

"In California we are on good terms with the principal Bennett people. These are Jacques Schlumberger and his wife, who came a few weeks ago to ask us if they could do movements with us, and gave $5000 for the film. And

Mrs. Stavely

Nyland people – Arlene Prinz. Depending on what happens in Paris and New York, it would be quite possible and unsurprising if our movements teaching came together with theirs in the next year or so.

"In any case, with Paul's [Reynard] – as far as I can see – complete approval, we are putting much emphasis on the movements and on selecting and training new assistants. We have several men, and the new women are quite young. I am avoiding married couples, (both man and wife as assistants.)

"Of course, I may be quite wrong about what happens, but in the meantime I feel some of the New York reactions are too personal, both for and against Wim and Pierre/Vivien and do not take enough account of the whole (unknowable) situation in USA.

"Besides Bennett and Nyland people, we have here the so-called Eden-West people, who have had help from Sherborne but were independent even in Bennett's lifetime. For the last 3 years they have been giving advertised movements demonstrations up and down the West Coast and attract pupils. We decided to send this letter to the local paper since we were advised that suing them – the performances are free – would not be effective.

"I am coming back to N.Y. next week – look forward to seeing you.

Yours with love   John

"P.S. Am told the letter to the paper has to be redrafted, so will show it to you later. JP"

(Left) Lord Pentland conferring with Jessmin in the Howarth's Manhattan apartment.

(Below) In California: Lord Pentland with Jacob Needleman (left) and Don Hoyt (right)

Immobile men figures are posed around the Hall as visitors enter.

The New York Gurdjieff Foundation, East 63rd. St.
(Below) The Foundation Movements Hall decorated for a January Thirteenth celebration with stage added to resemble the Study House at the Prieuré.

Alfred (above right) welcomes the guests explaining that the standing figures are experiencing a "Stop" exercise and the wall decorations are recreations of the Study House windows on which aphorisms were painted in a special coded script.

Final adjustments to costumes and the classes are ready to share their Movements work with the visitors. (Left to right) Roberta Neal, Ellen Dooling Draper, and Gerard Harris.

Lord Pentland talks with Mme. de Hartmann and Mme. de Salzmann (right)   (Far right) Dr. William Welch

Mme. de Salzmann confers with Jessmin (back to camera) as the class waits. (Front row left to right) Beatrice Sinclair, Davd Lewiston, Lise Etievant, pianist Annette Herter, (Standing) Marian Sutta and Henri Tracol.

Visiting day at Corey Lane, a Foundation property outside New York, where the children have their special activities. (Jessmin in foreground).

"Bon Voyage" party for Mme. de Salzmann aboard the *Queen Elizabeth*. (Left to right) Alfred Etievant, Margaret "Peggy" Flinsch, Jeanne de Salzmann (seated), Lady Lucy Pentland, Lise (Tracol) Etievant, Cora (Carlyle) Segal, Christopher Fremantle, Wim Nyland, William Segal (kneeling). Evelyn (Mrs. Maurice) Sutta, Louise Welch, Olga de Hartmann, and Illonka Karasz Nyland.

Mme. de Salzmann visiting the new N.Y. Foundation Movements Hall in 1955. (Front row left to right) Wesley Addy, Elizabeth Segal (Katz), Jojo Flinsch (Thatcher), Daphne Ripman (Matchelajovic), Evelyn Sutta and Lady Pentland.

Bill Welch   John Pentland   Tom Forman   Jacob Needleman   Christopher Fremantle   Jerry Brewster

Peggy Flinsch   Doro Dooling   Cora Segal   Lillian Firestone   Cynthia Pearce   Stanley Isaacs

Pierce Wheeler   Emil Hanna   Paul Reynard   Sheila Bura   André Enard   Beatrice Sinclair

Jimmy Wykoff and Peter Colgrove   Mildred Ripman   Dr. Jon and Mary Sinclair Rothenberg   Barbara and John Mills

Louise March   Vicky Orfaly (Fewsmith)   Olga de Hartmann and David Lewiston   Marielle and Bill Segal.

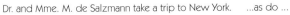

...Pauline de Dampierre ... Marthe de Gaigneron

...and
Henri
Tracol

Dr. and Mme. M. de Salzmann take a trip to New York.   ...as do ...

(Above) Michel takes time off in Manhattan to
visit a showing of Paul Reynard's paintings.
(Left) When Dushka visits Paris, Michel and
Josée join her for an evening at the *Auberge
de Yugoslavie* where she is known and asked
to join in with the musicians.

◆◆◆

Dushka
◆

In 1953, the Gurdjieff Foundation had been established in New York with headquarters on East 63rd St. in Manhattan. An old carriage house was chosen, in large part, I think, because the unobstructed ground floor could be rebuilt as a beautiful Movements hall. The basement housed changing rooms, a coffee shop and workshop, and the rest of the three-story building was divided into meeting rooms, a library and a dining room. On the top floor there was a small apartment which was offered to Alfred when he arrived from England a year or so later to assist Mother with the Movements teaching.

Alfred and I were both pretty poor as correspondents and yet we had remained the best of friends. But now it was I who was usually abroad and busy with my own activities. So I was happier than anyone when Lise Tracol also came to New York to work with Mother. She and Alfred were wonderfully suited and in 1958 were married, later had two daughters, Camille and Anne, and in addition to Movements teaching also became popular instructors at the French Institute. Mother and the two of them made a Movements teaching "troika" [three-person team] which older pupils still hold up as the criterion. It functioned superbly until Alfred's unexpected and premature death from cancer in the summer of 1967, after which Lise took her little girls and returned to France and the Etievant family home in Chambray. After cutting herself off from all old associations for a few painful years, Lise finally returned to Work activities in Paris, and currently teaches Movements in Lyons and other European cities... and proudly sends me photos of her grandchildren.

In 1957 Thomas de Hartmann died just before a concert of his compositions was to be presented at New York's Town Hall. The featured singer, Patricia Neway,

Alfred Etievant with wife Lise and their first daughter Camille.

(Above) The de Hartmanns a few days before his death when they were preparing the concert of his works with Patricia Neway (seen below rehearsing with the composer.)

and other artists performed the concert as planned in his memory.

The community at Mendham hadn't been able to continue with any validity after Mme. Ouspensky died in 1961.

The young people living there were marrying, starting families, or developing new professions and moving on. Fewer and fewer visitors went out to the Farm even on the weekends, and the efforts of a small group of pupils to continue it as a house of work were unsuccessful, especially as Tania (Mme. O.'s granddaughter) was anxious to start selling. She was the sole remaining heir to the property as well as all publishing rights to Ouspensky's books since her brother Lonia's death. Groups of people went out to help pack up, make provision for the animals, clear everything and soon the main house was sold, to be used, I understood, as a school, and later by a Chinese doctor and his colleagues.

Tania's marriage to Tom Forman hadn't survived long after

Tania Nagro by one of her horse trailers

(Above) Daphne Ripman marries Carlos Matchelajovic at Franklin Farms.
(Behind left...with cigarette...!) Nancy Pearson (right) Dorothy Darlington (and Rita Benson in back?)

After Daphne and Carlos move to Buenos Aires their newly formed group works in the basement of the esoteric bookstore run by Carlos who plays piano as Daphne teaches "The Forming Twos" just as she learned it from Jessmin in 1938 at Lyne in England..

her return from France and he moved to New York City, while she stayed in Mendham, keeping for her own use a house down near the barns. Into another small house called "The Turkey Cottage," she installed the last remaining residents, the elderly ladies who had nursed her grandmother, i.e. Margaret Capper, Nancy Pearson, Margaret Harper. and for a time, Dorothy Darlington, Miss [Robin] Dickson had returned to her native Scotland and Daphne Ripman had married and gone to South America with her husband, Carlos Matchelajovic.

Horses remained Tania's one real interest. She and I had sometimes gone together to ride at a nearby stable, the owner of which was a decent, simple, middle-aged man named Clarence Nagro. He and Tania joined forces boarding horses, teaching riding, competing in shows, and finally married. In subsequent years they managed to get much of the Franklin Farms property re-zoned for residential housing, and Tania, now widowed, lives nearby, no longer riding as much, but training and showing dogs.

Mevlevi "whirling" dervishes from Konya, Turkey

As for the other "calves," Marian, although acknowledged by us all in France as the most "serious about the Work," no longer attended Foundation activities or classes once her parents, Maurice and Evelyn Sutta, retired to Miami (where they started the first Florida groups). I didn't see her for years until she turned up in 1979 for the big Lincoln Center premier of the film *Meetings with Remarkable Men,* and Mother and I renewed contact with her.

Marian seemed at a low point then and in need of women friends. She had, in the interim, made a successful career for herself, and I had seen her pictured in financial publications as a "foremost securities' analyst." She told us about going one summer to the annual gathering of Dervishes at Konya in Turkey. There she met a young, local boy named Hussein Unger. He followed her back to the U. S. and she helped him finish his education and then get established in banking and married him. But she was beginning to have health problems when we met her again and although Hussein seemed very nice, attentive to her, and even did the serving when Mother and I were invited to supper, (unexpected from a Turkish husband), he later left her for a younger woman who would give him children. Marian's professional life deteriorated with her health and private life and after a pitiable couple of years during which she fought a form of Alzheimers, she, the youngest and brightest of the "calves," was the first to die.

Iovanna had returned to Taliesin and for a few years, pushed by her mother and with, I would guess, her father's resigned acceptance, gave Movements classes to the architectural apprentices. She had several marriages, a daughter who became a dancer, and in later life, I was sad to hear from mutual friends, addiction problems.

Iovanna LLoyd Wright

Petey, on the other hand, came away from her experience as a "calf," seemingly pretty untouched. In the first year or so afterwards, she returned to modelling and on a fashion shoot in the South of France met the leading French photographer, Jean Remy Chevalier, known to the world of fashion as "Cheval." Long accustomed to being lionized by glamorous and sophisticated French women, models, actresses and magazine publisher's wives, Cheval evidently found Petey's sweetness, ingenuousness, and "Americaness" irresistible. Much to everyone's surprise, including Petey's, he insisted on marrying her, and settling down to a sub-urban life just outside of Paris.

Their first child, Remy Jr., was such a beautiful boy that all their magazine friends insisted that Cheval do photo spreads of mother and son, but otherwise Petey kept rather separate from her husband's professional world and concentrated on her home and two more children, Alice and Cathy.

Until I gave up the French branch of Howarth Services, Petey and I would get together in Paris for Chinese lunches, cocktail parties, or, sometimes, at their country house in Louveciennes.

Now widowed and a grandmother, with two of her children opting for American lives, Petey is again spending most of her time in Westport, Connecticut and we are back in touch.

I was also happy to renew my friendship with Petey's half-brother, Paul Beekman Taylor, who recently retired as a literature professor in Geneva, Switzerland. He is producing interesting books and articles, such as ***Shadows of Heaven, Gurdjieff and Orage.*** Having his mother's diaries, and having lived with Jean Toomer's family and been close to the Orage family, he had valuable material to add to the "Gurdjieff literature."

Though Petey kept in touch with Mr. G.'s three nieces (his brother Dimitri's daughters), Luba was the only one of the family with whom I ever made any relationship. When I visited London I always went to her wonderful little restaurant, "Luba's Bistro" where we all sat on small beer kegs, elbow to elbow with all sorts of people. One time I shared a table with Randolph Churchill and Mme. Molyneux while Luba talked to us from the open kitchen, and invited us in to serve ourselves from simmering pots of tasty, mostly Russian, specialties.

But our best time together was one summer when Luba and I arranged to meet in Greece. She had driven down from London in a snazzy convertible. With the top down she and I would cruise around Athens or go to the beach — two oversized, sun-tanned charmers naughtily enjoying the local male attention we attracted, but always secure in the knowledge that her nice husband, Arthur Everitt, was waiting back at the hotel if any of our Greek admirers got too eager.

Luba had lived at Coombe Springs for a time, admired Bennett, was god-mother to his son George, and had been helped by Bennett's pupils to start her restaurant. So I was surprised when I began hearing about legal difficulties that "the Gurdjieff family" had started making for the leaders of the Work, (and for the now widowed Mme. de Hartmann who was fighting fiercely to retain control of the "Gurdjieff/de Hartmann" music).

Apparently, Luba wasn't doing anything to help resolve the problems. Even she, closer than the other relatives to people in the "Work," never really understood the activities, relationships, the reasons for the communal life, how pupils could work at all sorts of menial tasks for their own reasons, how funds were raised for materials that were needed but not to pay leaders and teachers. She and her sisters saw only the facade of a big "Gurdjieff organization." They didn't comprehend that this wasn't a profit-making business, but a school and the result of many people's unselfish work. They had a fantasy that their "Uncle George" must have accumulated a fortune somewhere that should have come to them when he died.

How did they get these ideas? I tried to understand.

I realized that Mr. Gurdjieff hadn't been able to bring out of Russia the surviving members of his family until a year or so after moving into the Prieuré. His mother had escaped to Tiflis with his younger brother Dimitri Ivanovitch, his wife Anna Grigorievna and their three daughters, Luba, Genia and Lida, a younger sister

M. et Mme. Jean "Cheval" Chevalier

(Above left) Remy Chevalier at home, (Above right) with his mother on a magazine cover, and (below) with "Auntie" Dushka who is more than ready to play her ukelele for him but ....?!

(Above) Another magazine cover with the Chevalier family including new daughter Cathy (Alice still to arrive.)

Luba Gurdjieff with husband Arthur Everett in their London restaurant, *Luba's Bistro*. (Below) Mr. and Mrs. Everitt in an Athens taverna drinking "*ouzo*" wth Dushka .

'Valya' young Valentin Anastasieff

Sophie Ivanovna with her husband Georgilibovitch Kapanadze, and Lucie, the daughter of another sister.

But, tragically, Gurdjieff's father, Ashogh Adash, and the rest of the family had remained in Alexandropol, then the capital of Armenia. When in 1915 the Turkish army invaded they were all massacred except for the ten-year-old Valentin "Valia" Anastasieff son of G.'s younger sister, Anna Ivanovna, and her husband Feodor Anastasieff. Somehow this boy managed to escape after witnessing everything from dangerous hiding places. Alone, with little money, he traveled on foot through snow, hid in trains, and managed to complete the long difficult journey to Tiflis to join his other relatives. He later recounted with gratitude, that at some point along the way, he was aided by American Red Cross representatives. Valia was included amongst the family members Gurdjieff finally managed to bring to Europe and as an adult he married a French woman, Sylvie, a cabaret singer, who is the one sometimes referred to as "La Anastasieff."

I can only suppose that those difficult war years that the relatives spent in Tiflis, and their lack of communication with Gurdjieff during that time, hardly prepared them for what they found when they were finally brought to a peaceful, prospering France. Suddenly they found themselves at the Prieuré! Of course they must have thought that their kinsman had become a very wealthy and powerful man to be the proprietor of such a luxurious chateau. They couldn't know what efforts had been necessary to acquire it, or how much work had been done by scores of pupils to reconstruct, furnish and decorate it — or have understood the planning and preparation that went into the demonstrations and lectures that attracted people there. All they saw were the results. Gurdjieff in these opulent surroundings with astonishing modern European comforts, (still unknown in the Caucasus), catered to by rich Americans, aristocratic Englishmen, and famous Russians, all of them, including many attractive women, obedient to his slightest command.

I don't have the impression that any of his family, except perhaps his father, had ever understood, or even been vaguely interested in what Gurdjieff was fascinated by as a youth and what he went searching for during the years he studied and travelled with his companions, the "Seekers of the Truth." It is understandable that girls in that time and place didn't have the same preparation. But how is it that his brother, Dimitri, only slightly younger, shared none of the same interests and completely missed out on the training and formation accorded Gurdjieff by his father and tutors?

Yet Dimitri was, in fact, capable and successful enough to have been the one who, according to his daughter Luba, was able and willing to finance Gurdjieff's early travels. He ran a cinema, a shoe store, and even, at one time, was mayor of Alexandropol. So when, years later, circumstances changed and Dimitri, now a refugee, arrived at the Prieuré with his family, disillusioned and dispossessed, it isn't surprising that Gurdjieff showed such patience and generosity to this "gambler-playboy" brother — much to the consternation, even indignation, of many of the newer Prieuré residents.

The family had also been out of touch when Gurdjieff returned from his travels in 1912 and began to lecture and teach in Moscow and St. Petersburg. They had no idea why people became his pupils and followers.

Even when installed at the Prieuré, since they didn't yet know any European languages, the family was unable to really communicate with the other residents, or join in conversation with the visitors. They evidently couldn't comprehend what Gurdjieff was doing with all those people, and were just confused and bored by the, to them, senseless sessions of discussions, music, readings, or even Movements (which, evidently, the children sometimes tried, but only as folk-dancing, or a game like "playing statues.") That situation never really seemed to change up to Gurdjieff's death.

Betsy Bonbright at a young age.

I felt uncomfortable and helpless to respond when Luba complained to me of the "bad treatment" the family received from all "those people who were profiting from their uncle and his books and music." She gave as an example how, when her mother was having physical and financial difficulties, Mme. de Salzmann would come out to visit "...in a blooming big fur coat with a ruddy great limousine and chauffeur!" I knew that Betsy Bonbright, an invalid American lady and devoted pupil of Jeanne's, kept the car and driver but was rarely able to go out. The rest of the time her car was put at the disposal of Jeanne or Michel, both of whom, together with hundreds of other dedicated people were working hard to keep the Gurdjieff work alive, and without whom there would be no royalties or income for the family at all.

On May 20, 1974 this letter was sent to Mother as one of the members of "Group One" at the N. Y. Gurdjieff Foundation by Lord Pentland the current Director.

"You all know, because Madame de Salzmann has often spoken of it, that for many years there have been misunderstandings between the Work and Mr. Gurdjieff's family in Paris.

"The family consists of Valya Anastasieff (the son of one of Mr. Gurdjieff's sisters) and his wife, Sylvie, the three daughters of Mr, Gurdjieff's other sister and brother, Leda, Luba and Xenia. Two of these nieces have sons, making a total of seven heirs.

(Above) CD put out by French singer Sylvie de Lille who, having married Gurdjieff's nephew Valentin ("Valia"), was sometimes known as "La Anastasieff"!

"Valya and Sylvie Anastasieff live in Paris where he owns a restaurant close to the Bourse, and they have been active as representatives of the heirs, seeking better terms and more active promotional activities from Janus, the publishing company started by Mr. Gurdjieff, which pays them royalties for the books and music. In this they are to some extent justified by recent laws in France which have reformulated the rights of the heirs of authors and composers. But we are advised that many of their claims, such as for compensation for the use of the family name Gurdjieff, are completely without legal justification, not only here but in England and France too. Two of the nieces live in London and over the years have become quite close to Bennett who was asked by Madame de Salzmann to help them after Gurdjieff's death.

John Pentland"

`* * * * *

CHAPTER 30

<u>LETTERS</u>

Dushka
◆

One of the few people Mother felt free to share really personal feelings with was her old friend and former pupil Rosemary Nott who was now living in London, and very active in the Work there. Although they rarely saw each other, they kept up a regular correspondence.

◆◆◆

Jessmin
◆

Dear Rosemary.....

I'm sorry that Jeanne was not more appreciative or encouraging about your recordings. You never told me much about them but I was so glad you were making them. And I hoped very much that you included Movement music, especially the Obligatories. No one plays them like you.

Of course, nowadays, the First Obligatories are not studied so much in the large centers: Paris, New York, London and San Francisco. But they are used by all the smaller groups, thousands of people, and are, alas, usually played for by amateurs who don't do the Movements well themselves and have never heard the music correctly played. Even our "senior" pianists here in New York fail in many ways. If they could only hear and learn from you... that, alone, would be worth having your recordings.

But, of course, there is this family difficulty. You know "la Anastasieff," (Valia's French wife who evidently never knew Mr. G.) already made a record of the First Obligatories... and we had to agree that these Movements and the music used at the Prieuré would be their property after three years, now soon to be up.

And Olga de Hartmann is still fighting with them about the music copyrights.

Her last move was to send me a message by Jeanne "that it would help her very much in her dispute with the nieces if she could cite Dushka as having a stronger claim than their's because of new inheritance laws in France."...!!!

Jeanne told me this at a hurried lunch in front of other people. I was so shocked after trying to behave discreetly, prevent gossip, and see that Mr. G.'s motives were understood and his personal privacy, as well as my own, respected, that I couldn't stomach Jeanne's being so "objective."

Why didn't she at once answer Olga, even if she was spitting and clawing like a tomcat, and say immediately "I'm sure Jessmin would never agree to such a thing."

After years of loyalty, I don't feel that I deserve this.

I'm certain it will turn out that Jeanne will be fair and

(Above) Rosemary Nott in her later years

helpful to you as far as she can without coming to blows with Olga, which she dare not do.

                                                All my love,   J.

◆ ◆ ◆

After Mother's death I was shown a touching note she wrote in answer to a plea for advice from one of her long-time pupils whose group-leader husband of 30 years apparently got a girl in his group pregnant,

     Mother replied:

Dushka
♦

◆ ◆ ◆

"Dear _ _ _ _ _ ,

     The other question you ask, about Mr. G. and his so-called "affairs," I am also not truly capable of answering.

     I do not believe, as many people do, that when a man reaches a high level of development, he may act towards others in any way he likes. But also I think it is probable that such a being still has the usual body functions and natural sexual needs.

     As far as I have seen, Mr. G. never acted out of his own weakness but sought to show each woman her biological state. He treated them with impartial kindliness and did not ever bind them to him emotionally, but sought to set them free. His imitators are not so conscious and so the results are messy.

     What more can I say? I wish you and your husband well, with all my heart.

     I do ask myself often whether we can truly accept to see ourselves as we really are, or instead, feeling something greater than ourselves, alternate between what we are and what we feel called upon to try to be. Do we not, out of vanity rather than self respect, take on Work tasks and responsibilities that are, as yet, beyond our powers to carry?

     We all face this difficulty. How to be modest, but not lazy. How to strive but not destroy. How to love, but not possess.

     We must just do our best and try to help each other.

                        With warmest affection to you all...   Jessmin

Jessmin
♦

◆ ◆ ◆

In the years that Mother was in charge of Movements at the Foundation one of her only escapes from oppressive New York summers was to sometimes go for a couple of weeks to cooler Switzerland where she and old friends would gather to hear Krishnamurti's "Saanen" talks. In July of 1968 she wrote to Rita Benson.

Dushka
♦

◆ ◆ ◆

Hotel Olden, Gstaad, Berne Oberland
My very dear Rita,

     K. [Krishnamurti] seems more "at home" here and emanates compassionate friendliness. The old crowds of 60-70 yr. old faithfuls are here and a number of younger campers. (He meets with the "under 40s" twice a week.) His talks have been not more than 50 minutes. Yesterday's on "How can I live rightly in this World?" going into the various so-called "right" actions, religious, patriotic, householder's, etc., etc. and showing that they all lead to conflict, then, giving a different meaning to "love," some hard truths about possessiveness, domination, self-fulfillment, search for pleasure, etc.The real message, not given in so many words though, being "Try

Jessmin
♦

to find out how to live every moment with real love (the greatest sensitivity and awareness...) Of course, this is nothing new to us but it comes over from him in a loving way."

July, 1971, My dearest Rita...

...I am deeply grateful to Krishnamurti, for, in listening to him I think I am beginning to be "quieter" and to stop thinking that things in myself, in work and world conditions, in other people, might be better changed. I am so willingly blind to FACTS! I won't try to tell you about his subject matter, for I would distort it. However, today I am awakened and moved by the first "dialogue." It was aimed mostly at the young people and he let them choose their subject from a number suggested. It finally came down to something like the question "can you, how do you, see the whole of life?" and he proceeded to lead them to the realization that the whole content of one's consciousness at any level, is conditioned, that we cannot see this completely —and so we and the whole of ordinary life must be in conflict.

Once this was pounded into people (he is more forceful than ever this year) he asked them/us: "Now - what do you do?" and again proved to them/us that they/we can "do" nothing, at the last moment saying in a way that was hardly heard: "Once there has been a complete deep realization that all one is, is a result of conditioning, that will bring of itself, another viewpoint on life.

Of course, you will read between the lines of my poor report, and, after all, we do know all this. However, for myself, I, honestly, have to say that I have not yet wiped the slate clean. Reflecting on all this very seriously..."

August:..

I talked with Jeanne twice, gave her Martin's message which she received with her nicest smile. She seemed to want to talk mainly about her own difficulties with the [Gurdjieff] family, and some mixup with Olga about Froma's [M. de Hartmann] being given more credit for the music, and she has asked me to go to Paris again, middle of October, same old carrot! I'll tell you more about it.

In any case it is understood that I stay in the background, and let Paul [Reynard] and the assistants work out the new Movements classes program, and Jeanne seemed to accept that I might enter into very few of the Foundation activities. I hope I made her trust that, altho' I am wearied of teachings (and wish to try to live more rightly) I am in no way disinterested in the Work, or the search, and want to be friendly and cooperative, but need to understand what "**real work**" truly requires of us.

Listening to Krishnamurti who manages to talk on the problems that concern us all, with a living freshness that is honest, simple and really amazing, I feel towards us all a kind of affectionate respect for the efforts made in such frustrating conditions.

I found that Tennyson, who sometimes says knowledgeable things, wrote: "self-reverence, self-knowledge, self-control, these three lead life to sovereign power" and it seems to me the first two, especially the first, in a right sense, are to be linked, as for the "power," for us, it surely means something different.

A warm hug to you both,   Lovingly,   Jessmin

◆◆◆

Dushka
◆

Mother finally retired from teaching at the Foundation in 1978. She continued working on the documentation and preservation of the Movements, and advising individual instructors, but felt that the two Frenchmen who had been sent over from Paris, Paul Reynard and André Enard, (both painters), should be left free to organize and direct the classes as they felt best.

Sometimes, I knew, she was strongly tempted to advise or help with situations that came up, but she always managed to keep herself from doing so!

She was, however, concerned about the preservation of certain Movements. Until Gurdjieff brought his new Movements to New York in 1949, she herself had taught for twenty-five years in America and England using only the more-than-sufficient repertoire that had been worked out so meticulously for the 1923-4 demonstrations. But these exercises and dances were rarely being taught now by anyone else, and Mme. de Salzmann always referred all questions about them to Mother.

Of the numerous Movements Gurdjieff created in later years, only forty-six (thirty-nine in France, seven more added during his last visit to the U. S.) did he acknowledge and announce as being completed and set. These also are not so very well known, because the large majority of them were immediately preserved in the first Movements film (in black and white made about 1951) before most of the current instructors were active.

As further films were made every few years, the Movements used were, of necessity, chosen from a third group, the many later creations that Mr. Gurdjieff was teaching, correcting and experimenting with, but hadn't yet completed. And these are what the newer instructors have experience in and are concentrating on, unconcerned that so much else may soon be lost.

Mother did regret, however, that Paul Reynard didn't share her vision or interest in training instructors, or accept her offers to hold seminars for out-of-town teachers. But the Welches were only too eager to pull her out of retirement, and, especially in the summers, she helped them organize periods of work in New York, Toronto and Nova Scotia, to which many leaders of other groups sent their Movements teachers and pianists so that "they could have contact with Mrs. Howarth."

As Mother wrote to Rosemary Nott:

◆◆◆

Jessmin
◆

"Monday, November 14:

...Here it is a cold sunny morning... quite quiet, for Dushka is still asleep and I am not dressing to go out.

Yesterday was my day to go up into New York State to see Wim Nyland's pupils, a really pleasant hour and three-quarters drive along the Parkways and through real country. As I have told you, I enjoy the Nyland pupils, young, earnest and so comradely together. The "Barn" is a wonderful large working space and they make it bearably warm in winter by putting up a kind of pliofilm tent which covers three-quarters of the space so that heaters keep things from getting too icy. They have already had snow there.

Things lump along here. Pentland had to go off for another month's so-called "rest" in California where he functions much more happily and independently than here. Cynthia [Pearce] went courageously to her group in Philadelphia and had to be brought back in an ambulance. She is indomitable, but I fear that she has not long to live.

You would hardly know us now, Group One having lost Alfred [Etievant], Annette [Herter], Cora Segal, and Stanley Spiegelberg. Ilonka [Karasz Nyland] and Edwin

The Chardavogne Barn.

(Above) Wim playing piano (usually improvisations).for his young pupils.

(Left) The interior of the barn.

Wolfe are out as well as Larry Morris. Now Rita [Romilly Benson] never comes to the Foundation and John [Pentland] and [Christopher] Fremantle are often ill... and Bill Segal often away. Fortunately Louise Welch and the Matthews sisters [Margaret "Peggy" Flinsch and Dorothy "Doro" Dooling] are energetic, Doro much more outgoing since she has had success with her magazine *PARABOLA*. [Tom] Forman is more responsible and there are a number of younger (!), that is to say, middle-aged men, a "Council"- who carry a lot.

(Above and below) Willem "Wim" Nyland

But I often think the real WORK would be more alive if only Jeanne would accept to allow the "organization" to be less demanding.

The Movements Seminar that I'd been preparing with Paul for months will dwindle to a daylong meeting with only New York instructors, assistants and pianists next Saturday.

Paul's agenda sounds interesting. He and Enard and the older instructors entitle their short sessions:

<u>Approach to Movement</u>
  Hearing and Listening (the pianists)
  Music and Movements
  Sound of Speech in Movements
  Tension and Relaxation
  Different Sources of Impulses in
    Movements
  (....and last, Group Leaders and Movements
    teachers together to discuss:)
    <u>The Relation of the Movements to the</u>
      <u>Work as a Whole.</u>

I look forward to it and am told I must not be only a silent spectator...!!
We'll see! I hope some day we'll face the question of how to teach better!
That's all the news. Be assured we all wish you well. Love from Rita, the Welches, Miss Darlington,.....

  ..and your Dushka.

Jessmin

◆◆◆

Dushka

◆

About this time Pamela ("P. L." Travers) wrote me from London.
"Dear Dushka,

  "My reason for sending you this letter and its enclosure not to your N.Y. apartment but by way of Louise is that I know if your Mother saw my writing or even an English stamp, she would, very naturally, ask about the letter. And then, hearing its contents, she might be displeased, anxious, worried and many other things that I know go on in her, - and I well understand them, - and she might protest and be difficult to persuade or insist on it going to the Foundation... and that I couldn't bear.

(Above) Mme. de Salzmann and her son Dr. Michel de Salzmann meet with Jessmin in the Howarth apartment and Dushka grabs the opporunity to snap them all together.

(Below) Louise Welch (Right) meets Jessmin for one of their lunches together in Manhattan.

P. L. "Pamela" Travers

"Your Father once said 'I have one good daughter.' Meaning you. And it is because of my love for him, as well as for my own dear friend, your Mother, that I enclose this cheque. It is my way of sending my heart to him and to her, this giving it to you. It is little enough but I wanted you to have a nest egg, especially now. If I left it in my will, the Inland Revenue would take a cut, and, oh, many things.

"I think it quite possible that your Mother will need comforts and things that make life a little easier. So, please, without saying anything to her, just toss it into your account or do something that you very much want to do. With my love... looking backward as well as forward.

You see the Gurdjieff Foundation is in a good state. It does not need this and I , have done my bit for it anyway, practically and symbolically. Here I am thinking of

Julie Andrews, Walt Disney, and P. L. Travers in 1964.

Years after her death and despite much other noteworthy work, Pamela Travers is still remembered primarily for her creation of Mary Poppins, the extraordinary "nanny". (Above) Pamela is shown in a recent issue of the *New Yorker* (Dec. 19, 2005) with Julie Andrews and Walt Disney.

human beings. I hate the idea of that Sylvie [Anastasieff] raking in shekels stemming from somebody she never even knew. I told Mme. de Salzmann long ago that I would not rest in my grave if a nephew, far less a nephew's wife, hauled in a net cast by me and got what should rightly go to my own darlings. And I am a bit mad at Luba of whom I am very fond, but who, I heard, said 'If there is anything going I want to be in on it,' instead of marching in and demanding something for you.

"On the other hand I have to remember the dignity with which your Mother has lived her life. Such a gesture might have hurt her properly fierce pride.

So dear, with love. You are always remembered. Put finger to lip and say nothing. A hen doesn't chatter to her Mother if somebody puts an egg under her wing.

"Another thing. Didn't he put you in charge of his tapes? Why couldn't a few private discs, unnamed, be made of some of them? I loved the ones, late ones, where he slapped the top of the instrument at the end. Whenever he did it, I felt that this was a message. And those 'Bravo Sophie's. And once a thunderclap sounded and he broke off playing and said 'Even elements compete!' How I would like to hear that one.

"You know... I always knew you have a gift for teaching the Movements. I was often in the class when you and Alfred were teaching at Colet Gardens. You might think about this. Teach Movements... but don't become a 'Teacher of Movements.'

"This distinction was made by a very perceptive person watching all the people at that Paris Conference. Your Mother has the right balance and is a Teacher of Movements... a very different matter.   All my love,   Pamela
*   * * * *

All through the years, before and after her retirement from the Foundation, Mother answered letters from near and far, from pupils and acquaintances. I'm sure she was always kind and tactful, but probably tried to keep people "grounded," simple, and practical. For instance, a young man we had known slightly years earlier evidently wrote her asking about forming and leading his own groups and she answered:

◆◆◆

Jessmin
◆   April 23rd, (1981?)

Your letter shows that, this time, you were able to see that your move "just happened!" This happens to us all many times for we seem to have recurring patterns.

Perhaps, the next time the cycle comes around, you will be forewarned from experience and be able to "put a spoke in the wheel" so to speak.

How to be able to live intentionally? One of the first requirements of our work is self-knowledge. Without this no deep understanding can come. We see that we cannot change our conditioning and our habitual ways of thinking and behaving just like that. But we can try to recognize them.

I think, even after years of search and study, one has to be simple about one's self-imposed tasks. We may fail discouragingly when attempting efforts beyond our powers. There are so many opportunities in ordinary life to try to remember and act, talk, move with attention and intention.

The work requires conditions for real work on oneself in the framework of everyday life.

I do not know your difficulty well enough to dare to advise you about ceasing to have a daily occupation. However from experience I do know that to assume responsibility for a group, which should be the greatest reminder for one's own work, can be exactly the opposite. One begins to think that one knows and can do. One is apt to become possessive or vain. One pretends to be a Teacher. Always for the sake of the pupils.

In any case, to test the ideas through practice, one needs to be in touch, each of us, with another link in the chain of Teaching which originated in Mr. Gurdjieff.

Think seriously before becoming responsible, on your own, for others' "spiritual development."

* * * *

New York, June 5

The Gurdjieff method begins with a systematic discipline of impartial self-observation, of attention to what one is doing, feeling and thinking. The aim is to reach a higher understanding and this depends upon one's attaining a new state of being.

You can always accumulate knowledge, or rather information at the level where one begins, but to reach a higher understanding you must first get to know, objectively, what you are at present. And then see whether you can live intentionally, developing the kind of attention - "unstrained constant awareness" - that is the key to higher consciousness.

* * * *

I realize the people you have written about, who turn to you, are possibly interested in a study. But each seems to have been conditioned differently and that makes it extremely difficult for them to be welded into a group to share and exchange. And I ask myself why each did not continue to study with the person he had met. "Window shopping" for THE Teacher is no good.

Try to find someone to lead you all. But abide by the conditions. Meetings must be serious and regular and there should be possibilities for other than reading and discussion.

Wishing you well.........

Hoping you can become more realistic...

Sincerely,

Jessmin Howarth

* * * * *

An Evening with Dushka

Our Jet-Set Gypsy in her own mini revue

CHAPTER 31

NAMES... THE PERFORMER... THE FBI... THE UN... CRUISE SHIPS

Dushka
♦

Throughout our lives there seem to have been confusions of names. Although for years Mother tactfully wore a plain ring on the third finger of her left hand, she always used her own last name "Howarth." As her father had asked her to perpetuate the family name O'Brien, she sometimes signed herself "Jessmin O'Brien Howarth."

When I began to be old enough to fill out forms on my own, at school and so on, I had to improvise. I knew nothing about my father or the name "Gurdjieff" but I had gathered vaguely that he had been some sort of teacher and his name was "George." As a result I learned to, and continue to this day, fill out: First name: Dushka Last Name: Howarth; Father's Name: George; Profession: Teacher; Mother's Maiden Name: O'Brien.

Even my own first name makes difficulties. I have to struggle with an unfamiliar signature, like a forger, whenever some document needs to be in accordance with my birth certificate, that legacy of my two dear godmothers. When I renew my passport I need all four sides of the little photo to squeeze in "Cynthia Ann Howarth AKA Dushka Howarth." "Also Known As" in France is translated as "*Dites*" [said to be]. I once spent many uncomfortable months in Paris accused of not having a legal "*Permis de Séjour*" [permission to reside]. The forms were finally discovered filed under "Dites Howarth."

So where did "Dushka" come from? I only know Mother always called me that. I was more surprised than anyone when just a few years ago someone said casually that Mother had admitted "it was a name Mr. Gurdjieff sometimes called her." I gathered long ago that "*dousha*" in Russian meant "soul," and the "ka" ending is the diminutive. But "little soul" is only used in Russian as we in English might use "honey" and is not a given name.

In 1949, with Mr. Gurdjieff, I had to accept being called "Sophie," "Sophia," or "Sophy" (I didn't even know how it should be spelled). Then most people forgot and I became a serious business-lady, Miss (or *Mlle.*) Howarth of Howarth Services.

At least there aren't many others with my same first name. Only my goddaughter and namesake in Venezuela, Boussik's seventh child who was adopted in Mexico. When she was small they called her "Dushkita." But now a young lady, she is the one called "Dushka," and when I visit, I'm relegated to being addressed as "Señora Dushka Grande."

I warned Boussik that it wasn't an easy name to grow up with. As a child I endured being called "dusty," "douche," etc., and during

Dushkita newly arrived from Mexico.

my years working with jazz musicians who couldn't be bothered with such a weird name, I became known, and was often introduced over the microphone, as "The Duchess." This really made poor Mother flinch. She said it sounded like the name of a gun-moll.

As a performer I began to find that the incongruous combination of Russian and English names caused confusion and questions. "A Greek-Russian father? Then it is 'Horvath?'" "No. That's Hungarian." So, emulating a long tradition of single-named celebrities, I dropped the "Howarth" part.

VARIETY
(February 19, 1969)
NEW ACTS

DUSHKA Songs, Guitar
Mins.45
Athena East, N.Y.

"Dushka, now singularly named, may be recalled by many in the theatrical trades as Dushka Howarth who used to come around with a batch of press releases. Apparently she believed some of the actor salaries that were quoted and decided to go into business for herself. As it happens, Dushka is a highly competent rhythmic singer who accompanies herself on the guitar.

"She is big physically and sings in the same vein. Her tunes are hearty and folksy. She handles several languages starting off with Greek which is appropriate for this spot, to songs of other countries whether they border the Mediterranean or not. She sets a spirit and an atmosphere. All that is lacking is a ballad done in a serious vein which she probably can essay as well.

"The lady would excel in specialized situations and in cafes which hanker for a change of pace. She performs exceedingly well, has a wholesome personality and a rather pretty face."

* * * *

Then some TV or nightclub emcee dreamed up a title for me which got repeated and used by the press, and henceforth I was condemned to be announced as...

"DUSHKA, 'THE JET-SET GYPSY'"

"'Dushka' is a versatile performer with a fascinating repertoire, an evident result of her unusual background. Of Greek, Russian and English descent, she has traveled widely and lived in Paris, London, Athens and various corners of the United States. Her dramatic and musical training was received in Europe, New York and Hollywood, and she studied guitar with Vicente Gomez, Alirio Diaz and Andres Segovia. A talented painter, she holds a Fine Arts Degree from Barnard College.

"Along with a wealth of intriguing folklore from all parts of the world, she has collected songs in fifteen languages, but is also a dedicated and knowledgeable enthusiast of authentic American jazz. Her introduction to 'the Broadway scene' was as a press agent and manager for other entertainers, many of them 'name' musicians including Nat 'King' Cole, the Glenn Miller Orchestra, and Lawrence Welk. Dushka's own performing career was launched when her former clients pushed her into entering the First International Guitar Festival competition. She walked off with the First Prize, accepted some of the European offers that followed and was soon enjoying great success abroad.

"Recently returned to America to fulfill concert, nightclub and television engagements, she makes her home in Manhattan where, despite a grueling schedule she also finds time to direct 'Howarth Services' a unique concern she originated in Paris which handles everything from travel arrangements and party catering to international public relations.

"TV viewers may recognize her as Betty Crocker's Italian housewife or Rheingold Beer's Greek singer, and a recently released series of LPs were recorded live at actual parties, Greek, Italian, Polish, Israeli, Irish etc. for which Dushka was 'hostess.' Under a variety of pseudonyms she has recorded cowboy songs, blues, radio jingles, even animal voices for children's records."

The *Athena East* supper club on Second Ave. in New York.   Dushka with the musicians and staff of the *Athena East*.

(Below) One of the *Athena East* publicity flyers.

(Above) Dushka leads the customers in a Greek folk dance.
(Below left) Greek Tourist Agency's Stellios Pappas drops by for dinner and a duet! (Right) Showtime!

ATHENA EAST
takes pride in announcing the
RETURN BY POPULAR DEMAND
of
THE INTERNATIONAL FAVORITE

Dushka

For a limited engagement beginning Monday, January 13
Shows 9:30 & 12:00 (Closed Sundays)

ATHENA EAST
1230 SECOND AVENUE (bet. 64th & 65th Sts.), NEW YORK, N. Y.
We recommend reservations: LE 5-5548

One difficulty of using such an ethnic name as "Dushka" is that it may suggest that you are a lot more Russian than is the case. Certainly whenever our cruise-ships docked in Russian ports, the authorities would sourly scrutinize my documents especially carefully, and once they even refused me permission to go ashore.

In New York also it could lead to incidents.

When I was working with Nick Papadakos as a "registered rep" I naturally never missed an opportunity to attend social functions hoping to cultivate potential clients. So one evening I dropped in on a meeting of the "International Friendship League." It was quite friendly and very international, and I noticed that my first name immediately attracted the attention of two good-looking, extremely well dressed young men. They spoke impeccable English, but on reading their cards, which they eagerly pressed on me, I saw that they were attachés to the Soviet Delegation to the UN.

Messrs. Vadim Kirilyuk and Boris Bukatiy were not only charming but they even seemed to react with interest when I teasingly suggested mutual funds as the perfect vehicle of capitalistic investing for them. At the end of the evening the two offered to escort me home. When I saw what a nice car they were driving, I began to think that they might really be potential investors. I figured that, considering the political uncertainty of the times, Russians working abroad might well wish to take the opportunity to set up an emergency nest egg in dollars.

So a month later, when two friends and I decided to give an international-style party together, I added to my part of the guest list — Vadim and Boris.

It was going to be a large, motley crowd (one of my friends worked at Radio Free Europe) but I foresaw no difficulties. In Paris, where I often gave equally mixed parties, I learned to circulate a descriptive guest list. This way people could seek out and cultivate, or on the contrary, identify and avoid, anyone whose professions or political affiliations meant something special to them. Since my gatherings always stressed food, drink, music and fun, there was little opportunity for differences of opinion or ideology, and often some profitable networking was accomplished.

This time also, the evening went smoothly. My pair of Russians were again super-charming, they sang us Slavic songs, gamely tried to learn a Greek folk dance, and flirted and chatted amusingly with everyone. Not our usual idea of "Bolshies."

A few weeks later, one of my co-hostesses called me to say she was giving her own party, invited me, and asked if I thought she should also invite the two Russians. I encouraged her: "Sure! We can always use a couple of unattached men."

So I was surprised when I arrived at her apartment to see that Boris had come alone without his usual side-kick. When I said to him: "What? No Vadim? Did he go back to Moscow?" Boris turned white and muttered : "How did you know that?"

For a moment I didn't even remember exactly what I had said, but seeing how concerned he suddenly looked, I just couldn't resist a mysterious: "Oh, I have my ways—." I would have thought nothing more of it, except as the evening progressed, so did Boris' vodka consumption, and several times he sidled up to me and hissed in my ear: "No! Really! How did you know?" And I just looked knowing.

A year or so went by and one day two FBI agents presented themselves at the desk of the Hotel Buckingham where Nick Papadakos and I had our offices. They telephoned up from the lobby asking if they might take me to lunch as they had some questions for me.

I agreed, but put them off for an hour during which Nick and I hurriedly tried to figure out which of our many strange acquaintances or business deals might be the object of FBI scrutiny. We thought of a couple of dozen possibilities! But, no! It turned out to be none of them.

When the two men (in identical, stuffy suits), an "Agent Fuchs" and his partner, picked me up, they escorted me on foot up Sixth Avenue. Our destination was not the St. Moritz or one of the other nice restaurants on Central Park South, but a bench at the entrance to the park, where they served me a hot-dog and orangeade from a vendor's cart. I did think, looking back, that, considering the taxes I pay, a Federal agency might have had a little less chintzy expense account!

Finally the agents explained that their inquiry concerned two Soviets who had been identified as the foremost recruiters of "subversives" active in the U.S.

Bingo! Boris and Vadim, of course! The FBI needed to follow up on all contacts they might have made and any results of their meetings.

I was glad to help, did my best to reconstruct the guest lists of both parties, and enthusiastically agreed to "cooperate with the FBI if I was ever again approached by any Russians...!" (They had promised to get together again to teach me some Russian songs even if they decided against the mutual fund.) Oh, fantasies of Mata Hari!

But it was when we compared in detail actual dates that we all suddenly realized why I had so discomfited Boris at the second party with all my teasing and mystery about Vadim and his return to Moscow.

Just twenty-four hours previous to that evening Agent Fuchs revealed, in a very hush-hush operation, Vadim had been arrested and, in exchange for a "KGB-detained" American "operative," had been deported to the USSR.

I never discovered how Boris avoided being involved, or what ultimately happened to him. Neither the Soviet Delegation nor the FBI contacted me again.

I sold mutual funds to lots of other people but had to learn my Russian songs from records.

Another time the name "Dushka" attracted attention was at a United Nations party.

Billie Biederman, who acted as my personal representative, had introduced me to another of her clients Bess Myerson, whose many activities at that time included helping the U. S. Mission to the UN give parties and receptions. One of these was a yearly event to which they invited all the other Missions. This time Bess asked me to come to dinner and then entertain.

I was known for my "international repertoire" and could present creditably I hoped, songs in many languages. But knowledgeable friends tactfully suggested that I limit my program to the three languages mainly used at the UN, *i.e.* English, French and Spanish. But I couldn't resist adding one of my Greek specialties (I admit I love to show off with those lively 7/8 or 9/8 rhythms), which then meant, in an effort to be internationally "politically correct," I had to follow it with something Turkish, of course.

Everything went very well and there was flattering applause as I laid aside my guitar and returned to my place at table. So I was surprised when my immediate neighbor, the attractive secretary of the current U.S. ambassador, James Roosevelt, groaned under her breath: "Oh no! Oh no! He's going to make trouble again."

Surprised, I looked up as a tall, dapper man strode across the floor and grabbed the microphone.

"That's the Russian ambassador, Federenko," she whispered to me. "He always makes difficulties on behalf of the Soviet Delegation, complaining that they are not properly received, given enough attention and so forth. What can it be this time?"

But I saw he had a nice smile and relaxed until I heard him say over the mike: "We wish to thank you for the pleasant dinner and the very nice entertainment — but — surely — with a name like Doooushka, the young lady can also give us a Russian song."

All heads swung around to our table to look at me. It seemed as though there was a special anxiety in the American faces, and my heart sank as I realized with horror that all the Russian songs I usually sang were old White Russian or gypsy things. These are popular in our cafés here and in Europe, but were, I had heard, strongly disapproved of by the Soviet régime. To do one of them under these circumstances would have been a bit like offering *Hava Nagila* to an Arab Delegation.

As everyone was pushing me back to the microphone, I was frantically searching my memory until it occurred to me that the recently popular *Moscow Nights*, since it was more modern, might be safe to do. The trouble was — I only knew two short verses of it. Would they be enough?

I dramatically strummed an introductory minor chord for a *very* long time. Not just to attract everyone's attention, but to fill up time. Then, taking a big breath, I started: "*Nye sleeshnyee...*" but three times slower than anyone else has ever sung it.

Federenko had walked back to his table but now remained standing by his chair. After a moment or two, Ambassador Roosevelt also stood up. (Afterwards he explained that it was the only protocol-correct thing he could do). Unfortunately, then the other delegates, seeing the two ranking ambassadors standing and hearing my lugubrious version of something in Russian, must have thought it was some kind of hymn or national anthem, and looking enquiringly at one another, started to stand up also.

Now I was really in trouble! Trying to keep the guitar going and pronounce the Russian lyrics correctly, I was also struggling to think of some alternate song to switch to. Visualizing my record albums I remembered one by the Red Army Chorus. Surely anything they sang would be suitable. Hadn't I started learning their *Kalinka*, because it was something audiences could join in on, clapping as the chorus gets faster and faster?

So I segued into that. Everyone gratefully sat down and started clapping along — including Federenko and Roosevelt. (Nothing like bringing your own applause!)

When afterwards I was introduced to Federenko and found him generous and easy to talk to, I admitted my difficulty in choosing the right songs for him and asked for suggestions. He staunchly insisted that *Moscow Nights* was his favorite and that I had done it justice. And *Kalinka* was always a winner. Then he screwed up his face and said: "But — as for gypsy songs —" and this very elegant and educated man wordlessly expressed his opinion with a grimace that on anyone else would have been a spit!

When he left a little later, Ambassador and Mrs. Roosevelt rushed over to me saying: "Oh, you don't know what you did." After a moment of panic, I realized they were just thanking me as they went on to explain.

Evidently there had long been tension and friction between the Soviet and U.S. Delegations to the UN. At a time when everyone was trying so hard to resolve the Cold War, openness and harmony would obviously have been greatly preferable. So Mr. and Mrs. James Roosevelt had recently been summoned to Washington for a series of high-level discussions aimed at resolving this problem. One result was an official request for the two of them to create a closer, personal relationship with their Russian counterparts.

(Above right) James Roosevelt (1907-1991) with his father "FDR" in 1934.

Accordingly, at the next UN social occasion, a reception followed by a buffet supper, the Roosevelts made a point of inviting Federenko to join them at their small table, and began asking him about his home, his family his years as a language specialist and so forth. Suddenly, in mid-sentence, his face stiffened, he stood up, and completely unlike the suave, polite politician he usually was, abruptly turned his back on them and strode away.

Shocked, the Roosevelts reported this incident to Washington and were ordered back there for detailed questioning. Every word and gesture was analyzed and discussed. Finally it seemed clear what had happened. Mrs. Roosevelt had the habit of wearing a large, "mushroom-shaped" ring on her right hand. At receptions where there might be a lot of hand shaking, she learned to switch it temporarily to her left hand to avoid getting pinched by it. Federenko had reacted so strongly precisely at the moment she noticed she still had her ring on the wrong hand and started to return it to its usual place. The FBI pointed out that the Russians often used a similarly shaped ring concealing a microphone when they secretly recorded conversations. It was decided that Federenko must have thought she was adjusting something similar, and that all the personal questioning had had an ulterior motive.

After that *faux-pas* everyone had been urgently trying to mend fences with little apparent success. That explained why the U.S. Mission people were so relieved when, for once, the Russians had no complaints, but in fact, even admitted to having enjoyed the evening.

And it also explained, I presume, the especially nice letter I received:

"*Dear Dushka,*

"*I cannot thank you enough for coming to my reception last Friday evening and*

UNITED STATES REPRESENTATIVE
ON THE ECONOMIC AND SOCIAL COUNCIL

May 23, 1966

Dear Dushka:

I cannot thank you enough for coming
to my reception last Friday evening and
for your wonderful performance. My guests
were all delighted with your singing and
the compliments do not cease.

Truly, I can think of no one more
worthy than you of the title "Miss United
Nations." Your rare talent for singing so
beautifully in the many languages that you
do merits this recognition.

I do hope that we will meet again soon.

With many many thanks again for helping to make my party such a success and
all best wishes for the future,

Sincerely,

JAMES ROOSEVELT

(Above) Ambassador Roosevelt's letter

Friday February 16, 1968

Evening

6:00   MIKE DOUGLAS—Variety
Hosts include Van Johnson;
TV personality Bess Myerson, Mrs. Rich-
ard Hughes, wife of the governor of New
Jersey; like rock 'n' rolling Perry Mark-
ers' Ban; and singer Dushka Haworth
Also a "talkie show (90 min.)

LAST 30 MINUTES -

DUSHKA sings a Mexican song, "Malaguena" in Spanish, and the Greek song, "Never On
Sunday", in Greek! DUSHKA, an American, sings in 17 different languages and has
appeared all over the world as an entertainer and a goodwill ambassador. BESS
describes DUSHKA's special contribution to Russian-American relations when DUSHKA
entertained a group of ambassadors at the UN. DUSHKA sings the Russian songs,
"Moscow Nights" and "Kalinka"

(Above) Listing of the Mike Douglas Show

for your wonderful performance. My guests were all delighted with your singing and the compliments do not cease.

"Truly, I can think of no one more worthy than you of the title "Miss United Nations." Your rare talent for singing so beautifully in the many languages that you do merits this recognition.

'I do hope that we will meet again soon.

'With many many thanks again for helping to make my party such a success, and all best wishes for the future,

Sincerely,

James Roosevelt"

Bess Myerson appeared on the Mike Douglas TV Show (February 16, 1968) as guest hostess, and talking about her experiences at the UN described my appearance there:

"Dushka really did more for international relations that night at the UN, than many ambassadors have been able to do in years."

So yes! I do sometimes wonder. What if, instead I had chosen a gypsy song?

One result of appearing on network TV shows like Mike Douglas, Girl Talk, etc. was that I began to be contacted for performing jobs outside New York. Performances were everything from college concert tours that I usually did with Frances Alenikoff and her dancers calling ourselves the "International Theater of Song and Dance" - (naturally I was the "Song" part) to summers on the "Borscht Circuit" (Jewish hotels in the Catskills and Poconos), casinos, outdoor weddings, "bar and bas mitzvahs," Girl Scout Jamborees, and all manner of clubs, not only jazz and night-clubs, but women's, men's, literary, golf, country, Rotary and Lion's clubs.

But on a grander scale were special performances that involved being flown to Paris for the Grand Opening of the new Hilton, to Hamburg for the Mercedes Benz convention, to Monaco for the Music Festival, and to Caesarea in Israel for a Club Med anniversary.

Even private parties in New York could hold some surprises like the time my Greek friend, singer Theresa Stratas, recommended me as entertainment for an elegant affair being held in someone's apartment. I was used to occasions like that. But this time it turned out that the hostess was on some committee for the Metropolitan Opera and was giving the party for the leading Met cast members, Zubin Mehta included.

As you can imagine, I encouraged a lot of audience participation for that one.

(Above) Conductor Zubin Mehta

(Above) Theresa Stratas in *La Boheme* at the "Met"

Incidentally, Zubin wouldn't sing along, but he did a really great job of finger snapping in time for *Never on Sunday* and clapping for the Russian and Flamenco things.

But what really suited me, I found, were cruise ships. The Bramson Office that provided entertainment for many different Shipping Lines and companies could keep me busy doing cruises all year long. They found my versatility, and applicable foreign repertoire, or American jazz and folk things, useful in many situations. I carried full orchestrations but, if necessary, could accompany myself on the guitar, and with Mother's help and theater-trained eye, I had developed an extensive, elaborate wardrobe. If the necessity arose I could even do my show in passable French, Greek or German. Most important of all in those confined, "fish bowl" conditions of shipboard life, I had no "bad habits!"

The first few times I did a cruise it just seemed like a paid vacation and I came back to New York ready for "work as usual." But it was beginning to be a slow period for entertainers and when my fellow performers exclaimed: "You mean that you've been working?" I agreed to be sent out again. Finally I settled in to what turned out to be almost fourteen years of cruising. Naturally it soon became less and less vacation, and more and more dreary work. Life aboard a ship becomes maddeningly restrictive and repetitious (I now understand fully the expressions "cabin fever" and "a golden prison"). It keeps you away from friends and family but doesn't provide an alternative social atmosphere, since the passengers are always coming and going and the officers and crew, whatever their nationality, are usually an insular, chauvinistic lot. (Who dreamed up "The Love Boat?') Even if your every show is a roaring success and you are treated like a prima donna, it is frustrating to a performer never to be reviewed or publicized to the outside world, and to realize that these enthusiastic audiences will soon disperse to their widespread homes and you have no hope of building them into a following.

One thing that helped me survive was not letting them keep me too long on any one ship, or repeating the same itinerary. I switched from Norwegian ships like the Vistafjord, Sagafjord, Viking Sea or Viking Sky, to Greek ones like the Golden Odyssey, Danae, Stella Solaris, Stella Oceanis, the German Hanseatic or Hamburg,

Aboard the Cruise ships....

..."tummeling" for the passengers.

the French Renaissance or Mermoz, or Italian-crewed ones like the Oceanic or Homeric, or others I have forgotten.

There were certainly advantages to cruise ship life. Once installed safely and comfortably aboard, I didn't have all the problems of getting to and from "gigs" with all my equipment, coping with sleazy agents and club owners, fighting with unrehearsed musicians, poor lighting and sound systems... all the usual vagaries of being a "solo girl act." I was nearly always greatly appreciated, and considering I had no expenses after the initial costs of my costumes and arrangements, I was well paid. In fact, for the first time in our lives, the Howarths were able to begin building a savings account and to put into practice some of the investing theories I had studied at General Securities.

Since I was rarely required to do more than two shows a week, I still had a lot of time on my hands, even after a lot of reading, rehearsing, sunbathing and polishing up my backgammon. As a result, I managed to ingratiate myself even more with everyone by doing extra socializing and hostessing among the passengers, or giving dance lessons to the officers, and English lessons to the crew. When we were in port, my salvation was to seek out the best beaches, snorkeling haunts, and ultimately, scuba-diving instructors. Or I might just relax with the rest of the staff on "Rockefeller Beach," our secret name for the ship's outdoor pool, which we appropriated as our own when, finally, all the passengers had gone ashore!

But mainly I filled my time taking "land tours."

The Shore Excursion Office was always asking for some of us on the staff to chaperone the passengers, so I proceeded to rack up enough sight-seeing for several life-times, such as: Elizabeth Taylor's house in **Puerto Vallarta,**... Gracie Field's house in **Capri**... Brazilian soccer star Pele's house in **Santos**... Grieg's house in **Norway**... Hamlet's castle in **Denmark**... The Duke of Windsor's residence in the **Bahamas**... Flipper's home in **Miami**'s Sea World... Diocletian's castle in **Split**...

Scuba-diving with the staff captain

With a *Fantasia* winner in Morocco.

When Jessmin joined Dushka for a summer cruise that stopped in Madiera, she didn't know she would have to go sledding!

King Farouk's summer palace in **Alexandria**...

I experienced panpipes in **Roumania**... bagpipes in **Edinburgh**... birimbaus in **Bahia**... charangos made out of an armadillo's shell in **Buenos Aires**... Greek bouzoukis in **Israeli** nightclubs... mariachis in **Athens**' Plaka... *al fresco* opera in **Rome**... amateurish presentation at **Leningrad**'s Kirov (all the regular company on a world tour)... midnight Christmas Mass with castanets in **Guatemala**... "bateria" drums all night long at **Rio**'s Carnival...

Tried baccarat in **Monte Carlo** (couldn't understand a thing)... craps in **St. Maarten** (won a lot following instructions from the ship's Catholic chaplain)... jai-lai in **Spanish** fronton (bets put in tennis balls and thrown down to courtside)...

Wondered at ancient brothels of **Ephesus**... and **Hamburg**'s modern Herbertstrasse... **Dutch Antilles** government-run prostitute compound "Campo Allegre..." **Pompeian** friezes... **Cairo**'s male belly-dancers... **Montevideo**'s cigar-smoking voodoo priestess... pot-smoking hippies in **Amsterdam**...

Noted Gaudi's Cathedral in **Barcelona**... the Duomo in **Milan**... St. Thomas' monastery on **Patmos**... the Sphinx by moonlight at **Giza**... Bahai Temple in **Haifa**... cliff-face hermits' caves in **Meteora**... the oracle's cave at **Delphi**... "Whirling Dervish" ceremony in an **Istanbul** high-school basketball court... **Jerusalem**'s wailing wall...

And, of course, the **Epidaurus** amphitheater (everybody whispering to check out the acoustics)... **Ecuador**'s equator (everyone being photographed by the "Middle Of The World" monument)... the remains of **Carthage**... being mobbed by begging toddlers in a **Senegalese** fishing village... the David in **Florence**... the Tower in **Pisa**... labyrinths at **Knossos**... There really are lace curtains everywhere in **Dublin**...!

Above the **Arctic Circle, Spitzbergen** in bright midnight sun we could pet the flying seabirds since they had no previous experience of humans...and loved sloths in **El Salvador**... vicuna in **Peru**... sailing into **Martinique** surrounded by hundreds of dolphins... baboons on the rock of **Gibraltar**... cows between hedges of flowering hydrangeas in the **Azores**... obese walruses sleeping on tiny fishing boats in **Mar de Plata**... valleys of butterflies... camels' halitosis in **Marrakesh**... riding donkeys on **Aegina**... mules on **Santorini**... slippery, grotesque, gory bull-fight in rain-soaked **Mexico City**... **Arabian** horses galloping at you amid smoking antique muskets at a **Moroccan** "Fantasia," followed by couscous dinner with everyone eating from a common dish, "fingers of the right hand only!"

Or tried grilled, ouzo-marinated octopus in **Skiathos**... bouillabaisse in **Villefranche**... turtlemeat hamburgers in **Guadeloupe**... Indonesian rijtafel on a house boat in **Aruba**... buffet lunch in **Chichen Itza** ("Never again, Montezuma!")... **Argentinian** gaucho-barbecued baby goats... exorbitant expresso in the **Piazza San Marco**... 25-cent entrées in **Teneriffe**... syrupy mint tea in **Tangiers** guarded by scores of bees... a bottling plant's twenty-seven kinds of sweet **Madeira** wine (ugh!)... **Iceland**'s only legal beer, non-alcoholic, (double ugh!)... buttery **Bulgarian** yoghourt... cheese sandwiches toasted over pits of molten lava in **Lanzarote**.... **Beirut** humus amazing with huge red radishes and fresh mint leaves...

...but found almost nothing edible in **Yalta**...

Visited nude beaches at **Mykonos**.... blue-tiled Turkish baths in **Agadir**... private swimming pools at **Acapulco**'s Las Brisas Hotel... the cable car up to **Caracas**... antique trolleys in **Helsinki**... bullock-drawn sleds in **Funchal**... hydrofoils in **Naples**... fiacres in **Alanya**...1500 gondolas in a **Venice** regatta...

Bargained for $10 oil paintings in **Port au Prince**... lavender and rosemary essences in **Dubrovnik**... Amazonian tribal fetishes from **Belem**... amber at the Intourist Shop in **Odessa**... orange liqueur from **Curaçao**... Zubrovka from **Gdynia**... postcards of the non-existent "Colossus" from **Rhodes**.... enormous enamel paella pans from Woolworth's in **Mallorca** (won't fit in our ovens)... a nargila (water pipe) from **Damascus**... bulging sacks of oregano from a **Corsican** market (very suspect to U.S. Customs)... **Heraklion**'s circular wedding bread, sculptured with fertility symbols and varnished for posterity, (warn any hungry friends you send it to)... caftans in **Casablanca**... gold-lurexed saris on the dock in **Trinidad**... embroidered "moles" from **San Blas** Indian women with gold rings in their noses... gold puzzle rings from **Kusadasi** (be sure to ask for an instruction booklet)... etc...

Cruise passengers' comments overheard on board

(I swear they are true and quoted verbatim.):

"No, dear, even if everyone else wants Second Sitting, we need to get into First Sitting or I won't be hungry for the Midnight Buffet."

"It's perfectly ridiculous. They insist I can't mail my cards and letters in any of these European ports with my own American stamps on them."

At last!... Her own posters!

On German TV backed by Jean-Pierre Faigle.

Shipboard colleague radio host Barry Gray.

Eleanore Steber, fellow diva!!

On the same show with her idol Segovia!

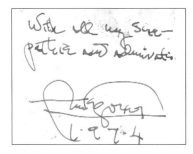

...but on the back of this photo of the two of them together, Segovia's kindly meant autograph just doesn't sound quite the same in English:"With all my simpathie [sic] and admiration"

After Dushla's show at Club Med, Agadir, a Moroccon dinner with friends including (Left) Boston Pops conductor John Williams and his wife. (Right) A duet!

The Robert Kleins.

With Barbara McNair. (right)

Carnaval night.

Mme de Salzmann in Caracas for Xmas.

(After several bus tours) "Why did they build the ruins so far from town?"

(Sailing into Istanbul) "The loudspeaker just said that we are now passing from the Dardanelles into the Bosphorus. But are we still at sea level?"

(Banana split on the lunch menu) "You've been so good about your diet up till now, dear, why not order one? After all, you need the potassium."

(The magician who opens our show comes off stage and warns us) "It's a real 'koan' audience out there tonight.!" (Most of us get it... the sound of one hand clapping!)

"Why do they call it the 'sixteen' chapel?"

"I guess the Captain is something like God. You rarely see him but it's nice to know he's up there."

"I loved that silver jewelry John brought me from Taxco. Is 'Acapulco gold' as good as they say?"

"We Spanish men treat our wives like cathedrals. Of course, we may also have a few chapels."

(After one of my usual "blockbuster" performances) "Very nice, dear. I hope they at least give you a discount on your cabin."

(Or...) "Our whole group wishes to complain to the Captain or someone. We think Dushka is wonderful. So why do they only stick her on at the tag end of the show?"

* * * * *

After one of Dushka's shows the ship's photographer tries to snap mother and daughter together. But this is why you see so many pictures of Dushka and relatively few of Jessmin. She always hated having her photo taken!

CHAPTER 32

MADAME OUSPENSKY

"...Of all the remarkable people I have met in my life, Madame Ouspensky stands out unique-
ly for her singleness of purpose and her unwavering pursuit of her aim...
"...She would never undertake anything beyond her own understanding and powers...
"...She said of herself: 'Madame is not a teacher. She always looks upon herself as a nursery
governess who prepares children for school.'" ...... (J. G. Bennett in *Witness*)

Jessmin
♦

Tatania Savitsky Nagro, (1983)
Franklin Farms, Mendham, New Jersey
Dear Tania,

Because I had my ninetieth birthday at the end of 1982, I felt I must make a
serious New Year resolution to try to do something soon about an idea I have had
for many years. So I am writing you and, through you, your mother.

There are a number of people still living who feel a loyal affection and deep
gratitude to your grandmother. And yet she is never given credit for her work and
help in nursing along those who studied with Mr. Ouspensky and later, due to her
guidance, with Mr. Gurdjieff.

I do wish something much more could be written about her contribution.
Certainly there is a risk that if people wrote about how and what they had learnt
from Mme. Ouspensky, it might become a collection of "testimonials." But I don't
see why it is not valid for people to express their indebtedness. And there should
exist many notes of the messages and book selections that came down from Madame's
room to be read at Sunday teas.

If your mother feels that she can agree to all this, I would eventually ask Jeanne
if she still has this material available and would offer it to any collection we can
make. It would contribute something serious and objective.

If I had your mother's permission I would feel it a privilege to write about this
to the many people I am still in touch with and I would like to help collate any
material and proofread it. I think I could manage to get enough money to have things
simply printed. Certainly, I have no intention of having any such collection sold.
Just to have enough copies to give one to each contributor and to the libraries in
Work Foundations.

I hope I could help with this before I get too old and fuzzyheaded to be of any
use. So, please, think about it.

Dushka sends her love and wishes you could meet oftener than once every two
or three years.

Always affectionately yours,

Jessmin

♦♦♦

There was apparently no further response to this letter and the project lan-
guished except for the following few scraps started by Mother.

Dushka
♦

◆◆◆

Jessmin
◆

Having felt, every time I came from her room, that whatever Madame said regarding the Work, organization, Mr. Gurdjieff, the house, or even individual people, was of general application and always connected with higher principles, I have decided to write down what and how I remember her conversations.

There exist photographs taken in 1922 at the Dalcroze studio in Paris. One shows Mr. G. sitting near the piano platform with Mme. O. beside him. [See Chapter 3] She said that her thus being "near" to Mr. G. was the result of chance and circumstance — that opportunities to have contacts with a "teacher" do not always come because they are "deserved"— that sometimes one was near Mr. G. for a time, and then another would have that place. She mentions Mme. de Hartmann as being one of the pupils who made the mistake of believing that she was irreplaceable. Her qualities of devotion, an essential capacity to live for another as evidenced by her constant service to her husband, unquestioning obedience, and nervous drive made her a very useful "secretary" for Mr. G. during one phase. But, later, other quite different persons filled this role: Elizabeth Gordon, Solita Solano, etc.

(Abover) Detail of the 1922 photo showing Mme. O. sitting beside Mr. G. (Below) An early photo of Sophie Grigorievna Ouspensky.

Mme. O. says that when she first met Mr. G. she felt that she was not "seeing" him as he was. She always had a realization that he was "different"— a being of a different order on a higher plane and that he was "acting" in ordinary life.

Speaking of "Juli Yussovna" [Gurdjieff's wife] Mme. O. said that, at first she was young and rather bewildered by the people who formed groups around Mr. G. So he asked Mme. O. to talk with her. He also, seemingly desirous of bringing his wife into the Work through the Movements, told her to practice standing in a modified Arabesque position, motionless for half an hour. She set herself to do this — first a few minutes at a time — then progressively longer, without, at first, comprehending any reason for making this effort.

Sometimes Mme. O. smilingly tells of her first encounter with "Jeanne Yulovna" [Mme. de Salzmann]. The original group who had worked with Mr. G. primarily on "ideas" and "inner exercises" were interested to hear later that Mr. G. was teaching Movements. At that time Mme. de S. had successful dance classes in Tiflis (where her husband was a stage designer and director at the Opera House). Mme. de S. brought her pupils to Mr. G. feeling that he was a truly great educator. Subsequently this group served as demonstration material.

Mme. O. was therefore interested in meeting this young woman who, she considered, had shown "right attitude" and direct perception. When she met Jeanne, she immediately moved toward her and greeted her. Jeanne looked at her and said: "But, do I know you?" Since then they have both often laughed together about this.

Mme. O. says that although, at first, it was difficult for the older group to understand Mr. G.'s work on Movements and his acceptance of "unprepared" pupils, later...

◆◆◆

Dushka
◆

It is such a pity that these rough notes were left uncompleted especially because that last sentence suggests just what I personally have always suspected, that the

Sophie Grigorievna Ouspensky

major reason for P.D. Ouspensky's differences, and eventual complete break with Gurdjieff was due largely to the increasing emphasis given to Movements. Mr. Ouspensky never seemed to understand or appreciate their role in the Work as it developed once they all left Moscow.

Boussik, who as a small child at the Prieuré loved being allowed to do Movements, told me she only once remembers seeing Ouspensky attempt the Movements —"very badly!" And it is extraordinary how his book *In Search of the Miraculous*, otherwise such a meticulous and faithful exposition of Mr. G.'s ideas, (at least as he espoused them in 1915!) makes almost no mention of, much less any indication of the importance of, Movements. What he does say shows a complete lack of understanding of this particular aspect of G.'s work. No wonder years later at Lyne he asked Mother: "Why do people do Movements?"

In Essentuki, March 1918, Ouspensky wrote: "... the principal part of the work which began at that time were the rhythmics to music and similar strange [sic] dances which afterwards led us to the reproduction of the exercises of various dervishes. G. did not explain his aims and intentions but according to things he had said before, it was possible to think that the result of these exercises would be to bring under control the physical body.

"...But my personal position [sic] in G.'s work began to change... I had nothing to say against G.'s methods except that they did not suit me... Of course, all that I had learned during those three years I retained... I went into a separate house and again began work on *A New Model of the Universe*.

"...G. left Essentuki. In the spring we learned that he was continuing work in Tiflis with new people and in a new direction, basing it principally on art, that is, on music, dance and rhythmic exercises.

"...During the year 1923 I went fairly often to Fontainebleau... G.'s own work during this time, that is, from 1922, was dedicated chiefly to the development of methods of studying rhythm and plastics... in spite of all my interest in G.'s work I could find no place for myself in this work nor did I understand its direction."

Mme. de Salzmann is quoted in Ravi Ravindra's journal as saying: "...Gurdjieff worked for years on ideas with Ouspensky. Then he shifted to direct work and Ouspensky wanted ideas and explanations which Gurdjieff refused. In part that is why Ouspensky left."

But I compare dates and written accounts and realize that although Ouspensky evidently encouraged some of his English pupils to help fund the acquisition of the Prieuré, it must have been a great shock to him that a bare year later (January of 1924) Gurdjieff was ready to gamble absolutely everything on taking his Movements people to America to give demonstrations. As G. himself wrote: he was only able to pay for the last travel expenses, because his mother, newly arrived from Tiflis, returned to him a valuable brooch he had once given her for safekeeping. So is it really just a coincidence that after years of indecision it was just that same month that Ouspensky returned to England and made the definitive, harsh announcement: "I have decided to break off all relations with Mr. Gurdjieff"?

Mme. O., on the other hand, had not only been active in Movements herself, (she was listed first on the list of instructors at the Prieuré followed by Jeanne de Salzmann, Olga Hinzenberg, and Elisaveta "Lily" Galumian), but it was she who manoeuvered her husband into accepting Mother's teaching of Movements at Lyne in England, then at Mendham in the U.S.

Moreover, if in 1949, she hadn't insisted on her Mendham pupils taking the long drive each night into the city where they made up the largest part of Gurdjieff's Movements classes and evening gatherings, his last trip to New York would never have succeeded as it did.

As she said: "All work begins with the control of attention, and in this connection much can be learned from the Movements."

Mme. Ouspensky agrees to pose for a photograph with the help of Mrs. Evans outdoors at Lyne Place in England.

I don't remember much about my own early visits as a schoolgirl to Lyne, the Ouspensky house in England, but when they came to the U.S. in the early Forties I often accompanied Mother out to "the Farm" in Mendham for visits, especially on weekends.

I knew nothing about "The Work" but I noticed that people seemed to be approaching various household tasks and farming chores in a special way. Of course some of them pontificated about "working consciously," so you can imagine my glee when one of the haughtier workers, an influential city-dweller, did in fact saw off the tree branch he was sitting on! And then there were interesting discussions and readings at mealtimes, especially at Sunday tea when there were the most visitors. For these occasions Mme. O. sent down excerpts from a wide variety of writings that she had carefully chosen out and grouped together to point up the universality of certain truths.

I finally broke down and asked Mother, "What are these people doing?"

Mother conferred with Mme. and I was given some things to read. They probably included Ouspensky's *Five Psychological Lectures*, a small booklet often used as introductory literature. I just remember that my reaction was, "Yes! That's true. Well, of course. But doesn't everybody know that?" Without my realizing it, Mother had evidently raised me with "Work" principles, and what now struck me as just common sense, was, I came to realize later, sadly less than common! In fact these were profoundly disturbing ideas to many people of more fundamentalist or provincial backgrounds. And how lucky I was to have as role models two such kind, practical, humorous sources of wisdom as Mother and Mme. Ouspensky!

Mme. O. had told me when I first came to Mendham to consider it my home and to join in anything that other people were doing, but only if and when I wished. But then, clever old lady that she was, she completely hooked my interest and participation by asking me to personally bring her reports and suggestions on what was going on. Of course, I gloried in that and even originated some big projects like converting the old dairy into a men's shower which everyone, especially the women, agreed greatly freshened the air at Sunday tea.

I considered that I had enough "women's work" at home, so I usually ended up outside with the men, especially Tom Forman and actor Wesley Addy (who also helped me find and bargain for my first and only little second-hand car.)

I joined them on the tractors, combines, and mowers, and soon with my hands calloused and engrained with machine grease, nails broken by bailing wire, I had to begin wearing long gloves in the city when I dressed up for press receptions, opening nights and the like.

Mme. O., like Mr. G., took food and cooking seriously. Even when she no longer actively supervised the kitchen as she had always done since before the days of the Prieuré, she still ordered, tasted and corrected the food. Except for some marvelous parties when we were treated to real Russian buffets, food at Franklin Farms was of necessity Spartan even on weekends when special efforts of hospitality were made for the big influx of guests. Mme O. just didn't have the funds necessary to do more.

She also never forgot her experiences in the Russian Revolution and worried about the state of the world and the future of the youngsters living with her. With no big freezers and only a musty root cellar in the garden, she instructed her "house people" to study other kinds of food preservation. They weren't too successful. One might spend hours in the dairy painfully hand-churning, and then come in to tea and be given lumps of a rather rancid product that had been stored for months while your day's work, all that beautiful, fresh butter, was salted down for future disappointing teas! And as for the wonderful, crisp green beans I picked — ! But, of course, nothing has ever tasted as good to me as the rather crudely textured, greyish bread that was made from wheat I had personally helped the men plough, plant, mow, stack, combine and mill.

Busy and frail though she was, I think Mme. O. enjoyed visits from young people with whom she could relax and not have to make the effort that earnest older pupils demanded of her, taking her slightest remarks as pronouncements to be engraved in stone for posterity. In any case, I was glad to be included with Tania and Lonia among those who had free access to her room.

It was extraordinary to witness how, though never leaving her bed, and seeing only a few chosen people whom she used as her eyes and ears, Mme. O. was able to tune in to, really understand and then influence each individual who came to Mendham, direct their activities and nurture their inner states.

Presiding calmly over a flurry of weekend organization, food planning, editing readings and dictating answers to personal questions, she would watch her various helpers with a twinkle in her eye. Only once do I remember seeing her upset.

Blanche Rosett, an elderly widow, had come out for the day on Sunday. Mme. O. somehow realized that she must have come by hired car, and was strongly critical that no one had remembered to send tea out to the driver waiting for hours in the back parking lot.

Another Sunday visitor, socialite Mrs. Hamilton Fish Armstrong, obviously had designs on one of the few eligible bachelors living at the farm, the tall and attractive Baron Ronimund von Bissing. (His mother, the Baroness von Bissing, a spunky relic from another era was a favorite of us all, and his sister, Tosca, became Mrs. Wolton.) Mrs. Armstrong hopefully invited him into Manhattan to an elaborate costume ball. When he reported this to Mme. O., she laughed and wickedly urged him to, of course, accept — but to take Tania, Lonia and me along as "chaperones!"

In those days I had nothing suitable to wear for such an occasion, but Mme. O. sent people scurrying down into her trunks in the storage basement, up into the attic, into their own closets, to gather together a borrowed black mantilla, a high Spanish comb, a long black dress, a beautiful black lace antique fan and flowers for my hair.

Finally satisfied (and I must say I did look gorgeous), Mme. sent me off with the others saying: "Remember, Dushka, always be Spanish lady — not Mexican girl!"

Not merely interested in and encouraging to my youthful ideas and ambitions, Mme. O. was also helpful practically. When it took so long to establish my business in Paris, she and Mother agreed that I should stick it out. And between them, I've never known how, they somehow sent me a check each month to keep me going.

In 1979 the Toronto group asked Mother to contribute some of her stories about Mme. O. to their publication, *A Journal Of Our Time*, which were included anonymously in the second issue under the title: *Wise Woman*.

◆◆◆

"WISE WOMAN

Jessmin
◆

"Once a number of us had the good fortune to live and work together, with the help of a wise woman. She also supported our wish to know ourselves.

"One day, having asked for, and listened to, what we had to say about our companions' behaviour, she said, 'How happy I would be if you saw yourselves as clearly as you think you see other people!'

"If one entered her room in a self-absorbed or inattentive state she would prick one into awareness by saying: 'Well, who is it in you who is talking to me now?'

"When people complained of the foibles of others as though they were crimes, she summed it up this way: 'For me, crime is making mountains out of molehills.'

"In advising us about our practical work together, she brought fundamental principles to our attention. She said, for example: 'If what you have made is not right, do not waste time and energy analysing and explaining — the material was not suitable — one worker was careless — others could not agree as to the best way to do it and so on. Just accept the fact that the job is botched and start over again.'

"Further, she read us the Russian fable about the four animals who had heard a nightingale sing and decided themselves to form a choir. When, on their first attempts to make music together, the result was cacophonic, they came to the conclusion that it must be necessary to sit in a certain formation. Said one: 'We should be in a straight row.' Another said: 'No, it must be a file, and I will lead.' They tried all ways and also experimented with sitting in a square. Nothing helped the sounds they produced to be agreeable. So, when they next saw the nightingale, they asked her why all their efforts led to nothing. She answered: 'To make music, you must first each be able to sing. Then it will not matter in what order you sit.'

"When she spoke of one of us who was apt to be too easily satisfied about her contribution to the general work and was rather officious and pompous, the wise woman said: 'Remember the fly who sat on the elephant's head in the procession and cried: Look how I lead the parade!'

"When people became proud or possessive about their 'positions,' she asked: 'Do you not see that your 'titles' and 'responsibilities' were given you as pegs on which to hang your self-study?'

"At the same time, she felt that we should respect the part more experienced people had played in making it possible for the ideas upon which our work was based to be transmitted. She described those people as pillars upholding the organization, trees rooted immovably in one place, able to serve as supports for climbing plants. 'But,' she added, 'the need is for living, growing branches.'

"The wise woman told us that when she first met her teacher, she was distressed because somehow she could not really 'see' him. She said she had had a great deal of experience in sizing up people — in fact, she rather prided herself on this intuition. But, although she watched this man constantly, '...like a cat at a mouse hole,' she could not sum him up. One day she realized that his very being was different from that of anyone she had ever met before.

"Of a period when he was putting many people to the test, exposing their weaknesses and arousing a great deal of emotional reaction, the wise woman said: 'He placed a number of pots on the fire to cook. One might boil over and put out the fire under it. Another might burn dry, another become lumpy. One might simmer until scum rose to the surface to be skimmed off. Possibly one or two would cook steadily and change into something nourishing and full of flavour. But only the cook knew what kind of meal he was preparing and when it would be ready.'"

◆◆◆

Dushka
◆

As Mother feared, the humanity, humor, and wisdom that she and Mme Ouspensky recognized and appreciated in each other is being lost through the years.

Just recently the current President of the NY Gurdjieff Foundation, Frank Sinclair, though a well-meaning man, published a book with these two revealing comments on the same page: "I, myself, never saw Madame Ouspensky alive." And, a little further down, "I have never been able to square Madame Ouspensky's well-documented authoritarianism with the search for truth."

Documented by whom? Another stranger who this extraordinary old lady didn't feel up to receiving in her bedroom?

So I am glad that another of the few people really close to Mme. O. (she cared for her during her last years), the late Daphne Ripman Matchelajovic, who led the large, active group in Buenos Aires, kindly sent me some of the notes she had made at Mendham from 1946-50. They bear witness to the kinds of conversations that took place in Mme.'s room as she chose readings, discussed people's questions and reacted to reports of the day's events. Here are some excerpts that I particularly treasure:

"Mme. said, 'If our aim is not formed, we are not in the work yet. If a man has aim he makes demands on himself — a man in the work knows what he wants, knows right from wrong and is determined to achieve his aim — hates sleep and desires to remember himself and takes everything relative to that.'

"Question: If one's aim is not formed yet and one cannot start work until one knows what one wants, it seems to be a circle. How can one get out?

"'It is a vicious circle but a way out does in fact exist. But for very few people. Only for those who realize that they are in a circle, have decision and determination to come out, and are willing to pay a high price to escape. You cannot come to consciousness unconsciously. If we see what we have not got we will know what we want — and what effort or payment we must make to get it.'

"We can always gauge how much we want something by the price we are willing to pay for it. Mme. describes us now as 'People without railway ticket who come up to the gate but who won't be let through.'

Daphne Ripman Matchelajovic at 90.

"Question: This house as arranged by Mme. seems to collect attention. If we use this house rightly it would help us to collect ourselves.

"In fact, Mme. finds that on the whole we have less attention and are less conscious than people in ordinary life. She says that 'today people in ordinary life have to have a certain degree of awareness, business people have to, they know they lose money if they don't, people in jobs have to be alert or they lose their jobs.' But we in this house can do things with impunity and therefore in fact Mme. finds most of the time we are on a level lower than people in ordinary life.

"'Making demands on oneself is not a question of activity. Some machines are made to be active.' To make demands on oneself, try to stop the machine in simple ways, which depends on whether one has energy.

"'It should already be clear that you cannot create energy. Necessary save energy, stop wastage. This is possible only if it is your heart's desire and you know what you want.'

"We had been told many times that we could not do. Mme. said, 'yes, in happenings, in momentum, impossible to do — only way of doing was by going against happenings, by stopping momentum. Aim is to be free to remember oneself. It is impossible to see anything or do anything without first stopping machine. She saw us as people without brakes. Even with car the first thing you check, before knowing what speed it goes at, are the brakes — while things were going at high speed, like a car going at high speed, no change of direction was possible.'

"'Everything depends on whether you really want, or you only think you do. Work is not living in house or coming into special conditions, or reading books, or coming to lectures or listening to readings. None of this leads in direction of work or aim from system point of view. People are divided in two categories — those who think and those who really want. If one really wants, one does.' God gives one free choice. No one forces you to do it. But your choice places you 'like the dog and the antelope, one goes for the bones and the other goes to the grass,' (in the anecdote it is carnal or spiritual). And all this has nothing to do with high ideas and imagination about yourself. Until one sees oneself as one is, and it may mean going many steps backwards from what one thought one was, one has no starting point.

"By ourselves we do not examine ourselves. We have to be made to see. If we then see 'it is like a thermometer, we can throw away thermometer or refuse to put it in our mouth but it is a fact. What we do with what we see is our business but facts exist, thermometer exists, temperature exists.'

"Before it is possible to work on attention a person must know why and what they want, to direct attention towards, because 'attention is like a tool, like a knife which can be used for right purpose or wrong purpose.'

"Analogy from Buddha reading: 'From the same food and the same circumstances the hornet produces poison and the bee produces honey.'

"'Directed attention supposes someone there to direct it – not just chariot without driver.'

"Where one's attention is caught, one becomes that thing and of the level of that thing. If one loses one's attention in this table one becomes this table. Collecting attention is bringing it back and bringing it into a definite place in oneself.

"Question: This feeling that one is nothing, to really feel it is a very rare thing.

"Mme. answered that 'you either have some feeling or have not. And what does it mean, nothingness? We come as beggar and we go as beggar. We have nothing, we have no consciousness, no 'I,' no will, are automatons. Question of seeing facts. Question of whether bigger 'Idea' exists for one or not. To be humble is natural, to be proud is absurd.'

"Realization must grow as man examines himself, observes. Mme. said for her 'big idea was that man was self-creative being, that exactly what one is depends on oneself.'

"Man has in his nature all things from God to devil. They all have their place and their 'note,' only which ones control is the question for us. 'Not question of abolishing lower, have pig in oneself – it isn't a question of killing pig, but keeping it in backyard.'

"Mme. also said she didn't want us to forget the parable of the talents, not to think that God had a sentimental attitude towards us. Those who had something could get more, but those who did not make use of what they had, would lose even what they had got. This was a principle and not sentimental."

* * * * *

Mme de Salzmann in later years

When Mme. Ouspensky died, on December 30, 1961, the following letter was received by the New York groups from Mme. de Salzmann in Paris:

"In the name of my relation with Madame Ouspensky, who was the nearest soul in my work, I wish to tell you this:

"Once more I recognize the truth I experienced in front of Mr. Gurdjieff's body, and which has become a certitude:

"There is no death... Life cannot die.

"The coating uses up, the form disintegrates, but life is – is always there – even if for us it is the unknown.

"We cannot know life.

"We can know life only after we know death. Death is the end – the end of everything known.

"And because we cling to the known, the unknown is a fearful thing.

"If we wish to know life, we need to die to the known and enter the unknown.

"We need to die voluntarily.

"We need to free ourselves from the known.

"In being free from the known, we can enter the unknown, the complete stillness where there is no deterioration, the only state in which we can find out what life is and what love is. As without that love we will never find the truth."

* * * * *

CHAPTER 33

A LAST SUMMER

"TO MRS. HOWARTH ON HER NINETIETH BIRTHDAY
FROM A PUPIL OF FORTY YEARS

Shuffling toward the classroom one by one,
Hurrying, lingering, loitering, meek as sheep,
Furtively glancing this way and that we come,
Passive as pillows - - - totally asleep.
But just around the screen a strange unease
Troubles our slumbers. Far off in her chair,
Erect, compact, our teacher sits at ease.
She vivifies the atoms of the air...
...and of our flesh. Slovenly chaos groans
As one by one the molecules awake.
Her beam illuminates our very bones
And shows us what we are until we ache,
And then amid our awkward strugglings
We scorn to change our joyous state with kings.
With love and gratitude... "
Martha Heyneman, author of *"The Breathing Cathedral"*

New York, August 20, 1984

To: Mr. & Mrs. Pierre Elliot,

c/o American Express, New Delhi, India

Dearest Vivien and Pierre,

Will this letter ever reach you, I wonder? The days have been flying by and I have lost count of the time you expected to stay in India. I do hope that the experience has come up to all your expectations and that you both have been able to keep well despite all the difficulties of changed conditions and high altitude.

I delayed writing partly because I thought I might hear from my "God-child...er...-man"...

♦♦♦

Mother is referring here to Phuntsok Tsering, a Tibetan refugee boy she had for years been sponsoring through school in Northern India.

Now almost grown, he had decided to study medicine, both Western and traditional Tibetan, because, as he wrote us, "my people will need both."

♦♦♦

...But a letter finally came only last week. Poor ambitious creature! He is upset because he only came out second in his class instead of getting the best marks. He is also fighting away, trying to get into some kind of medical training center. Of course, I don't know enough to judge rightly but I wish he could stay on in Dharmsala where he has people who know him and appreciate the serious way he works, and where, I think, there is still the possibility of studying at the school of medicine. Especially since I understand that if he is forced to go to another part of India with a lower altitude it may aggravate the tuberculosis that he, like many of his fellow refugees, is constantly battling.

Jessmin
♦

Dushka
♦

Jessmin
♦

Phuntsok Tsering, student

Patty Welch de Llosa

During the summer he is working in the Information Center there. They are trying to decide which alphabet to choose for some Tibetan publishing they now intend to do. Anyway, I hope you can meet. He would love to show you around. I would want you to enjoy some tiny pleasure after so kindly carrying to him for me such a big, heavy book as *Gray's Anatomy*. I'm sure he will be as grateful as I am.

News from here is meager for I am in touch with people only by telephone. The Americans and Londoners who spent a week *en famille* with Michel and Josée [de Salzmann] in Chandolin, their place in the Swiss Alps, seem to have been quite happy, but, maybe, a little surprised that any planning was not obvious. I'm glad if Michel can get to know our people better, for the usual Paris attitude towards all American efforts is one of disapproval.

How sad that although "identification" with one's teacher can help students to strive toward the ideal he sets, it also seems to make them forget that, beyond all else we need a true inner unity.

Our seminar in Armonk has just yesterday been cancelled because there has been a plague of ticks there, and in all Westchester and a number of serious cases of tick fever. So we have five days to reorganize and see how it can be accommodated in Nova Scotia.

Although I am rather afraid of not being able to cope with all the Movements teaching necessary, (Patty Llosa and Sheila Bura may not come up, but some of the Toronto people are good and can help).

I will be glad to have a change of air, and particularly pleased for Dushka who has devoted herself to me and all the household chores without respite since last November. We shall be away from 8/14 to 9/5.

With much love to you both always,

Jessmin

◆◆◆

Dushka

◆

The Elliots got to read this letter more than six months late, long after Mother's death. It was returned to me at our New York address marked "UNCLAIMED - RETURN TO SENDER." Also stamped on the envelope was the Indian Post Office's explanation for the delay: "Found in supposedly empty equipment." But how often do these sorts of incidents happen in India that it was necessary to have this lame excuse made up into a rubber stamp?

In 1985 I was happy to hear once more from Phuntsok. He wrote that the Dalai Lama had taken a personal interest in him and had arranged for him and one other boy to study Tibetan medicine in one of the last remaining places where it was still possible, a monastery in Mongolia. To prepare for this he was taking special courses in Tibetan culture and studying Mongolian with a monk visiting Dharmsala. He finished this letter with his usual exuberance, promising that when he was "a famous doctor" he would build a "Jessmin Howarth Hospital" in Mother's memory.

That was the last time I heard from him personally, but I recently read about a "Phuntsok Tsering" in an article from the magazine *India Abroad* sent me by Ravi Ravindra, a physics and religion professor in Dalhousie University, Nova Scotia. He and his wife, Sally, leaders of the group there, had once returned to India on a visit and Mother had asked them to look up and if possible, advise, Phuntsok. They enjoyed a pleasant visit with him, admired his pluck, and had even put him in touch with some of Ravi's influential Indian relatives. So they had been pleased to recognize a photo in this article identified as "Phuntsok Tsering, head-master of the Tibetan Children's Village."

His Holiness the 14th Dalai Lama, Tenzin Gyatso.

I don't know whether this is the same Phuntsok and if he became a medical doctor, but he is certainly helping to preserve his country's ancient traditions, as witnessed by the rest of this article:

"A 3,000-year-old healing system has become a crucial element of the exiled Tibetan Community's struggle to retain its identity. The herb-based Tibetan medicine, whose long exis-tence was virtually destroyed during the Chinese invasion of Tibet in the 1950s, is being revived vigorously by publicity-shy doctors in this Himachal Pradesh town. Since 1961 the Tibetan Medical and Astrological Institute (TMAI) has made a definite turn from near extinction. Said Dr. Namgyal Qusar, a researcher at TMAI, 'Although Tibetan medicine combines the best features of many other indigenous traditions, there are many unique features to it. One philo-sophical distinction is that 'it treats the patient and not the disease'. Traditionally our ancestors used to depend upon herbs and plants that are

From the *India Abroad* article showing Phunsok Tsering, (Upper right) headmaster of the Tibetan Children's Village.

found at much higher altitudes than what we have here. But over the years we have managed to make do with what we can get in the higher Himalayas at 15,000 feet or so." About 80 Tibetan doctors trained by TMAI offer treatment at 35 clinics throughout India.

"If TMAI offers an opportunity to the exiled community to learn about the advances their ancestors made in the higher studies, the Tibetan Children's Village (TCV) offers students what its headmaster Phuntsok Tsering calls 'Tibetanization'. 'While our curriculum adheres to what India's education authorities have officially lain down, we have introduced a serious degree of Tibetanization' Tsering said. There are about 2,000 students at TCV who study up to undergraduate levels. It offers dor-mitories and is considered the best school of its kind. 'Many of our students are recent arrivals from Tibet,' he said. 'As part of our Tibetanization campaign we ask the new refugee students to share their experience with those who were born here. We want them to grow up properly understanding Tibet and its history, and China's role in it.'"

Vivien Elliot wrote in *Impressions Magazine*, (Claymont, Virginia, 1985)

"Jessmin Howarth came into my life when I first started work on the Movements at the age of sixteen. I was going regularly to the Ouspensky's farm in Mendham, and on Friday evening I heard from upstairs strange, haunting piano music the like of which I had never heard before. My mother told me this was 'Movements' music. On Saturday there was a demonstration in white costumes so that I was fortunate to see them for the first time in this way. Afterwards I met Mrs. Howarth and Mrs. Nott (Stanley Nott's wife who played the piano). From then on I was devoted to Jessmin in a way I shall always treasure. For eight years she taught us the First and Second Obligatories, some of the dervish Movements such as the Forming Twos, the HoYa, the Warrior Dervish – a small repertoire but it was all we had in 1941.

"In the years to come there was a twenty-seven year gap in my contact with Jessmin, she lived in the States and I in England. From 1975 on I saw her regularly in New York and came to appreciate her irreplaceable qualities of impartiality, clarity of vision and her complete dedication to the work of Mr. Gurdiieff. Whenever I was in trouble she was an unfailing source of help, not necessarily of sympathy, but always she brought a balanced judgement to the situation. Her wisdom had an astringent quality that I found both welcome and bracing. She had, of course, a fund of stories of life at the Prieuré, of work with Mr. Gurdjieff, with the de Hartmanns, with Madame de Salzmann, and many, many others. She told me of a time during the war when Mr. Bennett had helped her over a difficult patch, and she always spoke of him with warmth and respect.

"Just before we left for India last summer, Pierre and I went to say good-bye, in one sense all my visits were goodbyes since at the age of ninety-two nothing is certain. She gave me a heavy medical textbook, *Gray's Anatomy*, to give to a Tibetan medical student in Dharamsala whom she had been sponsoring for several years. I promised to deliver it, and as I left, she guessed my unspoken question and said, 'Yes, dear heart, I'll be here when you get back.'

"She died without any warning a week before I returned to the States. I learnt of it by telephone and spent one afternoon walking as fast as I could along country lanes, tears streaming down my face. Even when my parents died I had not felt such grief. I had absolutely counted on seeing her upon my return and giving her the Tibetan cymbals I had brought back from Ladakh."

At the age of ninety-two, Mother was still very active. Her wit and intelligence were brighter than ever, but her body regrettably beginning to fail her. As she said herself, it was especially bitter for the dancer in her to have an arthritic knee, and for the musician in her to need help hearing. I did constant battle with her determined optimism and lifelong independence in an attempt to make her take care of herself. She didn't want her "doctor's appointments to use up Dushka's savings," and she was suspicious of everyone's reassurances that Medicare would cover most of it. She pooh-poohed the idea that anyone could do something about her knee: "after all, it was ninety-one years old!" But she was stymied when we pointed out that her other leg was just as old, and was perfectly all right.

It was even more difficult to talk her into the expense of a hearing aid, until one day she asked someone for news of her old friend Tom Forman. When they answered that he was, unfortunately, very sick and in hospital, she laughed gaily and said "Oh that's nice!" When I later told her what had happened, she was aghast and so mortified that she went right out and bought an aid. But only one! So it had to be turned up too high, often whistled, and picked up the clatter of dishes and silverware. Finally, a modest additional expense evened out her hearing with two aids and she was back in easy communication with people. At least until her pupils addressed her in what we always called "Work voices" those lugubrious mumbles some people affect thinking it denotes "inner remembering."

Even more than "Work voices," Mother was impatient with what she called "Work faces" and she would gently tease earnest pupils into being simpler and less pedantic or "holier than Thou," reminding them that they were working for themselves, not to impress anybody else, especially her.

Mother would have no one else share the apartment with her when I was away, and considering her age and the present state of New York City, I really felt she shouldn't live alone. So I retired and came home from my final cruise ship booking. I was hardly in the door when she wanted to tell me a story "while she remembered it." It had evidently really hit home with her, since, for once, she remembered it all, even the punchline:

"Three old ladies are sitting at a table together and one of them complains: 'Oh isn't it awful to be old. I have to wear this hearing aid and the crashing noises in the restaurant give me a headache. It's awful to be old!' The second old lady sighs: 'Oh, yes, I agree. I've developed arthritis in all my joints and the pain is terrible. It's awful to be old.' The third old lady says brightly: 'Well, I'm as old as either of you and I can hear perfectly well and have no arthritis.' - and she raps her knuckles on the wood of the table. A moment later she looks up at the door and calls out: 'Come in!'"

Mother and her closer friends like Bill and Louise Welch would sometimes sigh over the faintly ridiculous side of some of the overly solemn aspects of the Work. She didn't hesitate to repeat stories that some others in the hierarchy might have disapproved of.

For example, the occasion when a poor stranger found himself by accident one night, in the 63rd St. Foundation House. Evidently late for an appointment, he mistook the building for one just across the street, rushed in and was halfway up the stairs before the pupil acting as doorman stopped him. The stranger turned around and called out: "Sorry, pal, I was looking for the bar of the Illustrator's Club." But when he reached the foot of the stairs and glanced into the anteroom where people were sitting stiffly and seriously "preparing themselves" for their Movements class, his voice suddenly dropped, and flustered, he whispered, "Oh, I am *so* sorry! I didn't realize. Funeral Home, eh?"

Mother was complacent and humorous about her age. Another night in the Foundation a young man passing by dropped something and just watched as she bent to pick it up and hand it back to him. I was furious and railed at him, "After all she's over ninety, can't you pick up your own things?" Mother tugged at my arm and said softly: "Don't keep telling them how old I am." I blustered: "But, why not? You should be proud of it." As usual, she had the last word: "Yes, dear heart, but if you keep telling them how old I am, they'll know how old you are!"

Somewhere she came across an old seventeenth-century prayer attributed to "Anonymous," an unknown nun. It made such an impression on her, evidently expressing her own feelings, that she copied it out carefully by hand, and we put a decorative border around it and sent it to all her friends at Christmas:

"Lord, Thou knowest better than I know myself, that I am growing older, and will, some day, be old.

"Keep me from the fatal habit of thinking I must say something on every subject and on every occasion. Release me from craving to straighten out everybody's affairs.

"Make me thoughtful, but not moody; helpful, but not bossy. With my store of wisdom, it seems a pity not to use it all, but Thou knowest, Lord, that I want a few friends left at the end.

"Keep my mind free from the recital of endless details. Give me wings to get to the point. Seal my lips on my aches and pains. They are increasing, and love of rehearsing them is becoming sweeter as the years go by I dare not ask for grace enough to enjoy the tales of other's pains, but help me to endure them with patience.

"I do not ask for improved memory, but for growing humility and a lessening cocksureness when my memory seems to clash with the memories of others. Teach me the glorious lesson that sometimes I may be mistaken.

"Keep me reasonably sweet. I do not want to be a Saint, some of them are so hard to live with. But a sour old person is one of the crowning works of the Devil.

"Give me the ability to see good things in unexpected places... and talents in unexpected people. And give me, O Lord, the grace to tell them so. Amen."

> Alas!
>
> When Mr G. came on the scene
> He cast bright light where dark had been
> And when, in time, he came to die,
> His pupils all knew they must try
> To understand and share his work,
> A task they felt they might not shirk.
> It all began so gratefully
> But soon they acted hatefully,
> Each leader deemed he had no peer,
> He was the only one to hear
> The voice of conscience, sense his Being.
> (God rarely grants the gift of seeing)
> And so, while wishing to do right,
> We've ended in a tragic plight.
> How to escape the web we've spun
> Correct our faults, love everyone?

Jessmin, in her mischievous moods, sometimes couldn't resist writing what she called "doggerels" for her close friends.

(Left) This one was for Bill and Louise Welch.

In 1984 the summer plans had been for the Welch groups from New York and Canada to meet and work together in Armonk, the large house in Westchester used by the Gurdjieff Foundation. Mother was eager to go and was preparing to give several classes a day. I was dreading it for her because I knew the heat and humidity could be terrible there and though I could try following her around with an electric fan, I knew it would be draining for us all.

But plans were changed at the last moment. Earlier in the year, some of the young people who had gone out for weekends at Armonk came down with a strange, aching, flu-like condition. Dr. Welch recruited several young doctors in his groups to start telephoning each of the eighty or so people who had come out to Armonk at various times. They identified eleven cases of something none of us until then had ever heard of, "Lyme disease" named after a town not far away in Connecticut. Once identified and treated with antibiotics it can usually be cured, but it is difficult to diagnose. In fact, Dr. Welch resigned himself to a stiff old age for months before realizing that he, himself, was the twelfth case.

It was decided that it would be madness to expose so many people to this possible illness, especially the very young (there were to be special activities for children) and the very old who would be with us.

Hurried arrangements were made to move the whole seminar up to Halifax, Nova Scotia. Ravi Ravindra and his wife, Sally, lead the group up there and they have several buildings built along the shore, which are sufficient for such a gathering.

The only problem they foresaw was that between the two main houses there was a deep ravine made by a stream, difficult to get across. Knowing that Mother liked to be independent and free to go back and forth as she wished, the Canadians gathered a day early, purchased tools and stacks of lumber and worked together all night.

By the time we arrived the next day, they had designed and built a beautiful sixty-foot bridge that was safe and convenient for us all. It is still used, and is of course called the "Jessmin Bridge."

The weather was cool and refreshing, the sea air fragrant, the view of the bay and forests heavenly after New York City. Mother was active, healthy and happy and agreed to arrange a Movements teacher's seminar in New York in October.

Louise Welch and Jessmin in Halifax planning the day's program.

◆ ◆ ◆

New York, September 16, 1984   **Jessmin**
To Dushka, on her sixtieth birthday: ◆
Darling,

Fortunately, we both appear and feel younger than our ages so I can light-heartedly wish you a birthday full of love and joy and many Happy Returns.

Although you have been and are spared many of the bad happenings of life, I see that some of the best do not seem to come your way. But I watch you, since years, always making the best of what does happen, and that is a most admirable quality. Yet, where to draw the line between good-naturedly accepting jobs, relationships and conditions which are, one knows, not truly good enough, and holding out for what might be much more difficult and demanding?

Krishnamurti says that it is through comparing ourselves and our situation, and then competing with others, that we create most of the stresses and problems that make us confused and unhappy. I think you and I have realized that and I wish for you, with all my loving heart, that you should be free in yourself, and feel secure and have fun!

For my daughter—
my only reason for
having cared to go on
living for so long....

...and this is really quite true, even though you spend a lot of time nowadays, scolding and criticizing me.

Against that (and you probably have cause) I weigh your thought for me and the way you keep house for me and your feeling that, at least in the Movements teaching, I am still not quite senile!

So with LOVE——

Mum

◆◆◆

Dushka
◆

At St Peter's Church: (Above) The Ellington birthday buffet. (Below) Pastor John Gensel.

On the morning of October thirteenth, 1984, about thirty people flew to New York for Mother's Movements seminar.

Having completed detailed lists and class plans the night before, she was up early so that she could give me moral support as I initiated a new diabetic regime and gave myself my first insulin injection.

Then I helped her, as I often did for special occasions, with a more formal hair-do. A few moments later she simply leaned back and was gone, just as she would have wished it; in full involvement, no fuss, no trouble to anybody.

I found the folder containing brochures and advertisements that she had thoughtfully collected together to help us out in this contingency, and as she had indicated she wished, she was cremated very simply.

We buried her ashes under her favorite big tree at Armonk. (But I sometimes ponder why no one thought to warn me that reponsibles at the Foundation had already practically finalized the decision to sell that property.)

There was no funeral as such. The day of Movements work had gone on as planned with only a few people knowing why "Mrs. Howarth" wasn't there.

A week or so later Dr. and Mrs. Welch helped me arrange what was intended, specifically, not to be a memorial service but rather a "celebration of her life."

We decided to do it at St. Peter's Church (in the Citicorp building) where she had often accompanied me in the course of my twenty years of activities there as a committee member of their Jazz Ministry. Many still remembered her and the time when just the two of us, Mother and I, prepared and brought from home the large, elaborate buffet for four hundred people that climaxed a Duke Ellington Birthday Concert.

After an affectionate introduction, Pastor John Gensel, who had known and respected Mother, turned the whole occasion over to Dr. Welch and the hundreds of people, her friends and pupils, who had gathered from all parts of the country and stayed on afterwards for a cheerful gathering and generous supper in the living-room area.

Gurdjieff's music was played by pianists including Karel Backer and Stafford Ordahl who then listened appreciatively as our old friend Dick Hyman took time out from his tight schedule to contribute one of his extraordinary improvisations.

Larry Rosenthal flew in from Hollywood, rewriting on the plane his inspiring composition *Gloria* so that an amateur choir of about twenty of us could manage to learn and sing it effectively that afternoon.

* * * * *

SUMMERS IN HALIFAX, NOVA SCOTIA

University Professor Ravi Ravindra   Potter Sally Ravindra   Theater Director Andrei Serban

Summer "Work periods" at Halifax and Armonk usually included special activities for the children. (Below left to right) Munju Ravindra, Sally Ravindra, Kabir Ravindra, Jessmin, Amy Kahan, Ravi Ravindra and Gabrielle Sharpe.

The young people have their Movements class outdoors in Nova Scotia (center Marty Paloheimo), accompanied by Allan Pulker on flute and Dr. Chris Wertenbaker on guitar.

(Left) Mrs. Welch encourages evening relaxation so composer/pianist Laurence Rosenthal is roped into accompanying one of Dushka's "party stunts."

(Left) Pianist/painter Stafford Ordahl confers with Dr. Welch

In preparation for Mrs. Howarth's arrival in Nova Scotia, a bridge is rushed to completion.
(Below right) David Young. Walking at left center Gordon Winemaker.

PRISCILLA SMITH, of New York, practices her juggling act for her role of the clown in Andrei Serban's production of *The Clown of God*. The Toronto-based STS Experimental Theatre group will present the medieval legend at All Saints Cathedral, Halifax, next week.

(Fairfield-Fairfield)

New York producer directs Toronto players in church

By BRIAN UNDERHILL

The Clown of God, which considers the question, "How to live one's daily life out of the new; how best to submit oneself to higher forces—God," will be presented by Andrei Serban at All Saints Cathedral Wednesday to Friday, Aug. 5-8.

Serban, who is associated with the Lincoln Centre in New

with Indian Orthodox producer Dr. Lloyd Heise.

"I believe in the sacred; and we are all clowns," Priscilla said.

"The people involved with the performances are doing something completely on their own time. It is their form of worship.

"We are trying to take a serious religious theme and see

the lives of that of an ordinary dance, an original legend from Florence. The 13th century text went to Old French but has been translated and adapted by members of STS Experimental Theatre in consultation with Serban.

Asked in an interview in Toronto why he had chosen to do *The Clown of God* in Toronto

Nova Scotia newspapers carry stories about the production
"The Clown of God" with noted director Andrei Serban, and
script by Louise Welch.

(Above left) A photo of New York actress Priscilla Smith in the
title role of "poor orphan boy" who offers his juggling as a gift
to the Virgin Mary.
(Above right) Outdoor and indoor scenes from the production
which takes place at All Saints Cathedral. During most of the
piece, Neal Hoff manages to remain completely immobile as
the statue of the Virgin Mary until suddenly and miraculously
coming to life to bless the orphan boy!

(Right) Dr. and Mrs. Welch help supervise
rehearsals involving approximately eighty
adults and children from their groups in
New York, Toronto and Halifax.

(Above) Jessmin appreciating the new *Jessmin's Bridge*.

(Below) *Jessmin's Bridge* the next Canadian winter.

CHAPTER 34

"WHAT IN G.'S NAME...?!"

Dushka
♦

For almost six years after Mother died, her colleague Jeanne de Salzmann continued to be active and to travel between Europe and the US, thanks to the *Concorde*, often accompanied by Henri Tracol.

On the occasion of Mme. de Salzmann's hundredth birthday, Bill Segal and his second wife, Marielle, threw a big party for her in New York. While many of the guests sat around stiffly trying to look "conscious," she herself gaily smoked, drank champagne and chatted. Meanwhile, I happily snapped photos.

Jeanne de Salzmann in 1990.

Mme. de Salzmann with host William Segal on the occasion of her 100th birthday.

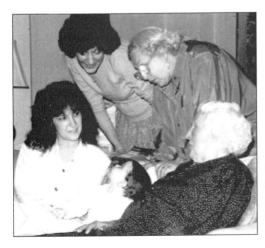

Five generations: (Right to left) Mme. Jeanne de Salzmann, her daughter Nathalie ("Boussik"), granddaughter Anne-Marie Grant, great granddaughter Gaby (Olivier's daughter) introducing her baby Amelie to her great, great grandmother!

(Above left) Dr. Michel de Salzmann on French TV in 1979.   (Right) Michel in 2001, his last year.

(Above) In the summers, Michel held "Work periods" in Switzerland or France.
At Beau Preaux, Michel's country house outside of Paris. James Ehlers from Philadelpha (right) carries one of the lunch tables while Eduardo Cordona from Paris, brings out his creation, a huge Spanish *paella* aided by helpers Michel (center), Anton Bluman from New York (to Michel's right), and John Cope from Philadelphia, while Ed Tupta from Cleveland snaps photos.

When Mme de Salzmann died on May 25, 1990, her son Michel was faced with the lonely and daunting task of heading the Gurdjieff Work internationally which he did until his own death on August 4, 2001.

Michel's son Alexandre had spent some time as an intern in a New York City hospital but then returned home to France to practice medicine, marry and start a family. Michel therefore, I like to think, had support nearby when he lost both his mother and his wife Josée within a few months.

Mother's death had started me on a huge archiving project reading, sorting and filing her personal writings and correspondence, and, especially, her precious Movements material — all those notes, photos, drawings, and various versions of music.

Dr. Alexandre de Salzmann

This study certainly renewed and reinforced my own faith in the value of the real, authentic Gurdjieff Movements, but also awakened in me an urgent necessity of seeing to it that Movements be preserved exactly as Mr. Gurdjieff had originally given them. It was obvious that destructive distortions and misunderstandings were creeping in and multiplying as time passes and memories fade. Really qualified instructors and musicians were becoming more and more rare, and the older, experienced teachers were dying off, leaving their insights and documentations to be ignored and scattered. I recognized a responsibility to preserve at least Mother's wealth of knowledge and understanding by setting up and making available her archives, transcribing tapes we made of her talks and classes, and disseminating and correcting notations, drawings, and music.

In 1986 Mme de Salzmann's daughter Boussik, (Senora Nathalie "de Etievan"), now responsible for the Work in South America, suggested that I return to Movements teaching and join her down there for four or five months of each year to help supervise or, as was often necessary, establish classes of Movements.

Years earlier, Boussik and her husband Jacques "Regis-Etievant" (Alfred's brother), had arranged the translation into Spanish and Portuguese of the dozen or so primary books of the Gurdjieff System. These had long been widely distributed, read and exhaustively discussed in groups that formed in various South American cities. Naturally, for most of these people there had been few possibilities to have meaningful personal contacts, indications for practical work, or the experience of Gurdjieff's physical exercises and "sacred dances."

So by now there were already more than 1500 potential Movements pupils!

I finally decided I could accept the awesome challenge of this responsibility, because I could carry with me, and refer to, my collection of Mother's written advice and material as backup to my own relatively limited personal experience. It was no real surprise that there was seldom a question or situation that couldn't be answered by directly quoting her written words or life experiences. Not that she was so omniscient (although it sometimes seemed as though she had been!), but because the same problems and doubts were evidently common to everybody, everywhere sooner or later. It was an impressive example of the universality

Nathalie de Etiievan ("Boussik") giving a lecture in Lima, Peru.

Emmy-winning guitarist/producer Flavio "Kike" Santander of Cali, Columbia being recruited as a Movements pianist by Dushka.

Music in the evening with Flavio and Dushka.

(Right) Dushka onferring with Hernan Areos, the "responsible" in Quito, Ecuador

Brazil's Dr. Marcel Horande (left) with Boussik (center) and Dushka lunching during a "special period" in Rio.

of our human experience. But the greatest revelation of all was to see meaningful results, immediate and profound effects of Movements, on all those people who had been reading and talking about "Ideas" for years.

It took time to create classes, train instructors, invent musical accompaniments since we often lacked pianos, and to cope with special conditions which even included government opposition: confiscation of materials, arrests of group members, cancellation of seminars, and so on. There was often dangerous social unrest: vicious bombings in Lima, kidnapping of group members in Chile, armed revolution during a Caracas seminar, murders at the Peru country house, cars often stolen during Rio meetings, general strikes and sudden military uprisings. We suffered through natural and physical problems like hurricanes, 120 degree heat, floods, earthquakes, power-line contamination, and primitive air and road transportation. Group poverty resulted in few decent meeting rooms or Movements halls, lack of privacy, poor ventilation, no air-conditioning, unfinished floors, no changing rooms, termite infested secondhand pianos, and mildewed books and music. Sometimes a parking lot was used, or the basement of a factory, back room of a restaurant, an office, greenhouse, or garage. Individual poverty meant few telephones for instructors or musicians, five hour bus trips to meetings, lack of Movements shoes, few pianos in homes or music lessons for children, sacrifices to purchase music books, and there was inadequate medical care for the many problems of cholera epidemics, high altitude sickness, unrefrigerated food, tropical fevers, drug addiction, poisonous snakes, spiders, scorpions, and malarial mosquitoes.

(Above) Dushka in South America working with Movements "responsibles", and (Below) At home receiving visitors in 2006.

Yet somehow we ended up with viable, useful classes, - some very meaningful work - and even, sometimes, exemplary execution!

From necessity and following Mother's example and suggestions, we had soon started organizing and training possible recruits as teachers, assistant instructors and musicians. And although this difficult but rewarding task required several years of coaxing, careful monitoring, stern correction, and appreciative encouragement, in the process we proved to ourselves (what many of the older Europeans may still deny) that it is indeed possible to develop in someone, even of apparently moderate gifts, if they are properly motivated, a useful ability to "pass on the Movements." That is to say it is possible to be able to convey a real understanding of the true aim and function of Movements, to sensitively select and cleverly schedule the specific exercises that will provide what those specific pupils need at that moment — to accurately, clearly (and concisely!) explain and demonstrate the physical positions and displacements demanded, and attentively supervise the group's continuing and consistent efforts to master them.

From this point of view it quickly became obvious that instructors needn't always be (in fact often shouldn't be), only those who happen to have "done" Movements well physically for years. Rather, they should be those who have come to an individual realization of the value of Movements for themselves personally, and have a true wish to help others have the same meaningful experience.

This all took on special meaning to me, as the more I looked back, the more I was personally convinced that in 1948 Mr. Gurdjieff already knew he hadn't much longer to live and was acting accordingly. Of course my own reasons for being so sure of this have to do in large part with his surprising and belated efforts to finally recognize his sons and daughters and bring us together at that time, but there is considerable other evidence to reinforce this belief.

Why during his last year or so, rather than intensify work with his long established groups, even his oldest Paris pupils, did Gurdjieff discontinue those meetings completely? He only talked individually with the few people he made responsible for practical matters, or in rare cases, out of concern to a supplicant with a real personal crisis. He did no more composing, lecturing, or writing although he strongly encouraged the work going on around him to complete the publishing plans for his own *All and Everything*, and Ouspensky's *Fragments*.

But he <u>did</u> give much of each day, and two or three hours every evening to Movements, creating, teaching and organizing how and by whom they would continue to be taught, authentically, in the various countries!

So what was he really preparing or hoping for? And how much of what he said then did even his closest people actually hear — and believe — and report accurately?

Apart from Movements, the only real participation open to all those followers who rushed to gather around him then were the ceremonial meals every day at midday and in the late evening after the long Movements sessions.

Many imagine these as occasions of serious philosophical discussion. Not at all!

There were certainly long moments of breathless silence as everyone at table strained to hear and understand Mr. G.'s soft comments in his special English that took a little getting used to. But most of our time was spent in howls of laughter. G.'s gift of mimicry and masterly comic timing infected everyone, old and young, of every nationality. He could point out situations and special characteristics in people with a wit that was sharp, but an attitude that was so warm and affectionate that although we all laughed in immediate recognition it was with the person, not at them.

Naturally, there was also much nervous tension, shyness, excitation, alcohol, unaccustomed food, and so on. At the end of the meal, therefore, when we all got up and crowded into the adjacent small room, we were ready for a complete change of atmosphere. He might take another cup of coffee or a cigarette as we got settled (and I prepared the tape recorder). But then he would lift up his little harmonium onto his lap, sometimes make a portentous introduction or an ironically flattering dedication, and begin to play. Everyone was immediately deeply attentive.

Sometimes, of course, to the embarrassment of us youngsters, there was a visiting hysteric who indulged in theatrical sighs or maudlin tears. But when G. finished playing, (and often then sat back to listen to a complete playback of my recording) there was dead silence. He might say a soft "Bravo, Sophie!" or often it was simply "*Amin!*" at which we would all rise and leave quietly and thoughtfully.

So these gatherings were, I believe, Mr. Gurdjieff's last effort, not so much to make an impression on the relatively few new people invited, but more especially to reaffirm and clarify for his older pupils definite projects and principles for the future. However veiled in humor or allegory this process might have been, he seemed to be trying to enlarge these people's timid, limited expectations for the Work, both for themselves and for the world at large, and to create and strengthen relationships between them, encouraging mutual appreciation, cooperation and joint constructive efforts.

Walter Driscoll

Projects that he often spoke of at table and clearly counted on to help preserve and spread his work internationally were public talks and concerts, open readings and active distribution of his books, impressive theater demonstrations of the Movements, and more.

It seems to me that these clear indications that he gave us have gradually been forgotten or simply shrugged off by most people otherwise faithful to the Work and carrying it on. Many such "responsibles" seem to react to what they see as the current notoriety of the names "Gurdjieff" and "Fourth Way" with withdrawal, a defensive insularity, even secrecy, instead of using it as an opportunity for the enthusiastic, altruistic sharing I believe Mr. Gurdjieff envisaged.

Obviously, the phenomenon aspect of the whole Gurdjieff story hasn't abated with time. Quite the contrary!

Walter Driscoll's *Annotated Bibliography* which was one of my original incentives for putting together this volume, will soon be reissued with another 1000 or so recent books and articles about Gurdjieff added to the original 1800.

I admit this continuing proliferation has evoked in me widely vacillating reactions. Driscoll himself recently told me that he considers "the Gurdjieff literature a vast compost heap out of which only a few nutritious vegetables and lovely flowers will now grow!"

At one moment I am pleased by the appearance of something like Martin Seymour-Smith's scholarly *The 100 Most Influential Books Ever Written, The History of Thought from Ancient Times to Today* that includes, even extols, Gurdjieff's *Beelzebub's Tales.*

But then somebody tells me about a *Gurdjieff Meditation and Coloring Book* (that actually turned out to be better than it sounded) or I'm sent reprints of the Gurdjieff section of *A Big Book of Weirdos...* or a thick script and ambitious cast recording of a misguided opus *Gurdjieff, A Crazy Wisdom Musical* (!), or an imaginative CD-ROM purporting to teach Movements.

Meanwhile, The Church of Conscious Harmony in Austin, Texas, is well established and has been actively and seriously functioning for years on Gurdjieffian principles. Rubin "Hurricane" Carter (often quoted saying: "Gurdjieff saved my life") with members of his groups have opened a Community Center, "The Way" in Georgia near Atlanta as their "tribute to Mr. Gurdjieff."

Simultaneously books and broadcasts describe "G." as "a present-day guru" in the same breath as Jim Jones or David Koresh, or equate the "Gurdjieff Work" with Scientology, Astrology, modern dance, martial arts, spiritualism, motivational training, distorted interpretations of the enneagram symbol, the Occult, devil worshipping, and so on. It never seems to end.

But a hopeful side of all this is that the continuing interest may yet result in answers to some of our many questions. Every once in a while we may still be able

(Above) The 1923 Demonstration at the Theatre des Champs Elysées? Perhaps one of the only actual photos existing, recently discovered in Paris, photographer unknown.

to add a little piece to the huge jig-saw puzzle that we are trying to put together to give us a better picture of Gurdjieff, the man and his message.

For instance, as I write this, Gert-Jan Blom in Holland sends me three tiny distorted photos that someone in France has just unearthed and believes may be photos (or stills from a motion picture film?) of an actual 1923 Movements demonstration.

I struggle with my computer to enlarge and clarify the fuzzy images so as to study them hoping that they will help us verify our present-day versions of those old but invaluable creations.

(Above) Brazilian friends start sending us photos of Rio apartment houses ("edificios") named after "Work" personalities.

(Above) Publisher Greg Loy and guest editor Don Hoyt (left) visit Dushka in New York to choose excerpts from the Howarth book to be included in Volume VII of the *Gurdjieff International Review.*

(Right) Some of the many recordings of Gurdjieff/de Hartmann music.

The Dutch State Radio Metropole orchestra records the Gurdjieff/de Hartmann *Oriental Suite.*

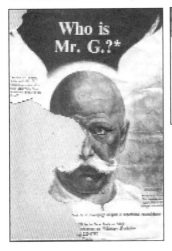

(Left and detail above) An E.J. Gold poster posted on lamp-posts throughout Manhattan saying "not G.I. Gurdjieff." It shows the carefully contrived "superficial resemblance!"
(Right) Another of Gold's masquerades, as a Sufi, in his publication *The Sufi Times.*
(Below left) Ruben "Hurricane" Carter with two young members of "THE WAY COMMUNITY CENTER" dedicated to Gurdjieff.

(Above) "Mr. G." on the cover of a French literary magazine.

I continue to investigate, observe and muse about the many emerging groups. For example I just got an invitation from the group in Beijing and videotapes of Movements classes in Moscow. There is widespread concertising and selling of endless new CDs of "Gurdjieff Music," films produced in Germany and elsewhere, stage adaptations of the books, TV documentaries and radio interviews, on-going and new periodicals concerning Mr. G. and the Fourth Way, (*The Gurdjieff International Review, The Gurdjieff Journal, Stopinder, Transformation*), further translations and publications of Work books (several versions in places like Russia and China are completely unauthorized and flaunt copyright laws) and so forth.

As one final example of the spreading of interest in Gurdjieff, I add a recent addition to my own scrapbook, to me a touching report from Mr. G's birthplace.

Several years ago I suddenly received "gifts and greetings from the people of Armenia." It seems that after the Soviets departed, Armenians felt a need to reclaim their national heroes, especially anyone like Gurdjieff who had been born in Armenia and then achieved recognition abroad. So one of their prominent film and TV producers, Avetik Melik-Sargasyan, eager to make contacts, asked to come to New York to meet with "Gurdjieff's daughter."

Thinking that everybody in the US groups would be as intrigued as I in this new evidence of interest in Gurdjieff, I let many people know, but nobody else took time out even to talk to this well-meaning man. I received copies of his completed films, TV shows, (of course, I don't understand the Armenian narration) newspaper clippings, and most tantalizing of all, I am following up on his promise to send us copies of those cylinder recordings of Gurdjieff's father Ashough Adash.

I did put Avetik in touch with Michael Pittman, a visiting professor from the US, and Carl Ulrich from the UK. This resulted in a "first annual Armenia Gurdjieff Conference" held in May of 2004. Successful, well-attended conferences have taken place every year since then and other active groups are forming there and in neighboring Georgia under the guidance of our friend Lillian Firestone.

Here is a part of the original material prepared by Avetik's Gyumri group:

"NOAH" INTELLECTUAL CREATIVE CENTER
G. I. GURDJIEFF - 2000

For more than 5 years the members of the "Gurdjieff group" at the Intellectual Creative Center "Noah" have been engaged in studying the life and activities of Gurdjieff whose birthplace was Gyumri, formerly Alexandropol. Before that there had been no exact information on Gurdjieff's birthplace, life and activities, especially during 1880 - 1907.

<u>The Armenian Gurdjieff Group has planned:</u>

1. Explore and study biographical data in historical or state archives.
2. Translate and publish Gurdjieff's books in Armenia.
3. Make a documentary film in two parts:
     Part 1. Gurdjieff's life and activities in Armenia.
     Part 2. Gurdjieff's travels about the world.
4. Study the musical inheritance of Ashough Adash, his father.
5. Establish relations between all the Gurdjieff centers of the world.

(Above) As Gurdjieff had requested, this stone, inscribed "I AM THOU, THOU ART I, ...etc." in Armenian now covers the grave of "Ashogh Adash" (G.'s father) which was finally located and marked by his pupils over fifty years after his death

(Right) Avetik Melik-Sargasyan (left) and other members of the Gyumri Gurdjieff group visit the gravesite.

(Left) The Kars Military Cathedral as it was when Gurdjieff was a boy and sang in the choir there and...

(Above) ...as it is now, spires removed, converted into a museum. by the Soviets.

Avetik Melik-Sargasyan and Dushka in one of the articles that appeared in Armenian publications.

6. Carry out the cultural program "Gurdjieff and Armenia" in all the countries visited by Gurdjieff.

* * * * *

<u>The Work Done by the Gyumri Gurdjieff Group:</u>

After a thorough study of the archive documents there has been a precise definition of Gurdjieff's date of birth [!], region, street and the house Gurdjieff and his family lived in in Gyumri.

In September 1999 the Gurdjieff group found the original gramophone recordings of Gurdjieff's father and other Ashoughs [bards] of Kars and Alexandropol in the Russian State Archive of Phonodocuments in Moscow.

Relations have been established between different Gurdjieff groups and centers.

GYUMRI AND THE REMARKABLE MEN OF GYUMRI

"Gurdjieff Days in Gyumri"

Project of the City Festivities

1. Life and activity of the world famous philosopher Gurdjieff in Armenia (publishing of the biographical book).

2. Making of a documentary film "Alexandropol-Kars-Ani" on the motives [sic] of the autobiography by Gurdjieff "Meetings With Remarkable Men."

3. Inauguration of the Armenian Gurdjieff Center.

4. Creating of the fund for Gurdjieff-Merkuroff library of art and philosophy.

[Sergei Dmitrievich Mercourov, or Merkuroff, born Oct. 21, 1888 in Alexandropol, was Gurdjieff's cousin and their two families were next door neighbors. Mercourov also had an early interest in

the occult and Eastern philosophy and it was by his "persistent efforts" in Moscow that P.D. Ouspensky was encouraged to meet Gurdjieff in 1915. He was famous in Russia as a sculptor, and took the death mask of Tolstoi in 1910. His statues and death mask of Lenin earned him the Order of Lenin in 1939.]

5. Inauguration of Gurdjieff memorial and street.

6. A visit of honor to the grave of Ashough Adash, Gurdjieff's father. [*Gurdjieff wrote that he "bid any of his sons, whether by blood or in spirit, to seek out this solitary grave, abandoned by force of circumstances... and there set up a stone with the inscription: I AM THOU, THOU ART I, HE IS OURS, WE BOTH ARE HIS, SO MAY ALL BE FOR OUR NEIGHBOUR." We believe it was American "Gurdjieffians" of Russian descent living in California who ultimately did this in the early 1970s.*]

7. Transportation of Gurdjieff's urn from Paris.

8. A historical excursion to the places where Gurdjieff lived and visited (Kumairi preserve, Jajur, etc.)

9. Receiving of delegation from foreign Gurdjieff Centers.

10. Scientific reports, seminars, readings on Gurdjieff's ideas and teaching.

11. City festivities "Gurdjieff Days in Gyumri" (Concerts of Ashoughs of the Gurdjieff Center and the city bands).

12. Bard (Ashough) Contests of Shirak. Restoring the historical tradition of "Ashough Majlis" (contests).

* * * * *

Pondering memories of Mr. Gurdjieff, his life and effect, and sharing them with all types of people in recent years I have been encouraged by a general heartfelt agreement and widespread wish to join any constructive efforts to preserve the "Gurdjieff Work" as we were all introduced to it originally. And as we have, since then, questioned it, worked with it, and proved it to ourselves as of inestimable value.

In fact, a group of us recently prepared the following letter to this effect:

TO OUR FRIENDS... PRESENT AND FUTURE:

More than fifty years have passed since that compassionate, special human being Mr. Gurdjieff left in our keeping a valuable teaching, with clearly defined principles, fresh stimulating ideas, and, most important, precise practical suggestions for living them.

But in recent years we have begun to see that elements of this priceless legacy are increasingly being allowed to deteriorate, become neglected or lost, and Mr. Gurdjieff's carefully considered, specific instructions are being ignored, misunderstood or misinterpreted. Distortions of "The Gurdjieff Ideas" and "The Fourth Way" proliferate in the public marketplace, and even the meticulously constructed and jealously guarded Movements are being deformed, forgotten, or used inappropriately.

A large number of people here and abroad don't just accept that "all this is inevitable" and share a sincere wish to preserve, practice and pass on Gurdjieff's teaching undistorted. We are now pooling our efforts in this direction.

P. D. Ouspensky warned long ago: "Ideas become distorted when people begin to invent their own explanations and theorize, but so long as they work sincerely and try to verify anything that comes into their minds, and work according to rules and principles, distortion is not at all necessary." (*A Record of Meetings*, p.367).

For such tangible materials as recordings, films, photos, letters, (and increasingly emerging treasures of unpublished exercise notations, music manuscripts, teaching suggestions, memoirs, etc.) **there are proven modern methods that can, and must, be used to arrest and reverse deterioration,** and sad to say, circumvent the possibilty of theft!

Once properly preserved and digitally copied, these items require a small fraction of the previous storage space, and as added insurance, can then be duplicated and distributed to other locales to ensure their safety, and longevity.

Such techniques also mean that without jeopardizing the irreplaceable originals, these materials can then be accessible to Foundation libraries and sanctioned Work groups for use in their activities, and, important to the future of the Work, to authorized Movements instructors, pianists, and group leaders for verification, arbitration and inspiration.

What started simply as numerous lengthy phone calls, countless e-mail exchanges and occasional personal visits has developed into an active community of like-minded people who we have called THE GURDJIEFF HERITAGE SOCIETY.

A nucleus was formed to protect and administrate the results of all this work, and various personal estates, assets, book rights, etc. Now there are already many encouraging first results, fruits of much research, on-going expert technical work, expenditures of time, energy and funds, sharing of personal experiences, and of course, many heated discussions and so on, but all in a climate of common goals, deep respect, warm humanity, and, hopefully, joy and satisfaction!

Legal advisors have suggested a more formal organization of the Society so this has been implemented. Non-profit corporation status will facilitate donations of funds but especially bequests of invaluable book collections and other Gurdjieff materials (tapes, photos, letters, etc.) which at present are often simply abandoned or discarded.

One of our first accomplishments followed upon our incredulous discovery that out of the approximately 3000 "Gurdjieff" books and articles currently available, (see *The Gurdjieff Annotated Bibliography*) the entire New York Public Library system contained only 61 examples (that did not even include *All and Everything*!)

Remembering that Mr. Gurdjieff wrote to us all in his Circular Letter January 13, 1949: **"I intend that the first series of my writings shall be made freely available without payment to all who are in need of their help"** we stepped in. So at our instigation and offer of cooperation, an extensive Gurdjieff division is now envisaged for the central research section of the NYPL. Randy Berenek and his recent successor John Bacon (Directors of "Planned Giving") and Beth Diefendorf ("Chief of Research Departments") have agreed to evaluate, coordinate and redirect materials to appropriate departments such as Research, Dance, Music, and Humanities. As extra copies of the major books are gathered, they will become available in lending branches and online.

A few of our other varied conservation projects include:

Full orchestral recordings of Gurdjieff's music. His *"Seid Dance," "Song of the Aisors," "Song of the Fisherwomen," "Duduki,"* and *"Tibetan Masked Dance,"* scored into an *"Oriental Suite"* by Thomas de Hartmann were beautifully recorded by the Metropole Orkest (Holland's public broadcasting orchestra) that also performed them live with Gurdjieff's *"Great Prayer"* in Amsterdam in June 2002, before an enthusiastic audience of 1500. The Gurdjieff Heritage Society had located and conserved the scores, acquired the proper permissions, and meticulously confirmed tempos from de Hartmann's own piano recordings, all in close cooperation with de Hartmann's heirs, Tom Daly Sr. and his son, Tom Daly, Jr.

Gert-Jan Blom, subsequently appointed Artistic Producer of the Metropole Orchestra and Musical Advisor of the Holland Festival, initiated and produced the entire project even recruiting outside financial support. The enthusiastic reception of this first work led to the even more important recording by the Metropole Orchestra of all the extraordinary orchestrations Gurdjieff himself wrote out or dictated in 1923 to be used in his first Movements Demonstrations. (Released in 2006 as: "Oriental Suite - Complete Orchestrations 1923-1924")

"Harmonic Development."
The Complete Harmonium Recordings.

As for <u>Gurdjieff's unique harmonium recordings,</u> although literally melting away with age, the original tapes were coaxed back from the Gurdjieff heirs. These, together with wire recordings made in New York, copies of missing tapes salvaged from amongst the effects of the late Tom Forman, from the NY Foundation's mildewed closets and private collections, were all salvaged, meticulously cleaned and data-based by Gert-Jan Blom. This urgent first step was accomplished only just in time, so that everything that Gurdjieff himself ever recorded could be saved for the future. A boxed set containing Blom's informative and well-illustrated book with 136 reconstituted recordings on two CD discs, and one MP3 with motion picture footage from 1949 was released in November 2004, under the title "Harmonic Development."

Gert-Jan Blom admires Gurdjieff's original harmonium when visiting Sylvie Anastasieff one of the Gurdjieff heirs now living in Spain.

<u>Definitive notes for the 39 MOVEMENTS</u> (actually 46 in total), those finished and set by Mr. Gurdjieff, are being scanned to CDs. Compiled and corrected during many summers of intensive cooperative work by Jeanne de Salzmann, Marthe de Gaigneron (the original note-taker), and Jessmin Howarth, these original notes (impeccably translated to English by J. Howarth) were confided to the NY Foundation and a copy sent to Mme. de Salzmann. However in 1984, when Mrs. Howarth died, they were not to be found in New York even after an extensive search was made! And sadly for the future neither have Mme. de Salzmann's copies surfaced!

With huge effort we recovered and reconstituted (from handwritten or carbon copies) most of these invaluable notations and a team is transferring them with verifying photos and other unique material to CDs for safe, practical storage. But there are still several lacking that we need help in locating.

Also being scanned onto CDs for preservation/storage and possible carefully considered sharing is <u>definitive material on the *Six Obligatories*</u> as noted by Jessmin Howarth, acknowledged by Mr. Gurdjieff and Mme de Salzmann as the final authority on all those earlier Movements. This collection includes notations, photographs, history and teaching material, (with special hints for beginners' classes, and "inhibition" exercises for advanced pupils), corrected music,and suggestions to pianists.

We have developed lively, mutually beneficial cooperation with the *Gurdjieff International Review* and other serious journals. We attempt on-going surveillance, investigation and documentation of (many of them dubious) "Gurdjieff" websites and investigate, and where justified, support other people's "Gurdjieff Work."

Although we refrain under present conditions, from giving out any "new material," we will correct what is already being used, go over notes and videos, make suggestions on projects like TV broadcasts, piano and choir recordings, and plans for public presentations. We personally maintain or are trying to renew contact with all who share our ethical and spiritual values, especially those who actively participated in the earlier days of the Gurdjieff Work, the Movements or music and theater activities.

We continue these and many other efforts, but warmly welcome suggestions, participation, criticism, materials, etc. from all of you.

As for a motto for us? Let's consider this one!

Almost a century ago the first written exposition of Mr. Gurdjieff's ideas appeared in the scenario for his ballet *The Struggle of the Magicians*. Since the climax and curtain line of this unique work is a memorable and meaningful blessing given by the White Magician, we have adopted it as our motto and will try to live up to it.

"May reconciliation, hope, diligence and justice be ever with you all."

And all say -

"Amen!"

Sincerely

Dushka Howarth
and all of us at the GURDJIEFF HERITAGE SOCIETY, Inc.
Website: www.gurdjieff-heritage-society.org

* * * * *

Dushka in New York, 2007

CHAPTER 35

THE LEGACY

Throughout her long life as a dedicated teacher and generous friend, Mother's constant concern was that her pupils and companions, young or old, be fulfilled and successful in both their everyday lives and their spiritual endeavors. She always made herself available to them, was a faithful correspondent, and although her modesty made her abhor "advice giving," her ability to listen with real interest, understanding, and above all, acceptance, evidently touched many people profoundly. To this day, they continue to contact me, enthusing about "Mrs. Howarth's kindness." (Cynic that I am by now, my usual inside reaction is, sadly, "in comparison to what and whom?")

As time passes and her old pupils and colleagues reevaluate all they learned from her, they realize the uniqueness of her dedication, and the modesty of her sincere wish to be helpful. Not as any kind of authority figure, group leader, or even "good example," but simply by pointing out what she believed had aided her personally in the Work, and specifically in the Movements.

So I felt that she had a legacy to leave us all, and that it might best be passed on by reiterating some of the heartfelt, lived-through convictions she expressed in numerous talks and letters. Here are a few.

Dushka
◆

◆ ◆ ◆

It is now over eighty years since Movements were first introduced to groups. This was when Mr. Gurdjieff was in Tiflis and visited a Dalcroze Eurhythmics class being taught by Mme. de Salzmann. He gave her pupils a number of exercises for attention and coordination. These later became obligatory for any people who wished to study with him, and we call them "the Obligatories."

Jessmin
◆

When, during the Revolution, he was able to escape from Russia with some of his pupils, Mr. G. also taught this group adaptations of Dervish Movements and Sacred Rituals which he had seen in Central Asia. In order to attract interest to his work, these Movements were shown to the public in Constantinople [Istanbul]. After two years, including some time spent in Berlin, he came to France, organized the Prieuré and there, with his Russian and some English pupils, prepared a much more extensive program of "Sacred Dances" first performed in December 1923 in Paris. But by the time I myself first met them all in my studio in 1922, his people already knew almost everything we others then learned and did in those demonstrations. (They didn't yet know "The Thirty Gestures" and the "Polyrhythm." Then others, like "The Men's Enneagram" and "The Lost Loves," were given in New York in 1924).

Since then these Movements have been preserved with the music he dictated to accompany them. In the summer of 1924, when Mr. G. had his almost fatal automobile accident, he gave up teaching and turned to the writing of *Beelzebub*. But those same Movements continued to be taught by myself and others and practiced regularly in New York by the Orage groups, then later in England by the Ouspensky groups, and in Paris by Mme. de Salzmann's group.

Just before the Second World War began, Mr. G. himself resumed teaching and carried on his work in Paris in spite of the German occupation. This was an extraordinary period. He created scores of exercises, combinations and sequences, mathematically calculated, designed to help sustain attention and to understand what we now call "sensation"; to provide shocks and new impressions, and to induce intentionally certain feelings and more "collected" states. A great number of these exercises he left with us here in New York in the spring of 1949 a few months before he died. And these Movements have been studied here ever since, as well as in many other countries.

This second body of work was not like the first which involved a limited program perfected during long years of meticulous preparation for public demonstrations. His interest had evidently turned to finding Movements which would arouse certain vibrations in people and bring about certain results. It was a period of immense energy and creativity. He brought new movements every single day. Some he continued on another day, some he changed, some were dropped altogether, and some he eventually set. These became the "Thirty-Nine," an extraordinary group of Movements, each greatly different in character, in its type of challenge and its result... with even the smallest gesture, degree of body tone, mental and emotional attitude precisely planned.

[Another seven movements were completed during Gurdjieff's 1949 visit to America and added to the series so that the "American Thirty-Nine" really total 46!]

And he didn't wish any notes to be made because, well, for many reasons which you can all imagine.

One person was disobedient and did make notes. Piles of notes. And after Mr. G.'s death Mme. de Salzmann asked her: "Will you go over your notes with Jessmin and see if anything can be rescued?" And the notes were very good. They showed how Mr. G. began, how he developed things and so on. However the rhythms and musical counts had to be added since this person knew no music at all.

Finally we worked them out together during many long summers of effort, and then reworked them with Mme. de Salzmann. She had played for all the classes when those Movements were given, could see what Mr. G. intended, and often had definite instructions from him. And so they were gradually saved. Mme. de S. also asked the whole first row of her Paris class, those who had worked the longest, to come together and make notes. One, a pianist, certainly understood the music part but was apt to make things more legato and soft than originally given, another understood the style of each movement better than anyone, but had no memory, etc., etc.

Thus many small changes have crept in. Sometimes because when a Movement was filmed we had to use less space on the sound stage than in a practice studio, (as happened in the change of steps in the "Tableaux"). Or because certain instructors experimented with variations (as, also, in the "Tableaux" where adding the multiplication can be reasonable and useful, but not if it makes such a complication that the tableaus themselves are sacrificed). Or, because people like Olgivanna Lloyd Wright believed that the Movements should be "developed" and encouraged her daughter, Iovanna, to add new groupings and otherwise "choreograph" them. And even John Bennett, much as he loved doing the Movements himself and valued them for his pupils, believed he could improve on them by designating specific "emotions" to be felt at certain places, adding Turkish or Arabic prayers, and so forth.

* * * *

AFTER WATCHING A BEGINNER'S CLASS
(JAN HUS HOUSE, New York, 1981)

Since so many of you are now embarking on the Movements, it seemed it might be appropriate to say something, both about their background or even about the way you do them.

I'm told that you are now beginning to study the Movements. How many lessons have you had? Four? Five?

Well! Doesn't it feel very interesting that Mr. Gurdjieff was not content to just give his system of ideas, but that he also brought a system of sacred dances, of "Movements?" And he made it very clear that the study of the ideas and the practice of the Movements were to be complimentary.

And if I think a little, I realize why it must be.

Certainly, when I first hear of the "Teaching" I am interested, uplifted, because I know Mr. G.'s aim was to help us develop consciousness and this gives us a purpose in life. We realize then, as some of his words have brought to us, that it is quite true: We are asleep in certain ways. We don't really know what we're doing, what we are thinking, what we are feeling. We are not aware. We don't live intentionally.

And when we realize that, something wishes to be able to live differently. And we try! We find that we really do need many, many reminders. We do need to wish very deeply and very continuously.

And then it is made possible for us to go into the Movements. And there we are under different conditions. We find that our habitual vocabulary of attitudes, movements, and gestures isn't required. We are asked to take positions and move in ways that many of us have never done before. And so there is a possibility of seeing, of knowing myself.

And as I "work," I realize that what I need is a very special kind of attention. With my HEAD I try to be clear. In the Movements, my head knows what the next attitude is supposed to be. It tries to help my body to get there directly. My BODY feels the different positions. It senses how it should be. It knows that it changes the tonicity of its muscles according to the various positions. So it has an attention as well as the head. And in myself I'm eager to do the Movements. I'm eager to learn what they can bring and so there's also an attention in the FEELING.

And when all of these are present, somehow I'm aware of all my energies being used in a right way. I feel myself collected. Somehow, a kind of life force in me is released and I can become more open, more sensitive, and perhaps receive impressions of a finer quality than usual.

Now! One thing I'll say to you. In the beginning in the Movements you will want to do them very well. And so you should, because these Movements are created in such a way that unless they are done absolutely exactly, the inner connections will not be linked, and the vibration that one looks for will not appear. But! If I grow too identified with how I do the Movements, and think only of executing the Movements very well - Ah, then I lose something.

It might be that even if I made a mistake, if I were able, at that very instant, to see myself. Not the mistake so much. Not to criticize myself, excuse myself, justify it, but really see HOW I AM AT THIS VERY INSTANT. **It's the act of seeing at this exact moment, of being aware at the moment one moves. THAT IS WHAT I MUST TRY TO DEVELOP!**

What I see — how I do — Yes, I learn from that. But if I can try to be alive and awake at the very instant that I move or speak — then I really am helping myself along the road to growing more conscious.

So try not to forget when you get enthusiastic about your Movements. Try to remember what it is you are really trying for — to develop and make grow.

I hope you all get a great deal from Movements. Most of us have. You'll find that, somehow, through your body and your feeling you'll begin to understand things in the system of ideas that might otherwise remain, perhaps, only theory.

◆ ◆ ◆

Dushka
◆

At a Movements seminar Mother was asked by one of the Canadian teachers:

"Mrs. Howarth, you once said that if all the complicated movements were lost, we could always work with the Obligatories. Can you say anything more about that?" She replied:,

◆ ◆ ◆

Jessmin
◆

You know, thinking about it after a long time, I realized that the Obligatories were really shocks.

In the First Obligatory you had to move suddenly. Instead of moving in a continuous way, you had to move from position, to position, to position. Now we have all grown accustomed to that, but in the beginning that was a very great shock. At least it taught us to represent to ourselves a position in advance and manage to take it absolutely definitely without having to adjust or anything.

The First March was done in a very Oriental kind of way. That also was something different for us. None of us were used to putting our arms down like this, sliding, travelling around our bodies.

In the Counting, for me the most important thing of it, besides the feeling that you're measuring with your body, is that — something we never do — you listen to your own voice. He gave us a new variation every single time. You had to speak in different languages. Sometimes you went slowly. Or very fast. Or in canon, or singing, or backwards. Sometimes he stopped the physical movements and you continued to sense them inside, or stopped the voices until he said to begin again and all together you knew exactly where you were.

The Note Values, I think one knows immediately what they could be used for. There's the trying to be aware of one's whole body sensation and be able in the midst of all that to move the arms, and the head, and legs, and at a certain instant, "strike the same note" with them all together.

The March Forward. Again, here were for us some very strange positions. I don't know if he ever said that, but we used to call them the "Buddha positions." One drops on the floor and everything.

As for the last one, the Mazurka, in the beginning I didn't take it very seriously, especially when M. de Hartmann told me that Mr. Gurdjieff claimed he took the music for that one from his guitar method! But later I saw its effect on people and the lesson to be learned. After working seriously through the other five exercises, as soon as they reached this light, springy, melodic dance, how difficult it was to maintain the special energy and attention that had been gradually generated. A real validation of Mr. Gurdjieff's warning, "the very first moment you have an opportunity to lose your attention – you will!"

* * * *

MESSAGE TO MOVEMENTS INSTRUCTORS AT THE END OF A SEMINAR
(GURDJIEFF FOUNDATION, New York, 1983)

Maybe you sometimes see, as I still so often do, that *the difficulty is to remind myself, with an ever-renewed passionate wish, to try to remember. To be present again and again in life and in the Movements classes.*

How to find useful "alarm clocks?" My wish for you is that when you go back to your homes and your classes you will feel that the way we have worked together here has provided you with a variety of means for working on your own.

When you learn a new Movement you face a challenge and you bring interest to it. Ask yourselves: Do you learn it with your head – picturing the positions, making mental notes of it? Or do you learn it through your body sensation – imitating the positions shown and so coming to feel the kind of tonicity needed to execute correctly what is given? *Try both ways, for Mr. Gurdjieff said one must, in the Movements, work with all three centers, in order to develop clarity of mind, depth of sensation, and vitality of interest.*

You have found that each center has its own kind of attention and when these three come together, in whatever proportions, a special state of total attentiveness appears.

At first, too, in your efforts to remain present you find yourself in a kind of solitude. But there one can, at times, set oneself to be aware of and feel with the other people working beside you. Every Movement when correctly executed sets up certain vibrations in each person. Many of them are so created that they bring about a definite result only when everyone in the class and every unit of the design is in harmony. When that result comes, you will all feel it.

In connection with self-study: To help one's right feeling and effort, remember why one came to the class, for what purpose the Movements are done, and how one has "slept" between lessons. REMEMBER THAT OPPORTUNITIES MAY COME IN THIS LESSON THAT MAY NEVER COME AGAIN. Try to use the Movements lesson as an opportunity for observing "one's creature" in a new activity and from a new viewpoint.

We are apt to imagine that, by practicing the Movements, we can quickly reach a "higher" state; we aim for a result. This may lead to identification with how well we execute the Movements. We forget that *it is the inner state of attentiveness and impartial watching that is essential*

Attention is energy, you exercise it and it is constantly renewed.

Sensation can be understood in many ways: Being aware of sense impressions before they are named and pigeonholed by the head. Or sensation can be the awareness of life in different parts, or the whole of one's body. It is this inner reservoir of vital force that we call upon each time we move with intention, with attention.

Try to realize that the impulse, the need for every movement comes from and is rooted in a state of inner stillness before it is seen on the outside.

If you can think, during Movements classes or elsewhere, of ways to remind yourself often to come back to your inner attention, write them down. At the Prieuré, we used either to carry these papers around with us, or place them somewhere where they would often catch our eyes. (I remember how Orage stuck them around his mirror.) You may find them useful in ordinary life too. Every moment of watching, of sensing, is a drop of energy transmuted.

Try to be simple about this. Start from where you are and how you are. Then demand more from yourselves.

* * * *

To you instructors: I've recapitulated all this process because I wish to call you to a renewed effort of study, ever active in searching for a deeper understanding of the teaching, to continue in a simple and honest appraisal of your function, and to bring thought to all you do.

You know, whenever there is a Movements instructors' seminar the first question is always, "How should I be in front of the class?"

I have to say to you something that may shock you all.

During a class you must put your own work behind you. I mean that your real effort must be to try to be centered enough to be sensitive to the manifestations of the class, the people in it, and altruistic enough to place their need before your own wish to use the activity as an exercise for yourself. The times that you have remembered to try for a state of over-all attentiveness will be your support. With simple and frequent "unstrained awareness" the personality becomes transparent, the essential wish to help others to profit shines through, and the head stops hogging one's energy.

The teacher's responsibility is to provide the challenge, to connect the physical activity with self-remembering. For this it is necessary to be very alert and alive in many different ways, capable of making each thing new, and approaching it from different points of view. You must never use the class just for your own work. They are not there for you to experiment with. They are not there to enhance your power or to try out your magnetism on. You are there to help them. *YOUR OWN WORK COMES BEFORE AND AFTER.*

You all need to work much more closely together. Your way of teaching must be your own, but your material must be exactly the same. You should check together conscientiously on every detail of the Movements you are passing on. It is quite shameful that the same exercise should be shown differently in different classes at the Foundation.

In a very few years, the older people who have struggled to prevent distortion of the Movements will be dead. You can continue your dedication to Mr. G.'s teaching by actively setting about the formation of a nucleus. You will try to exchange, share and stay all together, supporting each other's efforts, and so endeavor to preserve purity in teaching Mr. G.'s System of Movements.

Unless we always remember that *the Movements are sacred*, we shall not be able to collect all our attention and reach a state open to higher impressions and influences. We are trying, all together, each bringing his drop, to fill a reservoir of genuine consciousness.

* * * * *

GURDJIEFF'S MOVEMENTS

"...simply, a 'teacher of dancing,'"

Dushka
♦

Of course I have always taken as my criterion for giving a Movements class what I experienced personally in Mr. Gurdjieff's classes, reinforced by Mother's teaching suggestions to myself and others. So any criticisms I may sometimes have about present-day teachers and what takes place in their classes are, I admit it, most unfair, since I am comparing them to an impossible standard.

None of us, as Mother would gently remind us, are "Teachers" as Mr. G. was. We just have to do our best according to our own abilities and the quantity and quality of the material we have available to us to pass on. Varying conditions and types of pupils may sometimes excuse our experimenting (hopefully, however, carefully and modestly,) with different methods of accomplishing this "passing on." But the Movements themselves are inviolable. We must constantly study, compare and verify the authenticity of what we are giving the class. No one of us has the knowledge or an understanding of all the components, relationships and vibrations involved to meddle with Gurdjieff's Movements, add to them or adapt them in any way.

So I would like to offer here my own clear memories of how Mr. Gurdjieff gave us Movements during the last year-and-a-half of his life when this was the urgent focus of his failing energy.

In those memorable months we met together for several hours every night, in a rented hall, large mixed groups of from fifty to seventy people depending on the number of extra visitors who were permitted to squeeze in, to struggle valiantly at the back. In New York this was usually in one of the Carnegie Hall studios, often the mirrored studio of ballet master Igor Youskevitch (much to the surprise of his regular pupils who gaped at us from the doorways). In Paris, we used any of a variety of studios in the venerable Salle Pleyel, where puffs of dust often came out from between the floorboards if we did a lively foot rhythm.

I point this out as an example of Mr. G.'s constant practicality and economy. He didn't require his own "Movements Hall" in a "Foundation" edifice but used and adapted existing facilities according to numbers, circumstances, and availability.

Mr. G. himself would give the entire class (senior pupils might supervise practices) and he demonstrated all the positions himself clearly and exactly (he might support himself against the piano or something if he needed to raise a foot) specifying every detail, type of finger vibration, size of step, direction of the eyes, etc.

He carefully prepared everything in advance. He certainly didn't just improvise on the spot, one of many ridiculous misconceptions being circulated these days.

When the class could begin to attempt combining the many inner and outer elements he indicated so that he could study the total effect, and probably more importantly, the effects on each of us, he might then make changes or adjustments.

We never missed a single night unless Mr. G. announced a break of perhaps a few days when some of us joined him for a trip. The classes always lasted at least two hours, often three, and I think everyone agreed that the second hour onwards produced the best results.

Yet we never tired except, perhaps, when poorly conditioned thighs were learning to do deep knee-bends as steadily and evenly as Mr. G. required, because there was such variety and interest! It wasn't only the physical differences between the various exercises: slow or fast, light or heavy, relaxed or energetic, machine-like or lyric, rhythmic or rubato, controlled, or once, in the "Black Magic," abandoned. More important were the very different ways we were challenged: mentally, physically or emotionally, with immediacy or sustained endurance, or with familiarity or shocking newness, everything fresh and surprising.

What also refreshed and inspired us was that all the music was improvised so we never heard melodies repeated, or got so accustomed to them that we could lean on them to help the counts or as crutches to our memory.

Yes, we were always learning new Movements, straining with our minds to understand, remember and master the difficulties. And then, with the details finally clear in our heads, we naturally needed hours of work and correction to convert the instructions into precise body positions and displacements without losing track of inner exercises, etc. But this was a very coarse, rudimentary part of our work.

Much more meaningful were the precise complete repetitions of any of a whole repertoire of Movements that we had already learnt: really knew with our minds, bodies and feelings. Mr. G. would suddenly stop whatever we were doing and order us (by an identifying name or number) to do whichever of these he felt would provide just what we needed at that moment: physically, emotionally, or psychologically. After a moment to collect ourselves, tune in to the appropriate physical tonicity and posture, check which row and file we found ourselves in and our distance and relationship to the rest of the class, we were given a couple of measures of music to set the tempo, and expected to do the entire exercise without comment or interruption, remembering how and when to finish.

Sadly it seems to me that these days most classes don't have this kind of repertory of Movements to call upon. There is so much "teaching" and "learning" going on that there is little time left for really "doing" Movements, working with them often, in depth, and with increasing appreciation of what they can give. It should be obvious that it isn't important how many exercises one learns, or how quickly, but how one uses them. And Mr. Gurdjieff would never have condoned wanton waste of time and expenditure of energy spent on trying to figure out an unprepared instructor's unclear, inaccurate or vacillating instructions, or useless draining of physical strength, feats of endurance, mindless, deadening repetitions or feats of memory by rote, or anything of that sort.

But an IMMEDIATE, WHITE-HOT EFFORT to bring together "on-the-spot" learned and practiced physical and mental attitudes in a prescribed emotional climate — collecting and controlling one's energy — directing one's sensing into different parts of the body exactly as instructed – and, behind all this, and most important, OBSERVING THE WHOLE PROCESS – **THIS IS REALLY WORKING WITH MOVE-MENTS!**

We were never asked to start the class sitting in a lotus position (cross-legged on the floor). Rather, we used any time before Mr. G. arrived, practicing or clarifying any doubts we might have with whichever more experienced pupil led our particular file.

Nor did the first few minutes of any class consist of marching. We needed no concentrating of our attention or warming up, or whatever else some instructors nowadays use this stultifying opening for.

When Mr. G. entered the room, he verified that Mme. de Salzmann was at the piano, sometimes said something to her in Russian and started in immediately with intensive work.

We were at once intensely riveted on him, eyes and ears and especially minds opened. There was no question about being really awake, because we soon learned that when Mr. Gurdjieff taught us something new he would only show us each component once, maybe adding a grunted instruction. Even his older pupils in the front row weren't always sure they had understood exactly what he wanted and usually met together after the class to compare, or indeed often argue. Fortunately, after letting us struggle as best we could the next few times, he would then take pity on us and patiently correct us, even pulling out to the front one of the few who was moving correctly so that we could all see and emulate. From then on he allowed no deviations or inexactitude. He had carefully planned and worked out whatever he gave us and that is how he expected to see it done.

And there is one very important aspect of his giving of new exercises that has been forgotten. Sometimes, having given us a fascinating new Movement that we finally learnt and really did well, exactly as he had instructed, he would nevertheless stop us and say gravely: "No! Never again!" And that Movement was never done again. Ever! Evidently he was trying to create in us certain states and even with all his genius and experience he couldn't always be sure of the results of certain combinations of elements, and our various reactions to them. Surely essential lessons should be learned from this.

We should trust that Mr. Gurdjieff not only created, but proved out and tested our Movements so that we can now have entire confidence in them and his evident compassionate wish for us to profit and learn the maximum from them. This whole process of fine-tuning and bringing to a complete finalisation only certain exercises should always be kept in mind. Yes, we may have partial material on between two- and three-hundred of his later exercises that he was in the process of working on. But he only announced as finished – "you may continue to work with this" – forty-six of them. All the rest although very interesting to do, and maybe exciting and beautiful to watch in those films made by Mme. de Salzmann should be considered "unauthorized" and definitely only to be used with responsible caution.

But the full spectrum of those forty six added to the early Movements which were worked out for years before the first Demonstrations, (the Obligatories, the Work Dances, Women's Dances, etc.) make a huge variety of extraordinary exercises giving proven results when used as Mr. G. specified. So there is certainly no need for anyone to start inventing exercises of their own. This would be stupidly arrogant and ill-advised, if not downright perilous, considering the delicate, mysterious balances we are dealing with.

All of which certainly doesn't deny teachers the opportunity to be innovative and creative in finding ways to help a class learn. When working on a specific Gurdjieff Movement, the aim, character and purpose of which are truly understood, and "felt," by the instructor (and, just as important, the pianist) it can often be most helpful to invent variations, e.g. to explore how a certain section may be repeated often without the class "going to sleep." There may be details to work out, difficulties to overcome that are unique to those specific pupils. All kinds of carefully considered experimentation may be useful. But always, however long it may take to achieve, the ultimate goal should be kept in mind: **that** particular Movement, in its entirety including all the different series, repetitions, "intermedes," and inner work, and the exploring and reinforcing of its "essence" represented by its style, tempo, and tonicity,

To second guess Mr. Gurdjieff's intention is a dangerous precedent.

In the half-century that has passed since we worked personally with Mr. Gurdjieff we have seen more and more misconceptions develop around Movements, their use, validity, precise content, even their comparative authenticity considering the constant influx of ersatz imitations, and amateur "preparatory exercises."

When Mme. de Salzmann made Movements films in later years, she climaxed several of them with the moving spectacle of some of her oldest men pupils doing Mevlevi-type, "whirling dervish" turning. As a result many people have come to believe that this was a common part of the Movements repertoire. But only once during all our months of nightly classes with Mr. G. did he feel that we were ready and would benefit from trying this kind of turning. And he watched very carefully, walking among us and stopping us individually as we needed it. And maybe on two other occasions he gave the "arms out sideways" exercise under the same careful supervision.

People also begin to expect "stops" so often described in books as part of the daily work at the Prieuré where at any time Mr. G. might interrupt an individual's physical task or a group activity by calling out "***STOP!***" thus providing an opportunity for instantaneous, direct self-observation. But "stops" weren't used on us in 1949 except as a feature of one notable Movement, French #19, specifically constructed to give participants that experience and then chosen by Mr. Gurdjieff as the very first of the American series. But after all, we weren't the same kind of close-knit group of pupils working full time with Mr. Gurdjieff as was the case in the early years or at the Prieuré. We were a combination of different ages, nationalities, and degrees of preparation. Visitors of all sorts were constantly coming and going, only occasionally joining briefly into groups for special meals, manuscript readings, Movements, or even the automobile trips. And there was never a suggestion that anyone else but Mr. G. himself would know how and when to give a true, meaningful and safe "Stop." As Ouspensky quotes Gurdjieff saying: "The 'stop' exercise is considered sacred in schools. Nobody except the principal teacher or the person he commissions has the right to command a 'stop.'"

Because they are seen in films and demonstrations, the question of "costumes" often comes up. They weren't part of our Movements experience. We came to class in street clothes, but ones carefully chosen for comfort, cleanliness and modesty, and only used for Movements. Mother encouraged her classes to keep to white shirts or blouses and dark trousers or skirts. In that epoch, especially since we were sensitive to the old world attitudes still held by both Mr. G. and Mme. Ouspensky, we women never thought of wearing pants, not even to work outdoors at Franklin Farms. But fortunately, the ballerina styles in 1948 and 1949 were ideal for our purposes. We "calves," like the other women in the classes, all had three-quarter length circular skirts that we belted in at the waist over a cotton blouse, no tight tee-shirts, and we wore little flat shoes, no bare feet, they don't give the necessary security of stance. These skirts swirled out most satisfactorily when we turned and they permitted us to kneel and sit comfortably.

Only in the last few weeks of our time in France did Mr. G., probably still hoping to present a demonstration with us when we returned to the States, begin to have us all fitted for the white silk tunics and trousers now considered traditional as Movements costumes.

As for the Enneagram, yes, we saw drawings of it, heard it mentioned with respect as an age-old symbol, and we accepted that if one were advanced enough in the Work one might understand the wealth of esoteric Laws and Truths it represents. But it wasn't discussed or used in our everyday work. Our only exposure to it was on the few occasions when it had a function in certain Movements, as an inner exercise, or as the basis for intricate displacements and sequences. (This study does give one a hint of why Movements have been described as being a "book" that can be "read" by certain "initiates.")

(Above) An enneagram according to Gurdjieff. (The top of the triangle representing "9", then clockwise the outer points are "1"," 2", "3". etc.

Working in six files, we would sometimes be abruptly ordered by Mr. G. to think of ourselves "not as 1 2 3 4 5 6, but as 1 4 2 8 5 7."

Some of the older pupils tried to explain to us the origins of these particular numbers and their intriguing sequence.

One version of this as I myself now try to formulate it for someone else might be: When "One" (Unity), is divided by "Seven" (that special number occurring in many esoteric situations, including "the Octave") the result is 1 4 2 8 5 7 1 4 2 8 5 7 1 4... and so on, recurring to infinity. Multiplying this 1 4 2 8 5 7 sequence by two gives the result: 2 8 5 7 1 4 2 8 5 etc. (by three gives 428571, by four, 571428, etc...) always the same numbers in the same relationship.

The visual design of the Enneagram symbol appears when one makes a circle (representing "the Whole"), and divides it into nine (in Greek, *ennea*) equal segments, that are then numbered. Drawing straight lines joining 1 to 4, 4 to 2, 2 to 8, 8 to 5, 5 to 7, and back to 1, you have a symbolic visual representation of the continuous path of a recurring sequence, indicative of the dynamic, ever active "Law of Seven." When the remaining numbers, 3, 6 and 9 (all multiples of three),

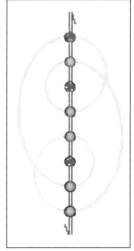

Another symbol representing the "142857" relationship as used in other traditions.

are joined by straight lines, one sees a perfect equilateral triangle that expresses the "Law of Three" with its references to "Affirming, Denying, Reconciling," or the Christian "Trinity," and so on.

But now the Enneagram has become big business. In 1994 in California there were nearly two thousand participants at the "First International Enneagram Conference." However a second Conference a couple of years later only drew about five hundred. Increasingly, nationwide store shelves, catalogues and Internet listings are filled with "Enneagram" books, tapes and videos sold as "aids to self-knowledge." Often these are promoted citing success with a particular group or profession, such as business executives, CIA agents, movie critics, farmers, lovers, "frocked" and "unfrocked" Catholics, and many others.

Usually, to establish an aura of authenticity, the name or portrait of Gurdjieff is linked in some way to these efforts. But these promoters have had practically no contact with Mr. G. or his Work, and the way in which they are using the Enneagram has little or nothing to do with what Mr. Gurdjieff was teaching. All the subtleties and interactions of "Great Laws" that the symbol was created to represent are ignored. Just the form (a circle enclosing intersecting lines) is used (misused!) as "a tool for self-study." Arbitrarily, certain "fixations," or "personality types," etc. have been invented (usually nine in number, one assigned to each segment of the circle), and then pupils are led through elaborate maneuvers supposedly helpful for studying human interactions, and personal relationships.

For example, particularly successful at commercializing the Enneagram have been Helen Palmer, Claudio Naranjo, and Oscar Ichazo, three rivals who, I see, have even taken each other to court for "misrepresenting" these misrepresentations!

The study of personality types, especially in relation to one's "essence" (what one has been born with) and how they relate, is certainly an interesting project. It is an important part of the Gurdjieff Work, but for me, it has little to do with these current pilferings. For myself, I always considered Mr. Gurdjieff's ceremonial "toasts to idiots" an opportunity to study personalities, my own and other people's.

Now, about "sittings!"

With Mr. Gurdjieff and for years after, we were guided to and achieved experiences of "sensation," "sensing," "directed attention," "finer impressions," "controlling energy or breathing," "hearing our own voices" (musically or when repeating special words, phrases, or numerical sequences). Always and only these things were done with us in the context of Movements.

We made intense practical efforts under strict discipline with little verbalization or opportunity for imaginings or "psychic" experiences. So it is surprising, even horrifying, to some of us nowadays to see the increasing proliferation and dependency on "conducted group sittings."

Certainly individual "sitting," "meditation," or "centering," whatever form it takes, is a valuable, widely used practice that Mr. Gurdjieff also suggested at various times, to certain individuals, or special small groups whom he knew intimately, but in silence, working for oneself! Today's "group sittings" may involve large gatherings of people of all types and degrees of experience, and are often "given," *(i.e.* narrated or talked through).

In 1949, we certainly never saw or heard about anything like that. And Mother, until the end, never advocated or used anything similar. Quite the contrary! She often pointed out how one needed to prove to oneself what might until then have been just words, something plausible-sounding read in books! That this was a primary, unique and essential function of Movements, to really experience with all of oneself what otherwise remained just verbal or intellectual concepts.

So we could hardly have imagined a roomful of people sitting immobile to attend to, not even their own inner selves, but to someone else's effort to express in often clumsy words what each should be experiencing or striving for.

The first indication I had of the full impact of this new trend happened when Lord Pentland was still alive.

Every year since 1949, on the anniversary of Mr. Gurdjieff's death, groups all over the world try to come together on October 29th to participate in a traditional Greek Orthodox Memorial Service. One year Lord Pentland asked me to handle the usual arrangements in New York with the little Russian church on 2nd Street, where we had often gone before. However, this year the 29th fell on a Friday and the only time the beautiful old church with its wonderful choir of real Russian voices was available was evidently "Impossible!" "Quite unacceptable!" to Lord Pentland and the Foundation's Group One. It would have conflicted with the weekly Friday night "sitting" at the Foundation!!

So the service never took place!

This emphasis on the extreme importance of "sittings" in the Gurdjieff Work only began years after Mr. Gurdjieff's death when Mme. de Salzmann accompanied William Segal on a trip to Japan. She returned with an increased interest in Zen practices, concepts like "*hara*," etc. some of which she evidently thought might offer something fresh to her older pupils. But I'm sure that she, of all people, who spent over seventy years of her life working to preserve the Movements and their use in Mr. Gurdjieff's System, never intended that "sittings" be accorded the importance they are increasingly given nowadays, especially since this is often at the expense of time and attention being given to Movements. Movements, we know, if taught and worked on in the correct way, can truly give real results, tastes of direct, profound, inner experience unadulterated by mental and verbal interference.

It seems to me a sad omen for the future that at certain official "International Conferences" on the Gurdjieff Work that have been held in recent years, no mention has been made, much less a study of, Movements and their place in Gurdjieff's Teaching. Yet, invariably scheduled are two, three, or four long "sittings" each day.

I wouldn't be true to my parentage, my personal experience, or my honest conviction if I didn't point this out.

* * * * *

<u>POSTSCRIPT 2</u>

GURDJIEFF'S MUSIC

"The question of music... should in reality be like a beacon light for the correct understanding of one of the aspects of truth." (G.I.Gurdjieff in "Meetings with Remarkable Men")

Dushka
♦

Music had a large place in Gurdjieff's life from his childhood as a chorister to his last year's daily recording of his lap harmonium.

Of course, best known is the period during the 1920s when he composed orchestral music to be used for the Movement Demonstrations. When he was writing *All and Everything*, he turned to pieces for piano. His aide in those years was the classically trained Thomas de Hartmann, who completed the harmonizations and scoring and did most of the actual notation.

Thirty years later Lonia Savitsky recorded Thomas de Hartmann playing some of these pieces on the old piano in the livingroom at Franklin Farms in Mendham, New Jersey. With clever modern digitizing these recordings have been preserved and were released on CD and cassette. At one moment, the pianist stops playing and one hears de Hartmann's heavily accented voice say in faltering English:

"I can't help to tell something about Georgei Ivanovich, till we understand why Georgei Ivanovich put always great weight on music.

"He himself played and he also composed. If we compared [sic] with the music of all the religions we can see that music played a great role, a great part in, so to say, religious service. But after the work of Georgei Ivanovich we can understand it more, we can understand it better that music helps to concentrate oneself, to bring oneself to an inner state where we can assume the greatest possible emanations.

"That is why music is just the thing which helps you to see higher.

"In this regard, I will just play - "

Some people, not only out of loyalty to Mme. de Hartmann, but in their effort to give due credit to M. de Hartmann for his real contribution to what is now known as "The Gurdjieff/de Hartmann Music," have, I feel, now erred in the other direction. They make it seem as if all Mr. Gurdjieff was capable of was to whistle a few melodies and de Hartmann did all the rest by himself.

But it must be remembered that not only was Mr. G. exceptionally gifted musically, an inheritance from his famous "ashough" father, but he did receive considerable training and experience dating back to his years at the Kars Military Cathedral, as a member of their prestigious choir.

He must already have been a particularly adept and accurate reader of music as he describes how Dean Borsch, a noted composer, would ask him to "sing some canticle he had just composed, to verify the transcription for voices." (*Meetings with Remarkable Men*, page 54).

De Hartmann attests to Gurdjieff's skill on the guitar, recounting how the first Movements classes were accompanied, not by his own piano playing, but by Mr. G.

playing guitar, "which he did very well."

Boussik remembers Mr. Gurdjieff at the Prieuré accompanying Movements on a big oriental drum, (probably a "daff," like a huge tambourine without the cymbals), held upright in front of him resting on his palms while just his fingers played light, intricate rhythms.

And Gurdjieff in his *Third Series* describes himself earning his way when fleeing into the Transcaspian region "...with the help of a mouth harmonica I then played, I confess, not badly."

Personally, never having heard him actually play anything except his little lap harmonium, I was especially curious and once at a Work gathering asked Mme. de Salzmann if Mr. Gurdjieff had played the piano. I think we were all surprised at her vehemence when she exclaimed: "But yes! In fact the first time I ever saw him, before I met him, he was sitting playing the piano in the Tiflis Opera House. I had had a lot of training and realized that he wasn't a schooled pianist, but what and how he was playing was so interesting and impressive that I never forgot!"

The creativity and special character of both the orchestral music for the Movements Demonstrations and the piano solos from the Twenties also attest to Gurdjieff's active participation. One has only to compare them to de Hartmann's own work through the years. All de Hartmann's training was classical and European. As he himself confesses, it was only when they were all in the Caucasus and Mr. Gurdjieff sent him out specifically to listen and study local mid-Eastern music that he began to understand and correctly notate what Mr. G. was passing on to him.

De Hartmann also credits Mr. G. with some of the most interesting effects in the orchestrations and actually describes him writing out on manuscript specific parts for certain instruments which he explained were needed to achieve special vibrations, harmonic effects or voicings.

This musical sensitivity and skill clarified for me the incident that Mother had described when she was writing about the first time Gurdjieff and his people came to her Paris studio in 1921. I recalled how it wasn't Mother's approval as a noted dancer and choreographer that most concerned Mr. G. The first thing he asked her, with de Hartmann listening near by, was whether she had understood the music. The fact that she did and could count out the tricky rhythms ensured her immediate acceptance by both men.

I myself have only gradually come to a full realization of how important the correct musical accompaniment is for profound work with the Movements. Mother was always stressing it, but I never fully appreciated what she meant until I proved it for myself in the fifty or so different classes I worked with all around South America. During my more than ten years down there I saw the extraordinary effect of music on every kind of participant: beginner, advanced, young, old, athletic, infirm, and every personality type, nationality, religious background and degree of education.

Yes, one learns to show accurately, and explain positions, displacements, and sequences. A good teacher can even suggest helpful inner work and attitude; but not even the clearest exposition and the most perfect demonstration can evoke true feeling, a specific mood, and therefore the desired inner and outer tonicity, as can the right music.

This is why I have tried in recent years to remind people that they should be knowledgeable and discriminating about Movements music. It is not all of the same quality, or usefulness to a class.

The only music that Gurdjieff ever specified should be played for his Movements were the orchestrations he himself dictated and worked out with de Hartmann for the first demonstrations in 1923. He was greatly concerned with the effects of different instruments, their individual tones and special vibrations, not so much on the ears of the audience, but much more importantly, on different parts of the performers' bodies. His music was exactly "right" in every way to help inspire the necessary physical responses.

In 1999, I joined forces with a dedicated Dutch musician/producer/technician Gert-Jan Blom and we began extensive "Gurdjieff music preservation," beginning with saving Mr. Gurdjieff's harmonium recordings. Gert-Jan had a long affiliation with the Dutch State Radio Organization as producer and researcher included programs dedicated to lesser known composers (e.g. Ferde Grofe, Raymond Scott,and others.) These works were played and recorded by the Metropole orchestra, a popular ensemble of fifty first-class musicians. After first recording de Hartmann's *Oriental Suite*, the enthusiastic Metropole orchestra asked for and recorded Gurdjieff's entire l923 (Paris) and 1924 (America) programs, and even helped fund the immense job of copying the parts.

In *Our Life with Mr Gurdjieff*, Thomas de Hartmann describes how when they arrived in America in 1924 Mr. G. couldn't afford the 36-piece orchestra he had used in Paris. So for the demonstrations in New York's Lesley Hall de Hartmann was told to quickly rearrange all the music for "five good Russian musicians with whom Mr. Gurdjieff could communicate," who would play violin, cello, double-bass, clarinet and percussion, with de Hartmann himself directing from the piano. Actually the final scores we located to record in 2005 proved to be for eight musicians. Apparently, flute and a second violin were added for the New York performances.

 Obviously a big orchestra is impractical for our present-day classes, but a few instruments could add immeasurably to the tonal richness. so I searched for many years, until we finally unearthed and now have available those reductions for a small group. We should be able to find eight good musicians in various Work centers to recreate the original effect. It will be an extraordinary experience for present-day pupils to hear the "right" music "live"and move to it.

Unfortunately, the Movements used in those early demonstrations are rarely taught, in fact, they are almost forgotten nowadays, superseded by newer things. And Gurdjieff's music for them, intended as it was for a big orchestra, is poorly represented by the sparse piano versions still used by classes everywhere, which were, perhaps merely de Hartmann's sketchy reminders to himself as he conducted. But these will be greatly improved when they are compared and renotated to more closely conform to the original orchestral versions. Many of us are working on this and it's not just an optimistic dream any more!

 For years after the 1924 Demonstrations and his return from America, and due to his serious automobile accident, Mr. G. gave no more Movements or the music for them. However, for a time, until de Hartmann left the Prieuré, the two men worked together on piano solos. But in 1949, these latter were never played or even mentioned in my presence. Mr. Gurdjieff himself had apparently abandoned them back in the Twenties. Until the end he never seems to have encouraged anyone to play this piano music. It wasn't scheduled to be published or recorded.

So I have found it hard in recent years to understand the exaggerated resurgence of interest and continual concertising and recording of the "Gurdjieff/de Hartmann Piano Music," as these pieces are now known. Yes, I enjoy and value them when they are played, one at a time, in a quieting moment before I concentrate on listening to a reading from *Beelzebub*. This is how most of them were originally intended to be used and Tom Daly, the de Hartmann's heir and executor, working from the manuscripts, did his best to help me identify which pieces go with which chapter. Unfortunately, we were able to attribute only a few with certainty. But to lump these disparate short pieces all together into a program for a public concert, especially when played by (why do I so often find myself having to resort to this placating expression?) "well-meaning amateurs," for they are certainly not easy to perform well, no, I was not enthusiastic.

However, many years after he broke off all contact with Gurdjieff, Thomas de Hartmann himself, evidently esteeming this music, copyrighted in 1956 masterful orchestrations of five of these pieces ("Seid Dance," "Song of the Aisors," "Song of the Fisherwomen," "Duduki," and "Tibetan Masked Dance") sensitively grouped together as an *"Oriental Suite."* When, in 2001, we located this suite and it was performed and recorded excellently by the Metropole Orchestra, I loved it!

For those of us working with Movements it must be remembered that after the demonstrations in 1923-4 were completed, all subsequent Movements that Mr. G. created and introduced to classes were accompanied solely by improvisation at the piano (mostly with amazing skill and understanding by Jeanne de Salzmann.) Until he died, nothing was composed for use with these later exercises (although some people like Helen Adie did try to note down by memory some of Mme. de Salzmann's improvised melodies.)

Of all his newer Movements, Mr. G. evidently considered only a small number complete and fixed. When he was sure they met his criteria, and there were no more adjustments to be made, he would announce to the class: "This now you may continue to work with," and it was added to the list and given the next number. Rarely he might refer to something with an identifying name, date, or category such as "march," "prayer," "multiplication," "canon," "dance," "machine group," "dervish," or "sensation exercise." But other people in ensuing years have often given their own inaccurate names to exercises. Many of these have stuck and encouraged distortion. For example what most people now call "The Pointing Dervish" and often do violently, was originally a neat, controlled quiet exercise known simply by its number, French 5 or American 2, in which one was helped to be centered by singing a long sustained note — certainly no stamping and leaping!

At the time of his death Mr. G. had worked out in France, and definitively set, thirty-nine completed exercises known simply as "The Thirty-Nine," and he also set another seven Movements which are included in "the American series." These were understood to be "the new exercises" for which, when he was dying, Gurdjieff suggested de Hartmann be recruited to compose accompaniments. Of course, Gurdjieff never lived to hear or approve of any of these compositions, and sometimes, regrettably, in spite of de Hartmann's enduring talent and sincere effort, the difference between them and the early music, made in direct collaboration with Mr. G., is regrettable.

In this case, de Hartmann had the additional obstacle of composing without seeing any of the exercises actually performed by a group of participants. He worked with just one or two of the older French pupils who came out to his small living room in Garches, the Paris suburb where the de Hartmanns lived. These pupils attempted to describe and demonstrate the subtle and complicated sequences but sometimes they lacked the musical training, clarity, or precise memories necessary. Thus there are some mistakes needing to be corrected in the printed editions of this music.

The de Hartmanns were already in Canada before Thomas completed the last six or seven of his Movements compositions, such as "Adam and Eve," "Amin," "Dur Rud," etc. and these he based purely on detailed descriptions and rhythmic charts that Mother wrote out and sent to him by mail. Since he and Mother shared such a similar expertise in music, understanding of its effects on the body and mind, and long experience with Gurdjieff, the results were surprisingly good. In fact, these pieces are amongst de Hartmann's best both musically and for the work of a class.

In the 1950 London demonstration described in Alfred's letter to me, see Chapter 23, except for the Obligatories, the major part of the program was chosen from the "Thirty-Nine" and played for by de Hartmann debuting his new compositions. We really regret that the filming they did had no soundtrack to preserve his playing. A few months later, after yet another experimental demonstration at London's Fortune Theatre, Mme. de Salzmann organized the first movements film. Made in Paris in black and white it featured approximately the same repertoire, but other pianists recorded de Hartmann's music for the soundtracks.

Differences between the French "Thirty-Nine" and the American numbering system have often caused confusion. Why are there two different sets of numbers? When Alfred arrived in New York in 1948, he taught us the new movements he had learned in France in a definite planned order. He was never an innovator or independent thinker when it came to Mr. Gurdjieff or the Movements. So this order was undoubtedly carefully planned by Gurdjieff himself and listed as given. Thus we have "the American numbers." When Mr. G. arrived and started teaching the class, he added seven totally new and complete movements, for which de Hartmann never wrote music, although others tried with varied success. That's how we finish up with 46 exercises in the "American Thirty-Nine!"

Of course when Mr. Gurdjieff died a huge number (over 300?) of other Movements were still "in progress," being changed and worked on, to Mme. de Salzmann's improvised accompaniment. Therefore they had no set music. But during the thirty-five or so years after the first Movements film was made, Mme. de Salzmann put together other films (seven or eight of them) salvaging and piecing together many of the incomplete Movements. Some of these are extremely interesting and beautiful, but it should be remembered, and instructors should point out, that Mr. Gurdjieff himself had not finished them or authorized their use.

For these later films, not wishing to personally play on the sound-tracks as she had done when the Movements were first given, Mme. de S. found and supervised others to provide music: composers and pianists like Edouard Michael, Alain Kremski, and Yvette Grimaud. Since she knew just what tempos and effects were needed, in, most cases she got them.

Some of this film music was transcribed and distributed in handwritten form, some of it later printed, but much of it is difficult to read and technically beyond our average class pianists. Again, some is naturally better than the rest.

Just to add to the confusion, mixed in with the class music used in some cities there are misguided attempts by anonymous beginners and more "well-meaning amateurs" which have somehow gotten preserved and continue to be circulated through the years.

The same pattern holds true in regard to recordings of the rest of the "Gurdjieff/de Hartmann" music. Some (notably, of course, Mr. de Hartmann's) are excellent but others are a travesty. Some are by recognizable names like jazz pianist Keith Jarrett who sold thousands of albums and others are by amateurs such as Sylvie, the wife of Gurdjieff's nephew. Even sincere, talented professionals may be led astray by uncorrected and/or inadequate manuscripts, misprints in published music or questionable attributions of authorship.

Recordings

Keith Jarrett Plays Gurdjieff's Hymns

By JOHN ROCKWELL

Keith Jarrett is a well-known jazz pianist who has taken, of late, to venturing into the classical realm both on records and in concert. But his latest disk conforms to neither of these categories, and counts as perhaps his most unusual recorded project thus far.

Its peculiarities start with its very title, "G.I. Gurdjieff: Sacred Hymns." That would seem to mean that this is a recording of music composed by someone named Gurdjieff. Which is apparently what it is, except that these scores are now copyrighted under the name of Thomas De Hartmann.

Gurdjieff was a curiously practical mystic who emerged from the Near East after World War I and established a center for spiritual studies near Paris that attracted considerable attention in the European intellectual community in the 20's. Gurdjieff and his posthumous followers have generally been a secretive lot; theirs was a society of the elect that didn't sully itself with proselytizing. It was also a bitterly fractious band of true believers who were forever splitting off from one another and squabbling among themselves.

For whatever reason, the non-mystical world has heard more of Gurdjieff in the past few years. There have been several books; there has been Peter Brook's film, "Meetings with Remarkable Men" and now there is this record.

Gurdjieff was not musically trained in the traditional Western sense; De Hartmann, a disciple, was. Gurdjieff would hum or pick out melodies and then De Hartmann would transcribe and arrange them. Thus some of their music is really by Gurdjieff, some is a collaboration and some is by De Hartmann, dedicated to Gurdjieff and composed in his spirit. Yet for reasons having mostly to do with who got what royalties, much of the music has been recopyrighted under De Hartmann's name.

In any case, whatever the copyrights say, the Sacred Hymns that Mr. Jarrett plays are reportedly by Gurdjieff. The music will separate the believers from the non-believers, perhaps; to this sympathetic but skeptical soul, it has its simple charms. This is primarily meditative music, with modal harmonies, songful melodies and chordal accompaniment, curiously akin to the scores of Alan Hovhaness. But sometimes the music becomes rhythmically complex; Gurdjieff was always one for hiding complexity under a veneer of simplicity, and vice versa.

The prevailing mood is rapt and innocent, and may strike musicians as simplisitic. Yet ultimately, music of this sort often works if the performer conveys conviction, and Mr. Jarrett plays these pieces with seeming devotion and an intensity that doesn't trouble the limpidiness. And the sound of his piano has been captured by ECM's engineers in a resonant and compelling way.

One of the first public recordings of the "Gurdjieff/de Hartmann music" is reviewed in the *New York Times* .

Mother once warned her assistant teachers: "The music that was written at Mr. Gurdjieff's dictation, de Hartmann's arrangement, was made at the same time each movement was given. I would only say for myself that there is very little music that has been composed since Mr. G. and de Hartmann worked together that the pupils can rely on completely to have the same inner vibration that they are struggling for."

So *Caveat Emptor*, especially Movement instructors and pianists, and discriminating listeners!

* * * * *

POSTSCRIPT 3

GURDJIEFF'S "SALAD"

Dushka
♦

Although Mr. G. liked to have by his place at table a big pile of fresh herbs, dill, parsley, tarragon, and so forth, which he distributed to special guests, his meals rarely included what we would term a salad. What he called his "salad" was a soupy, highly seasoned mixture of raw vegetables that was nearer to a chunky "gazpacho." Ripe tomatoes, cucumbers, onions, dill pickles, herbs and spices were marinated to a thick consistency, redolent of fresh dill, fruit juices and gingery chutney. It was usually offered in a small bowl and was especially succulent with the smoothing, soothing addition of *smetana* [sour cream].

The "salad" was certainly a gastronomic and exotic treat, in its various forms, for it was never exactly the same. But nowadays it has become associated in many people's minds with memorable Gurdjieff incidents, personal experiences with him, or stories repeated, and it begins to take on an almost legendary reputation. As a result there have been many (to my mind, usually mistaken,) attempts to recreate it, because even if one does manage to find the perfect basic ingredients, achieve just the right balance of flavors and textures, judge the timing of the marinating — ?

And then — when the people you are making it for treat it like some sort of sacrament, the partaking of which will aid them on the path to consciousness — !

Or worse yet, at the other extreme, as new generations come along, there are youngsters present who don't understand what this strange cupful is and save it for dessert?!

All right — so much for my personal reservations! But I confess, I myself do sometimes bother to make it at home — because I love it!

Once at the Hotel Wellington in 1949, Mr. G. had us make a big jar of "salad" and because we had no refrigerator, it was put to marinate on a windowsill. It slipped and fell down a dozen floors, crashing, (thank goodness!) not onto the busy sidewalk, but onto the solid covering over the *m*ain entrance. Happily, no one was hurt, and despite a loud noise, it was ignored. But for months the resultant red splash was visible from the front windows, evoking gruesome imaginings in many a hotel guest.

Then when Mr. Gurdjieff left New York to return to Paris, a great quantity of carefully imitated "salad" was proudly and lovingly prepared for him, sealed in a large earthenware crock and delivered to his first-class cabin aboard the "Queen Mary." In mid-ocean, reacting badly to several days of warmth and engine vibration, it finally exploded with copious and horrendous results to Cunard's walls and furnishings.

A year or so ago, I was eagerly awaiting the publication of *Luba Gurdjieff, a Memoir with Recipes* that Mr. G.'s niece had told me she was writing.

Knowing she had worked in the kitchen at the Prieuré, I naturally hoped that she would give, finally, an authentic version of the recipe in print to which I could refer anyone else who asks how to make "The Salad."

But when her book came out I found that my dear cousin had decided to concentrate on the dishes she perfected during many years in London running her famous "Luba's Bistro." Oh, she mentions briefly that: "This salad seems to be famous all on its own," but then cops out with: "We had something like it lots of times, not for big occasions but when somebody was coming, somebody new to impress, you know. My Uncle would say in a big whisper, 'That is my salad.' He used to come into the kitchen and make it himself. He was tasting all the time. Valya and I and my auntie used to cut, cut, cut, and give to him. You can't have a recipe for it. It costs the earth! You put anything you can find in that thing" and she recalls variations and additions: radishes, nuts, seeded green olives, chopped prunes, capers, apples, even "some tomato ketchup brought from England because we couldn't find any in France."

Luba, Gurdjieff's niece, with husband Arthur Everitt in front of her successful London restaurant *Luba's Bistro*.

In 1962 the New York Gurdjieff groups tried to make "The Salad" for a January Thirteen celebration. Lise (Tracol Etievant), now a Movements teacher at the Foundation had experienced working in Mr. Gurdjieff's Paris kitchen and was on hand to supervise the process with many dedicated helpers.

My godmother Annette Herter stood by noting carefully the procedure they followed to make three hundred forty-six cup-size servings for the evening at the Foundation, plus thirteen generous portions to be sent out to Mendham for people left on duty there. Here is what she wrote down:

"RECIPE FOR MR. GURDJIEFF'S SALAD

(Note: The, so to say, 'center of gravity' is the specially marinated dill pickle and that dill juice. Only real Greek or Armenian places have this because they make it for themselves, and it has to be ordered in advance...)

TO BUY:
10 large Bermuda onions (chopped or grated)
60 at least, firm but ripe tomatoes (diced large) with their juice
10 medium cucumbers (diced large)
40 specially marinated dill pickles, medium-sized (diced small)
4 quarts of the juice of these pickles
3 large bunches of fresh parsley
A good quantity of fresh dill
2 quarts of grapefruit juice
2 quarts of good apple juice
4 quarts of real chutney (Mr. G. used authentic Major Grey)
3 small jars of Dijon or other strong mustard
1 pound fine granulated sugar
Seasoning: Salt, pepper (black and hot, red in powder), imported paprika and curry powder.

We worked in two teams. Each team used a plastic baby bathtub and put into their tub exactly the same quantities (half the total) of the ingredients in the same order. When everything was in, the contents of both tubs were transferred to porcelain (not metal) bowls and kept in a very cold place overnight and for the following day. It was served that evening in glass cups with spoons.

Sometimes, at the Wellington, Mr. Gurdjieff let us add twelve hard-boiled eggs cut in small pieces. He himself measured out everything with his hands except for the liquids which he measured with his eyes. We used to keep the leftover, if any, in an earthenware jug. It does ferment, but in a really cold place can be kept quite a few days."

* * * *

Well – yes – Thank you godmother Annette –This recipe may – in talented, conscientious hands – with suitably ripe ingredients – and someone with a flair for mathematics to adjust quantities (if you don't need exactly three hundred fifty-nine portions!) – aided by experienced veterans with experienced palates for tasting and correcting – etc. etc. etc– give respectable results.

It can be used as a base.

But my personal experience in making the salad and trying to live up to old taste and texture memories is that nowadays sensible adjustments need to be made.

Our American raw vegetables and fruits have too little flavor, especially in January, and give up too much liquid during the marinating. As a precaution, I personally replace the fruit juices and sugars that are listed, with undiluted frozen fruit juice concentrate. Pineapple or cranberry also work well besides the grapefruit or apple mentioned. I have never had to add any liquid after the marinating. In fact I even keep ready additional tomato concentrate to thicken the "sauce" and extra dill leaves, coarsely chopped, for last minute adjustments of texture as well as flavor and aroma. It must never be watery.

Most of the ingredients should blend into an opaque, liquid type of purée, Someone said recently: "Oh, kind of like a *salsa*!" but I guess it depends which kind of *salsa* you're used to. But the "body" of the salad should be recognizable, toothsome pieces of tomato and cucumber, so don't dice these too small since the marinating will shrink and soften them a lot. Try for half- to three-quarter inch pieces.

Since "ripe but firm tomatoes" aren't always so easy to find, I suggest a larger number of the smaller "plum tomato" variety which usually have a pleasant taste and hold up better to the hours of marinating, just as large watery cucumbers don't keep their texture as well as crisp fresh gherkins, or "Kirbys."

Ideally, as ripeness is so important, one should buy extra quantities in advance, let them ripen, and carefully discard bad ones.

Thirty years ago they may have needed those "special home-made dill pickles" and they were difficult to find, but now very respectable substitutes are available in most big supermarkets. They'll be still better if treated for several days by adding extra handfuls of fresh dill that can then be retrieved, chopped up and added to the final mixture.

Bermuda onions? Whatever happened to them? No matter! Sweet Spanish or Vidalia onions are fine.

Most important, expensive though it is in the supermarket, one just can't stint on **real Major Grey chutney** or a very cleverly copied homemade substitute, or a half-and-half mixture of both. But I found it possible to order large jars very reasonably from a wholesaler. After all, economy as well as quality was characteristic of Mr. G.'s hospitality and generosity.

Authentic Major Grey chutney contains large firm slices of green mango in a thick syrup. So it is a good idea to empty the jars into a bowl and then, with big scissors, cut those slices into fine, small pieces so as to distribute them throughout each spoonful. It is their gingery piquancy that gives a subtle heat and depth of flavor. It is much preferable to the palate-numbing amounts of mustard or cayenne pepper used by some eager but inexperienced cooks being guided by "old timers" who may, I'm sorry to say, no longer have much taste sensitivity.

This aromatic spiciness is wonderful when a generous amount of sour cream is stirred into it. For large groups, since these days some people avoid cream, I suggest putting a single generous dollop on each serving which can then be blended in or put aside as wished, topped with a decorative sprig of fresh dill.

So your list of ingredients should include, per serving, a good tablespoon of sour cream and a piece of dill, washed, dried and trimmed, to be added at the last minute. Note: Two- or three-inch pieces of crusty French bread are a welcome accompaniment.

It isn't always easy to achieve the cold temperature needed for the night's marinating, but be warned, don't put your salad outside unattended in winter. If it freezes, you will have a useless unpleasant mush.

On one of my trips to South America, remembering that the US customs allow Americans to bring home one bottle of "booze" duty free, I figured that from Brazil, the land of coffee, the obvious souvenir would be a real Brazilian coffee liqueur. But amazingly I couldn't find one anywhere. They don't produce it but import from Europe something made by Bols, or Kahlua from Mexico.

Since our Work groups down there are always in need of funds, I immediately suggested that this could be a good money-making project for them: make and sell, especially to tourists at the airport, their own local brand of *"Licor de Caffe."*

I don't think they really believed me or ever even tried it, but my experimenting for them developed a recipe which is luscious, quick and easy, and very inexpensive to make. The only costly ingredient is good vanilla.

My friends all ask for it at Christmas or as their "hostess gift" when they invite me.

So here's how:

SIMPLE IMITATION KAHLUA

or

<u>DUSHKA'S COFFEE LIQUEUR</u>

Boil two cups of strong coffee (Of course to the Brazil Group I specified real Brazilian coffee, but any good one will do) **with four cups of sugar until it is slightly viscous. Add another cup of hot coffee in which you have dissolved two ounces of instant coffee. If you use a whole vanilla bean, add it now. Let cool.**

When quite cool, add two cups of the cheapest, tasteless vodka or brandy, and mix well. If you decided to use vanilla essence, add about three tablespoons now and *Caramba!* you already have about a bottleful ready to enjoy. If you use a real vanilla bean you'll have to wait for about a month for your mix to steep.

So recycle some bottles, multiply the recipe as needed, design a catchy name and label, and go into business!

An additional sales gimmick for Americans might be a variation I once tried for an elderly Italian couple who loved my "product" but had been told by their doctor to cut down their caffeine intake. So for them at Christmas I made a few bottles following my usual recipe but substituted ***decaffeinated supermarket coffee,*** both regular grind for brewing and powdered instant, and it worked out just fine.

We could use a sugar substitute and advertise "Diet Kahlua"! ...or...??

As Mr. Gurdjieff often said:"Send me nine percent!"

* * * * *

APPENDIX 1

"FOR MY DAUGHTER AT CHRISTMAS"

Dearest Dushka,

    You have asked me how it came about that my brother Wallace and I were left in the charge of foster parents when we were small.

    To answer I can only tell the little I know about our parents and our guardians. This is really very little, scraps of conversation, not always well understood, heard during childhood.

    I have no recollection whatsoever of my mother. The grown-ups used to hold her up to me as a "little saint." They said she was born in the Shetland Islands and that her father was a fine musician, pupil of the Norwegian violinist Ole Bull. Her maiden name being Annie Garssen, she probably had Scandinavian forbears. She must have been left alone early in life, something was mentioned about two older sisters having died of consumption. In any case, she trained as a nurse, a calling which, in those days, was considered only a little above the status of a domestic servant.

    It seems that my father used to say, and be frowned upon for doing so: "My wife and I were raised only forty miles away from each other, (in Yorkshire). We met first when she was a probationer at the Huddersfield Hospital. We ran into each other again on a ship when she was accompanying a patient to Egypt. And, Lo and Behold, who should I find again in Australia but Annie? So we really had to get married."

    I have a photograph of them both taken in Sydney, possibly at the time of their wedding about 1888. Mother looks very young and trim. She has a sweet face. She half-sits so as to look taller, has her parasol firmly planted on the ground. She gives an impression of shyness and calm.

    About our father, John Henry Crossley Howarth (there are scores of Howards in the South, and Howarths in the North of England) I know a little more. He was born in Halifax, Yorks. His mother was one of the Crossleys, a large prosperous family, who were wool merchants. His father died when he was a baby. Father's mother married again, a man named O'Brien. Father always had wished my brother Wallace to add Crossley to his name, while I was supposed to add O'Brien to mine.

◆◆◆

    She did do this years later but only when, as a "single mother," she evidently felt it necessary to simulate a "maiden" name!

◆◆◆

    The stepfather already had a son, Charles O'Brien, who, according to my guardians, exerted a very bad influence on his younger stepbrother.

    Although father studied medicine in Edinburgh (where he first knew our guardian), he seems to have practiced very little as a doctor. His stepbrother became

Jessmin
◆

Dushka
◆

Jessmin
◆

(Above) Dr. John Henry Crossley Howarth.
(Right) Dr. Howarth with his wife Annie (née Garssen), probably in 1888 at the time of their wedding in Sydney, Australia.

1897, Yorkshire, England, In Dr. Sutcliffe's conservatory.

(Standing at back) Mrs. Sutcliffe, "Tanta," the guardian's wife.

(Seated) Mrs. Burgess, the governess.

(Standing at right) Jessmin, five years old.

(Seated in front) Wallace, Jessmin's brother, with the dog Topsy.

a "government contractor" which meant, I think, that he traveled extensively, purchasing supplies and equipment of all kinds for the British government. He evidently often persuaded father to go off with him. That probably explains why father was in Australia about 1888.

I suspect that he must have found this a good way of making money. Certainly it was not through doctoring that he was able, ten years later, to leave enough money to educate my brother and me and provide a nest egg for each of us when we came of age.

Our parents went to Johannesburg, South Africa, in 1890, just before Wallace was born. Mother seems to have officiated as Matron in a hospital there for five years or so. (An oil painting used to exist, a portrait of her in a very becoming uniform, a bunch of keys at her waist and a sheaf of papers in her hand.)

When my brother's sixth birthday was approaching, (I was two years younger), our parents must have begun to take thought for his education and be concerned about our being so much in the company of native houseboys. I was told that they decided to return to England and asked my guardian to find them a home near him on the Lancashire coast. This he did, and I gathered later that he had hoped my father as well as my mother, would work with him in his infirmary for which he saw a great future.

But mother evidently exhausted herself preparing for the move. When she insisted upon nursing one of the servants who had a fever, she caught it, and died.

So father brought us to England in the late summer of 1896. He did not stay long, just got us settled in with my guardians and hurried back to South Africa. I did not see him again for four years, and then I did not at first recognize or welcome him.

In the meantime, Wallace and I had been separated, a move on our guardians' part which we bitterly resented. It was all my fault. I must have been a pestiferous brat. I early decided that I did not like England and being cared for by strange white women. So I pretended not to be able to understand or speak English. Wallace and I talked in a language of our own - Zulu, Kaffir, Africaans? I don't know. People soon grew exasperated at having to call upon my brother to interpret. So he, poor delicate six-year-old, was packed off to Brighton "for his health." His so-called school was really a place where a number of children of "Colonials" were boarded. Fortunately a friend of my father lived nearby and often took Wallace home for weekends. When Wallace was ten and came north he told me how lonely he had been although everyone was kind. He was always retiring afterwards.

Father's visit in 1900 was again brief. He spoilt me terribly. I was given all kinds of treats, new dresses, a necklace, a tricycle, a bracelet, and any small things I asked for. He told my guardian that this time he really would settle his affairs quickly and come back. After a few months we heard that he had died, from an attack of fever.. From the letter, which I saw later, it could be guessed that he had ruined his health drinking. My guardians were charitable enough to make excuses for him, saying that he "just never could face life without Annie."

The O'Brien stepbrother was again in disgrace. He was supposed to take charge and settle father's affairs in Africa. As far as business matters were concerned, he seemed to have done so. But our guardians were shocked when the only personal possessions he had shipped to them were: a Chinese vase, an unframed painting, my mother's Bible, two fans, and her squirrel fur cape (which provided the lining for my winter coats some years later!)

Now, about my guardians: "Uncle," Dr. Wallace Sutcliffe, when not visiting patients or the infirmary, was busy with his flowers, a consuming passion. He had four greenhouses, one for orchids, another where he grew tomatoes and grapes (rare in the North of England), and the others for young plants and his chrysanthemums and roses. He was always experimenting with grafts trying to get a new flower. He was a Town Councilor and chairman of the Horticultural Society (which explains why, at the Annual Show, I had to be dressed up and present a bouquet to the "Lady Something or Other" who opened the proceedings). He had become interested in mental diseases and inspected some Insane Asylums at intervals, telling lurid anecdotes about the inmates, which I took as if they were characters in fairy tales.

So, all in all, we hardly ever saw him. He did share a love of music with his wife Mary, who we called "Tanta." He encouraged us all to learn an instrument and to sing. In fact, there were times when he insisted upon our performing. These were the Sundays when nurses from the infirmary were invited two by two to have "High Tea" with us.

I must tell you that in those days, "High Tea" in the North of England was an unbelievable spread, what we would nowadays call a "Cold Buffet," taking the place of Sunday tea and supper. On the table would be set: roast chicken, boiled ham, veal and egg aspic pie, sardines, potted shrimps, home-baked white and raisin bread, scones, honey in the comb, jam, rock buns, shortbread, currant and mint pasties, lemon curd tarts, chocolate biscuits, stewed fruit and Devonshire cream. Then, to top it all off, one of the rich fruit and nut cakes with almond (marzipan) icing, which his patients were always bringing to my guardian. He considered these unwholesome and would not allow the younger people a crumb of them, but would press them on the guests and tell Tanta to give the nurses large wedges to take with them.

To work up an appetite everyone was taken on a tour: first, of the little aviary where a number of small birds, Java sparrows, parakeets, canaries etc., could always be seen. The Botanical Gardens sent these up to be cared for by Tom, our gardener, who was crazy about birds and nursed any invalids back to health. Next, through the greenhouses, and when each had received a bunch of flowers, back indoors to be urged by Tanta (who took great pride in her "Yorkshire Teas") to taste a little of everything and eat far too much.

After this, Uncle would call for music. Queenie, (an older girl living with us then), would be at the piano and struggle through *Rustle of Spring*, or one of the easier Strauss Waltzes. I would scrape away on my violin *Blue Bells of Scotland, With Variations.* or Handel's *Largo*. Tanta would consent to try a song, something sad like *Men must work and women must weep and the harbor bar is moaning*. Or, more ambitious, Braga's *Angel's Serenade*, on which we collaborated. I provided the violin obligato representing the angelic choir and Tanta sang for the dying invalid.

Then Uncle would tell us to join him in some rousing ballad or he would ask us to sing in parts *Sweet and Low*, and *All Through the Night*. If the guests were young, he would allow us choruses of popular songs, such as *You are my honey, honeysuckle; I am the bee.*

Otherwise, we had to take our music lessons seriously. I practiced an hour a day wherever I might be and was taken to every concert of interest held in the town.

As for Tanta, she was strange. How she came to marry this husband I cannot imagine. She had evidently kept house for her father, a schoolmaster, since she was fifteen, and even when she married she had to put up with this elderly parent living in her new home for many years. He was, somehow, omnipresent even after his death. He had filled the walls of the house with quite dreadful oil paintings in heavy gilded frames: copies of landscapes and still-lifes. I shall never forget one horror that hung opposite my place at table in the dining room. It depicted a frowzy old couple: "Darby and Joan" with wrinkled faces and lumpily gnarled hands, sitting close together in front of a plate on which was laid a very dead kipper and, of all things, an apple.

Tanta's problem, I realized later, was her sorrow at having had a miscarriage when thrown from the pony cart during her first pregnancy. She was always somewhat hysterical afterwards. Having no child of her own, she persuaded her husband and her father to let her bring up one of the Italian stableman's pretty daughters, Queenie. Then she sent for a distant relative's girl to keep Queenie company. Soon after, two teen-age boys were put in her charge during their holidays, and, finally, my brother and I were added.

She never enjoyed young people, for she had been the pampered companion of an older husband as well as her father. But, she was kind to me, as the youngest, and worried a great deal about my winter colds, caused, she thought, by the change of climate from the South African warmth.

I know it amuses you to have me list the layers of clothes she insisted on my wearing, so here goes: First, winter and summer my chest and back were covered with a flannel "chest protector!" Then came a Jaeger woolen "under combination" reaching from neck to knees. Next, a gray twill bodice with accordian pleats over what were hoped would eventually become breasts, thus this was called a "developer." It had rows of buttons to attach suspenders for long woolen stockings. Two pairs of panties (drawers), one cotton and the other serge, if I was wearing dark clothes, or embroidered linen if I had on lighter ones... a flannel slip, and on top, a starched cotton one called a petticoat. To venture outdoors I had to put on, over my serge or cotton middy blouse and pleated skirt, another cross-over chest protector, and in winter a lined coat with silk muffler, bonnet, woolen gloves, gaiters. And, in cold weather, a fur neckpiece and a muff... and, of course, always high-buttoned or laced boots, "to keep one's ankles from thickening!"

Tanta, like all Yorkshire people was manic about cleanliness, especially about her person. She had had installed a cistern to hold rain water with which she always washed her face, using a little "Pear's" soap on a clean piece of flannel. Her hair was also washed with rain water and eggs, her scalp rubbed between the biweekly shampoos with a cloth moistened in water to which a few crumbs of rock ammonia had been added. I must say that this care paid off for she had the clearest, finest textured skin I have ever seen, and her hair, brushed for half an hour at a time reached below her waist.

She must have had some sad complexes. I could be punished for having a hole in my stocking, not for untidiness but for immodesty. She never mentioned anything to me about menstruation. When it came about, she enjoined silence and privacy

Four-year-old Jessmin newly arrived and outfitted in England, 1896.

Jessmin (Right) as the boy at Mrs. Mackies dancing school...

...and (Below)
 as Red Riding Hood

...and in 1900: Eight years old and all dressed up for her father's visit.

upon me. I had to sew my own sanitary napkins, rinse them in cold salt water, wash and boil them myself. I was glad to get to boarding school where our laundry was taken care of and where I was not constantly told not to lean against my chair back, not to take off my gloves in any public conveyance, and always to put on clean under-things if I had to travel at all "in case of an accident!"

Her favorite pastime was to go on Cook's Tours and collect picture postcards from foreign countries, many albums of them. She took me with her to Scotland, Wales and Holland.

Tanta also joined the Bronte Society and took me to Haworth to see where the writers had lived. But she never allowed me to read any of their books!

But kinder and more understanding than our guardian and his wife, were the two Austrian women my brother and I called fondly "Kitchen-M." That was because one of them, our pretty brunette parlormaid, was Kätchen, and her companion, the grizzled, bony cook, was Emma. They were inseparable, so we believed them mother and daughter.

It was to Emma that I turned when I was irked beyond endurance by the long Kate Greenaway dress it was judged "quaint" for me to wear. We would slip into the back garden and she would carefully pin up the frustrating garment. Then away I would gallop to creep under the appletree and savor a ripe greengage plum and a Petit Beurre biscuit (unforgettable combination!) produced from Kätchen's special tea caddy, sniffing the tart smell of crushed nasturtium leaves, watching the beetles, ants and caterpillars in enchanted quiet, until a warning hiss from Emma would call me in to be unpinned and become presentable again.

And when, with winter, it was believed sensible to shut me in my room for weeks at a time, because all the provincial ladies in the north of England believed that a child born in South Africa must not be exposed to changes of temperature — it was Kätchen who would come in bringing a breath of frosty outdoors into the thick euca-lyptus atmosphere, and, her cheeks glowing, tell me tales of skiing and sledding in the Tyrol. These gave me happy pictures to mull over during the wheezy nights as, itching from flannel chest protector and sweltering in camphorated oil, I'd listen to the steam kettle and watch the light patterns cast on the ceiling by the oil heater cover, and long to be grownup and cast off Jaeger underwear and be free to sport in the snow.

My brother, too, although two years older and already developing a protective mask from life in school would come to Kitchen-M with his problems: "Was it true what the gardener said, that if he combed his hair regularly with a lead curry comb, it would lose its carroty brightness?" and "How could you answer chaps who insisted you must be a Boer if you came from Johannesburg?"

The only points on which we both disagreed with Kätchen (who was, before her time, a fanatic about natural foods, the simple life and *Muller* exercises) were her insistence on cold sponge baths followed by prickly loofah frictions, and exposure to the sun whenever possible. (This last we both hated because of the inevitable aftermath of crops of freckles.) "Health is Beauty," Kätchen would say, "and don't be like these old fuddyduddies here who let their bodies go moldy under all those clothes." Which led me, at least, into strange imaginings about any visitors, espe-cially the women, who dressed at that period in layers of silk and braided broadcloth with fur, or flounces of dotted swiss, long gloves and complicated Queen Alexandra hairdos.

Outwardly, or, perhaps more correct to say, on the other side of the baize door of the butler's pantry (so-called, although we never had a butler), Kätchen and Em were paragons of correct house-retainer behavior, their caps and aprons starched, their shoes squeakless, their faces meek. They moved to an unvarying schedule. We knew it was noon when Kätchen was sighted carrying her can of hot water upstairs to change from her pink and white striped cotton to her black, and four o'clock when Em did the same. Window blinds were drawn up to exactly the same level every morning, and lowered in every room at the same time every late afternoon.

In the dining room, my guardian insisted that the waitress sit by the sideboard between courses. When I ate at the big table, I kept my eyes on Kätchen, for we had a secret language. If she crossed her ankles and put her head in the air, this meant: "Never mind! It will soon be over."

I should explain that since I was, by seven years, the youngest of the six children under my guardian's care, no one else suspected my mealtime sufferings, the discomfort of chilled legs dangling from too high a chair, the struggle to swallow greyish oatmeal. Kätchen would draw in it and write letters in syrup on it for me, so that I could down it a little at a time, otherwise it would be placed in front of me at the beginning of the next meal. Or the glass of port wine prescribed for after lunch. Kätchen would set me, each day, a certain number of little sips or big gulps and count soundlessly as I drank it.

She heartily agreed with some of my guardian's strange prescriptions, one being that I must rest in the stable after lunch. (The taste of Madeira still is associated for me with the smell of horses.) And another, that all beds must be left opened during the days, with the windows wide, then, at dusk, each bed received its flannel-wrapped "back stone," a piece of slate heated in the oven, and all windows were tightly closed, not one breath of air allowed in until we were up and dressed next morning.

But Kätchen and Em disapproved very strongly of other aspects of my education. There would be shakings of the head, pursing of the lips, and mutterings in German, and sympathetic pats on my head, on the days when I had been fretted more often than usual by admonitions to "look at my Table Manners Reminder." This was a large card with Gothic script propped up in front of my plate, with numbered rules of **Correct Behavior for the Small Child When Dining with its Parents**. Of course, it began with **Children may be seen, but not heard.**" There were other gems. I still am apt to start if someone suddenly says, "Number Three," i.e. "**Wipe the mouth before and after drinking.**" Then there was: "**Bread must be buttered on the plate, not in mid-air**," or "**Avoid all appearance of struggling with your food,**" and, most involved of all: "**Do not seek to dislodge particles of food from the teeth with the tongue.**"

Also, when my punishment was to sit still in a small, darkened room (supposedly calming for a high-strung child) and I would work myself into a catatonic state of wordless sulks, it was Kätchen who would disobey and come to me, tickle me and laugh me back to normalcy.

On afternoons when the older ones were out, it was heaven to be allowed in the kitchen, to pet the cat who always had her kittens in the bottom drawer of the china dresser, to watch the parrot, who was "older than I" dancing on his perch with irritation when the table was scrubbed with sand, to make my own toast with a long toasting fork in front of the range, and to dice it myself ready for supper's bread and milk.

It was a haven where my brother dared not tease me, even if I tied a shawl around my close-cropped head, pretending it was the long hair I wished so much to have. Such a satisfying gesture to pretend to toss it proudly over my shoulder!

We felt there that Kätchen and Em loved each other and loved us, although they never hugged or kissed us. I can't remember that they talked very much. Em would rock in her chair, telling her rosary and Kätchen would read the medical journals thrown out by my guardian.

It was surely to Kätchen that I owed a happy adolescence. She had evidently watched me and once, when he was home for awhile, enlisted my brother's aid to persuade me to give up certain taboos with which I hedged around my indoor existence: "Never step on the bottom stair even if they do say you make too much noise jumping." "Never turn your back on the dried and varnished devil-fish (one of the curios hanging halfway up the front staircase) even if everyone who sees you says, 'Child! Why do you have that irritating habit of climbing stairs backwards? One day you'll slip and hurt yourself.'" "And always say 'Thank you, Maria' to the lamp on the landing."

Kätchen understood that, if left alone, I sprang into bed and undressed between the covers, because I was frightened by the creakings of the huge wardrobe, whose old wood made a fuss adjusting to changes of temperature. And indeed, she was the only person who knew that I hid often behind the bushes where there was a climbable wall separating the stable entrance from the vegetable garden... because I could talk then to the stable man's little daughter, the only girl of my own age that I knew.

Also, after various stomach upsets, and unexplained naughtiness, it was Kätchen who found out that I would rather go constipated and headachy and hide myself and lie than use one of the lavatories where the mahogany closet seat was massive and the tank heavy above one's head. The water, being treated with Condy's fluid, ran a purplish pink and gurgled loudly with swishes and groans when flushed. I was convinced (Goodness knows what stories I'd heard) that someone was bleeding to death in there.

So, finally, when Kätchen had won my guardian's confidence by helping in emergencies in his surgery and filling out prescriptions, work which she found much more congenial than sweeping and dusting, she cornered him one day and spilled out all that she thought was unhealthy in their treatment of me. She thus brought about my being packed off at age ten to be a boarder at the Eversley House School on Cambridge Road in Southport.

I hardly saw her and Em again, for soon afterwards they left England.

Three years later I was sent to school in Wales (Dr. Williams School in Dolgelly, Merionshire). I've often told you how wonderful the singing was there. Seemingly all the Welsh have magnificent voices and the ability to find for themselves and carry rich, full harmonies. I worked at my violin there, maybe the music inspired me, but, also, I was allowed to skip things I didn't want to do if it was in order to practice.

When I was approaching seventeen I was asked to come back and keep Tanta company since my guardian had to go away for three months. All the other young people who had lived with them had left; one killed in an accident, two married, one studying in London, my brother living with a friend both being coached to enter Law Courses.

I began with all kinds of ideals, intending to give Tanta breakfast in bed, with a flower on the tray, to share books with her, and go with her to parks and concerts. I did not succeed. She refused every attention, spied on everything I did, and drove the maid crazy complaining that things were dirty.

We would set out for some appointment and she would stop obstinately on the doorstep, sending for rags and the brass polish because the doorknocker was not shined to her liking. She was always driving me to go and practice my violin, but terrified my poor teacher (a musician who came all the way from Liverpool for two or three pupils) by sitting in at my lessons and snorting every time he touched my hand to correct a position.

When my guardian returned, he at last realized that his wife was in a bad state. So, arrangements were made for me to go to study music in Germany early in 1911.

I begin to understand how lonely the poor woman must have been. I can grow sick with remorse about how we all neglected her once we were out of the house.

It is true that my brother and I were shocked and a little disgusted when, on Wallace's coming of age, we were shown her years of accounting. Every Christmas present, birthday cake, every little treat had been carefully listed and paid out of our patrimony. But this did not excuse our never visiting or writing Tanta later.

Though, I did once call on her when I went back from Germany. She found fault with everything I did or said. "Why had I not put up my hair?" "Why was I not wearing a nice navy blue coat and skirt?" "Was it true that there were young men in my music classes?" and so on...

I never saw her again and now my heart aches for my unkindness. After all, she cared for us, in her own way, for years. What brutes adolescents can be!

* * * * *

APPENDIX 2

Gurdjieff: an Original Teacher

by J. Walter Driscoll and George Baker

taken from the

Gurdjieff International Review

Gurdjieff was an abrupt awakener. Since his death in 1949, his ideas, teachings, writings, music and contemplative dances or gymnastics called 'Movements' continue to provide opportunity for essential insight in the never-ending, moment by moment struggle for self-knowledge and self-understanding. Gurdjieff summons us to transformation by showing how to focus our attention on the reality of our inner being and the outer life it attracts.

On January 13, 1949, Gurdjieff was in New York City and announced (on what proved to be his last birthday,) his decision to publish *Beelzebub's Tales to His Grandson*. This was a complete departure from the practice he had followed for almost four decades of expounding his teaching orally and circulating his writings privately. He died on October 29 of that year, hardly a week after receiving the publisher's proofs for *Beelzebub's Tales*.

* * * *

Little is certain about Gurdjieff's early life. We cannot even be sure of the simple fact of his birth date. According to various biographers he was born between 1866 and 1877, of a Greek father and an Armenian mother in Alexandropol which is now Gyumri, formerly Leninakan, in what was Soviet Armenia. He grew up in this war-torn frontier area of the Caucasus, which for generations has been a melting pot of cultures, religions and races from the East and the West. Gurdjieff was deeply influenced by his father's wisdom and the ancient oral traditions he preserved as an 'ashokh' or storyteller and troubadour.

Privately educated for both medicine and the Eastern Orthodox priesthood, but equally interested in science and technical specialization, Gurdjieff found that neither conventional religion nor scientific knowledge by themselves answered his insatiable and unrelenting questions about the world he observed in daily life and particularly about paranormal phenomena. Even as a youth he was driven by the intimation that authentic understanding of life's meaning and purpose was possible. He became convinced that a key to understanding the significance of organic and human life lay within ancient traditions that survived in the Middle East. Determined to find at any cost the surviving traces of this ancient wisdom, he attracted a group of like-minded men and women who shared in the search. Calling themselves "The Seekers of Truth" they launched expeditions into the Middle East, India, Tibet and Central Asia, and made contact with little known monastries, religious schools and wise men. Gurdjieff would later tell the story of this period of search for understanding that manifests as what he calls "a 'spiritualizing factor' enabling" him to "comprehend the incomprehensible," in his autobiography *Meetings with Remarkable Men*.

After more than two decades of repeated search, disappointment and eventual discovery, Gurdjieff appeared in Moscow in 1912 with a powerful. comprehensive teaching. There he started to gather followers and attract the attention of a few influential people. Among these was the author and lecturer P. D. Ouspensky whose brilliant and original *Tertium Organum* had established him as a major philosopher. They met in Moscow during the spring of 1915. Ouspensky quickly recognized that what Gurdjieff presented surpassed what he had known before. He studied intensively with Gurdjieff for three years until they were driven from Russia by the Bolshevik revolution. He eventually left Gurdjieff and established his own groups but recorded this early period in his systematic and vividly detailed notes that were eventually published as *In Search of the Miraculous.*

In addition to Ouspensky, the Russian composer Thomas de Hartmann with his wife Olga and the Finnish psychiatrist Leonid Stjoernval were among those who rallied around Gurdjieff in Russia. Moved by what Gurdjieff's teaching helped them to realize, they followed him through the maelstrom of the revolution on a three month trek across the forbidding Caucasus Mountains to Tiflis

There they were joined by the artist Alexandre de Salzmann and his wife Jeanne in 1919, who helped stage the first public performance of the Movements that June. They lived in Constantinople for a little over a year until August 1921. After a further series of moves through Europe, they settled in France where Gurdjieff established his "Institute for the Harmonious Development of Man," at the Chateau de Prieuré in Fontainebleau, during October of 1922. The de Hartmanns later described the inner and outer adventures of this period in their autobiographical *Our Life With Mr. Gurdjieff* (1964, revised 1983 and 1992).

The Prieuré was the scene of intense activity and Gurdjieff attracted many new people, chiefly from England where Ouspensky was lecturing. By January 1924 Gurdjieff had sufficiently established his Institute to travel to the United States on the first of several visits. There he gave private talks, and students from the Prieuré gave demonstrations of his Movements exercises in major cities. In response to the interest expressed by several groups of Americans, Gurdjieff appointed A. R. Orage, the renowned English editor and critic who had been studying at the Prieuré for over a year, as his representative in New York City. Shortly after his return to France, Gurdjieff suffered a near fatal automobile accident in early July 1924.

As he recuperated, Gurdjieff began writing the three volume series he titled *All and Everything.* Within a year he distributed to his students the first installments of *Beelzebub's Tales*, the first volume of the *All and Everything Series.* This book came to provide Gurdjieff with a vast and epic platform for the transmission of his ideas. One observer has called it "the first truly comprehensive modern myth." *Beelzebub's Tales* became one of the continuing focal points of Gurdjieff's groups. He issued a provisional mimeographed typescript in 1930, but amendments, based in part on his observation of listeners' responses to oral readings, continued for a few more years.

Gurdjieff evidently intended *Beelzebub's Tales* to play a central role in the continuation of his oral teaching. The seemingly pompous but truly "friendly advice" that he gives on the opening page of *Beelzebub's Tales* to "Read each of my written expositions thrice," is a harbinger of the next thousand plus pages. For the first few readings *Beelzebub's Tales* is safeguarded by a deliberately excessive and rigorously frustrating obscurity. But behind the bulwark of confusing terms and tangential associations in interminable sentences, the attentive reader cannot help but be touched by Gurdjieff's concern to transmit to others a complete and contemporary rendering of ancient wisdom for the fulfillment of human life and its undeveloped possibilities.

Repeated reading and careful study reveal that Gurdjieff's compassionate thought remains consistently at the same level from the first page to the last and that in embracing the whole human situation, it cuts across all the tidy categories into which ordinary modern thought is usually divided. We usually analyze our thinking about human life into such categories as psychology, cosmology, and metaphysics. In *Beelzebub's Tales*, Gurdjieff sweeps away these categories and looks at humanity as we are and from a level which sees us psychologically, cosmologically, metaphysically and in terms of our spiritual possibilities, all simultaneously and as potentially integrated beings. By persistent and attentive reading or listening to *Beelzebub's Tales*, without trying to comment or interpret prematurely with our mechanical thinking, shallow feelings or habitual associations and reactions, progressively deeper meanings, knowledge and understanding gradually emerge in the form of direct perceptions as the author intended.

During the early 1930s Gurdjieff undertook the writing of the Second Series of *All and Everything* titled *Meetings with Remarkable Men*. In this work he employed a medley of autobiography, allegory, parable, proverb and travelogue to transmit the story of his childhood, education, travels and thoroughly vivid portraits of his companions in the search for understanding. It is the only account we have of the first half of Gurdjieff's life and as he says, serves "to acquaint the reader with the material required for a new creation and to prove the soundness and good quality of it." Also in the early '30s Gurdjieff began work on what he called the 'Third Series' of *All and Everything* titled, *Life Is Real Only Then, When "I Am."* Although it is fragmentary, this final work offers essential insight into Gurdjieff's teaching, methods and inner life.

Gurdjieff stopped writing in May of 1935. He continued to work intensively and unobtrusively with individuals and small groups, mainly in Paris and New York, throughout the 1930s and 1940s. During the same period, Ouspensky was leading his groups in London and New York in the strictest privacy. A few months after Ouspensky's death in October 1947, his manuscript of *Fragments of an Unknown Teaching* was submitted by Mme. Ouspensky to Gurdjieff, who warmly approved it and advised her to publish. In this book, Ouspensky provides a lucid and systematic account of the 'fragments of an unknown teaching' he received from Gurdjieff and the impact it had on his development. It appeared in October 1949, with the title *In Search of the Miraculous*. This occurred a few weeks before Gurdjieff's death and was followed in February 1950 by the publication of *Beelzebub's Tales*.

* * * * *

<u>APPENDIX 3</u>

Dushka
 ♦

This would usually be the place of an "Index" I suppose.

But since this is not one of those "scholarly tomes" but a personal collection of memories and recountings, quotations and photographs, I'll just list the many people and places, ordinary and extraordinary, that you will find in these pages:

Ashish, Sri Madhava (Alexander
Phipps
Benson, Rita Romilly
Besant, Annie
Besinger, Curtis
Best, Mary Ann
Bestor, Don
Bettis, Valerie
Bhagwan (see Rajneesh,/Osho)
Bharati, Sri Govindananda
             (see Baba, Shivapuri)
Biddle, Mrs. Anthony
Biederman, Billie
Binet, Jean
Bing, Suzanne
Bissing, Baroness (von)
Bissing, Ronimund (von)
Bissing, Tosca (von) (Mrs. Aubrey
                    Wolton)
Blanch, Arnold
Blanchard, Dominique
Blanchard, Pierre
Blavatsky, Helene Petrovna (Mme.)
Blom, Gert-Jan
Blouet, Max
Bluman, Anton
Blythe, Ann
Bohm, David
"Bonbon, Monsieur" (Gurdjieff,
                    G.I.)
Bonbright, Elizabeth "Betsy"
Bontemps, Arna
Borsh, Father Dean
Bothwell, Johnny
Bouquet, Romain
"Boussik" (see Salzmann, Natalie de)
Bowyer, E.C.
Bragdon, Claude
Brandwein, Rowland
Brays, The
Brewster, Jerry
Brook, Peter
Brown, Allan
Bruckiner, Anton
Buber, Martin
Buchwald, Art

Buckle, Richard
Buddha
Bukatiy, Boris
Bura, Shiela
Burley, Dan
Butlin, Billy

Caldwell, Helen
Caldwell, Jon
Calloway, Cab
"Calves, The"
Campbell,Charles
Campbell, Joseph
Campbell, Mrs. Patrick
Campendank, Heinrich
Camus, Albert
Capper, Margaret
Carlisle, Una Mae
Carlyle, Cora (Mrs. William Segal)
Carmichael, Hoagy
Carney, Matt
Carroll, Nancy
Carroll, Robert Todd
Carton, Dr. Paul
Caruso, Dorothy
Caruso, Enrico,
Caruso, Gloria
Casa, (Casadesus) Robert
Casadesus, Henri
Cassini, Prince Oleg
Castle, Lee
Cayla, Odile
Chadwick, Major
Chaliapine
Chenevière, Jacques
Chevalier,Eve (see Petey Taylor)
Chevalier, Jean Remy "Cheval"
Chevalier, Remy
Cheverdian (see Lily Galumian)
Child, Julia
Chogyal, Tenzing "T. C."
Churchill, Randolph
Claparode, Edouard
Clark, Fred
Claustres, Solange (Lubchansky)
Clayton, "Commander"

Subuh, Pak
Sudan, Club
Sullivan, Barry
Sullivan, Ed
Sutcliffe, Mrs. Mary "Tanta"
Sutcliffe, Dr. Wallace
Sutta, Elihu
Sutta, Evelyn
Sutta, Marian
Sutta, Maurice
Swingle, Ward
Sykes, James
Sylvie (see Anastasieff, Sylvie)
Symphony Sid

Tabor, Jim
Tafel, Edgar
Taliesin
Taniev
Tart, Charles T.
Taylor, Billy
Taylor, Edith (Mrs, Cesar Zwaska)
Taylor, Eve "Petey"
Taylor, Paul Beekman
"TC" [Tenzin Choegyal, the Ngari
            Rinpoche)
Tchekovitch, Tcheslaw
Teasdale, Brother Wayne
Tessenow, Henri
Tessier, Valentine
Tharp, Twyla
Thatcher, Mrs. Lew (see Flinsch,
            Jojo)
Thevanaz, Paulet
Thompson, Susan
Thurman, Wallace
Tiflis (Tblisi)
Tilley, Basil
Tilley, Irene (Mrs. Basil Tilley)
Tito, Marshall
Tobey, Mark
Toomer, Nathan Eugene "Jean"
Toscanini, Arturo
Tracol, Henriette (see Lannes,
            Mme.)
Tracol, Henri

Tracol, Lise (Mme. Alfred Etievant)
Travers, P.L. "Pamela"
Trevor, Claire
Truman, Pres. Harry S.
Tsering, Phuntsok
Tsopei, Corinne
Tupta, Ed
Tyabji, Raihana
Tyndall, Doris
Tyndall, Mrs.

Unanue, Roberto
Unger, Mrs. Hussein (see Sutta,
                        Marian)

V., Alex
V., Dushan
Valnieff, Irina (Mrs. Hoare)
van Pallandt, Baron
Vandis, Tito
Varese, Edgar
Vartaped, (see Komitas)
Vaysse, Jean
Venuta, Benay (Mrs. Fred Clark)
Vithaldas, Yogi
Vogel, Speed
Val, Nicholas de (see Stjernval,
                        Nikolai)

Walker, Dr. Kenneth
Walker, Ray "The Fake Sheik"
Wallace, Babe
Walrand, Eric
Washington, Peter
Webb, James
Welch, Louise
Welch, Patty (see Patty de Llosa)
Welch, Dr. William "Bill"
Welk, Lawrence
Wells, Joe T.
Wertenbaker, Dolphie George
West, Dorothy
West, Mae
Wheeler, Barbara Mills
Whee;er, Pierce
Whitcomb. Donald and Lillian

BIBLIOGRAPHY

ANDERSON, MARGARET, *The Fiery Fountains*, Rider & Co.,   1953

BECHHOFER-ROBERTS, C.E., T*he World Today* (London), June   1924

BEKE, GEORGE LATURA, *Digging Up The Dog*, Indications Press,   2005

BELL, DR. MARY C., *Gurdjieff International Review*, Summer,   1998

BENNETT, JOHN G, & ELIZABETH, *Idiots in Paris*, Coombe Springs Press, 1980

BENNETT, J.G., *Witness*, Hodder & Stoughton,   1962

BOWYER, E. C., *Daily News*, (London), Feb. 19.   1923

BUCKLE, RICHARD, *Diaghilev*, Atheneum, New York   1984

COLLIN, RODNEY, *The Theory of Conscious Harmony*, By The Way Books, 1958

DE ROPP, ROBERT, *Talks by Madame Ouspensky* Logos Press,   1978

DRISCOLL, WALTER J. AND THE GURDJIEFF FOUNDATION OF CALFORNIA, *Gurdjieff, An Annotated Bibliography*, Garland Publishing, New York   1985

DREYFUS, JACK *A Remarkable Medicine Has Been Overlook*ed. New York, Continuum, 1997

GURDJIEFF, G. I *Beelzebub's Tales to his Grandson*, London, Routledge and Kegan Paul, 1950

"   *The Struggle of the Magicians*, Capetown, The Stourton Press,   1957

"   *Meetings with Remarkable Men*, London, Routledge & Kegan Paul, 1963

"   *Life is Real Only Then, When 'I Am'*, New York, Triangle Editions,   1975

HAMILTON, ROSEMARY, *Hellbent for Enlightenment*, Ashland, Oregon White Cloud Press, 1998

HANDS, RINA, *Diary of Madame Egout pour Sweet*, Two Rivers Press, Aurora, Oregon, 1991

de HARTMAN, THOMAS and OLGA, *Our Life with Mr. Gurdjieff*, Arkana, Penguin Books, 1992

HULME, KATHRYN, *Undiscovered Country*, Little Brown & Co. Boston   1966

KAPUR, TRIBHUWAN, *Quest for Realisation, J. Krishnamurti, The Bhagavad Gita and G. I. Gurdjieff*. New Dawn, New Delhi, 1999

LANNES, HENRIETTE, *Inside a Question*, Paul H. Compton Ltd.,   2002

LOCKSPEISER, EDWARD, *Debussy*, Dent, London1936; Revised   1951, 1964

"   "   *Debussy, His Life and Mind* ,Vol.11, Cassell,   1965

LUYTENS, MARY *Krishnamurti: The Years of Enlightenment*, Farrar, Straus, Giroux New York, 1983

Krishnamurti: The Years of Fulfilment,   "   "

MAIRET, PHILIP, *A.R. Orage, A Memoir*, University Books, New York, 1966

MOORE,JAMES, *Gurdjieff, The Anatomy of a Myth*, Element Books Limited, 1991

Gurdjieff and Mansfield, Routledge& Kegan Paul, London, 1980

NEEDLEMAN, JACOB & BAKER, GEORGE, Editors *Gurdjieff, Essays and Reflections on the Man and his Teaching*, New York, Continuum, 1996

NOTT, C.S., *Teachings of Gurdjieff*, Routledge and Kegan Paul,   1961

"   " *Journeys Through This World*, Routledge and Kegan Paul,   1969

O'SULLIVAN, VINCENT *Katherine Mansfield, Selected Letters*, Oxford University Press,New York, 1989

OUSPENSKY, P.D. *In Search of the Miraculous* London, Routledge and Kegan Paul, 1950

The Psychology of Man's Possible Evolution, London, Hodder & Stoughton, 1951

PATTERSON, WILLIAM PATRICK, *Struggle of the Magicians*, Arete, Fairfax, Calif.

                                  Taking With The Left Hand,   "   1998

      "   "   *The Rope*   "   "

PATWARDHAN, SUNANDA, *A Vision of the Sacred: My Personal Journey with Krishnamurti,* Edwin House Publishing, 1999

PETERS, FRITZ *Boyhood with Gurdjieff.* Gollancz. 1964

"   *Gurdjieff Remembered,* Gollancz, 1965

"   *Balanced Man: A Look at Gurdjieff Fifty Years later,* Wildwood House, 1979

POPOFF, IRMIS, *Gurdjieff: His Work on Myself...with Others...for the Work,* Vantage, New York 1969

PRIESTLEY, J.B. *Man and Time,* Doubleday & Co.Inc., New York, 1964

RAJNEESH, BHAGWAN SHREE, *The New Man:* Cologne, West Germany, Neo-Sannnyas Int

WEBB, JAMES, *The Harmonious Circle: The Lives and Work of G. I. Gurdjieff, P.D. Ouspensky and their Followers,* Thames and Hudson, 1980

RAVINDRA, RAVI, *Heart Without Measure,* Shaila Press, Halifax, Nova Scotia, 1999

"   "   *Krishnamurti, Two Birds On One Tree,* Quest Books, London 1995

REGISTRES 4: *Jacques Copeau, Les Registres du Vieux Colombier,* 2, America Éditions Gallimard, 1984

RIPMAN, HUGH BROCKWILL, *Search for Truth,* Washington D.C. Forthway Center, Palisades Press,1999

SAXTON, JOSEPHINE, *Group Feast,* Doubleday Science Fiction, 1971

SEYMOUR-SMITH, MARTIN, *100 Most Influential Books Ever Written,* Carol Publishing Group, 1998

SINCLAIR, FRANK R. *Without Benefit of Clergy,* Xlibris, 2005

STAVELEY, A.L. *Memories of GURDJIEFF,* Two Rivers Press, Aurora, Oregon, 1978

STORR, ANTHONY, *Feet of Clay, A Study of Gurus* Free Press Paperbacks, New York, 1997

SRI ANIRVAN and LIZELLE REYMOND, *To Live Within, Teachings of a Baul,* Coombe Springs Press, 1984

TAFEL, EDGAR, *Apprentice to Genius:Years with Frank Lloyd Wright,* Dover Publications, N. Y., 1979

TAYLOR, PAUL BEEKMAN, *Shadows of Heaven,* Samuel Weiser, York Beach, ME, 1998

"   "   "   *Gurdjieff and Orage,* Weiser Books,   "   "   2001

TILLEY, BASIL, *Letters from Paris and England 1947-1949*, privately printed at the Phene Press 1981

VAYSSE, JEAN, *Toward Awakening* San Francisco, Harper & Row, 1979

WALKER, KENNETH, *Venture with Ideas*, London: Jonathan Cape, 1951

"   "   *A Study of Gurdjieff's Teaching,* Samuel Weiser, New York, 1974

          Tomorrow   New York, Winter 1952-3

WASHINGTON, PETER, *Madame Blavatsky's Baboon,* Martin Secker & Warburg, Ltd. London, 1993

WEBB, JAMES, *The Harmonious Circle: The Lives and Work of G. I. Gurdjieff,*
               P.D.Ouspensky and their Followers, Thames and Hudson, 1980

WELCH, LOUISE, *Orage with Gurdjieff in America,* Routledge & Kegan Paul, London
                            Boston,   1982

WELCH, WILLIAM J. *What Happened in Between; A Doctor's Story,* George
                         Braziller, New York, 1972

WILSON, COLIN, *Rudolf Steiner,* The Aquarian Press   1985
    "   "   *G.I. Gurdjieff,*   "   "

WOLFE, EDWIN, *Episodes with Gurdjieff,* Far West   1987

ZUBER, RENE, "*Who Are You, Monsieur Gurdjieff?,*" Routledge & Kegan Paul, 1980